LEGAL RESEARCH
AND WRITING

Paralegal Titles from Delmar Publishers

Legal Research, Steve Barber, Mark A. McCormick, 1996
Wills, Estates, and Trusts, Jay H. Gingrich, 1996
Criminal Law and Procedure, 2E, Daniel E. Hall, 1996
Introduction to Environmental Law, Harold Hickok, 1996
Civil Litigation, 2E, Peggy N. Kerley, Joanne Banker Hames, Paul A. Sukys, 1996
Client Accounting for the Law Office, Elaine M. Langston, 1996
Law Office Management, 2E, Jonathan S. Lynton, Terri Mick Lyndall,
    Donna Masinter, 1996
Foundations of Law: Cases, Commentary, and Ethics, 2E, Ransford C. Pyle, 1996
Administrative Law and Procedure, Elizabeth C. Richardson, 1996
Legal Research and Writing, David J. Smith, 1996

Legal Research and Writing, Carol M. Bast, 1995
Federal Taxation, Susan G. Covins, 1995
Everything You Need to Know About Being a Legal Assistant, Chere B. Estrin, 1995
Paralegals in New York Law, Eric M. Gansberg, 1995
Ballentine's Legal Dictionary and Thesaurus, Jonathan S. Lynton, 1995
Legal Terminology with Flashcards, Cathy J. Okrent, 1995
Wills, Trusts, and Estate Administration for Paralegals, Mark A. Stewart, 1995
The Law of Contracts and the Uniform Commercial Code, Pamela R. Tepper, 1995
Life Outside the Law Firm: Non-Traditional Careers for Paralegals,
    Karen Treffinger, 1995

An Introduction to Paralegal Studies, David G. Cooper, Michael J. Gibson, 1994
Administrative Law, Daniel E. Hall, 1994
Ballentine's Law Dictionary: Legal Assistant Edition, Jack G. Handler, 1994
The Law of Real Property, Michael P. Kearns, 1994
Ballentine's Thesaurus for Legal Research and Writing, Jonathan S. Lynton, 1994
Legal Ethics and Professional Responsibility, Jonathan S. Lynton,
    Terri Mick Lyndall, 1994
Criminal Law for Paralegals, Daniel J. Markey, Jr., Mary Queen Donnelly, 1994
Family Law, Ransford C. Pyle, 1994
Paralegals in American Law: Introduction to Paralegalism, Angela Schneeman, 1994
Intellectual Property, Richard Stim, 1994

Legal Writing for Paralegals, Steve Barber, 1993
Administration of Wills, Trusts, and Estates, Gordon W. Brown, 1993
Torts and Personal Injury Laws, William R. Buckley, 1993
Survey of Criminal Law, Daniel E. Hall, 1993
The Law of Corporations, Partnerships, and Sole Proprietorships,
    Angela Schneeman, 1993

LEGAL RESEARCH AND WRITING

David J. Smith

Harford Community College
Bel Air, Maryland

Delmar Publishers

I⟨T⟩P An International Thomson Publishing Company

Albany · Bonn · Boston · Cincinnati · Detroit · London · Madrid · Melbourne
Mexico City · New York · Pacific Grove · Paris · San Francisco · Singapore · Tokyo
Toronto · Washington

NOTICE TO THE READER

Background by Jennifer McGlaughlin
Design by Douglas J. Hyldelund

Delmar Staff:

Acquisitions Editor: Christopher Anzalone
Developmental Editor: Jeffrey D. Litton
Project Editor: Eugenia L. Orlandi

Production Coordinator: Jennifer Gaines
Art & Design Coordinator: Douglas J. Hyldelund
Cover Design: Linda DeMasi

COPYRIGHT © 1996
By Delmar Publishers
a division of International Thomson Publishing Inc.

The ITP logo is a trademark under license.

Printed in the United States of America

For more information, contact:

Delmar Publishers
3 Columbia Circle, Box 15015
Albany, New York 12212-5015

International Thomson Editores
Campos Eliseos 385, Piso 7
Col Polanco
11560 Mexico D F Mexico

International Thomson Publishing Europe
Berkshire House 168 - 173
High Holborn
London WC1V7AA
England

International Thomson Publishing GmbH
Königswinterer Strasse 418
53227 Bonn
Germany

Thomas Nelson Australia
102 Dodds Street
South Melbourne, 3205
Victoria, Australia

International Thomson Publishing Asia
221 Henderson Road
#05 - 10 Henderson Building
Singapore 0315

Nelson Canada
1120 Birchmount Road
Scarborough, Ontario
Canada M1K 5G4

International Thomson Publishing - Japan
Hirakawacho Kyowa Building, 3F
2-2-1 Hirakawacho
Chiyoda-ku, Tokyo 102
Japan

1 2 3 4 5 6 7 8 9 10 XXX 01 00 99 98 97 96

Library of Congress Cataloging-in-Publication Data

Smith, David J.
   Legal research and writing/David J. Smith
    p. cm.
   Includes index.
   ISBN 0-8273-6355-9
   1. Legal research—United States. 2. Legal composition.
  I. Title.
KF240.S6 1996
340'.072073—dc20

95-19601
CIP

DEDICATION

This book is dedicated to those who, like my late father, devote their lives with quiet yet determined voice to making this world a more peaceful and compassionate place.

Delmar Publishers' Online Services

To access Delmar on the World Wide Web, point your browser to:
http://www.delmar.com/delmar.html
To access through Gopher: gopher://gopher.delmar.com
(Delmar Online is part of "thomson.com", an Internet site with information on
more than 30 publishers of the International Thomson Publishing organization.)
For more information on our products and services:
email: info@delmar.com
or call 800-347-7707

CONTENTS

IIII CHAPTER 4:   Primary Law Finders and Verification 69

IIII CHAPTER 5:   Secondary Sources of Law 113

IIII CHAPTER 6:   Computers and Other Technology 150

IIII CHAPTER 7:   Proper Identification: Citation 170

IIII CHAPTER 8: Basic Legal Analysis 202

IIII CHAPTER 9: Strategies for Research 231

PART II
LEGAL WRITING

IIII CHAPTER 10: Introduction to Legal Writing 257

ⅢⅢ CHAPTER 11: Legal Writing Mechanics and Style 277

ⅢⅢ CHAPTER 12: Correspondence 320

IIII CHAPTER 15: Pleadings, Motions, and Discovery 434

IIII CHAPTER 16: Litigation Memoranda and Appellate Briefs 482

▐▌ Appendices

DELMAR PUBLISHERS INC.

 AND

LAWYERS COOPERATIVE PUBLISHING

ARE PLEASED TO ANNOUNCE THEIR PARTNERSHIP TO CO-PUBLISH COLLEGE TEXTBOOKS FOR PARALEGAL EDUCATION.

DELMAR, WITH OFFICES AT ALBANY, NEW YORK, IS A PROFESSIONAL EDUCATION PUBLISHER. DELMAR PUBLISHES QUALITY EDUCATIONAL TEXTBOOKS TO PREPARE AND SUPPORT INDIVIDUALS FOR LIFE SKILLS AND SPECIFIC OCCUPATIONS.

LAWYERS COOPERATIVE PUBLISHING (LCP), WITH OFFICES AT ROCHES-TER, NEW YORK, HAS BEEN THE LEADING PUBLISHER OF ANALYTICAL LEGAL INFORMATION FOR OVER 100 YEARS. IT IS THE PUBLISHER OF SUCH REKNOWNED LEGAL ENCYCLOPEDIAS AS **AMERICAN LAW REPORTS, AMERICAN JURISPRUDENCE, UNITED STATES CODE SERVICE, LAWYERS EDITION,** AS WELL AS OTHER MATERIAL, AND FEDERAL- AND STATE-SPECIFIC PUBLICATIONS. THESE PUBLICATIONS HAVE BEEN DESIGNED TO WORK TOGETHER IN THE DAY-TO-DAY PRAC-TICE OF LAW AS AN INTEGRATED SYSTEM IN WHAT IS CALLED THE "TOTAL CLIENT-SERVICE LIBRARY®" (TCSL®). EACH LCP PUBLICATION IS COMPLETE WITHIN ITSELF AS TO SUBJECT COVERAGE, YET ALL HAVE COMMON FEATURES AND EXTENSIVE CROSS-REFERENCING TO PROVIDE LINKAGE FOR HIGHLY EFFICIENT LEGAL RESEARCH INTO VIRTUALLY ANY MATTER AN ATTORNEY MIGHT BE CALLED UPON TO HANDLE.

INFORMATION IN ALL PUBLICATIONS IS CAREFULLY AND CONSTANTLY MONITORED TO KEEP PACE WITH AND REFLECT EVENTS IN THE LAW AND IN SOCIETY. UPDATING AND SUPPLEMENTAL INFORMATION IS TIMELY AND PROVIDED CONVENIENTLY.

FOR FURTHER REFERENCE, SEE:

AMERICAN JURISPRUDENCE 2D: AN ENCYCLOPEDIC TEXT COVERAGE OF THE COMPLETE BODY OF STATE AND FEDERAL LAW.

AM JUR LEGAL FORMS 2D: A COMPILATION OF BUSINESS AND LEGAL FORMS DEALING WITH A VARIETY OF SUBJECT MATTERS.

AM JUR PLEADING AND PRACTICE FORMS, REV: MODEL PRACTICE FORMS FOR EVERY STAGE OF A LEGAL PROCEEDING.

AM JUR PROOF OF FACTS: A SERIES OF ARTICLES THAT GUIDE THE READER IN DETERMINING WHICH FACTS ARE ESSENTIAL TO A CASE AND HOW TO PROVE THEM.

AM JUR TRIALS: A SERIES OF ARTICLES DISCUSSING EVERY ASPECT OF PARTICULAR SETTLEMENTS AND TRIALS WRITTEN BY180 CONSULTING SPECIALISTS.

UNITED STATES CODE SERVICE: A COMPLETE AND AUTHORITATIVE ANNOTATED FEDERAL CODE THAT FOLLOWS THE EXACT LANGUAGE OF THE STATUTES AT LARGE AND DIRECTS YOU TO THE COURT AND AGENCY DECISIONS CONSTRUING EACH PROVISION.

ALR AND ALR FEDERAL: SERIES OF ANNOTATIONS PROVIDING IN-DEPTH ANALYSES OF ALL THE CASE LAW ON PARTICULAR LEGAL ISSUES.

U.S. SUPREME COURT REPORTS, L ED 2D: EVERY REPORTED U.S. SUPREME COURT DECISION PLUS IN-DEPTH DISCUSSIONS OF LEADING ISSUES.

FEDERAL PROCEDURE, L ED: A COMPREHENSIVE, A-Z TREATISE ON FEDERAL PROCEDURE—CIVIL, CRIMINAL, AND ADMINISTRATIVE.

FEDERAL PROCEDURAL FORMS, L ED: STEP-BY-STEP GUIDANCE FOR DRAFTING FORMS FOR FEDERAL COURT OR FEDERAL AGENCY PROCEEDINGS.

FEDERAL RULES SERVICE, 2D AND 3D: REPORTS DECISIONS FROM ALL LEVELS OF THE FEDERAL SYSTEM INTERPRETING THE FEDERAL RULES OF CIVIL PROCEDURE AND THE FEDERAL RULES OF APPELLATE PROCEDURE.

FEDERAL RULES DIGEST, 3D: ORGANIZES HEADNOTES FOR THE DECISIONS REPORTED IN FEDERAL RULES SERVICE ACCORDING TO THE NUMBERING SYSTEMS OF THE FEDERAL RULES OF CIVIL PROCEDURE AND THE FEDERAL RULES OF APPELLATE PROCEDURE.

FEDERAL RULES OF EVIDENCE SERVICE: REPORTS DECISIONS FROM ALL LEVELS OF THE FEDERAL SYSTEM INTERPRETING THE FEDERAL RULES OF EVIDENCE.

FEDERAL RULES OF EVIDENCE NEWS

FEDERAL PROCEDURE RULES SERVICE

FEDERAL TRIAL HANDBOOK, 2D

FORM DRAFTING CHECKLISTS: AM JUR PRACTICE GUIDE

GOVERNMENT CONTRACTS: PROCEDURES AND FORMS

HOW TO GO DIRECTLY INTO YOUR OWN COMPUTERIZED SOLO PRACTICE WITHOUT MISSING A MEAL (OR A BYTE)

JONES ON EVIDENCE, CIVIL AND CRIMINAL, 7TH

LITIGATION CHECKLISTS: AM JUR PRACTICE GUIDE

MEDICAL LIBRARY, LAWYERS EDITION

MEDICAL MALPRACTICE—ALR CASES AND ANNOTATIONS

MODERN APPELLATE PRACTICE: FEDERAL AND STATE CIVIL APPEALS

MODERN CONSTITUTIONAL LAW

NEGOTIATION AND SETTLEMENT

PATTERN DEPOSITION CHECKLISTS, 2D

QUALITY OF LIFE DAMAGES: CRITICAL ISSUES AND PROOFS

SHEPARD'S CITATIONS FOR ALR

SUCCESSFUL TECHNIQUES FOR CIVIL TRIALS, 2D

STORIES ET CETERA—A COUNTRY LAWYER LOOKS AT LIFE AND THE LAW

SUMMARY OF AMERICAN LAW

THE TRIAL LAWYER'S BOOK: PREPARING AND WINNING CASES

TRIAL PRACTICE CHECKLISTS

2000 CLASSIC LEGAL QUOTATIONS

WILLISTON ON CONTRACTS, 3D AND 4TH

FEDERAL RULES OF EVIDENCE DIGEST: ORGANIZES HEAD-NOTES FOR THE DECISIONS REPORTED IN FEDERAL RULES OF EVIDENCE SERVICE ACCORDING TO THE NUMBERING SYSTEM OF THE FEDERAL RULES OF EVIDENCE.

ADMINISTRATIVE LAW: PRACTICE AND PROCEDURE

AGE DISCRIMINATION: CRITICAL ISSUES AND PROOFS

ALR CRITICAL ISSUES: DRUNK DRIVING PROSECUTIONS

ALR CRITICAL ISSUES: FREEDOM OF INFORMATION ACTS

ALR CRITICAL ISSUES: TRADEMARKS

ALR CRITICAL ISSUES: WRONGFUL DEATH

AMERICANS WITH DISABILITIES: PRACTICE AND COMPLI-
ANCE MANUAL

ATTORNEYS' FEES

BALLENTINE'S LAW DICTIONARY

CONSTITUTIONAL LAW DESKBOOK

CONSUMER AND BORROWER PROTECTION: AM JUR PRAC-
TICE GUIDE

CONSUMER CREDIT: ALR ANNOTATIONS

DAMAGES: ALR ANNOTATIONS

EMPLOYEE DISMISSAL: CRITICAL ISSUES AND PROOFS

ENVIRONMENTAL LAW: ALR ANNOTATIONS

EXPERT WITNESS CHECKLISTS

EXPERT WITNESSES IN CIVIL TRIALS

FORFEITURES: ALR ANNOTATIONS

FEDERAL LOCAL COURT RULES

FEDERAL LOCAL COURT FORMS

FEDERAL CRIMINAL LAW AND PROCEDURE: ALR ANNOTA-
TIONS

FEDERAL EVIDENCE

FEDERAL LITIGATION DESK SET: FORMS AND ANALYSIS

PREFACE

The overall goal of this book is to prepare students for employment where basic paralegal duties are expected. These duties include conducting basic case law and statutory research; drafting correspondence; developing various documents, including instruments and pleadings; and preparing legal memoranda. The impetus for my writing this book was my frustration in locating a text that covered these essential concepts in a comprehensive, yet unintimidating fashion that could be used on the community college level.

Besides an overall emphasis on fundamental skills, this book does some things not seen elsewhere. First, it looks at legal research and writing as a process—a continuum, if you will. The results of nearly all legal research will be submitted in written form. Additionally, few documents, even the simplest letters, do not require some basic research. I want students to understand that research and writing must be treated as two parts of a whole; the success of one always depends on the other.

Secondly, this book has features not found in other texts. Though the sources of paralegal ethical guidance include NFPA and NALA codes, attorneys employing paralegals look to the ABA and state bar opinions for insight. Occasionally excerpts from bar opinions are provided, mostly in the chapters dealing with legal writing, to illustrate ethical dilemmas that arise in paralegal practice. In addition, a variety of tips have been collected from practicing legal assistants. These tips consist of pragmatic advice that can be used either in employment or in school. They often take the form of "shortcuts" for getting things done quickly and efficiently. A good shortcut can save time, effort, and client fees. This is certainly a laudable ambition for a paralegal. Both features bring a necessary dose of reality to the book.

The glossary terms and definitions that appear throughout the book (and cumulated in the glossary at the end of the book) give students a handy reference without the need to consult a separate text. Terms marked with a dagger are from *Ballentine's Legal Dictionary and Thesaurus;* these provide standard, general definitions to give the student a grounding in typical legal terminology. More subject-specific definitions, tailored by me for the context of this text, also help students in particular areas.

This text follows *The Bluebook* for citation style. Thus, for example, "Lawyer's Edition" is cited consistent with that authority as it stood at the time of publication of this text.

Legal research is considered as a three-step process. The steps include: (1) understanding the problem, (2) understanding the law, and (3) conducting legal research. The process is introduced in Chapter 2 and applied to a typical fact pattern. Though the application might seem overwhelming at that point, it is important for students to understand early on how theory can be put into practice. The process is revisited in Chapter 9 when research strategies are discussed.

Legal writing is also viewed as a three-step process. The steps consist of: (1) identifying the document's purpose, audience, and constraints; (2) developing a structure and draft; and (3) editing and rewriting. These steps are introduced in Chapter 10. I make a point of integrating previously introduced legal research concepts when considering legal writing.

During the writing of this text, the American Association for Paralegal Education (AAfPE) developed certain competencies for paralegal programs. I have attempted to address the legal research and legal writing skills that the AAfPE recommends that students obtain in paralegal education.

It is my hope that this text will prove to be a useful addition to the body of work in the field of legal research and writing. By understanding my goals and philosophy, I hope you are better prepared to use it.

David J. Smith

ACKNOWLEDGMENTS

This book would not have been possible without the advice, encouragement, technical support, and editorial assistance of my wife Lena. As an attorney, she offered her substantive knowledge of the field. As a teacher, she considered what would work with students and what would not. As a business owner, she provided real-life experiences to use as examples in the book. As a friend, she was candid about my work when appropriate while always being mindful of my fragile ego. As a mother, she assumed more than her share of responsibility for our son Lorenzo, thus allowing me to work. Finally, as a wife she provided the comfort and love that an author needs when enduring the loneliness and frustration associated with writing. This book is as much a result of her efforts as it is of mine.

Of course countless others have assisted, often indirectly. Though I am a teacher, lawyer, and possibly writer, my most important roles in life are those of father, husband, and son. Those individuals who lessened the burdens associated with these roles have my undying gratitude. These individuals include my mother and father, my mother and father-in-law, my sister, my brother-in-law, and in many ways my son. He especially was willing to accept a less than adequate job as father, maybe realizing (as much as one can at age 21 months) the importance of this work to me.

Many other friends and family members assisted in the production of this book. Susan Wheeler and Kathi Weinel assisted with typing the manuscript. Patty Ferraris, Barb Petr, Jim Vale, Ruth Harrison, Norbert Lechner, Bob Bearden, Anita Merrill, Larry Vencill, Linda Henry, Alison Robinson, Kelley McDonald, Susan Terlep, my colleagues at Harford Community College, and countless others offered insights, examples, paralegal tips, and encouragement in writing this text.

Most importantly, I would like to thank my students. I have gotten the better of the bargain. By imparting to each student a modest amount of learning, I gained an abundance of confidence, experience, knowledge, and wisdom. The sum and substance of their contribution is in this text.

I am also grateful for the support of Delmar. I entered this venture somewhat skeptical of my chances of success. At every point along the way, I received only encouragement. In particular, Jay Whitney, Glenna Stanfield, Chris Anzalone, Judy Roberts, and Jeff Litton deserve special thanks. Graphics West and Brooke Graves deserve thanks for final editing and production.

Finally, my heartfelt thanks goes to the following individuals who reviewed my work. The offering of their various perspectives only improved my work.

Cheryl Kirschner, Esq.
  Bentley College
  Boston, MA

Norman Holt, II, J.D.
  Daytona Beach Community College
  Daytona Beach, FL

Gwynne Hutton, J.D.
  State Technical Institute
  Memphis, TN

Dolores Grissom
  Samford University
  Birmingham, AL

Christopher Sadler
  Denver Paralegal Institute
  Denver, CO

Frances McClean
  Dyke College
  Cleveland, OH

Jeanne Maxwell
  Athens Area Technical College
  Athens, GA

Elizabeth Sullivan
  Phillips Jr. College
  Birmingham, AL

Chanda Miller
  Des Moines Area Community College
  Des Moines, IA

C. Suzanne Bailey, J.D.
  Auburn University at Montgomery
  Montgomery, AL

Anneta Buster, J.D.
  Johnson County Community College
  Overland Park, KS

Gary Glascom
  Cedar Crest College
  Allentown, PA

||||

CHAPTER 1

OVERVIEW OF LEGAL RESEARCH AND WRITING

Introduction

Paralegal, legal assistant, legal technician, paralegal assistant: Each of these titles describes an individual who, though not a lawyer, assists attorneys in their day-to-day professional activities. The responsibilities of lawyers include a myriad of tasks, including representing clients, negotiating agreements, preparing documents, conducting research, and offering advice. Ethically, paralegals are permitted to assist in any areas that do not constitute the practice of law. Though the *practice of law* has never been clearly defined, it is generally accepted to mean the functions that center around legal representation, such as appearing with clients in court, and providing legal advice, such as informing clients of their legal rights. As a consequence, the role of the paralegal can best be described in the negative; all other legal tasks are, in many cases, permitted.

Researching the law in response to legal problems and presenting the results in written form are essential to providing legal services. This book is about these two important areas: legal research and legal writing. The critical importance of these areas is illustrated by the fact that many attorneys justify the employment of paralegals solely because of the need for assistance in research and writing. Since the 1960s, attorneys and their professional associations, such as the **American Bar Association** (ABA), have encouraged the employment of paralegals to help improve the quality of legal services. In a report issued by the ABA in August 1968, the following was recommended:

> That the legal profession recognize that there are many tasks in serving a client's needs which can be performed by a trained, nonlawyer assistant working under the direction and supervision of a lawyer;

> That the profession encourage the training and employment of such employees ... .

Today, lawyers understand and appreciate the important contribution that legal assistants make to the legal profession, particularly in the area of legal research and writing.

Legal Research and Writing as a Process

Legal research and writing can be thought of as a process. A *process* is defined as a particular method of doing something involving a number of steps or operations. For instance, cooking is a process. It involves a number of steps, including identifying a need, finding an appropriate recipe, procuring ingredients,

---

LEGAL TERMS

American Bar Association †   The country's largest voluntary professional association of attorneys, commonly referred to as the ABA. Its purposes include enhancing professionalism and advancing the administration of justice.

assembling these ingredients in a particular fashion, and then presenting the results in an appealing way.

The process of legal research and writing is quite similar. It consists of identifying a legal problem, determining a plan to answer the problem, procuring the resources necessary to answer the problem, analyzing the legal principles found in these sources, and then, finally, presenting the results in an acceptable form.

Both cooking and legal research and writing are continuums. You would not think of making an exquisite meal without considering how it should be presented. Likewise, serious research cannot be conducted without considering the appropriate written form it should take. Though maybe not consciously, while cooking the chef considers the way in which the dish will be offered. During legal research, as a paralegal you must be conscious of the written form your final product will take.

About This Book

The course in which this text is used is likely to be offered at the commencement of your paralegal education. This book is designed to dispel the mystery of the law, and legal knowledge is not presumed. Each chapter builds on the previous one. Terms are defined and redefined. Finally, both legal research and legal writing are considered as logical three-step processes. By approaching the subjects in this way, self-confidence, so necessary when learning about a new area, will come easily.

This book is premised on the belief that to understand legal research and writing, you must see its practical applications. Consequently, this book, through its paralegal practice situations and paralegal tips, considers specific day-to-day duties found in typical legal settings.

The research tasks you may be assigned in an office vary. It is not uncommon for an attorney to request a paralegal to define a specific word or locate a particular law on short notice. More complicated tasks often involve considering a factual scenario, determining the legal problem that arises from it, and locating a legal answer.

A variety of documents are produced in a legal practice. Legal assistants today play a role in the production of most forms of legal writing. Preparing correspondence is an area in which paralegals have long played a predominant role, but paralegals are now being used more frequently to draft documents related to litigation and business transactions. Finally, paralegals' analytical and writing abilities are now being put to use to produce substantive legal memoranda.

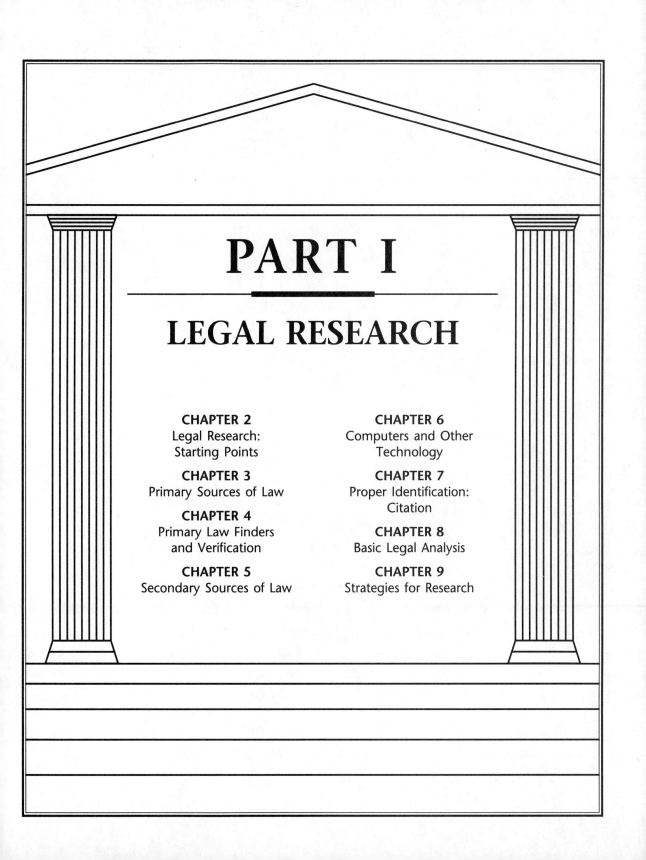

PART I

LEGAL RESEARCH

CHAPTER 2

LEGAL RESEARCH: STARTING POINTS

OVERVIEW

Legal applications are not limited to the courtroom and law office. Daily situations in which you are involved have legal significance. This significance will not likely seem apparent until something goes wrong—the merchandise you purchase breaks, or the service you paid for is inadequate. In these situations, a legal problem arises. The answer to the problem is referred to as a *legal remedy.*

Whether the legal remedy you seek is achieved will depend on the legal authority that is applied. *Legal authority* is the power to command or act, stated as a specific rule. There are two forms of authority in law: *mandatory authority,* which must be followed, and *persuasive authority,* which need only be considered. The goal of legal research is to locate authority that allows or supports the legal remedy desired by the attorney's client.

Locating legal authority can be a frustrating process. As a paralegal, you need to be patient, careful, and persistent in your efforts, and employ a creative yet ethical approach. Researching is not a matter of the quantity of your work, but its quality.

Legal research is conducted in law libraries. The most comprehensive law libraries are found in law schools. Most undergraduate colleges and universities have legal collections. Court-affiliated and bar association libraries exist in most areas. Every state has a state-supported library located in the state capital. Most government agencies and public interest associations also have library collections. Finally, all law offices have some form of a library, the size of which depends on the size of the firm. Larger libraries are administered by a law librarian. This person and the other library staff can be valuable resources.

Research can be accomplished by utilizing a three-part plan. In Step One, a full understanding of the legal problem and its ramifications is determined. Step Two focuses on an understanding of the law that might apply to the problem. Finally, in Step Three, actual techniques of legal research are employed.

PARALEGAL PRACTICE SITUATION

You are employed as a senior paralegal in a medium-sized law firm. Your responsibilities include not only working for a senior **partner**, but also overseeing the work of other paralegals. Michael Ortega was recently hired as a legal assistant for two **associates**. One of his first tasks was to conduct preliminary research on the issue of whether a criminal defendant's constitutional rights were violated when the police failed to provide him with the opportunity to speak to his lawyer after arrest. For you, this would be a simple matter to research (the starting point would be the Sixth Amendment of the U.S. Constitution).

After an afternoon of researching in the local bar library, Michael has approached you for assistance. He apparently has not located an answer. He is frustrated and afraid that his failure to find an answer might result in his dismissal. After reassuring him that that would not happen, you give him general advice about researching and working in the library.

--- LEGAL TERMS ---

partner [†]   A member of a partnership.

associate [†]   A person engaged in the practice of law with another attorney or attorneys, but not as a partner or member of the firm.

Legal Problems, Authority, and Remedies

Applications of the law can be seen both in and out of the courtroom and law office. Common, everyday occurrences have legal significance. For example, students report to the first day of class, the instructor is present, and the semester begins. Even in this rather simple situation, legal relationships are formed and duties created. Students pay tuition and as a consequence enter into a **contract** with the college. The instructor is an **agent** of the college. As such, she represents the college and acts on its behalf. Accreditation was previously granted to the institution, permitting it to grant degrees. Here concepts of contract, agency, and education law are present.

At first the legal ramifications of common factual situations may not be obvious. The significance will certainly be lost on those who lack legal training.

If something goes wrong, however, and a legal problem arises, then those who participated in the situation suddenly are concerned. The phrase *legal problem* is generic. Within a legal specialty, a more specific term or phrase would be used. In **tort** law, a legal problem might be characterized as **negligence**. In contract law, the phrase **breach of contract** might be used. The term **crime** is used in criminal law. A basic understanding of these areas is necessary to identify the appropriate term or phrase.

Now suppose that the students show up for class (for which they have already paid), but the instructor decides at the last minute not to teach the course. Additionally, the college is unwilling to hire a new instructor. Pursuant to contract law, the agreement between the college and students has been breached by the college. What can the students do about it? Can they get their tuition refunded? Can they compel the college to hire a new instructor? How can the students be compensated for the lost knowledge they believe they would have gained from the course? The answers to these questions are referred to as *legal remedies*.

Legal research is just another form of problem solving. In a dispute between a brother and sister over a toy, the problem may be solved by the father interceding and ordering the children to share. His judgment may be based on instinct

---

LEGAL TERMS

contract [†] An agreement entered into, for adequate consideration, to do, or refrain from doing, a particular thing.

agent [†] One of the parties to an agency relationship, specifically, the one who acts for and represents the other party, who is known as the *principal*. The word implies service as well as authority to do something in the name of or on behalf of the principal.

tort [†] A wrong involving a breach of duty and resulting in an injury to the person or property of another.

negligence [†] The failure to do something that a reasonable person would do in the same circumstances, or the doing of something a reasonable person would not do.

breach of contract [†] Failure, without legal excuse, to perform any promise that forms a whole or a part of a contract, including the doing of something inconsistent with its terms.

crime [†] An offense against the authority of the state; a public wrong, as distinguished from a private wrong; an act in violation of the penal code; a felony or a misdemeanor.

EVERYDAY OCCURRENCES AS LEGAL PROBLEMS

Common Occurrence	*Legal Significance*
Students arrive for class	No legal problem
Instructor does not show up	Legal problem: Breach of contract
Students are mad. What are their options?	What are students' legal remedies?
▪ Refund tuition	▪ Restitution
▪ New instructor	▪ Specific performance

Legal research conducted to locate appropriate authority

Rule applied to determine/ support appropriate remedy

or a previously established family rule that all toys are to be shared. He has applied a rule to achieve a remedy just as a judge does in a courtroom. A legal remedy is reached as a result of the application of **legal authority**.

Legal authority is the power to command or act. It is often stated as a specific rule. For the father, the rule might be:

When siblings fight over a toy, the toy is shared.

Legal authority takes two forms: mandatory and persuasive. **Mandatory authority** must be applied and followed by a court. When mandatory authority is presented to a judge, she must follow its mandates. **Persuasive authority**, in contrast, is used to convince and influence a judge. A court considering it has the option of either applying the authority or not. Locating appropriate authority is crucial to supporting the request for a particular legal remedy. In court the judge frequently asks the lawyer requesting a certain legal remedy, "What is your authority?" Understandably, then, finding supporting authority is important.

In the problem the students faced, determining that a breach of contract (the legal problem) exists and that possible legal remedies include a refund (called **restitution**) or a new instructor (called **specific performance**) requires knowledge of contract law. A general understanding of contract principles might not be

---

LEGAL TERMS

legal authority † 1. The power of the law to require obedience. 2. Precedent.

binding (mandatory) authority † Previous decisions of a higher court or statutes that a judge must follow in reaching a decision in a case.

persuasive authority † Authority that is neither binding authority nor precedent, but which a court may use to support its decision if it chooses.

restitution † In both contract and tort, a remedy that restores the status quo. Restitution returns a person who has been wrongfully deprived of something to the position he or she occupied before the wrong occurred; it requires a defendant who has been unjustly

adequate; you might have to conduct extensive legal research to locate the specific legal authority applicable in this situation. Although it might seem as easy as getting from A to B, it is not. Legal research involves using numerous resources and techniques to find the appropriate answer. This is the object of Chapters 2 through 9 of this book: teaching the methods of legal research.

Paralegal Requirements

Like other forms of research, legal research is an extensive undertaking. At times, you will find it frustrating and tiring. These feelings at first will be due to intimidation at the variety and complexity of legal resources: libraries, books, periodicals, and computers. However, as you become more experienced you will gain confidence. As a result you will become a proficient researcher.

Patience will be required; researching can be time-consuming. In a society where the quickest or fastest is valued, it might be difficult to see the virtues of taking your time. A patient researcher is careful. A careful researcher is a valued and indispensible member of a legal team.

Along with patience, it will be necessary for you to be persistent in your efforts. Legal authorities are not easily located. Like a detective, you will follow many false leads or occasionally go down a dead-end road. You will be required to push on, always developing new theories and considering other possibilities.

Creativity is required in research. Looking at unusual, nontraditional sources is a form of creativity. Conventional methods can only go so far. This is not to say that convention is bad, just that it is conventional—what everyone else does. Sometimes it is equated with a minimum level of acceptable effort. You should go beyond convention. Explore old books and new books, newspapers and periodicals; consider interviews. A creative mind will improve your work attitude, research skills, and final results.

Creativity, though, does not mean doing what is unethical. Some forms of legal research violate professional rules of conduct. Cheating and stealing are never acceptable in legal research.

Often instructors give legal research assignments that require students to share resources. Hiding texts, removing pages, or marking them would all constitute unethical behavior. In a practice setting, if you are aware that colleagues need a particular book, hiding it would unquestionably be inappropriate conduct. Rather, you should assist them in finding the resource. Your efforts

---

LEGAL TERMS

enriched at the expense of the plaintiff to make the plaintiff whole, either, as may be appropriate, by returning property unjustly held, by reimbursing the plaintiff, or by paying compensation or indemnification.

specific performance [†] The equitable remedy of compelling performance of a contract, as distinguished from an action at law for damages for breach of contract due to nonperformance.

will be remembered. The next time you are in a pinch, you will be able to count on them for help.

Plagiarism is defined as taking another's writing and passing it off as your own. To avoid plagiarism, one must refer to the source of the material. In law, this is called **citation**. Whenever legal authority is used, be it in oral argument or writing, acknowledgment of the source is required. To do otherwise is a form of stealing. Just the same, some materials are designed to allow you to use and copy without providing citation. For example, books that contain forms for drafting documents can be copied without the need for citation. With experience, you will come to know which sources must be cited and which need not.

In any situation, if you sense that what you are doing may be wrong, find out from your superior the correct and proper way to proceed. If this is not possible, see if your local or state bar association has a "hotline" set up to answer ethical questions anonymously.

SIDEBAR   **HAVE AN ETHICS QUESTION? CALL ABA ETHICSearch**

The American Bar Association provides an ethics research service called ETHICSearch. Should an attorney (or paralegal) have an ethical question, she can contact this service either by telephone, mail, or fax. She will receive citations to ABA ethics rules, ABA and state ethics opinions, and other relevant material that answers the dilemma. Most inquiries are handled within 24 hours. ETHICSearch can be reached by contacting the Center for Professional Responsibility, American Bar Association, 541 North Fairbanks Court, Chicago, IL 60611-3314. The telephone number is (312) 988-5323.

Finally, do not confuse quantity with quality. Finding the most is not necessarily finding the best. A common complaint of beginning legal research students is: "I spent all day in the library and I have nothing to show for it." Research is not a matter of showing, it is a matter of learning. Those same students who tested many unworkable theories and resources made mental notes and as a result will not repeat the same mistakes. In the beginning, you might tend to collect everything without evaluating it as to quality. As you advance, your evaluation techniques will improve. You will soon know when research material should be saved or discarded.

Legal Research Settings

Often specialized libraries are created for particular types of research. There are medical libraries for medical research and art libraries for art research. In legal

---

LEGAL TERMS

citation †   Reference to authority (a case, article, or other text) on a point of law, by name, volume, and page or section of the court report or other book in which it appears.

research, a law library is the research setting. The size of a law library can vary. Some can be large and institutional-looking, as in a law school; others are small and informal, as in a solo lawyer's office. In fact, a library can be whatever you define it as. One good book, under some circumstances, could be a complete library.

The most comprehensive law libraries are found at law schools. Most states have at least one public law school, and most large metropolitan areas have both private and public law schools. If the library is state-supported, it is required to be open to the general public. Most users of these libraries will be law students, attorneys, and paralegals.

Most undergraduate colleges and universities have legal collections as part of their general libraries. Your institution likely has a legal collection sufficient enough to support a paralegal program. Although it may not be as comprehensive as a law school library, it nevertheless will contain the most frequently used legal resources.

SIDEBAR

IS YOUR LIBRARY A FEDERAL DEPOSITORY LIBRARY?

Many libraries participate in the U.S. Government Printing Office's Depository Library Program (see Figure 2-1). This program was established by Congress to allow the public free access to publications of the federal government. About 1,400 libraries are designated as depository libraries by congressional appointment. These libraries receive government documents free of charge, on the condition that they make these materials available to the general public. The types of material available range from consumer information, such as gardening and nutrition tips, to formal laws and regulations. To locate the depository library in your area, contact your Congressperson's office or write to the Superintendent of Documents, 732 N. Capitol St., NW, Washington, D.C. 20401. The telephone number is (202) 512-1119.

FIGURE 2-1 Depository library seal

Court-affiliated and bar association libraries exist in most counties and cities. Once they were restricted to the use of attorneys and judges. Today, paralegals and other legal professionals are free to utilize them. The extensiveness of the library collection may in large part depend on the size of the jurisdiction or bar association.

State-run law libraries usually exist in the state capital. They are often set up to assist legislators and government officials in their work (see Figure 2-2). These libraries maintain and update all legal documentation relevant to the state.

Most government agencies and public interest associations have library collections, although usually they are restricted to employees within that particular organization. The focus of the collection will be in the agency's specialty. For instance, at the Environmental Protection Agency, the library will focus on environmental law matters.

Your first experience in a library may be at a private law firm. In large firms, a large computer-assisted library may exist. In smaller firms, the library may double as a conference room or reception area. Often solo practicing lawyers will pool their resources and share a library.

Besides these locations, law libraries can be found in correctional institutions (to assist inmates who represent themselves and others, sometimes called **jailhouse lawyers**) and private industry (to assist attorneys, known as **general counsel**, who are employed by businesses). See Figure 2-3. Finally, legal resources can also be found in public libraries.

Library Etiquette

Larger libraries will be administered by a professional law librarian. Most librarians today have either a law degree or a graduate degree in library science. This person is responsible for the upkeep and operation of the library and its staff. No one knows the library as well as the librarian. Thus, it is important to have a good rapport with the librarian and the library staff—they can be a great resource in a pinch! In fact, some libraries prefer that you ask questions rather than aimlessly wander around. Just the same, do not inundate the staff with questions that you could answer with a little effort.

Some larger libraries give tours of their facilities. It is likely that you will tour your local bar association or law school library during the course of your paralegal education. If offered, take advantage of this opportunity. Unfortunately, paralegal programs can rarely provide the depth of research materials that a full-service law library can.

LEGAL TERMS

jailhouse lawyer   An inmate who represents himself or herself or assists other inmates in legal matters.
general counsel   The chief attorney in the legal department of a business.

BACKGROUND/STRUCTURE/MISSION

THE MARYLAND STATE LAW LIBRARY,

established by the State Legislature in 1826 and now a part of the Judicial branch of State Government, is located on the first floor of the Courts of Appeal Building on Rowe Boulevard, adjacent to the Department of Natural Resources complex in Annapolis, Md. (see map) The legal authority for this information facility appears in §§ 13–501 to 13–504 of the Courts & Judicial Proceedings Article of the Annotated Code of Maryland.

The primary function of the State Law library, with an in-house collection approaching 300,000 volumes and easy electronic access to literally millions of informational resources outside the collection, is to support the research activities of the State's two appellate courts and court-related units of the Judiciary. In addition, a wide variety of information services are extended to the Executive and Legislative branches and the public.

The Library encourages use of its services and resources by all citizens. Of particular interest are the specialized informational materials encompassing the law, federal and state government publications, and state and local histories.

S E R V I C E S

The information specialist performs many functions which may be categorized as services extended to his/her community of users. Among the services provided by professionals at the library are:

☐ REFERENCE ASSISTANCE

Reference librarians provide several levels of informational service to clientele. In addition to providing directional assistance, staff will aid users (on site, by phone or letter) with suggestions for beginning and advanced research techniques using the various indexes and updating tools and automated guides that provide access to the collections. The library's, *Guidelines for Information Service to the Public*, qualifies the level of service and limits giving any legal advice on law-related inquiries. Specialty areas of reference assistance include:

■ Expertise in identifying Maryland statutory legislative history sources/steps in intent research

■ Instruction in the use of the collection, including new technologies (CD and online), used as access points to retrieve substantive information.

■ Specialized literature searches and compilation of bibliographies and pathfinders

☑ MATERIALS CIRCULATION / INTERLIBRARY LOAN

Direct borrowing of materials by the public is currently prohibited by statute, however appellate court and state agency personnel may borrow items not identified as reference resources.

Established interlibrary loan procedures do allow for the borrowing of some library materials by the public. An efficient, on-line networking system turns the library into an electronic gateway in which staff can provide timely retrieval of information not available in our own collection. On-line access to over 15 million book records through OCLC and millions of journal articles greatly enhances the breadth of research possibilities.

☑ PHOTOCOPYING / TELEFACSIMILE

Coin operated copying facilities are available for all library users at very reasonable rates. Debit cards for copying may be purchased. The large microforms collection can be accessed from three microfilm/fiche reader printers. A detailed state-

ment of policy on photocopy services/costs is available at the library.

The library's telefacsimile (fax) machine is available for use by the court and library in responding to requests for information.

☑ PUBLICATIONS / RESEARCH AIDS

In response to perceived information needs of the user, the library issues a variety of publications in the form of bibliographies, checklists, pathfinders, and recent acquisition lists. These materials are available for free distribution or sale. Please inquire.

☑ TOURS / EDUCATIONAL LECTURES

Library reference staff will conduct tours which include orientation to the various specialized law, local history and government information collections. Educational lectures on various aspects of conducting basic legal research are available to individuals as well as small school/university classes or civic organizations.

FIGURE 2-2   Maryland State Law Library services. (Courtesy of Maryland State Law Library as composed by Fishergate Press, Annapolis, MD.)

LOCATIONS OF LAW LIBRARIES

Law schools

Colleges and universities

Courts

Bar associations

State government

Government agencies

Public interest associations

Law firms

Correctional institutions

Private industry

Public libraries

FIGURE 2-3 Locations of law libraries

If you are unsure as to whether you may use a specific library, seek permission first. You may have to sign in with a security guard or show identification. Once in, be polite and tactful. Dress appropriately and obey all library rules. As a paralegal, you will be spending many working hours in the library. By starting your career off properly, you will ensure that your research experiences are successful ones.

A Research Plan: An Introduction

Suppose that, on your first day of work, you are presented with the following memorandum:

MEMO

TO: Paralegal
FROM: Attorney
DATE: Today
RE: Marriage Issue

The firm has represented Tom Ricardo for the past seven years in various business matters. He and his wife Gail have been happily married for one year. They were married before a deputy clerk at the local county courthouse. Recently, an article appeared in a newspaper indicating that the deputy clerk had no authority to perform marriages [see Figure 2-4]. He and his wife are in a panic, believing they were not married properly. Were they? See what you can find out. Look everywhere. I need an answer by tomorrow!

Many Howard County marriages may be off to false start

Howard Co. marriages may be off to false start

❝If we have to do it again, it should be on Howard County's bill.❞

— JIll Huston,
recently married

By Norris P. West
Evening Sun Staff

Last June, Mark A. Cochran, 29, of Columbia, married the former Shelby Armstrong. And now, because the Howard County Circuit Court employee who married them was not sworn in as a deputy clerk as required by law, the Cochrans' marriage could be invalid.

Mark Cochran, expressing some anger, said he would not take the vows again unless he is told his marriage is invalid.

"I only live a few minutes away and I don't mind going back and doing it again. But in my mind, I was married on that day," said Cochran, a member of the Army who has been stationed in the Baltimore area for the past year.

He said he recalled that the deputy clerk who performed the marriage ceremony recited the official words from memory and told them she had performed "hundreds" of weddings. He said he was disturbed that officials did not ensure that she was given authority to do her job.

"You make lifetime decisions

See WEDDINGS, A4, Col. 1

FIGURE 2-4 Newspaper article on marriage impediment. (Reprinted: Courtesy *The Baltimore Sun*. By: Norris P. West.)

Of course, at first you might be just as panicked as the Ricardos! However, once you have a plan to resolve their problem, your anxiety will subside. In this section we discuss how to develop and then apply such a plan. The plan is covered only briefly here, but we will revisit the subject in Chapter 9 after you have gained knowledge of the tools utilized in conducting legal research.

A proper plan involves applying the following three steps.

STEP ONE requires a full understanding of the legal problem and its ramifications. To start with, you might ask: Why is this matter so important? Could not the Ricardos just live together thinking they were married? Consider if the following were true:

- Mr. and Mrs. Ricardo are having marital problems. They are considering separation and divorce. If they are not legally married, how does this affect a divorce proceeding? How would property be divided? Could Mrs. Ricardo obtain **alimony** without being married?

- Mr. and Mrs. Ricardo have a minor child. If the Ricardos were never married, is the child legitimate? Could he, as a consequence, be denied various benefits such as Social Security?

As you can see, one person's legal problem might create unanticipated consequences for others.

Before you start working, it is important to find out exactly why you are conducting research. If you are unclear after examining the information given, go back and ask more questions. If you are unable to ask additional questions of your supervisor or the client, it will be up to you to get a handle on the problem, based on the facts available. This involves identifying the relevant facts and analyzing them. Early in your career, it will be more difficult for you to determine the "why." If you do not have a detailed understanding of the legal specialty—in this case, **family law**—it will be even more difficult.

Acquiring a basic understanding of the law is the focus of STEP TWO. It will be important for you to obtain an understanding of the law dealing with the formation of marriages. A general text on family law in your jurisdiction or a legal encyclopedia might be a good starting point. You might have to look up unfamiliar terms or concepts in a law dictionary. Usually you will only have to apply this step once, the first time you deal with a marriage issue. Afterward, you will be much more knowledgeable about the law of marriage.

STEP THREE deals with the actual techniques of legal research. Where do you go? What is the significance of what you locate? What do you do with the authority located? Once the legal remedy has been determined, your job will be to find the legal authority to support that legal remedy. Legal authority can be physically located in primary or secondary law sources.

LEGAL TERMS

alimony [†]   Ongoing court-ordered support payments by a divorced spouse, usually payments made by an ex-husband to his former wife.

family law [†]   Area of the law concerned with domestic relations.

Primary sources of law consist of decisions by courts, statutes passed by legislatures, administrative regulations enacted by agencies, and constitutions. Chapter 3 is devoted to a complete understanding of primary law. There are also various primary law finders, which can be used to assist in locating the law. These are discussed in Chapter 4.

Secondary sources of law are sources that discuss and explain the law. They can also assist in finding appropriate authority and understanding the law. Chapter 5 is devoted to understanding secondary law. Techniques that can be employed in using all types of resources are discussed in Chapter 9.

Recall that mandatory authority consists of rules that must be followed, as opposed to persuasive authority, which is only advisory. The strongest support for a legal remedy is found in mandatory authority. Only primary law can act as mandatory authority. The ultimate goal of your research, then, is to locate mandatory authority in primary law. The characteristics of mandatory and persuasive authority are discussed in Chapter 8.

Applying the Steps: A Typical Problem

The application of the three research steps to the following typical factual situation may seem confusing at first. It is done so that you can get a complete picture of legal research. Consider re-reading this section as you cover relevant sections of the book. This problem is revisited in Chapter 8.

STEP ONE requires an understanding of the problem. The Ricardos are happily married, but it is upsetting to them that they could have been living together and had a child without being married. If they are not married, they would like to be legally married as soon as possible. By carefully reading the memo, you can determine that the central question to research is whether the ceremony was legal. For purposes of the example, assume the Ricardos live and were married in Maryland.

STEP TWO requires a basic understanding of the law of marriage. This can be approached from a national or a state perspective. National secondary sources of law (that is, those discussing authority from all jurisdictions) might include:

1. *American Jurisprudence 2d* (a legal encyclopedia);
2. *Corpus Juris Secundum* (a legal encyclopedia);
3. *Domestic Relations* by Homer H. Clark, Jr. (a specialized source known as a hornbook).

In addition, there might be Maryland resources that could be helpful in understanding the law of marriage. One good source would be John F. Fader II and Richard J. Gilbert's *Maryland Family Law* (a hornbook). When you have a choice, state resources will be more relevant and to the point. However, any of these resources would give you a basic understanding of the law of marriage. In your research, you would want to focus on the requirements of a marriage ceremony.

In STEP THREE, you search for an answer. You must consider two questions. What is the legal problem? What is the legal remedy the client desires? The problem has been established: failure to comply with the requirements of marriage. Your job would be to locate the legal authority that supports the desired remedy. The Ricardos' legal remedy might be no more than reassurance that their marriage is valid. Your search would take you to primary law, primary law finders, and secondary law sources. Primary law finders, such as digests and American Law Reports, and secondary sources, such as encyclopedias and hornbooks, are the best starting points. A secondary source of law would give you an understanding of marriage requirements with references to primary law, whereas a primary law finder will point you directly to controlling primary law. Using primary law finders in this situation would lead you to a constitution, a statute, and a case opinion. A secondary source of law applicable here would be an opinion of a state attorney general.

Statutory law would be found in the Annotated Code of Maryland. Section 2-406 of the volume on family law states:

(a) *Authorized officials.*—A marriage ceremony may be performed in this State by:

* * *

...
(3) any deputy clerk designated by the county administrative judge of the circuit court for the county.

Constitutional law, as found in the Maryland Constitution, art. IV, § 26, provides that to perform the duties of deputy clerk, an individual must be appointed and sworn in by the chief clerk. Once his term expires he must be reappointed and sworn in; otherwise, he is no longer a deputy clerk but a court employee. Let us assume that in the Ricardos' situation, the facts occurred in just that way. The deputy clerk at the time of the ceremony was only an employee.

The court decision of *Knapp v. Knapp*, 149 Md. 263, 131 A. 329 (1925), a form of primary law known as **case law**, would also be considered. In *Knapp*, the court determined that marriages are to be upheld if the parties had a reasonable belief that the person officiating the ceremony was authorized to do so. This was the belief of the Ricardos.

All of these primary law sources—Annotated Code of Maryland, the Maryland Constitution, and *Knapp v. Knapp*—must also be given mandatory effect because they emanate from Maryland. They constitute the "law" and must be followed.

──────────────── **LEGAL TERMS** ────────────────

statutory law [†]   Law that is promulgated by statute, as opposed to law that is promulgated by the judiciary.

constitutional law [†]   The body of principles that apply in the interpretation, construction, and application of the Constitution to statutes and to other governmental action. Constitutional law deals with constitutional questions and determines the constitutionality of state and federal laws and of the manner in which government exercises its authority.

case law [†]   The law as laid down in the decisions of the courts in similar cases that have previously been decided.

However of the three, the *Knapp* case is the most crucial. In the American legal system, courts have the right to interpret other forms of primary law. They also have the right to create legal rules based on principles of fairness in the absence of primary law (called *common law,* which is addressed in Chapter 3).

A secondary law source that would be helpful is the Opinions of the Attorney General of Maryland. Part of an **attorney general**'s responsibility is to issue advisory opinions on legal questions. In an opinion dated September 25, 1990, he concluded that marriages performed under circumstances of those of the Ricardos are valid. In part he said:

> [I]t is our opinion that an employee of the clerk's office is not authorized by Maryland law to perform marriages unless, at the time of the marriage, that individual is a duly appointed and sworn deputy clerk who has been designated by the county administrative judge to perform marriages. Nevertheless, marriages performed by an employee of the clerk's office who reasonably appears to be a deputy clerk with authority to perform marriages are valid.

This opinion is only persuasive; however, read together with the *Knapp* decision, it further supports the position that the Ricardo marriage is valid.

The question as to validity of the Ricardo marriage is solved. The fact that there might have been an impediment in the ceremony does not affect the legitimacy of their marriage. In this simple situation, you were able to apply the three-step process to locate a solution.

THREE-STEP PROCESS

STEP ONE: Understanding the Problem
- Are the Ricardos legally married?
- If not, is their child legitimate?
- Do they have to remarry?

STEP TWO: Understanding the Law
- Use encyclopedias and hornbooks to get an understanding of marriage requirements

STEP THREE: Conducting Legal Research
- Constitutional law: mandatory authority
- Statutory law: mandatory authority
- Case law: mandatory authority
- Attorney general opinion: persuasive authority

LEGAL TERMS

attorney general † The chief law officer of the nation or of a state. The attorney general is responsible for representing the government in legal actions with which it is concerned, and for advising the chief executive and other administrative heads of the government on legal matters on which they desire an opinion.

Summary

- Everyday occurrences have legal significance.

- When a legal problem arises, a legal remedy must be found.

- Finding legal remedies is the essence of legal research.

- Legal remedies are found in the application of rules of law called legal authority, which can be mandatory or persuasive.

- Legal research is difficult and time-consuming. As a researcher you must be patient, persistent, creative, and ethical.

- While researching, you should not confuse quantity with quality.

- Legal research is generally done in a law library. Law libraries can be found in law schools, colleges and universities, courts and bar associations, public and private agencies, state government, and law offices.

- Larger libraries are staffed by librarians. It is always helpful to have good rapport with the librarian.

- If you are unsure whether you can use a library, seek permission first. It is important in using a library that you be polite and tactful, dress properly, and obey all rules.

- Effective legal research involves utilization of a three-step plan. Step one requires a full understanding of the legal problem and its ramifications; step two requires a basic understanding of the applicable law; step three involves the application of techniques of legal research.

Review Questions

1. What are the benefits of a creative approach to conducting research?

2. What would constitute unethical research?

3. List the various places where law libraries can be found.

4. What is the three-step plan for conducting legal research?

5. Define generally primary sources of law, secondary sources of law, and primary law finders.

Chapter Exercises

1. Find and visit the nearest bar association or law school library in your jurisdiction. Spend some time walking around and exploring. If possible, arrange a tour through the librarian.

2. Is your school library a federal depository library? If it is, talk to the government records librarian about the resources it contains. If your library is not a depository library, locate the nearest one.

3. While in a law library, ask the librarian to assist you in locating primary law and secondary resources on marriage in your jurisdiction.

4. Consider the following situation:

> During a class discussion in a state-supported community college, a male student makes a comment that appears to denigrate women. He also uses a racial epithet to describe the instructor. Other students want to take action against the student.

> Determine the legal problem that exists in this situation. What could be possible legal remedies? Can you determine any legal authority that might guarantee the rights of the offensive student or protect the offended students?

IIII

CHAPTER 3

PRIMARY SOURCES
OF LAW

CHAPTER OUTLINE

OVERVIEW

Recall that in Chapter 2 a father needed to apply a rule to obtain a result that he felt was necessary under the circumstances. A rule applied to settle a legal matter is referred to as *legal authority.* To constitute legal authority, the rule must emanate from the government. These rules are collectively referred to as *primary law.*

Historically, the sovereign had the ultimate power to decide what constituted the law. The command of the sovereign was to be followed without question, under pain of punishment. As a result, representative government evolved in most countries having monarchs, in response to potential abuses by sovereigns. With representative government, the monarch's ability to command was limited, and in some cases ended completely, by a legislature elected by the people.

The United States was founded on the principle of representative government. This was in large measure a response to the abuses to which Americans were subjected under the rule of the British king. In the United States there is, of course, no monarch; rather, the government, consisting of the executive, legislative, and judicial branches, is the sovereign. The members of these branches are ultimately controlled by the people through the ballot box. What these branches command is primary law.

Primary law is divided into four major categories. First and foremost is the document that created the government, whether state or federal: its *constitution.* A constitution does not produce laws the way other parts of government do. Instead, its terms and provisions are read and interpreted by the judicial branch to determine meaning and appropriate application. Should a change be desired in its terms, it is up to the legislative branch to initiate such a change. It is in a constitution that the other parts of government are created, defined, and given power to create laws.

Among other things, a constitution provides for a legislative body to act on the will of the people. This body passes laws, called *statutes,* reflecting the collective expectations of society. Statutes are located in publications called codes. These laws constitute a second form of primary law.

To effectuate the plans of the executive branch, legislative bodies on both the state and federal levels create agencies to implement the details of major legislation. To operate effectively, agencies must develop rules and regulations to carry out their mandates. These *administrative regulations* often affect the lives of citizens more than statutes.

Case law is primary law created by courts. Judges have the responsibility for interpreting constitutions and as a result must consider whether other laws violate constitutional language. In addition, legal problems are presented to judges, who decide these matters in written case opinions. These case opinions are located in reporters.

These are the major areas of primary law. In addition, there are several other forms that can be consulted. *Rules of court* are developed by courts to govern judicial procedure. *Executive orders* are issued by the president or other chief executives. Finally, *treaties* are written agreements entered into between the United States and other nations. All of these types of law are addressed in this chapter.

PARALEGAL PRACTICE SITUATION

You have recently been hired as a paralegal in a newly formed small general-practice law firm. The emphasis of the firm's work is mostly state practice. The office consists of two attorneys, a secretary, and you. Your employers were previously with a large regional firm. After several years, they decided to strike out on their own. When they departed, they were not able to take with them books and other library materials.

During their years of practice, they did not purchase many books personally, but instead relied on the employing firm's resources.

You have been assigned the immediate task of developing a list of suggested primary law sources to form the basis of a new library collection. Consider what texts you feel would be appropriate to purchase. Your list and justification for each purchase should be submitted to the attorneys for final consideration.

Primary Law Defined

To find and read the law, you must locate and understand sources of primary law. These sources can be viewed as the command of the sovereign. Because there is no king or queen in the United States, the *sovereign* is the various branches of state and federal governments. When an appendage of the government "speaks," law is created. Governments speak chiefly through constitutions, statutes, administrative regulations, and case opinions. The basic function of primary law is to guide government officials, administrators, legislators, and judges in making legal decisions. Primary sources of law can be divided into four major categories.

The Constitution of the United States and the constitutions of each state make up the first category of primary law. A **constitution** sets the basic structure of government. It describes governmental powers and limits through its establishment of executive, legislative, and judicial branches. Many local municipalities, such as towns, cities, and counties, are governed by a form of a constitution called a **charter**.

Each state legislature and Congress has as its chief responsibility the creation of laws. Legislatures enact laws in direct response to needs of their constituencies. Once a proposed law, known as a **bill**, goes through the complete lawmaking process, it is called a **statute**. In addition to state and federal legislatures, other local governmental bodies, such as city, town, and county councils, periodically enact laws called **ordinances**.

LEGAL TERMS
---

constitution [†]   1. The system of fundamental principles by which a nation, state, or corporation is governed. A nation's constitution may be written or unwritten. A nation's laws must conform to its constitution. A law that violates a nation's constitution is unconstitutional and therefore unenforceable. 2. The document setting forth the fundamental principles of governance.

charter [†]   The basic law of a city or town.

bill [†]   A proposed law, presented to the legislature for enactment; i.e., a legislative bill.

statute [†]   A law enacted by a legislature; an act.

ordinance [†]   A law of a municipal corporation; a local law enacted by a city council, town council, board of supervisors, or the like.

Every federal and state government agency has the power and responsibility to create laws to govern their activities. These laws are referred to as **administrative regulations**.

In the United States, laws are also developed by judges considering legal problems brought before them. The written decisions of judges considering legal problems are referred to as **case law**. Case law, also called *case opinions* or *decisions,* consists of decisions of courts on the federal and state levels.

In addition, **rules of court, treaties,** and **executive orders** are considered primary law. Rules of court are developed by courts to govern judicial procedures. Treaties are agreements entered into between the United States and other countries. The president negotiates treaties, but the U.S. Senate must ratify them. A chief executive, such as the president or a governor, has the right to issue executive orders. These are proclamations of powers left to his or her discretion by a constitution or statute.

Common Law and Precedent

To fully appreciate the role of case law, you must understand the concept of **common law**. The United States is considered a common law country. This is a consequence of its acceptance, at the time of independence, of the process of developing laws and legal principles that existed in Great Britain. Other common law countries include Canada, Australia, India, and New Zealand.

As a common law country, the laws made and fashioned by judges are of paramount importance. This is because, in the absence of other forms of primary law that might control, court-fashioned legal rules are created to settle legal matters. The source of these rules are traditions and customs based on fairness to the "common" person.

These judge-made laws are subsequently followed by other judges when dealing with factually similar cases. This is called following **precedent**. To employ

--- LEGAL TERMS ---

administrative regulation   A law enacted by an agency, sometimes referred to as a *rule.*

case law [†]   The law as laid down in the decisions of the courts in similar cases that have previously been decided.

rules of court [†]   Rules promulgated by the court, governing procedure or practice before it.

treaties [†]   A formal written agreement between two or more nations with respect to matters of common concern. The Constitution requires ratification, by a two-thirds vote of the Senate, of all treaties between the United States and foreign countries.

executive order [†]   An order issued by the chief executive officer of government, whether national, state, or local.

common law [†]   1. Law found in the decisions of the courts rather than in statutes; judge-made law. 2. English law adopted by the early American colonists, which is part of the United States' judicial heritage and forms the basis of much of its law today.

precedent [†]   Prior decisions of the same court, or a higher court, which a judge must follow in deciding a subsequent case presenting similar facts and the same legal problem, even though different parties are involved and many years have elapsed.

precedent means to invoke the doctrine of **stare decisis**, which in Latin means "standing by the decision." The application of common law principles through stare decisis promotes the even-handed application of justice, because people in similar situations are treated similarly. This is the cornerstone of the administration of justice.

BRANCHES OF GOVERNMENT AND PRIMARY LAW

Form of Primary Law	Branch of Government
Constitutions	All branches consider, but judiciary interprets
Statutes	Legislatures
Administrative regulations	Agencies (created by the executive and legislative branches)
Case law	Judiciary

Constitutional Law

The fundamental law of a nation or state is called its *constitution.* As previously indicated, its purpose is to describe the branches of government, as well as to define governmental powers and limitations. Most constitutions, in addition, guarantee personal liberties and freedoms. In the United States, every state and the federal government has a constitution. Generally, constitutions are written in far less detail than other forms of primary law, such as statutes, regulations, or cases. As a result, the interpretation of their provisions is often the subject of judicial and political debate. The study of constitutions is referred to as *constitutional law.*

Federal Constitution

The **United States Constitution** was written in the summer of 1787 and ratified when ultimately approved by New Hampshire on June 21, 1788. It went into effect, replacing the **Articles of Confederation**, on March 4, 1789. In viewing its contents, found in Appendix A, note that it is divided into a preamble

---

LEGAL TERMS

stare decisis † [Latin for] "standing by the decision." Stare decisis is the doctrine that judicial decisions stand as precedents for cases arising in the future. It is a fundamental policy of our law that, except in unusual circumstances, a court's determination on a point

(which you might have memorized in elementary school) and seven articles. Article I deals with the legislative branch (Congress); Article II covers the executive branch (Presidency); Article III concerns the judiciary (federal courts); Article IV covers the states; Article V deals with the amendment process; Article VI deals with debts, constitutional authority, and oaths; and Article VII deals with the ratification process. The U.S. Constitution has been amended twenty-seven times; the last time was in May 1992 with the passage of Amendment 27 (which prohibits congressional pay raises from taking effect until after an election).

The first ten amendments to the U.S. Constitution are referred to as the **Bill of Rights**. Rights such as freedom of speech, freedom of religion, freedom from illegal search and seizure, and the protection against self-incrimination are guaranteed in the Bill of Rights.

The U.S. Constitution is by far the easiest source of primary law to locate. It can be found in dictionaries, encyclopedias, and almanacs. Most likely you have several copies in your home already and do not realize it. It is also located in publications containing federal and state statutes, known as *codes*.

State Constitutions and Local Charters

All state constitutions are patterned after the U.S. Constitution. Although there has been only one federal Constitution for more than 200 years, many states have had several constitutions in the course of their history. Maryland, for instance, has had four; the first was written in 1776, the second in 1851, the third in 1864, and the current one in 1867. Each new constitution was written in response to a change in public sentiment.

Some state constitutions afford more protections to their citizens than the U.S. Constitution. The **Equal Rights Amendment**, for example, was never **ratified** by the states and thus is not included in the U.S. Constitution. This

─────────────────── **LEGAL TERMS** ───────────────────

of law will be followed by courts of the same or lower rank in later cases presenting the same legal issue, even though different parties are involved and many years have elapsed.

Constitution of the United States † The fundamental document of American government, as adopted by the people of the United States through their representatives in the Constitutional Convention of 1787, as ratified by the states, together with the amendments to that Constitution.

Articles of Confederation † The document that governed the confederation of the original 13 states before the Constitution was adopted. It formed a mere association of states, not the union of states into a nation, which the Constitution created.

Bill of Rights † The first 10 amendments to the United States Constitution. The Bill of Rights is the portion of the Constitution that sets forth the rights which are the fundamental principles of the United States and the foundation of American citizenship.

Equal Rights Amendment † A proposed constitutional amendment, passed by Congress in 1972, which failed for lack of ratification by three-fourths of the states. The proposed amendment, generally referred to as the ERA, provided that "equality of rights under the law shall not be abridged by the United States or any state on account of sex."

ratify † To give approval; to confirm.

amendment has, however, been enacted by a number of state governments and appears in their state constitutions. Illinois is one such state.

IIII

Equal Rights Amendment (Illinois)
Art. 1   **CONSTITUTION OF 1970**

§ 18. No Discrimination on the Basis of Sex
The equal protection of the laws shall not be denied or abridged on account of sex by the State or its units of local government and school districts.

Local units of government, such as cities, towns, and counties, have documents similar to constitutions called *charters*. Permission to write a charter is given by the state legislature and is called **home rule**.

Role of Judicial Review

Under the doctrine of **judicial review**, all forms of primary law (in particular statutes and administrative regulations) are subject to review and interpretation by the courts. A constitution (whether of the United States or a state) is said to be the ultimate law of the land. As such, judges may find laws contrary to constitutional provisions and void them. This is referred to as the doctrine of **unconstitutionality**.

The process of judicial review may also result in constitutional provisions being given meanings that might not be apparent at first glance. For example, the right of privacy guarantees freedom of choice in matters of sexual reproduction. The words "right of privacy" are not located in the text of the U.S. Constitution. However, through interpretations of the First, Third, Fourth, Fifth, and Ninth Amendments, the U.S. Supreme Court, in the seminal case of *Griswold v. Connecticut*, 381 U.S. 479, 85 S. Ct. 1678, 14 L. Ed. 2d 510 (1965), determined that such a protection could be found by implication. As a result of judicial review, courts often create new legal principles through their interpretation of constitutional provisions.

LEGAL TERMS
---

home rule [†] The right of a city, town, or county to self-government with respect to purely local matters. A state's constitution may or may not confer such a right upon its cities and towns.

judicial review The power of courts to review decisions of another department or level of government.

unconstitutional [†] 1. In conflict with the Constitution of the United States. 2. In conflict with a constitution. 3. Not grounded in or based upon the Constitution or a constitution.

STEPS IN CONSTITUTIONAL RESEARCH

1. Determine if case is a state or federal matter.

2. If state matter, locate state constitution.

3. If federal matter, locate U.S. Constitution.

4. Locate and read appropriate constitutional provision.

5. If annotated version, review case annotations.

Constitutional Research

As a paralegal, you will rarely spend time researching constitutions. Exceptions might be if you are employed by an organization such as the American Civil Liberties Union (ACLU), whose purpose is to defend the protections granted under the Bill of Rights, or by a criminal law practice where the constitutional rights of defendants are at issue.

In constitutional research, more emphasis is placed on reading case law interpreting constitutional provisions than on the document itself. The starting point in constitutional research is determining whether the U.S. Constitution (for a federal issue) or a state constitution (for a state issue) is applicable. Reviewing the document itself is the next step. If you already have some knowledge in a constitutional area or topic, review the text of the constitution briefly. Constitutions often have indexes that help speed the review. Some constitutions are **annotated**. In these versions, case summaries (called *annotations*) appear after a provision, interpreting that provision. If you are reviewing an annotated version, read through the annotations.

Statutory Law

The primary responsibility of Congress is to pass federal laws, known as statutes. Congress consists of two houses, the Senate and the House of Representatives. On the state level, legislatures are set up similarly and perform the same function. With the exception of Nebraska, all states have bicameral legislatures consisting of a senate and an assembly or house. Federal and state legislatures meet for periods called **sessions**.

──────────── **LEGAL TERMS** ────────────

annotated [†]   Containing explanatory comments.

session [†]   1. As opposed to a "term," the time when a court, legislature, or other body is actually meeting or sitting for the purpose of conducting its business. A court that is sitting, or a legislature that is meeting, is said to be in session. 2. Synonymous with "term," i.e., the entire period during a particular year in which a court sits to conduct its business.

How a Bill Becomes a Law

A bill must pass both houses of the legislature before it is presented to the chief executive for signature. This is known as the **enactment** process. This process includes referral of the bill to a committee (or subcommittee) for consideration and hearings, issuance of a committee report on the bill, floor debate, and voting. This process must be completed in both chambers. Differences between the versions put forth by each house must be resolved by a **conference committee** consisting of members from both chambers. Only a small percentage of all proposed legislation ever becomes statutory law. Most proposals are defeated during committee review. Passage by both houses, however, does not guarantee that the bill will become law.

The final step consists of signature by either the governor or the president, or legislative override. Bills that pass both houses are sent to the chief executive for approval (signature), disapproval (**veto**), or nonaction (**pocket veto**). Should there be a veto, the legislature may be able to **override** by a vote of both bodies (generally two-thirds of each house). If an override is achieved, the bill becomes law. At that point, it is designated as either a public law or a private law and is assigned a number reflecting the order in which it was passed. Bills that affect the general welfare are known as **public laws**. Those which deal with specific constituent matters are known as **private laws**. Only a small percentage of bills are private laws. Only public laws become part of a statutory code.

A bill that becomes law is referred to first as a **slip law**, because of the form of its first appearance, and then as a **session law**. The law is first issued on a

---

LEGAL TERMS

enactment [†]   1. A statute. 2. The process by which a legislative bill becomes law.

conference committee [†]   A meeting of representatives of both houses of a legislature to resolve differences in the versions of the same bill passed by each, by working out a compromise acceptable to both bodies.

veto [†]   The refusal of the executive officer of government to approve a bill passed by the legislature. A veto by the executive nullifies the bill unless the legislature is able to override the veto by the constitutionally required number of votes. In the case of a presidential veto, the requirement is two-thirds of the members of both houses of Congress.

pocket veto [†]   The veto of a congressional bill by the president by retaining it until Congress is no longer in session, neither signing nor vetoing it. The effect of such inaction is to nullify the legislation without affirmatively vetoing it. The pocket veto is also available to governors under some state constitutions.

override [†]   To exercise one's authority or will so as to nullify the action of another or others.

public law [†]   1. Body of law dealing with the relationship between the people and their government, the relationship between agencies and branches of government, and the relationship between governments themselves. 2. A statute dealing with matters that concern the community as a whole.

private law [†]   1. The rules of conduct that govern activities occurring among or between persons, as opposed to the rules of conduct governing the relationship between persons and their government. 2. A private statute.

slip law   A statute issued in single sheet form and published shortly after it has been issued by the legislature.

session laws [†]   The collected statutes enacted during a session of a legislature.

FORMS OF A LEGISLATIVE LAW

Bill	Before enactment
Slip law	After passage
Session law	After compilation of slip laws in *Statutes at Large* or state source
Statute	Compiled in federal code (U.S. Code, USCA, USCS) or state code

single sheet (a "slip" of paper) or as a pamphlet. Federal session laws are afterwards collected chronologically in ***Statutes at Large***, published by the U.S. Government Printing Office. *Statutes at Large* also includes presidential executive orders, proposed constitutional amendments, and an index to the session. Both private and public laws are found here. (See Figure 3-1.) Similar publications exist on the state level. For instance, the publication *Acts of Alabama* is a state equivalent of *Statutes at Large*. *Statutes at Large* is not, however, an effective research source, because you must know the year of the enactment to use its index. Thereafter, public session laws are compiled in topically divided codes.

Background information about federal law can be found in *United States Code Congressional and Administrative News* (USCCAN) (see Figure 3-2). A West publication, USCCAN is published to mirror volumes of the *Statutes at Large*. It provides legislative committee reports, presidential proclamations, executive orders, and other materials that focus on **legislative history**. It first appears as a monthly advance sheet and is then put in permanent bound volumes at the end of a session. Legislative history as a method of determining statutory intent is discussed in Chapter 8.

Anatomy of a Statute

To better understand a statute, it is helpful to look at its component parts. The statute considered is 39 U.S.C.A. § 3003, a section of the *U.S. Code Annotated* dealing with mail that is sent to a fictitious name or address (see Figure 3-3).

───────────────────────── **LEGAL TERMS** ─────────────────────────

Statutes at Large [†]   An official publication of the federal government, issued after each session of Congress, which includes all statutes enacted by the Congress and all congressional resolutions and treaties, as well as presidential proclamations and proposed or ratified amendments to the Constitution.

legislative history [†]   Recorded events that provide a basis for determining the legislative intent underlying a statute enacted by a legislature. The records of legislative committee hearings and of debates on the floor of the legislature are among the sources for legislative history.

PUBLIC LAW 95–118—OCT. 3, 1977　　　　91 STAT. 1067

Public Law 95–118
95th Congress

An Act

To provide for increased participation by the United States in the International Bank for Reconstruction and Development, the International Development Association, the International Finance Corporation, the Asian Development Bank and the Asian Development Fund, and for other purposes.

Oct. 3, 1977
[H.R. 5262]

Be it enacted by the Senate and House of Representatives of the United States of America in Congress assembled,

International financial institutions. U.S. participation, increase.

TITLE I—PURPOSE AND POLICY; DECLARATION OF CONGRESSIONAL INTENT IN RESPECT TO CONTINUED PARTICIPATION OF THE UNITED STATES GOVERNMENT IN INTERNATIONAL FINANCIAL INSTITUTIONS FOSTERING ECONOMIC DEVELOPMENT IN LESS DEVELOPED COUNTRIES

SEC. 101. (a) It is the sense of the Congress that—

22 USC 262c.

(1) for humanitarian, economic, and political reasons, it is in the national interest of the United States to assist in fostering economic development in the less developed countries of this world;

(2) the development-oriented international financial institutions have proved themselves capable of playing a significant role in assisting economic development by providing to less developed countries access to capital and technical assistance and soliciting from them maximum self-help and mutual cooperation;

(3) this has been achieved with minimal risk of financial loss to contributing countries;

(4) such institutions have proved to be an effective mechanism for sharing the burden among developed countries of stimulating economic development in the less developed world; and

(5) although continued United States participation in the international financial institutions is an important part of efforts by the United States to assist less developed countries, more of this burden should be shared by other developed countries. As a step in that direction, in future negotiations, the United States should work toward aggregate contributions to future replenishments to international financial institutions covered by this Act not to exceed 25 per centum.

(b) The Congress recognizes that economic development is a long-term process needing funding commitments to international financial institutions. It also notes that the availability of funds for the United States contribution to international financial institutions is subject to the appropriations process.

TITLE II—INTERNATIONAL BANK FOR RECONSTRUCTION AND DEVELOPMENT

SEC. 201. The Bretton Woods Agreements Act (22 U.S.C. 286 et seq.) is further amended by adding at the end thereof the following new section:

Capital stock increase, authorization.

FIGURE 3-1 Sample page from *Statutes at Large*

LEGISLATIVE HISTORY
P.L. 95–118

INTERNATIONAL BANK FOR RECONSTRUCTION AND DEVELOPMENT

P.L. 95–118, see page 91 Stat. 1067

House Report (Banking, Finance and Urban Affairs Committee) No. 95–154, Mar. 31, 1977 [To accompany H.R. 5262]

Senate Report (Foreign Relations Committee) No. 95–159, May 13, 1977 [To accompany H.R. 5262]

House Conference Report No. 95–544, July 28, 1977 [To accompany H.R. 5262]

Senate Conference Report No. 95–363, July 26, 1977 [To accompany H.R. 5262]

Cong. Record Vol. 123 (1977)

DATES OF CONSIDERATION AND PASSAGE

House April 6, September 16, 1977

Senate June 14, July 27, September 21, 1977

The Senate Report and the House Conference Report are set out.

SENATE REPORT NO. 95–159

[page 1]

The Committee on Foreign Relations, to which was referred the bill (H.R. 5262) to provide for increased participation by the United States in the International Bank for Reconstruction and Development, the International Development Association, the International Finance Corporation, the Asian Development Bank and the Asian Development Fund and for other purposes, having considered the same, reports favorably thereon with an amendment and an amendment to the title and recommends that the bill as amended do pass.

[page 5]

PURPOSE OF THE BILL

The purpose of this bill is to support the economic development of the less developed world by maintaining a flow of capital to these countries through the multilateral financial lending institutions. The bill achieves this purpose by authorizing additional appropriations for six development lending institutions in which the United States has participated for a number of years: the International Bank for Reconstruction and Development (IBRD), the International Finance Corporation (IFC), the International Development Association (IDA), the Asian Development Bank (ADB), the Asian Development Fund (ADF), and the African Development Fund (AFDF). As a group these institutions are referred to as international financial institutions (IFIs).

2670

FIGURE 3-2 Sample page from *U.S. Code Congressional and Administrative News.* (Reprinted with the permission of West Publishing Company.)

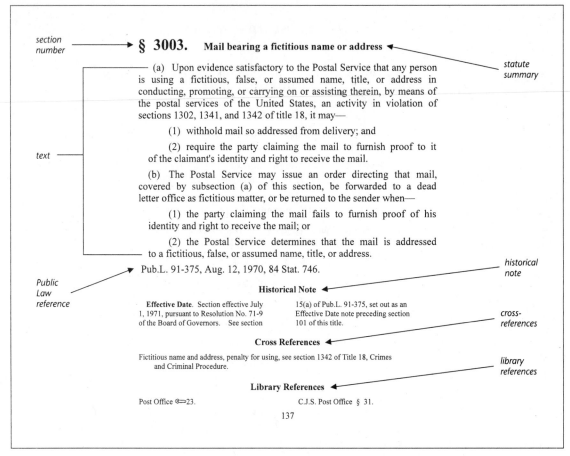

section number

§ **3003.** **Mail bearing a fictitious name or address**

statute summary

(a) Upon evidence satisfactory to the Postal Service that any person is using a fictitious, false, or assumed name, title, or address in conducting, promoting, or carrying on or assisting therein, by means of the postal services of the United States, an activity in violation of sections 1302, 1341, and 1342 of title 18, it may—

(1) withhold mail so addressed from delivery; and

(2) require the party claiming the mail to furnish proof to it of the claimant's identity and right to receive the mail.

text

(b) The Postal Service may issue an order directing that mail, covered by subsection (a) of this section, be forwarded to a dead letter office as fictitious matter, or be returned to the sender when—

(1) the party claiming the mail fails to furnish proof of his identity and right to receive the mail; or

(2) the Postal Service determines that the mail is addressed to a fictitious, false, or assumed name, title, or address.

Pub.L. 91-375, Aug. 12, 1970, 84 Stat. 746.

historical note

Public Law reference

Historical Note

Effective Date. Section effective July 1, 1971, pursuant to Resolution No. 71-9 of the Board of Governors. See section

15(a) of Pub.L. 91-375, set out as an Effective Date note preceding section 101 of this title.

cross-references

Cross References

Fictitious name and address, penalty for using, see section 1342 of Title 18, Crimes and Criminal Procedure.

library references

Library References

Post Office ⟜23.

C.J.S. Post Office § 31.

137

FIGURE 3-3 39 U.S.C.A. § 3003. (Reprinted with the permission of West Publishing Company.)

Statute Summary and Section Number The section number of the statute, 3003, and its summary, "Mail bearing a fictitious name or address," are considered first. If the statute's summary is detailed, you will have a basic overview of its coverage. However, summaries often are general, uninformative, or poorly designed. Never let the summary limit your understanding of a statute.

Text The body of the law follows. This is the text of the statute. Most laws are subdivided alphabetically and then numerically, as in the sample in Figure 3-3. An analysis of this statute is the focus of Chapter 8.

Public Law Reference "Pub.L. 91-375, Aug. 12, 1970, 84 Stat. 746" appears at the end of the statute. This tells you where the original version of the law can be found in *Statutes at Large* and the date of its enactment. Pub. L. 91-375 is a chronological number given to the law by Congress; in this case, it was the

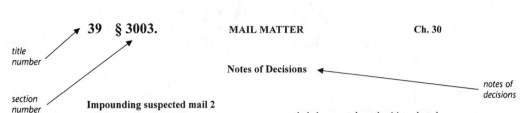

39 § 3003.   MAIL MATTER   Ch. 30

title number

Notes of Decisions

notes of decisions

section number

Impounding suspected mail 2
Rules and regulations 1

1. Rules and regulations

The Postmaster General may adopt measures and issue instructions to prevent the Post Office Department [now United States Postal Service] from being made a means for the accomplishment of an unlawful purpose by fraud on the public. 1868, 12 Op.Atty.Gen. 399.

The Post Office Department [now United States Postal Service] has authority to make a regulation which will prevent the Department from being prostituted to purposes of fraud, and order nondelivery of letters addressed to persons under names which are known to have been assumed as part of a system to defraud the public, but the fraudulent intent ought to be very clear before order is enforced. 1860, 9 Op.Atty.Gen. 454.

2. Impounding suspected mail

Where individual, in administrative hearing, attempted to identify himself with company, whose mail was being im-

pounded by postal authorities, but he conceded that while he nominally owned the company, its business was controlled by third party, the Postmaster General was justified in concluding that company had not been satisfactorily identified, and Postmaster General was justified in continuing to have the company's mail impounded pending termination of administrative hearing to determine whether mails were being used unlawfully by a person using a fictitious name. Barel v. Fiske, D.C.N.Y.1954, 136 F.Supp. 751.

The Postmaster General had authority to impound suspected mail matter pending decision of question whether mails were being used unlawfully. Id.

Where Post Office Department [now United States Postal Service] claimed to have probable cause to believe that dealer in pictures and publications was conducting an unlawful business through the mails, Postmaster General could make an order impounding dealer's mail prior to a determination that dealer was guilty of a violation of law. Stanard v. Olesen, D.C. Cal.1954, 121 F.Supp. 607.

FIGURE 3-3   *(continued)*

375th law passed by the 91st Congress. "84 Stat. 746" is the reference assigned by *Statutes at Large*.

Historical Note   The historical note information is helpful in determining legislative history. In this example, the date when the provision was approved by the Board of Governors of the U.S. Postal Service is provided.

Cross References   Cross-references list other statutes that should be read in conjunction with this statute. 18 U.S.C.A. § 1342 discusses the penalties for using a fictitious name or address. To fully understand § 3003, read all the cross references as well.

Library References   Library references indicate secondary sources of law that discuss or refer to the subject statute. In this statute, a reference is made to West's Topic and Key Number System and a section of *Corpus Juris Secundum* (CJS), a legal encyclopedia. Referring to either might be helpful in interpreting the statute.

Notes of Decisions   In notes of decisions, case annotations are indicated. These are summaries of decisions of courts that have interpreted the code provision. Occasionally, summaries of attorney general opinions might be included, as they are in this illustration.

Typically, the notes are divided by topical categories—in this example, "Impounding suspected mail" and "Rules and regulations." The longer and more complex the statute, the more likely it is that annotations will be divided by subject matter. Statutory law can never be fully understood until the annotations have been reviewed. Whenever possible, it is best to read the cases themselves in their entirety.

Pocket Parts   Finally, make sure to check the pocket part of the code to determine if there are any recent statutory changes or new annotations. Checking the pocket part for this volume does not reveal any new information.

Federal Codes

On the federal level, the official code is the **United States Code** (see Figure 3-4). It is divided into fifty titles that correlate to different functions of the federal government (see Figure 3-5). Besides the statutes themselves, the U.S. Code often includes amendment notes and cross-references. The best method of locating a statute in the U.S. Code is by using its general index, which is located in several volumes. Each section of the U.S. Code includes a reference to the law's source in the *Statutes at Large*. Additionally, the U.S. Code contains tables converting code references to public law and *Statutes at Large* numbers.

Besides the *U.S. Code,* both the West Publishing Company and Lawyers Cooperative Publishing (LCP) produce unofficial annotated versions of the U.S. Code. West's is called *U.S. Code Annotated* and is referred to as USCA (see Figure 3-6(a)). LCP's is called *U.S. Code Service* and is referred to as USCS (see Figure 3-6(b)). Each is a multivolume set using the same reference numbering system as the U.S. Code. As annotated codes, each contains case summaries of judicial decisions interpreting each statute. In addition, research references are included. Both also have indexes that make them easy to access.

West's USCA follows the same format as the U.S. Code, though it is more widely used than the U.S. Code. This is in large part because it contains features that are not in the original code. These include library references, references to

---
LEGAL TERMS

United States Code [†]   The official codification of the statutes enacted by Congress.

Page 27   TITLE 22—FOREIGN RELATIONS AND INTERCOURSE   Page 26

§ 261. Policy as to settlement of disputes and disarmament

It is declared to be the policy of the United States to adjust and settle its international disputes through mediation or arbitration, to the end that war may be honorably avoided. It looks with apprehension and disfavor upon a general increase of armament throughout the world, but it realizes that no single nation can disarm, and that without a common agreement upon the subject every considerable power must maintain a relative standing in military strength.

(Aug. 29, 1916, ch. 417, 39 Stat. 618.)

SHORT TITLE OF 1977 AMENDMENT

Section 1 of Pub. L. 95-118, as added by Pub. L. 97-35, title XIII, § 1361(a), Aug. 13, 1981, 95 Stat. 745, provided that: "This Act [enacting sections 262c, 262d, 262e to 262g-3, 282i, 284n, 285s, 285t, 286e-1f, and 290-10 of this title, repealing sections 283y, 284m, and 290g-9 of this title, and enacting provisions set out as notes under 262c and 282i of this title] may be cited as the 'International Financial Institutions Act'."

FIGURE 3-4 Sample page from United States Code

WESTLAW (a form of computer-assisted legal research, discussed in Chapter 6), references to federal administrative law, and annotations.

Lawyers Cooperative's USCS also follows the same format as the U.S. Code. Its textual language, though, follows the form as published in the *Statutes at Large.* This differs from *U.S. Code Annotated,* which follows the exact language in the U.S. Code. This is important because, when there is a conflict between the language of the U.S. Code and the *Statutes at Large,* the latter controls. As an LCP publication, *U.S. Code Service* provides research references to other LCP publications, such as American Law Reports (ALR), and references to federal administrative regulations.

State and Local Codes

State codes are also considered either *official* or *unofficial.* A code published by or under government authority is considered official. Many states have given permission to private publishing companies to produce their codes, sometimes with government authority as official codes, and sometimes without as unofficial codes (see Figure 3-7). Most state codes are annotated. Besides

TITLES OF UNITED STATES CODE

*1. General Provisions.

2. The Congress.

*3. The President.

*4. Flag and Seal, Seat of Government, and the States.

*5. Government Organization and Employees; and Appendix.

†6. [Surety Bonds.]

7. Agriculture.

8. Aliens and Nationality.

*9. Arbitration.

*10. Armed Forces; and Appendix.

*11. Bankruptcy; and Appendix.

12. Banks and Banking.

*13. Census.

*14. Coast Guard.

15. Commerce and Trade.

16. Conservation.

*17. Copyrights.

*18. Crimes and Criminal Procedure; and Appendix.

19. Customs Duties.

20. Education.

21. Food and Drugs.

22. Foreign Relations and Intercourse.

*23. Highways.

24. Hospitals and Asylums.

25. Indians.

26. Internal Revenue Code.

27. Intoxicating Liquors.

*28. Judiciary and Judicial Procedure; and Appendix.

29. Labor.

30. Mineral Lands and Mining.

*31. Money and Finance.

*32. National Guard.

33. Navigation and Navigable Waters.

‡34. [Navy.]

*35. Patents.

36. Patriotic Societies and Observances.

*37. Pay and Allowances of the Uniformed Services.

*38. Veterans' Benefits.

*39. Postal Service.

40. Public Buildings, Property, and Works.

41. Public Contracts.

42. The Public Health and Welfare.

43. Public Lands.

*44. Public Printing and Documents.

45. Railroads.

*46. Shipping; and Appendix.

47. Telegraphs, Telephones, and Radiotelegraphs.

48. Territories and Insular Possessions.

*49. Transportation; and Appendix.

50. War and National Defense; and Appendix.

---

*This title has been enacted as law. However, any Appendix to this title has not been enacted as law.
†This title was enacted as law and has been repealed by the enactment of Title 31.
‡This title has been eliminated by the enactment of Title 10.

FIGURE 3-5 Titles of the United States Code

§ 261. Policy as to settlement of disputes and disarmament

It is declared to be the policy of the United States to adjust and settle its international disputes through mediation or arbitration, to the end that war may be honorably avoided. It looks with apprehension and disfavor upon a general increase of armament throughout the world, but it realizes that no single nation can disarm, and that without a common agreement upon the subject every considerable power must maintain a relative standing in military strength.

(Aug. 29, 1916, c. 417, 39 Stat. 618.)

HISTORICAL AND STATUTORY NOTES

Short Title
1977 Act. Section 1 of Pub.L. 95–118, as added by Pub.L. 97–35, Title XIII, § 1361(a), Aug. 13, 1981, 95 Stat. 745, provided that: "This Act [enacting sections 262c, 262d, 262e to 262g–3, 262m to 262p–5, 282i, 284n, 285s, 285t, 286e–1f, and 290g–10 of this title, repealing sections 283y, 284m, and 290g–9 of this title, and enacting provisions set out as notes under 262c and 282i of this title] may be cited as the 'International Financial Institutions Act'."

LIBRARY REFERENCES

American Digest System
   Arbitration of international disputes, see International Law ☞13.
Encyclopedias
   Arbitration of international disputes, see C.J.S. International Law § 61.

WESTLAW ELECTRONIC RESEARCH

International law cases: 221k [add key number].
See, also, WESTLAW guide following the Explanation pages of this volume.

FIGURE 3-6(a)   Sample page from *U.S. Code Annotated.* (USCA reprinted with the permission of West Publishing Company.)

case annotations, these codes also include many of the same editorial enhancements as USCA and USCS.

Finally, ordinances passed on the local level are also found in codes. These codes, for the most part, are not annotated. Sometimes they are compiled in looseleaf binders.

How to Use a Code

Because the sources of the federal code are divided into fifty titles, the most obvious method of using each is by locating the correct title volume which houses the particular statute you are interested in. Unfortunately, this method presumes that you are thoroughly familiar with the coverage of the various

§ 261.   Policy as to settlement of disputes and disarmament

It is hereby declared to be the policy of the United States to adjust and settle its international disputes through mediation or arbitration, to the end that war may be honorably avoided. It looks with apprehension and disfavor upon a general increase of armament throughout the world, but it realizes that no single nation can disarm, and that without a common agreement upon the subject every considerable power must maintain a relative standing in military strength.

(Aug. 29, 1916, ch 417, 39 Stat. 618.)

RESEARCH GUIDE

Am Jur:

45 Am Jur 2d, International Law § 11.

Law Review Articles:

Assistance Rendered by the United States in Proceedings Before International Tribunals. 62 Colum L Rev 1264.

Procedural Status of the Individual Before Supernational Judicial Tribunals. 41 Det LJ 284.

American Lawyer and the International Court of Justice. 3 Santa Clara Law 3.

National Sovereignty, International Cooperation, and the Reality of International Law. 10 UCLA L Rev 739

FIGURE 3-6(b)   Sample page from *U.S. Code Service*

titles. Realize that the title scheme was developed in the 1920s when the U.S. Code was first published. The subjects of current laws do not always fit easily into this scheme. If you use this method, make sure to peruse the table of contents preceding each title before you examine the code provisions themselves.

All three forms of the federal code have general indexes. Chapter 9 introduces different research techniques for developing terms that can assist in accessing a code through its index.

In addition, both USCA and USCS have specialized tables that assist in locating particular statutes. The most helpful are the popular names tables and cross-references to the *Statutes at Large.* Many acts are given a particular name, such as the Freedom of Information Act, a federal statute providing for public access to public records. A popular names table would reveal that this law is located at title 5, § 552 of either the U.S. Code, *U.S. Code Annotated,* or *U.S. Code Service.*

Most state and local codes follow a format similar to that of federal codes. They are divided into titles and then each title is subdivided. As with federal codes, the most popular method of researching is by using the code's index.

West's

S M I T H – H U R D

ILLINOIS

Compiled Statutes Annotated

Constitution

of the

State of Illinois

Article 1

WEST PUBLISHING CO.
ST. PAUL, MINN.

FIGURE 3-7 Typical state code. (Reprinted with the permission of West Publishing Company.)

STEPS IN USING A CODE

---

1. Determine whether your case is a local, state, or federal matter.
2. If local or state, choose appropriate code.
3. If federal, choose either U.S. Code, USCA, or USCS.
4. Select best method:
   - Title method: review titles to find most appropriate
   - Index method: access index through terms/phrases (illustrated in Chapter 9)
   - Popular names tables: if you know statute's popular name

---

Federal and state codes are updated in two ways. On an annual basis, **pocket part** supplements are provided for each volume of a code. Each supplement is placed in the back of the corresponding volume. Once a pocket part has become too large, the entire volume will be replaced. When conducting research, it is critical to review the pocket part, to make sure that the law you are researching has not been amended or repealed.

Regulatory Law

Administrative regulations are rules governing administrative agencies. Because they deal with the day-to-day operations of an agency, they are usually written in great detail. Agencies are found at all levels of government: federal, state, and local. Though agencies are not provided for constitutionally, they are often referred to as the fourth branch of government, because of their size and impact on American life.

When Congress and state legislatures create agencies, the agencies are given authority to promulgate rules and regulations to carry out their mission. To ensure this, agencies are also permitted to hold hearings to enforce and monitor their regulations.

Prior to its passage by an agency, a proposed regulation must go through the **rulemaking** process. This includes the requirement that all proposals be published in the *Federal Register* or a similar state register.

--- LEGAL TERMS ---

pocket part   A periodically published pamphlet that supplements a bound volume. It is placed in a "pocket" in the back of a volume.

rulemaking †   The promulgation by an administrative agency of a rule having the force of law, i.e., a regulation.

Federal Register †   An official publication, printed daily, containing regulations and proposed regulations issued by administrative agencies, as well as other rulemaking and

STEPS IN REGULATORY RESEARCH

1. Determine whether your case is a state or federal matter.

2. If state, choose appropriate state register or regulatory compilation.

3. If federal, go to *Federal Register* (if rule is not yet approved) and to C.F.R (if approved).

4. Review *CFR Index and Finding Aids* or *Index of CFR* by using terms/phrases (illustrated in Chapter 9).

5. Use LSA pamphlet and C.F.R. Parts Affected table to note changes.

6. If unsuccessful, contact particular agency.

The *Federal Register* (see Figure 3-8) has been published since 1936. It is a chronological source of proposed regulations, executive orders, and other documents. The overall mission of this publication is to comply with the notice and comment requirements of the **Administrative Procedure Act** (APA), a federal statute governing the implementation of federal regulations. This law requires that the general public have notice of the proposed law and an opportunity to comment in writing or at a hearing before enactment.

Once a federal agency has complied with the APA, the final regulation is published in the **Code of Federal Regulations** (C.F.R.). C.F.R. was first published in 1938. It consists of 50 titles in more than 200 paper volumes, which are revised and reissued periodically (see Figure 3-9). Organizationally, it is divided into titles and chapters. Approximately one-quarter of the pamphlets are replaced each calendar year. The regulations are arranged according to their subject matter, which generally corresponds to titles of the U.S. Code.

C.F.R. can be accessed through its *CFR Index and Finding Aids* volume or the *Index of CFR*, published by the Congressional Information Service (CIS). Once you locate a provision, you must use the latest "List of Sections Affected" (LSA) pamphlet and the C.F.R. "Parts Affected" tables in the latest *Federal Register* volumes to determine if the regulation has been affected by a subsequent regulation or rulemaking. Because regulations change rapidly, sometimes the best way to locate and verify a particular provision is by contacting the relevant agency.

The relationship between the *Federal Register* and C.F.R. is similar to that between the *Statutes at Large* and the U.S. Code. The original forms of regulations

─────────── **LEGAL TERMS** ───────────

other official business of the executive branch of government. All regulations are ultimately published in the Code of Federal Regulations.

Administrative Procedure Act [†]   A statute enacted by Congress that regulates the way in which federal administrative agencies conduct their affairs and establishes the procedure for judicial review of the actions of federal agencies. The Act is referred to as the APA.

Code of Federal Regulations [†]   An arrangement, by subject matter, of the rules and regulations issued by federal administrative agencies; commonly referred to as the CFR or abbreviated as C.F.R.

65514 **Federal Register** / Vol. 58, No. 238 / Tuesday, December 14, 1993 / Rules and Regulations

DEPARTMENT OF HEALTH AND HUMAN SERVICES

Food and Drug Administration

21 CFR Parts 16 and 1270

[Docket No. 93N–0453]

Human Tissue Intended for Transplantation

AGENCY: Food and Drug Administration, HHS.

ACTION: Interim rule; opportunity for public comment.

SUMMARY: The Food and Drug Administration (FDA) is issuing an interim rule to require certain infectious disease testing, donor screening, and recordkeeping to help prevent the transmission of AIDS and hepatitis through human tissue used in transplantation. The regulations are effective upon publication. FDA is taking this action in response to growing concerns that some human tissue products are being offered for transplantation use without even the minimum donor testing and screening needed to protect recipients against human immunodeficiency virus (HIV) infection and hepatitis infection. The new regulations require all facilities engaged in procurement, processing, storage, or distribution of human tissues intended for transplant to ensure that minimum required infectious disease testing has been performed and that records documenting such testing for each tissue are available for inspection by FDA. The regulations also provide authority for the agency to conduct inspections of such facilities and to detain, recall, or destroy tissue for which appropriate documentation is not available.

DATES: *Effective Date:* The interim rule is effective December 14, 1993. *Comments:* Written comments by March 14, 1994.

ADDRESSES: Submit written comments to the Dockets Management Branch (HFA–305), Food and Drug Administration, rm. 1–23, 12420 Parklawn Dr., Rockville, MD 20857.

FOR FURTHER INFORMATION CONTACT: Steven F. Falter, Center for Biologics Evaluation and Research (HFM–635), Food and Drug Administration, 1401 Rockville Pike, suite 200N, Rockville, MD 20852–1448, 301–594–3074.

SUPPLEMENTARY INFORMATION:

I. Background

There has been a growing concern about the risk of transmission of hepatitis or HIV-related disease through transplantation of human tissue. Many forms of human tissue are currently subject to Federal regulation. FDA has regulated blood and blood products for decades under the Federal Food, Drug, and Cosmetic Act and the Public Health Service Act (PHS Act). Further, the agency recently published a notice on the application of current statutory authorities to human somatic cell therapy and gene therapy products (58 FR 53248, October 14, 1993). Somatic cell therapy products are defined as autologous, allogenic, or xenogeneic cells that have been propagated, expanded, selected, pharmacologically treated, or otherwise altered in biological characteristics ex vivo to be administered to humans and applicable to the prevention, treatment, cure, diagnosis, or mitigation of disease or injuries. Gene therapy products are defined as products containing genetic material administered to modify or manipulate the expression of genetic material to alter the biological properties of living cells.

Other human tissues have been regulated by FDA on a case-by-case basis, as a public health need was identified. Tissues that the agency has already regulated under the Medical Device Amendments of 1976 (Pub. L. 94–295) include: Corneal lenticules (corneas used to correct rather than restore vision), dura mater allografts (brain membrane material), heart valve allografts, skin and bone products that are processed in ways other than to only reduce infectivity or preserve tissue integrity, and preserved umbilical cord vein grafts.

The National Organ Transplant Act of 1984 (Pub. L. 98–507, (42 U.S.C. 273 *et seq.*)), as amended, provides for Federal oversight of the organ transplant system. The Health Resources and Services Administration (HRSA) and the Health Care Financing Administration (HCFA) within the Department of Health and Human Services (DHHS) currently administer programs related to organ transplantation. In June 1991, DHHS published proposed rules governing performance standards for organ procurement organizations (56 FR 28513, June 21, 1991). The organ transplant system currently includes: Liver, heart, lung, kidney, and some pancreas transplants. Organ transplants are characterized by the fact that the organs receive oxygen and nutrients in the ultimate recipient through the original vascular structures.

Under 42 U.S.C. 274e, it is unlawful to buy or sell a human organ for use in transplantation. Transactions prohibited by this provision include: Sale of a human (including fetal) kidney, liver, heart, pancreas, bone marrow, cornea, eye, bone, skin, or any subpart. Human tissues that are subparts of the listed organs are included within the scope of the prohibition. Reasonable payments associated with removal, transportation, implantation, processing, preservation, quality control, and storage of an organ or with certain donor expenses are not prohibited.

The National Heart, Lung, and Blood Institute, within the National Institutes of Health of HHS, administers the contract for the National Marrow Donor Program, for which standards were established by the Transplant Amendments Act of 1990 (Pub. L. 101–616), and has published a related notice (58 FR 4961, February 7, 1991).

II. Human Tissue Banking

These various programs have, however, left one area of substantial activity without direct or active Federal oversight. Generally, this subject matter consists of musculoskeletal and integumentary materials that may be recovered from living or cadaveric donors. Specifically, these materials largely consist of bone, ligaments, tendons, fascia, cartilage, corneas, and skin that are used in the treatment of bond disease, orthopedic injuries, ligamentous and joint complaints, degenerative skeletal disease, blindness due to corneal opacification, and burn wounds. Tissue donation may be associated with organ procurement. In that event, a HCFA-certified organ procurement organization is likely to have interacted with the donor or the donor's family. Tissue banks may also recover tissue based on referrals of donor availability from other domestic sources, such as medical examiners' offices and hospitals. Medical examiners' offices and hospitals may also directly recover the tissue and send it elsewhere for processing and distribution. In addition, tissue may be recovered from foreign sources.

Currently, industry estimates are that over 280,000 patients annually receive bone, skin, or other integumentary transplants. Additionally, nearly 42,000 patients receive cornea transplants. Annual revenues for tissue banking generally may approach $100 million. Representatives of industry have noted the increasing commercialization of tissue banking.

In part based upon the absence of comprehensive national oversight, there has been concerted effort within the private sector to develop voluntary quality assurance programs. In 1976, the tissue banking industry established the American Association of Tissue Banks (AATB) to develop a voluntary

---

FIGURE 3-8 Sample page from *Federal Register*

Food and Drug Administration, HHS

§ 1250.96

designed and constructed as to be easily cleaned. The jet of a drinking fountain shall be slanting and the orifice of the jet shall be protected by a guard in such a manner as to prevent contamination thereof by droppings from the mouth. The orifice of such a jet shall be located a sufficient distance above the rim of the basin to prevent backflow.

(b) Ice shall not be permitted to come in contact with water in coolers or constant temperature bottles.

(c) Constant temperature bottles and other containers used for storing or dispensing potable water shall be kept clean at all times and shall be subjected to effective bactericidal treatment after each occupancy of the space served and at intervals not exceeding one week.

§ 1250.86 Water for making ice.

Only potable water shall be piped into a freezer for making ice for drinking and culinary purposes.

§ 1250.87 Wash water.

Where systems installed on vessels for wash water, as defined in § 1250.3(n), do not comply with the requirements of a potable water system, prescribed in § 1250.82, they shall be constructed so as to minimize the possibility of the water therein being contaminated. The storage tanks shall comply with the requirements of § 1250.83, and the distribution system shall not be cross connected to a system carrying water of a lower sanitary quality. All faucets shall be labeled "Unfit for drinking".

§ 1250.89 Swimming pools.

(a) Fill and draw swimming pools shall not be installed or used.

(b) Swimming pools of the recirculation type shall be equipped so as to provide complete circulation, replacement, and filtration of the water in the pool every six hours or less. Suitable means of chlorination and, if necessary, other treatment of the water shall be provided to maintain the residual chlorine in the pool water at not less than 0.4 part per million and the pH (a measure of the hydrogen ion concentration) not less than 7.0.

(c) Flowing-through types of salt water pools shall be so operated that complete circulation and replacement of the water in the pool will be effected every 6 hours or less. The water delivery pipe to the pool shall be independent of all other pipes and shall originate at a point where maximum flushing of the pump and pipe line is effected after leaving polluted waters.

§ 1250.90 Toilets and lavatories.

Toilet and lavatory equipment and spaces shall be maintained in a clean condition.

§ 1250.93 Discharge of wastes.

Vessels operating on fresh water lakes or rivers shall not discharge sewage, or ballast or bilge water, within such areas adjacent to domestic water intakes as are designated by the Commissioner of Food and Drugs.

CROSS-REFERENCE: For Environmental Protection Agency's regulations for vessel sanitary discharges as related to authority under the Federal Water Pollution Control Act, as amended (33 U.S.C. 1314 et seq.), see 40 CFR part 140.

[40 FR 5624, Feb. 6, 1975, as amended at 48 FR 11432, Mar. 18, 1983]

§ 1250.95 Insect control.

Vessels shall be maintained free of infestation by flies, mosquitoes, fleas, lice, and other insects known to be vectors in the transmission of communicable diseases, through the use of screening, insecticides, and other generally accepted methods of insect control.

§ 1250.96 Rodent control.

Vessels shall be maintained free of rodent infestation through the use of traps, poisons, and other generally accepted methods of rodent control.

PARTS 1251–1269—(RESERVED)

PART 1270—HUMAN TISSUE INTENDED FOR TRANSPLANTATION

FIGURE 3-9 Sample page from Code of Federal Regulations

§ 1270.1

1270.15 Recall and destruction of human tissue.

AUTHORITY: Secs. 215, 311, 361, 368 of the Public Health Service Act (42 U.S.C. 216, 243, 264, 271).

SOURCE: 58 FR 65520, Dec. 14, 1993, unless otherwise noted.

§ 1270.1 Scope.

(a) The regulations in this part apply to banked human tissue and to establishments or persons engaged in the recovery, processing, storage, or distribution of banked human tissue.

(b) Regulations in this chapter as they apply to drugs, biologics, devices or other FDA-regulated commodities do not apply to banked human tissue, except as specified in this part.

§ 1270.3 Definitions.

(a) *Act* for the purpose of this part means the Public Health Service Act, section 361 (42 U.S.C. 264).

(b) *Banked human tissue* means any tissue derived from a human body, which:

(1) Is intended for administration to another human for the diagnosis, cure, mitigation, treatment, or prevention of any condition or disease;

(2) Is recovered, processed, stored, or distributed by methods not intended to change tissue function or characteristics;

(3) Is not currently regulated as a human drug, biological product, or medical device;

(4) Excludes kidney, liver, heart, lung, pancreas, or any other vascularized human organ; and

(5) Excludes semen or other reproductive tissues, human milk, and bone marrow.

(c) *Vascularized* means containing the native vasculature which continues to carry blood after transplantation.

(d) *Donor* means a human being, living or dead, who is the source of tissue for transplantation.

(e) *Recovery* means the obtaining from a donor of tissue that is intended for use in human transplantation.

(f) *Processing* means any activity to prepare, preserve for storage, and/or remove from storage to assure the potency, quality and/or sterility of human tissue for transplantation.

(g) *Distribution* includes any transfer of human tissue from one establishment or individual to another establishment or individual (including importation), whether or not such transfer is entirely intrastate and whether or not possession of the tissue is taken.

(h) *Storage* means holding tissue in any facility other than the facility at which the tissue is to be implanted.

(i) *Quarantine* means the identification of banked human tissue as not suitable for transplantation or the holding of banked human tissue in an area clearly identified as being for quarantine.

§ 1270.5 Donor testing and screening.

(a) Donor blood specimens shall be tested for the following communicable disease serological markers by tests approved for such uses by the Food and Drug Administration:

(1) Human immunodeficiency virus-1 antibody (anti-HIV-1);

(2) Human immunodeficiency virus-2 antibody (anti-HIV-2);

(3) Hepatitis B surface antigen (HBsAg); and

(4) Hepatitis C virus antibody (anti-HCV).

(b) Such infectious disease testing shall be performed by a laboratory appropriately certified under the Clinical Laboratories Improvement Act of 1988 (CLIA).

(c) Banked human tissue shall be quarantined or accompanied by records indicating that the donor's blood has been tested and found negative in approved tests for anti-HIV-1, anti-HIV-2, HBsAg, and anti-HCV.

(d) Banked human tissue shall be quarantined from donors who, within 48 hours prior to taking the blood sample, have been transfused with four or more units of blood, blood components, colloids or crystalloids in adults, or any transfusions within 48 hours in children under 12 years of age, unless:

(1) A pretransfusion blood sample is available for infectious disease testing; or

(2) An adequate algorithm is used to ensure that there is not hemodilution sufficient to alter test results.

(e) Determination that a donor of banked human tissue intended for transplantation is suitable shall in-

FIGURE 3-9 *(continued)*

are housed in the *Federal Register,* much like the original forms of statutes are in the *Statutes at Large.* The difference is that regulations in the *Federal Register* are only proposed, whereas statutes in the *Statutes at Large* have been enacted.

Most states have a procedure similar to that of the federal government for the enactment of administrative regulations. This includes a regulatory depository similar to C.F.R.

Case Law

Legal principles created by court are referred to as *case law.* This form of primary law is fashioned by judges who review legal disputes and then reach decisions based on common law or statutory or constitutional interpretation.

The Reporting Process

For a case opinion to be considered primary law that another court can rely on as precedent, the decision must be published. To say a case is published is another way of saying that it is located in a **reporter**. Reporters are multivolume collections of court decisions of a particular jurisdiction, court, or geographic area. They form the backbone of legal research because of their importance in locating case law principles.

Only reported decisions from appellate courts can be used as precedent. All jurisdictions have either court rules, statutes, or case law that permit only reported cases to act as precedent.

||||

Maryland Rule 8-114 Unreported Opinions

(a) Not authority.—An unreported opinion of the Court of Appeals or Court of Special Appeals is neither precedent within the rule of stare decisis nor persuasive authority.

Soon after a court renders a publishable decision, the case is published as a **slip opinion.** Like a statute slip law, a slip opinion appears as a pamphlet.

The law is then published in a booklet called an **advance sheet.** An advance sheet can be thought of as a collection of slip opinions. It reports cases adjudicated

--- LEGAL TERMS ---

reporters [†] Court reports, as well as official, published reports of cases decided by administrative agencies.

slip opinion [†] A single judicial decision published shortly after it has been issued by the court and well before it is incorporated into a reporter.

advance sheets [†] Printed copies of judicial opinions published in loose-leaf form shortly after the opinions are issued. These published opinions are later collected and published in bound form with the other reported cases which are issued over a longer period of time.

since the last reporter was published. It contains cases issued over a short period of time (a week, a month, or several months) and is paginated in the same fashion as the reporter it is published in "advance" of.

All reporters present cases in chronological fashion. One volume typically contains cases for a specific period of time: a year, a session of the court, or several months. A case is identified by its **citation**. Many reporters also give the citation of the same case in another reporter. This is known as a **parallel citation**.

Reporters contain decisions of state and federal courts. If a court publishes its own reporter, it is referred to as an *official reporter*. Many states, such as Ohio, Oregon, and Wisconsin, publish reporters of their appellate courts. Other states, like Oklahoma, Rhode Island, and Wyoming, have ceased publishing their own reporters, considering it more practical to permit publication through a private company. The primary unofficial reporter publisher is West Publishing Company. West long ago concluded that it could compete successfully with the official reporters by publishing the same cases, but in a user-friendly fashion. Today, West publishes the decisions of all fifty states and all federal courts as part of its National Reporter System (described in more detail later). West reporters include editorial enhancements along with the text of each opinion. For this reason, most legal researchers prefer using West reporters.

Besides producing state reporters, West publishes a number of federal court reporters. These include decisions from the U.S. Supreme Court, U.S. Courts of Appeals, and U.S. District Courts.

Anatomy of a Case Opinion

As you now know, *case law* is the written result of a court's deciding an actual legal controversy. The particular matter is frequently referred to as the **case at bar**. When one of the parties to the dispute, either the plaintiff or the defendant, believes that the trial court's decision was unfair or incorrect, it may appeal that decision to a higher court.

At the appeals court level, the parties are generally referred to as **appellant** or **petitioner** (the party who took the appeal) and **appellee** or **respondent** (the party responding to the appeal). The appeals court is required to review the record of the lower court and reach an independent decision.

To illustrate the parts of an opinion, the Maryland case of *Stuart v. Board of Supervisors* is considered. See Figure 3-10.

––––––––––––––––––––––––––––––––– **LEGAL TERMS** –––––––––––––––––––––––––––––––––

citation [†]   Reference to authority (a case, article, or other text) on a point of law, by name, volume, and page or section of the court report or other book in which it appears.

parallel citation [†]   A citation to a court opinion or decision that is printed in two or more reporters.

case at bar   The legal matter that is before the court.

appellant (petitioner) [†]   A party who appeals from a lower court to a higher court.

appellee (respondent) [†]   A party against whom a case is appealed from a lower court to a higher court.

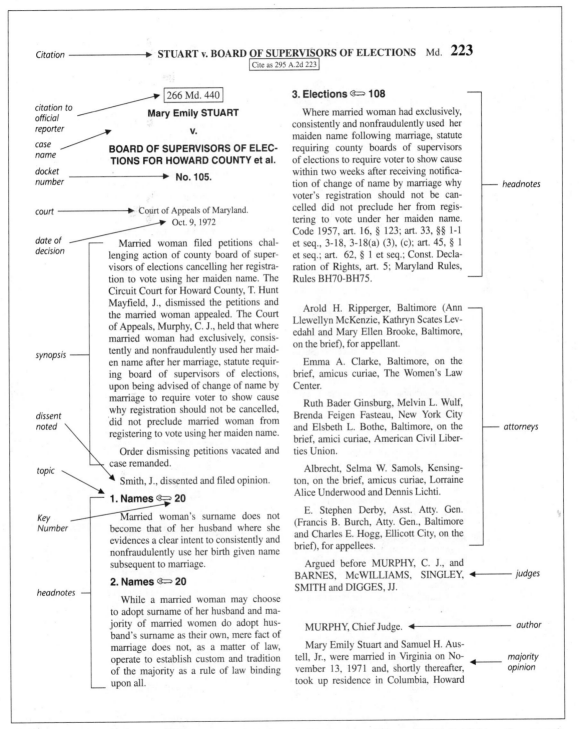

Citation

STUART v. BOARD OF SUPERVISORS OF ELECTIONS Md. **223**

Cite as 295 A.2d 223

citation to official reporter

266 Md. 440

Mary Emily STUART

case name

v.

BOARD OF SUPERVISORS OF ELECTIONS FOR HOWARD COUNTY et al.

docket number

No. 105.

court

Court of Appeals of Maryland.

date of decision

Oct. 9, 1972

synopsis

Married woman filed petitions challenging action of county board of supervisors of elections cancelling her registration to vote using her maiden name. The Circuit Court for Howard County, T. Hunt Mayfield, J., dismissed the petitions and the married woman appealed. The Court of Appeals, Murphy, C. J., held that where married woman had exclusively, consistently and nonfraudulently used her maiden name after her marriage, statute requiring board of supervisors of elections, upon being advised of change of name by marriage to require voter to show cause why registration should not be cancelled, did not preclude married woman from registering to vote using her maiden name.

Order dismissing petitions vacated and case remanded.

dissent noted

Smith, J., dissented and filed opinion.

topic

1. Names ⟨≈⟩ 20

Key Number

Married woman's surname does not become that of her husband where she evidences a clear intent to consistently and nonfraudulently use her birth given name subsequent to marriage.

2. Names ⟨≈⟩ 20

headnotes

While a married woman may choose to adopt surname of her husband and majority of married women do adopt husband's surname as their own, mere fact of marriage does not, as a matter of law, operate to establish custom and tradition of the majority as a rule of law binding upon all.

3. Elections ⟨≈⟩ 108

Where married woman had exclusively, consistently and nonfraudulently used her maiden name following marriage, statute requiring county boards of supervisors of elections to require voter to show cause within two weeks after receiving notification of change of name by marriage why voter's registration should not be cancelled did not preclude her from registering to vote under her maiden name. Code 1957, art. 16, § 123; art. 33, §§ 1-1 et seq., 3-18, 3-18(a) (3), (c); art. 45, § 1 et seq.; art. 62, § 1 et seq.; Const. Declaration of Rights, art. 5; Maryland Rules, Rules BH70-BH75.

headnotes

Arold H. Ripperger, Baltimore (Ann Llewellyn McKenzie, Kathryn Scates Levedahl and Mary Ellen Brooke, Baltimore, on the brief), for appellant.

Emma A. Clarke, Baltimore, on the brief, amicus curiae, The Women's Law Center.

Ruth Bader Ginsburg, Melvin L. Wulf, Brenda Feigen Fasteau, New York City and Elsbeth L. Bothe, Baltimore, on the brief, amici curiae, American Civil Liberties Union.

attorneys

Albrecht, Selma W. Samols, Kensington, on the brief, amicus curiae, Lorraine Alice Underwood and Dennis Lichti.

E. Stephen Derby, Asst. Atty. Gen. (Francis B. Burch, Atty. Gen., Baltimore and Charles E. Hogg, Ellicott City, on the brief), for appellees.

Argued before MURPHY, C. J., and BARNES, McWILLIAMS, SINGLEY, SMITH and DIGGES, JJ.

judges

MURPHY, Chief Judge.

author

Mary Emily Stuart and Samuel H. Austell, Jr., were married in Virginia on November 13, 1971 and, shortly thereafter, took up residence in Columbia, Howard

majority opinion

FIGURE 3-10 *Stuart v. Board of Supervisors.* (Reprinted with the permission of West Publishing Company.)

224 Md.   295 ATLANTIC REPORTER, 2d SERIES

*majority
opinion*

County, Maryland. In accordance with the couple's oral antenuptial agreement, Stuart continued, after the marriage, to use and be exclusively known by her birth given ("maiden") name and not by the legal surname of her husband.

On March 2, 1972, Stuart undertook to register to vote in Howard County in her birth given name. After disclosing to the registrar that she was married to Austell but had consistently and nonfraudulently used her maiden name, she was registered to vote in the name of Mary Emily Stuart.

On March 16, 1972 the Board of Supervisors of Elections for Howard County notified Stuart by letter that since under Maryland law "a woman's legal surname becomes that of her husband upon marriage," she was required by Maryland Code, Article 33, § 3-18(c) to complete a "Request for Change of Name" form or her registration would be cancelled. Stuart did not complete the form and her registration was cancelled on April 4, 1972.

Stuart promptly challenged the Board's action by two petitions filed in the Circuit Court for Howard County, the first entitled "Petition to correct [the voter] registry," and the second "Petition to restore name to registry of voters in Howard County." In each petition Stuart maintained that she was properly registered to vote in her birth given name, that being her true and correct name; that under the English common law, in force in Maryland, a wife could assume the husband's name if she desired, or retain her own name, or be known by any other name she wished, so long as the name she used was not retained for a fraudulent purpose; and that since the only name she ever used was Mary Emily Stuart the Board had no right to cancel her voter registration listed in that name.

The petitions were consolidated and an evidentiary hearing was held before Judge T. Hunt Mayfield on May 8, 1972. Evidence was adduced showing that the oral antenuptial agreement between Stuart and

Austell that she would retain her maiden name was a matter of great importance to both parties. Stuart testified that her marriage to Austell was "based on the idea that we're both equal individuals and our names symbolize that." There was evidence that prior to the marriage lawyers were consulted on the parties' behalf who indicated that Stuart had the right to retain her own name after the marriage. Stuart testified, and Austell corroborated her testimony, that she would not have gotten married "if * * * [the marriage] would have jeopardized my name." She testified that after the marriage she continued to use her own name on charge accounts, on her driver's license and Social Security registration and in "every legal document I've ever had." "Everybody" she said, "knows me by the name Mary Stuart."

There was evidence showing that the practice of the Board requiring a married woman to use the surname of her husband dated back to 1936; that the practice was a uniform one throughout the State and was adopted to provide some trail of identification to prevent voter fraud; that if a married woman could register under different names the identification trail would be lost; and that the only exception permitted to the requirement that married women register under their husbands' surnames was if the name was changed by court order.

By opinion filed May 10, 1972, Judge Mayfield concluded "that a person may adopt and use any name chosen in the absence of fraudulent intent or purpose"; that the use by Stuart of her maiden name was without fraudulent intent or purpose; that it is the law of Maryland that "the use by the wife of the husband's surname following marriage, while the same have been initially based upon custom and usage, is now based on the common law of England, which law has been duly adopted as the law of this State"; that under the provisions of the ode, Article 33, § 3-18(a)(3) clerks of courts, as therein designated, are required to notify

FIGURE 3-10 *(continued)*

STUART v. BOARD OF SUPERVISORS OF ELECTIONS Md. 225
Cite as 295 A.2d 223

Boards of Supervisors of Elections of the "present names" of females over the age of eighteen years residing within the State "whose names have been changed by marriage"; that by subsection (c) of § 3-18, the Boards, upon being advised of a "change of name by marriage," are required to give notification "that such * * * change of name by marriage * * * has been reported to the board, and shall require the voter to show cause within two weeks * * * why his registration should not be cancelled"; that § 3-18 appeared "to be in conformity with the common law," as espoused in such cases as People ex rel. Rago v. Lipsky, 327 Ill.App. 63, 63 N.E.2d 642 (1945) and Forbush v. Wallace, 341 F.Supp. 217 (M.D.Ala.1971), aff'd per curiam 405 U.S.970, 92 S.Ct. 1197, 31 L.Ed.2d 246 (1972); that the "statutory requirements [of § 3-18] are in accordance with the law which says that upon marriage the wife takes the surname of her husband"; that the provisions of § 3-18 do not deprive Stuart of her right to use her maiden name, nor of her right to vote, but require only that she "register to vote under her 'legal' name, * * * based upon the broad general principle of the necessity for proper record keeping and the proper and most expedient way of identifying the person who desires to vote."[1]

From the court's order denying her petitions to correct the voter registry and

to restore her name thereto, Stuart has appealed. She claims on appeal, as she did below, that a woman's surname upon marriage does not become that of her husband by operation of the common law in force in Maryland and that nothing in the provisions of § 3-18(a)(3) and (c) mandates a contrary result.

What constitutes the correct legal name of a married woman under common law principles is a question which has occasioned a sharp split of authorities, crystallized in the conflicting cases of State ex rel. Krupa v. Green, 114 Ohio App. 497, 177 N.E.2d 616 (1961), relied upon by Stuart, and People ex rel. Rago v. Lipsky, *supra*, adopted by the lower court as its principal authority for denying the petitions. *Green* approved the voter registration of a married woman in her birth given name which she had openly, notoriously and exclusively used subsequent to her marriage, and held that she could use that name as a candidate for public office. The court held:

"It is only *by custom,* in English speaking countries, that a woman, upon marriage, adopts the surname of her husband in place of the surname of her father." *Id.* 177 N.E.2d at 619 (Emphasis in original.)

Lipsky refused to allow a married woman to remain registered to vote under her birth given name on the basis of

1. In pertinent part, § 3-18(a)(3) and
    (c) provides:

    "(a) *Reports to be made by certain public agencies.*—Reports to the board shall be made by the several officials in Baltimore City at least once each month, and in the several counties, by the last days of January and July in each year, as follows:

       *   *   *   *   *

    "(3) The clerk of the Court of Common Pleas in Baltimore City and the clerk of the circuit court for each county shall file with said respective boards the former and present names of all female residents of said city or county, as the case may be, over the age of
    295 A.2d-15

twenty-one years, whose names have been changed by marriage since the date of the last such report.

   *   *   *   *   *

"(c) *Notification to show cause before cancellation.*—Whenever the * * * change of name by marriage * * * is reported as above provided, the board shall cause to be mailed to the address of such voter * * * a notification that such * * * change of name by marriage * * * has been reported to the board, and shall require the voter to show cause within two weeks * * * why his registration should not be cancelled. * * *"

FIGURE 3-10 *(continued)*

226 Md.   295 ATLANTIC REPORTER, 2d SERIES

"* * * the long-established custom, policy and rule of the common law among English-speaking peoples whereby a woman's name is changed by marriage and her husband's surname becomes *as a matter of law* her surname." *Id.* 63 N.E.2d at 645 (Emphasis supplied.)

Cases tending to support the rationale of *Green* are Lane v. Duchac, 73 Wis. 646, 41 N.W. 962, 965 (1889); Rice v. State, 37 Tex.Cr.R. 36, 38 S.W. 801, 802 (1897); Succession of Kneipp, 172 La. 411, 134 So. 376, 378 (1931); State ex rel. Bucher v. Brower, Ohio Com.Pl., 7 Ohio Supp. 51, 21 Ohio Op. 208 (1941); Wilty v. Jefferson Parish, 245 La. 145, 157 So.2d 718, 727 (1963) (Sanders, J., concurring). Cases tending to support the *Lipsky* theory are Chapman v. Phoenix National Bank, 85 N.Y. 437, 449 (1881); In re Kayaloff, 9 F.Supp. 176 (S.D.N.Y.1934); Freeman v. Hawkins, 77 Tex. 498, 14 S.W. 364, 365 (1890); Bacon v. Boston Elevated Ry. Co., 256 Mass. 30, 152 N.E. 35, 36 (1926); Wilty v. Jefferson Parish, *supra,* 157 So.2d at 723-724 (Hamlin, J.); Forbush v. Wallace, *supra,* 341 F.Supp. at 221-222.[2]

[1,2] We think the lower court was wrong in concluding that the principles enunciated in *Lipsky* represent the law of Maryland. We have heretofore unequivocally recognized the common law right of any person, absent a statute to the contrary, to "adopt any name by which he may become known, and by which he may transact business and execute contracts and sue or be sued." Romans v. State, 178 Md. 588, 597, 16 A.2d 642, 646. In the context of the name used in an

automobile liability insurance contract, we approved the consistent nonfraudulent use by a married woman of a surname other than that of her lawful husband in Erie Insurance Exchange v. Lane, 246 Md. 55, 227 A.2d 231. Citing with approval Everett v. Standard Acc. Ins. Co., 45 Cal.App. 332, 187 P. 996 (1919), we summarized its holding as follows:

"The court * * * held that because the insured had been known as Everett for twenty-two years before the policy was issued, a representation that his name was Everett was not a misrepresentation, although his name before had been Cowie, since a man may lawfully change his name without resorting to legal proceedings and by general usage or habit acquire another." *Erie* 246 Md. at 62-63, 227 A.2d at 236.

If a married woman may lawfully adopt an assumed name (which, in *Erie,* was neither her birth given name nor the name of her lawful husband) without legal proceedings, then we think Maryland law manifestly permits a married woman to retain her birth given name by the same procedure of consistent, nonfraudulent use following her marriage. In so concluding, we note that there is no statutory requirement in the Code, in either Article 62 (Marriages) or Article 45 (Husband and Wife), that a married woman adopt her husband's surname.[3] Consistent with the common law principle referred to in the Maryland cases, we hold that a married woman's surname does not become that of her husband where, as here, she evidences a clear intent to consistently and nonfraudulently use her birth given name subsequent to her marriage.

---

2. The three-judge District Court in *Forbush* upheld the constitutionality of the Alabama regulation, based on Alabama case law, that a married woman's legal surname is that of her husband, requiring that she use her husband's surname in obtaining a driver's license. The Supreme Court's affirmance was without opinion and since it was based upon Alabama common law, differing from

that of Maryland, it is not constitutional authority binding upon us in applying the common law rule in force in Maryland.

3. Compare Hawaii Rev.Stat., Title 31, § 574-1 (1968): "Every married woman shall adopt her husband's name as a family name." Hawaii appears to be the only state with a statutory provision determinative of the issue.

FIGURE 3-10   *(continued)*

STUART v. BOARD OF SUPERVISORS OF ELECTIONS Md. **227**
Cite as 295 A.2d 223

Thus, while under *Romans,* a married woman may choose to adopt the surname of her husband—this being the long-standing custom and tradition which has resulted in the vast majority of married women adopting their husbands' surnames as their own—the mere fact of the marriage does not, as a matter of law, operate to establish the custom and tradition of the majority as a rule of law binding upon all.

[3] From a study of the English authorities cited to us by the parties and amici curiae, we believe the rule we enunciate today is founded upon the English common law incorporated into the laws of Maryland by Article 5 of the Maryland Declaration of Rights. The question of English common law was considered by the Ohio Court of Appeals in State ex rel. Krupa v. Green, *supra,* 177 N.E.2d at 619:[4]

"In England, from which came our customs with respect to names, a woman is permitted to retain her maiden surname upon marriage if she so desires.

"M. Turner-Samuels, in his book on 'The Law of Married Women' at page 345, states:

'In England, custom has long since ordained that a married woman takes her husband's name. This practice is not invariable; not compellable by law. * * * A wife may continue to use her maiden, married, or any other name she wishes to be known by. * * *'

He cites the following cases as authority for his statement: Fendall v. Goldsmid (1877) 2 P.D. 263; Dancer v. Dancer (1948) 2 All E.R. 731; Chipchase v. Chipchase (1939) P. 391; Chipchase v. Chipchase (1942) P. 37, distinguished; Sullivan v. Sullivan (1818) 2 Hag.Con. 238, 161 E.R. 728, 27 Digest 49, 279; Wakefield v. Mackay (1807) 1 Hag.Con. 394, 1 Phillim. 134, n."

Other English text writers have expressed a similar view of English law:

"In England (followed by the United States of America) practice has crept in, though apparently comparatively recently, for a woman upon marriage to merge her identity in that of her husband, and to substitute his name for her father's acquiring the new surname by repute." C. Ewen, A History of British Isles 391 (London 1931)

To the same effect see 19 Halsbury's Laws of England 829 (3d 1957):

"1350. Assumption by wife of husband's name. When a woman on her marriage assumes, as she usually does in England, the surname of her husband in substitution for her father's name, it may be said that she acquires a new name by repute. The change of name is in fact, rather than in law, a consequence of the marriage. * * * " (Footnotes omitted.)

Under the common law of Maryland, as derived from the common law of England, Mary Emily Stuart's surname thus has not been changed by operation of law to that of Austell solely by reason of her marriage to him. On the contrary, because of her exclusive, consistent, nonfraudulent use of her maiden name, she is entitled to use the name Mary Emily Stuart unless there is a statute to the contrary. Romans v. State, *supra.* We do not think that the provisions of Article 33, § 3-18(a)(3) and (c), heretofore set forth, require that a married woman register to vote in the surname of her husband unless her name has been changed by legal proceedings under Maryland Rules BH70-BH75, and Article 16, § 123 of the Annotated Code of Maryland, as claimed by the Board. We are unable to attribute to that Section, even with the aid of a long-standing and uniform administrative practice, such an effect in derogation of the common law. See MacBride v. Gulbro, 247 Md. 727,

---

4. People ex rel. Rago v. Lipsky, *supra,* contains no reference to English law.

FIGURE 3-10 *(continued)*

228 Md.   295 ATLANTIC REPORTER, 2d SERIES

234 A.2d 586; Gleaton v. State, 235 Md. 271, 201 A.2d 353; Mayor and City Council of Baltimore v. Baltimore Gas and Electric Company, 232 Md. 123, 192 A.2d 87.[5]

Nothing in the language of § 3-18(a)(3) or (c) purports to compel *all* married women to register to vote in their husbands' surname. Since Mary Emily Stuart did not undergo a "change of name by marriage," this Section merely requires her to show cause to the Board that she consistently and nonfraudulently used her birth given name rather than her husband's surname following marriage. Although no show cause hearing was held in this case because, as found by the lower court, Stuart had difficulty in contacting the Chairman of the Board, two things are abundantly clear on the record before us: (1) that a show cause hearing, had one been held prior to the critical date specified by the Board, would not have resulted in the registration of Mary Emily Stuart in her maiden name, in light of the uniform practice of the Board, supported by an opinion of the Attorney General of Maryland dated April 7, 1971, and the statements of counsel for the Board at oral argument of the appeal; and (2) that Mary Stuart has amply demonstrated sufficient cause that her registration not be cancelled by proof adduced at the trial, and accepted by the court, that she has consistently and openly, with no intent to defraud, used the name Mary Emily Stuart as her sole and exclusive name after her marriage to Samuel Austell. In view of the impending closing of the voter registration books prior to the November 1972 election, we shall direct that the court below promptly order the Board to restore the name of Mary Emily Stuart to the registry of voters in Howard County. Of course, in so doing, the Board may make whatever cross-reference notation to the fact of Stuart's marriage to Austell that it thinks administratively feasible to meet the avowed needs of voter identification and prevention of dual registrations. See State ex rel. Krupa v. Green, *supra,* 177 N.E.2d at 618.

In light of our disposition of the common law issue, we find it unnecessary to reach the constitutional issues raised by the appeal.

Order dismissing petitions vacated; case remanded for the passage of an order in accordance with this opinion; costs to be paid by appellees. Mandate to issue forthwith.

SMITH, Judge.

I would affirm.

dissenting opinion

I do not see a constitutional issue in this case other than that of judicial legislation.

The issue is not under what name one might prefer to permit a woman to register to vote, but what the General Assembly meant by "name" insofar as a married woman is concerned in its enactment of the laws relative to registration.

We start out with two bases, Article 8 of the Maryland Declaration of Rights

---

5. The first election law dealing with the name of married women was enacted as part of the permanent general registration of voters in Baltimore City. It provided for notification to the Board by the Clerk in Baltimore City similar to the present § 3-18(a)(3) and further provided that "Whenever, after an original registration, a person shall change his or her name, such person shall be required to re-register; * * *." Laws of 1937, ch. 77 § 29-0.

In 1945, Article 33 was repealed and a new Article 33 enacted. The notification provision was extended statewide, but without express provision for cancellation and re-registration. Laws of 1945, ch 934, § 28(c).

In 1959 the provision was added that in the event of change of name by marriage, the voter would be given an opportunity to show cause prior to cancellation. Laws of 1959, ch. 287 § 43(g).

Minor changes, not here relevant, were made by Laws of 1967, ch. 392 and Laws of 1972, ch. 10.

FIGURE 3-10   *(continued)*

STUART v. BOARD OF SUPERVISORS OF ELECTIONS   Md.   **229**
Cite as 295 A.2d 223

providing "[t]hat the Legislative, Executive and Judicial powers of Government ought to be forever separate and distinct from each other," and the oft expressed doctrine that the construction placed upon a statute by administrative officials soon after its enactment is strong, persuasive influence in determining the judicial construction and should not be disregarded except for the strongest and most urgent reasons. Williams v. Associated Professors of Loyola College, 257 Md. 316, 329, 263 A.2d 5 (1970); F. & M. Schaefer Brewing Co. v. Comptroller, 255 Md. 211, 218, 257 A.2d 416 (1969); John McShain, Inc. v. Comptroller, 202 Md. 68, 73, 95 A.2d 473 (1953); and Smith v. Higinbothom, 187 Md. 115, 132-133, 48 A.2d 754 (1946). When the General Assembly revised the election laws by the enactment of Chapter 392 of the Acts of 1967 it eliminated from the statute a specific provision relative to name. However, there is included a form with "Last Name," "First Name" and "Middle Name or Initial" appearing on it. Code (1971 Repl. Vol.) Art. § 33, § 3-13(a) provides for prospective voters "to answer in the presence of the registrars all questions required on the registration forms." The provision in Code (1957) Art. 33, § 23(c) for entering "[t]he name and age of every applicant" is but little different from the requirement of Code (1939) Art. 33, § 19 that "[u]nder the column 'Name'" should be entered "the name of the applicant, writing the surname first, and full given or Christian name after," which came into the Maryland law under § 15 of Chapter 22 of the Acts of 1882, apparently our first registration law, which became Code (1888) Art. 33, § 14.

Prior to the adoption of the 19th Amendment to the Constitution of the United States women were not permitted to vote in Maryland, Leser v. Board of Registry, 139 Md. 46, 114 A. 840 (1921), the provisions of Article 1, § 1 of the Constitution of Maryland limiting suffrage to males not having been eliminated until the adoption of a constitutional amendment by Maryland voters in 1956. It would seem that the General Assembly took special cognizance of women and their right to vote when it enacted Chapter 299 of the Acts of 1924, which became Code (1924) Art. 33, § 19, providing that "[a] female applicant for registration as a voter [should] not be required to state her exact age, but it [should] be sufficient for said applicant to state, in answer to any and all questions relating to her age, that she [would] be at least 21 years of age on the regular election day next succeeding the day of registration," a provision which remained in Article 33 until it was revised by Chapter 934 of the Acts of 1945. It chose to remain silent upon the subject of name, however, from which one might infer tacit approval of the prevailing practice.

In 1921, prior to the day of the so-called "permanent registration" now in effect, when a person once registered in a given election district or precinct could continue to vote there notwithstanding the fact that he might move to some other address in that election district or precinct, Attorney General Alexander Armstrong was asked whether a woman who had registered and voted the preceding year and had since married was entitled to vote at a coming or subsequent election under the name which she bore at the time of registration. In 6 Op. Atty. Gen. 188 (1921), he replied in the affirmative, saying that the only ground upon which the right to vote might be challenged was that the person offering to vote was not a registered voter of the district or precinct in which application was made. He further said:

"The case of a woman whose name has been changed by marriage is analogous to that of a person who has, since registration, changed his or her residence to some other residence within the district or precinct. In each of these instances no change of the registration books is necessary." Id. at 189.

FIGURE 3-10   *(continued)*

It is interesting to note that in 1931 the Attorney General was asked to advise "as to the proper name to be used by a Catholic Sister or a Brother in a religious order when registering for voting purposes." In 16 Op. Atty. Gen. 144 (1931), he replied:

"The law requires the giving of the correct legal name, and until a person's name has been changed in the manner provided by law, this name should be given when applying for registration purposes." *Id.* at 144.

2 Bishop, Marriage, Divorce and Separation § 1622 (1891), states:

"The rule of law and custom is familiar, that marriage confers on the woman the husband's surname."

Like statements are to be found in 57 Am. Jur.2d Name § 9 (1971), relied upon by the trial judge, and 65 C.J.S. Name § 3 c (1966). *See also* on the subject Annot., 35 A.L.R. 413 (1925).

In re Kayaloff, 9 F.Supp. 176 (S.D.N.Y.1934), is interesting in this regard. There a married woman was seeking naturalization. She was a musician "known professionally by her maiden name." She feared that she might possibly suffer financial loss if her naturalization certificate showed her surname to be that of her husband. She saw another problem in that a discrepancy would exist between her musical union card and her naturalization certificate. The court, after stating that "[t]he union card should conform to the naturalization certificate rather than that the latter should yield to the union card," said:

"Under the law of New York, as pronounced in Chapman v. Phoenix National Bank, 85 N.Y. 437, a woman, at her marriage, takes the surname of her husband. 'That,' it was there said, 'becomes her legal name, and she ceases to be known by her maiden name. By that name she must sue and be sued, make and take grants and execute all legal documents. Her maiden surname is absolutely

lost, and she ceases to be known thereby.'" *Id.* 9 F.Supp. at 176.

The exact point here involved was before the court in People ex rel. Rago v. Lipsky, 327 Ill.App. 63, 63 N.E.2d 642 (1945). Antonia E. Rago, admitted to the bar of Illinois in 1938, married Mac-Farland in 1944. She was admitted to practice under the name of Rago in the federal courts in Chicago and before the Supreme Court of the United States, in addition to the Illinois courts. She practiced under the name of Rago. She claimed that her husband expressly approved of her plans to continue her practice of law and her other business affairs under the name of Rago. She sought to register under that name and challenged a provision of the Illinois law which provided that any registered voter who changed her name by marriage should "be required to register anew and authorize the cancellation of the previous registration." In holding that she was obliged to register under her married name, the court said:

"Notwithstanding petitioner's contention to the contrary, it is well settled by common-law principles and immemorial custom that a woman upon marriage abandons her maiden name and takes the husband's surname, with which is used her own given name." *Id.* 327 Ill. at 67, 63 N.E.2d at 644.

The courts in *Kayaloff* and in *Lipsky*, as have many of the authorities, relied upon Chapman v. Phoenix Nat'l Bank of City of New York, 85 N.Y. 437 (1881). There Verina S. Moore had married a man by the name of Chapman. The question actually before the court was the propriety of notice given after her marriage to an individual described as "Ver. S. Moore." The court there said:

"Her name was then, and for more than three years had been, Verina S. Chapman. For several centuries, by the common law among all English

FIGURE 3-10   *(continued)*

STUART v. BOARD OF SUPERVISORS OF ELECTIONS Md. **231**
Cite as 295 A.2d 223

speaking people, a woman, upon her marriage, takes her husband's surname. That becomes her legal name, and she ceases to be known by her maiden name. By that name she must sue and be sued, make and take grants and execute all legal documents. Her maiden surname is absolutely lost, and she ceases to be known thereby." *Id.* 85 N.Y. at 449.

I am not impressed by the comment, citing Romans v. State, 178 Md. 588, 597, 16 A.2d 642 (1940), that a person has a common law right, absent a statute to the contrary, to "adopt any name by which he may become known, and by which he may transact business and execute contracts and sue or be sued." Rather, the question is, as I see it, what the General Assembly meant in the registration laws when "name" was mentioned.

It is conceded by all concerned that the uniform practice in Maryland has been for a married woman to register under the surname of her husband. This is in accordance with what I understand to be the authorities on the subject of name. It certainly is in accordance with custom. Therefore, I believe that to permit a married woman to register under a surname other than that of her husband she must either go through the process of having her name changed or the General Assembly must so provide. A holding to the contrary is in my humble opinion judicial legislation which is forbidden by the Maryland Declaration of Rights.

FIGURE 3-10 *(continued)*

Citation   The citation for the reported opinion is found at the top of page. The citation consists of the volume of the *Atlantic Reporter, 2d* (295), the abbreviation of the reporter name (A.2d), and the page on which the opinion begins (223). If you are looking at an unofficial reporter, often the citation to the official reporter for the same case will be presented as well. In the *Stuart* case, it is; 266 Md. 440, or volume 266 of *Maryland Reports*, page 440.

Case Name   This is the most identifiable portion of the opinion. Here, the full names of the parties are provided. Additionally, the litigation status of the parties may be indicated: appellant and appellee. If it is not, as in this case, the first party is presumed to be the appellant and the second party the appellee. This section is also called the caption.

Docket Number   Next the court indicates the internal administrative number that it has assigned to the case. This number is not to be confused with a citation.

Court Name   The name of the court deciding the opinion is indicated next. Many state appeals courts are divided in divisions or parts. This would be noted as Part I, Part II, Civil Division, and the like.

Date of Decision   Next the date of the decision is indicated. This is important in that the effective date of any legal precedents in the case will be "law" only on that date. In addition, the date the case was argued before the court sometimes is noted.

Synopsis   If you are reading an opinion reported by West Publishing Company, a short paragraph summarizing the opinion, known as a *synopsis*, follows the case information. In a non-West format, it may be referred to as a *case summary* or *syllabus*. Provided also at this point is a short statement indicating the court's ultimate decision in the case. In the *Stuart* case, the order of the trial court dismissing the case was **vacated** and the case was **remanded**.

Dissenting Opinion   If there is a dissenting opinion, it will be noted here. In this case, Judge Smith filed a dissent. The dissenting opinion itself follows the majority opinion.

Headnotes   **Headnotes** were developed as an aid to research. Essentially, they are paragraph summaries of the major legal principles of the case. In a West opinion, the headnotes are prepared by editors at West. West publications also include references to West's Topic and Key Number System. There are three headnotes in the Stuart case; two dealing with "names" and one dealing with "elections."

Attorneys   The names of the lawyers who argued the case are listed next. This information is useful should you desire to contact these attorneys about the particulars of the case. In addition to counsel for appellant and appellees, representation is indicated for the Women's Law Center and the ACLU. Both filed "friend of the court" or *amicus curiae* briefs in this matter.

Judges   The judges who heard the case are indicated next.

Author   The judge who wrote the opinion is identified. This opinion was written by Chief Judge Murphy.

Opinion   Finally, the text of the opinion is provided. After reviewing a matter, the judges come to a decision as to the outcome. One judge then is assigned to put that decision in writing. Because it is here that legal principles are located, this

---
LEGAL TERMS
---

vacate [†]   As applied to a judgment, decree, or other order of a court, to annul, set aside, void, or cancel.

remand [†]   n. The return of a case by an appellate court to the trial court for further proceedings, for a new trial, or for entry of judgment in accordance with an order of the appellate court. v. To return or send back.

headnote [†]   A summary statement that appears at the beginning of a reported case to indicate the points decided by the case.

amicus curiae [†]   [Latin for] "Friend of the court." A person who is interested in the outcome of the case, but who is not a party, whom the court permits to file a brief for the purpose of providing the court with a position or a point of view which it might not otherwise have. An amicus curiae is often referred to simply as an *amicus*.

is the most important part of the opinion. As part of the text, judges indicate the reasoning they used in reaching their decision. In a sense, this is the court's justification for its ruling. Analysis of an opinion is addressed in Chapter 8.

Appellate panels are usually comprised of three or more judges. In this case the panel was made of up of six judges. The position of a majority of the judges is the **majority opinion**. Should a judge disagree, he may draft either a **dissenting opinion** or a **concurring opinion**. In a concurring opinion, he disagrees with the reasoning of the majority but not the final outcome. A dissenting judge, however, disagrees with both the reasoning and the outcome. A **per curiam opinion** is one written jointly by the entire majority rather than a single judge.

Federal Court Reporters

The U.S. Supreme Court is the highest court in the land. It is the court of the last resort for the federal courts and for state courts on issues of federal law. Appellate review is by the court granting a writ of **certiorari**. On average, the Supreme Court receives about 5,000 requests for writs per year, but only about 5 percent of these cases are granted review.

Located in Washington, D.C., since 1800, the Supreme Court consists of nine Justices who meet starting the first Monday of October each year. The term runs until late spring.

The official reporter of the Supreme Court is *United States Reports,* first published in 1790. At its inception, it was published as a private venture, but it became official in 1817. A little-known fact is that the first volume contained decisions from several Pennsylvania state courts instead of the U.S. Supreme Court. As with all reporters, the cases are compiled chronologically. Approximately three or four volumes of U.S. Reports are added every year.

------------------------------ LEGAL TERMS ------------------------------

majority opinion [†]   An opinion issued by an appellate court that represents the view of a majority of the members of the court.

dissenting opinion [†]   A written opinion filed by a judge of an appellate court who disagrees with the decision of the majority of judges in a case, giving the reasons for his or her differing view. Often a dissenting opinion is written by one judge on behalf of one or more other dissenting judges.

concurring opinion [†]   An opinion issued by one or more judges which agrees with the result reached by the majority opinion rendered by the court, but reaches that result for different reasons.

per curiam opinion [†]   An opinion, usually of an appellate court, in which the judges are all of one view and the legal question is sufficiently clear that a full written opinion is not required and a one- or two-paragraph opinion suffices.

certiorari [†]   *(Latin)* A writ issued by a higher court to a lower court requiring the certification of the record in a particular case so that the higher court can review the record and correct any actions taken in the case which are not in accordance with the law. The Supreme Court of the United States uses the writ of certiorari to select the state court cases it is willing to review. Commonly referred to as "cert."

United States Reports [†]   The official court reports of the decisions and opinions of the Supreme Court of the United States.

In addition, Supreme Court cases are published in two unofficial reporters. These are West's *Supreme Court Reporter* and Lawyers Cooperative Publishing's *United States Supreme Court Reports, Lawyer's Edition.*

The *Supreme Court Reporter* began publication in 1882. It does not include cases reported by *United States Reports* prior to that date. Each opinion is reported with editorial enhancements such as West headnotes with references to the Topic and Key Number System.

Lawyer's Edition, as it is called, contains all Supreme Court decisions since the court's inception. Its editors include editorial summaries and headnotes to ALR digests. An interesting feature of this publication is that the briefs counsel used in arguing their cases are presented. This gives the researcher an understanding of the legal arguments presented before the court. See Figure 3-11.

Like *United States Reports,* both are published first as biweekly advance sheets. In addition, on their spines they include references to corresponding volumes in *U.S. Reports.* A pagination system called **star paging** is used to help the reader in an unofficial reporter locate the same page in the official source.

Two additional unofficial Supreme Court reporters are worth noting. *United States Law Week* is published weekly by the Bureau of National Affairs (BNA) as a loose-leaf service. It is usually the fastest publisher of Supreme Court opinions. A publication similar to this is the *United States Supreme Court Bulletin,* published by Commerce Clearing House (CCH).

The intermediate federal appeals courts are known as the United States Courts of Appeals, commonly referred to as the circuit court. This court hears cases originating from the United States District Courts, the federal trial court. There are 94 district courts, each apportioned geographically into one of 11 circuits. Separate circuits also exist for the District of Columbia and for special federal courts, bringing the total to 13 (see Figure 3-12).

There is no official reporter to publish decisions of the United States Courts of Appeals. West in 1880 initiated its *Federal Reporter* to publish decisions of that court. It went into its second series in 1932, and its third series in 1993.

Also in 1932, West launched its series, the *Federal Supplement,* to report selected U.S. District Court decisions. Both are set up similar to the *Supreme Court Reporter.*

West also publishes specialized court reporters such as *Federal Rules Decisions, Bankruptcy Reporter, Military Justice Reporter, Federal Claims Reporter,* and the *Veterans Appeals Reporter.* All of these reporters are part of West's National Reporter System.

State Court Reporters

In the late 19th century, the West Publishing Company developed its **National Reporter System**. In addition to specialized federal reporters, regional

---
LEGAL TERMS

star paging   A pagination system to help a reader in an unofficial report locate the same page in the official report.

National Reporter System   West's systematic reporting of decisions from all state appellate courts and many federal courts.

510   U. S. SUPREME COURT REPORTS   14 L ed 2d

*[381 US 479]
*ESTELLE T. GRISWOLD et al., Appellants,

v

STATE OF CONNECTICUT

381 US 479, 14 L ed 2d 510, 85 S Ct 1678

[No. 496]

Argued March 29, 1965. Decided June 7, 1965.

SUMMARY

A Connecticut statute made the use of contraceptives a criminal offense. The executive and medical directors of the Planned Parenthood League of Connecticut were convicted in the Circuit Court for the Sixth Circuit in New Haven, Connecticut, on a charge of having violated the statute as accessories by giving information, instruction, and advice to married persons as to the means of preventing conception. The Appellate Division of the Circuit Court affirmed and its judgment was affirmed by the Supreme Court of Errors of Connecticut. (151 Conn 544, 200 A2d 479.)

On appeal, the Supreme Court of the United States reversed. In an opinion by DOUGLAS, J., expressing the views of five members of the Court, it was held that (1) the defendants had standing to attack the statute, and (2) the statute was invalid as an unconstitutional invasion of the right of privacy of married persons.

GOLDBERG, J., with whom WARREN, Ch.J., and BRENNAN, J., concurred, joined the opinion of the Court, elaborating in a separate opinion the view that the Fourteenth Amendment concept of liberty protects those personal rights that are fundamental, and is not confined to the specific terms of the Bill of Rights.

HARLAN, J., concurred in the result, expressing the view that the statute violated basic values implicit in the concept of ordered liberty.

WHITE, J., also concurred in the result, on the ground that the statute as applied to married couples deprived them of "liberty" without due process of law, as that concept is used in the Fourteenth Amendment.

BLACK and STEWART, JJ., dissented in separate opinions, each joining in the other's opinion. They expressed the view that the statute violated no provision of the Federal Constitution, BLACK, J., particularly emphasizing that there is no constitutional right of privacy.

FIGURE 3-11 Sample page from *United States Supreme Court Reports, Lawyer's Edition*

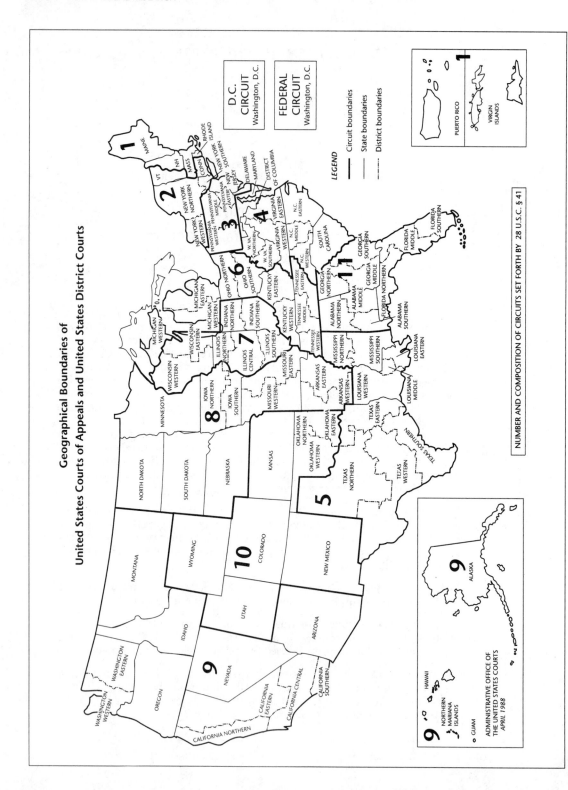

FIGURE 3-12   Federal court circuits and districts map

reporters were established to publish court decisions from the various states in a particular region. The first regional reporter was the *North Western Reporter.*

The regional reporters contain the decisions of all state and District of Columbia appellate courts. Each reporter's name corresponds to the region of the country it serves (see Figure 3-13). For instance, the *South Eastern Reporter* contains decisions from the states of West Virginia, Virginia, North Carolina, South Carolina, and Georgia. However, this pattern is not always followed rigorously. For instance, Kansas is in the *Pacific Reporter,* though it might seem more appropriate in the *South Western Reporter.* This may be because when the *Pacific Reporter*

FIGURE 3-13 National Reporter System map

was created in 1884, Kansas was considered part of the "west" and thus was identified with Pacific-region states such as California.

All reporters are now in their second series, denoted by "2d." In addition, due to the amount of litigation in California, Illinois, and New York, West publishes individual reporters for these states. These reporters are formatted exactly like the regional reporters, except that they contain decisions from only one state.

West also extracts cases from the regional reporters and publishes individual reporters for several states. Because the regional reporters contain cases for several states, purchasing an individual West state reporter gives the user the advantage of the West system at a lower cost.

Of course, many states continue to publish their own official reporters for their appellate courts. At one time all states did so; now many have ceased publishing their own reporters (often for economic reasons) and permit West to take on the responsibility.

Other Sources of Primary Law

Rules of court govern the activities of state and federal courts. Examples include rules of practice for civil, criminal, probate, or appellate procedure. Most states have a separate publication containing court rules. Federal court rules are found in the United States Code and the unofficial code versions.

Agreements that the United States enters into with other nations are called *treaties*. The texts of treaties entered into before 1950 are located in the *Statutes at Large*. Since 1950, treaties have been published in a chronological federal government publication known as *United States Treaties and Other International Agreements* (UST).

Finally, *executive orders* are laws issued by a chief executive pursuant to statutory or constitutional authority. Federal executive orders are published in the *Federal Register*.

Summary

- When a branch of government commands, it creates primary law.

- Constitutions, statutes, administrative regulations, and case law are the major categories of primary law.

- Common law consists of legal principles created by courts when there is an absence of other primary law. These precedents are then applied by judges in other factually similar cases. This is the principle of stare decisis.

- The fundamental law of a nation or state is called its constitution. The U.S. Constitution was written in 1787. Its first 10 amendments are known as the Bill of Rights.

- All states have constitutions based on the federal Constitution.

- A charter serves as the constitution of a local municipality.

- Through the process of judicial review, laws can be found by the courts to be contrary to a constitution and declared void.

- Legislative bodies generally consist of two houses. A bill must pass both houses before it can be submitted to the chief executive for signature.

- The first form of a statutory law is a slip law. Statutes are also published in session law publications.

- The permanent depositories of statutes are called codes. The official federal code is the United States Code. *U.S. Code Annotated* and *U.S. Code Service* are unofficial codes.

- Every state either publishes or gives authority to a private company to publish its code.

- Administrative regulations are rules governing administrative agencies. A proposed regulation must comply with the rulemaking process, which includes publication, before it becomes law. Federal regulations are located in C.F.R.

- Only the published decisions of appellate judges are considered precedent. These decisions or case law are located in reporters. Prior to compilation in a reporter, decisions are published as slip opinions and in advance sheets.

- When a government unit publishes or gives authority to a private company to publish its reporter, that reporter is said to be official. Privately published reporters are unofficial. The most popular unofficial reporter publisher is the West Publishing Company.

- Understanding the component parts of a case is critical to the research process. The most important part is the majority opinion, because it contains the legal principles that can be applied in other cases.

- *United States Reports* is the official reporter of the U.S. Supreme Court. Unofficial reporters include the *Supreme Court Reporter* and *Lawyer's Edition*.

- The intermediate federal appeals courts are the United States Courts of Appeals. The opinions of these courts are published in West's *Federal Reporter*. Selected decisions of the United States District Courts are published in the *Federal Supplement*.

- In the National Reporter System, the states are divided into regions. Regional reporters, the primary unofficial state reporters, publish the appellate decisions of state courts.

- Many states publish their own official reporters.

- Rules of court are generally located in state and federal codes.

- Federal executive orders are published in the *Federal Register*.

- Treaties since 1950 are located in *United States Treaties and Other International Agreements*.

Review Questions

1. Name several common law countries other than the United States.

2. What are the primary purposes of a constitution?

3. Define the concept of judicial review.

4. Explain the process that a bill goes through to become a statute. What are the president's options once a bill reaches him or her?

5. Name the official and unofficial federal codes. Who publishes them?

6. Why must a proposed federal regulation be published in the *Federal Register?* What is the relationship between the *Federal Register* and CFR?

7. What is an advance sheet?

8. What is the difference between official and unofficial reporters?

9. What is the difference between a dissenting opinion and a concurring opinion?

10. Why are West versions of case law often preferred over non-West versions?

Chapter Exercises

1. Locate your state constitution in your state code. Has your state enacted a form of the Equal Rights Amendment?

2. Determine the name of your state regulatory publication. Compare it with CFR. Is it set up similarly? How is it different?

3. What are the names of your state's appellate courts? Does your state still publish its own reporters?

4. Locate the case of *Griswold v. Connecticut,* 381 U.S. 479, 85 S. Ct. 1678, 14 L. Ed. 2d 510 (1965) in any reporter that covers the U.S. Supreme Court. "U.S." stands for *U.S. Reports,* "S. Ct." stands for the *Supreme Court Reporter,* and "L. Ed. 2d" represents the *Lawyer's Edition, Second Series.* The first number stands for the volume; the second is the page on which the case begins. (These concepts are covered in Chapter 7.) Why did Justice Douglas believe that various amendments created a "right to privacy"? What did he mean by the word "penumbra"? Read the concurring and dissenting opinions. What are the authors' reasons for disagreement with the majority?

5. Carefully read the *Stuart v. Board of Supervisors* opinion in Figure 3-10. The majority spends considerable time discussing English common law. Why is this important? Is a woman required to take her husband's name in England? Judge Smith, in his dissent, takes the position that the majority has violated the Maryland Declaration of Rights (a portion of the Maryland Constitution). What are his reasons?

CHAPTER 4

PRIMARY LAW FINDERS AND VERIFICATION

OVERVIEW

The focus of this chapter is understanding the tools that can be used to locate primary law. In addition, an important source for verifying the law's accuracy will be introduced. The amount of law is vast. Utilizing resources that can assist in finding the correct case opinion, statute, or other primary law and verifying its accuracy is critical to efficient and effective research.

First to be examined is *American Law Reports* (ALR), published by Lawyers Cooperative Publishing Company (LCP). ALR is a multivolume publication that reports selected cases of importance. Included with each case is a comprehensive discussion and analysis of the subject of the case called an *annotation*.

Digests are also considered. Locating cases in West's National Reporter System can be facilitated by understanding and using West's Topic and Key Number System. A *key number* is a permanent number assigned to a particular legal principle represented in a case by a headnote. This number is in turn assigned to a digest topic name. These headnotes are compiled in a digest by their key numbers and topic names.

Finally, Shepard's/McGraw-Hill publishes *Shepard's Citations,* a series specifically designed for primary law location and verification. Shepard's is also used to fill in the time gaps between the reporting of a case, enactment of a statute, and passage of a regulation, and the present. During these periods, legal principles are subject to changes or new interpretations, and you must be aware of these changes. Further, Shepard's can be used in locating and verifying additional primary law as well as secondary sources interpreting primary law.

In addition, there are other tools for locating primary law. Some of these resources, such as annotated codes, have already been discussed. Others that will be discussed in future chapters include computer-assisted legal research (CALR) (Chapter 6) and secondary sources such as encyclopedias, treatises, and periodicals (Chapter 5).

PARALEGAL PRACTICE SITUATION

You have been assigned the immediate task of locating primary law in your state in support of the **equitable parent doctrine**.

Peter Houck and his wife Jeanne have been having marital difficulties. As a result, Peter retained your law firm. He believes that his wife is also seeking counsel. Last week he moved out of their home and into a motel.

Prior to Peter's leaving, Jeanne admitted to having had an affair about seven years ago. She told Peter that their son Michael is not his child but rather the child of the man she was involved with at the time. Jeanne has threatened to prove this by way of **HLA blood testing** and then, with this information in hand, fight Peter for custody. Understandably, Peter is quite upset. He considers Michael his child and wants custody of him.

LEGAL TERMS

equitable parent doctrine   A doctrine that permits a nonbiological parent to be considered a natural parent when certain circumstances exist between parent and child, including mutual acknowledgment of their relationship.

HLA testing [†]   Abbreviation of human leukocyte antigen testing. An HLA blood test is a paternity test.

The associate for whom you work remembers learning about the concept of an equitable parent in law school. In such a situation a parent might be given the rights of parenthood even though he or she is not biologically related to the child.

Your job is to determine whether the equitable parent concept is recognized in your state and whether it might apply in this situation.

Importance of Location

Locating a primary law principle is an obvious prerequisite before applying it in a legal document or arguing it before a court. Recall that judges often ask attorneys in court about their authority. Consequently, location is critical to research, because of authority's role in legal advocacy. It is important that the attorney locate, read, and understand the authority, be it case opinion, statute, administrative regulation, or constitutional provision, that supports her proposition. Understanding the following tools will assist you in finding all forms of primary law, but particularly case opinions, the most often cited form of law.

American Law Reports

An excellent yet underappreciated primary law finder is **American Law Reports** (ALR). ALR has a hybrid look to it; in one way it is a reporter (and thus primary law), and in another way it appears to be an encyclopedia or treatise (both secondary law sources). The starting point in ALR is its **reported case**. An opinion is selected by ALR editors because it is representative of an important legal principle. The discussion that follows, called an **annotation**, is an in-depth analysis of the principle from a national perspective. In the process, every other form of primary law that has considered the principle is collected and analyzed as well.

LEGAL TERMS

American Law Reports   A primary law finder and reporter published by Lawyers Cooperative Publishing Company. It is commonly known as ALR.

reported case [†]   A case which has been published.

annotation [†]   1. A notation, appended to any written work, which explains or comments upon its meaning. 2. A commentary that appears immediately following a printed statute and describes the application of the statute in actual cases. Such annotations, with the statutes on which they comment, are published in volumes known as annotated statutes or annotated codes. 3. A notation that follows an opinion of court printed in a court report, explaining the court's action in detail.

Overview

Published by Lawyers Cooperative, ALR was first released in its present form in 1919. ALR had evolved from several previous annotated reporters—*American Decisions, American Reports, American State Reports,* and *Lawyer's Reports Annotated*—all published in the late 1800s. In these reporters, leading cases were fully reported, followed by annotations such as now appear in ALR.

Today ALR is published in more than 500 volumes covering 6 different series, with each volume containing between 10 and 20 cases. Every series spans a specific period of time: *A.L.R.,* 1919 to 1948 (commonly referred to as *A.L.R.* (1st)), 175 volumes; *A.L.R.2d,* 1948 to 1965, 100 volumes; *A.L.R.3d,* 1965 to 1980, 100 volumes; and *A.L.R.4th,* 1980 to 1992, 90 volumes. The current series, *A.L.R.5th,* already has more than 28 volumes. Lawyers Cooperative also publishes *A.L.R. Fed.,* which contains federal cases reported since 1969. Federal cases before that date are included in the appropriate ALR series.

To fully appreciate ALR, you must understand its basic philosophy. Its editors believe that only a small percentage of the total number of cases reported each year are of importance to the legal community. Most cases reported deal with firmly established legal points. The thrust of ALR is to publish only cases that affect current legal principles by making changes or establishing a new legal trend. The reported case is the starting point for the annotation that follows it (except in *A.L.R.5th*). The length of an annotation can be from a few pages to more than 100 pages. ALR's significance and utility are in its annotations.

Paralegal Tip

Many paralegals mistakenly think that ALR will not address issues in their particular state. Unfortunately, it is often bypassed for secondary sources of law such as encyclopedias and hornbooks. However, most trend-setting cases and issues are likely reprinted and discussed in ALR. In the annotations, all states considering new principles are discussed. When dealing with an issue that is uncommon, unusual, or just new, ALR is an excellent starting point.

Component Parts

To fully appreciate and understand an ALR entry, it is necessary to examine the component parts of one.

To begin with, the editors make the decision to publish a case of legal importance. In our example, the published case is the Michigan Court of Appeals opinion of *Atkinson v. Atkinson,* 160 Mich. App. 601, 408 N.W.2d 516, 84 A.L.R.4th 643 (1987) (the name of the case is followed by its full parallel citation). During a divorce action, the wife established that her husband was not the biological father of their son. Based on this fact, the court awarded custody to the wife and denied visitation to the husband. On appeal, the Michigan Court of Appeals held that in a case in which a husband's nonpaternity is shown, the doctrine of equitable parenthood might be applied. Provided certain circumstances exist, a husband could be accorded the rights of a natural parent. These circumstances would include the fact that the husband and child acknowledged their relationship as father and son, that the mother cooperated in the development of this relationship, and that the husband desired to have the rights and responsibilities (including financial support) of a parent.

ALR reported this case because of its significance in establishing a new right for nonbiological fathers. However, for the researcher, the "gold mine" is in the annotation following the case. Here, the equitable parent doctrine is considered from a national perspective. By reading the annotation, you can comprehend the full impact of the principle. References to cases in other jurisdictions that have considered the same theory are included in the annotation.

The *Atkinson* case is reported in *A.L.R.4th* (see Figure 4-1). Besides a full parallel citation to the case, two important research devices are provided in the beginning. First is a short statement indicating the primary legal issue dealt

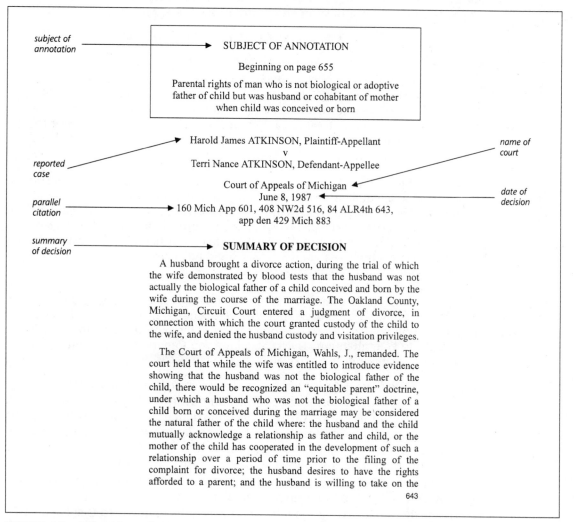

subject of annotation

SUBJECT OF ANNOTATION

Beginning on page 655

Parental rights of man who is not biological or adoptive father of child but was husband or cohabitant of mother when child was conceived or born

reported case

Harold James ATKINSON, Plaintiff-Appellant

v

Terri Nance ATKINSON, Defendant-Appellee

name of court

Court of Appeals of Michigan
June 8, 1987

date of decision

parallel citation

160 Mich App 601, 408 NW2d 516, 84 ALR4th 643, app den 429 Mich 883

summary of decision

SUMMARY OF DECISION

A husband brought a divorce action, during the trial of which the wife demonstrated by blood tests that the husband was not actually the biological father of a child conceived and born by the wife during the course of the marriage. The Oakland County, Michigan, Circuit Court entered a judgment of divorce, in connection with which the court granted custody of the child to the wife, and denied the husband custody and visitation privileges.

The Court of Appeals of Michigan, Wahls, J., remanded. The court held that while the wife was entitled to introduce evidence showing that the husband was not the biological father of the child, there would be recognized an "equitable parent" doctrine, under which a husband who was not the biological father of a child born or conceived during the marriage may be considered the natural father of the child where: the husband and the child mutually acknowledge a relationship as father and child, or the mother of the child has cooperated in the development of such a relationship over a period of time prior to the filing of the complaint for divorce; the husband desires to have the rights afforded to a parent; and the husband is willing to take on the

643

FIGURE 4-1 ALR subject of annotation and summary of decision

with in the annotation, called the subject of annotation. After the caption of the opinion, the editors provide a summary of decision. Read both to obtain a quick overview of the equitable parent doctrine.

Following are headnotes from the case. These headnotes, unlike the ones discussed in Chapter 3, are classified for ALR digests. The purpose of the headnotes is the same here as in a West reporter—to summarize the legal principles from the case. ALR headnotes, however, have limited utility because they do not correspond to those of West's digests and National Reporter System. The headnotes are followed by the names of counsel representing the parties (see Figure 4-2) and then the fully reported case opinion (see Figure 4-3).

The annotation then follows. First in the annotation is the Total Client-Service Library References, abbreviated TCSL. This is a coordinated legal research system consisting of Lawyers Cooperative units (which are national in scope) related to the subject of the annotation. See Figure 4-4.

THE TOTAL CLIENT-SERVICE LIBRARY

A Modern Legal Information System

A thoroughly modern and coordinated legal research system called the Total Client-Service Library (TCSL) has been created by Lawyers Cooperative Publishing ... . The TCSL represents the first successful attempt in over a century to develop a new system of legal research that is specifically designed to meet the needs of the modern lawyer.

* * *

Each of the TCSL publications may be used independently. But legal problems are seldom one-dimensional. Rarely will you find a case which can be considered "just a tort problem" or "simply a matter involving contracts or trial practice." However, under the pressure of the legal curriculum, many students tend to think in these terms and approach the matter at hand by the first aspect which presents itself—an approach that could prove disastrous if the other aspects of the problem are not investigated.

The unique strength of the TCSL is the way it functions as an integrated system. No matter how you approach your legal research—no matter which handle of the problem you grasp first—the other facets of the problem are automatically brought to your attention. The TCSL allows you to pursue each avenue of research to whatever degree adequately meets your needs.

From *The Living Law: A Guide to Modern Legal Research* (1992). See Figure 4-5.

Next in the annotation is the *scheme,* an outline of the entire annotation. At this point, you might be directed to a particular concept to research. The scheme is especially helpful if you already have an understanding of the equitable parent doctrine.

The alphabetized index follows. Here, the entire annotation is broken down by detailed subject matter (see Figure 4-6). Once inside the annotation, this is the most efficient way of looking up a particular point.

This is then followed by the table of jurisdictions represented (see Figure 4-7). This is important to the researcher who is looking for authority in states other

ATKINSON V ATKINSON
160 Mich App 601, 84 ALR4th 643

84 ALR4th

A.L.R.
volume
number

responsibility of paying child support. The court held that the husband in this case was entitled to be treated as a natural father under the doctrine of equitable parent where: the child was conceived and born during the parties' marriage; the husband and child had always had a close and affectionate father-son relationship; the husband was the only father that the child had ever known and was active in the child's life; the husband desired to have the relationship continue and to have the rights accorded to a father, along with the responsibility of supporting the child; and the wife had acknowledged at trial that the husband had related to the child as a father and that the wife had waited until answering a question in interrogatories filed by the husband in the divorce action before asserting that the husband was not the child's biological father.

headnotes

———

HEADNOTES
Classified to ALR Digests

Children Out-of-Wedlock § 1; Evidence § 1170 — putative parent's right to rebut legitimacy of child

1. Although the burden of proof is high, a putative parent may rebut the legitimacy of a child born to a couple during their marriage, and, accordingly, the wife is entitled to offer evidence in a divorce proceeding that the husband is not the biological father of the couple's child.

Divorce and Separation § 5 — court's authority — determination of parenthood

2. In divorce actions, the court may determine whether the husband is the father of the wife's child.

Evidence § 558 — divorce action — wife's challenge to husband's paternity of child — admissibility of HLA test

3. It is within the power of a court in a divorce proceeding, wherein the wife alleges that the husband is not actually the biological father of her child, to order the father to submit to a human leukocyte antigen (HLA) blood test in order to determine the paternity of the child born during the marriage, since it is a natural extension of the "best evidence" rule that a mother challenging the father's

paternity should be allowed to present her best evidence (just as a father who denies paternity is allowed to present his best evidence), the HLA test is extremely reliable in determining the parentage of a child, and it is the court's role to determine the parentage of minor children.

Estoppel and Waiver § 34.8 — equitable estoppel — general elements

4. Equitable estoppel arises when one causes another, by acts, representations, or silence, intentionally or through culpable neglect, to believe in the existence of some material fact and to detrimentally rely on the existence of such fact.

Estoppel and Waiver § 49 — divorce proceeding — estoppel of wife from denying husband's paternity of child

5. Although equitable estoppel may be applied to a divorce proceeding, equitable estoppel does not apply to bar a wife from asserting in a divorce proceeding that the husband is not the biological father of the wife's child where her claim that the husband is not the biological father is made early in the proceedings, and, thus, a representation by the wife of the husband's paternity upon which the

page
number

FIGURE 4-2 ALR headnotes and appearance of counsel

84 ALR4th   ATKINSON V ATKINSON
160 Mich App 601, 84 ALR4th 643

husband may have relied could not have existed.

Evidence § 1391 — admissibility of results of HLA blood test — sufficiency of foundation

6. The foundation requirements for the admission of human leukocyte antigen (HLA) test results in a paternity action are that the blood tested is in fact that of the defendant, the plaintiff, and the child, and that the test results are based on reliable blood samples, and this foundation includes the establishment of a chain of identification from the time the blood samples are taken to the time the samples are analyzed, either by direct or circumstantial evidence.

Evidence § 1391 — HLA blood test results — admissibility in divorce proceeding on issue of child's paternity — sufficiency of foundation

7. A sufficient foundation is laid in a divorce proceeding for the admission of human leukocyte antigen (HLA) blood test results, for purposes of establishing the wife's contention that the husband is not the biological father of her child, where a medical technologist has testified from personal knowledge as to the identification and labeling procedures for blood samples, and as to the procedures used when samples are taken out of the locked box in which they are kept, and sufficient evidence is presented to show that the blood samples are those of the parties and of the child in question and that the HLA blood tests are reliable and relevant evidence.

Parent and Child § 13 — doctrine of equitable parent — husband who is not biological father of wife's child

8. There exists a doctrine of "equitable parent," under which a husband who is not the biological father of a child born or conceived during the marriage may be considered the natural father of that child for purposes of determining custody and visitation rights upon divorce, where: the husband and the child mutually acknowledge a relationship as father and child, or the mother of the child has cooperated in the development of such a relationship over a period of time prior to the filing of the complaint for divorce; the husband desires to have the rights afforded to a parent; and the husband is willing to take on the responsibility of paying child support.

[Annotated]

Divorce and Separation §§ 118, 120; Parent and Child § 3 — duty of support and right to custody and visitation — necessity of biological relationship — exceptions

9. It is generally recognized that biological parents are obligated by law to maintain and support their children, and implicitly coupled with this duty is the right to custody or visitation, while, when there is no biological relationship between a putative father and a child from which a support obligation may arise, the reciprocal right to custody or visitation similarly does not arise because the putative father is not treated as a "parent" under the Child Custody Act; however, this general rule is subject to exceptions and it is recognized by the court that a person who is not the biological father of a child may be considered a "parent" against his will, and is consequently burdened with the responsibility of the support of this child, where he marries a woman knowing that she is carrying a child who may or may not be his offspring and thereafter holds himself out as the father and supporter of the child for some time, and it is a logical extension of this rule to recognize that under certain circumstances, a person who is not the biological father of a child may be considered a parent when he desires such recognition, is willing to support the child, and wants the reciprocal rights of custody or visitation afforded to a parent.

[Annotated]

645

FIGURE 4-2   *(continued)*

Divorce and Separation § 118 — custody and visitation — treatment of husband as equitable parent though he is not biological father

10. A husband is entitled to be treated in a divorce proceeding as the "equitable parent" of a child for purposes of custody and visitation, notwithstanding that the wife has proved that the husband is not the biological father of the child, where: the child was conceived and born during the parties' marriage; the husband and child have always had a close and affectionate father-son relationship; the husband is the only father that the child has ever known and has been active in the child's life; the husband desires to have the relationship continue and to have the rights accorded to a father, along with the responsibility of supporting the child; and the wife has acknowledged at trial that the husband related to the child as a father and that the wife had waited until answering a question in interrogatories filed by the husband in the divorce action before asserting that the husband was not the child's biological father.

[Annotated]

Descent and Distribution § 28 — intestate succession — doctrine of equitable adoption

11. There is recognized in the law of intestate succession the doctrine of "equitable adoption," under which an implied contract to adopt is found when a close relationship, similar to a parent-child relationship, exits between a child and the deceased, and, as a result, the child has a right to share in the deceased's estate, and under this doctrine a child was the heir of his mother's husband where the husband believed the child to be his, treated the child as his, and wished to continue to do so, notwithstanding that it had been proved during divorce proceedings that the husband was not the biological father of the child.

Divorce and Separation § 118 —

child custody — best interest of child as major concern

12. The best interest of the child is the major concern of any custody determination.

Appeal and Error § 533; Divorce and Separation § 82 — award of attorneys' fees to enable party to carry on or defend divorce action — trial court discretion — standard of appellate review

13. Necessary and reasonable attorneys' fees may be awarded to enable a party to carry on or defend a divorce action, and a trial court's award of such fees will not be disturbed on appeal absent an abuse of discretion; there was no abuse of discretion where a divorce court had ordered a husband to pay $3,500 of the wife's attorney's fees since there was a sufficient showing that the wife was in need of financial assistance in order to defend the divorce action where the husband's yearly income was approximately $55,000, the wife's yearly income was approximately $9,600, the husband's attorneys' fees amounted to $46,000, and the wife's fees were $20,000, at the time of trial.

Appeal and Error § 807; Evidence § 852 — exclusion of expert testimony for failure to list witness — reversible error

14. A husband in a divorce proceeding who was dissatisfied with the hearing of a referee to whom the issue of child custody had been referred, and who had requested a de novo hearing as authorized by statute, should have been permitted to call at the de novo hearing a psychologist who had evaluated the child and who was to offer expert testimony as to the psychological damage that separation from the husband would cause the child, notwithstanding the wife's objection that the husband had not given notice that this expert testimony would be offered, since there is no requirement in the court that rules that a party must supply a

FIGURE 4-2 *(continued)*

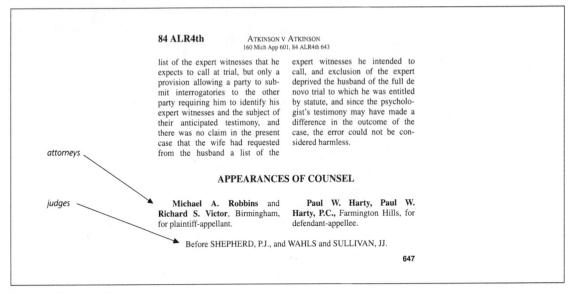

84 ALR4th   ATKINSON V ATKINSON
160 Mich App 601, 84 ALR4th 643

list of the expert witnesses that he expects to call at trial, but only a provision allowing a party to submit interrogatories to the other party requiring him to identify his expert witnesses and the subject of their anticipated testimony, and there was no claim in the present case that the wife had requested from the husband a list of the expert witnesses he intended to call, and exclusion of the expert deprived the husband of the full de novo trial to which he was entitled by statute, and since the psychologist's testimony may have made a difference in the outcome of the case, the error could not be considered harmless.

attorneys

judges

APPEARANCES OF COUNSEL

Michael A. Robbins and **Richard S. Victor**, Birmingham, for plaintiff-appellant.

Paul W. Harty, Paul W. Harty, P.C., Farmington Hills, for defendant-appellee.

Before SHEPHERD, P.J., and WAHLS and SULLIVAN, JJ.

647

FIGURE 4-2   *(continued)*

than Michigan. Because *A.L.R.4th* is supplemented annually, you are also warned at this point to check the pocket parts for later cases.

Finally, the annotation text, starting with the scope, is presented (see Figure 4-7). The scope delineates the subject of the annotation. It also indicates if an earlier annotation has been superseded. A related matters section provides informative references to areas related to the equitable parent doctrine in other ALR volumes. For instance, to research the subject of awarding attorney fees in a parent-nonparent custody case, you would turn to volume 45 of *A.L.R.4th,* page 212. In the summary and comment, the author of the annotation provides his analysis about the subject, as well as a comprehensive summary. This is followed by a detailed discussion of the equitable parent doctrine from a national perspective. (See Figure 4-8.) It is in this section that other cases considering the principle are noted and analyzed. This is the "meat" of the annotation and will most likely be the largest part.

In several ways, each series of ALR has undergone improvements in updating and style. With the exception of *A.L.R.* (1st) and *A.L.R.2d,* pocket parts are published annually for annotation revision. *A.L.R.2d* is updated through its *Later Case Service* volumes, which are themselves updated with pocket parts. *A.L.R.* (1st) is updated through a series called *ALR Blue Book of Supplementary Decisions.*

In *A.L.R.5th,* the most significant change is that the leading cases are reported in the back of the volume, separate from the annotation. This change recognizes the importance of the annotations. Also, the TCSL is published after the scheme (now called the *article outline*). The table of jurisdictions represented is now called the *jurisdictional table of cited statutes and cases.* To help in understanding the features of *A.L.R.5th,* LCP publishes a handy free pamphlet, *How to Use ALR 5th.*

ATKINSON V ATKINSON   **84 ALR4th**
160 Mich App 601, 84 ALR4th 643

OPINION OF THE COURT

majority opinion

WAHLS, Judge.

Plaintiff, Harold J. Atkinson, appeals as of right from an Oakland Circuit Court judgment of divorce. The issues on appeal generally involve the award of custody of the couple's child to defendant, Terri N. Atkinson, the denial of visitation privileges to plaintiff, the award of attorney fees to defendant, and the refusal of the trial court to allow the testimony of an expert witness. We hold that a wife may establish the nonpaternity of a husband in a divorce action through use of blood testing, but that, notwithstanding the fact that the husband is not the biological father of a child born during the marriage, the husband may acquire rights of paternity under the theory of "equitable parent" and the analogous doctrine of "equitable adoption."

The parties were married on March 1, 1973. The only child of the marriage, James Baird Atkinson (Baird), was born on August 1, 1981. Defendant left the marital home with Baird on February 5, 1985, and, in March, 1985, plaintiff filed for divorce. During the divorce proceeding, defendant contended that plaintiff was not the biological father of Baird and plaintiff vigorously argued that he was Baird's father. The trial court awarded defendant custody of Baird and attorney fees and denied plaintiff custody and visitation privileges.

Plaintiff's first argument is that he should not have been compelled to submit to a human leukocyte antigen (HLA) blood test to determine the paternity of a child he has always treated as his own.

[1] The issue of whether the court in a divorce case may compel the husband to submit to blood testing in order to determine whether he is the biological father of a child born during the marriage has never been addressed by a Michigan appellate court. Originally, Michigan adhered to Lord Mansfield's Rule, which prohibited testimony by either spouse in a divorce action that showed a child born during the marriage to be illegitimate. *Serafin v. Serafin*, 401 Mich. 629, 258 N.W.2d 461 (1977). However, Michigan shifted away from that prohibition in *Serafin*, wherein the Supreme Court determined that the policy reasons behind Lord Mansfield's Rule of reducing the number of public charges and preserving family peace and harmony were no longer viable. The Court noted that illegitimacy is not held in such low regard as it use to be, and that state and federal laws now serve to lessen

648

FIGURE 4-3 Portion of *Atkinson v. Atkinson* as reprinted in ALR

Accessing ALR

Though ALR can be accessed through direct reference to its annotations, the best way is through the *ALR Index*. This separate, six-volume set provides comprehensive coverage for all ALRs (except *A.L.R.* (1st)) and the *Lawyer's Edition*.

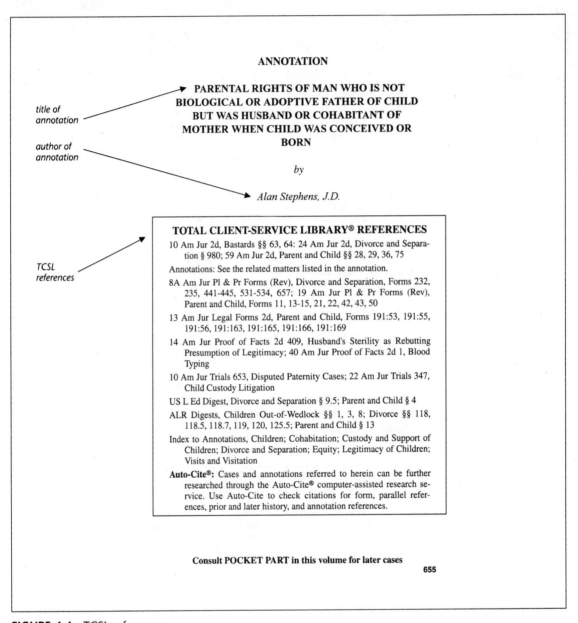

Figure content:

ANNOTATION

title of annotation

PARENTAL RIGHTS OF MAN WHO IS NOT BIOLOGICAL OR ADOPTIVE FATHER OF CHILD BUT WAS HUSBAND OR COHABITANT OF MOTHER WHEN CHILD WAS CONCEIVED OR BORN

by

author of annotation

Alan Stephens, J.D.

TCSL references

TOTAL CLIENT-SERVICE LIBRARY® REFERENCES

10 Am Jur 2d, Bastards §§ 63, 64: 24 Am Jur 2d, Divorce and Separation § 980; 59 Am Jur 2d, Parent and Child §§ 28, 29, 36, 75

Annotations: See the related matters listed in the annotation.

8A Am Jur Pl & Pr Forms (Rev), Divorce and Separation, Forms 232, 235, 441-445, 531-534, 657; 19 Am Jur Pl & Pr Forms (Rev), Parent and Child, Forms 11, 13-15, 21, 22, 42, 43, 50

13 Am Jur Legal Forms 2d, Parent and Child, Forms 191:53, 191:55, 191:56, 191:163, 191:165, 191:166, 191:169

14 Am Jur Proof of Facts 2d 409, Husband's Sterility as Rebutting Presumption of Legitimacy; 40 Am Jur Proof of Facts 2d 1, Blood Typing

10 Am Jur Trials 653, Disputed Paternity Cases; 22 Am Jur Trials 347, Child Custody Litigation

US L Ed Digest, Divorce and Separation § 9.5; Parent and Child § 4

ALR Digests, Children Out-of-Wedlock §§ 1, 3, 8; Divorce §§ 118, 118.5, 118.7, 119, 120, 125.5; Parent and Child § 13

Index to Annotations, Children; Cohabitation; Custody and Support of Children; Divorce and Separation; Equity; Legitimacy of Children; Visits and Visitation

Auto-Cite®: Cases and annotations referred to herein can be further researched through the Auto-Cite® computer-assisted research service. Use Auto-Cite to check citations for form, parallel references, prior and later history, and annotation references.

Consult POCKET PART in this volume for later cases

655

FIGURE 4-4 TCSL references

It was introduced in 1986 and was designed to replace a number of smaller indexes. The index contains an alphabetical listing of both factual and legal terms, in turn divided by subject with references to specific ALR volumes. An important feature of the index is the table of laws, rules, and regulations, which indicates where statutory and other noncase law are referenced in ALR.

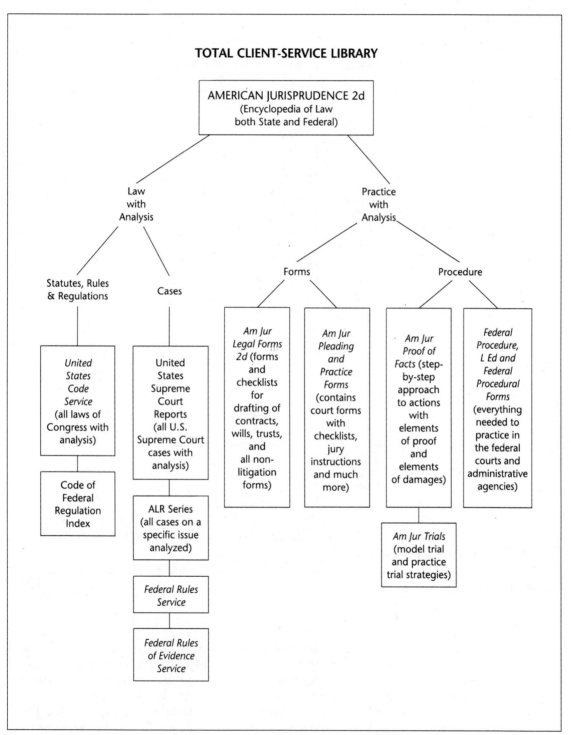

FIGURE 4-5 Total Client-Service Library chart

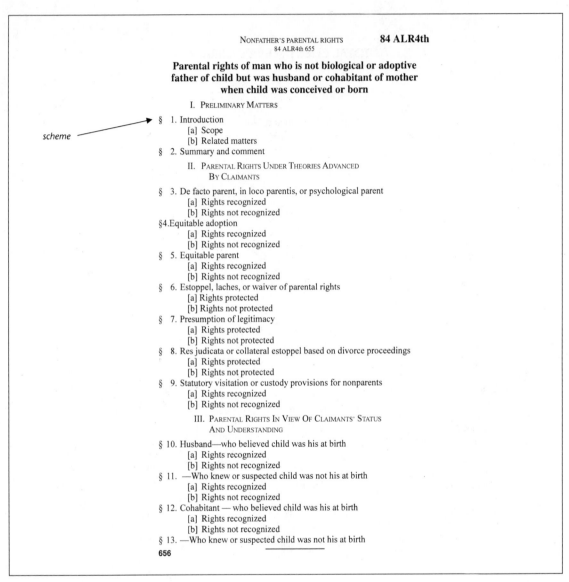

FIGURE 4-6   ALR scheme and index

LCP publishes digests accompanying each ALR series. They are classified into more than 400 alphabetically arranged topics. Each topic reproduces the headnotes from the cases reported. There is one digest for *A.L.R.3d, 4th, 5th,* and *Fed.;* another for *A.L.R.2d;* and another for *A.L.R.* (1st).

Finally, Lawyers Cooperative provides a hotline for ALR questions, 1-800-527-0430. Through this service you can find out about cases too recent to be published in the annotations or pocket parts.

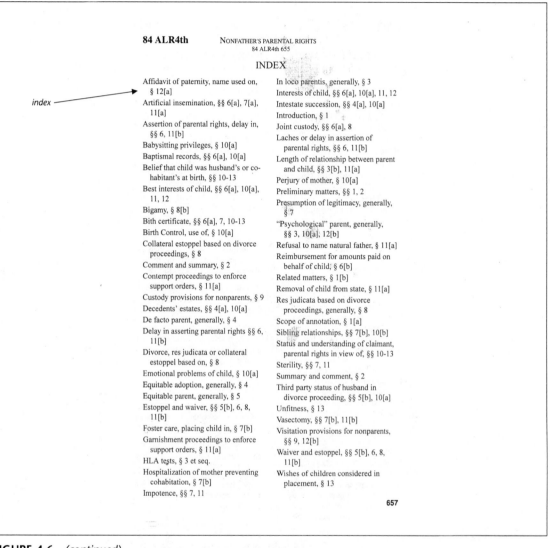

index →

84 ALR4th   NONFATHER'S PARENTAL RIGHTS
84 ALR4th 655

INDEX

Affidavit of paternity, name used on,
    § 12[a]
Artificial insemination, §§ 6[a], 7[a],
    11[a]
Assertion of parental rights, delay in,
    §§ 6, 11[b]
Babysitting privileges, § 10[a]
Baptismal records, §§ 6[a], 10[a]
Belief that child was husband's or co-
    habitant's at birth, §§ 10-13
Best interests of child, §§ 6[a], 10[a],
    11, 12
Bigamy, § 8[b]
Bith certificate, §§ 6[a], 7, 10-13
Birth Control, use of, § 10[a]
Collateral estoppel based on divorce
    proceedings, § 8
Comment and summary, § 2
Contempt proceedings to enforce
    support orders, § 11[a]
Custody provisions for nonparents, § 9
Decedents' estates, §§ 4[a], 10[a]
De facto parent, generally, § 4
Delay in asserting parental rights §§ 6,
    11[b]
Divorce, res judicata or collateral
    estoppel based on, § 8
Emotional problems of child, § 10[a]
Equitable adoption, generally, § 4
Equitable parent, generally, § 5
Estoppel and waiver, §§ 5[b], 6, 8,
    11[b]
Foster care, placing child in, § 7[b]
Garnishment proceedings to enforce
    support orders, § 11[a]
HLA tests, § 3 et seq.
Hospitalization of mother preventing
    cohabitation, § 7[b]
Impotence, §§ 7, 11

In loco parentis, generally, § 3
Interests of child, §§ 6[a], 10[a], 11, 12
Intestate succession, §§ 4[a], 10[a]
Introduction, § 1
Joint custody, §§ 6[a], 8
Laches or delay in assertion of
    parental rights, §§ 6, 11[b]
Length of relationship between parent
    and child, §§ 3[b], 11[a]
Perjury of mother, § 10[a]
Preliminary matters, §§ 1, 2
Presumption of legitimacy, generally,
    § 7
"Psychological" parent, generally,
    §§ 3, 10[a], 12[b]
Refusal to name natural father, § 11[a]
Reimbursement for amounts paid on
    behalf of child, § 6[b]
Related matters, § 1[b]
Removal of child from state, § 11[a]
Res judicata based on divorce
    proceedings, generally, § 8
Scope of annotation, § 1[a]
Sibling relationships, §§ 7[b], 10[b]
Status and understanding of claimant,
    parental rights in view of, §§ 10-13
Sterility, §§ 7, 11
Summary and comment, § 2
Third party status of husband in
    divorce proceeding, §§ 5[b], 10[a]
Unfitness, § 13
Vasectomy, §§ 7[b], 11[b]
Visitation provisions for nonparents,
    §§ 9, 12[b]
Waiver and estoppel, §§ 5[b], 6, 8,
    11[b]
Wishes of children considered in
    placement, § 13

657

FIGURE 4-6   *(continued)*

Digests

Another useful resource in researching case law is the use of a **digest**. Headnotes from case opinions are grouped together in alphabetically arranged topics

—————————————————— LEGAL TERMS ——————————————————

digest [†]   A series of volumes containing summaries of cases organized by legal topics,
subject areas, and so on. Digests are essential for legal research. ... Digests cover virtually all
cases ever decided in the United States; some digests are limited to specific jurisdictions or to
specific fields in the law. Digests are updated continuously to ensure that they are current.

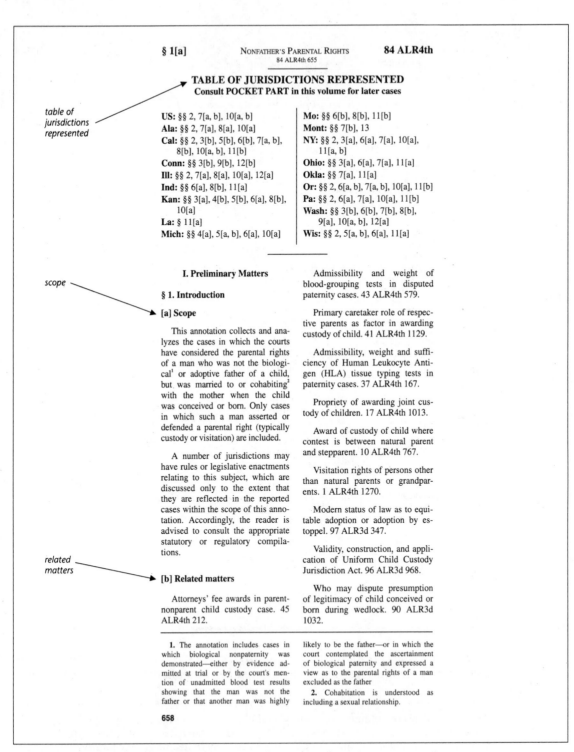

table of
jurisdictions
represented

§ 1[a]   NONFATHER'S PARENTAL RIGHTS   **84 ALR4th**
                        84 ALR4th 655

TABLE OF JURISDICTIONS REPRESENTED
Consult POCKET PART in this volume for later cases

US: §§ 2, 7[a, b], 10[a, b]
Ala: §§ 2, 7[a], 8[a], 10[a]
Cal: §§ 2, 3[b], 5[b], 6[b], 7[a, b],
    8[b], 10[a, b], 11[b]
Conn: §§ 3[b], 9[b], 12[b]
Ill: §§ 2, 7[a], 8[a], 10[a], 12[a]
Ind: §§ 6[a], 8[b], 11[a]
Kan: §§ 3[a], 4[b], 5[b], 6[a], 8[b],
    10[a]
La: § 11[a]
Mich: §§ 4[a], 5[a, b], 6[a], 10[a]

Mo: §§ 6[b], 8[b], 11[b]
Mont: §§ 7[b], 13
NY: §§ 2, 3[a], 6[a], 7[a], 10[a],
    11[a, b]
Ohio: §§ 3[a], 6[a], 7[a], 11[a]
Okla: §§ 7[a], 11[a]
Or: §§ 2, 6[a, b], 7[a, b], 10[a], 11[b]
Pa: §§ 2, 6[a], 7[a], 10[a], 11[b]
Wash: §§ 3[b], 6[b], 7[b], 8[b],
    9[a], 10[a, b], 12[a]
Wis: §§ 2, 5[a, b], 6[a], 11[a]

I. Preliminary Matters

§ 1. Introduction

[a] Scope

This annotation collects and analyzes the cases in which the courts have considered the parental rights of a man who was not the biological[1] or adoptive father of a child, but was married to or cohabiting[2] with the mother when the child was conceived or born. Only cases in which such a man asserted or defended a parental right (typically custody or visitation) are included.

A number of jurisdictions may have rules or legislative enactments relating to this subject, which are discussed only to the extent that they are reflected in the reported cases within the scope of this annotation. Accordingly, the reader is advised to consult the appropriate statutory or regulatory compilations.

[b] Related matters

Attorneys' fee awards in parent-nonparent child custody case. 45 ALR4th 212.

Admissibility and weight of blood-grouping tests in disputed paternity cases. 43 ALR4th 579.

Primary caretaker role of respective parents as factor in awarding custody of child. 41 ALR4th 1129.

Admissibility, weight and sufficiency of Human Leukocyte Antigen (HLA) tissue typing tests in paternity cases. 37 ALR4th 167.

Propriety of awarding joint custody of children. 17 ALR4th 1013.

Award of custody of child where contest is between natural parent and stepparent. 10 ALR4th 767.

Visitation rights of persons other than natural parents or grandparents. 1 ALR4th 1270.

Modern status of law as to equitable adoption or adoption by estoppel. 97 ALR3d 347.

Validity, construction, and application of Uniform Child Custody Jurisdiction Act. 96 ALR3d 968.

Who may dispute presumption of legitimacy of child conceived or born during wedlock. 90 ALR3d 1032.

---

1. The annotation includes cases in which biological nonpaternity was demonstrated—either by evidence admitted at trial or by the court's mention of unadmitted blood test results showing that the man was not the father or that another man was highly

likely to be the father—or in which the court contemplated the ascertainment of biological paternity and expressed a view as to the parental rights of a man excluded as the father

2. Cohabitation is understood as including a sexual relationship.

FIGURE 4-7 ALR table of jurisdictions, scope, related matters, and summary and comment

84 ALR4th   Nonfather's Parental Rights   § 2
84 ALR4th 655

Proof of husband's impotency or sterility as rebutting presumption of legitimacy. 84 ALR3d 495.

Effect, in subsequent proceedings, or paternity findings or implications in divorce or annulment decree of in support or custody order made incidental thereto. 78 ALR3d 846.

Modern status of maternal preference rule or presumption in child custody cases. 70 ALR3d 262.

Statute of limitations in illegitimacy or bastardy proceedings. 59 ALR3d 685.

Presumption of legitimacy of child born after annulment, divorce, or separation. 46 ALR3d 158.

Child's wishes as factor in awarding custody. 4 ALR3d 1396.

Determination of paternity, legitimacy, or legitimation in action for divorce, separation, or annulment. 65 ALR2d 1381.

Material facts existing at the time of rendition of decree of divorce but not presented to court, as ground for modification of provision as to custody of child. 9 ALR2d 623.

Constitutional principles applicable to award or modification of custody of child—Supreme Court cases. 80 L Ed 2d 886.

summary and comment

§ 2. Summary and comment

A man who is not the biological or adoptive father of a child about whom he has developed parental feelings, either because he originally believed the child to be his or because of an agreement with the mother about raising the child together, is confronted in an attempt to assert or defend his parental rights in opposition to the mother with a powerful presumption that the child's welfare is best served by being in the custody of a natural parent (10 Am Jur 2d, Bastards § 63; 59 Am Jur 2d, Parent and Child §§ 28, 29), whose wishes concerning visitation are also given considerable weight by the courts (59 Am Jur 2d, Parent and Child § 36). On the other hand, such a man who is married to the mother and enjoys her support in his defense of his parental rights may have an advantage against his challenger—typically the natural father —because of the courts' inclination to protect the marital union.[3] The

3. See, for example, John M. v Paula T. (1990, Pa) 571 A2d 1380.

659

FIGURE 4-7 *(continued)*

STEPS IN USING ALR

1. Using terms and phrases, search ALR Index (illustrated in Chapter 9.)

2. Turn to appropriate ALR entry.

3. Review subject of annotation and summary of decision for an overview.

4. Read reported case.

5. Review scheme and index for relevant topic.

6. Check table of jurisdictions represented for other states.

7. Read annotation.

8. Check pocket parts for updates.

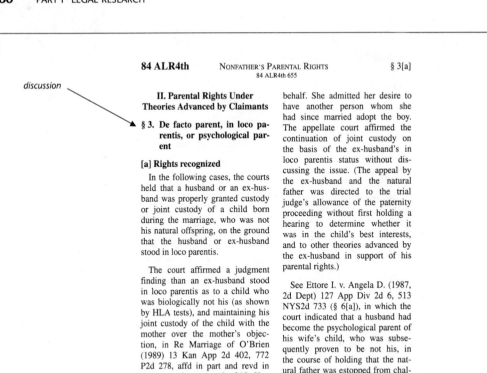

discussion

II. Parental Rights Under Theories Advanced by Claimants

§ 3. De facto parent, in loco parentis, or psychological parent

[a] Rights recognized

In the following cases, the courts held that a husband or an ex-husband was properly granted custody or joint custody of a child born during the marriage, who was not his natural offspring, on the ground that the husband or ex-husband stood in loco parentis.

The court affirmed a judgment finding than an ex-husband stood in loco parentis as to a child who was biologically not his (as shown by HLA tests), and maintaining his joint custody of the child with the mother over the mother's objection, in Re Marriage of O'Brien (1989) 13 Kan App 2d 402, 772 P2d 278, affd in part and revd in part on other grounds 245 Kan 591, 783 P2d 331. The mother testified that near the time of conception she had engaged in sexual intercourse with both her future husband and another man; when the child was born 6 months after the parties' marriage, she decided that her husband was the father. She claimed to have begun to suspect that he was not the father when the boy reached the age of 3½, after the divorce and after the joint custody subsequently obtained by her ex-husband had continued for 6 months; she informed both her ex-husband and the other man of her suspicion and then filed a paternity action, from which she was dismissed but which was allowed to proceed on the child's behalf. She admitted her desire to have another person whom she had since married adopt the boy. The appellate court affirmed the continuation of joint custody on the basis of the ex-husband's in loco parentis status without discussing the issue. (The appeal by the ex-husband and the natural father was directed to the trial judge's allowance of the paternity proceeding without first holding a hearing to determine whether it was in the child's best interests, and to other theories advanced by the ex-husband in support of his parental rights.)

See Ettore I. v. Angela D. (1987, 2d Dept) 127 App Div 2d 6, 513 NYS2d 733 (§ 6[a]), in which the court indicated that a husband had become the psychological parent of his wife's child, who was subsequently proven to be not his, in the course of holding that the natural father was estopped from challenging the husband's paternity.

In Nelson v Nelson (1983, Franklin Co) 10 Ohio App 3d 36, 10 Ohio BR 44, 460 NE2d 653, a divorce action filed by the wife, the court held that temporary and permanent custody of a child born during the marriage had been properly granted to the husband notwithstanding the parties' stipulation that the boy was not the husband's biological child, under the rationale that the husband stood in loco parentis to the child after accepting his wife's adultery and raising the boy for 12 years as his own son. The court referred to a long-standing rule that a man who marries a woman who is pregnant by another man consents to

663

FIGURE 4-8 ALR discussion of equitable parent doctrine

and then organized into numerical subdivisions within each topic. These headnotes are then published in books called *digests*. Each digest series covers a specific jurisdiction, region, subject matter, or period of time. Though Lawyers Cooperative publishes digests to be used with ALR, West digests are the most well known and most frequently used.

West Digests

Recall that the West Publishing Company reports all appellate cases issuing from state and federal courts. Because of this unique role, West has been able to develop a digest system based on its reporters. This is referred to as the *Topic and Key Number Digest System.*

The basis of this system is more than 400 different key topics. In every digest, these topics are arranged alphabetically, from "Abandoned and Lost Property" to "Zoning and Planning." These topics are then divided into subtopics, each of which is assigned a key number. West defines a *key number* as "a permanent, or fixed number given to a specific point of case law." Conceptually, the system is explained as follows:

> The Key Number System may be understood easily by remembering how to locate a house within your city. Each street in your city represents one of the digest topics. On each street there are many houses each having a number corresponding to a key number. This means that both the topic (street) and key number (house number) are necessary to locate a particular house.

> Every time a case is decided on a certain point of law, the digest paragraph dealing with that point is delivered to the house assigned to that point of law. Therefore, every house will have delivered to it digest paragraphs from all cases that have dealt with its assigned point of law.

From *West's Law Finder* (1991). See Figure 4-9.

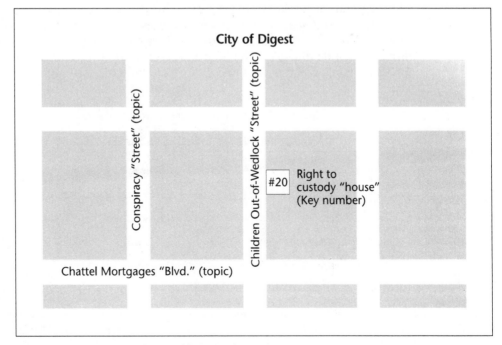

FIGURE 4-9 Concept of topical key number system

As part of the reporting process, editors at West thoroughly read and analyze every case submitted to them by state appellate and federal courts. They then create headnotes for every significant principle of law found in an opinion. Each headnote is then published at the beginning of the West opinion from which the headnote was taken, as well as in applicable digests.

As part of its American Digest System, West publishes a variety of digests. First and foremost is the *General Digest,* which collects and publishes headnotes from every appellate court in the country. It is the most current source of headnotes. A new volume is published approximately each month. The *General Digest* is currently in its eighth series.

To review a certain key number, the researcher would have to search every volume of the *General Digest.* To help in consolidation, West in 1906 published its first *Decennial Digest,* covering headnotes of the *General Digest* for the period of 1897 to 1906. Since then, every 10 years West has published a *Decennial Digest.* Starting with the *Ninth Decennial Digest,* West decided to issue the decennial digest in two parts, each covering five years. For example, the *Ninth Decennial Digest* is divided between Part I, 1976 to 1981, and Part II, 1981 to 1986. The *Tenth Decennial Digest* is the most recent.

For cases prior to 1896, West has published the *Century Digest.* Cases reported from 1658 (the year of the first reported American case) to 1896 are contained here. The *Century Digest* does not employ the key number system. Rather, a modified numbering system is used, although this system can be cross-referenced into the key number system.

As a practical matter, you will spend of most of your time using one of West's state regional or jurisdictional digests. This is because the vast majority of legal problems are state-based. West publishes digests for four of its regional reporters—Atlantic, North Western, Pacific, and South Eastern (see Figure 4-10)—but recently discontinued its digest for the Southern region. It also publishes separate digests for every state, except Nevada and Utah. The states of North and South Dakota are

VARIOUS NONSTATE DIGESTS PUBLISHED BY WEST

Digest Name	Coverage
Supreme Court Digest	Cases from the *Supreme Court Reporter*
Federal Digest	Cases from all federal courts
Bankruptcy Digest	Cases from the *Bankruptcy Reporter*
Military Justice Digest	Cases from the *Military Justice Reporter*
Claims Court Digest	Cases from the *Federal Claims Reporter*
Merit Systems Protection Board Digest	Cases from the *United States Merit Systems Protection Board Reporter*

WEST'S
NORTH WESTERN DIGEST
2d

Volume 5A

CHATTEL MORTGAGES—CONSPIRACY

ST. PAUL, MINN.

WEST PUBLISHING CO.

FIGURE 4-10 Sample title page of digest. (Reprinted with the permission of West Publishing Company.)

combined in the *Dakota Digest*. The *Virginia and West Virginia Digest* contains both states. There is also a *District of Columbia Digest,* which covers cases emanating from Washington, D.C. State digests report all state cases, as well as federal cases originating in the U.S. District Court within that state. State and regional digests are updated through annually issued pocket parts. West also publishes 13 additional digests on specialized and federal matters.

How to Use a Digest

To understand how to properly use a digest, take another look at the case of *Atkinson v. Atkinson,* 160 Mich. App. 601, 408 N.W.2d 516, 54 A.L.R.4th 643 (1987). To assist in your understanding, the West version of the opinion is provided in Figure 4-11.

Known Case Methods

Assume that in the course of your research you came across a reference to *Atkinson.* After locating and reading the entire opinion, you realize that the principle in headnote no. 6, "Children Out-of-Wedlock 20," discusses the equitable parent doctrine and is helpful to your client. Assume further that you are not in Michigan but in a state that is in the North Western region. Here, the topic and key number can assist in your search for authority in your state.

Situated after the *North Western 2d* series in the library would be West's *North Western Digest 2d*. To locate the topic "Children Out-of-Wedlock," you could peruse the spines of the volumes. "Children Out-of Wedlock" would be in volume 5A "Chattel Mortgages – Conspiracy." You would turn to your topic. Then, using key number 20, you would locate the *Atkinson* headnote by finding "Mich. App. 1987" (see Figure 4-12). On that page, you would find headnotes from other regional cases dealing with the same or similar issue. Remember, too, that you could use *any* West digest to access this topic. Finally, you will need to check the pocket part of the digest for more recent cases.

Alternatively, each digest provides a table of cases (see Figure 4-13). By using the *North Western Digest 2d*'s table of cases, you would locate a reference to *Atkinson v. Atkinson* Child 20. This is a reference to "Children Out-of-Wedlock 20." You would then turn to that digest entry. If you knew only the name of the case (and had not read it), you could use this second method.

Topic Method

If you do not know a case, you could use the topic approach. However, West provides a caveat about using this method: "Do not rely on your own judgment in Topic selection until you are thoroughly familiar with the Key Number Classification System." Accordingly, for a new researcher, this is probably not the best method to use.

516 Mich.   **408 NORTH WESTERN REPORTER, 2d SERIES**

appeal bars defendant from raising it after remand or on appeal. We will not address this issue since for reasons stated in this opinion collateral estoppel does not apply.

The trial court is reversed and the cause of action against defendant Roper is remanded for trial.

160 Mich.App. 601

Harold James ATKINSON,
Plaintiff-Appellant,

v.

Terri Nance ATKINSON,
Defendant-Appellee.

Docket No. 93215.

Court of Appeals of Michigan.

Submitted Nov. 17, 1986.

Decided June 8, 1987.

Released for Publication July 17, 1987.

In divorce action, the Circuit Court, Oakland County, Richard D. Kuhn, J., denied visitation privileges to husband after human leukocyte antigen blood test supported wife's claim that husband was not father of minor child, conceived and born during marriage. On husband's appeal, the Court of Appeals, Wahls, J., held that: (1) wife was entitled to offer evidence that husband was not biological father of child, despite presumption of legitimacy which attaches to children born during marriage; (2) trial court had authority to order husband to submit to human leukocyte antigen blood test to determine paternity of child born during marriage; (3) doctrine of equitable estoppel did not apply to prevent court from ordering husband to submit to blood test; (4) blood test results were properly admitted; and (5) husband was entitled to reconsideration of right to custody and

visitation under "equitable parent" doctrine.

Remanded.

1. Witnesses ⬳54

Wife was entitled to offer evidence that husband was not biological father of minor child, in divorce proceeding, though child was born during marriage and husband had treated child as his own.

2. Children Out-of-Wedlock ⬳58

Court has power, in divorce case, to order individual to submit to human leukocyte antigen blood test in order to determine paternity of child born during marriage, in light of reliability of test.

3. Estoppel ⬳52(4)

Equitable estoppel arises when one causes another, by acts, representations, or silence, intentionally or through culpable conduct, to believe in existence of some material fact and to detrimentally rely on existence of such fact.

4. Divorce ⬳86
   Estoppel ⬳87

Although generally applicable in divorce proceedings, doctrine of equitable estoppel did not apply to prevent trial court from ordering husband to undergo human leukocyte antigen blood testing in order to determine whether he was natural father of minor child born during marriage, where wife's claim that husband was not biological father was made early in divorce proceedings and thus, representation by wife of husband's paternity upon which husband may have relied could not have existed.

5. Evidence ⬳150

Results of husband's human leukocyte antigen blood test was properly admitted as evidence in divorce proceeding, regarding paternity of minor child born during marriage where appropriate foundation was laid prior to admission through testimony by medical technologist regarding identification and labeling procedures for blood samples, and through evidence that blood samples were those of parties involved, and that blood test results were reliable and relevant.

FIGURE 4-11 Regional reporter version of *Atkinson.* (Reprinted with the permission of West Publishing Company.)

6. Children Out-of-Wedlock ⇐20

Under doctrine of "equitable parent," husband, who is not biological father of child born or conceived during marriage, may be considered natural father of that child where husband and child mutually acknowledge relationship as father and child, or mother of child has cooperated in development of such relationship over period of time prior to filing of complaint for divorce, husband desires to have rights afforded to parent, and husband is willing to take on responsibility of paying child support.

7. Children Out-of-Wedlock ⇐20

Although husband was not biological father of minor child who was conceived and born during marriage, as evidenced by results of human leukocyte antigen blood tests, husband was nevertheless entitled to consideration of his claim to custody or visitation rights as child's "equitable parent" where husband and child had close and affectionate father-son relationship, husband was only father child ever knew, denial of custody or visitation rights was not in child's best interest, and husband was willing to take on responsibility of child support.

8. Divorce ⇐227(1)

Trial court did not abuse its discretion in ordering husband to pay $3,500 of wife's attorney fees incurred in divorce action, where husband's income was approximately $55,000 per year while wife's income was only $9,600 per year and at time of trial, husband's attorney fees amounted to $46,-000 and wife's were $20,000.

9. Divorce ⇐145

Trial court erred in divorce action, in refusing to permit psychologist to testify as to psychological damage that separation from man who child believed was his father would cause minor child, on basis that husband did not provide name of expert witness to mother prior to trial, where mother did not request that such witnesses be listed, through interrogatories. MCR 2.302(B)(4)(a)(i).

Michael A. Robbins and Richard S. Victor, Birmingham, for plaintiff-appellant.

Paul W. Harty, P.C. (by Paul W. Harty), Farmington Hills, for defendant-appellee.

Before SHEPHERD, P.J., and WAHLS and SULLIVAN, JJ.

WAHLS, Judge.

Plaintiff, Harold J. Atkinson, appeals as of right from an Oakland Circuit Court judgment of divorce. The issues on appeal generally involve the award of custody of the couple's child to defendant, Terri N. Atkinson, the denial of visitation privileges to plaintiff, the award of attorney fees to defendant, and the refusal of the trial court to allow the testimony of an expert witness. We hold that a wife may establish the nonpaternity of a husband in a divorce action through use of blood testing, but that, notwithstanding the fact that the husband is not the biological father of a child born during the marriage, the husband may acquire rights of paternity under the theory of "equitable parent" and the analogous doctrine of "equitable adoption."

The parties were married on March 1, 1973. The only child of the marriage, James Baird Atkinson (Baird), was born on August 1, 1981. Defendant left the marital home with Baird on February 5, 1985, and, in March, 1985, plaintiff filed for divorce. During the divorce proceeding, defendant contended that plaintiff was not the biological father of Baird and plaintiff vigorously argued that he was Baird's father. The trial court awarded defendant custody of Baird and attorney fees and denied plaintiff custody and visitation privileges.

Plaintiff's first argument is that he should not have been compelled to submit to a human leukocyte antigen (HLA) blood test to determine the paternity of a child he has always treated as his own.

[1] The issue of whether the court in a divorce case may compel the husband to submit to blood testing in order to determine whether he is the biological father of a child born during the marriage has never been addressed by a Michigan appellate court. Originally, Michigan adhered to

FIGURE 4-11 *(continued)*

518 Mich.   **408 NORTH WESTERN REPORTER, 2d SERIES**

Lord Mansfield's Rule, which prohibited testimony by either spouse in a divorce action that showed a child born during the marriage to be illegitimate. *Serafin v. Serafin*, 401 Mich. 629, 258 N.W.2d 461 (1977). However, Michigan shifted away from that prohibition in *Serafin*, wherein the Supreme Court determined that the policy reasons behind Lord Mansfield's Rule of reducing the number of public charges and preserving family peace and harmony were no longer viable. The Court noted that illegitimacy is not held in such low regard as it use to be, and that state and federal laws now serve to lessen arbitrary distinctions formerly made between legitimate and illegitimate children. *Id.*, 636, 258 N.W.2d 461. See *Hackley v. Hackley*, 426 Mich. 582, 586, 395 N.W.2d 906 (1986). The Court also acknowledged the viability of the strong presumption of legitimacy that attaches to children born during a marriage, and held that this presumption may only be rebutted by clear and convincing evidence. *Serafin, supra*, 401 Mich. 636, 258 N.W.2d 461. In other words, although the burden of proof is high, a putative parent may now rebut the legitimacy of a child born to the couple during their marriage. Accordingly, defendant was entitled to offer evidence that plaintiff is not the biological father of Baird.

Plaintiff asserts that the trial court acted pursuant to the Paternity Act, M.C.L. § 722.711 *et seq.;* M.S.A. § 25.491 *et seq.,* in ordering him to submit to the test, and that since the purpose of the act is to provide for the support of minors, it was error to force him to submit to the test in this case. There is no indication in the trial court's order, however, that it was acting pursuant to the Paternity Act when it ordered the test. Furthermore, it is now well-established that in divorce actions the court may determine whether the husband is the father of the wife's child. M.C.L. § 552.16; M.S.A. § 25.96; *Lynch v. Lynch*, 127 Mich. App. 34, 35, 338 N.W.2d 413 (1983); *Gonzales v. Gonzales*, 117 Mich.App. 110, 114, 323 N.W.2d 614 (1982).

[2] As noted above, in most cases where paternity of a minor child is at issue, the putative father is claiming that he is not the biological father and consequently not responsible for the child's financial support. Such was the case in *Serafin, supra,* where the Court stated:

"In our view the public peace and respect for the law are enhanced, not by arbitrarily assigning the duty of support to a man who is not the father of the child, *but by allowing him to contest paternity by his best evidence.*" 401 Mich. 635, 258 N.W.2d 461 (emphasis added).

Similarly, in *Shepherd v. Shepherd*, 81 Mich.App. 465, 470, 265 N.W.2d 374 (1978), this Court held that the plaintiff husband, who was challenging his paternity, should be able to present "his potential best evidence" to overcome the presumption of legitimacy; the results of blood grouping tests were therefore admissible. It is thus a natural extension of the "best evidence" rule that a mother challenging the father's paternity should also be allowed to present her best evidence. The HLA test is extremely reliable in determining the parentage of a child. See *In re Flynn*, 130 Mich.App. 740, 760, 344 N.W.2d 352 (1983). This reliability, coupled with a mother's right to present the best evidence and the court's role of determining the parentage of minor children, leads us to the conclusion that it is within the court's power in a divorce case to order an individual to submit to an HLA blood test in order to determine paternity of a child born during the marriage.

[3, 4] Plaintiff also relies on the doctrine of equitable estoppel in arguing that he should not have been compelled to undergo the HLA testing. Equitable estoppel arises when one causes another, by acts, representations, or silence, intentionally or through culpable neglect, to believe in the existence of some material fact and to detrimentally rely on the existence of such fact. *Nygard v. Nygard*, 156 Mich.App. 94, 401 N.W.2d 323 (1986). Although this theory may be applied to a divorce proceeding, equitable estoppel does not apply here. Defendant's claim that plaintiff is not

FIGURE 4-11 *(continued)*

Baird's biological father was made early in the proceedings. Thus, a representation by defendant of plaintiff's paternity upon which plaintiff may have relied could not have existed. *Id.; Johnson v. Johnson,* 93 Mich.App. 415, 419, 286 N.W.2d 886 (1979). See *Hackley, supra,* 426 Mich. at 596, 395 N.W.2d 906.

[5]   Plaintiff's second contention is that the trial court erred in admitting the HLA blood test results because an insufficient foundation was laid. We disagree. The foundation requirements for the admission of HLA test results in a paternity action are that the blood tested was in fact that of the defendant, the plaintiff, and the child, and that the test results were based on reliable blood samples. *Willerick v. Hanshalli,* 136 Mich.App. 484, 488, 356 N.W.2d 36 (1984). This foundation includes establishing a chain of identification from the time the blood samples were taken to the time the samples were analyzed, either by direct or circumstantial evidence. *Id.; Zyskowski v. Habelmann,* 150 Mich.App. 230, 244–245, 388 N.W.2d 315 (1986), *lv. gtd.* 426 Mich. 865 (1986).

In the present case, a medical technologist testified from personal knowledge as to the identification and labeling procedures for blood samples, and as to the procedures used when samples are taken out of the locked box in which they are kept. Sufficient evidence was presented to show that the blood samples were those of the parties and of Baird and that the HLA blood tests were reliable and relevant evidence. *Zyskowski, supra;* MRE 406.

[6]   Plaintiff's third argument is that the trial court erred in treating him as a third party because of the absence of a biological relationship between Baird and himself, rather than treating him as a parent due to the close father-son relationship the two shared, in deciding custody and visitation. In making this argument, plaintiff asks us to adopt the doctrine of "equitable parent." This is a novel request. However, we find ample support in granting the request, especially in the present circumstances. Therefore, we adopt the doctrine of "equitable parent" and find that

a husband who is not the biological father of a child born or conceived during the marriage may be considered the natural father of that child where (1) the husband and the child mutually acknowledge a relationship as father and child, or the mother of the child has cooperated in the development of such a relationship over a period of time prior to the filing of the complaint for divorce, (2) the husband desires to have the rights afforded to a parent, and (3) the husband is willing to take on the responsibility of paying child support. We hold that the husband may be considered the "equitable parent" under these circumstances and remand this case in order to allow the circuit court to reevaluate custody and visitation, treating plaintiff as a natural parent of Baird.

The first thing we have considered in deciding to adopt this new doctrine is that the Child Custody Act "is equitable in nature" and its provisions are to be liberally construed, M.C.L. § 722.26; M.S.A. § 25.-312(6). Therefore, a basis for fashioning an "equitable parent" doctrine is present.

Turning to the case law interpreting this act, it is generally recognized that biological parents are obligated by law to maintain and support their children. *West v. West,* 241 Mich. 679, 684, 217 N.W. 924 (1928); M.C.L. § 722.3; M.S.A. § 25.244(3); M.C.L. § 722.1(b); M.S.A. § 25.244(1)(b). Implicitly coupled with this duty is the right to custody or visitation. In this case, however, there is no biological relationship from which a support obligation may arise, *Magarell v. Magarell,* 327 Mich. 372, 376, 41 N.W.2d 898 (1950); *Nygard v. Nygard, supra.* The reciprocal right to custody or visitation similarly does not arise because plaintiff is not treated as a "parent" under the Child Custody Act. See *Johnson, supra.*

[7]   However, we have recognized exceptions to this rule of first finding a biological relationship before imposing a support obligation. One exception is found in *Johnson, supra.* In that case, the plaintiff husband married defendant wife knowing that she was carrying a child who may or may not have been his offspring. Plaintiff

FIGURE 4-11   *(continued)*

husband thereafter held himself out as the father and supporter of the child for several years. This Court noted:

> "Plaintiff assumed the status of father of this child when the child was born and continued as such for ten years until he amended his divorce complaint at trial. As the child was born during the marriage while the parties lived together as husband and wife, it was not necessary for plaintiff to go through adoption proceedings. Conversely, after plaintiff has represented himself as the father of this child for nine to ten years, he may not now say that he was not.

> "On the facts of this case the Court is compelled to hold that plaintiff is estopped by his conduct to deny paternity of this child." *Johnson, supra,* 93 Mich. App. at 419–420, 286 N.W.2d 886.

See *Nygard, supra.* In other words, we recognize that a person who is not the biological father of a child may be considered a "parent" against his will, and consequently burdened with the responsibility of the support for the child. By the same token, in being treated as a parent, he may also receive the right of custody or visitation. It is the logical extension of *Johnson* to recognize that, under certain circumstances, a person who is not the biological father of a child may be considered a parent when he desires such recognition and is willing to support the child as well as wants the reciprocal rights of custody or visitation afforded to a parent. Such circumstances are present here. Baird was conceived and born during the parties' marriage. Plaintiff and Baird have always had a close and affectionate father-son relationship. Plaintiff is the only father Baird has ever known and is active in Baird's life. He desires to have the relationship continued and to have the rights accorded to a father, along with the responsibility of supporting the child. Defendant acknowledged at trial that plaintiff related to Baird as a father and that she waited until answering a question in interrogatories filed by plaintiff in the instant divorce action before asserting that plaintiff was not Baird's biological father. Under this set of facts, plaintiff is clearly entitled to

be treated as a natural father under the doctrine of "equitable parent." Therefore, we are remanding for reevaluation of custody and visitation consistent with this decision.

In addition, the doctrine of "equitable adoption" provides support for plaintiff's requested relief. Michigan has long recognized the doctrine of "equitable adoption" in intestate succession. *Wright v. Wright,* 99 Mich. 170, 58 N.W. 54 (1894). Under this doctrine, an implied contract to adopt is found when a close relationship, similar to parent-child, exists between a child and the deceased. *Id.* See also *Steward v. Richardson,* 353 F.Supp. 822, 825 (E.D. Mich.1972). As a result, the child has a right to share in the deceased's estate. That doctrine has been codified in M.C.L. § 700.111; M.S.A. § 27.5111. Thus, Baird is plaintiff's heir. It is only logical that a person recognized as a natural parent in death should have the same recognition in life. The parent-child relationship here is similar to that found in equitable adoption situations. Therefore, a legal relationship akin to the doctrine of "equitable adoption" is present.

Furthermore, let us not forget that the best interest of the child is the major concern of any custody determination. M.C.L. § 722.25; M.S.A. § 25.312(5); *Hackley, supra,* 426 Mich. at 597, 395 N.W.2d 906. Plaintiff was married to Baird's mother when Baird was conceived and born. He has been a father to Baird in all respects. Following the parties' separation, he remained active in Baird's day-care program, school, and church. In fact, it appears that it was quite a shock for both plaintiff and Baird when it was revealed during the divorce proceedings that plaintiff was not Baird's biological father. Given such a close relationship, it is unlikely that forbidding plaintiff from having custody or visitation rights is in Baird's best interest.

[8] Plaintiff's fourth argument is that the trial court abused its discretion in ordering plaintiff to pay $3,500 of defendant's attorney fees. Necessary and reasonable attorney fees may be awarded to en-

FIGURE 4-11   *(continued)*

PROVIDENCE HOSP. v. MORRELL Mich. **521**
Cite as 408 N.W.2d 521 (Mich.App. 1987)

able a party to carry on or defend a divorce action. *Zecchin v. Zecchin*, 149 Mich.App. 723, 732, 386 N.W.2d 652 (1986). MCR 3.206(A). A trial court's award of attorney fees will not be disturbed on appeal absent an abuse of discretion. *Vaclav v. Vaclav*, 96 Mich.App. 584, 593, 293 N.W.2d 613 (1980).

We find no abuse. Plaintiff's income is approximately $55,000 per year. Defendant's income is approximately $9,600 per year. Plaintiff's attorney fees amounted to $46,000, and defendant's were $20,000, at the time of trial. There was a sufficient showing that defendant was in need of financial assistance in order to defend this divorce action.

Plaintiff's fifth argument is that the trial court erred in refusing to allow the expert testimony of Dr. Haynes. We agree.

The issue of custody was referred to the Oakland County Friend of the Court for a referee hearing. Plaintiff was dissatisfied with the referee hearing and requested a de novo hearing pursuant to M.C.L. § 552.-507(5); M.S.A. § 25.176(7)(5).

[9] At trial, plaintiff called as his first witness Dr. Jack Haynes, who had performed a psychological evaluation of Baird. Dr. Haynes was to testify as to the psychological damage that separation from plaintiff would cause Baird. Defendant objected on the ground that plaintiff had not given notice that Dr. Haynes' expert testimony would be offered. The trial court sustained defendant's objection, stating that "[t]he Court's not going outside of the hearing which they had in front of the Friend of the Court." The court also refused to rule that Dr. Haynes could testify later in the trial.

There is no requirement in the Michigan Court Rules that a party must supply a list of the expert witnesses that the party expects to call at trial. A party may

"through interrogatories require another party to identify each person whom the other party expects to call as an expert witness at trial, to state the subject matter about which the expert is expected to testify, and to state the substance of the facts and opinions to which the expert is expected to testify and a summary of the grounds for each opinion." MCR 2.302(B)(4)(a)(i).

There is no claim in the present case that defendant requested from plaintiff a list of the expert witnesses that plaintiff intended to call. The trial court erred in refusing to admit the testimony of Dr. Jack Haynes, and deprived plaintiff of a full de novo trial. Dr. Haynes' testimony may have made a difference in the outcome of this case. Therefore, the error cannot be considered harmless.

Remanded.

FIGURE 4-11 *(continued)*

5A N W D 2d—85   **CHILDREN OUT–OF–WEDLOCK**   ☞20

For references to other topics, see Descriptive-Word Index

showing that it would be in best interests of the child.—Gay v. Cairns, 298 N.W.2d 313.

Acknowledged father of illegitimate child established that it would be in child's best interests to allow visitation.—Id.

Iowa App. 1986. While natural father originally had right to have dispositional order vacated on basis that he had not received statutory notice of the proceedings, right was waived when natural father voluntarily appeared by way of intervention and acquiesced in jurisdiction for ten months. I.C.A. §§ 232.1 et seq., 232.38, 232.103.—In Interest of J.F., 386 N.W.2d 149.

Discovery after entry of original dispositional order of natural father's ability to provide stable environment for his child constituted sufficient change in circumstances and warranted modification of original dispositional order so as to allow transfer of custody to natural father.—Id.

Failure to serve natural mother with reasonable notice of proceedings to modify or vacate dispositional order to allow natural father custody of child did not constitute reversible error where natural mother was aware that court would consider transfer of custody either by vacating or modifying dispositional order, and she had fair opportunity to present evidence on that issue. I.C.A. §§ 232.102, 232.103, subd. 3.—Id.

Mich. 1978. Putative father's parental rights are subject to termination only after father is afforded notice and an opportunity to be heard. M.C.L.A. § 710.36.—Matter of Barlow, 273 N.W.2d 35, 404 Mich. 216.

Putative fathers who have established no custodial relationship with child, and who have provided no support for mother or child prior to notice of hearing, may have their parental rights terminated if court finds, after examining father's fitness and ability to properly care for child, that it would not be in best interests of child to grant custody to him. M.C.L.A. §§ 710.21 et seq., 710.39.—Id.

Parental rights of putative fathers who have established some kind of custodial or support relationship prior to notice of hearing are subject to termination only by proceedings under general jurisdictional provisions of Probate Code. M.C.L.A. § 712A.1 et seq.—Id.

In proceedings to terminate parental rights of putative fathers who have established some kind of custodial or support relationship prior to notice of hearing, judgment should not turn upon a showing or failure to show that putative father is unfit, but should be based on showing of best interests of child. M.C.L.A. § 712A.1 et seq.—Id.

Youth and marital status of putative father are not evidence of either an incapacity or disinclination to assure that child will receive adequate care and supervision. M.C.L.A. § 710.21 et seq.—Id.

Possibility that there may be a better home somewhere, be it natural mother's or an adoptive one, yet unidentified or unidentifiable, is not evidence but rather mere speculation and conjecture that it would not be in best interests of child to award custody to natural father. M.C.L.A. § 710.21 et seq.—Id.

In termination of parental rights proceeding, putative father is not required to prove that an unknown home would not be a better one than that which he is prepared to provide child. M.C.L.A. § 710.21 et seq.—Id.

In the absence of evidence indicating natural father's home would not be a good one for child, there is no basis for finding that it would not be in best interests of child to award custody to natural father. M.C.L.A. § 710.21 et seq.—Id.

Mother's preference that infant be raised in mother's own faith should not be given controlling weight in deciding whether to terminate natural father's parental rights, all other things being equal. M.C.L.A. §§ 710.21 et seq., 710.39(1).—Id.

In termination of parental rights proceeding, lower court's conclusion that it would not be in best interests of child to award custody to natural father was not supported by record. M.C.L.A. §§ 710.21 et seq., 710.39(1).—Id.

Mich.App. 1987. Under doctrine of "equitable parent," husband, who is not biological father of child born or conceived during marriage, may be considered natural father of that child where husband and child mutually acknowledge relationship as father and child, or mother of child has cooperated in development of such relationship over period of time prior to filing of complaint for divorce, husband desires to have rights afforded to parent, and husband is willing to take on responsibility of paying child support.—Atkinson v. Atkinson, 408 N.W.2d 516, 160 Mich.App. 601, appeal denied.

Although husband was not biological father of minor child who was conceived and born during marriage, as evidenced by results of human leukocyte antigen blood tests, husband was nevertheless entitled to consideration of his claim to custody or visitation rights as child's "equitable parent" where husband and child had close and affectionate father-son relationship, husband was only father child ever knew, denial of custody or visitation rights was not in child's best interest, and husband was willing to take on responsibility of child support.—Id.

Mich.App. 1985. In a rehearing under adoption code [M.C.L.A. § 710.64] sought by putative father who had previously denied paternity, a probate court did not err in failing to articulate on record its application of factors evaluating best interests of child. M.C.L.A. § 710.39(1).—Matter of Koroly, 377 N.W.2d 346.

Mich.App. 1980. Putative father, who was not married to natural mother, had standing to litigate his claim for visitation rights. M.C.L.A. § 722.24.—Raleigh v. Watkins, 293 N.W.2d 789, 97 Mich.App. 258.

Child Custody Act standards were properly utilized in considering putative father's petition for visitation rights with his alleged son. M.C.L.A. §§ 722.21 et seq., 722.23.—Id.

Award of visitation rights to natural father, who was not married to mother and whose relationship with mother had terminated before child was born, was not against the great weight of the evidence where father was apparently a fit parent and testimony indicated that the child was cheerful, stable and would ultimately benefit from his visits; lack of psychological ties between father and son did not deprive father of visitation rights, especially in view of limited opportunity to cultivate such bond. M.C.L.A. §§ 722.21 et seq., 722.23, 722.28.—Id.

Mich.App. 1977. Evidence supported findings of probate court, in proceedings to terminate parental rights of unwed father, that father had neither established custody or relationship with child nor provided any support or care for mother or child prior to being served with notice of hearing. M.C.L.A. §§ 722.23, 722.25.—Matter of Barlow, 260 N.W.2d 896, 78 Mich.App. 707, reversed 273 N.W.2d 35, 404 Mich. 216.

Probate court did not abuse its discretion when it terminated unwed father's parental rights in his child on finding that child's best interests would not be served by granting custody to father. M.C.L.A. §§ 710.39(1), 722.23, 722.25.—Id.

FIGURE 4-12 Sample page from *North Western Digest 2d*. (Reprinted with the permission of West Publishing Company.)

N W D 2d—35

References are to Digest Topics and Key Numbers

ATTORNEY

242.1(4); Infants 132, 178, 243, 246, 253; Witn 214.5, 219(1).

Atkins v. Baxter, Iowa, 423 NW2d 6.—Int Liq 289, 312.

Atkins v. Department of Motor Vehicles 192 Neb 791, 224 NW2d 535—Const Law 287.3.

Atkins v. Department of Social Services 92 MichApp 313, 284 NW2d 794—Admin Law 4, 453, 469; Asyl 3; Const Law 287.2(1).

Atkins v. Diggles, Wis, 85 NW2d 454, 1 Wis2d 549—B & L Assoc 3.2, 3.3.

Atkins v. Jones & Laughlin Steel Corp 258 Minn 571, 104 NW2d 888—Const Law 249(4).

Atkins v. Outside Inn, Iowa, 423 NW2d 6. See Atkins v. Baxter.

Atkinson, Application of, Minn, 291 NW2d 396—Statut 210; Weap 1, 2, 12.

Atkinson, Matter of, MinnApp, 443 NW2d 864, review den—Const Law 48(1), 48(6); Mental H 2, 45.

Atkinson v. Atkinson, MichApp, 408 NW2d 516, 160 MichApp 601, appeal den.—Child 20, 58; Divorce 86, 145, 227(1); Estop 52(4), 87; Evid 150; Witn 54.

Atkinson v. DeBraber, MichApp, 446 NW2d 637, 180 MichApp 236, appeal den.—App & E 1064.1(1); Schools 147.

Atkinson v. Diocese of Bismarck, ND, 500 NW2d 203. See Diocese of Bismarck Trust, Matter of.

Atkinson v. Farley, MichApp, 431 NW2d 96, 171 MichApp 784.—Damag 50.10, 56.10, 149; Pretrial Proc 624, 679, 681.

Atlanta Intern. Ins. Co. v. Bell, Mich, 475 NW2d 294, 438 Mich 512.—Atty & C 26, 64; Subrog 1.

Atlanta Intern. Ins. Co. v. Bell, MichApp, 448 NW2d 804, 181 MichApp 272, appeal gr in part 465 NW2d 916, 435 Mich 862, rev 475 NW2d 294, 438 Mich 512.—Atty & C 21.5(5), 64, 105; Plead 246(2).

Atlantic Bottling Co. v. Iowa Dept. of Revenue, Iowa, 385 NW2d 565.—Tax 1243, 1245, 1342.

Atlantic Educ. Ass'n v. Atlantic Community School Dist., Iowa, 469 NW2d 689.—Labor 178, 434.5, 434.8, 435; Schools 147.32.

Atlantic Mut. Ins. Co. v. Judd Co., Minn, 380 NW2d 122.—Decl Judgm 392; Insurance 435.24(4), 514.9(1), 514.21(1), 675; Stip 17(1).

Atlantic Mut. Ins. Co. v. Judd Co., MinnApp, 367 NW2d 604, review gr, aff 380 NW2d 122.—Costs 194.26; Insurance 435.22(3), 514.11, 514.21(1), 675.

Atlantis Exp., Inc. v. LL Transport Services, Inc., MinnApp, 481 NW2d 79, review den.—Carr 4, 192; Commerce 85.33.

Atlas Coal Co. v. Jones, Iowa, 61 NW2d 663, 245 Iowa 506—Estop 52.15.

Atlas Farm & Indus. Bldg. Co., Inc. v. Siegler, MichApp, 355 NW2d 654. See Lumber Village, Inc. v. Siegler.

Atlas, Ltd. v. Kingman Warehouse Co. VIII, Iowa, 357 NW2d 584.—Parties 51(2), 51(3); Plead 353; Trial 3(3).

Atlas Mini Storage, Inc. v. First Interstate Bank of Des Moines, N.A., Iowa App, 426 NW2d 686.—Banks 191.15, 191.30.

Atlas Ready-Mix of Minot v. White Properties, Inc, ND, 306 NW2d 212—App & E 854(1); Contracts 143(2), 147(1), 156, 176(1, 2), 202(1), 312(4); Damag 15, 62(4), 120(7), 163(1), 176; Evid 370(1), 383(7), 448; Tax 1245.

Atlas Steel & Wire Corp. v. L & M Const. Chemicals, Inc., Neb, 321 NW2d 64, 212 Neb 16.—App & E 931(1), 931(3), 1008.1(10), 1008.2.

Atokad Agr. and Racing Ass'n v. Governors Of the Knights of Ak-Sar-Ben, Neb, 466 NW2d 73, 237 Neb 317.—App & E 151(1), 544(1), 548(1), 554(1), 1064.1(1); Contracts 15, 16, 236, 238(2), 353(7); Interest 39(2.15), 39(2.30); Judgm 185(2); Trial 141, 142, 203(1).

Atrium Village, Inc. v. Board of Review, Johnson County, Iowa, Iowa, 417 NW2d 70.—Tax 203, 204(2), 241.2.

Attard v. Adamczyk, MichApp, 367 NW2d 75, 141 MichApp 246.—Costs 194.44; Judgm 181(3); Parent & C 2(17).

Attoe v. Madison Professional Policemen's Ass'n 79 Wis2d 199, 255 NW2d 489—Assoc 5; Labor 764; Plead 34(1), 36(2), 193(5).

Attoe v. Rural Mut Ins Co 83 Wis2d 341, 265 NW2d 281—Death 58(1); Neglig 135(9).

Attorney Fees, Petition of, Minn, 279 NW2d 366—Work Comp 1983.

Attorney Fees and Partial Reimbursement for Attorney Fees Pursuant to M.S. 176.081, In re Petition of, Minn, 350 NW2d 873.—Work Comp 1983.

Attorney General, In re, MichApp, 341 NW2d 253, 129 MichApp 128.—Courts 207.1; Crim Law 124, 132.

Attorney General, Petition of, Mich, 369 NW2d 826, 422 Mich 157.—Admin Law 357.

Attorney General v. Ambassador Ins. Co., MichApp, 421 NW2d 271.—Garn 40, 106; Insurance 8.

Attorney General v. American Way Life Ins. Co., MichApp, 465 NW2d 56, 186 MichApp 679.—Insurance 9.

Attorney General v. Ankersen, MichApp, 385 NW2d 658.—Carr 77; Corp 306, 324; Em Dom 2(1), 2(1.1), 2(5); Equity 65(1), 65(2); Estop 52.15, 62.2(1), 62.2(2); Evid 546; Health & E 32; Land & Ten 149; Lis Pen 24(2); Mast & S 310; Nuis 10, 78; States 112.1(2).

Attorney General v. Ballenger, MichApp, 378 NW2d 607, 145 MichApp 811. See Ballenger v. Cahalan.

Attorney General v. Blue Cross & Blue Shield of Michigan, MichApp, 424 NW2d 54.—Escheat 2, 3; States 18.51.

Attorney General v. Bruce, Mich, 369 NW2d 826, 422 Mich 157. See Atty. Gen., Petition of.

Attorney General v. Bruce, MichApp, 335 NW2d 697, 124 MichApp 796, aff Petition of Atty Gen, 369 NW2d 826, 422 Mich 157.—Hosp 3, 6; Statut 190.

Attorney General v. Clinton County Drain Com'r 91 MichApp 630, 283 NW2d 815. See People ex rel Attorney General v. Clinton County Drain Com'r.

Attorney General v. Consumers Power Co., MichApp, 508 NW2d 901, 202 MichApp 74, appeal gr Kelley v. Consumers Power Co, 521 NW2d 14, appeal held in abeyance 526 NW2d 917.—Electricity 16(1); Fish 6; Land & Ten 275; States 18.3, 18.33, 18.39, 18.73.

Attorney General v. Diamond Mortg. Co., Mich, 327 NW2d 805, 414 Mich 603.—Cons Prot 5, 31; Quo W 3; Venue 36.

Attorney General v. East Jackson Public Schools, MichApp, 372 NW2d 638, 143 MichApp 634.—Schools 55, 164.

Attorney General v. Hermes, MichApp, 339 NW2d 545, 127 MichApp 777.—Conversion 3; Fish 12, 17; Game 3½; Indians 1, 2, 6(1), 32.5(1), 32.10(1, 2, 7, 8); Trover 1, 2, 32(1), 44, 46.

Attorney General v. Insurance Com'r of State of Mich., MichApp, 323 NW2d 645, 117 MichApp 186.—Insurance 11.2, 11.3, 11.4, 11.7; Work Comp 1063.

Attorney General v. John A. Biewer Co., Inc., MichApp, 363 NW2d 712, 140 Mich 1, appeal den.—App & E 893(2), 895(2), 1009(1); Evid 333(1), 351, 356; Health & E 25.5(2), 25.7(23), 25.7(24), 25.15(2); Nuis 85; Statut 190, 241(1); Witn 37(2).

Attorney General v. Lake States Wood Preserving, Inc., MichApp, 501 NW2d 213, 199 MichApp 149, appeal den 511 NW2d 686, reconsideration den 512 NW2d 846.—Admin Law 412.1; App & E 842(2), 1008.1(5), 1009(1); Health & E 25.7(6.1), 25.7(17.1), 25.7(20).

Attorney General v. Lapeer Community Schools, MichApp, 372 NW2d 638, 143 MichApp 634. See Attorney General v. East Jackson Public Schools.

Attorney General v. Michigan Public Service Com'n 412 Mich 385, 316 NW2d 187. See Kelley v. Michigan Public Service Com'n.

Attorney General v. Michigan Public Service Com'n, MichApp, 520 NW2d 636, 206 MichApp 290.—Gas 14.3(3), 14.4(1), 14.5(7), 14.6; Pub Ut 120, 162, 167, 168, 194, 195.

Attorney General v. Michigan Public Service Com'n, MichApp, 333 NW2d 131, 122 MichApp 777.—Electricity 11.3(4), 11.3(6), 11.3(7).

Attorney General v. Michigan Public Service Commission 93 MichApp 596, 287 NW2d 1. See Cities of Grosse Pointe Part, Highland Part, Grosse Pointe Woods, Harper Woods, Royal Oak, Livonia, Ann Arbor, Inkster, and Warren v. Michigan Public Service Commission.

Attorney General v. Michigan Public Service Commission 88 MichApp 633, 278 NW2d 702. See Consumers Power Co v. Michigan Public Service Commission.

Attorney General v. Oakland County, MichApp, 335 NW2d 654, 125 MichApp 157.—Offic 100(1).

Attorney General v. Piller, MichApp, 514 NW2d 210, 204 MichApp 228.—Costs 194.16, 194.25.

Attorney General v. Piller Land Co., MichApp, 514 NW2d 210, 204 MichApp 228. See Attorney General v. Piller.

Attorney General v. Professional Psychological Consultants, Inc., MichApp, 341 NW2d 141, 128 MichApp 564. See Search Warrant on 5000 Northwind Drive, Ste. 200, East Lansing, In re.

Attorney General v. Public Service Com'n, Mich, 420 NW2d 81, 430 Mich 33. See Association of Businesses Advocating Tariff Equity (A.B.A.T.E.) v. Public Service Com'n.

Attorney General v. Public Service Com'n, Mich, 414 NW2d 687.—Pub Ut 192.

Attorney General v. Public Service Com'n, MichApp, 527 NW2d 533, 208 MichApp 248. See Association of Businesses Advocating Tariff Equity v. Public Service Com'n.

Attorney General v. Public Service Com'n, MichApp, 472 NW2d 53, 189 MichApp 138.—Electricity 11.8(1), 11.3(6); Pub Ut 119, 147, 194, 195.

Attorney General v. Public Service Com'n, MichApp, 455 NW2d 724, 183 MichApp 692.—Statut 223.1; Tel 834, 335.

Attorney General v. Public Service Com'n, MichApp, 448 NW2d 806, 181

For Later Case History Information, see INSTA-CITE on WESTLAW

FIGURE 4-13 Table of cases from a digest. (Reprinted with the permission of West Publishing Company.)

If you feel that you have sufficient understanding of digest topics, you would proceed as follows. First, select the most appropriate topic name. A complete topic listing is found in the front of each digest volume. There West also provides an outline of the law, which arranges digest topics into seven divisions. This can also be helpful in locating a topic name. Then turn to the topic and review the topic analysis (see Figure 4-14). Locate your subtopic name and key number there. Then locate other cases in the digest by turning to the appropriate pages.

Descriptive Word Method

The final method used is the most popular, the descriptive word method. Here you use popular catchwords and phrases to describe specific legal terms of art. Every digest has a *descriptive word index* containing thousands of words that are tied to specific topics and key numbers. West suggests, when using this method, that you break down a legal problem into five component parts: (1) parties; (2) places and things; (3) basis of action or issue; (4) defenses; and (5) relief sought. For example, in the paralegal practice situation, you could use:

1. *Parties:* Husband, father, parent, child, infant.
2. *Places and things:* Marriage, family.
3. *Basis of action:* Divorce, custody, visitation, illegitimacy.
4. *Defenses:* Nonpaternity.
5. *Relief sought:* Custody, paternity, visitation.

The disadvantage of this method is that using it demands a thorough understanding of family law and litigation. You have to know what a defense is, the various types of relief that are available, and the types of actions that could be brought. Obtaining a strong footing in family law would be a prerequisite to employing this method.

This and other methods based on developing word lists are further discussed in Chapter 9. One of the other methods that does not require extensive substantive knowledge could be used in lieu of the descriptive word method. Once you had a list of appropriate terms, you would apply these words in the descriptive word index, which you hope will lead you to digest entries for a case such as *Atkinson.*

Digests are critically important tools in finding case law. However, when using digests you can become dependent on reading headnotes rather than the cases themselves. Remember, headnotes represent an editor's opinion of the important legal principles in a case. An editor can be wrong. Furthermore, you cannot achieve a complete appreciation of the case unless you fully understand the facts. You will not grasp the practical applicability of the legal principles in the case unless you understand the factual scenario they come from.

Two publications may help in using West digests. The 76-page publication *West's Law Finder* (1994) provides a comprehensive discussion of West's digests. *Sample Pages* (3d ed. 1986) contains pages from digests with explanation. Both are available free of charge from West.

CHILDREN OUT–OF–WEDLOCK

SUBJECTS INCLUDED

Persons born out of wedlock and their rights and disabilities in general

Custody, support, protection and legitimation of such children

Legal proceedings for determination of questions of status, ascertainment of paternity, and enforcement of liabilities for support

SUBJECTS EXCLUDED AND COVERED BY OTHER TOPICS

Social welfare laws, provisions for children, see SOCIAL SECURITY AND PUBLIC WELFARE

Testamentary provisions, see WILLS

For detailed references to other topics, see Descriptive-Word Index

---

Analysis

I. STATUS IN GENERAL, ☜1–19.

II. CUSTODY, SUPPORT, AND PROTECTION, ☜20–29.

III. PATERNITY PROCEEDINGS, ☜30–79.

IV. PROPERTY, ☜80–90.

I. STATUS IN GENERAL.

 ☜1. Who are bastards, illegitimate, or out-of-wedlock; name and status.
  2. Evidence.
  3. —— Presumption of legitimacy.
  4. —— Burden of proof.
  5. —— Admissibility.
  6. —— Sufficiency.
  7. Proceedings to repudiate child.
  8. Legitimation.
  9. —— In general.
  10. —— Legislative act.
  11. —— Marriage of parents.
  12. —— Recognition or acknowledgment.
  13. —— Judicial proceedings.

II. CUSTODY, SUPPORT, AND PROTECTION.

 ☜20. Right to custody.
  21. Duty to support.
  22. Contracts for support.
  23. Neglect to support.
  24. Concealment of birth and death.

FIGURE 4-14 Digest's topic analysis. (Reprinted with the permission of West Publishing Company.)

METHODS OF USING DIGESTS

1. Known Case Methods
   - Read headnote in case.

     Review digest spines for topic.

     Turn to topic.

     Using key number, locate case.

     Locate other cases on page.
   - Turn to table of cases.

     Using case name, locate reference to topic and key number.

     Turn to topic and key number in digest.

2. Topic Method
   - Review list of topics in front of digest.

     Select most appropriate topic.

     Turn to topic.

     Using topic analysis, locate subtopic and key number.

3. Descriptive Word Method
   - Develop list of terms/phrases (illustrated in Chapter 9).

     Apply terms/phrase to descriptive word index.

     Locate reference to topic and key number.

     Turn to topic and key number in digest.

Shepard's Citations

During the course of research, you may find a reported case that stands for a certain legal principle. Unfortunately, that case is quite old, and you want to locate a newer, more recent reported case for use in a legal document or oral argument. Or you may need to determine if the legal principles in a case or statute have been affected by a subsequent reported case opinion. Both goals can be achieved through the use of a *citator,* the most noted of which is **Shepard's Citations**, published by Shepard's/McGraw-Hill (see Figure 4-15).

LEGAL TERMS

Shepard's Citations   A citator published by Shepard's/McGraw-Hill.

FIGURE 4-15
Sample title page from Shepard's. (Reproduced by permission of Shepard's/McGraw-Hill, Inc. Further reproduction of any kind is strictly prohibited.)

SHEPARD'S
NORTHWESTERN REPORTER
CITATIONS

A COMPILATION OF CITATIONS
TO
ALL CASES REPORTED IN THE NORTHWESTERN REPORTER

THE CITATIONS
which include affirmances, reversals and dismissals by higher state courts and by the United States Supreme Court

APPEAR IN

NORTHWESTERN REPORTER
UNITED STATES SUPREME COURT REPORTS
LAWYERS' EDITION, UNITED STATES SUPREME COURT
    REPORTS
SUPREME COURT REPORTER
FEDERAL CASES
FEDERAL REPORTER
FEDERAL SUPPLEMENT
FEDERAL RULES DECISIONS
BANKRUPTCY REPORTER
CLAIMS COURT REPORTER
MILITARY JUSTICE REPORTER
ATLANTIC REPORTER
CALIFORNIA REPORTER
NEW YORK SUPPLEMENT
NORTHEASTERN REPORTER
PACIFIC REPORTER
SOUTHEASTERN REPORTER
SOUTHERN REPORTER
SOUTHWESTERN REPORTER
AMERICAN BAR ASSOCIATION JOURNAL

and in annotations of

LAWYERS' EDITION, UNITED STATES SUPREME COURT REPORTS
AMERICAN LAW REPORTS

also in Vols. 1–283 Illinois Appellate Court Reports, Vols. 1–19 Ohio Appellate Reports and Vols. 1–101 Pennsylvania Superior Court Reports

FIFTH EDITION - - - - - - - - - - - - - - - - - VOLUME 2 (PART 5) 1993

SHEPARD'S/McGRAW-HILL, INC.
COLORADO SPRINGS
COLORADO 80921-3630
(719) 488-3000

Purposes of Shepard's

The primary function of Shepard's is to serve as a locator and reviewer. As a locator, Shepard's indexes reported cases that support a proposition found in a known case. These indexes are national in scope. In your search process, Shepard's will reveal other cases and secondary sources of law that have discussed the known case or the principles established by that case. As a reviewer, Shepard's allows you to verify whether the legal propositions in the case are still current law—that is, if they have been overturned. Shepard's also helps you determine whether other courts have modified the known case's principles. It also reviews other noncase law, especially statutes, to determine how they have been interpreted by courts.

Shepard's is published as sets of books accompanying every reporter and code, both official and unofficial, federal and state. As a result, Shepard's has two primary applications, one to cases and another to statutes. As a researcher, you will more often use Shepard's for cases.

How to Shepardize a Case

Assume you are once again researching the case of *Atkinson v. Atkinson,* 160 Mich. App. 601, 408 N.W.2d 516, 84 A.L.R.4th 643 (1987). You are still interested in the principle illustrated in headnote no. 6, dealing with the equitable parent doctrine. As it is now several years beyond 1987, you must determine whether the principle is still "good law." The first step is to determine whether the case was appealed to the Michigan Supreme Court (the Michigan Court of Appeals is the intermediate appellate court) or the U.S. Supreme Court and the result, if any. If the case was reversed, it could no longer be used as authority. A second important consideration is whether the *Atkinson* case was overruled by another court in a subsequent case. The process of finding these answers is referred to as **shepardizing**.

The known case in Shepard's is referred to as the **cited case**. Subsequent cases considering the cited case are called **citing cases**. The first step is to locate the appropriate starting point in Shepard's. In this example, you could choose from either Shepard's *Michigan Citations* or Shepard's *Northwestern Reporter Citations.* Both provide the same information, but the first is based on official reporters and the second on unofficial West reporters.

A Shepard's series typically contains one or more bound maroon volumes, a gold paperback annual supplement, a red paperback supplement, and a newsprint advance sheet. To ensure that every set is complete, the cover page of each lists what each set should contain. See Figure 4-16.

For our example, we will use the *Northwestern Reporter Citations.* The cited case is located in volume 408, so the first place to check is the bound book that first includes that volume. From this point, check each paperback and bound supplement for that volume, in sequential order, to the present.

Before going further, the concepts of history and treatment must be understood. Remember that one of the purposes of shepardizing is to determine whether the cited case itself has been considered by the Michigan Supreme Court or the U.S. Supreme Court. This is part of the *history* of the case. The history will often be noted if the case is from an intermediate appellate court. *Treatment* of

--------- **LEGAL TERMS** ---------

shepardizing [†]   Using a citator.

cited case   A known case that is being shepardized.

citing case   A case located through shepardizing that makes reference to principles from the cited case.

VOL. 91   MAY, 1995   NO. 10

Shepard's

Northwestern

Reporter

Citations   ANNUAL CUMULATIVE SUPPLEMENT

(USPS 656970)

IMPORTANT

Do not destroy the May 1995 gold paper-covered **Annual** Cumulative Supplement.

WHAT YOUR LIBRARY SHOULD CONTAIN

1993 Bound Volume, Vol. 1 (Parts 1-5)*
1993 Bound Volume, Vol. 2 (Parts 1-5)*
*Supplemented with:
  –May, 1995 Annual Cumulative Supplement Vol. 91 No. 10

DESTROY ALL OTHER ISSUES

SEE "THIS ISSUE INCLUDES" ON
PAGE III

Presenting New Supplementation Style

Please see inside

SHEPARD'S
McGRAW-HILL

FIGURE 4-16 Sample cover page from Shepard's. (Reproduced by permission of Shepard's/McGraw-Hill, Inc. Further reproduction of any kind is strictly prohibited.)

the case is how the cited case has been "treated" by citing cases. The case could have been criticized, distinguished, or followed. There are, in fact, ten different forms of treatment. Both treatment and history are indicated by abbreviations. A listing of these abbreviations appears at the beginning of the Shepard's volume you are using (see Figure 4-17).

Reading Shepard's entries can at first be an intimidating experience. References to citing cases and other authority are indicated by an abbreviation system that is unique to Shepard's. If you do not wear glasses now, you will after using Shepard's for some time!

You are now ready to shepardize *Atkinson v. Atkinson.* Having located the appropriate starting volume, the volume number of the *North Western Reporter*

ABBREVIATIONS—ANALYSIS
CASES

History of Case

a	(affirmed)	Same case affirmed on appeal.
cc	(connected case)	Different case from case cited but arising out of same subject matter or intimately connected therewith.
D	(dismissed)	Appeal from same case dismissed.
m	(modified)	Same case modified on appeal.
r	(reversed)	Same case reversed on appeal.
s	(same case)	Same case as case cited.
S	(superseded)	Substitution for former opinion.
v	(vacated)	Same case vacated.
US	cert den	Certiorari denied by U. S. Supreme Court.
US	cert dis	Certiorari dismissed by U. S. Supreme Court.
US	reh den	Rehearing denied by U. S. Supreme Court.
US	reh dis	Rehearing dismissed by U. S. Supreme Court.
US	app pndg	Appeal pending before the U. S. Supreme Court.
Lv	app den	Leave to appeal denied (Michigan cases only).

Treatment of Case

c	(criticised)	Soundness of decision or reasoning in cited case criticised for reasons given.
d	(distinguished)	Case at bar different either in law or fact from case cited for reasons given.
e	(explained)	Statement of import of decision in cited case. Not merely a restatement of the facts.
f	(followed)	Cited as controlling.
h	(harmonized)	Apparent inconsistency explained and shown not to exist.
j	(dissenting opinion)	Citation in dissenting opinion.
L	(limited)	Refusal to extend decision of cited case beyond precise issues involved.
o	(overruled)	Ruling in cited case expressly overruled.
p	(parallel)	Citing case substantially alike or on all fours with cited case in its law or facts.
q	(questioned)	Soundness of decision or reasoning in cited case questioned.

FIGURE 4-17 Shepard's abbreviations—analysis page (cases). (Reproduced by permission of Shepard's/McGraw-Hill, Inc. Further reproduction of any kind is strictly prohibited.)

2d—408—is used to direct us to the appropriate page. On that page, the first page number of the opinion—516—leads us to the first Shepard's entries for *Atkinson.* See Figure 4-18.

After the name of the case, you will notice two references in parentheses. The first, 160McA601, is a citation to the same case in the *Michigan Appellate Reports;* 160 is the volume number, McA represents the Michigan Court of Appeals, and 601 is the page number. The second is a reference to the case in *A.L.R.4th.* These are both parallel citations. The notation "lv app den in 429 Mch 884" refers to the fact that the Michigan Supreme Court denied consideration to one party in the case. This is an example of history.

Following this, the principle in headnote no. 6 of *Atkinson,* was "distinguished" in "d 426 NW^6 766." The small elevated "6" indicates that the citing case was only interested in headnote 6 of *Atkinson.* The opinion was then "followed" (without limiting it to a headnote), as noted by "f 431 NW 64." These are examples of treatment. Note that in the citing cases, the page reference is not the first page of the citing case, but rather the page on which *Atkinson* is mentioned.

If the case is significant, it might be used by other states as persuasive authority. Here cases are cited from Wisconsin, California, New Jersey, and New York. HCC § 2.05 refers to a section of Haralambie, *Handling Child Custody Cases* (1989), a Shepard's publication on family law. Finally, there are several references to ALRs that have discussed *Atkinson.*

In that Shepard's accounts for a period of time up through the present, checking all supplements becomes critical. In checking the gold-covered supplement, we notice additional citations for Iowa, Colorado, Florida, Illinois, Rhode Island, West Virginia, and Nebraska (see Figure 4-19). All of these states have at least considered the *Atkinson* case.

As a result of this search, you have located recent cases from Michigan and other states discussing the equitable parent doctrine as developed in *Atkinson v. Atkinson.* In the event you desire a more recent case to reference, you now have several. More importantly, you know that the principle is still good law in Michigan.

Shepardizing Other Sources of Law

You will on occasion be required to shepardize statutes. The process is similar to that of shepardizing cases. Rather than notations covering history and treatment, abbreviations are designated for either form of statute or operation of statute by courts and legislatures.

The statute editions of Shepard's cover citations to the federal and state constitutions, U.S. Code, state codes, court rules, and selected municipal charters and ordinances. Shepard's Citations lists every case in which a form of noncase law was been cited, applied, or construed. It also provides information regarding the effects of subsequent legislation.

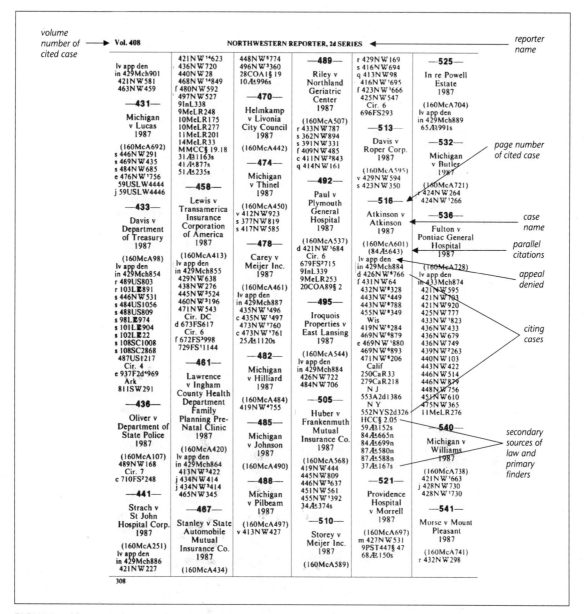

FIGURE 4-18 Sample page from Shepard's. (Reproduced by permission of Shepard's/McGraw-Hill, Inc. Further reproduction of any kind is strictly prohibited.)

The exact form of the statute will vary with the jurisdiction. You should check the abbreviations—analysis page in the beginning of each unit of Shepard's to determine the form (see Figure 4-20).

If you wanted to shepardize a statute discussed in the *Atkinson* case—for instance, the Paternity Act, Mich. Comp. Laws § 722.711—you would turn to the

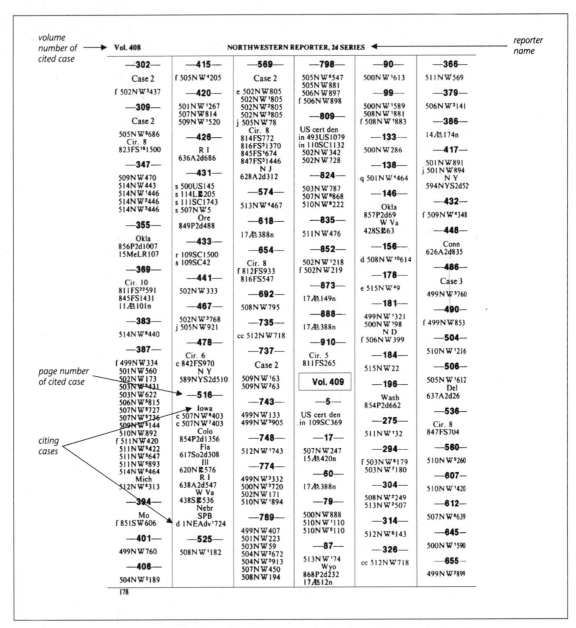

FIGURE 4-19 Sample page from Shepard's supplement. (Reproduced by permission of Shepard's/McGraw-Hill, Inc. Further reproduction of any kind is strictly prohibited.)

relevant page in Shepard's Citations for Michigan statutes, as indicated by the statute number (see Figure 4-21). There you would find a list of all cases that have considered the law since its inception (including *Atkinson*) listed by their official and unofficial cites. The page reference will be to the page in the case

ABBREVIATIONS—ANALYSIS

Form of Statute

Amend.	Amendment		J.R.	Joint Resolution
Appx.	Appendix		No.	Number
Art.	Article		p	Page
C or Ch.	Chapter		¶	Paragraph
CA	Code Amendments		P. L.	Public Law
Cl.	Clause		Res	Resolution
C. R.	Concurrent Resolution		§	Section
Ex. Ord.	Executive Order		St.	Statutes at Large
Ex. or			Stand.	Standard
Ex. Sess.	Extra Session		Subd.	Subdivision
GRP	Governor's Reorganization Plan		Sub ¶	Subparagraph
			Subs. or Subsec.	Subsection

Operation of Statute

Legislative

A	(amended)	Statute amended.
Ad	(added)	New section added.
E	(extended)	Provisions of an existing statute extended in their application to a later statute, or allowance of additional time for performance of duties required by a statute within a limited time.
GP	(granted and citable)	Review granted and ordered published.
L	(limited)	Provisions of an existing statute declared not to be extended in their application to a later statute.
R	(repealed)	Abrogation of an existing statute.
Re-en	(re-enacted)	Statute re-enacted.
Rn	(renumbered)	Renumbering of existing sections.
Rp	(repealed in part)	Abrogation of part of an existing statute.
Rs	(repealed and superseded)	Abrogation of an existing statute and substitution of new legislation therefor.
Rv	(revised)	Statute revised.
S	(superseded)	Substitution of new legislation for an existing statute not expressly abrogated.
Sd	(suspended)	Statute suspended.
Sdp	(suspended in part)	Statute suspended in part.
Sg	(supplementing)	New matter added to an existing statute.
Sp	(superseded in part)	Substitution of new legislation for part of an existing statute not expressly abrogated.

Judicial

C	Constitutional.		V	Void or invalid.
U	Unconstitutional.		Va	Valid.
Up	Unconstitutional in part.		Vp	Void or invalid in part.

FIGURE 4-20 Shepard's abbreviations—analysis page (statutes). (Reproduced by permission of Shepard's/McGraw-Hill, Inc. Further reproduction of any kind is strictly prohibited.)

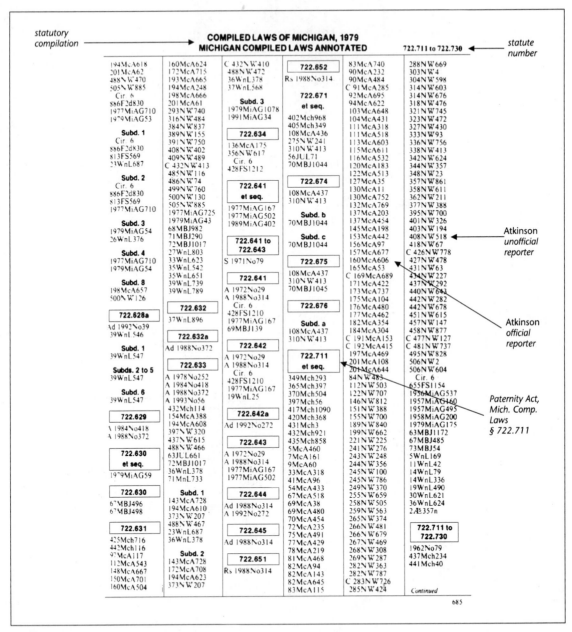

FIGURE 4-21 Sample page from Shepard's (statutes). (Reproduced by permission of Shepard's/McGraw-Hill, Inc. Further reproduction of any kind is strictly prohibited.)

that refers to the act, rather than the first page of the case. You would still need to check the gold, red, and newsprint supplements to that volume.

Finally, Shepard's publishes a number of specialty citators. These include *Acts and Cases by Popular Names*, *Code of Federal Regulations*, and *Law Review Citations*.

Shepard's publishes an excellent reference booklet, *How to Shepardize* (1993), which can be obtained free of charge. In addition, an instructional video, *Introduction to Shepardizing*, is both useful and entertaining.

STEPS IN SHEPARDIZING A CASE

---

1. Determine the known case, called the *cited case.*
2. Based on the cited case, locate appropriate starting volume of Shepard's.
3. Turn to the page of Shepard's where the cited case volume is located.
4. Locate the cited case page number.
5. Find name of cited case and parallel citation(s).
6. Review citing cases for history and treatment.
7. Locate other noncase-law references.
8. Continue the same process in paperback and bound supplements up to present.

Other Law Finders

Besides ALR, West Digests, and Shepard's, primary law can be located through other research resources, such as secondary sources. These include encyclopedias, law review articles, and treatises, as discussed in Chapter 5. Also, computer-assisted legal research (CALR) was envisioned primarily as a method of locating cases. CALR is discussed fully in Chapter 6.

Summary

- Lawyers Cooperative Publishing publishes the American Law Reports series (ALR).

- In ALR, leading cases are fully reported, followed by monographs called annotations describing other cases that are similar.

- There are five published series of ALR; the most current is *A.L.R.5th.*

- The philosophy of ALR is that only a small portion of the total number of reported cases are of importance to the legal community. Only these cases become ALR reported cases and form the basis of annotations.

- A digest is a categorized collection of headnotes. The most noted digests are those published by West Publishing Company.

- The basis of West's digests is the Topic and Key Number System.

- A key number is a permanent number given to a specific point of case law. Once a point of law is extracted from a case, it is put in the form of a headnote and is assigned a key topic and number. These topics are then alphabetically arranged in digests.

- Shepard's Citations is a citator system used to locate and review case law, as well as other forms of primary authority and some secondary sources of law.

- Through shepardizing, the researcher can determine if a case is still good law and how it has been construed by other courts. The judicial interpretation of statutes can also be determined.

- Other primary law finders include encyclopedias, law review articles, and computer-assisted legal research (CALR).

Review Questions

1. What are the purposes of an ALR annotation?

2. Since 1969, where have annotations for federal law been located?

3. What can be determined by the ALR table of jurisdictions represented?

4. In what ways is *A.L.R.5th* different from other ALR editions?

5. Define a key number.

6. Why is the *Decennial Digest* now divided into two parts?

7. What are the four regional digests published by West?

8. In Shepard's Citations, what is a cited case?

9. List the typical volumes of Shepard's.

10. What is meant by treatment of a case in Shepard's?

Chapter Exercises

1. Using either ALR or a West digest, determine whether the equitable parent theory is recognized in your state.

2. Shepardize *Griswold v. Connecticut* (Figure 3-11) and *Stuart v. Board of Supervisors* (Figure 3-10). What did you find?

3. Locate a volume of *A.L.R.5th*. Look up and read any annotation. Were there cases from your jurisdiction in the annotation?

‖‖‖

CHAPTER 5

SECONDARY
SOURCES OF LAW

CHAPTER OUTLINE

Encyclopedias

Law Outlines

Textbooks

Restatements

Uniform Laws and Model Acts

Periodicals

Looseleaf Services

Law Dictionaries, Thesauri, and
   Related Resources

Legal Directories

Attorney General Opinions

OVERVIEW

Secondary sources of law are works that either comment on or analyze the law. Many types of secondary sources will seem familiar to you—encyclopedias, professional magazines, and textbooks, to mention a few. Others, such as hornbooks and law reviews, are unique to the legal profession. For the paralegal, understanding the purposes and proper usage of secondary sources is critical to competent research.

The principal importance of these sources is to help you better understand legal principles. Unfortunately, constitutions, case law, statutes, and administrative regulations are not written with the novice legal researcher in mind. Primary law is frequently hard to comprehend and as a result is difficult to apply to factual scenarios. Alternatively, secondary sources often excel at objectively looking at a complicated legal doctrine, breaking it down, and explaining it clearly and succinctly. For this reason, extensively utilizing secondary sources in research will assist you in understanding primary law.

On a theoretical level, secondary sources help analyze and explain the justification for primary law. Authors often accomplish this through interpreting the law in light of its social impact. Considering the historical basis of the law is another useful technique. Providing insight as to the development of the law results not only in better understanding, but also in an appreciation of the societal forces at work in creating laws.

On an applications level, many secondary law sources take the form of practice guides. These works focus on *how* to accomplish a certain task rather than the esoteric *why* it is done. A well-developed guide or checklist found in such a work can be invaluable if you are working in an unfamiliar area. Many secondary sources are written with this application in mind.

Most of all, primary law can be discovered through the use of secondary sources. In this way, these resources act like the finding tools discussed in Chapter 4. Many are well annotated, so that cases and statutes can be easily located and examined. Because the goal of legal research is to locate primary law to support a legal position, secondary source materials often become a logical starting point.

Encyclopedias are among the most utilized secondary sources. There are encyclopedias with a national focus, such as *Corpus Juris Secundum* and *American Jurisprudence 2d,* and locally focussed ones, such as *Maryland Legal Encyclopedia* and *Ohio Jurisprudence 3d.*

Because they are published at frequent intervals, legal periodicals are often consulted in legal research. These include law reviews, professional journals, newsletters, and legal newspapers.

Textbooks, Restatements, Uniform Laws, Model Acts, and legal dictionaries are also widely considered secondary sources. These and other resources are all examined in this chapter.

PARALEGAL PRACTICE SITUATION

Your state legislature recently enacted a statute permitting the **battered spouse syndrome** to be used as a **defense** to certain **capital offenses** such as murder. You are employed as a paralegal in the county **public defender's** office and have been assigned the task of determining whether this law could be used to assist a client, Eva Popolus,

---

LEGAL TERMS

battered spouse (woman) syndrome [†]   A psychological condition in which a woman commits physical violence against her husband or mate as a result of the continued

who has been charged with the murder of her husband. At present, there is no case law interpreting this act.

Your supervisor intends to use **expert testimony** to prove the syndrome. He would like you to provide him with materials that will help him in his preparation. As this is a new law, your understanding of it is limited. He has suggested that you review secondary sources of law.

Encyclopedias

As a rookie researcher, the first secondary source of law you should become familiar with is a **legal encyclopedia**. These legal counterparts of standard encyclopedias are written in narrative form and are arranged alphabetically by subject matter. Most legal encyclopedias attempt to discuss the entire body of law. Because they reference case law and statutes through the use of footnotes, they serve as excellent primary law finders. Possibly because of their similarity to standard encyclopedias, many feel comfortable using them and as a result begin researching there.

Generally speaking, encyclopedias only cover broad concepts in a somewhat cursory manner. Thus, their research utility is, at times, limited. They do not attempt to analyze or evaluate the material; they simply discuss it noncritically. Encyclopedias provide a basic description of the applicable principle and then direct you to its primary source location.

There are three legal encyclopedias of note. *Corpus Juris Secundum* (CJS), published by the West Publishing Company, and *American Jurisprudence 2d* (Am. Jur. 2d), published by Lawyers Cooperative Publishing, are the two national legal encyclopedias written for the legal professional. A third encyclopedia, the *Guide to American Law* (also published by West), is written for the

---

LEGAL TERMS

physical or mental abuse to which he has subjected her. The courts are split with respect to the admissibility of expert testimony ... to prove the psychological effects of continued abuse.

defense [†] In both civil and criminal cases, the facts submitted and the legal arguments offered by a defendant in support of his or her claim that the plaintiff's case, or the prosecution's, should be rejected. The term "defense" may apply to a defendant's entire case or to separate grounds, called affirmative defenses, offered by a defendant for rejecting all or a portion of the case against him or her.

capital crime (offense) [†] A crime punishable by death.

public defender [†] An attorney appointed by the court to represent indigent persons in criminal cases.

expert testimony [†] The opinion evidence of an expert witness; the testimony of a person particularly skilled, learned, or experienced in a particular art, science, trade, business, profession, or vocation who has a thorough knowledge concerning such matters that is not possessed by people in general.

legal encyclopedia An encyclopedia devoted to legal matters and subjects.

layperson. In addition, various state and specialty encyclopedias are published by West, Lawyers Cooperative, and other smaller publishing houses.

Corpus Juris Secundum

Corpus Juris Secundum (CJS), Latin for "body of law, second," was first published in the 1950s to replace West's original *Corpus Juris* (CJ), started in 1936. CJS covers all federal and state American jurisprudence. The encyclopedia encompasses 433 topics in more than 100 blue-bound volumes. Since 1961, it has included cross-references to West's Topic and Key Number System. This way, additional cases can be found by cross-referencing to West digests. Cumulative pocket parts are published annually. Periodically, outdated and revised volumes are replaced with newer volumes.

CJS can be accessed by one of three methods. The first is the *index method* (also called the *fact method*). You must first come up with a list of phrases or terms that describe the legal problem (see Chapter 9). You then check these words in CJS's general index. This will lead you to a particular volume and subject section of CJS. For example, in looking up "husband and wife" in the index and finding "battered spouse syndrome," you are referred to "Crim L § 1067" (see Figure 5-1). This notation leads you to the text of CJS to find a discussion on the topic.

The second technique is referred to as the *topic analysis method* (also referred to as the *outline method*). Here, you determine first which one of CJS's 433 topics best addresses your problem. After determining the appropriate topic, you turn to the analysis page, which is at the beginning of the title (see Figure 5-2). A review of this outline leads to the appropriate legal point.

The third method involves using CJS in conjunction with another West publication, *Words and Phrases*. Set up like an encyclopedia, and covering 90 volumes, *Words and Phrases* is actually a form of a dictionary. The major difference is that a definition here can cover several pages. The definitions also refer directly to language from primary law. A word located in *Words and Phrases* can be cross-referenced in the general index of CJS.

American Jurisprudence 2d

The *American Jurisprudence* series began in 1936; the title denotes "all the law of America." Its present version, Am. Jur. 2d, began in 1962. It presently contains more than 120 green volumes. All 425 topics are cross-referenced to ALR and the TCSL. Like CJS, it is supplemented with replacement volumes and annual pocket parts. Lawyers Cooperative's philosophy of considering only selected cases is continued in Am. Jur. 2d. Whereas CJS attempted until recently to cite every case on a particular point of law, Am. Jur. 2d selectively chooses only representative cases to cite (CJS now cites only representative cases). Also, Am. Jur. 2d places more of an emphasis on statutory law than does CJS.

HUSBAND

HUSBAND AND WIFE—Continued
Animals—Continued
Notice of vicious tendencies, weight and sufficiency of
evidence, **Anim § 227**
Offspring, title to property, **Anim § 9**
Vicious animals, notice, personal injuries, instructions to
jury, **Anim § 231**
Annulment of Marriage, generally, this index
Antenuptial Contracts, generally, this index
Appeal and Review, generally, this index
Arbitration,
Domestic relations arbitration agreements, **Arbit § 162**
Granting award, **Arbit § 110**
Armed forces, see **Title Index to Armed Services**
Arrest,
Civil actions, arrest in, privileges and exemptions, **Arrest
§ 85**
Removing wife from highway, **Sher&C § 49**
Arson, husband or wife as owner of house, **Arson § 17**
Assault and battery,
Communication of venereal disease to spouse, marital
rights no defense, **Asslt&B § 85**
Defense of spouse, **Asslt&B § 22**
Criminal assault, **Asslt&B § 93**
Domestic violence, **Asslt&B § 62**
Intimacy with accused's wife, provocation, defense, crimi-
nal assault, **Asslt&B § 86**
Sexual assault or battery, marital exception, **Asslt&B § 85**
Wife, right of action, vagrancy, **Vag § 2**
Assets, value and duty to disclose, **Hus&W § 222**
Assignments,
Patents, **Pat § 224**
Undivided one-half interest in realty, proceeds of sale,
assignability of right, **Assign § 19**
Wage assignments, spouse joining in, **Assign § 44**
Associations,
Actions against association, **Assoc § 45**
Personal injuries, class actions, **Assoc § 48**
Attachment, this index
Attorney and client, generally, see **Title Index to Attorney and
Client**
Automobile liability insurance, coverage, declaratory judg-
ments, **Decl Jdg § 66**
Avoidance, transactions between husband and wife, **Hus&W
§ 95**
Banks and banking,
Burden of proving ownership of deposits made jointly,
Banks § 327
Certificate of deposit, payment of, **Banks § 316**
Checks of husband on wife's account, liability of bank
paying, **Banks § 353**
Deposits,
Joint names,
Declaratory judgments, **Decl Jdg § 106**
Priority of claim on insolvency, **Banks § 530**
Parties to action for recovery of, **Banks § 325**
Personal property, joint bank accounts, **Hus&W § 39
et seq.**
Savings bank, rights in respect to, **Banks § 994**
Transactions between husband and wife, gift of bank
deposits, **Hus&W § 104**
Joint account, irrevocability of right to withdraw balance,
Banks § 286
Married women's liability as stockholders, **Banks § 74**
National bank stock, **Banks §§ 594, 605**

HUSBAND AND WIFE—Continued
Banks and banking—Continued
National bank stockholders' liability, judgment for assess-
ment against wife alone, **Banks § 614**
Ownership of deposit, **Banks § 1019**
Savings bank deposits, withdrawals, **Banks § 1003**
Battered spouse syndrome, expert testimony concerning, **Crim ◄
L § 1067**
Bequest, community or separate property, **Hus&W § 136**
Bigamy, generally, this index
Bills and notes,
Advancement by husband to pay notes secured by mort-
gage as volunteer, subrogation, **Subrog § 38**
Defense, **Bills & N § 506**
Delivery of instrument to husband for wife, sufficiency,
Bills & N § 78
Illegality of consideration based on agreements or trans-
actions affecting, **Bills & N § 154**
Maker, averment as to in declaring against indorser or
assignor, **Bills & N § 585**
Married women, accommodation paper, power to exe-
cute, **Bills & N § 739**
Pleading relationship in action on wife's note, **Bills & N
§ 592**
Prior indorser, right of indorser to set up, **Bills & N
§ 241**
Promise of wife to live with husband, sufficiency as
consideration, **Bills & N § 151**
Purchaser taking with constructive notice of, **Bills & N
§ 329**
Transactions between husband and wife, contracts,
Hus&W § 89
Borrowing money, community property, property as communi-
ty or separate, **Hus&W § 131**
Breach of promise to marry, negligence claim against para-
mour, **Hus&W § 118**
Breach of the peace, security to keep the peace on behalf of
husband, **Brch of P § 19**
Brokers,
Ability to perform, time of earning compensation, **Brok
§ 154**
Compensation, person liable, issues, proof and variance,
Brok § 207
Defective title, compensation, **Brok § 160**
Real estate brokers, **Brok § 7**
Refusal to complete contract, compensation, **Brok § 162**
Stockbrokers, authority, **Brok § 48**
Building and loan associations, savings and loan associations,
and credit unions, shareholders, transfer of interest,
B&L Assn § 42
Burglary,
Breaking and entering, consent, **Burg § 24**
Title to property, **Burg § 38**
Indictment, **Burg § 67**
Issues, proof and variance, **Burg § 77**
Stolen property issues, proof and variance, **Burg
§ 80**
Cancellation, marriage settlements, **Hus&W § 86**
Cancellation of instruments, rescission, see **Title Index to:
Cancellation of Instruments; Rescission**
Children, Infants, generally, this index
Choice of domicile, right to choose, **Hus&W § 8**
Choses in action, personal property, **Hus&W § 34 et seq.**
Claims, community or separate property, mutual claims,
Hus&W § 159 et seq.

562

FIGURE 5-1   CJS index of "Crim Law § 1067" and CJS text page. (Reprinted with the permission of West
Publishing Company.)

§ 1067   CRIMINAL LAW

pact.[15] Defendant may not present evidence that the victim was not suffering from rape trauma syndrome where the state has not first introduced evidence that the victim was suffering from rape trauma syndrome.[16]

c. Battered Woman's Syndrome

Battered woman's syndrome is a suitable subject for explanation through expert testimony; it assists the trier of fact in evaluating the reasonableness of both the use of force and the degree of force used in a case involving the recognized circumstances of self-defense.

Battered woman's syndrome is a subject beyond the ken of the average juror, and thus is suitable for explanation through expert testimony,[17] at least where it relates to defendant's claim of self-defense.[18] Indeed, where a psychologist is qualified to testify about battered wife syndrome and defendant establishes her identity as a battered woman, expert evidence on battered wife syndrome must be admitted since it may have a substantial bearing on the woman's perceptions and behavior at the time of the killing.[19]

The function of evidence of the battered woman syndrome is merely to assist the trier of fact in evaluating the reasonableness of both the use of force and the degree of force used in a case involving the recognized circumstances of self-defense.[20] Such testimony is irrelevant unless there is a sufficient factual basis for the allegation that defendant was a battered woman.[21]

d. Sexual Abuse of Children; Battered Child Syndrome

Expert testimony describing the reactions of typical child victims of sexual abuse is admissible, and so is testimony regarding battered child syndrome.

It is within the trial court's discretion to admit qualified expert testimony describing psychological and emotional characteristics typically observed in sexually abused children.[22] Expert testimony describing the reactions of typical child victims of sexual abuse is admissible if it will assist the jury in deciding whether or not the alleged abuse occurred.[23] So, too, in appropriate factual circumstances, testimony regarding battered child syndrome is admissible when given by a properly qualified expert witness.[24]

The syndrome indicates that a child found with certain types of injuries has not suffered those injuries by accidental means.[25] A diagnosis of battered child syndrome is often indicated when a child's injuries do not jibe with the history given by the parent.[26] A properly qualified expert medical witness, therefore, may appropriately explain the syndrome to the jury and express his opinion that the victim suffers from it.[27]

The courts must weigh carefully the probative value against the potential for undue prejudice that may be created by the use of the term "battered child syndrome."[28] The term should not be applied broadly or as a generalization.[29] The expert should be able to testify in detail regarding the nature of the child's injuries and

---

15. Ohio—State v. Whitman, 475 N.E.2d 486, 16 Ohio App.3d 246, 16 O.B.R. 269.

16. Kan.—State v. McQuillen, 689 P.2d 822, 236 Kan. 161, appeal after remand 721 P.2d 740, 239 Kan. 590.

17. U.S.—Fennell v. Goolsby, E.D.Pa., 630 F.Supp. 451.

N.J.—State v. Kelly, 478 A.2d 364, 97 N.J. 178.

S.C.—State v. Hill, 339 S.E.2d 121, 287 S.C. 398.

Wash.—State v. Kelly, 685 P.2d 564, 102 Wash.2d 188.

Substantial scientific acceptance

Theory underlying battered woman syndrome had gained substantial scientific acceptance and expert testimony thereon would be helpful in dispelling jury's possible misperceptions about women in battering relationships, and in countering any "common sense" conclusions that woman was free to leave husband and thus was admissible.

Kan.—State v. Hodges, 716 P.2d 563, 239 Kan. 63, appeal after remand 734 P.2d 1161, 241 Kan. 183.

18. Fla.—Terry v. State, App. 4 Dist., 467 So.2d 761, petition denied 476 So.2d 675.

Kan.—State v. Hodges, 716 P.2d 563, 239 Kan. 63, appeal after remand 734 P.2d 1161, 241 Kan. 183.

N.Y.—People v. Torres, 488 N.Y.S.2d 358, 128 Misc.2d 129.

19. Me.—State v. Anaya, 438 A.2d 892, appeal after remand 456 A.2d 1255.

20. Wash.—State v. Walker, 700 P.2d 1168, 40 Wash.App. 658, reconsideration denied; review denied.

21. U.S.—Fennell v. Goolsby, E.D.Pa., 630 F.Supp. 451.

22. Minn.—State v. Myers, 359 N.W.2d 604.

23. Or.—State v. Hansen, 728 P.2d 538, 82 Or.App. 178, affirmed in part, reversed in part on other grounds 743 P.2d 157, 304 Or. 169.

24. Ariz.—State v. Moyer, App., 727 P.2d 31, 151 Ariz. 253.

Conn.—State v. Dumlao, 491 A.2d 404, 3 Conn.App. 607.

Utah—State v. Tanner, 675 P.2d 539.

25. Conn.—State v. Dumlao, 491 A.2d 404, 3 Conn.App. 607.

26. Conn.—State v. Dumlao, 491 A.2d 404, 3 Conn.App. 607.

27. U.S.—U.S. v. Bowers, C.A.Ga., 660 F.2d 527.

Ala.—Eslava v. State, Cr.App., 473 So.2d 1143.

Ariz.—State v. Poehnelt, App., 722 P.2d 304, 150 Ariz. 136.

Conn.—State v. Dumlao, 491 A.2d 404, 3 Conn.App. 607.

28. Ariz.—State v. Moyer, App., 727 P.2d 31, 151 Ariz. 253.

Conn.—State v. Dumlao, 491 A.2d 404, 3 Conn.App. 607.

29. Conn.—State v. Dumlao, 491 A.2d 404, 3 Conn.App. 607.

FIGURE 5-1 *(continued)*

CORPUS JURIS SECUNDUM

CRIMINAL LAW

Analysis

I. **INTRODUCTION,** §§ 1–7

II. **NATURE OF CRIME,** §§ 8–30
- A. IN GENERAL, §§ 8–18
- B. POWER TO DEFINE AND PUNISH CRIME, §§ 19–23
- C. SOURCES OF CRIMINAL LAW, §§ 24–30

III. **ELEMENTS OF CRIME,** §§ 31–45

IV. **DEFENSES AND CIRCUMSTANCES BARRING PROSECUTION OR CONVICTION GENERALLY,** §§ 46–95
- A. GENERAL CONSIDERATIONS, §§ 46–54
- B. OFFICIAL ACTION OR MISCONDUCT, §§ 55–77
  1. *General Considerations,* §§ 55–57
  2. *Entrapment,* §§ 58–63
  3. *Selective Prosecution or Discriminatory Enforcement,* §§ 64–66
  4. *Prosecutorial Vindictiveness,* §§ 67–77
- C. IMMUNITY AND COMPELLED TESTIMONY, §§ 78–86
- D. OTHER PARTICULAR MATTERS, §§ 87–95

V. **CAPACITY TO COMMIT, AND RESPONSIBILITY FOR, CRIME,** §§ 96–113
- A. GENERAL CONSIDERATIONS, §§ 96–98
- B. INSANITY, §§ 99–108
- C. INTOXICATION; USE OF DRUGS OR NARCOTICS, §§ 109–113

VI. **ATTEMPTS AND SOLICITATION,** §§ 114–126

VII. **PARTIES TO OFFENSES,** §§ 127–148
- A. GENERAL CONSIDERATIONS, §§ 127–129
- B. PRINCIPALS, §§ 130–136
- C. ACCESSORIES, §§ 137–142
- D. PROSECUTION AND PUNISHMENT, §§ 143–148

See also descriptive word index pamphlet

XXVII

FIGURE 5-2 CJS criminal law analysis page. (Reprinted with the permission of West Publishing Company.)

Both the topic analysis and index methods of research can be used in Am. Jur. 2d. If you know the topic, you can locate the volume containing that topic and review the topic outline. However, the most common method is by using the index method (see Figure 5-3).

Am. Jur. 2d includes a separate volume called the "Table of Statutes and Rules Cited." The *U.S. Code Service,* C.F.R., the Federal Rules of Procedure, the Federal Rules of Evidence, and various uniform laws are cross-indexed to the body of Am. Jur. 2d here. The *New Topic Service* started in 1973 contains new topics not yet incorporated into the main volumes. The *Desk Book* is a separate volume that functions as a legal almanac of various legal information. It includes statistical information, medical diagrams, and historical documents. Finally, Lawyers Cooperative also publishes a separate student textbook titled *Summary of American Law,* which is keyed to and summarizes Am. Jur. 2d.

Guide to American Law

Published by West, the *Guide to American Law* is directed toward the layperson. More than 5,000 legal and law-related topics are covered in 12 volumes. Annual yearbooks are also published. It is written in an easy-to-read style and contains biographical and historical information on matters not likely to be found in either CJS or Am. Jur. 2d. (See Figure 5-4.) For instance, if you need background information on the life of a Supreme Court Justice, the *Guide to American Law* would be a good resource. If you have no background on your topic, this is a good place to start your research to obtain some general familiarity.

State and Specialty Encyclopedias

A number of state law encyclopedias are published by West, Lawyers Cooperative, and other smaller companies. These encyclopedias cover case and statutory law emanating from one particular state.

In Illinois, Maryland, and Michigan, West publishes state encyclopedias similar in style to CJS (see Figure 5-5). Lawyers Cooperative (with its sister company Bancroft-Whitney) publishes encyclopedia sets in the style of Am. Jur. 2d for California, Florida, Illinois, Kentucky, Massachusetts, New York, Ohio, Pennsylvania, and Texas. The Michie Company publishes encyclopedias for Tennessee and a combined series for Virginia and West Virginia. Callaghan & Company of Wilmette, Illinois, publishes one for Michigan, and the Harrison Company of Norcross, Georgia, publishes an encyclopedia for Georgia. For researchers in these states, going to a state encyclopedia can save time and effort. In most legal research situations, ample state mandatory authority will exist controlling the outcome of your case. If your choice is between a national encyclopedia and a state one, the state one is better because it will provide only state authority. If you use CJS or Am. Jur. 2d, much of your time will be spent sifting through authorities from other states.

GENERAL INDEX

For assistance using this Index, call 1-800-527-0430

FIGURE 5-3 Index and text pages from Am. Jur. 2d

§ 194   EXPERT AND OPINION EVIDENCE   31A Am Jur 2d

- The lack of specific intent may not be inferred from evidence of the mental disorder, and it is insufficient to only give conclusory testimony that a mental disorder caused an inability to form a specific intent.
- The opinion must contain an explanation of how the mental disorder had this effect.[25]

§ 195. Battered woman syndrome

The courts are in disagreement as to whether the battered woman syndrome, a condition in which a woman who is subjected to continued physical and or mental abuse by her husband or companion refuses to tell anyone of the situation based on a fear of increased aggression against herself, but who often engages in an act of physical violence against her husband or companion in the name of self-defense, is a proper subject for expert testimony. Numerous courts hold that such expert testimony is admissible,[26] stating in support of its admissibility, for example, that it may be used to prove the nature and effect of continued abuse of a woman just as expert testimony is used to prove the standard mental state of hostages, prisoners of war, and others under long-term life-threatening situations.[27] There are a number of other courts, however, holding that expert testimony is inadmissible regarding the battered woman syndrome,[28] stating that such evidence is inadmissible upon a finding that: (1) it is irrelevant and immaterial to the issue of whether the defendant acted in self-defense at the time of the incident; (2) the subject of the expert testimony is within the understanding of the jury; (3) the battered woman syndrome is not sufficiently developed, as a matter of common accepted scientific knowledge, to warrant testimony under the guise of expertise; and (4) its prejudicial impact outweighs its probative value.[29]

25. State v Edmon, 28 Wash App 98, 621 P2d 1310, review den 95 Wash 2d 1019.

26. Hawthorne v State (Fla App D1) 408 So 2d 801, petition den (Fla) 415 So 2d 1361 and later proceeding (Fla App D1) 470 So 2d 770, 10 FLW 1406; Smith v State, 247 Ga 612, 277 SE2d 678, 18 ALR4th 1144, on remand 159 Ga App 183, 283 SE2d 98; Pruitt v State, 164 Ga App 247, 296 SE2d 795; People v Minnis (4th Dist) 118 Ill App 3d 345, 74 Ill Dec 179, 455 NE2d 209; State v Hundley, 236 Kan 461, 693 P2d 475; Commonwealth v Rose (Ky) 725 SW2d 588, cert den (US) 98 L Ed 2d 80, 108 S Ct 122; State v Anaya (Me) 438 A2d 892, later app (Me) 456 A2d 1255, habeas corpus proceeding (CA1 Me) 781 F2d 1, 19 Fed Rules Evid Serv 1190; State v Allery, 101 Wash 2d 591, 682 P2d 312; State v Walker, 40 Wash App 658, 700 P2d 1168, review den 104 Wash 2d 1012; State v Kelly, 33 Wash App 541, 655 P2d 1202, review gr 100 Wash 2d 1001; State v Steele (W Va) 359 SE2d 558.

Annotation: 18 ALR4th 1153.

Mather, The Skeleton in the Closet: The Battered Woman Syndrome, Self-Defense, and Expert Testimony. 39 Mercer L. Rev. 545-89, Winter 1988.

A Trend Emerges: A State Survey on the

Admissibility of Expert Testimony Concerning the Battered Woman Syndrome. 25 J Fam L 373, 1986-87.

27. State v Hundley, 236 Kan 461, 693 P2d 475.

28. Ibn-Tamas v United States (Dist Col App) 455 A2d 893; State v Necaise (La App 5th Cir) 466 So 2d 660; State v Thomas, 66 Ohio St 2d 518, 20 Ohio Ops 3d 424, 423 NE2d 137, later proceeding (CA6 Ohio) 728 F2d 813, affd 474 US 140, 88 L Ed 2d 435, 106 S Ct 466, 3 FR Serv 3d 436, reh den 474 US 1111, 88 L Ed 2d 933, 106 S Ct 899 and (not followed on other grounds by United States v Bernhardt (CA9 Hawaii) 840 F2d 1441, cert den (US) 102 L Ed 2d 379, 109 S Ct 389) and (not followed by Greenhow v Secretary of Health & Human Services (CA9 Cal) 863 F2d 633, CCH Unemployment Ins Rep ¶ 14403A); Buhrle v State (Wyo) 627 P2d 1374.

Annotation: 18 ALR4th 1153.

The Unreliability of Expert Testimony on the Typical Characteristics of Sexual Abuse Victim. 74 Geo LJ 429, December, 1985.

29. State v Thomas, 66 Ohio St 2d 518, 20 Ohio Ops 3d 424, 423 NE2d 137, later proceeding (CA6 Ohio) 728 F2d 813, affd 474 US 140, 88 L Ed 2d 435, 106 S Ct 466, 3 FR Serv

200

FIGURE 5-3   *(continued)*

DOUBLE JEOPARDY

DOUBLE CRIMINALITY See Extradition, International.

DOUBLE ENTRY □ A bookkeeping system that lists each transaction twice in the ledger. □

Double-entry bookkeeping is a method whereby every transaction is shown as both a DEBIT and a CREDIT. This is done through the use of horizontal rows and vertical columns of numbers. The reason for the use of this bookkeeping method is that if the total of horizontal rows and vertical columns is not the same, it is easier to find mistakes than when the records are kept with only a single ENTRY for each item.

DOUBLE INDEMNITY □ A term of an IN-SURANCE policy by which the insurance company promises to pay the insured or the BENEFICIARY twice the amount of coverage if loss occurs due to a particular cause or set of circumstances. □

Double indemnity clauses are found most often in life insurance policies. In the case of the accidental death of the insured, the insurance company will pay the beneficiary of the policy twice its face value. Such a provision is usually financed through the payment of higher premiums than those paid for a policy that entitles a beneficiary to recover only the face amount of the policy, regardless of how the insured died.

In cases where the cause of death is unclear, the insurance company need not pay the proceeds until the accidental nature of death is sufficiently established by a PREPONDERANCE OF EVIDENCE. A beneficiary of such a policy may sue an insurance company for breach of contract to enforce his or her right to the proceeds, whenever necessary.

DOUBLE INSURANCE □ Duplicate protection provided when two companies deal with the same individual and undertake to indemnify that person against the same losses. □

When an individual has double insurance, he or she has coverage by two different insurance companies upon the identical interest in the identical subject matter. If a HUSBAND AND WIFE have duplicate medical insurance coverage protecting one another, they would thereby have double insurance. An individual can rarely collect on double insurance, however, since this would ordinarily constitute a form of UNJUST ENRICHMENT, and a majority of insurance CONTRACTS contain provisions that prohibit this.

DOUBLE JEOPARDY □ A doctrine that prohibits a person from facing a second TRIAL for the same criminal offense following an acquittal or conviction in the original proceeding. □

[Milan], 1396

1396

Alberico of Meda, maker of spurs, must give—Credited to the account of Marco Serrainerio on folio 6 on March 6—[for money] which he [Marco] paid to him
£ 9 s.— d.—
Item—[credited] to said Marco on folio 6 on March 11—[for money] deposited for Filippo, his [Alberico's] brother, in [the bank of] Paolino of Osnago
£ 15 s.— d.—
Item—[credited] to Giovanni of Dugnano, on folio 8 on March 24—[for money] which he [Giovannino] ordered to be given him [Alberico or Filippo?] in [the bank of] Andrea Monte   £ 18 s.— d.—
Item—[credited] to Marco Serrainerio, on folio 6 on May 13—[for money] deposited in [the bank of] Mano, [son] of Ser Jacopo   £ 15 s.— d.—
Item—paid in his behalf on the aforesaid day to Pietrino Bazuella—posted in the cash account on folio 23 £ 10 s.— d.—
Item—for the [balance] posted to the credit account of the joint profit [of the partnership] on folio 20 on January 3, 1397
£ 4 s.8 d.—
[Total £71 s.8]

1396

He [Alberico] must have— Debited to the account of Merceries on folio 15 on February 24—for 6 dozen fine jeweled spurs, at £ 4 s.10 imperial per dozen, amounting to
£ 27 s.— d.—
Item, posted as above, for 6 dozen small fine jeweled spurs, at s.54 per dozen
£ 16 s.4 d.—
Item, posted as above, for 6 dozen Cordovan spurs, at s.48 per dozen, amounting to
£ 14 s.8 d.—
Item, posted as above, for 4 dozen spurs with a prick, at s.26 per dozen, amounting to   £ 5 s.4 d.—
Item, posted as above, for 4 dozen quality spurs with thick arms, at s.23 per dozen
£ 4 s.12 d.—
Item, posted as above, for 4 dozen spurs of medium quality, at s.20 per dozen
£ 4 s.— d.—
[Total £ 71 s.8]

© 1995, Columbia University Press. Reprinted by permission

The earliest surviving examples of double-entry bookkeeping derive from fourteenth-century Italy. The maker of spurs who made these entries in 1396 kept his accounts in pounds (£), shillings (s), and pence (d). These monetary units were used as moneys of account throughout medieval and renaissance Europe although local units of currency also existed.

Double jeopardy is a constitutional guaranty. The Fifth Amendment provides "nor shall any person be subject for the same offense to be twice put in jeopardy of life or limb; . . ." This protection is extended to state prosecutions through the Due Process Clause of the Fourteenth Amendment as a result of the decision of the Supreme Court in *Benton v. Maryland*, 395 U.S. 784, 89 S.Ct. 2056, 23 L.Ed.2d 707 (1969). The doctrine does not apply to civil lawsuits but only to criminal prosecutions. In most JURISDICTIONS, the grade of the offense, whether a MISDE-MEANOR or a FELONY, is unimportant.

Jeopardy means the danger of conviction and punishment faced by a person accused in a criminal action. Double jeopardy is designed to protect an accused from the hazards of more than one trial and the possibility of multiple convictions for an alleged offense. It prevents the government from unduly harassing an accused. The principle underlying the doctrine is that a state should not repeatedly attempt to convict a person of the same crime. Double jeopardy alleviates a continuing state of anxiety and insecurity over the possibility of repeated prosecutions. The accused should not incur the embarrassment, expense, and ordeal of constant prosecutions for the same offense. Moreover, repeated prosecutions unjustly increase the likelihood of finding an innocent person guilty of a crime.

FIGURE 5-4 Page from *Guide to American Law*. (Reprinted with the permission of West Publishing Company.)

West's

MARYLAND

LAW ENCYCLOPEDIA

*Based on Maryland Statutes; Case Law, State
and Federal; Attorney General Opinions
and Law Reviews*

VOLUME 7

COURTS — CRIMINAL LAW § 360

ST. PAUL, MINN.

WEST PUBLISHING CO.

FIGURE 5-5 Title page from *Maryland Legal Encyclopedia.* (Reprinted with the permission of West Publishing Company.)

Lawyers Cooperative also publishes *Federal Procedure, Lawyer's Edition.* Similar in style to Am. Jur. 2d, this 80-chapter work emphasizes federal procedure law. Another specialty encyclopedia is *Fletcher's Cyclopedia of the Law of Private Corporations.*

STEPS IN USING A LEGAL ENCYCLOPEDIA

1. Determine which encyclopedia best suits your needs. If researching a matter of state law, a state encyclopedia is best.
2. If using CJS or a West state encyclopedia, employ one of three methods:
   - Index method

     Determine terms/phrases to describe problem (illustrated in Chapter 9).

     Check terms/phrase in index.

     Go to references in CJS or state encyclopedia.
   - Topic method

     Determine which topic addresses the problem.

     Turn to topic analysis page.

     Go to references within topic.
   - *Words and Phrases* method

     Go to *Words and Phrases.*

     Locate terms/phrases that describe problem.

     Go to references in CJS or state encyclopedia..
3. If using Am. Jur. 2d or other non-West encyclopedia, use index method or topic method.
4. Check the pocket part for updates.

Law Outlines

Popular with law students, **law outlines** are integrated paperback summaries of general legal principles and concepts. The demand for them stems from an emphasis placed on preparing course outlines as a law school study method. Like encyclopedias, they summarize the law and refer to cases and other supporting authority. However, they cover legal topics in less depth than encyclopedias. For this reason, they should be avoided as a research tool. They serve only to give a quick background in a major legal area or in a major specialty area such as torts or contracts. The most recognized are *Emmanual Law Outlines,* Gilbert's *Law Summaries, Legalines,* and West's *Black Letter Series.*

───────────── **LEGAL TERMS** ─────────────

law outline   A paperback summary of general legal principles.

Textbooks

Legal textbooks can take a number of varied and different forms. Traditional textbooks consist of scholarly works by eminent legal authorities, such as casebooks, hornbooks, and treatises. Consumer-oriented books include Nutshells, handbooks, and self-help books.

Nutshells

West addresses a variety of topics in its popular Nutshell series. Nutshells are concise, inexpensive paperbacks containing the essential legal principles of a specific area of law. Because of their low price, they are popular with both law and paralegal students. Nutshells are available in any legal area imaginable, from AIDS law to water law (see Figure 5-6).

Accounting & Law	Constitutional Analysis	Evidence	Insurance Law	Legal Negotiation	Sea, Law of the
Administrative Law	Constitutional Federalism	Family Law	Intellectual Property-Patents,	Legal Research	Secured Transactions
Admiralty	Constitutional Law	Federal Disability Law	Trademarks & Copyright	Legal Writing	Securities Regulation
Agency-Partnership	Consumer Law	Federal Estate &	International Business	Legislative Law & Process	Sex Discrimination
AIDS Law	Contract Remedies	Gift Taxation	Transactions	Local Government Law	Sports Law
Alternative Dispute	Contracts	Federal Income Taxation of	International Human Rights	Mass Communications Law	State Constitutional Law
Resolution	Corporations	Corporations & Stockholders	International Law, Public	Medical Malpractice	State & Local Taxation &
American Indian Law	Corrections & Prisoners'	Federal Income Taxation of	International Taxation	Negotiable Instruments and	Finance
Antitrust Law & Economics	Rights	Individuals	Introduction to Law Study &	Check Collection	Tax Procedure and
Appellate Advocacy	Criminal Law	Federal Income Taxation of	Law Examinations	Oil & Gas Law	Tax Fraud
Art Law	Criminal Procedure	Partners and Partnerships	Introduction to the Study &	Personal Property	Torts
Banking & Financial	Debtor-Creditor Law	Federal Jurisdiction	Practice of Law	Pretrial Litigation	Trial Advocacy
Institutions	Employee Benefit Plans	Federal Rules of Evidence	Judicial Process	Products Liability	Trial & Practice Skills
California Civil Procedure	Employment Discrimination	First Amendment Law	Jurisprudence	Professional Responsibility	Unfair Trade Practices
Civil Procedure	Energy and Natural	First Trial	Juvenile Courts	Real Estate Finance	Uniform Commercial Code
Civil Rights	Resources Law	Government Contracts	Labor Arbitration Law &	Real Property	Uniform Probate Code
Coastal and Ocean	Environmental Law	Health Care Law and Ethics	Practice	Regulated Industries	Water Law
Management	Estate Planning	Historical Introduction to	Labor Law	Remedies	White Collar Crime
Community Property	Estates in Land and Future	Anglo-American Law	Land Use	Sales and Leases of Goods	Wills & Trusts
Comparative Legal Traditions	Interests	Immigration Law &	Landlord & Tenant Law	Schools, Students &	Workers' Compensation &
Conflicts	European Community Law	Procedure	Legal Interviewing &	Teachers, Law of	Employee Protection
		Injunctions	Counseling		

FIGURE 5-6 List of Nutshell titles

Casebooks

Textbooks include law school texts generally referred to as **casebooks**. As the name implies, these texts contain excerpts from cases with commentary, analysis, and questions. In legal education, casebooks are the primary instrument of instruction, referred to as the "casebook method." They have, however, two major limitations as secondary sources. First, only edited versions of

---

LEGAL TERMS

casebook †   A book containing court decisions and other materials in a specific field of law, used for teaching law students.

cases are provided. This is because law school instructors only focus on an opinion's major principles. Because unrelated principles and facts are removed, the cases are often difficult to understand. Secondly, a casebook can go several years without a revision. Consequently, their substance is often dated.

Handbooks and Manuals

Practitioners' **handbooks** and **manuals** are developed as practice guides. They are written from a nuts-and-bolts perspective, with few case or statutory references. Many state bar-affiliated organizations publish handbooks. For example, the Maryland Institute for the Continuing Professional Education of Lawyers (MICPEL) publishes handbooks and manuals for the state legal community. Handbooks and manuals typically include checklists, practice tips, and litigation strategy discussions. A specific type of handbook that includes sample documents, called a *formbook,* is discussed in Chapters 14 and 15.

Self-Help Books

Self-help books are the newest form of legal textbook on the market today. They became popular in the 1980s with books designed to assist the general public in do-it-yourself **probate**, business planning, and divorce. Your local bookstore probably has an ample supply of these texts. Though often providing good general information, they do not deal with the nuances of state law, and thus have limited utility. One of the major publishers in this field is Nolo Press of Berkeley, California, which publishes books on areas such as tenant rights, change of name, traffic court procedure, and dog law.

Treatises

A **treatise** is a specific type of textbook. It differs from other resources in that it covers a topic in much greater depth than a standard textbook. A treatise is said to "treat" the subject. This includes interpretation as well as criticism of a legal subject, which results in virtually complete exploration and analysis.

A treatise's title may give the impression of single authorship. Though most were originally written by an eminent authority in the field, subsequent editions are usually revised by teams of authors. Famous treatises include *Page on Wills, Powell on Real Property,* and *Corbin on Contracts.*

LEGAL TERMS
---

handbook   A "nuts-and-bolts"-oriented practice guide, often prepared by a bar association.

manual †   Written directions for performing a certain task or certain work.

self-help book   A book designed to explain legal procedures to nonlawyers.

probate †   1. To prove a will to be valid in probate court. 2. To submit to the jurisdiction of the probate court for any purpose.

treatise †   A book that discusses, in depth, important principles in some area of human activity or interest.

Hornbooks

Some treatises are referred to as **hornbooks**. (The name is taken from the term given to the school tablets with handles used at one time; see Figure 5-7.) Whereas treatises may be in several volumes, hornbooks are generally in one volume. West has developed a hornbook series on numerous areas of law. Noted West hornbooks include *Prosser and Keeton on the Law of Torts* and *McCormick on Evidence*. Hornbooks are useful one-stop resources of secondary law. If one has been written in the area you are researching, it should be consulted.

The Hornbook

Dr. Johnson described the hornbook as "the first book of children, covered with horn to keep it unsoiled." Pardon's *New General English Dictionary* (1758) defined it as "A leaf of written or printed paper pasted on a board, and covered with horn, for children to learn their letters by, and to prevent their being torn and daubed."

It was used throughout Europe and America between the late 1400s and the middle 1700s.

Shaped like an old-fashioned butter paddle, the first hornbooks were made of wood. The paper lesson the child was to learn was fastened to the wooden paddle and covered with a piece of horn. The transparent strip of horn was made by soaking a cow's horn

in hot water and peeling it away at the thickness of a piece of celluloid. The horn was necessary to protect the lesson from the damp and perhaps grubby hands of the child. Hornbooks commonly contained the alphabet, the vowels, and the Lord's Prayer. Later hornbooks were made of various materials: brass, copper, silver, ivory, bronze, leather, and stone.

As the art of printing advanced, the hornbook was supplanted by the primer in the book form we know today. Subsequently, West Publishing Company developed its "Hornbook Series", a series of scholarly and well-respected one volume treatises on particular areas of law. Today they are widely used by law students, lawyers and judges.

FIGURE 5-7 Discussion on the hornbook. (Reprinted with the permission of West Publishing Company.)

LEGAL TERMS

hornbook †   A book that explains the fundamental aspects of an area or field of the law in basic terms. A hornbook is usually concise.

Restatements

A group of prominent American legal scholars, lawyers, judges, and law professors founded the **American Law Institute** (ALI) in 1923. The primary objective of the ALI has been to work toward reducing complexity and uncertainty in the law. The vehicle to accomplish this is the publication of **Restatements** of the common law. Each Restatement is a statement of the law as it should be interpreted and applied by the judiciary.

Between 1923 and 1944, Restatements were published for the laws of agency, conflicts of laws, contracts, judgments, property, restitution, security, torts, and trusts. After 1952, a second series of Restatements was published in many of the same areas, plus foreign relations and landlord and tenant. Since 1986, the ALI has worked on new Restatements dealing with the law governing lawyers and unfair competition. The Restatements are cited frequently as persuasive authority. Unfortunately, they never achieved the prominence desired by the ALI. The Restatement that has achieved the most success has been the *Restatement (Second) of Torts,* which is often considered by judges in reaching decisions. See Figure 5-8.

The Restatements 1st series is indexed through a one-volume index. In Restatements, 2d series and now 3d series, each Restatement has its own index.

Uniform Laws and Model Acts

There has long has been a desire to achieve statutory uniformity among the states. As to the common law, this has been attempted through the Restatements. In statutory law, this has been tried through the development of **Uniform Laws**. Early in this century, the American Bar Association passed a resolution requesting that each state and the District of Columbia adopt a law providing for the appointment of commissioners from all the states to meet,

---

LEGAL TERMS

American Law Institute (ALI) † A nonprofit organization committed to clarifying legal principles and standardizing them throughout the country. Its best-known work [is] the Restatement of the Law ... .

Restatement of the Law † A series of volumes published by the American Law Institute, written by legal scholars, each volume or set of volumes covering a major field of the law. Each of the Restatements is, among other things, a statement of the law as it is generally interpreted and applied by the courts with respect to particular legal principles.

Uniform Laws † Model legislation prepared and proposed ... by the [National Conference of Commissioners] on Uniform State Laws, the purpose of which is to promote uniformity throughout the country with respect to statutes governing significant areas of the law. Many Uniform Laws are adopted by many, most, or all of the states, with variations from state to state.

FIGURE 5-8 Title page of the *Restatement (Second) of Torts.* (Reprinted with the permission of the American Law Institute.)

RESTATEMENT OF THE LAW
SECOND

TORTS 2d

As Adopted and Promulgated

BY

THE AMERICAN LAW INSTITUTE
AT WASHINGTON, D.C.

May 25, 1963 and May 22, 1964

APPENDIX

Volume Through June, 1984

§§ 310–402

Citations to the Restatement from 1976 through June, 1984

ST. PAUL, MINN.
AMERICAN LAW INSTITUTE PUBLISHERS
1986

discuss, and develop uniform laws in various legal areas. This group collectively is called the **National Conference of Commissioners on Uniform State Laws.**

The commissioners meet once a year to consider drafts of proposed uniform laws. Once they approve a law, they lobby state legislatures to adopt it. More

---

National Conference of Commissioners on Uniform State Laws A group of legal scholars whose purpose is to develop uniform statutory law.

than 200 uniform laws have been approved by the National Conference. The greatest success has been the passage of the **Uniform Commercial Code (UCC)**, which has been passed in full or in part by all 50 states and the District of Columbia. In all, about 150 different Uniform Laws have been enacted by at least one state (see Figure 5-9). Most states make changes in the proposed law to fit their particular needs. If a state has enacted a Uniform Law, it can be found in that state's code.

If a drafted act has a reasonable probability of enactment, the National Conference will designate it as a Uniform Law. Otherwise, it will be denoted a **Model Act**. An example of a Model Act is the Model Penal Code, which deals

---

SELECTED UNIFORM LAWS AND MODEL ACTS

Uniform Laws

Uniform Acknowledgment Act

Uniform Anatomical Gift Act

Uniform Arbitration Act

Uniform Child Custody Jurisdiction Act

Uniform Commercial Code

Uniform Enforcement of Foreign Judgments Act

Uniform Gifts to Minors Act

Uniform Limited Partnership Act

Uniform Law on Notarial Acts

Uniform Probate Code

Model Acts

Model Business Corporation Act

Model Interparty Agreement Act

Model Joint Obligations Act

Model Land Sales Practices Act

Model Penal Code

FIGURE 5-9 List of selected Uniform Laws and Model Acts

— LEGAL TERMS —

Uniform Commercial Code † One of the Uniform Laws, which has been adopted in much the same form in every state. It governs most aspects of commercial transactions, including sales, leases, negotiable instruments, deposits and collections, letters of credit, bulk sales, warehouse receipts, bills of lading and other documents of title, investment securities, and secured transactions.

Model Act A statute developed by the National Conference of Commissioners on Uniform State Laws.

with crimes and punishments. All Uniform Acts passed by the National Conference can be found in West's *Uniform Laws Annotated, Master Edition.*

Periodicals

The two primary distinguishing characteristics of legal periodicals are that they are published at regular intervals—daily, weekly, monthly, or quarterly—and that they typically take a paperback or magazine form. They are a good source for evaluating the legal market (employment and new products), legal scholarship (articles on new trends and developments), and legal events (meetings and conferences).

Periodicals are frequently geared to a specific legal professional group and its needs. For instance, specialty sections (family law, criminal law, general practice, etc.) of the ABA publish periodical materials for their members. The Young Lawyers Division publishes *Barrister* magazine, which focuses on the practices of younger attorneys. Other publications have a more general focus. An example is the *ABA Journal,* a magazine designed for all legal professionals.

Probably the most significant function of periodicals is to keep the legal profession current on recent changes in the law. This points to the major strength of periodicals: because they are published at short intervals, they are usually the most current source of legal developments.

Legal periodicals usually fall into four groups: law reviews, bar association and paralegal publications, newsletters, and legal newspapers. Most periodicals can be found through the *Index to Legal Periodicals* published by the H.W. Wilson Company.

Law Reviews

All of the 177 ABA-approved and several of the 31 nonapproved law schools publish **law reviews**. Their unique feature is that they are, by and large, controlled by student editorial boards. Most are published on a quarterly basis. Though most law reviews are general in focus, many schools publish specialty law reviews treating one particular subject area exclusively.

The feature articles, called *comments,* are written by either law professors or prominent attorneys. (See Figure 5-10.) In addition, students write case, book, or subject reviews known as *notes.*

In addition, some law schools publish magazine-like journals. Rather than having a scholarly focus, these publications discuss the more practical aspects of practicing law. Like law reviews, they are governed by student-run editorial

---

LEGAL TERMS

law review [†]   A publication containing articles by law professors and other authorities, with respect to legal issues of current interest, and summaries of significant recent cases, written by law students. ... Another name for a law review is law journal or legal periodical.

MERCER LAW REVIEW

VOLUME XXXIX
1988

The Skeleton in the Closet: The Battered Woman Syndrome, Self-Defense, and Expert Testimony

by Victoria Mikesell Mather*

I. INTRODUCTION

The common practice of wife beating is a 'skeleton in the closet' of many families today.[1] In recent years, however, the public has focused much attention on the phenomenon of the battered woman, bringing the battering relationship and its consequences to the forefront of American social consciousness. The numbers are staggering: FBI statistics show that a husband or boyfriend beats a woman in the United States approximately every eighteen seconds;[2] other sources estimate that somewhere between two and six million women will be beaten by their mates each year;[3] and experts believe that between one-half and two-thirds of all marriages will experience at least one battering incident during the relationship.[4] The figures are somewhat speculative since wife beating is still

---

* Assistant Professor of Law, St. Mary's University School of Law. University of Illinois (B.S., 1978; J.D., 1981; LL.M., 1987).

The author extends special thanks to her research assistant, Peter Goebel, for his careful and patient work.

1. The author uses the terms wife and woman interchangeably in this Article because many female victims of battering are not married to their abusers, but live with them.

2. A wide range of such statistics are cited in Moore, *Editor's Introduction*, in BATTERED WOMEN 7, 13-14 (D. Moore ed. 1979), in J. FLEMING, STOPPING WIFE ABUSE 330-32 (1979), and in D. MARTIN, BATTERED WIVES 11-14 (1976).

3. Waits, *The Criminal Justice System's Response to Battering: Understanding the Problem, Forging the Solutions*, 60 WASH. L. REV. 267, 273 (1985) (citing *Wife Beating: The Silent Crime*, TIME, Sept. 5, 1983, at 23); and G. GOOLKASIAN, CONFRONTING DOMESTIC VIOLENCE: A GUIDE FOR CRIMINAL JUSTICE AGENCIES 7 (1986) [hereinafter CONFRONTING DOMESTIC VIOLENCE]. Both authors were drawing from a study by M. STRAUS, R. GELLES & S. STEINMETZ, BEHIND CLOSED DOORS: VIOLENCE IN THE AMERICAN FAMILY 32-33 (1980) [hereinafter BEHIND CLOSED DOORS].

4. *See, e.g.*, L. WALKER, THE BATTERED WOMAN ix (1979) [hereinafter THE BATTERED

545

FIGURE 5-10 Law review page. (Reproduced with the permission of the publisher. Further reproduction without permission is strictly prohibited.)

boards. An example is *The Law Forum* published by the University of Baltimore School of Law.

Bar and Paralegal Publications

The most abundant periodicals are bar publications. Because of their format, most are indistinguishable from ordinary magazines. Examples include journals of attorney associations, widely read by all legal professionals. Examples include the previously mentioned *ABA Journal* and the National Bar Association's *NBA Magazine*. The widely read *American Lawyer,* at one time a legal newspaper, has now evolved into a magazine and is published monthly.

In addition, state associations and larger city and county associations publish journals for their membership. For example, the Maryland State Bar Association publishes the *Maryland Bar Journal.* The journals of smaller associations take the appearance of newsletters. An example is *The Advocate,* published by Baltimore County, Maryland Bar Association. Indicated previously was the fact that all ABA membership sections publish journals. Some of these include the *Family Law Quarterly* (a scholarly law review-like journal) and the *Family Advocate* (a magazine-like journal), both published by the ABA Section on Family Law.

In addition, several useful publications for paralegals are on the market today. These magazines publish articles of particular interest to paralegals; information on employment trends, new technology, and professional meetings is commonly featured.

Legal Assistant Today is published monthly by James Publishing in Costa Mesa, California. It features a news and trends section focusing on state paralegal activity, as well as regular columns on research, technology, writing, and career advice. It is the most widely read paralegal magazine.

The *National Paralegal Reporter* is the official magazine of the **National Federation of Paralegal Associations** (NFPA). Distributed quarterly, the magazine's offices are in Kansas City, Missouri. Its most important function is in communicating policies, events, meetings, and other news about NFPA.

The **National Association of Legal Assistants** (NALA) publishes *Facts and Findings* on a quarterly basis. NALA headquarters are located in Tulsa, Oklahoma.

LEGAL TERMS

National Federation of Paralegal Associations (NFPA) † An association of paralegal and legal assistant organizations nationwide whose purpose is to enhance professionalism and the interests of those in the profession, as well as to advance the administration of justice. Among its other undertakings, NFPA has established the "Affirmation of Responsibility," a code of professional conduct for paralegals and legal assistants, and provides continuing education and assistance in job placement.

National Association of Legal Assistants (NALA) † A national organization of legal assistants and paralegals whose purpose is to enhance professionalism and the interests of those in the profession, as well as to advance the administration of justice generally. Among its other undertakings, NALA has established a "Code of Professional Responsibility" for paralegals and legal assistants and provides professional certifications, continuing education, and assistance in job placement. A person who receives certification through NALA is entitled to so indicate by the use of "CLA" (Certified Legal Assistant) after his or her name.

Like NFPA's magazine, it focuses mostly on conveying information to members about NALA activities.

Newsletters

Various specialty newsletters are published on a monthly or weekly basis. These include two from the Internal Revenue Service: The *Internal Revenue Bulletin* and the *Tax Practitioner Newsletter*. Countless others are published by private publishers. Many are published on the state level for specific legal specialty areas (see Figure 5-11). The source of the most current information in a technical legal specialty is a newsletter. If the firm you are employed by emphasizes only one area of law, it likely subscribes to a newsletter service in that area.

Legal Newspapers

The most current sources of general legal information are legal newspapers. Located in major metropolitan areas, most legal newspapers are either wholly or substantially devoted to legal matters and are published daily, Monday through Saturday. Examples include the *Los Angeles Daily Journal* and the *New York Law Journal*. The *National Law Journal, Legal Times,* and *Lawyers Weekly USA* are weekly published newspapers with a national focus.

Legal newspapers, especially those with a local focus, feature recently published case opinions, information on court hearings (called **court calendars**), notices of professional meetings, professional announcements, official legal notices, and articles on legal personalities, local issues, and new technology. (See Figure 5-12.) For attorneys and paralegals, reading the local legal newspaper should be a daily requirement. The *Index to Legal Periodicals* can be used when looking for an appropriate legal newspaper article.

Looseleaf Services

Specialization in the legal field created a need for publications that could be quickly and easily updated. Originally these **looseleaf services** were limited to areas that were greatly affected by government regulation. Because tax regulations change rapidly, tax law was the first area to employ the use of looseleaf services. Thereafter services began appearing in the areas of labor, antitrust, and

--- **LEGAL TERMS** ---

(court) calendar [†]   A list of cases ready for the court to dispose of, whether by trial or otherwise ... also referred to as a *docket*.

looseleaf service   A specialized form of legal publication used in areas subject to rapid change.

$\overline{F}$Maryland
AMILY LAW Monthly

January 1991

1 Md. Fam. L. M. (1991)

INSIDE

Ignorance may not
be bliss for unwed,
uninformed fathers

3

A free hand
for masters

8

Implied waiver
of jury on paternity

9

In brief

Calendars	4,7
Court of Appeals	4
Certiorari petitions	5
Ct. of Spec. App.	8,9
Unreported opinions	10
Agency action	19
Index	20

Goodwill of solo practice ruled indivisible in divorce
Split decision bars spouse from share in firm she helped build

In a ruling of questionable durability, a deeply divided Court of Appeals declared last month that the goodwill generated by a solo law practitioner is entirely too personal to be divisible as marital property at time of divorce.

And, the court reasoned, in a long-awaited decision in *Prahinski v. Prahinski,* ___ Md. ___ (No. 88-62, filed Dec. 6, 1990), the result doesn't change even if the non-lawyer spouse played a dominant role in developing that practice because state rules of professional conduct bar non-lawyers from participating in or benefitting in any direct way as partners in law practices. See synopsis at p. 4, full text at p. 13.

The decision, which affirms the result reached in a lower court ruling in *Prahinski v. Prahinski*, 75 Md. App. 113, 540 A.2d 833 (1988), addresses only the rights of *lawyers'* spouses, but it is likely to have a decisive impact on claims

See full text at page 13

raised by the spouse of any professional who practices on his or her own.

The 4-3 majority opinion authored by Judge Harry Cole came under sharp attack from dissenters, led by Judge Lawrence Rodowsky, who accused the majority of applying wooden principles to yield a result that runs contrary to the (Continued on page 4)

Case tests marital property status of joint-titled gift

It's a clash of form and substance that has been lurking between the lines of the Marital Property Act ever since its inception in 1978, when lawmakers first agreed to recognize the notion of marital property then voted to exclude from its reach items "acquired by inheritance or gift from a third party."

The question, which the Court of Appeals has decided to take up in a case to be argued this spring, *Pope v. Pope,* No. 90-104, is whether a gift jointly titled to husband and wife from a blood relative of one of the parties to the marriage falls within that exclusion, codified at Fam. Law 8-201(e)(2), or is, by consequence of the donor's titling, transformed im- (Continued on page 5)

In the Court of Special Appeals

Employer contribution proves key to fair valuation of vested pension

Although precedent on alternative methods for valuation of pensions is laced with modifiers such as "flexible" and "elastic," in characterizing approaches that trial courts may take, there are limits to the manner in which that discretion may be exercised once pension rights have vested, the Court of Special Appeals announced last month in *Imagnu v. Wodajo,* ___ Md. App. ___ (No. 90-283, filed Dec. 4, 1990). See synopsis at p. 9.

In what is likely to serve as a benchmark against which to measure the fairness of future decisions on spousal pension rights, the court effectively foreclosed the option of

valuing the pension at time of divorce based solely on the husband's contributions plus accrued interest -- one of three methods that have been expressly endorsed by the state's highest court for purposes of determining the interest of the non-covered spouse -- when the pensioner has already fully vested and is eligible to retire, and the non-covered spouse has presented competent evidence in support of an alternative method of valuation.

Without purporting to look beyond the facts of the particular case, a three-judge panel of the court concluded in a unanimous opinion authored by Judge Theodore Bloom that the "contribu- (Continued on page 9)

Estranged spouse ordered to share lottery spoils

Lottery winnings may be a unique form of marital property, but they're not too special to be divvied up with an estranged spouse at time of divorce, the Court of Special Appeals ruled last month.

In a reported decision that drew wide publicity because it dealt with the exotic and rela- (Continued on page 6)

FIGURE 5-11 State-focussed newsletter. (Reproduced with the permission of the publisher. Further reproduction without permission is strictly prohibited.)

SATURDAY, SEPTEMBER 16, 1995

THE DAILY RECORD

MARYLAND LAWYER

Volume 211
Number 216
50 cents per copy

Serving the
public daily
since 1888

◆ DIGEST ◆

RULINGS

CIVIL PROCEDURE, JUDGMENTS: *John H. Shenasky, II et al. v. Sandra E. Gunter et al.*, CA No. 12, Sept. Term, 1995 Sept. 12, 1995. Where damages at trial are not set, the judge's order is not a final, appealable judgment. As such, an appeal can be ruled premature. p. 5.

PROFESSIONAL RESPONSIBILITY, ALCOHOLISM: *Attorney Grievance Commission of Maryland v. Samuel F. Kenney*, CA Misc. No. 25, Sept. Term, 1994 July 5, 1995. An attorney whose professional breaches were directly attributable to alcoholism may avoid disbarment. p. 5.

STATE REGULATIONS, SCOPE OF, APPELLATE REVIEW: *The Insurance Commissioner of the State of Maryland, et. al. v. The Equitable Life Assurance Society of the U.S.*, CA No. 26, Sept. Term, 1993 Sept. 11, 1995. Both the circuit court and the insurance commissioner, who first decided the controversy, considered the wrong statutes within Maryland's Insurance Code in reaching their decisions. As such, the case must be remanded for reconsideration before any Court of Appeals can review the constitutional issues. p. 5.

CRIMINAL LAW, LASER SPEED DETECTION: *David Ellis Goldstein v. State of Maryland*, CA No. 94, Sept. Term, 1994 Sept. 7, 1995. Despite the General Assembly's rejection of a statutory amendment specifically making laser readings admissible, measuring speed by laser technology is generally accepted within the scientific communitiy and laser readings are admissible. p. 6.

CONSTITUTIONAL LAW, SEARCH AND SEIZURE: *In re: Albert S.*, CSA No. 2079, Sept. Term, 1994 Sept. 8, 1995. An off-duty police office must comply with the Fourth Amendment when acting under color of police authority. p. 6.

EVIDENCE LAW, PRIOR INCONSISTENT STATEMENTS: *Macley Dumornay v. State of Maryland*, CSA No. 2075, Sept. Term, 1994 Sept. 8, 1995. An audiotaped, prior inconsistent statement of a witness may be admitted in a criminal trial as substantive evidence against a defendant. p. 7.

FAMILY LAW, RETROACTIVE COURT ORDERS: *Pamela W. Doser v. John C. Doser*, CSA No. 2032, Sept. Term, 1994 Sept. 7, 1995. An entry or order of *nunc pro tunc* is to be granted only to correct a record improperly entered due to clerical error, not to correct a judicial error or to adjust a failure to have a matter resolved quickly. p. 7.

FAMILY LAW, ADOPTION/GUARDIANSHIP: *In Re: Adoption/Guardianship No. 11137 in the Circuit Court for Montgomery County*, CSA No. 1924, Sept. Term, 1994 Sept. 7, 1995. Any words that indicate that a natural parent does not intend to relinquish his or her rights to the child, if found by a

SEE DIGEST PAGE 3

INSIDE

COURT REPORTS

FEATURES

House of Ruth's Amanda Owens, a victim's advocate, is on the front line when domestic abuse victims reach to the court system for help. Owens says the mission of her office is to "demystify" the legal process for those trying to break ties with their abusers.

Seeking Quick Refuge: Court Orders Protect Abuse Victims

District Court 'Ex Parte' Orders Prove Primary Weapons in the Battle To Help Battered Partners: Advocates Say Benefits Outweigh Abuses

BY JANE BOWLING
Daily Record Legal Affairs Editor

As this week's tragic car bombing in Essex showed, domestic abuse victims can face escalated violence when they decide to leave their abusers.

For many in Maryland, the first steps away from an abusive relationship lead to impromptu district court hearings for civil "*ex parte*" orders — temporary orders from the judge requiring an alleged abuser to stay away from the victim, issued solely on the abuse victim's word.

The victims, mostly — but not exclusively — women, fill out a simple petition and are called before the judge to answer questions about their situation. The whole process takes only an hour or so.

The judge's order, which can force an alleged abuser to vacate a shared home and award custody of children to the victim, lasts only a week and carries no effect until police personally deliver it to the alleged abuser.

A hearing scheduled seven days after the *ex parte* proceeding gives the accused an opportunity to have a say before the temporary order is converted to a full-scale 200-day protective order.

It's a process intentionally designed to offer legal solutions to people without lawyers. And the legislation that governs *ex parte* proceedings has been amended in recent years to make it more accessible to more victims of abuse.

At one time only married people were covered by the statute, but now former spouses, people who have children together and any pair who've lived together for at least 90 days, including homosexual couples and parents and children, are covered.

The 200-day final protective order gives the domestic violence victim time to choose a course of action — whether it's divorce, finding a job, filing a civil suit — and put it into effect with some legal protection against the abuser's interference.

12,000 each year

A trip to the city's district courts — particularly on Monday morning, when a weekend's worth of violence can first be addressed — almost guarantees a front-row view of the wide use *ex parte* orders are given.

According to District Court Chief Judge Robert F. Sweeney, about 12,000 *ex parte* petitions are handled by the district courts each year — about 90 percent of the statewide total. That's up from the 2,000-3,000 cases they handled when the orders first became available about a decade ago.

SEE SEEKING PAGE 17

Caregivers' Role in Abuse Help To Grow

BY JESSICA HALL
Daily Record Business Writer

Health workers serve on the front lines of domestic violence — treating the cuts, bruises and broken bones. But often these wounds are only viewed as physical ailments and not part of a larger, widespread problem.

However, a statewide effort called the Maryland Physicians' Campaign Against Family Violence aims to train medical personnel to take a more active role in identifying and eliminating domestic abuse.

"Often, doctors and nurses deal with the injury. But there's no linkage that it could be violence-related," said Roseanne

SEE CAREGIVERS PAGE 19

FIGURE 5-12 Legal newspaper. (Reproduced with permission of the publisher. Further reproduction without permission is strictly prohibited.)

securities law. Today, services exist in all areas, including family law, criminal law, and environmental law.

There are basically two types of looseleaf services. In a *cumulative service,* new material is added at the end of the volume. This new material, called the supplement, does not replace current pages. In an *interfiled service,* the volume is updated by replacing superseded pages with revised pages. In other words, new pages are inserted where appropriate within the book, rather than simply added at the end. Many looseleaf services have characteristics of both types. Both types generally use a three- or five-ring binder.

The material provided for supplementation in either cumulative or interfiled services is published weekly, biweekly, monthly, quarterly, or yearly, depending on the type of service. The actual format of the service varies with the subject matter. For instance, those areas of the law greatly affected by statute usually follow a statutory format; that is, the topics are arranged by statute. If case law is the basis, then a subject matter format is normally followed.

Major publishers of looseleaf services include Commerce Clearing House (CCH), the Bureau of National Affairs (BNA), Research Institute of American (RIA), and Prentice-Hall Information Services. *Legal Looseleafs in Print,* published annually, can be consulted to locate a particular looseleaf service.

Law Dictionaries, Thesauri, and Related Resources

A standard English dictionary provides word origin, meanings, forms, and uses of a particular word or term. Some, in fact, are excellent sources for finding legal words. In a basic sense, a **law dictionary** is no different except that the words have particular legal meanings. Many of these legal words have Latin, French, or old English origins.

The best known law dictionary is *Black's Law Dictionary* compiled by Henry Campbell Black in 1891. Subsequent editions were published in 1910, 1933, 1951, 1957, 1968, 1979, and 1990. The major features of *Black's* include definitions, pronunciations, selected citations to cases, a table of abbreviations, the U.S. Constitution, a time chart of the U.S. Supreme Court, an organizational chart of the U.S. government, and a table of British rulers. *Black's* is available in a standard edition, a deluxe edition, and an abridged paperback edition. (See Figure 5-13.)

The second most consulted dictionary is *Ballentine's Law Dictionary.* Originally prepared by James A. Ballentine in 1916, it has been revised three times in 1923, 1948, and 1969. Its major features include definitions, pronunciations, selected citations to cases and *Lawyer's Edition,* ALR, Am. Jur., and Am. Jur. 2d.

LEGAL TERMS

law dictionary   A dictionary devoted to legal terms.

BLACK'S
LAW DICTIONARY®

Definitions of the Terms and Phrases of
American and English Jurisprudence,
Ancient and Modern

By

HENRY CAMPBELL BLACK, M. A.

ABRIDGED SIXTH EDITION

BY

THE PUBLISHER'S EDITORIAL STAFF

Coauthors

JOSEPH R. NOLAN

Associate Justice, Massachusetts Supreme Judicial Court

and

JACQUELINE M. NOLAN–HALEY

Associate Clinical Professor,
Fordham University School of Law

———

Contributing Authors

M. J. CONNOLLY
Associate Professor (Linguistics),
College of Arts & Sciences, Boston College

STEPHEN C. HICKS
Professor of Law, Suffolk University
Law School, Boston, MA

MARTINA N. ALIBRANDI
Certified Public Accountant, Bolton, MA

ST. PAUL, MINN.
WEST PUBLISHING CO.
1991

FIGURE 5-13 Title page from *Black's Law Dictionary.* (Reprinted with the permission of West Publishing Company.)

Recently, Lawyers Cooperative and Delmar Publishers published *Ballentine's Law Dictionary—Legal Assistant Edition* by Jack G. Handler, Jr. This is an excellent resource for new paralegals.

Other dictionaries (all published by West) include *Oran's Dictionary of the Law,* written for the nonlawyer; *Bouvier's Law Dictionary,* last published in 1914 and therefore considerably outdated; and Statsky's *Legal Thesaurus/Dictionary.*

In addition to Statsky's publication, several other legal thesauri have been published. These include Cochran's *Law Lexicon* and Burton's *Legal Thesaurus.* A new addition is Jonathan Lynton's *Ballentine's Thesaurus for Legal Research and Writing,* published by LCP and Delmar. This publication includes LCP's *The Living Law: A Guide to Modern Legal Research,* a comprehensive resource of all Lawyers Cooperative publications and how they are used.

Another word-finding publication has previously been mentioned: *Words and Phrases.* If a headnote from a case opinion defines a legally significant term, it is published alphabetically by that term in *Words and Phrases.*

Legal Directories

A **legal directory** is customarily a list of practicing attorneys, other legal service providers, and certain important federal, state, and local court and government information in a particular area. Many state bar associations publish their own directories. These are helpful when making legal referrals. For job hunters, they are critical in the search for potential employers.

The most renowned legal directory is the *Martindale-Hubbell Law Directory.* National in scope, this multivolume set is divided by state, with listings arranged alphabetically. Each volume of *Martindale-Hubbell* contains two parts. The first section is brief and contains a listing arranged by city and town of all practicing attorneys. The larger second section consists of paid attorney listings. Here attorneys purchase space to publish information, including their addresses, telephone and fax numbers, areas of practice, biographies, and representative clients. In separate volumes following the attorney listings, *Martindale-Hubbell* provides summaries of the law of each state, Canadian provinces, and selected nations. Also included are Model Acts and Uniform Laws. These volumes are called *law digests* (see Figure 5-14).

Other directories of note include West's *Legal Directory,* Macmillan's *Who's Who in American Law,* and Legal Directories Publishing's *United States Lawyers Reference Directory.* Martindale-Hubbell also publishes the *Bar Registry of Preeminent Lawyers,* an abridged edition of its regular directory.

--------------------------------- **LEGAL TERMS** ---------------------------------

legal directory   A resource containing lists of attorneys as well as other useful legal information.

QUEBEC LAW DIGEST

Revised for 1984 edition by

McMASTER MEIGHEN, Advocates, Barristers and Solicitors of the Montreal Bar.

(C. C. indicates Civil Code of Lower Canada; C. C. Q. indicates new Civil Code of Quebec (see topic Statutes, infra.); C. P. indicates Code of Civil Procedure; R. S. Q. indicates Revised Statutes of Quebec 1977; S. Q., followed by the year, indicates an annual statute of Quebec; O. C. Q., followed by the number and date, indicates an Order of the Lieutenant-Governor in Council. Citations refer to articles of the codes and to chapters and sections of statutes. See Statutes, infra.)

ABSENTEES:

Definition.—Those who, having a domicile in Quebec, have disappeared without anyone having received intelligence of their existence. (C. C. 86). See also Death.

Care of Property.—If it be necessary to provide for the administration of the property of an absentee a curator may be appointed on the advice of a family council homologated by the court or by one of its judges or by the prothonotary. The powers of such curator extend to acts of administration only, and he cannot alienate, pledge or hypothecate the property of the absentee. (C. C. 87s). See topic Guardian and Ward, subhead Curators.

Succession to Property.—The presumptive heirs of a person who has ceased to appear at his domicile or place of residence and has not been heard of for a period of five years may obtain authority to take provisional possession of his property on giving security for their due administration of it. This possession becomes absolute when the absence has continued for 30 years from the day of the disappearance or from the latest intelligence received or if 100 years have elapsed since the birth of the absentee. (C. C. 93s).

Escheat.—See topic Descent and Distribution, subhead Irregular Successions; also topic Wills, subhead Unclaimed Legacies.

ACCORD AND SATISFACTION:

By a contract known as "Transaction," parties may terminate a law suit already begun or prevent future litigation by means of concessions or reservations made by one or both of them. Transaction has, between the parties, authority of a final judgment but except for error of law, it may be annulled for same causes as contracts generally. (C. C. 1918s).

Dation en paiement (giving in payment) is an act by which a debtor gives a thing to his creditor who consents to accept it in payment of a sum due. It is equivalent to a sale of the thing and makes party giving it liable to same warranty. (C. C. 1592).

ACKNOWLEDGMENTS:

Instruments not executed in authentic form (i.e., before notary of Province) are normally proved by affidavits of subscribing witnesses. Courts of Justice Act (R. S. Q. c. T-16) states that such affidavits may be taken by following officers:

Alternative to Acknowledgment or Proof.—No statutory provision.

Within the Province.—Persons appointed by Minister of Justice as Commissioners for Oaths for a particular district; prothonotaries or clerks of a court of justice or their deputies; mayors and clerks or secretary-treasurers of every municipality; rectors or ministers of religion authorized to keep registers of civil status in any territory not erected to a municipality; practising advocates and notaries; and justices of the peace.

Without the Province.—Persons appointed by Minister of Justice as Commissioners for Oaths for Province of Quebec; agents-general or delegates-general of Quebec; notaries public under their hand and official seal; mayors or chief magistrates of any city, town or borough; judges of a superior court in any province of Canada, or in any other British territory; any consul, vice-consul, temporary consul, pro-consul or consular agent of Canada or of Her Majesty.

Commission for Oaths.—Commissioners for Oaths for particular judicial district or for Province of Quebec are appointed for term of five years. Commissions may be renewed for further period of five years. Persons administering oaths in capacities similar to Commissioners for Oaths retain their powers while holding their office or while practising their profession, as case may be. (O. C. Q. 940, 1966).

Married Women.—There are no special requirements concerning acknowledgments by married women.

Effect.—Instrument acknowledged or proved according to law may be read in evidence and used in any court of province. See topics Deeds; Records.

Authentication.—See topic Notaries.

Fees.—Authorized fee for instrument executed before a notary $2 per signature; customary fee for certificate of Board of Notaries authenticating signature of notary of the province, $2.

Forms.—None prescribed. The following may be used:

Forms

Individual:

I, ..., residing at No. .... Street, in the City of ......, in the State of ......, being duly sworn do depose and say: I was present and did see ...... of ...... to me personally known to be the person described in and who executed the within (deed, power of attorney, etc.), sign and execute the same. The signature ...... is in the handwriting of the said ...... and was subscribed to the within .... in my presence and in that of the other subscribing witness.

And I have signed ....

Sworn before me at ...... this ...... day of ...... 19..... (Signature and title of officer administering oath).

Corporation:

I, ... of ...... being duly sworn do depose and say: I was present, and did see ...... of ...... the president, and ...... of ...... the secretary of (name of corporation), to me personally known to be the persons described in and who executed the within (deed, power of attorney, etc.) on behalf of the said company, sign and execute the same and affix thereto the seal of the company. The signatures ...... and ...... are in the handwriting of the said ...... and ...... respectively, and were subscribed to and the seal of the said company was affixed to the within ...... in my presence and in that of the other subscribing witness.

And I have signed ....

Sworn to before me at ...... this ...... day of ...... 19..... (Signature and title of officer administering oath).

ACTIONS:

There has never been any distinction between law and equity in Quebec; civil action is purely and simply judicial prosecution of legal civil right.

Commencement.—Except in certain specified cases, action is instituted by means of writ of summons in name of Sovereign, prepared by plaintiff or his attorney, endorsed by prothonotary upon payment of judicial stamps. Causes of demand must be stated in writ or in a declaration annexed thereto. Ordinarily, defendant has ten days from date of service to appear. (C. P. 110s).

Parties.—Any inhabitant of Quebec may be sued in its courts for fulfilment of obligations contracted by him at home or abroad. (C. C. 28). Subject to ordinary rules of jurisdiction (C. P. 68s), aliens, although not resident in Quebec, may be sued in its courts for fulfilment of obligations contracted by them even in foreign countries (C. C. 27). Correlative right of appearing as plaintiffs is conferred upon nonresidents by C. P. 57, 58.

Whoever brings an action at law, whether for enforcement of right which is not recognized or is jeopardized or denied, or otherwise to obtain judgment upon existence of a legal situation must have sufficient interest therein and free exercise of his rights. Person who has not free exercise of his rights must be represented in manner provided by laws which govern his status and capacity or by Code of Civil Procedure. Irregularity resulting from failure to be so represented can be remedied retroactively at any stage of case even in appeal. (C. P. 55s).

Class Actions.—When several persons have a common interest in a dispute, any one of them may appear in judicial proceedings on behalf of them all, if he holds their mandate. (C. P. 59). Any group of persons associated for pursuit of a common purpose which does not possess a civil personality and is not a partnership within meaning of civil code may defend an action at law taken against it and may also, if it is an association of employees within meaning of labour code, institute legal proceedings. (C. P. 60).

By Act respecting Class Action (1978 S.Q., c. 8) Code of Civil Procedure amended by adding Book Nine (arts. 999 to 1051). Former Book Nine becomes Book Ten. Class action may be brought in any matter which is not small claim and Superior Court has exclusive jurisdiction. Bringing of class action requires authorization of court obtained on motion. Applicant must, inter alia, establish that persons on whose account he acts have in common identical, similar or related questions of law or fact to bring and court must ascertain that person to whom it ascribes status of representative is in position to represent members of group adequately. Judgment on motion describes members of group, identifies questions to be dealt with collectively. Notice to members published and delay provided for members to advise they wish to be excluded from group. Action must be brought within three months of authorization. Decision binding on members of group who did not give notice of exclusion. Pleno jure appeal lies to Court of Appeal.

Act also creates "Fonds d'aide aux recours collectifs" fund to ensure financing of class actions. Contains rules for granting of assistance, rights and obligations of fund and recipients, right of appeal from refusal to grant assistance to Provincial Court.

Intervention.—There are two types of intervention, voluntary and forced.

Voluntary intervention occurs when any person interested in action between other parties or whose presence is necessary to represent incapable party, may intervene therein at any time before judgment, by means of declaration served on all parties. Voluntary intervention is termed aggressive when third party asks for acknowledgment of right against other parties; it is termed conservatory when third party wishes to represent or to assist one of parties in his action. (C.P. 208s).

See Topical Index in front part of this volume.

1

FIGURE 5-14 Page from *Martindale-Hubbell Law Digest.* (Reproduced with the permission of the publisher. Further reproduction without permission is strictly prohibited.)

Attorney General Opinions

When government officials (usually the president or a governor) have a question concerning a statute or regulation, they may request a formal or informal opinion from the attorney general of that government entity. The opinions of attorneys general, though a voice of the government and therefore appearing to be primary law, are in fact classified as a secondary source of law because they are advisory in nature. The written opinions of the attorneys general of the United States are published in the *Opinions of the Attorneys General of the United States.*

The need for formal attorney general opinions has been greater on the state level. Nearly every state publishes the opinions of its attorney general in either slip opinions or bound volumes (see Figure 5-15).

Paralegal Tip

Do not overlook the most obvious, yet often forgotten, secondary source of law—another individual. In the course of research projects, it might be appropriate to interview individuals with specialized knowledge in an area. This could be conducted in person or by telephone. Of course, proper credit to the individual is required.

Summary

- One of the most commonly used secondary law source is a legal encyclopedia. The two major encyclopedias for the legal profession are West's *Corpus Juris Secundum* (CJS) and Lawyers Cooperative's *American Jurisprudence 2d* (Am. Jur. 2d). The *Guide to American Law,* published by West, is directed toward the nonlegal professional. West, Lawyers Cooperative, and several other companies publish state-specific legal encyclopedias.

- Law outlines, popular with law students, are integrated paperback summaries of legal principles and concepts.

- Textbooks include Nutshells, casebooks, handbooks and manuals, self-help books, treatises, and hornbooks.

- In an effort to help reduce complexity and uncertainty in the law, the American Law Institute (ALI) began publishing Restatements of the law in 1923. To date, Restatements have been published for 11 different areas of law.

- The National Conference of Commissioners on Uniform State Laws is responsible for developing Uniform Laws and Model Acts.

- Legal periodicals include law school reviews, bar and paralegal journals, newsletters, and legal newspapers.

- Looseleaf services were developed in response to the need for specialization in the practice of law. There are two types of looseleaf services: cumulative services and interfiled services.

OPINIONS OF THE ATTORNEY GENERAL-STATE OF MARYLAND

CLERKS OF THE COURT — DEPUTY CLERKS — MARRIAGES —
MARRIAGES PERFORMED BY EMPLOYEE AFTER EXPIRATION OF
APPOINTMENT AS DEPUTY CLERK ARE NONETHELESS VALID.

September 25, 1990

The Honorable Merritt Pumphrey, Clerk
Circuit Court for Howard County

You have requested our opinion concerning the validity of marriages performed by an employee of your office. Specifically, you ask if marriages performed since 1986 by an employee who was, prior to 1986, a deputy clerk designated to perform marriages are valid even if the employee was not reappointed and resworn after the 1986 election.

For the reasons given below, we conclude that the marriages performed by the employee are entirely valid. The couples married by this employee need take no further action whatever.

I

Authority of Designated Deputy
Clerks to Perform Marriages

Section 2-406 of the Family Law Article ("FL" Article) provides:

A marriage ceremony may be performed in this State by:

  (1) any official of a religious order or body authorized by the rules and customs of that order or body to perform a marriage ceremony;

  (2) any clerk; or

  (3) any deputy clerk designated by the county administrative judge of the circuit court for the county.[1]

*   *   *   *

CITE AS: 75 Opinions of the Attorney General ___ *(1990)*
            [Opinion No. 90-045 (September 25, 1990)]

OP-Original   -51-
RULES SERVICE CO.   COPYRIGHT, 1991   BETHESDA, MD.

FIGURE 5-15 Maryland Attorney General opinion. (Further copies of the Opinions of the Attorney General and other legal publications can be obtained from Rules Service Company. Contact Kim at (301) 424-9402.)

OPINIONS OF THE ATTORNEY GENERAL-STATE OF MARYLAND

A deputy clerk is a person appointed by the clerk of a circuit court pursuant to Article IV, §26 of the Maryland Constitution and confirmed by the judges of that court.[2] A deputy clerk, once appointed and confirmed, is required to take the oath of office prescribed by §2-104(b) of the Courts Article. The oath of office is a prerequisite to qualifying for the office of deputy clerk. *See* Article 1, §10 of the Constitution.

A deputy clerk's term of office is concurrent with that of the elected clerk, other than in Washington County; a deputy clerk is subject to reappointment by the clerk, in the exercise of the clerk's discretion and subject to confirmation of the judges, and must be resworn at the beginning of the clerk's new term of office. *See* 43 *Opinions of the Attorney General* 119 (1958). *See also O'Leary v. Shipley*, 313 Md. 189, 191 n. 1, 545 A.2d 17 (1988).

When the clerk elects not to reappoint and reswear an individual to a new four-year term as a deputy clerk, that person, if he or she continues in the clerk's employment, becomes an "employee" of the clerk and no longer qualifies as a "deputy clerk." Since the county administrative judge has no authority to designate someone other than a deputy clerk to perform marriages, a designation properly made when an individual was a deputy clerk is no longer effective after the individual ceases to be a deputy clerk, whether by reason of resignation, retirement, failure to be reappointed to a new term, or any other termination of the status of deputy clerk.

Therefore, an employee of the clerk's office is not authorized to perform marriages under FL §2-406 unless, at the time the marriage is performed, the person is a duly qualified deputy clerk who has been designated by the county administrative judge to perform marriages.[3]

II

Validity of Marriages Performed
by Non-Deputized Employee of Clerk

Although, as stated in Part I above, an employee of the clerk's office who is not a duly appointed and sworn deputy clerk is not authorized under Maryland law to perform marriages, any marriage performed by the employee under apparent authority to do so is nonetheless valid. This conclusion is firmly rooted in both Maryland case law and sound public policy favoring the validity of marriage.

FIGURE 5-15 *(continued)*

OPINIONS OF THE ATTORNEY GENERAL-STATE OF MARYLAND

In *Knapp v. Knapp,* 149 Md. 263, 131 A. 329 (1925), the Court of Appeals held that a marriage performed by one who reasonably appeared to be a minister was valid despite complete absence of authority in fact. While this case was decided at a time when Maryland law required a religious ceremony and before the law expressly authorized a civil ceremony performed by a clerk or designated deputy clerk, the rationale of the case is unquestionably applicable to a marriage performed by a person who reasonably appears to be a designated deputy clerk.

In upholding the marriage performed by the supposed minister, the Court relied on the law of public officers and stated as follows:

> The law has long recognized that because of this inability of the public to go behind apparent authority, dealings of supposed officers, who are in fact not qualified, must be given effect nevertheless. "Third persons who have occasion to deal with a public officer and to rely upon his acts, finding a person in the apparent possession of the office and ostensibly exercising its functions lawfully and with the acquiescence of the public, can neither be expected to know, nor to investigate, in every instance, his title to the office or his eligibility to election to it. As to them, he must be held to be what he appears to be, the lawful occupant of the office. This rule is demanded by public policy as the only one affording protection to the public." ... And the reason for that rule applies with even more force to a case of marriage before an unauthorized minister.

149 Md. at 268 (citations omitted). Because the marriage by a supposed minister in *Knapp* was upheld by the Court on the basis of the law of apparent authority of supposed public officers, it necessarily follows that the validity of a marriage by a supposed public officer (a deputy clerk) is also upheld by the same decision. *See* Stranhorn, *Void and Voidable Marriages in Maryland and Their Amendment,* 2 Md. L. Rev. 211, 221 (1938) ("[T]he case of *Knapp v. Knapp* decided that, even if the celebrant lacked appropriate authority, if the parties acted on the belief that he had it the marriage is valid.").

The case of *Knapp v. Knapp* has never been overruled or modified. In fact, *Knapp* simply affirmed a longstanding principle upholding marriages entered into upon the reasonable belief of the parties that the person officiating over the ceremony had been authorized to do so. *See Farley v. Farley,* 94 Ala. 501, 10 So. 646 (1891); *Haggin v. Haggin,* 35 Neb. 375, 53 N.W. 209 (1892); *Holder v. State,* 35 Tex. Crim. 19, 29 S.W. 793 (1895). *See also* Uniform Marriage and Divorce Act, 9A U.L.A. §206(d) at 166-67.

FIGURE 5-15 *(continued)*

OPINIONS OF THE ATTORNEY GENERAL-STATE OF MARYLAND

Additionally, Maryland cases have held that failure to comply with certain other statutory requirements concerning marriage does not invalidate the marriage. For example, in *Feehley v. Feehley*, 129 Md. 565, 99 A. 663 (1916), the Court of Appeals rejected a contention that failure to secure a marriage license as required by law rendered a marriage void. Furthermore, in 1974, the Court of Special Appeals had occasion to address the effect of a marriage performed with a license procured by fraud. *Picarella v. Picarella*, 20 Md. App. 499, 361 A.2d 826 (1974). Despite the fraud, the court applied the reasoning of the *Feehley* decision to find the marriage valid. Both the *Feehley* and *Picarella* decisions rested upon the theory that "'[i]n contracts of marriage there is an interest involved above and beyond that of the immediate parties. Public policy requires that marriage should not be lightly set aside.'" 20 Md. App. at 504, (quoting *Oswald v. Oswald*, 146 Md. 313, 126 A. 81 (1924)).

The *Picarella* court, citing *Feehley*, noted that the Maryland Code nowhere provides that a marriage contracted in violation of its licensing provisions is invalid:

> "In view of the important considerations of morality and legitimacy involved, it is manifestly a sound and just rule of construction the statues providing for marriage licenses are not held to have the effect nullfying, for non-compliance with their terms, a marriage valid at common law, unless such an intention is plainly disclosed. ... [±] statutory provision for license to marry should not be regarded as mandatory, and vital to the validity of a marriage, in the absence of a clear indication of a legislative purpose that it should be so construed."

20 Md. App. at 512-13 (quoting *Feehley*, 129 Md. at 568-69).

This same reasoning must apply when construing the statutory provision governing who may perform marriages in Maryland. If the General Assembly had intended that marriages performed in violation of FL §2-406 would be invalid, it could have expressly so provided. In fact, when the General Assembly did intend such a consequence, that intent was expressly stated. For example, FL §2-202 governing marriages within certain degrees of relationship clearly states, "[a]ny marriage performed in this State that is prohibited by this section is void."[4] By contrast, the law does not provide that a marriage is invalid if performed by someone who does not satisfy the requirements of §2-406(a).

OP-Original
RULES SERVICE CO.

-54-
COPYRIGHT, 1991

BETHESDA, MD.

FIGURE 5-15 *(continued)*

OPINIONS OF THE ATTORNEY GENERAL-STATE OF MARYLAND

III

Conclusion

In summary, it is our opinion that an employee of the clerk's office is not authorized by Maryland law to perform marriages unless, at the time of the marriage, that individual is a duly appointed and sworn deputy clerk who has been designated by the county administrative judge to perform marriages. Nevertheless, marriages performed by an employee of the clerk's office who reasonably appears to be a deputy clerk with authority to perform marriages are valid.

/ s /   J. JOSEPH CURRAN, JR.
Attorney   General

/ s /   JULIA M. FREIT
Assistant   Attorney   General

/ s /   JACK SCHWARTZ
Chief Counsel
Opinions and Advice

FIGURE 5-15 *(continued)*

- The meaning of a legal term can best be found through a legal dictionary. *Black's* and *Ballentine's* are the two major law dictionaries.

- Legal directories are usually lists of practicing attorneys, other legal service providers, and certain important federal, state, and local government information. The *Martindale-Hubbell Law Directory* is the most renowned directory.

- In response to a request for interpretation of a specific statute or regulation, an attorney general will provide a formal written opinion.

Review Questions

1. Describe how to use CJS and Am. Jur. 2d.

2. In Am. Jur. 2d, what is provided in the "Table of Statutes and Rules Cited"?

3. Why might someone use the *Guide to American Law*?

4. What is the major limitation on using a law outline for research?

5. Who publishes the Nutshell series?

6. How is a treatise different from other legal textbooks?

7. Where did the term *hornbook* originate?

8. What is the primary objective of the American Law Institute?

9. What is the National Conference of Commissioners on Uniform State Laws? What are their responsibilities?

10. List the various types of legal periodicals.

11. Who publishes *Facts and Findings?*

12. Why might you want to consult a legal newspaper over other legal periodicals when conducting legal research?

13. Describe the two types of looseleaf services.

14. Besides word meanings, what other information is found in a law dictionary?

15. Why would a job hunter want to consult a legal directory like *Martindale-Hubbell?*

16. Are attorney general opinions primary or secondary law?

Chapter Exercises

1. Locate and review an edition of the legal newspaper serving your area. What are its features?

2. Locate a practitioner handbook or manual published in your state on the battered spouse syndrome. Does it assist in answering the problem in the paralegal practice situation?

3. If you were responsible for purchasing secondary source materials for a firm, what would you purchase and why? Would it make a difference if the firm specialized in criminal law?

4. Locate the *Martindale-Hubbell Law Directory*. In the law digest, look up the Model Rules of Professional Conduct. These are the ethical guidelines that govern attorneys. Read Rule 5.3. What is the effect on a firm partner if a paralegal steals from a client and the partner could have stopped the theft?

5. Review the Selected Uniform Laws and Model Acts in Figure 5-10. Research your state's statutory law to determine which Uniform Acts have been enacted. The Uniform Commercial Code has been accepted in every state in some form. The other laws most likely passed by a state are the Uniform Child Custody Jurisdiction Act and the Uniform Gifts to Minors Act. Study each to determine their coverage.

6. Reconsider the paralegal practice situation from Chapter 4. Using the most appropriate encyclopedia, research the equitable parent doctrine. (If you use the index method, you will want to read Chapter 9 first.) Using the *Index to Legal Periodicals*, determine if there are any law review articles on the subject.

7. Study the Opinion of the Attorney General in Figure 5-15. The opinion is the same one discussed in Chapter 2, which answered the Ricardo problem. Did the attorney general consider any secondary sources of law? (You may have to review Chapter 7 on citation before you can answer this question.)

‖‖‖
CHAPTER 6

COMPUTERS AND OTHER TECHNOLOGY

OVERVIEW

As in nearly every other professional field, recent advances in technology have affected the practice of law. Law office management, litigation support, and document preparation in particular have undergone considerable change as a result of the introduction of computers and other forms of technology. However, the most revolutionary transformations have been in legal research. Today, students of the law are instructed as to the most effective ways of harnessing computers to expedite the location of legal authority. This use has come to be known as computer-assisted legal research (CALR).

CALR made its appearance in the 1970s with the introduction of first LEXIS, by Mead Data Central, and then WESTLAW, by West Publishing Company. Both systems consist of large databases of primary law and secondary source materials, which the researcher can access via personal computer or workstation. Although competitors have emerged since their introduction, WESTLAW and LEXIS are by far the most popular and comprehensive systems.

The basic components of CALR consist of a microcomputer, a modem, and an open telephone line. To conduct a search for primary or secondary sources of law, you must first develop a *query,* an instruction to the computer to look in the database for occurrences of specific words in a legal source. CALR is quicker and more comprehensive than manual legal research, but it is also expensive. To reduce this expense, you must plan carefully before beginning your research.

CALR has also improved the process of legal authority location and verification. Shepard's Citations is now offered online as part of LEXIS and WESTLAW. In addition, both companies have their own citator programs: AUTO-CITE offered by LEXIS, and INSTA-CITE offered by WESTLAW. Shepard's PreView and Quick*Cite* are also citators on WESTLAW. LEXCITE is a citator available on LEXIS.

Another technological advance in the legal field has been the application of CD-ROMs to legal research. Similar to those used for audio recordings, a CD-ROM disc can permanently store large amounts of information that can be read by optics. Reporters, codes, and other legal material can now be accessed on CD-ROM using a personal computer equipped with a CD-ROM drive.

Microtext formats have been used in the legal environment for many years. This noncomputer-based technology was used in the past to store client files and administrative records. More recently, however, due to the overwhelming quantity of legal materials published, microtexts are beginning to replace books. Microfilm places images on reels or cassettes of film. Microfiche places the images on celluloid library cards; one microfiche card can store one volume of a reporter. They have become a necessity where office space is at a premium.

Attorneys are generally required to attend continuing education courses in order to maintain their licenses. Many of these programs, frequently offered by bar associations, are recorded on audiocassettes. Video is also being used to explain many of the "how-tos" of legal research.

Today, all law schools incorporate CALR and other technological advances into their curriculum. Most attorneys, however, are reluctant to permanently discard their books for computers, disks, and microfilm. There continues to be a high reliance on the hardcopy version of the law. There are three probable reasons for this. First, most attorneys practicing today are from the pre-computer age and cannot easily be retrained to accommodate new technological advances. However, this trend may change as more computer-literate students enter law school. Secondly, the availability of and exposure to new technology is limited to larger law firms and law schools. This is in part due to the third reason, namely, that the use and set-up fees for CALR, CD-ROM products, and microtext applications are relatively expensive.

PARALEGAL PRACTICE SITUATION

Your firm recently received a large fee as a result of the settlement of a major **medical malpractice** case. For some time, the senior partners have desired to make technological improvements in the way research is conducted in the office; at present the library is exclusively book-based.

You have been assigned the task of reviewing the various computer-based and other new research options on the market today. After your study, you will make a report and recommendation to the partners.

Computer-Assisted Legal Research

Like manual research, the aim of **computer-assisted legal research** (CALR) is to locate primary law to serve as authority for specific legal positions. CALR accomplishes this electronically without the need to research individual volumes of reporters, codes, texts, or journals.

The basic theory behind CALR is the ability to access a legal database through the use of key words. In 1960, several health law organizations sponsored a computer research demonstration before the American Bar Association. All state statutes dealing with hospital regulations were collected into an IBM mainframe computer. Each state statute was broken down by the computer into individual words. Significant words were then logged into the system, which searched within the database for particular statutes that mentioned these words. Though successful in theory, in practice this particular system turned out to be both expensive and slow. The central concept of using key words to search a database was, however, carried on by other CALR systems, most notably WESTLAW and LEXIS.

Basic equipment is necessary to engage in CALR. You must have access to a microcomputer or an adapted workstation, a modem, and an open telephone line. The purpose of the modem is to convert the signals a computer produces into analog signals that can be transmitted over a telephone line. Most microcomputers (often referred to as PCs) can be adapted to CALR use. However, both WESTLAW and LEXIS provide their own workstations to service subscribers. On the other end of the telephone line is a host computer that operates the

---

LEGAL TERMS

medical malpractice [†]   A physician's negligent failure to observe the appropriate standard of care in providing services to a patient; also, misconduct while engaging in the practice of medicine. Like legal malpractice, medical malpractice is a tort if it causes injury.

computer-assisted legal research   Known as CALR, a method of research utilizing computers and databases.

particular information service. To get online, the user must call an access service that connects to the database. See Figure 6-1.

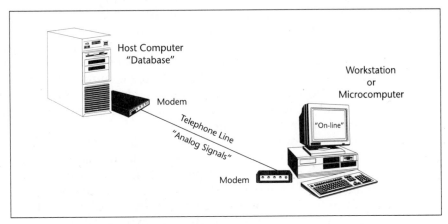

FIGURE 6-1   The process of CALR

Once you are online, actual research can begin. The basic vehicle for this is called a *word search,* otherwise referred to as a *query.* A *query* is an instruction to the computer to examine a database for all occurrences of specific words or terms. In response, and depending on the database, all cases, statutes, regulations, or other materials containing the key words are located.

The following is not a substitute for a detailed discussion on the proper use of a particular CALR database. Both WESTLAW and LEXIS have excellent material available for teaching the proper use of their systems. These materials include West's booklets *Discovering WESTLAW: The Essential Guide* (5th ed. 1995); *WESTLAW Database List* (1994); West's subscribers-only newsletter, *Password;* and Reed Elsevier's (the recent purchasers of LEXIS) booklets *Learning LEXIS: A Handbook for Modern Legal Research* (1996) and *LEXIS-NEXIS: Directory on Online Services* (1995). However, there are general guidelines which can be used regarding both services.

Basic Steps in CALR

Of foremost importance in CALR is advance planning. The high user cost is the most obvious reason for this. Depending on the service, online fees are charged either by the hour or per search. Although rates may vary depending on which system is used, charges may run as high as $200 for an hour's work. These costs are almost always passed directly on to the client. Because of the competitive legal marketplace, bringing down client fees is a goal of every office.

First designate what database you desire to search. These components can be thought of as jurisdictions, regions, or types of sources, such as a particular state, group of states, federal law, or type of periodical. Then decide how you wish to retrieve and review your findings. You can read the material on the screen (called *reading online*), have the material printed, or obtain only the citations to your findings and then follow up with manual research.

The most critical aspect of your research is the determination of the key words to use to form your query. There are two ways to do this. One uses terms and connectors, referred to as *Boolean logic;* the other uses nonlegal words and phrases, sometimes referred to as *natural language*. See Figure 6-2. Of the two, the terms-and-connectors method is more common. This method involves the determination of both primary words and possible synonyms of those words. Many legal resources provide recommended queries when researching a particular area of law. See Figure 6-3.

To make your Boolean query complete, you need to add expanders, of which there are two types. The first, a *root expander,* is a character that enables the computer to retrieve multiple words with the same root. The second, a *universal character,* represents one letter or number and enables a computer to retrieve words with minor variations. For example, in both LEXIS and WESTLAW, the exclamation point "!" is the root expander. When applied to the search "crim!", both systems would produce "criminal," "criminology," "criminalistic," "criminalization," and "criminologist." The universal character is the asterisk, "*". Using the query "crime*", both WESTLAW and LEXIS would locate "crimes."

Finally, to show relationships between terms, *connectors* can be used. Common connectors include "&" to indicate two phrases or terms within the same document, "/n" to indicate a phrase or term within a certain number of words

---

WESTLAW

Boolean query

      SUCCESSOR/3 CORPORATION COMPANY /P LIAB! /P

      CLEAN UP /P HAZARDOUS TOXIC CHEMICAL /5 WASTE

      DUMP

WIN query

      IS A SUCCESSOR CORPORATION LIABLE FOR THE CLEAN-UP OF HAZARDOUS WASTE?

LEXIS

Boolean query

      ADOPT! AND CHILD! W/P PARENT AND CHILD

FREESTYLE query

      WHEN CAN BIOLOGICAL PARENTS REGAIN CUSTODY OF THEIR ADOPTED CHILD?

FIGURE 6-2   Examples of Boolean and natural-language word search methods. (Reprinted with the permission of West Publishing Company.)

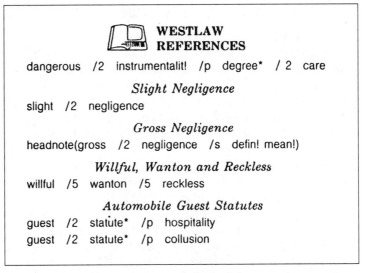

WESTLAW REFERENCES

dangerous /2 instrumentalit! /p degree* / 2 care

Slight Negligence

slight /2 negligence

Gross Negligence

headnote(gross /2 negligence /s defin! mean!)

Willful, Wanton and Reckless

willful /5 wanton /5 reckless

Automobile Guest Statutes

guest /2 statute* /p hospitality

guest /2 statute* /p collusion

FIGURE 6-3   Boolean recommended search in secondary source

of another phrase or term, and "or" to indicate alternate phrases or terms. See Figure 6-4.

One of the benefits of CALR is that you can change your plan—that is, make new query variations—as you progress. You may need to make your query more restrictive or less restrictive, depending on your initial findings.

Connector	Usage
OR	Used to find documents in which one or both of the words linked by "or" appear
	Example
	prosecutor OR state's attorney
&	Used to find documents in which words appear in same document
	Example
	unreasonable & fourth amendment
/n	Used between two phrases/terms expected to appear within a specified number of phrases/terms of each other
	Example
	visitation /10 custody

FIGURE 6-4   Common CALR connectors

Advantages and Disadvantages

When compared to manual research, there are both advantages and disadvantages to CALR. CALR is quicker and more comprehensive because it is possible to search many databases at once. However, it is rather expensive, both in initial subscription cost and in online time. For these reasons, you must be fairly knowledgeable in the most expedient yet thorough methods of using CALR. It must be kept in mind that the costs connected with CALR are usually passed directly on to the client. As a paralegal, you have an ethical duty to minimize research costs for clients. This requires extensive planning prior to starting a search or utilizing manual non-CALR research methods. The costs of your CALR training should never be charged to a client.

When available, the use of CALR is tempting. Because it is quick, does not require physical searching, and current, many legal professionals automatically choose CALR over manual methods of research. In the course of a research project, however, it should be approached cautiously. Not only is it expensive, but it may also be overwhelming. Unless the search developed is precise, you will retrieve an overabundance of material. In that case, you will be left with too many options and will have done little to focus your research. Overall, it is best to use CALR at the end of a research task. In this way, it confirms the authority that you have found through manual research and provides material you might have missed. Also, by that point your research has become focussed, so it will not be difficult to develop precise queries. See Figure 6-5.

Other forms of research are based on searching for applicable legal principles or facts similar to your problem. CALR is based on selecting words that might appear in a legal source. If you choose the wrong word, you can miss cases and statutes critical to your effort. For instance, if your Boolean query consisted of the word "dog," because it deals with liability for injuries a third party might suffer, a case opinion that used the word "canine" would not be found.

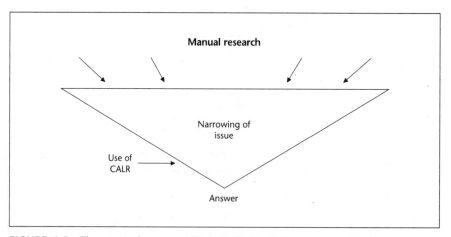

FIGURE 6-5 The research process "inverted triangle"

LEXIS

In 1966, the Ohio State Bar Association and the Data Corporation launched a joint project to form a full-text legal research computer system. They called their system Ohio Bar Automated Research or OBAR. Data Corporation was acquired by Mead Data Central of Dayton, Ohio, in 1968. The success of this effort led Mead Data Central to independently launch LEXIS in 1973. Finally, in late 1994, Mead Data Central was purchased by the Anglo-Dutch publishing company, Reed Elsevier. Today, Reed Elsevier has more than 707,000 subscribers to LEXIS and its full-text news and business information service, NEXIS. They are offered as a package and referred to collectively as LEXIS-NEXIS.

Through LEXIS, the entire unedited text of statutes, cases, and regulations can be accessed. Originally, LEXIS contained a few limited databases including major federal laws and laws from only Ohio and New York. Today, LEXIS contains more than 11 million statutes, cases, and agency decisions, including opinions of the U.S. Supreme Court, the U.S. Courts of Appeals, the U.S. District Courts, and the U.S. Court of Claims. It also contains the United States Code, C.F.R., and the *Federal Register*. On the state level, LEXIS contains the texts from the appellate courts of all 50 states. LEXIS also contains databases of English, French, and Canadian law, as well as materials from Australia, New Zealand, Ireland, and Scotland.

Subscribers to LEXIS can obtain access through a dedicated UBIQ, Super UBIQ, or LEXIS Deluxe workstation or personal computer 24 hours a day (except from 2:00 A.M. to 10:00 A.M. EST on Sundays). Once online, the user transmits an identification number to designate to which account the time should be charged. At that point, a search can begin. See Figure 6-6.

The LEXIS database is divided into specialized "libraries," such as state libraries, a law review library, and libraries devoted to areas of law such as tax, banking, and energy. Libraries are in turn divided into "files." Each file is divided into "documents" and each document into "segments," with each split yielding increasingly more specialized areas. See Figure 6-7.

A recent feature on LEXIS is a word-searching method called *FREESTYLE*. With FREESTYLE the researcher can use nonlegal terms and phrases to search for legal materials. LEXIS in 1995 introduced a speech-recognition system for retrieval of materials on LEXIS, called LEXVOICE. It works with either a FREESTYLE or a Boolean word search.

LEXIS is the only source of various non-West publications (many of which are published by Lawyers Cooperative), including ALR and the *Lawyer's Edition*. LEXIS also features the online citator, AUTO-CITE. Other LEXIS features include LEXIS Financial Information Services, which provides business and financial news; LEXIS Country Information Service, which contains international news; Associated Press Political Service, which contains information on elections, political issues, polls, and candidates; and LEXPAT, which contains patent and trademark information.

Should your school or firm not have LEXIS, you might consider contacting them directly. Often they will provide a tutorial package that includes disks to

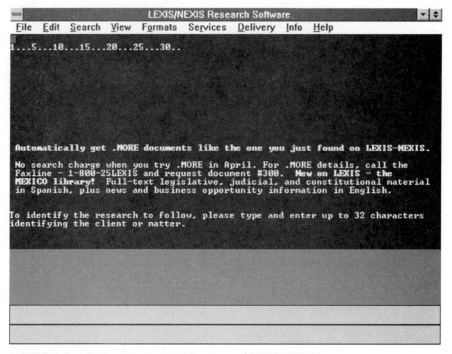

FIGURE 6-6   LEXIS entry screen. (Courtesy of LEXIS-NEXIS.)

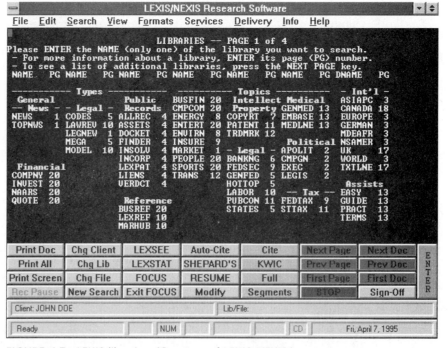

FIGURE 6-7   LEXIS libraries. (Courtesy of LEXIS-NEXIS.)

demonstrate the system. LEXIS-NEXIS can be contacted at LEXIS-NEXIS, P.O. Box 933, Dayton, OH 45401-9964. Their customer service telephone number is 1-800-543-6862.

WESTLAW

In 1975, West Publishing launched its computer-assisted legal research system, *WESTLAW*. At first it differed from LEXIS in that it did not contain full texts, but rather only headnotes taken from West's Topic and Key Number System. Today, however, WESTLAW contains the full text from the U.S. Supreme Court, the U.S. Courts of Appeals, the U.S. District Courts, and the U.S. Court of Claims, as well as state case law. It also contains the U.S.C.A., C.F.R., and the *Federal Register.* In addition, its international collection includes European Community, Chinese, Polish, and Russian materials. WESTLAW's total databases presently total about 5,000.

WESTLAW can be accessed through a WALT PC (West's Automated Law Terminal) or more than 200 different types of personal computers 24 hours a day, 7 days a week. Once online, the WESTLAW logo appears on the screen (see Figure 6-8). The user is then required to transmit a password. At this point, the user must select the appropriate database in which to run a search.

The WESTLAW database directory is divided into general materials, topical materials, texts and periodicals, citators, directories, services, and specialized

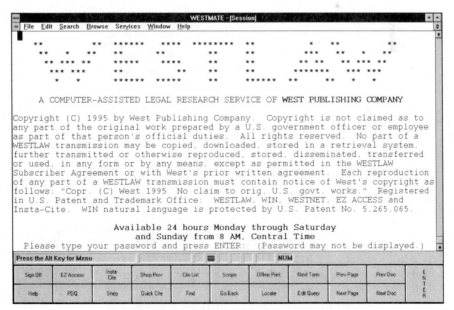

FIGURE 6-8 WESTLAW logo screen. (Reprinted with permission of WESTLAW.)

materials. Each database is in turn divided into smaller units. General materials, for example, include state and federal case law, statutes, regulations, and historical materials. Also found within general materials are news and information, and DIALOG materials. Topical materials are catalogued in more than 30 different specialty areas, such as tax, education, and international law. Law reviews, bar journals, and newspapers are included in texts and periodicals. Citators include Insta-Cite, *Shepard's On-Line, Shepard's PreView,* and Quick*Cite.* Specialized material includes databases provided from other sources, such as the American Bar Association, Dow Jones News/Retrieval, the Bureau of National Affairs (BNA), and the *Restatements.* See Figure 6-9.

In 1992, WESTLAW introduced a research method that allows the user to employ natural language to retrieve legal materials. West calls this method *WIN,* an acronym for "WESTLAW Is Natural." West and Kolvox Communications, Inc. of Toronto, Ontario, in 1994 introduced *LawTALK,* which permits WESTLAW subscribers to search by voice command. With LawTALK, users can dictate into a computer microphone which then translates the voice into WESTLAW commands. The researcher starts by giving the command "wake up" and ends by saying "go to sleep." LawTALK is used with WESTMATE, West's specialized software for using WESTLAW.

WESTLAW can be contacted at West Publishing, 620 Opperman Drive, Eagan, MN 55123-1396. The customer service number is 1-800-WESTLAW (1-800-937-8529).

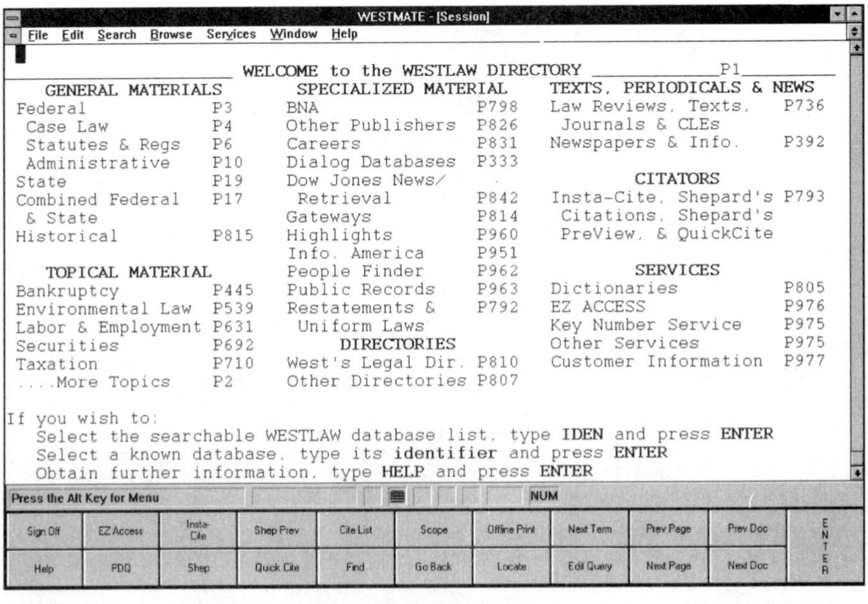

FIGURE 6-9 WESTLAW directories. (Reprinted with permission of WESTLAW.)

Sidebar   **WESTLAW and LEXIS Have the Fax for You**

Through West Publishing's WEST*fax,* you can obtain immediate hard copies of case law, statutes, and other legal materials through your fax machine. West has publicized this as an inexpensive alternative to WESTLAW.

LEXIS has a similar service called LEXIS EXPRESS. Expert researchers will search LEXIS-NEXIS for nonsubscribers and then send the documents retrieved, by fax, to the requester.

Other Major Databases

There are a number of other research databases and systems available to the legal community besides LEXIS and WESTLAW.

NEXIS

In 1979, *NEXIS* was launched by Mead Data Central as the nonlegal complement to LEXIS. NEXIS contains more than 2,400 full-text sources for a wide range of nonlegal information, including more than 750 newspapers (e.g., *The New York Times, The Washington Post,* and *The Los Angeles Times*), magazines (e.g., *Business Week, Fortune,* and *The Economist*), newsletters, wire services (e.g., Associated Press, Reuters, and Agence France-Press), and broadcast transcripts (e.g., *The NewsHour*). It also carries Cable News Network and National Public Radio news and features. In addition, the annual reports of thousands of public corporations can be accessed through NEXIS.

MEDIS

LEXIS-NEXIS also distributes *MEDIS,* a medical database, as part of a subscription to LEXIS-NEXIS. Here textbooks, journals (e.g., *Journal of the American Medical Association*), as well as pharmacology and other medical information can be retrieved through its database. MEDIS can be particularly helpful to a law firm specializing in medical malpractice or personal injury matters.

DIALOG

Very popular with colleges and universities, *DIALOG* is distributed by Dialog Information Services, Inc. It provides many of the same sources as NEXIS, as well as various standard encyclopedias, trade journals, and newsletters. DIALOG allows access to the Congressional Research Service, which provides information on business matters, copyrights, engineering, medicine, patents, trademarks, science, and other subjects. Also accessible are various financial reports, including Dun & Bradstreet. As indicated previously, DIALOG is available on WESTLAW.

The ABA's Legal Technology Resource Center for Technology Assistance

The American Bar Association has created the Legal Technology Resource Center (LTRC). Often this center is a good starting point in collecting and evaluating information on technological options for a firm. The LTRC consists of four programs: the Technology Clearinghouse, Market Research, the LawTech Center and Electronic Communications.

The Technology Clearinghouse is a one-stop source for information on software, hardware, services, and publications. For a modest fee, the Clearinghouse provides packets on a variety of areas affected by technology, including case management, document management, general law automation, and litigation support.

Market Research is a survey research program designed to collect and disseminate technological data and to identify industry trends. The LTRC has completed surveys that explore automation issues in various office settings.

The LawTech Center is an educational facility where lawyers and paralegals can test office automation products without pressure to subscribe to or purchase them. Materials available include applications for calendar/docket control, CD-ROMs, citation checking, CALR (including LEXIS and WESTLAW), and word processing. The LawTech Center is located at ABA headquarters, 750 North Lake Shore Drive, Chicago, IL 60611-3314.

Finally, Electronic Communications consists of resources available through the ABA Network. There are two major components of the ABA Network: ABA Information and Resources, which provides access to information on legal resources through its World Wide Web site on the Internet (http://www.abanet.org/); and Personal Phone Consultation, which consists of one-on-one assistance in understanding online services.

The LTRC can be reached by telephone at (312) 988-5465 or through e-mail at ltrc@attmail.com.

How About Surfing the Internet?

The services available on the Internet, a worldwide network of computer networks, are growing exponentially. Although limited originally for government and educational use, today more than half of the U.S. Internet addresses are for private citizens. It is estimated that as of 1994, there were nearly 2 million host computers connecting 20 million users in the United States. Approximately 15,000 new users join the Internet each day.

To use the Internet, you must have a computer, modem, and telephone line, just as with CALR. A mouse (an input device used to move the cursor on the monitor) is also helpful. Access is usually accomplished through a commercial access provider. Once on the Internet, you are assigned an address. With an address, you can perform a multitude of tasks, including sending and receiving electronic mail (e-mail), participating in topical discussion groups (listservs and newsgroups), and retrieving data from a myriad of databases. For the legal researcher, the possibilities are endless.

The latest Internet inventions are hypertext linkage and the World Wide Web. Hypertext linkage is abbreviated http:// (meaning hypertext transport protocol). Through http://, the author of a document can set up certain words or graphics in a document as push-button links to another document or computer. The World Wide Web (WWW or Web) is a service that makes information available across the Internet. It uses hypertext to allow browsers to connect one Web location or site to another. Web sites typically include professional associations, education institutions, government agencies, and private industry. Web sites of particular interest to paralegals include:

Web Site	Web Address	Materials Available
NFPA	http://www.paralegals.org/	NFPA resources
ABA Network	http://www.abanet.org/	ABA network resources
Library of Congress	http://thomas.loc.gov/	Federal congressional materials and resources (See Figure 6-10)
Legal Information Institute at Cornell University	http://www.law.cornell.edu/	U.S. Supreme Court decisions

All sites provide links to other legal materials and resources on the Internet through hypertext.

CALR Online Citators

With the ability to locate primary law through computer access came the application of this technology to the process of citation location and verification. This led to the development of several commercial, computer-operated citation services.

Shepard's On-Line

Shepard's/McGraw-Hill has developed an online version of *Shepard's Citations,* available on WESTLAW and LEXIS, that is quicker than using the bound volumes. One benefit of using *Shepard's On-Line* is that the bound volumes and pamphlet lists of citing cases are automatically merged for each cited case. The specific technique required for accessing Shepard's depends on the CALR system that carries it. *Shepard's PreView* will shepardize recent cases appearing

In the spirit of Thomas Jefferson,
a service of the U.S. Congress through its Library.

Full Text of Legislation
Full text of all versions of House and Senate bills searchable by keyword(s) or by bill number.
>   103rd Congress Bills
>   104th Congress Bills

Full Text of the Congressional Record
Full text of the daily account of proceedings on the House and Senate Floors searchable by keyword(s).
>   Congressional Record for the 103rd Congress
>   Congressional Record for the 104th Congress
>   Congressional Record Index for the 103rd Congress (1994)
>   Congressional Record Index for the 104th Congress

Hot Legislation
Major bills receiving floor action in the 104th Congress as selected by legislative analysts in the
Congressional Research Service.
>   Hot bills by topic
>   Hot bills by popular and/or short title
>   Hot bills by number/type
>   Hot bills enacted into law
>   Hot bills under Congressional consideration this week.

The Constitution of the United States
The full text of the Constitution and its amendments, searchable by keyword

How Our Laws Are Made Edward F. Willett, Jr., House Law Revision Counsel
An explanation of the lawmaking process from the origin of a legislative proposal through its publication as
a law.

House of Representatives Gopher
Directory information for House of Representatives members and committees; House of Representatives
yearly calendar, latest daily committee hearing schedules, the current week's House floor schedule; visitor
information.

House of Representatives Constituent E-Mail and U.S. Senate Constituent E-Mail
E-mail directories for selected House and Senate members and committees.

U.S. House of Representatives Audit
Office of the Inspector General Financial Statements and Performance Reports, July 18, 1995.

Senate Gopher
Frequently Asked Questions (FAQs) about Senate Internet services for constituents (e-mail, gopher, ftp),

FIGURE 6-10 THOMAS Web site screen

Committee and Member documents (searchable).

C-SPAN (Cable-Satellite Public Affairs Network)
C-SPAN Gopher provides program schedules, Congressional information, FEC Reports, Supreme Court information and historical government documents. C-SPAN Web Server offers program and events schedules, Campaign '96 info, and other political resources.

Visit the Library of Congress World Wide Web <u>Home Page</u>
Select <u>LOCIS</u> for Federal legislation summary and status.
Select <u>Indexes to Other World Wide Web Services</u> for additional information on the <u>Legislative Branch</u>, the <u>Executive Branch</u>, and <u>State and Local Government</u>.

Visit the Library of Congress Gopher <u>LC MARVEL</u>
Select <u>U.S. Congress</u> for additional legislative information; select <u>Government Information</u> for additional U.S. federal and state/local government resources.

<u>**Thomas Usage Statistics**</u>

Send comments on this service to thomas@loc.gov

FIGURE 6-10   *(continued)*

in advance sheets of the National Reporter System. This is available, however, only on WESTLAW. The publication *How to Shepardize* (1993) explains in detail the various computer-based methods of accessing Shepard's.

AUTO-CITE

In 1982, Lawyers Cooperative introduced AUTO-CITE, a system designed to verify the accuracy and validity of citations. It is available on LEXIS-NEXIS. AUTO-CITE permits the user to verify the case, check the current validity of the case, and review prior and subsequent history.

AUTO-CITE focuses on later developments in the same litigation (appeals, rehearings) and on cases affecting the precedential authority of the case. After the user enters the name of the citation, that case, parallel citations, and the names and citations of related cases are shown, with the effect of each subsequent decision noted. AUTO-CITE provides references to ALR and *Lawyer's Edition.* AUTO-CITE also offers CheckCite, a software program designed to check citations in a brief or document. Finally, LEXCITE can be used to find citations to cases, including parallel citations within LEXIS case law documents.

INSTA-CITE

West's case history and citation verification system, called *INSTA-CITE,* was developed in 1983 and is available on WESTLAW. Using the same method of entering cases as AUTO-CITE, INSTA-CITE provides prior and subsequent history of decisions from federal courts from 1754 to the present, and state court decisions from the court's inception to the present. INSTA-CITE also provides parallel citations (with an obvious emphasis on West's National Reporter System), precedential treatment, and citation verification information. INSTA-CITE also provides references to citations in CJS.

WESTLAW also offers Quick*Cite,* which automatically retrieves cases not yet appearing on Shepard's PreView. West's automated citation check software is called WEST*Check.*

Both INSTA-CITE and AUTO-CITE are updated more rapidly than either printed or online *Shepard's Citations.* However, *Shepard's Citations* exceeds both in scope and breadth of coverage.

CD-ROM

CD-ROM (meaning "compact disc-read only memory") is the newest technological addition in legal research. Through the use of optical technology (laser beams), large quantities of data can be stored on a small disk. Approximately 250,000 to 500,000 pages of text, or about 100 to 125 books, can be contained on one disk. The accessor need only have a personal computer with a CD-ROM disk drive.

West was the first publisher to heavily develop CD-ROM legal products. As part of its CD-ROM library, West offers materials on federal practice and procedure, including *Federal Rules Decisions, Federal Reporter,* U.S.C.A., *Supreme Court Reporter,* and *Federal Supplement,* as well as extensive state materials.

Lawyers Cooperative offers its CD-ROM LawDesk series. LCP has developed CD-ROMs for many of its publications, including *Am. Jur. Pleading and Practice Forms,* Am. Jur. 2d, and U.S.C.S.

Martindale-Hubbell started publishing its directory on CD-ROM in 1990. Information Access Corporation publishes LegalTrac on CD-ROM. This contains the *Legal Resource Index,* a good source of legal periodicals. The Research Institute of America (RIA) now puts out the *Internal Revenue Manual* on CD-ROM. Also, Commerce Clearing House (CCH) offers many of its tax materials on CD-ROM.

Other publishers have followed, including the Michie Company, Prentice-Hall, and Matthew Bender. Smaller publishers are making their market by putting out specialized practice materials and state law products. CD-ROM technology is now on the market for practice materials for nearly all states.

CD-ROM products have definite advantages. The most obvious benefit is space-saving. A law firm with limited library space can purchase a few CD-ROM disks that are equivalent to a room full of reporters. In addition, over a long period of time, purchasing reporters in CD-ROM version will be cheaper than buying them in book form.

There are, however, also shortcomings. The most important is that once a CD-ROM is created, it is fixed, like a book. In a sense, it is never as completely up-to-date as WESTLAW and LEXIS are. The only practical way of updating is the issuance of a new disk.

Microtext

The discussion of *microtext* includes two forms of information storage: microfilm and microfiche. Both have been used for several years for storing client and administrative files. Recently, however, due to the voluminous amounts of legal material available, publishers are distributing books and reporters in microtext form.

Microfiche places images on a celluloid library-catalog-sized card. The researcher needs a fiche reader or a combination reader/printer. Today libraries frequently purchase fiche publications, and many state and federal agencies store public documents on microfiche. West offers Ultra Fiche editions of units of the National Reporter System. This presently covers only the first series, but is now expanding into the second series.

Microfilm places images on reels or cassettes of film containing miniature pictures of printed pages. Like microfiche, it is commonly utilized by government agencies.

Video and Audio Recordings

Most bar associations offer continuing legal education (CLE) programs for their members. In addition, a number of private companies have gotten into the continuing education business. The business of offering post-law-school courses to attorneys has greatly increased due to the fact that almost every state now requires practicing attorneys to take annual courses to maintain their licenses to practice.

An example of such a private company is the ALI. Besides developing the Restatements, this organization offers a full array of programs for practitioners. Most of their programs are on audiocassette. This organization's programs are national in scope.

Most CLE associations furnish cassettes of their programs along with printed materials. These audio recordings can be played by attorneys and paralegals at home or in a car's cassette player.

In addition, some companies have attempted to provide educational materials on video. West publishes a series of short videotape segments entitled *Introduction to Legal Research.* Video recordings of this nature generally focus on the process (how to do it) rather than results (specific legal authority). They can be extremely helpful for someone unfamiliar with how to accomplish a specific task. You might consult the ABA's *Video Law Seminars Catalog,* published periodically, to locate a video appropriate for your needs. ABA video topics include antitrust law, computers and law, environmental and natural resources law, and law office management.

Paralegal Tip

When considering the purchase of new technology, be it CALR or other forms, keep in mind the following five rules:

1. *Never acquire equipment or services that cannot be serviced adequately.* Imagine the nightmare you would face if, after you purchased expensive equipment or services, the seller went out of business and no other company would service the product. It is always a good idea to consider a company's reputation when making a purchasing decision. Also, companies that can be easily contacted and/or are local are better than those that are hard to reach and/or out-of-state.

2. *Rent, do not buy, when the technology is expensive and subject to change.* When considering acquiring or upgrading equipment, keep in mind that what is new today is outdated tomorrow. Fax machines purchased only a few years ago are now not sufficient for current needs.

3. *Acquire compatible and complementary equipment.* Make sure your machines and software can "talk" to each other. It is more costly to retrofit equipment to be compatible than to have purchased the right components in the first place.

4. *Personally test everything.* If possible, borrow the equipment or software. Almost all computer software companies have tutorials that can be borrowed demonstrating the service.

5. *Include the operator in the decision-making process.* Often decisions are made by supervisors who have an unrealistic expectation of staff capabilities. Making decisions without involving the ultimate user is the fastest way to lower morale in an office and bring about work alienation. Attorneys should always take the secretary or paralegal with them when they go to the computer store or meet with vendors.

Summary

- Computer-assisted legal research (CALR) is the ability to search a database for primary law and secondary sources through the use of key words, via word searches or queries.

- To conduct CALR, the researcher needs a microcomputer, modem, and open telephone line.

- Though CALR is quicker and more comprehensive than manual research, it is also more costly. Also, unless the query is precise, an overabundance of material will be retrieved.

- The two major CALR systems are LEXIS, developed by Mead Data Central, and WEST-LAW, developed by West Publishing.

- Other databases useful to the legal practitioner include NEXIS, MEDIS, and DIALOG.

- Computerization has also resulted in the development of several online citators, including Shepard's On-Line, AUTO-CITE, and INSTA-CITE.

- Many publishers, including West and LCP, now publish primary law and secondary sources on CD-ROM.

- Microtext includes microfilm and microfiche. Microfiche places images on a celluloid library-catalog-sized card. Microfilm places the images on film reels or cassettes.

- Many bar associations and private continuing education associations offer their programs on audiocassettes.

- Video recordings are now used to explain research "how-tos."

Review Questions

1. What basic equipment is needed to perform CALR?

2. What is a query?

3. What is a connector? Provide an example.

4. What are FREESTYLE and WIN?

5. Name the nonlegal companion database to LEXIS.

6. Name the three major online citation services.

7. What does CD-ROM stand for?

8. List several materials now on CD-ROM.

9. What are the two types of microtext?

Chapter Exercises

1. Survey your local bar. Of the two primary CALR services, LEXIS and WESTLAW, which is the most popular? Why?

2. Investigate whether state materials in your jurisdiction are available on CD-ROM. Have a company sales representative set up a demonstration.

3. Does your school library obtain any federal publications on microtext? Which ones?

4. For most small law firms today, do you think the advantages of employing CALR outweigh the disadvantages? Why?

5. Contact the agency in your state that registers and regulates business organizations. Find out if they keep their records on microtext.

IIII

CHAPTER 7

PROPER IDENTIFICATION: CITATION

OVERVIEW

You have mastered the difficult task of locating legal authority. Now you will be expected to properly reference it when you use it in a legal document. In nonlegal writing, a *reference* to a source includes the information necessary to verify and locate it: the author's name, the name of the source, the publisher, and the year published. Depending on the particular application, there may be a specific format to be followed, such as that recommended in *The Chicago Manual of Style* (14th ed. 1993). The reference can be indicated at the bottom of the page as a footnote, at the end of the chapter or work as an endnote, or even as a parenthetical or citation sentence within the text. Proper referencing is critical to good scholarship.

The need to reference sources is also crucial in the legal profession. Each and every legal assertion must be supported by legal authority. This means providing a reference to that legal authority by giving a citation. As with a nonlegal reference, a *citation* is descriptive information about a specific source.

Because of the importance of precedent in our legal system, accurate citation of sources is important. It is essential to substantiate your legal position; the person reviewing the authority must know that the legal principle was not created out of thin air. It follows, then, that an understanding of citation is important to accurately conveying the results of research.

In that every proposition must be supported by either mandatory or persuasive legal authority from either primary law or a secondary source, citations can take up much of the space in research-based legal documents. Recall the case of *Stuart v. Board of Supervisors* from Chapter 3. If you were to give complete citation for that source, it would be:

> Mary Emily Stuart, appellant, versus the Board of Supervisors of Elections for Howard County and the State of Maryland, appellees, located in volume 266 of the *Maryland Reports* on page 440 and volume 295 of the *Atlantic Reporter, Second Series* on page 223, issued on October 9, 1972.

If you intended to use a legal point from this case in your document, you would have to indicate the citation as shown here. To provide all of this information is both time- and space-consuming, however. The same problem exists when referencing other sources of legal authority. For these reasons, citation systems have evolved that reduce citations to commonly accepted abbreviations. By employing a citation system, the case citation is reduced to *Stuart v. Board of Supervisors,* 266 Md. 440, 295 A.2d 223 (1972).

The standard for citation is *The Bluebook: A Uniform System of Citation* (15th ed. 1991). Recently, though, an alternative system, *The University of Chicago Manual of Legal Citation* (1989), has emerged to challenge the preeminence of the *Bluebook.* Though both are discussed, because of its dominance the emphasis here is on the *Bluebook.*

For the paralegal, the sources most frequently cited are constitutions, case opinions, statutes, administrative regulations, and secondary sources, such as encyclopedias, textbooks, law reviews, bar association journals, and newspapers. Citation to these sources is the focus of this chapter. However, the more time you spend as a paralegal, the greater the possibility that you will need to cite to an antiquated treatise, obsolete treaty, or unpublished thesis. A thorough understanding of citation will be critical to using these sources.

A note of caution is provided. Confidence in the ability to properly cite can be achieved only after many years of practice. The limited exposure presented in this chapter cannot serve as a substitute for diligently employing the citation system required in your jurisdiction. Only if you constantly challenge yourself can you become a master of citation.

PARALEGAL PRACTICE SITUATION

Your supervising attorney has called you into her office. The firm employs law students as clerks on a part-time basis. Recently, Dominic Martin, a first-year law student, completed a draft of a research memorandum on the issue of whether an ambulance service can be held liable for the death of a person when the service arrives late. Unfortunately, Dom has not been instructed in the proper use of citation. Your attorney would like you to verify and correct the citations in his memo.

Goals of Effective Citation

One primary purpose of citation systems is to abbreviate what would otherwise be long, complex references to legal authority. This has added importance in complicated legal writing such as case law. Consider the excerpt taken from *Stuart v. Board of Supervisors* shown in Figure 7-1. The court in this paragraph is listing cases supporting differing views on whether a woman must, as a matter of law, take on her husband's name in voter registration or may do so as matter of custom.

If the citations had not been abbreviated, the paragraph would have been considerably longer. The overall result would have been an opinion that was very difficult to read and understand.

A second goal of citation is help in location. Proper citation enables the reader to quickly and accurately find the location or multiple locations of a particular authority. This becomes particularly important when it is necessary to support or oppose a specific proposition or argument. In the hectic pace of a legal practice, it is critical to quickly locate cited sources. If the citation is inaccurate,

---

Cases tending to support the rationale of *Green* are Lane v. Duchac, 73 Wis. 646, 41 N.W. 962, 965 (1889); Rice v. State, 37 Tex.Cr.R. 36, 38 S.W. 801, 802 (1897); Succession of Kneipp, 172 La. 411, 134 So. 376, 378 (1931); State ex rel. Bucher v. Brower, Ohio Com.Pl., 7 Ohio Supp. 51, 21 Ohio Op. 208 (1941); Wilty v. Jefferson Parish, 245 La. 145, 157 So.2d 718, 727 (1963) (Sanders, J., concurring). Cases tending to support the *Lipsky* theory are Chapman v. Phoenix National Bank, 85 N.Y. 437, 449 (1881); In re Kayaloff, 9 F.Supp. 176 (S.D.N.Y.1934); Freeman v. Hawkins, 77 Tex. 498, 14 S.W. 364, 365 (1890); Bacon v. Boston Elevated Ry. Co., 256 Mass. 30, 152 N.E. 35, 36 (1926); Wilty v. Jefferson Parish, *supra*, 157 So.2d at 723–724 (Hamlin, J.); Forbush v. Wallace, *supra*, 341 F.Supp. at 221–222.

FIGURE 7-1 Excerpt from *Stuart v. Board of Supervisors*. (Reprinted with the permission of West Publishing Company.)

the credibility of the attorney offering the authority will suffer in the eyes of the judge and colleagues. Ultimately, if you assisted that attorney, you will be held responsible and your competence questioned.

The *Bluebook,* the Maroon Book, and State Variations

First published in 1926, *The Bluebook: A Uniform System of Citation* is the leading authority on legal citation. It was first compiled and is now updated by the editors of the law reviews of Columbia, Harvard, the University of Pennsylvania, and Yale law schools; the Harvard Law Review Association is its publisher. The 15th edition of the *Bluebook,* a 343-page, spiral-bound book with a blue cover, was issued in 1991.

The citation recommendations of the *Bluebook* are divided between those for law reviews and those for other forms of legal writing. The overall emphasis, however, is on law reviews (most likely due to the *Bluebook*'s editorship). The contents include an overview; basic guidelines for court documents and legal memoranda citations (called "practitioners' notes"); a detailed discussion of the rules of citation and style; citation for primary and secondary materials; citation for foreign and international materials; and tables and abbreviations. The front and back inside covers provide quick references for law reviews, court documents, and legal memoranda. This feature of the book is probably the most useful for the novice researcher.

More than any other function, the *Bluebook* provides consistency in citation within the legal profession. Acting as a benchmark, judges, lawyers, professors, and paralegals all measure citation according to *Bluebook* standards. This system is employed, with some variation, by most legal publishing companies and most state and federal courts. The *Bluebook* is by far the most comprehensive citation system. In addition to guidance for printed materials, it provides citation formats for such nonlegal sources as songs, movies, and interviews.

The *Bluebook* provides only a suggested style of citation and thus is only a reference book. It has long been criticized as being overly technical, confusing, and therefore difficult to use. Though the *Bluebook* is followed by most of the legal community, due to its perceived weaknesses, other guides to citation have evolved. (See Figure 7-2.)

Paralegal Tip

The *Bluebook* is not a user-friendly reference—paralegals may find its organization perplexing and frustrating. To make use easier, most users extensively mark up, tab, and paper-clip its contents. You should early on determine the provisions that you are most likely to use, particularly in the state-designated areas. These portions should be tabbed for quick access. By making the *Bluebook* easier to use, you will make learning proper citation a better experience.

The Bluebook

A
Uniform
System
of
Citation

Fifteenth Edition

**Compiled by the editors of the Columbia
Law Review, the Harvard Law Review,
the University of Pennsylvania Law
Review, and The Yale Law Journal.**

FIGURE 7-2   Title pages from two citation manuals. (Reprinted with the permission of the publisher. Further reproduction without permission is strictly prohibited.)

The major competitor to the *Bluebook* is *The University of Chicago Manual of Legal Citation,* commonly referred to as the "Maroon Book" because of its maroon

THE UNIVERSITY OF CHICAGO
MANUAL OF LEGAL CITATION

EDITED BY

THE UNIVERSITY OF CHICAGO
LAW REVIEW
AND
THE UNIVERSITY OF CHICAGO
LEGAL FORUM

1989

THE LAWYERS CO-OPERATIVE
PUBLISHING COMPANY
BANCROFT-WHITNEY COMPANY
AND
MEAD DATA CENTRAL, INC.

FIGURE 7-2   *(continued)*

cover. It is published jointly by Lawyers Cooperative Publishing, Bancroft-Whitney, and Mead Data Central. Based on a 1986 law review article written by federal judge Richard A. Posner, it was released in 1989. Rather than venture into the exact details of every applicable legal authority, the Maroon Book provides an overall philosophy of citation that stresses efficiency and practicality. For instance, even though it requires parallel citation for cases, the researcher has discretion to eliminate some forms of redundant citation. Its most obvious difference from the *Bluebook* is the abolition of the period as part of most citations. Overall, the Maroon Book gives the user discretion to develop citation forms he feels are appropriate in the particular situation. At only 63 pages, it is considerably shorter than the *Bluebook*. The Maroon Book is most criticized for what it is not; it is far less comprehensive than the *Bluebook* and omits many of the citation applications provided for in the *Bluebook*.

COMPARISON OF *BLUEBOOK* AND MAROON BOOK STYLES

BLUEBOOK Rule	Maroon Book Rule
Constitutions	
U.S. Const. art. III, § 1	US Const, Art I, § 1
Statutes	
13 U.S.C. § 23 (1988)	13 USC § 23 (1988)
Regulations	
21 C.F.R. § 1270.1 (1994)	21 CFR § 1270.1 (1994)
Cases	
Mapp v. Ohio, 367 U.S. 643 (1961)	*Mapp v. Ohio,* 367 US 643 (1961)
Secondary Sources	
Victoria Mikesell Mather, *The Skeleton in the Closet: The Battered Woman Syndrome, Self-Defense, and Expert Testimony,* 39 Mercer L. Rev. 545 (1988)	Victoria Mikesell Mather, *The Skeleton in the Closet: The Battered Woman Syndrome, Self-Defense, and Expert Testimony,* 39 Mercer L Rev 545 (1988)

It is difficult to predict whether the Maroon Book will overtake the *Bluebook* in popularity. Many scholars feel that the more streamlined and simplistic approach of the Maroon Book will soon gain acceptance by more law reviews—the first step in challenging the *Bluebook*'s preeminence. Only time will tell.

Because it is still the standard in the profession, the examples in this chapter are based solely on the *Bluebook* system of citation.

In addition, a number of states and even courts have developed their own citation systems. Most are based on local modifications of the *Bluebook*. The states include California, Florida, Louisiana, Maine, Michigan, New Jersey, New York, Ohio, Pennsylvania, Tennessee, and Texas. If you are employed in one of these states, an understanding of the state's citation system will be necessary. The best way to locate a state-developed citation system is by checking for a law review article on the topic.

Citing Constitutions

Occasionally, you may have the opportunity to cite to either a federal or state constitutional provision. Your chances increase if you are working in a field that relies heavily on constitutional law.

A citation to the U.S. Constitution would appear as in these examples:

EXAMPLE

U.S. Const. art. I, § 4   [to the main text]

U.S. Const. amend. XVI   [to the 16th amendment]

Citing to a state constitutional provision (see Figure 7-3) is similarly done:

EXAMPLE

Ill. Const. art. I, § 18   [to a provision of the Illinois Constitution]

Consult *Bluebook* Rule 11 for a detailed analysis of constitutional citation.

FIGURE 7-3
Components of a citation to a constitution

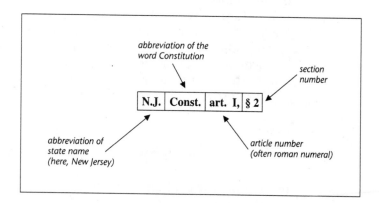

Citing Statutes

Statutory law is one of the most frequently researched forms of primary law. Few legal issues can be resolved without consulting state or federal codes. On the state level, citation style varies greatly. This is because there is a variety of publishers of state codes, each using a different format. Citation on the federal level, in contrast, is fairly consistent. The U.S. Code, the official source, and *U.S. Code Annotated* and *U.S. Code Service,* unofficial sources, all use similar citation formats.

State Statutes

Though citation format for states, the District of Columbia, and other U.S. jurisdictions vary greatly, each citation will include (not necessarily in this order):

1. Number of the code title, chapter, or article
2. Name of the subject volume (if in a subject volume)
3. Abbreviation for the code
4. Section of the code
5. Date of the edition of the code (or supplement)
6. Name of the publisher (generally only if an unofficial version).

The variations among jurisdictions can be seen by considering a few citation examples. A typical citation to a section of the Annotated Code of Maryland would appear as:

EXAMPLE

Md. Code Ann., Fam. Law § 7-103 (1991)

This is a reference to the statute in Maryland that discusses the grounds for divorce. "Md. Code Ann." is the abbreviation for the Annotated Code of Maryland. "Fam. Law" is an abbreviation for the subject volume, Family Law. In Maryland, the code is divided between consecutively numbered articles over several volumes, and subject volumes containing all laws relating to one topic. The symbol "§" stands for section. The title and section numbers, as well as the year of the edition, are also indicated.

The corresponding law in Massachusetts would be cited as follows:

EXAMPLE

Mass. Ann. Laws ch. 208, § 1 (Law. Co-op. 1981)

In Virginia, the citation would be:

EXAMPLE

Va. Code Ann. § 20-91 (Michie 1995)

As you can see, all three citations include the name of the code, title (or chapter) and section number, and year of the edition of the code. The only additional information is the name of publisher (see Figure 7-4). You will have to consult your state table in the *Bluebook* to cite correctly.

State statutes also appear in session law compilations similar to *Statutes at Large.* Consult *Bluebook* Rule 12.4 and your state table to determine the proper method of citing to a session law. Be warned: many state codes say "Cite this volume as ... " or "This law may be cited as ... ." These suggested abbreviations

FIGURE 7-4
Components of a citation to a state code

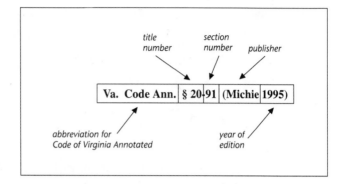

are not official and may be incomprehensible or misleading to anyone not already familiar with that jursidiction's law.

STATE CODE CITATION FORMATS
(cited according to the *Bluebook*)

State	*Code*
Alabama	Ala. Code § x (19xx)
Alaska	Alaska Stat. § x (19xx)
Arizona	Ariz. Rev. Stat. Ann. § x (19xx)
Arkansas	Ark. Code Ann. § x (Michie 19xx)
California	Cal. [subject] Code § x (West 19xx) or Cal. [subject] Code § x (Deering 19xx)
Colorado	Colo. Rev. Stat. § x (19xx) or Colo. Rev. Stat. Ann. § x (West 19xx)
Connecticut	Conn. Gen. Stat. § x (19xx) or Conn. Gen. Stat. Ann. § x (West 19xx)
Delaware	Del. Code Ann. tit. x, § x (19xx)
District of Columbia	D.C. Code Ann. § x (19xx)
Florida	Fla. Stat. ch. x.xxx (19xx) or Fla. Stat. Ann. § x (West 19xx) or Fla. Stat. Ann. ch. x.xxx (Harrison 19xx)
Georgia	Ga. Code Ann. § x (19xx) or Ga. Code Ann. § x (Harrison 19xx)

State	*Code*
Hawaii	Haw. Rev. Stat. § x (19xx)
Idaho	Idaho Code § x (19xx)
Illinois	Ill. Rev. Stat. ch. x, para. x (19xx) or Ill. Ann. Stat. ch. x, para. x (Smith-Hurd 19xx) or Ill. Comp. Stat. ch. x, act x, § x (19xx) or [ch.] ILCS [act]/[§] (Smith-Hurd 19xx)
Indiana	Ind. Code § x (19xx) or Ind. Code Ann. § x (Burns 19xx) or Ind. Code Ann. § x (West 19xx)
Iowa	Iowa Code § x (19xx) or Iowa Code Ann. § x (West 19xx)
Kansas	Kan. Stat. Ann. § x (19xx) or Kan. [subject] Code Ann. § x (Vernon 19xx)
Kentucky	Ky. Rev. Stat. Ann. § x (Baldwin 19xx) or Ky. Rev. Stat. Ann. § x (Michie/Bobbs-Merrill 19xx)
Louisiana	La. Rev. Stat. Ann. § x (West 19xx) or La. [subject] Ann. art. x (West 19xx)
Maine	Me. Rev. Stat. Ann. tit. x, § x (West 19xx)
Maryland	Md. Code Ann., [subject] § x (19xx) or Md. Ann. Code art. x, § x (19xx)
Massachusetts	Mass. Gen. L. ch. x, § x (19xx) or Mass. Gen. Laws Ann. ch. x, § x (West 19xx) or Mass. Ann. Laws ch. x, § x (Law. Co-op. 19xx)
Michigan	Mich. Comp. Laws § x (19xx) or Mich. Comp. Laws Ann. § x (West 19xx) or Mich. Stat. Ann. § x (Callaghan 19xx)
Minnesota	Minn. Stat. § x (19xx) or Minn. Stat. Ann. § x (West 19xx)
Mississippi	Miss. Code Ann. § x (19xx)

State	Code
Missouri	Mo. Rev. Stat. § x (19xx) or Mo. Ann. Stat. § x (Vernon 19xx)
Montana	Mont. Code Ann. § x (19xx)
Nebraska	Neb. Rev. Stat. § x (19xx)
Nevada	Nev. Rev. Stat. § x (19xx) or Nev. Rev. Stat. Ann. § x (Michie 19xx)
New Hampshire	N.H. Rev. Stat. Ann. § x (19xx)
New Jersey	N.J. Rev. Stat. § x (19xx) or N.J. Stat. Ann. § x (West 19xx)
New Mexico	N.M. Stat. Ann. § x (Michie 19xx)
New York	N.Y. [subject] Law § x (McKinney 19xx) or N.Y. [subject] Law § x (Consol. 19xx) *Note:* New York also has "uncompiled laws," which are published by McKinney and Consolidated.
North Carolina	N.C. Gen. Stat. § x (19xx)
North Dakota	N.D. Cent. Code § x (19xx)
Ohio	Ohio Rev. Code Ann. § x (Anderson 19xx) or Ohio Rev. Code Ann. § x (Baldwin 19xx)
Oklahoma	Okla. Stat. tit. x, § x (19xx) or Okla. Stat. Ann. tit. x, § x (West 19xx)
Oregon	Or. Rev. Stat. § x (19xx)
Pennsylvania	x Pa. Cons. Stat. § x (19xx) or x Pa. Cons. Stat. Ann. § x (19xx) or Pa. Stat. Ann. tit. x, § x (19xx)
Rhode Island	R.I. Gen. Laws § x (19xx)
South Carolina	S.C. Code Ann. § x (Law. Co-op. 19xx)
South Dakota	S.D. Codified Laws Ann. § x (19xx)
Tennessee	Tenn. Code Ann. § x (19xx)
Texas	Tex. [subject] Code Ann. § x (West 19xx) or Tex. Rev. Civ. Stat. Ann. art. x (West 19xx) or Tex. [independent code] Ann. art. x (West 19xx)

State	Code
Utah	Utah Code Ann § x (19xx)
Vermont	Vt. Stat. Ann. tit. x, § x (19xx)
Virginia	Va. Code Ann. § x (Michie 19xx)
Washington	Wash. Rev. Code § x (19xx) or Wash. Rev. Code Ann. § x (West 19xx)
West Virginia	W. Va. Code § x (19xx)
Wisconsin	Wis. Stat. § x (19xx) or Wis. Stat. Ann. § x (West 19xx)
Wyoming	Wyo. Stat. § x (19xx)

* Many states break down their codes by subject matter rather than title number. Where this is done, [subject] is indicated.

Federal Statutes

Citation to federal statutory law will either be to the *Statutes at Large* or to a form of the U.S. Code. A cite to the U.S. Code would appear as follows:

EXAMPLE

13 U.S.C. § 21 (1988)

This refers to title 13 of the U.S. Code, section 21. The edition of the code is 1988. However, the researcher could also cite to USCS or USCA (see Figure 7-5):

EXAMPLE

13 U.S.C.S. § 21 (Law. Co-op. 1978)
13 U.S.C.A. § 21 (West 1990)

FIGURE 7-5
Components of a citation to a federal statute

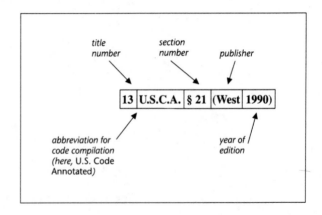

In that the *Statutes at Large* is the original form of the laws passed by Congress, periodically you might want to cite to the law in that form. For instance, a recently enacted statute might not appear in the U.S. Code, but will likely have a *Statutes at Large* reference:

EXAMPLE

Goals 2000: Educate America Act, Pub. L. No. 103-227, 108 Stat. 125 (1994)

Review *Bluebook* Rule 12 and Table 1 for a detailed understanding of statutory citation.

Local Ordinances

At times, it will be necessary to cite to county, city, or other local ordinances (see Figure 7-6). Direction on citing to an ordinance can be found in *Bluebook* Rule 12.8.2. A citation to the Harford County, Maryland, Code would appear as follows:

EXAMPLE

Harford County, Md., Code § 58-1 (1986)

FIGURE 7-6
Components of
a citation to a
local ordinance

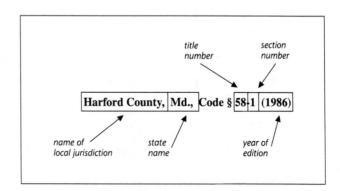

Citing Administrative Regulations

All states and the federal government have administrative regulatory compilations. Most states publish an administrative register similar to the *Federal Register*. Consult *Bluebook* Rule 14 or the appropriate state table for citations to administrative regulations.

State Regulations

As with state statutory law, citation to state administrative law varies from jurisdiction to jurisdiction. If a state has an administrative register like the *Federal Register,* all administrative laws will first be published there. A citation to the *Maryland Register* would appear as follows:

EXAMPLE

13 Md. Reg. 1155 (1986)

This refers to volume 13, page 1155 of the 1986 edition of the *Maryland Register.* (See Figure 7-7.)

FIGURE 7-7
Components of
a citation to a state
administrative register

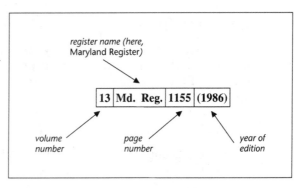

State regulations in their final form are located in administrative compilations (see Figure 7-8). It is possible that the publication itself will recommend a citation format in citing the source. In Maryland, regulations are found in the Code of Maryland Regulations. COMAR, as it is known, recommends that citation to it be done in the following fashion:

EXAMPLE

COMAR 09.30.67.01 (1982)

This translates to COMAR, title 9, subtitle 30, chapter 67, regulation 1.

FIGURE 7-8
Components of
a citation to a state
administrative code

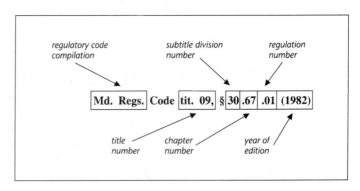

However, the *Bluebook* requires that the citation appear as:

EXAMPLE

Md. Regs. Code tit. 09, § 30.67.01 (1982)

It seems, at least with state regulations, that the non-*Bluebook* alternative might be more efficient for those who know what state is involved.

Federal Regulations

Federal administrative regulations first appear in the *Federal Register* and then, upon approval, in C.F.R.. The format of a citation in the *Federal Register* is similar to that employed on the state level:

EXAMPLE

56 Fed. Reg. 48,976 (1991)

Citation to C.F.R. is similar to that for the U.S. Code.

EXAMPLE

41 C.F.R. § 51 (1993)

This refers to title 41, section 51 of the 1993 edition of the Code of Federal Regulations. See Figure 7-9.

FIGURE 7-9
Components of citations to federal administrative regulations (*Federal Register* and C.F.R.)

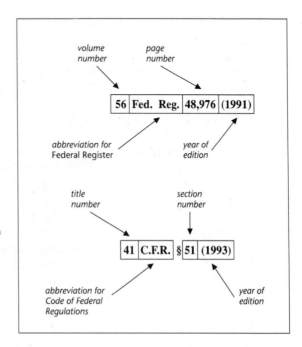

Citing Cases

Case law must always be considered in legal research. Even when the legal problem necessitates analysis of other forms of primary law, case law always plays a critical role in interpreting these other sources.

State Cases

A basic, standard case citation to a state appellate decision will contain the following elements:

1. Name of the case (or caption)
2. Volume reporter number
3. Name of the reporter
4. Page number
5. Year the decision was issued.

Here is an example:

EXAMPLE

Fairbanks v. McCarter, 330 Md. 39 (1993)

Case Name

The first part of the citation is the case name. This is also called the caption. In our example, the parties are appellants Richard M. Fairbanks and his wife Rebecca Fairbanks, and appellee James F. McCarter, Jr. The appellant is listed first, followed by the appellee. The parties are separated by "v." meaning *against* or *versus.* When individuals are the parties, only last names are used. A spouse is abbreviated *et ux.* and multiple parties *et al.* However, neither abbreviation is used in the citation itself—only in the information found on the first page of the opinion. When a litigant is a business entity, the *Bluebook* allows you to drop duplicative terms. For instance, if one party is the Western Broadcast Company, Inc., you would be permitted to indicate Western Broadcast Co. If a party is a state government, just the name of the state is used, if referring to a case outside of the state from which it emanated; and "State," "People," or "Commonwealth" if referring to a case within the state from which it emanated. If a party is the federal government, "United States" is the proper form, rather than "U.S." Finally, when the matter deals with a guardianship or a juvenile matter, only one name might be indicated such as *In re Gault,* which means "in the matter of the minor child Gault."

If possible, case names should be italicized. Unfortunately, many offices do not have italics as a word processing option. The acceptable *Bluebook* alternative is to underscore the names of the parties. See *Bluebook* Practitioners' Note 1 for a discussion of this option.

Reporter Volume Number

The case name is followed by a comma, a space, then a number indicating the volume number of the official reporter in which the case is located. In the *Fairbanks* case, 330 is the volume of the *Maryland Reports*.

Name of Reporter

Next follows an abbreviation for the name of the official reporter. The *Fairbanks* case is in fact housed in two reporters, the *Maryland Reports* (Md.), the official source, and *Atlantic 2d* (A.2d), the unofficial source.

Most decisions on the state level are published in more than one reporter. Such a case is said to have a **parallel citation**. A parallel cite, as mentioned before, is a reference to another reporter in which the same opinion is published.

EXAMPLE

Fairbanks v. McCarter, 330 Md. 39, 622 A.2d 121 (1993)

If you are preparing a document for a state court, the citation to cases decided by the courts of that state (not other states) must be in parallel form. The official citation must appear before the unofficial one. In all other situations, cite only to the relevant regional reporter (i.e., from West's National Reporter System) and provide information about the court and state issuing the case.

EXAMPLE

Fairbanks v. McCarter, 622 A.2d 121 (Md. 1993)

Several jurisdictions, including Rhode Island and Wyoming, no longer publish their own reporters. Rather, they rely exclusively on the National Reporter System to report their cases. The format for citation in those jurisdictions in all applications is the same as in the previous example.

EXAMPLE

Foianni v. Brinton, 855 P.2d 1238 (Wyo. 1993)

Because Wyoming no longer publishes its own reporter, the researcher need only cite to the *Pacific 2d* reporter of the National Reporter System. The name

──────────── **LEGAL TERMS** ────────────

parallel citation †   A citation to a court opinion or decision that is printed in two or more reporters.

of the state court is identified in parentheses with the date. Use the *Bluebook* state tables to find the correct abbreviation for the court.

Page Number

The page on which the opinion begins is indicated after the abbreviation for the reporter. In the *Fairbanks* case, 39 is the page on which the opinion begins in *Maryland Reports;* 121 is the page on which the opinion begins in *Atlantic 2d.*

Year of Decision

To verify that the case used contains legal principles that are still applicable, it is important to know the year the opinion was decided. In the example, 1993 is the year.

Locating a Parallel

Because state case law is so frequently cited in the state in which the law is applied, you will need to locate parallel citations. Provided there is a known citation, a number of different techniques are available for accomplishing this.

The easiest source for a parallel cite is the opinion itself. Generally, opinions in the National Reporter System provide the parallel citation. The official citation is located at the very beginning of the case, above the caption—although it may not be in *Bluebook* format. See Figure 7-10.

The table of cases found in the West digest containing the decisions of the court publishing the opinion is a second source for parallel citation. The Shepard's Citations edition that reviews the opinion is also a source. The first entry, found in parentheses in Shepard's, is the parallel citation. See Figure 7-11.

Finally, West publishes two sources, the *National Reporter Blue Book* and the *Blue and White Books,* that provide parallel citations.

Pinpoint Cites

At times, you might provide more than just one page number, such as:

EXAMPLE

Fairbanks v. McCarter, 330 Md. 39, 46, 622 A.2d 121, 125 (1993)

In this case, you have directed the reader to a specific page in the reporter called a **pinpoint cite**. When used, the *Bluebook* requires that this be done for both sources.

Figure 7-12 shows the components of a state case citation.

LEGAL TERMS

pinpoint cite A citation to a particular page in a report.

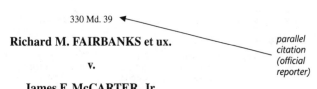

330 Md. 39

Richard M. FAIRBANKS et ux.

v.

James F. McCARTER, Jr.

No. 125, Sept. Term, 1992.

Court of Appeals of Maryland.

March 31, 1993.

parallel citation (official reporter)

Maternal grandparents brought actions against father, seeking visitation rights. The Circuit Court Dorchester County, Richard D. Warren, J., denied petition, and grandparents appealed to Court of Special Appeals. Granting certiorari on its own motion prior to intermediate appellate review, the Court of Appeals, Murphy, C.J., held that: (1) mother, as well as father, should have been joined in action, and (2) grandparents petitioning for visitation with their grandchildren are not obliged to support their claim by alleging and proving existence of exceptional circumstances justifying such visitation but, rather, outcome of petition lies within sound discretion of trial court, guided exclusively by best interests of grandchild

Remanded for further proceedings.

McAuliffe, J., filed concurring opinion.

FIGURE 7-10 Parallel citation in *Fairbanks v. McCarter.* (Reprinted with the permission of West Publishing Company.)

Federal Cases

The components of federal case citations are the same as for state case citations. Citation of federal case law will usually be to the U.S. Supreme Court, U.S. Court of Appeals, or the U.S. District Court. *Bluebook* Table 1 should be consulted for citation to all federal courts, including specialized courts such as the U.S. Bankruptcy Court and the U.S. Court of Claims.

A typical U.S. Supreme Court citation would appear as follows:

EXAMPLE

Griswold v. Connecticut, 381 U.S. 479 (1965)

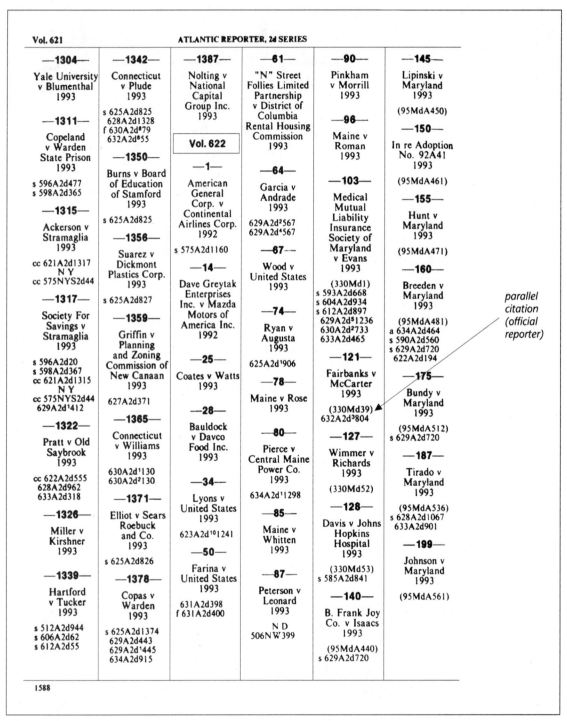

Vol. 621	ATLANTIC REPORTER, 2d SERIES				
—1304— Yale University v Blumenthal 1993	**—1342—** Connecticut v Plude 1993 s 625A2d825 628A2d1328 f 630A2d879 632A2d855	**—1387—** Nolting v National Capital Group Inc. 1993	**—61—** "N" Street Follies Limited Partnership v District of Columbia Rental Housing Commission 1993	**—90—** Pinkham v Morrill 1993	**—145—** Lipinski v Maryland 1993 (95MdA450)
—1311— Copeland v Warden State Prison 1993 s 596A2d477 s 598A2d365	**—1350—** Burns v Board of Education of Stamford 1993 s 625A2d825	**Vol. 622** **—1—** American General Corp. v Continental Airlines Corp. 1992	**—64—** Garcia v Andrade 1993 629A2d²567 629A2d⁴567	**—96—** Maine v Roman 1993 **—103—** Medical Mutual Liability Insurance Society of Maryland v Evans 1993	**—150—** In re Adoption No. 92A41 1993 (95MdA461) **—155—** Hunt v Maryland 1993
—1315— Ackerson v Stramaglia 1993 cc 621A2d1317 N Y cc 575NYS2d44	**—1356—** Suarez v Dickmont Plastics Corp. 1993 s 625A2d827	s 575A2d1160 **—14—** Dave Greytak Enterprises Inc. v Mazda Motors of America Inc. 1992	**—67—** Wood v United States 1993 **—74—** Ryan v Augusta 1993	(330Md1) s 593A2d668 s 604A2d934 s 612A2d897 629A2d⁵1236 630A2d²733 633A2d465	(95MdA471) **—160—** Breeden v Maryland 1993 (95MdA481) a 634A2d464 s 590A2d560
—1317— Society For Savings v Stramaglia 1993 s 596A2d20 s 598A2d367 cc 621A2d1315 N Y cc 575NYS2d44 629A2d¹412	**—1359—** Griffin v Planning and Zoning Commission of New Canaan 1993 627A2d371	**—25—** Coates v Watts 1993 **—28—** Bauldock v Davco Food Inc. 1993	625A2d¹906 **—78—** Maine v Rose 1993 **—80—** Pierce v Central Maine Power Co. 1993	**—121—** Fairbanks v McCarter 1993 (330Md39) ◄ 632A2d³804 **—127—** Wimmer v Richards 1993	s 629A2d720 622A2d194 **—175—** Bundy v Maryland 1993 (95MdA512) s 629A2d720 **—187—** Tirado v Maryland 1993
—1322— Pratt v Old Saybrook 1993 cc 622A2d555 628A2d962 633A2d318	**—1365—** Connecticut v Williams 1993 630A2d¹130 630A2d²130	**—34—** Lyons v United States 1993 623A2d¹⁰1241	634A2d¹1298 **—85—** Maine v Whitten 1993	(330Md52) **—128—** Davis v Johns Hopkins Hospital 1993	(95MdA536) s 628A2d1067 633A2d901 **—199—** Johnson v Maryland 1993
—1326— Miller v Kirshner 1993	**—1371—** Elliot v Sears Roebuck and Co. 1993 s 625A2d826	**—50—** Farina v United States 1993 631A2d398 f 631A2d400	**—87—** Peterson v Leonard 1993 N D 506NW399	(330Md53) s 585A2d841 **—140—** B. Frank Joy Co. v Isaacs 1993 (95MdA440) s 629A2d720	(95MdA561)
—1339— Hartford v Tucker 1993 s 512A2d944 s 606A2d62 s 612A2d55	**—1378—** Copas v Warden 1993 s 625A2d1374 629A2d443 629A2d¹445 634A2d915				

parallel citation (official reporter)

1588

FIGURE 7-11 Page from Shepard's Citations, showing parallel citation. (Reproduced by permission of Shepard's/McGraw-Hill, Inc. Further reproduction of any kind is strictly prohibited.)

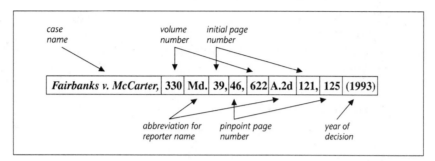

FIGURE 7-12 Components of a citation to a state case, with pinpoint cites

It contains the same elements as a state citation, except that there is no parallel citation. Disagreement exists as to the appropriate method of citation to the U.S. Supreme Court. *Bluebook* rules do not contemplate citation to parallel, unofficial reporters. However, in most practice settings, attorneys and judges expect U.S. Supreme Court decisions to be parallel-cited. With parallel citations, the reference would be:

EXAMPLE

> *Griswold v. Connecticut,* 381 U.S. 479, 85 S. Ct. 1678, 14 L. Ed. 2d 510 (1965)

The *Griswold* case can thus be found in volume 381, page 479 of the *U.S. Reports*; volume 85, page 1678 of the *Supreme Court Reporter*; and volume 14, page 510 of the *United States Supreme Court Reports, Lawyer's Edition, Second Series.* The decision was decided in 1965. The space-saving benefits of using a citation system should be obvious now.

Remembering that one of the primary goals of citation is to enable the reader to locate the case, citing to all sources is clearly practical. Should the reader not have the *U.S. Reports* at his disposal, providing him with other locations becomes all the more important. Consequently, you should provide parallel citations to the *Supreme Court Reporter* and *Lawyer's Edition.*

A citation to a decision of the U.S. Court of Appeals would appear as:

EXAMPLE

> *Young v. New York City Transit Authority,* 903 F.2d 146 (2d Cir. 1990)

Because the *Federal Reporter* is the only reporter of decisions of this court, there is no parallel citation. In addition to the year of the decision, the circuit (one of 13) from which the case emanated is indicated. In this case, it is the Second Circuit, which sits in New York City.

Finally, there are times when you will cite to the federal trial court—the U.S. District Court. An example is:

EXAMPLE

> *Murphy v. Ford,* 390 F. Supp. 1372 (W.D. Mich. 1975)

The only source of decisions for the U.S. District Court is the *Federal Supplement* reporter. In parentheses, you indicate the year of the decision as well as the court from which the decision emanated (here, the Western District Court of Michigan).

Complex Citations

Consider the following example of a citation taken from the *Bluebook*:

EXAMPLE

Jackson v. Metropolitan Edison Co., 348 F. Supp. 954, 956–58 (M.D. Pa. 1972), *aff'd,* 483 F.2d 754 (3d Cir. 1973), *aff'd,* 419 U.S. 345 (1974).

Here is what appears to be a series of citations. The citations, in fact, all refer to the same case at different stages of litigation. First, the case at the U.S. District Court level—348 F. Supp. 954, 956–58 (M.D. Pa. 1972)—is cited, then at the U.S. Court of Appeals—483 F.2d 754 (3d Cir. 1973)—and finally at the U.S. Supreme Court—419 U.S. 345 (1974). In complex citations, each separate segment will include explanatory phrases indicating prior or subsequent history and/or the weight of authority of judicial decisions. The most commonly used phrase—*aff'd*—tells the reader that a higher court has affirmed the decision of a lower court.

Citation to case law on both state and federal level can be complicated. When in doubt, consult Rule 12 and Table 1 of the *Bluebook*. Figure 7-13 reviews the elements of federal citations.

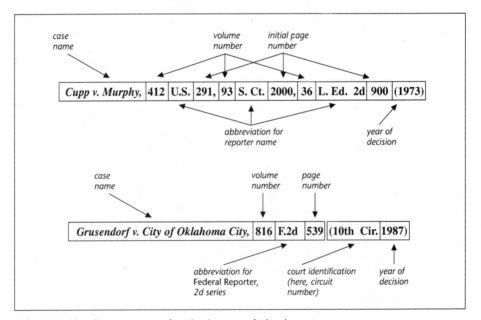

FIGURE 7-13 Components of a citation to a federal case

HOW ABOUT A PUBLIC DOMAIN CITATION SYSTEM?

The U.S. Department of Justice has proposed the development of a citation system for case law that would bypass the need to use West's National Reporter System. At present, users of federal and state case law are often required to cite cases from West-owned reporters. The idea would be to develop a **public domain** database that would contain both state and federal opinions. The database's citation system would not require the use of certain publications or formats (i.e, the National Reporter System). The database could be accessed through the Internet. Consumer groups support the proposition because they feel that the government, not West, should report its own case opinions. Through government reporting, public access is guaranteed. Presently, publishers have to obtain permission to use certain portions of West's version of case opinions, such as pinpoint cites. West Publishing opposes the proposition, seeing it as a waste of taxpayer dollars and arguing that the present system works. West also points out that access to opinions is already available to the public through state law libraries.

Several states are not waiting to see what the federal government does. Louisiana, in 1993, became the first to adopt its own public domain citation system for its case law. The new format uses the case name, date of issue, and docket number, with pinpoint cites to the slip opinion. Wisconsin is considering implementing a similar system, possibly as early as 1996. Florida and South Dakota are also studying the issue.

Citing Secondary Sources

Books, encyclopedias, journals, law reviews, and newspapers are the most frequently cited secondary sources of law. Because secondary source citation guidelines vary greatly, only general rules are covered here. For most secondary sources, the *Bluebook* quick reference is a good starting point. Further detailed understanding can be obtained by reviewing *Bluebook* Rules 15–17.

Encyclopedias

Citing to encyclopedias in court documents is frowned upon. Remember, encyclopedias reference primary law within their text. In this way, encyclopedias serve as case finders. It is primary law that is needed to support a legal proposition. If the document is not for litigation, though, citing to an encyclopedia may be helpful. The elements of a citation to a legal encyclopedia include:

1. Volume number of the encyclopedia
2. Abbreviated name of the encyclopedia
3. Title of the subject in the encyclopedia

—————————— **LEGAL TERMS** ——————————

public domain †   In copyright law, a literary composition or other work that has not been copyrighted or with respect to which the copyright has expired.

4. Section number within the subject or topic
5. Date of publication of the volume or supplement.

Typical examples for both CJS and Am. Jur. 2d appear as:

EXAMPLE

> 53 C.J.S. *Libel & Slander* § 2 (1987)
> 50 Am. Jur. 2d *Libel & Slander* § 2 (1970)

Textbooks

Texts, especially treatises, can be helpful in explaining legal propositions. Book citations (see Figure 7-14) typically contain:

1. Name of the author as it appears in the publication
2. Title of the book
3. Particular page, section, or paragraph that is being cited
4. If the book is in other than its first edition, the edition number
5. Publication date.

An example is:

EXAMPLE

> O.J. Coogler, *Structured Mediation in Divorce Settlement* 56 (1978)

If there is more than one volume of the publication, this is noted before the name of the author.

EXAMPLE

> 2 Milton R. Friedman, *Friedman on Leases* § 27.1 (3d ed. 1990)

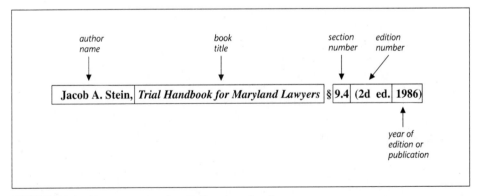

FIGURE 7-14 Components of a citation to a book

Law Reviews

Recall that law reviews are scholarly works providing in-depth analysis of a particular topic or legal issue. There may be occasions when this analysis should be brought to a court's attention. Consequently, they are sometimes cited in court documents. Law review citations typically include:

1. Name of the author as it appears in the publication
2. Title of the article
3. Volume number of the law review
4. Abbreviated name of the law review
5. Page on which the article begins
6. Year of publication.

Consider the following example and Figure 7-15:

EXAMPLE

Marshall A. Leaffter, *Protecting United States Intellectual Property Abroad: Toward a New Multilaterialism,* 76 Iowa L. Rev. 273 (1991)

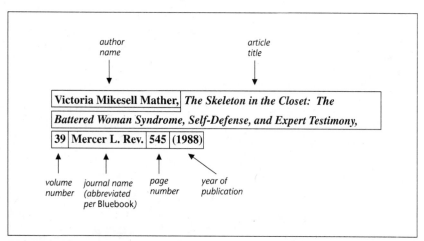

FIGURE 7-15   Components of a citation to a law review article

Journals and Other Periodicals

In noncourt documents, journal articles are often cited to show new legal trends. A citation to a nonconsecutively paginated journal would include:

1. Name of the author as it appears in the publication
2. Name of the article
3. Name of the journal

4. Date of issue

5. Page number referenced within the journal, following the word "at."

The following is an example. See also Figure 7-16.

<u>*EXAMPLE*</u>

James Walsh, *The U.N. at 50: Who Needs It?,* Time, Oct. 30, 1995, at 72

A consecutively paginated journal would be cited similarly to law review article.

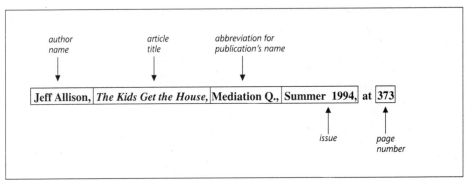

FIGURE 7-16   Components of a citation to a nonconsecutively paginated journal

Newspapers

In large metropolitan areas, legal newspapers can be excellent sources of information. National legal newspapers are also available for research consideration. Citation to a newspaper would take the following form:

<u>*EXAMPLE*</u>

Murry White, *The TV Producer and the First Amendment,* Legal Times, Dec. 6, 1993, at 62

Citing Interviews

Periodically, when conducting preliminary research, it may be necessary to interview clients, witnesses, and others who have important information pertaining to your case. A cite to an interview would take the following form:

<u>*EXAMPLE*</u>

Interview with the Honorable Henry Bone, Judge, Circuit Court for Hogan County, in Rome, Wis. (Nov. 1, 1995)

Short Citation

Once you have provided a complete citation in a document, should you need to further cite that particular source, the *Bluebook* permits you to use a short form of the citation.

The most common short citation is the use of *id.* in legal documents, especially memoranda. *Id.* is an abbreviation for the Latin term *idem,* meaning "previously referred." It may be used after any legal authority. If a previous authority is identical to the authority needed for the next cite, and immediately precedes the source needing a cite, then *id.* by itself will be sufficient. If the page or section is different, then *id.* with an indication of the new page or section is required. See Figure 7-17. Consult *Bluebook* Practitioners' Note 4 and Rule 4 for a more detailed understanding of the use of *id.*

In addition, the *Bluebook* allows you to use a shortened version of a complete citation rather than *id.* when citing case law. For example, the case of *Fairbanks v. McCarter,* 330 Md. 39, 46, 622 A.2d 121, 125 (1993) (with pinpoint cites) could be subsequently cited as:

> *Fairbanks,* 330 Md. at 46, 622 A.2d at 125
> *or*
> 330 Md. at 46, 622 A.2d at 125
> *or*
> *Id.* at 46, 622 A.2d at 125.

There are two categories of licensees: a bare licensee, and licensee by invitation, or social guest. *Fitzgerald v. Montgomery County Board of Education,* 25 Md. App. 709, 336 A.2d 795 (1975). A person privileged by consent for his own purpose or convenience to enter the property of another is considered a bare licensee. *Mech v. Hearst Corp.,* 64 Md. App. 422, 496 A.2d 1099 (1985). A bare licensee takes the property as he finds it and is owed no duty by the owner except that of not being wantonly injured. *Id.*

A licensee by invitation or social guest takes the premises as the owner use it. The legal duty owed by the owner is to take care of his guest as he takes care of himself or members of his family. He must exercise reasonable care to make the premises safe for his guest or he must warn him of known dangerous conditions that cannot be reasonably discovered by and which, in fact, are not discovered by the guest. *Bramble v. Thompson,* 264 Md. 518, 287 A.2d 265 (1972).

Finally, a trespasser is one who intentionally or without consent enters upon the property of other. The only duty owed by the property owner is that of not wantonly injuring the intruder. *Id.* at 522, 287 A.2d at 267.

FIGURE 7-17 Use of *"id."*

The *Bluebook,* in Practitioners' Note 4, provides guidance for short citation of all legal sources.

Short citation can also be employed by using the Latin term *supra,* meaning "above." *Supra* can be used when the authority has been fully cited previously though not immediately preceding; *id.* should be used if the authority is immediately preceding. Only in exceptional situations should *supra* be used with primary law authority. It should be restricted to secondary sources. The use of *supra* is discussed in *Bluebook* Rule 4.2.

Two popular other short citation forms are the use of "hereinafter" and *infra. Infra* means "below" in Latin. It is used to direct the reader to a source that will appear later in the document. It is discussed in *Bluebook* Rule 3.6.

For authority that might be awkward to cite with *supra,* the word "hereinafter" may be placed after the original citation before a special shortened form of the original cite. An example is:

EXAMPLE

Marshall A. Leaffter, *Protecting United States Intellectual Property Abroad: Toward a New Multilaterialism,* 76 Iowa L. Rev. 273 (1991) [hereinafter *Leaffter*]

The use of "hereinafter" is covered in *Bluebook* Rule 4.2.

Signals

Citations are frequently introduced by words and phrases called **signals**. These words indicate how the writer wants the reader to consider the authority being cited. Examples include *"e.g.,"* meaning "this authority states the proposition; other authorities also state the proposition, but citation to them would not be helpful or is not necessary" and *"contra,"* meaning "this authority states the contrary." Consult *Bluebook* Rules 1.2–1.4 to understand and apply signals.

Unwritten Rule of Exceptions

As has been mentioned, *Bluebook* conformance is pervasive within the legal profession. The Maroon Book has positioned itself as the citation format of choice for those discontented with the *Bluebook*'s overly technical format.

Even though one of these two systems may be the standard in a given office, attorneys create exceptions to these rules. This may be due to convenience,

---

LEGAL TERMS

signal   A phrase indicating how a writer wants a reader to consider an authority.

technological shortcomings, or local custom. Like the rule for **hearsay** (which you will learn about in an evidence course), citation rules are replete with exceptions, which make them seem more like Swiss cheese than uniform systems. The exception regarding parallel citation to the U.S. Supreme Court is one. Another is the use by many attorneys and judges of "sec." or "section" in lieu of "§", because many typewriters and word processors cannot produce that symbol. A third is the use of "blank" lines in case citations to indicate missing or unavailable volume or page number information. You must learn the local exceptions so that you can better serve your employer's needs.

Summary

- The goals of effective citation are to abbreviate references to legal authority and to provide information necessary to locate a particular reference.

- Use of the citation system developed in *The Bluebook: A Uniform System of Citation* assists in achieving these goals.

- Due to the highly technical nature of the *Bluebook, The University of Chicago Manual of Legal Citation* (Maroon Book), with its emphasis on efficiency and practicality, has emerged as an alternative citation system.

- Citations to constitutional provisions include a reference to the article and section or amendment.

- State statute citations include code title number, name of the subject volume, abbreviation for the state code, section of the code, year of the edition or supplement, and (if unofficial) publisher.

- Federal statutory citations include the number of the title, abbreviation for the source, section number, year of the edition or supplement, and (if unofficial) the publisher.

- State case citations include the name of the case, reporter volume number, name of the reporter, page number, and year the decision was issued. The citation will generally include a reference to both the official reporter and an unofficial regional reporter, known as a parallel citation.

- If citation is made to a case of the U.S. Supreme Court, the *Bluebook* forbids parallel citation. However, in practice most writers will provide it.

- Citations to cases from the U.S. Courts of Appeals must always indicate the circuit from which the case emanated.

- Citation to secondary sources is usually limited to books, encyclopedias, journals, law reviews, and newspapers.

––––––––––––––––––––––––––––– **LEGAL TERMS** –––––––––––––––––––––––––––––

hearsay † The testimony of a witness as to a statement made to him or her outside of court, or made to someone else who told [the witness] what was said, that is offered in court to prove the truth of the matter contained in the statement.

- Encyclopedia citations include volume number, abbreviated name of the encyclopedia, title of the subject, section number, page number, and date of publication.

- Book citations include the name of the author, title of the book, page number cited, edition number (if it is not the first), and the publication date.

- Journal, law review, and newspaper citations are similar to book citations.

- The *Bluebook* provides methods for employing short citations for all types of legal authority.

- A signal indicates how the writer wants the reader to consider an authority.

- Notwithstanding *Bluebook* and Maroon Book rules, citation variations exist in the legal profession. Often they are determined by local custom.

Review Questions

1. What are the two goals of effective citation?

2. Who publishes the *Bluebook*? The Maroon Book?

3. What is the philosophical perspective behind the Maroon Book?

4. If you are using a Pennsylvania Supreme Court case in a document submitted to a New Jersey court, would you need to parallel cite?

5. What is the *Bluebook* rule regarding parallel citation to the U.S. Supreme Court? How is that rule varied in practice?

6. Is it necessary to indicate the publisher of USCA or USCS in a citation to those sources?

7. When citing to a book, when would you indicate its edition?

8. When is the use of *id.* appropriate in citation?

9. What is a signal?

Chapter Exercises

Using *Bluebook* citation rules, complete the following exercises. You may have to refer to specific state and periodical tables.

1. Unscramble the following citations.
   a. Constitution, art. II, U.S. § 1.
   b. U.S.C.S., § 1, (Law. Co-op. 1978), 16.
   c. 34 Conn. App. 866, *Squeglia v. Squeglia*, 644 A.2d 378 (1994).
   d. *Palko v. Connecticut*, (1937), 302 U.S. 319.
   e. *New Balance in the Rights of Creditors and Debtors: The Effect on Maryland Law*, Charles M. Tatelbaum, (1973), 2 U. Balt. L. Rev. 236.

2. Place the following information in correct citation form.

    a. Lois Grato, appellant, versus Louis Grato, appellee; located at volume 272 of the New Jersey Superior Court Reports, page 140; and volume 639 of the Atlantic Reporter, second series, page 390; issued in 1994.

    b. Author: S.C. Gwynne; Article title: Guilty, Innocent, Guilty; Publication: *Time;* publication date: Jan. 16, 1995; Page 38.

3. Correct the following citations.

    a. *Allstate Insurance Company versus Robinson,* 645 Atl.2d 591 (D.C.App. 1994).

    b. 42 United States Code § 3412 (May, 1970)

    c. William P. Statsky, *The Education of Legal Paraprofessionals: Myths, Realities, and Opportunities,* vol. 24 Vanderbilt Law Review 1083 (1971).

CHAPTER 8

BASIC LEGAL ANALYSIS

CHAPTER OUTLINE
Legal Analysis of Case Law
Legal Analysis of Statutory Law
Legal Analysis of Ordinances
Legal Analysis of Administrative Law
Legal Analysis of Constitutional Law
IRAC Method of Analysis

OVERVIEW

You should not confuse the ability to describe, use, and cite authority with the ability to study and analyze legal principles. As a paralegal, you must be able to carefully study principles as they appear in cases, statutes, and other forms of primary law. *Legal analysis* is the process of identifying and understanding legal principles and then applying those rules to particular factual situations. This chapter introduces the fundamentals of legal analysis.

It is important to recall that our legal system is based on common law. In a common law system, the courts are given significant responsibility for determining the meaning of the law. This is done through the interpretation of various forms of primary law. Through the power of judicial review, judges interpret statutes, administrative regulations, constitutional provisions, and the decisions of other judges. These written interpretations, known as *case opinions,* constitute mandatory or persuasive authority. As a result, much of legal analysis centers around understanding case law.

Statutes are also the focus of legal analysis. This is because of the important, constitutionally mandated role that legislative bodies play in producing laws. Legislatures are charged with crafting laws that reflect the public will. Unfortunately, the legislative enactment process often results in poorly written laws that are difficult to understand. In many instances, it is necessary for the courts to step in to determine a statute's meaning.

Before beginning case law research, you must fully understand the facts in the assigned legal problem. The actual sources of these facts might include client interviews, witness statements, or documents such as hospital records or police reports. Understanding the facts is vital because the essence of case law research requires locating cases with similar factual circumstances. A case with like facts will often deal with issues similar to those in the problem being researched.

The legal issue is posed as a question. The answer to this question will be governed by a legal principle located in a case opinion known as a *holding.* Understanding the relationship between facts, issues, and holdings is the key to case law research.

Case briefing is a way of summarizing case law. It provides a full understanding of the opinion and efficiently conveys its essential points to your colleagues. A suggested format for briefing a case in a clear, concise, and user-friendly manner is discussed and examined in this chapter.

Statutory law analysis is also examined. Statutes are generally written to anticipate a comprehensive set of circumstances. As mentioned, the process of legislative enactment may result in statutes that are poorly written and complex. This greatly hampers one's ability to comprehend the meaning of a law. Breaking a statutory provision down into its component parts can help you to understand its purpose and application.

Legal analysis is critical to an understanding of ordinances, administrative regulations, and constitutional provisions. In this chapter, legal analysis of each of these forms of primary law is examined. Administrative regulations and ordinances are drafted similarly to statutes, and thus an analysis comparable to statutes is appropriate. Constitutional provisions appear simple and straightforward, but in fact are difficult to analyze, because of the role courts play in interpreting and establishing the meanings of these provisions.

Finally, a method of analysis taught in law school, known as *IRAC,* is introduced. IRAC is an acronym for issue, rule, application/analysis, and conclusion. It is particularly useful when answering a legal problem in writing.

PARALEGAL PRACTICE SITUATION

Your firm has been retained by Marie Connolly and her daughter, Roxanne, regarding injuries they sustained about two weeks ago at a neighborhood playground. Marie and her 24-month-old daughter were approached by a German shepherd owned by Joan and Kevin Johnson. The dog, though on a leash, leaped out and attacked Roxanne. She was rushed to a local hospital where she required 100 stitches to repair her right cheek and ear.

The incident caused Marie, though physically uninjured, to become "a nervous wreck." She has recently started seeing a psychiatrist for her problems.

Your attorney would like you to conduct research to determine if an action can be brought against the Johnsons for Marie's mental injuries. (Holding them responsible for Roxanne's injuries should not be difficult.) He would like you to focus your research on the theory of **strict liability**.

Legal Analysis of Case Law

Facts, Issues, Reasoning, and Holdings

Application of the principle of *stare decisis* on the state level requires that the decisions of state appeals courts be followed as precedent by lower appeals and trial courts within the same jurisdiction. In addition, a decision of the U.S. Supreme Court binds all lower courts, both federal and state. Because the courts must follow the precedent, the decision is **mandatory** or **binding authority**. In contrast, state courts need only consider, but are not required to follow, decisions from other states. These decisions have only persuasive effect on the courts that consider them. (These concepts are discussed later in this chapter.)

To better understand how precedent is applied, let us reconsider the example from Chapter 2 of two children fighting over use of a toy. There, the father needed to determine the proper rule to apply to achieve the result he desired—peace in the family.

Similarly, a court's ultimate task is to determine relief for the parties, called the **judgment** of the court. The judgment solves the basic legal problem for the parties: who wins, who loses, the amount of money awarded. In most instances, the judgment is also the remedy requested in part or in full by a party on the trial or appeals level.

LEGAL TERMS

strict liability [†]   Liability for an injury whether or not there is fault or negligence; absolute liability. The law imposes strict liability in product liability cases.

binding (mandatory) authority [†]   Previous decisions of a higher court or statutes that a judge must follow in reaching a decision in a case.

judgment [†]   1. In a civil action, the final determination by a court of the rights of the parties, based upon the pleadings and the evidence; a decision. 2. In a criminal prosecution, a determination of guilt; a conviction.

To reach a judgment, the court goes through a process of considering various authorities or rules. With the father, the rule was:

> When siblings fight over a toy, the toy is shared.

The rule itself embraces certain factual conditions (siblings that are fighting) together with a specific result that takes place (sharing the toy). The rule is very precisely applied. If the necessary facts do not exist, the rule would not apply. For example, this rule would not be used with nonsiblings fighting or to nonfighting siblings.

A legal rule generally includes factual conditions and a specific result, as in the following:

1. (FACTS) A married individual showing an inclination and having the opportunity to have sexual relations with one other than his or her spouse (RESULT) has committed **adultery** by **circumstantial evidence**.

2. (FACTS) When two individuals own real estate as **joint tenants** (RESULT), each is entitled to the other's rights in the property upon the other's death (called the **right of survivorship**).

If one of these statements was found in a case opinion, it would be referred to as a **holding**. The holding is the *ratio decidendi,* or, translated from Latin, "the reason for the decision." When courts develop or apply a holding, a very specific outcome is achieved. When the holding is applied to a specific case at bar, it could result in the granting of a divorce or the awarding of ownership of a piece of land to one individual over another. The particular result (i.e., one spouse gets a divorce, or one party gets the land) is the judgment.

As a guide in reaching a judgment, a court looks to other case opinions dealing with similar factual situations and issues. This process (see Figure 8-1), often recorded in the opinion, is referred to as the court's **reasoning**. The reasoning is an explanation of why and how the court answered the legal issues in the way it did—in other words, its justification for deciding in a certain way.

LEGAL TERMS

adultery [†]   Sexual intercourse by a married person with a person not his or her spouse.

circumstantial evidence [†]   Facts and circumstances from which a jury or a judge may reason and reach conclusions in a case.

joint tenancy [†]   An estate in land or in personal property held by two or more persons jointly, with equal rights to share in its enjoyment. The most important feature of a joint tenancy is the right of survivorship, which means that upon the death of a joint tenant the entire estate goes to the survivor (or, in the case of more than two joint tenants, to the survivors, and so on to the last survivor).

right of survivorship [†]   In the case of a joint tenancy or a tenancy by the entirety, the entitlement of the surviving tenant, upon the death of the other, to hold in his or her own right whatever estate or interest both previously shared.

holding [†]   The proposition of law for which a case stands; the "bottom line" of a judicial decision.

reasoning   As found in a case opinion, a court's analysis and justification for a specific holding.

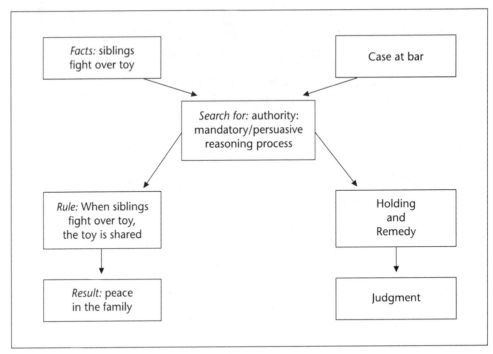

FIGURE 8-1 Flow chart of legal analysis

Mandatory versus Persuasive Authority

A case containing facts identical to the case at bar and espousing favorable legal principles is said to be **on all fours** with the client's case. It is rare, however, to find a case that matches so closely. In most situations, attorneys locate cases that are close and emphasize their similarities and play down their differences with the case at bar. The court, in turn, evaluates and analyzes the cases offered by the attorneys. If a case constitutes mandatory authority, the principles contained in it must be followed by the court. The holdings in the case offered must be applied to the facts at hand. Consequently, the same result as in the researched case will be reached in the case at bar.

For a case to be considered mandatory authority, the following conditions must be met.

First, the facts of the case opinion and the facts in the case at bar must be similar. Only those that are considered **key facts** are included in this consideration. Key facts are those that are essential to the court in reaching its decision. Or, thinking of it in another way, the prerequisite facts were not present to bring about the desired result. As an example, consider a divorce action in which

──────────────── **LEGAL TERMS** ────────────────

on all fours † Refers to a judicial opinion in a case that is very similar to another case, both with respect to the facts they involve and the applicable law.

key facts Facts that are essential for a court in reaching its decision.

a husband is suing his wife on the grounds of **desertion**. The fact that the wife is of Japanese descent is immaterial to the court's determination of desertion. However, the fact that the wife has been living in Japan for the past several years without her husband might be a key fact.

Second, the rule of law applied in the prior case opinion must be applicable to the case at bar. A sufficient knowledge of substantive legal areas of law (i.e., tort law, contract law, criminal law) is the best aid in making this determination. For instance, a rule dealing with adultery would not apply to a case involving facts that show only desertion.

The last condition is that the case opinion come from a jurisdiction that has binding authority on the case at bar. Within a state system, there may be one or more appellate courts, a **general jurisdiction** trial court and a **limited jurisdiction** trial court. Higher courts always exert mandatory authority on lower courts. Thus, holdings emanating from a state supreme court would be mandatory authority in all lower courts of the same state.

REQUIREMENTS OF MANDATORY AUTHORITY

1. Key facts in case opinion and case at bar are similar.
2. Rule of law applied in case opinion is applicable to case at bar.
3. Case opinion is from a jurisdiction that has mandatory effect on case at bar.

In contrast, an appellate court opinion from one state cannot be used as mandatory authority in a different state. It would be considered only **persuasive authority**. For instance, an opinion from the Pennsylvania Supreme Court would only be persuasive authority to a trial court in Oregon. A court looking at the case at bar might consider the rule of law from another state's court, but is under no compulsion to follow it.

As you recall, the federal court system includes the U.S. Supreme Court, the U.S. Courts of Appeals, the U.S. District Courts, and various miscellaneous limited jurisdiction courts, such as the U.S. Bankruptcy Court and the U.S. Tax Court.

LEGAL TERMS
---

desertion [†]   As a ground for divorce, a voluntary separation of one of the parties to a marriage from the other without the consent of or without having been wronged by the second party, with the intention to live apart and without any intention to return to cohabitation.

court of general jurisdiction [†]   Generally, another term for trial court; that is, a court having jurisdiction to try all classes of civil and criminal cases except those which can be heard only by a court of limited jurisdiction.

court of limited jurisdiction [†]   A court whose jurisdiction is limited to civil cases of a certain type or which involve a limited amount of money, or whose jurisdiction in criminal cases is confined to petty offenses and preliminary hearings. A court of limited jurisdiction is sometimes called a court of special jurisdiction.

persuasive authority [†]   Authority that is neither binding authority nor precedent, but which a court may use to support its decision if it chooses.

A decision of the U.S. Supreme Court is mandatory authority in all federal courts and in state courts when federal issues are involved. Decisions of the U.S. Courts of Appeals are only mandatory for the district courts within their circuits. For instance, the U.S. District Court of Maryland is under the jurisdiction of the U.S. Court of Appeals for the Fourth circuit. It is required to follow decisions emanating from that court, but may merely consider decisions from other circuits. See Figure 8-2.

If the court is unable to locate mandatory authority, it will consider and weigh the relative merits of various persuasive authorities. This, of course, encompasses the consideration of cases from jurisdictions other than the one in which the case at bar is taking place. Usually, a state court will look to neighboring states that have dealt with the same matter it is considering. A U.S. District Court will look outside of its circuit to decisions from other U.S. Courts of Appeals. This evaluation process will be found in the opinion's reasoning.

Situations in which other states' case law is considered often arise when courts are dealing with issues that have not been previously addressed in their jurisdiction. Matters arising out of new legal areas, such as AIDS-related issues, new family law controversies such as surrogacy and in-vitro fertilization, and legal issues impacting computer technology, are often dealt with by courts for the first time. In these cases of **first impression**, courts will look to the case law of other jurisdictions that have dealt with similar facts to guide them in applying their decision-making powers. Generally, both parties offer legal theories from outside jurisdictions to prove their opposing positions. The court evaluates each argument and sides with the position it finds most convincing.

Mootness and Dictum

Each case holding is based on an issue that the court is addressing at that moment. There are times when a court will choose not to resolve an issue raised by the parties. For instance, a court might have to decide whether a particular party can bring a lawsuit (referred to as **standing**) and the type of relief the party is entitled to. If the court decides that the party is not entitled to bring the suit, the issue of relief cannot be decided. Alternatively, suppose that the party can bring the lawsuit, but obtains nonjudicial relief before the court can decide the issue. For instance, a car owner sues a manufacturer requesting a refund because his car is defective. Before the court can decide the issue, the manufacturer agrees to provide the refund. The issue is then said to be **moot**: it cannot

――――――――――――――― **LEGAL TERMS** ―――――――――――――――

first impression †   Phrase referring to a case that has not arisen before and that is without precedent to govern it.

standing to sue †   The legal capacity to bring and to maintain a lawsuit. A person is without standing to sue unless some interest of his or hers has been adversely affected or unless he or she has been injured by the defendant. The term "standing to sue" is often shortened simply to "standing."

moot †   Of no actual significance.

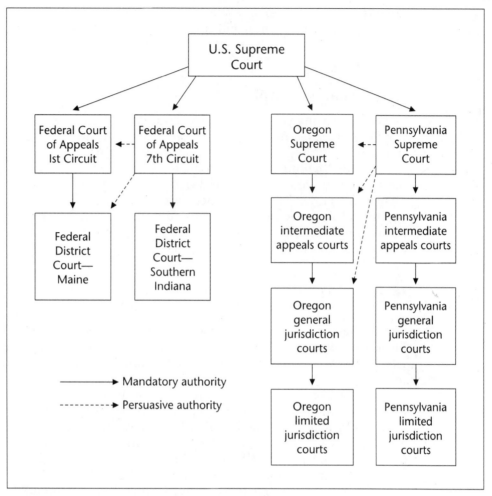

FIGURE 8-2 Mandatory and persuasive authority

or will not be decided by the court. In these situations, you must continue to research to locate a case in which the issue you are researching has been addressed by a court.

Additionally, judges often make legal statements that appear to be holdings but are actually irrelevant to the issues presented. This is called *dictum* (or plural **dicta**). Every holding must respond to an issue. If in the course of researching a case, you find a holding without a corresponding issue, it is probably dictum. Dictum does not serve as precedent or have legal significance; it is merely judicial

---

LEGAL TERMS

dicta † Plural of dictum, ... short for the Latin term *obiter dictum*. Dicta are expressions or comments in a court opinion that are not necessary to support the decision made by the court; they are not binding authority and have no value as precedent.

commentary. Unfortunately, many attorneys use dictum to bolster a legal position. To do this is unethical and is severely criticized by judges.

Legal Analysis Applied

When starting your research, it is critical that you determine the legal issues from the facts presented. Your goal is to locate case law that has similar fact patterns and addresses the same issues as the case at bar.

Consider the situation concerning the Ricardos from Chapter 2. To review the facts, Maryland residents Tom and Gail Ricardo have been married for one year. They were married by a deputy clerk at the local county courthouse. Because the deputy did not have the prerequisite authority to perform marriages, the Ricardos now have reason to believe that they were not properly wed. The legal issue can be stated as follows:

> When parties are married and they, as well as the officiating clerk, believe that the official had the proper authority to perform the ceremony, but it is later found that no such authority existed, is the marriage valid?

This rather long and cumbersome question is the formal technique of *stating a legal issue,* often used in law school. For purposes of expediency and efficiency, the facts of the case can be assumed and the issue stated simply as: Is the marriage valid?

Once the key facts are understood and the issue stated, the search can begin for a case opinion with similar facts and issues. Some *context facts* can also be considered. Context facts—names of parties, dates, and places—humanize the situation and as a consequence make for more interesting reading. Employing the three-step process from Chapter 2 (addressed again in Chapter 9) would lead you to the Maryland case of *Knapp v. Knapp,* 149 Md. 263, 131 A. 329 (1925).

In *Knapp v. Knapp,* relatives of the deceased John Knapp litigated the disposition of his **estate**. On one side were John's blood relatives, headed by Joseph H. Knapp (probably his father or brother, we do not know for sure). On the other side was John Knapp's widow, Mary M. Knapp. Joseph H. Knapp made the argument that because the minister who married the Knapps did not have proper authority, Mary Knapp was not married to John Knapp and could not be his widow. As a result, Mary was not entitled to a **widow's allowance** from his estate. Of course, Mary Knapp responded that she was legally married to John Knapp. The issue the court wrestled with was whether the Knapps were husband and

---
──────────────── **LEGAL TERMS** ────────────────

estate † 1. The right, title, and interest a person has in real or personal property, either tangible or intangible. Estates in real property (estates in land or landed estates) include both freehold estates … and estates less than freehold. … 3. The property left by a decedent; i.e., a decedent's estate.

elective share (widow's allowance) † In some states, the share a surviving spouse may elect to take in the estate of the deceased spouse.

wife at the time of John's death. It would appear that the court's resolution of this case might affect the Ricardo matter.

The necessary key and context facts found in the *Knapp* opinion are as follows. The minister, Leland W. Windsor, signed the marriage certificate as pastor of Cummins Memorial Reformed Episcopal Church. The marriage was celebrated at Rev. Windsor's home. Though he honestly believed he had received permission from his superiors to conduct marriages, a bishop of his church testifying at the *Knapp* trial indicated that Rev. Windsor's "connection with the church did not, in fact, authorize him to celebrate marriage or any other ceremony."

Nonetheless, the court held that persons married by a minister they believe to have authority to marry them are validly married, provided there was a ceremony. There was a ceremony in the *Knapp* case (as there was in the Ricardo case). The Knapps believed that Rev. Windsor had appropriate authority and therefore, according to the court, they had a valid marriage.

KNAPP
v.
KNAPP
149 Md. 263, 131 A. 329 (1925)
(Maryland Court of Appeals)
December 9, 1925

BOND, C.J. A supposed will of John Knapp, deceased, which had been probated, and under which the appellees had been appointed ... as executors, was afterwards set aside ... by appellants.

* * *

Three objections have been pressed.

* * *

The remaining, or third, objection ... is the important one in the case. An allowance of $75 to Mary M. Knapp as widow of the deceased ... is contested on the ground that she was not validly married to the deceased. Testimony taken on this objection showed that a license in due form was procured, and that the marriage was celebrated by a certain Leland W. Windsor, who signed the return certificate as pastor of the Cummins Memorial Reformed Episcopal Church. The marriage was celebrated at Windsor's home. It appears that Windsor ... had received authority to ... celebrate marriages from [the] Apostolic Church of Philadelphia. ... It declared him authorized to celebrate marriages. Because of a lack of regular ministers, he was invited to preach in two churches in

Baltimore ... [one being] the Cummins Memorial Reformed Episcopal Church. The officials of this latter church invited him to preach in their pulpit, and he did so for over a year and a half. He was called pastor of the church, and the congregation understood that he was a minister. The defendant, Mary M. Knapp, was a member of the congregation. Windsor testifies that he believed himself authorized to perform the marriage ceremony, and that he did actually marry five couples during the time he occupied the pulpit. ... The parties to this last marriage [John and Mary Knapp] ... assumed that Windsor was qualified to perform the ceremony, believed themselves duly married, lived together as husband and wife, and were recognized as such. ... But the bishop of the Reformed Episcopal Church testifies that Windsor was not accepted by him or by the church officials as the regular pastor of the Cummins Memorial Church, and that his connection with the church did not, in fact, authorize him to celebrate marriages ... and it was denied that his connection with the Apostolic Church and his certificate from elders of that church constituted him an ordained minister ... .

* * *

The requirement of a religious ceremony in Maryland is fixed, and this court has not the slightest disposition to relax it. But can it be the rule that a marriage solemnized with a religious ceremony by one who to all appearances is authorized to solemnize marriages, whom the parties believe, and have every reason to believe, authorized, may still be invalid because of some flaw in the title of the supposed minister, or complete absence of authority in fact? If so, then the validity of marriages in the state must remain open to question despite all the parties may do to assure validity, for few can look up the orders of apparent ministers, and fewer still can pass judgment on them. Only an unescapable mandate would justify construing the law to intend such a thing. The law has long recognized that, because of this inability of the public to go behind apparent authority, dealings of supposed officers, who are in fact not qualified, must be given effect nevertheless.

* * *

[W]e hold that under the law of Maryland the marriage now questioned was valid ... .

Order affirmed.

Here the court applied the principle of **apparent authority** to find the marriage valid. The authority to perform an act is not actually granted by the superior, but by all appearances seems to have been granted. Often it is created as a result of the failure of a superior to properly oversee the activities of a subordinate. In such a situation, the authority is said to exist. To find otherwise would cause hardship on innocent persons acting based on the authority (in this case, the Knapps).

The key facts in the *Knapp* case are the same as those in the Ricardo case. More importantly, the central issue the court dealt with—whether the marriage was valid—is clearly the same. Because the *Knapp* case is from the Maryland Court of Appeals (the state's supreme court), it would be mandatory authority in this matter and thus control the outcome in the Ricardo case. Consequently, the Ricardo marriage would be held valid. See Figure 8-3.

Case Briefing

The process of case analysis is greatly assisted by *case briefing.* The word **brief** has three different meanings in legal practice. The first refers to a document filed at the trial court level for the purpose of persuading the court of the correctness of a certain legal position. This is referred to as a **trial brief**. To avoid confusion, sometimes this document is called a *trial memorandum.* However, a

---

LEGAL TERMS

apparent authority [†] Authority which, although not actually granted by the principal, he or she permits his or her agent to exercise.

brief [†] 1. A written statement submitted to a court for the purpose of persuading it of the correctness of one's position. A brief argues the facts of the case and the applicable law, supported by citations of authority. 2. A text that an attorney prepares to guide him or her in the trial of a case. Called a *trial brief,* it can include lists of questions to be asked of various witnesses, points to be covered, and arguments to be made. 3. An outline of the published opinion in a case, made by an attorney or a paralegal for the purpose of understanding the case.

trial brief Either a memorandum submitted to court or a text that an attorney prepares to guide him or her at trial.

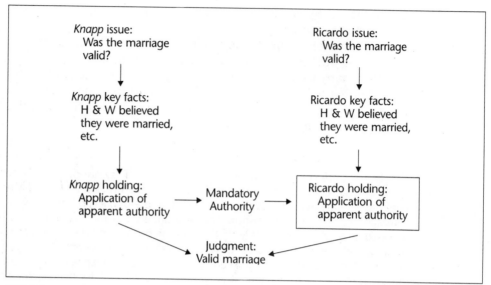

FIGURE 8-3 Application of authority

trial brief also can be a game plan for the trial; when it functions in this way, it is not submitted to the court. As strategy guidelines, it will include questions to ask of witnesses, points to be considered, and arguments to be made at trial. The second type of brief is the **appellate brief**, a formally structured document. Should a party feel that a trial court erred, the party could take an appeal. An appellate brief lays out the legal arguments that form the basis of the appeal; one is filed by the appellant and one by the appellee. (Trial and appellate briefs are addressed in Chapter 16.)

Finally, a **case brief** is an objective summary of the important points in a case opinion. It includes a concise summary of the facts, issues, reasoning, and holdings, as well as other aspects of a case. It is an internal document seen only by those working in the firm. To better understand case briefs, it is important to appreciate the reasons for briefing in the first place.

One important purpose for briefing a case is to assist in understanding the case. To brief a case, you must first thoroughly read the opinion. This takes the form of active reading. That is, you must comprehend not only with your eyes, but also with your hand by making margin notes and underlining important points. Studies have shown that better comprehension is achieved when note-taking is done in combination with reading.

A second reason for briefing is that the brief becomes a record of the case on which another can rely. The briefs of a researcher with a solid reputation will

---

LEGAL TERMS

appellate brief A formal structured document filed in an appeals court by either appellant or appellee.

case brief A concise, objective summary of a case opinion.

be sought out by co-workers. Utilizing a good "briefer" can save time and energy for an attorney.

Full comprehension of the case is required to prepare a brief. This can be accomplished only by a careful reading of the opinion. Before beginning, read the case from start to finish, headnotes and all. Never succumb to the temptation to read only the headnotes. Remember, a complete appreciation of the case's legal principles is not possible without an understanding of the facts that gave rise to the legal problem.

Paralegal Tip

Canned briefs are commercially marketed case briefs. They are particularly popular with law students who, under great stress and pressure, succumb to their use. Relying on a canned brief poses several serious risks. Recall that the purpose of briefing is not only to provide a summarization of the case, but also to help you understand the case fully. This second goal is thwarted if you do not physically go through the process of briefing. In addition, a brief you produce will use your language and shorthand; a canned brief will not. You might be required to brief the brief in order to understand it! Finally, when you brief a case you are likely to do it with the client's legal position in mind. You will look for things (concepts, facts, principles) that are important to your case. A canned brief is not produced with your client in mind. As a result, it will likely include points that are not relevant to your case, and may omit some that are.

At first, reading cases will be a frustrating experience. Read with a good legal dictionary at hand. Jot down unfamiliar words, concepts, and legal theories with the intention of further studying them. It is a good practice to read the case several times before beginning the briefing process.

There is no universal format for briefing. Some law firms may have an established form, but in most instances, each paralegal develops her own method. Generally, all briefs, at the very least, include the following major components, as illustrated in our brief of the case of *Douglas v. Fulis,* 138 N.H. 740, 645 A.2d 76 (1994).

Case Identification

First, it is important to accurately, though concisely, identify the case opinion for the reader at the top of the page.

Citation

The identification is followed by the full citation, including the parallel citation. Phrases such as *et al.* and *et ux.* can be dropped. Some courts use "and another" to mean both. In the *Douglas* case, the phrase "Individually and as Father and Next Friend of Lindsay Douglas" is dropped. First and middle names are also superfluous. The names of the parties must be reduced to their most essential parts.

Robert DOUGLAS, Individually and
as Father and Next Friend of
Lindsay Douglas
v.
Kimon FULIS and another.
No. 93–571.
Supreme Court of New Hampshire.
Aug. 1, 1994.

Father whose child was attacked by dog sued dog owners under statute imposing strict liability on owners or keepers for damage done by their dogs, seeking to recover for mental and emotional injuries incurred as result of witnessing dog attack his child. The Superior Court, Rockingham, Gray, J., granted defendants' motion to dismiss. Father appealed. The Supreme Court, Brock, C.J., held that statute was not intended to cover bystander's claim for emotional distress.

Affirmed and remanded.

1. Animals ⬅️ 74(1)
Statute imposing strict liability on owners or keepers for damage done by their dogs does not confer right of action on all persons indiscriminately, but rather, must be given reasonable interpretation. RSA 466:19.

2. Statutes ⬅️ 222
Statutes are not to be construed as changing common law unless that intention is clearly expressed.

3. Damages ⬅️ 51
Statute imposing strict liability on owners or keepers for damage done by their dogs was not intended to cover bystander's claim for emotional distress. RSA 466:19.

Nicholas R. Aeschliman, Portsmouth, by brief and orally, for plaintiff.

Devine, Millimet & Branch, P.A., Manchester (Richard E. Mills, on the brief and orally), for defendants.

BROCK, Chief Justice.

The plaintiff, Robert Douglas, individually and as father and next friend of Lindsay Douglas, brings this interlocutory appeal from an order of the Superior Court (*Gray,* J.) dismissing one count of his writ of summons. The plaintiff seeks recovery, pursuant to RSA 466:19 (Supp. 1989) (current version at RSA 466:19 (1992)) (the statute), for mental and emotional injuries incurred as a result of witnessing the defendants' dog attack his daughter. The plaintiff argues that the trial court erred in dismissing the count for failure to state a cause of action. We affirm.

In August 1989, the plaintiff and his three-year-old daughter, Lindsay Douglas, were at a neighborhood playground. Defendant Laurie Fulis and her daughters were walking their family's golden retriever on a leash through the same playground. After the Douglases approached the dog, it attacked and bit Lindsay, causing lacerations and permanent scars on her face, ear, and head. The plaintiff, who was standing next to his daughter, saw and heard the attack. After Lindsay and the dog were separated, the plaintiff rushed Lindsay to the hospital where she received medical treatment.

The plaintiff brought a three-count action in tort against Kimon and Laurie Fulis, the owners of the dog, based solely on RSA 466:19. Counts I and II sought recovery for personal injuries sustained by Lindsay and for medical expenses incurred on her behalf. In count III, the plaintiff sought recovery for mental and emotional injuries he allegedly suffered as a result of witnessing the attack. The plaintiff did not allege negligence on the part of the defendants. The trial court granted the defendants' motion to dismiss count III, and this interlocutory appeal followed.

On an appeal from an order granting a motion to dismiss, we "assume the truth of both the facts alleged in the plaintiff's pleadings and all reasonable inferences therefrom as construed most favorably to the plaintiff. If the facts as alleged would constitute a basis for legal relief, the motion to dismiss should be denied." *Collectramatic, Inc. v. Kentucky Fried Chicken Corp.,* 127 N.H. 318, 320, 499 A.2d 999, 1000 (1985).

The plaintiff contends that the trial court misinterpreted RSA 466:19 by denying him a right of recovery for mental and emotional injuries suffered as a bystander. He argues that his cause of action was intended under the "broad language" of the statute. We disagree. RSA 466:19 states:

> "Any person to whom or to whose property damage may be occasioned by a dog not owned or kept by him shall be entitled to recover such damage of the person who owns or keeps the dog, or has it in his possession, unless the damage was occasioned to him while he was engaged in the commission of trespass or other tort. A parent or guardian shall be liable under this section if the owner or keeper of the dog is a minor."

The statute, in substantially identical form, was enacted nearly 150 years ago. *See* Laws 1851, ch. 1124. We have consistently held that the reason for the enactment of the statute "was to obviate the difficulty of showing the owner's knowledge of the vicious propensities of the dog as required at common law." *Allgeyer v. Lincoln,* 125 N.H. 503, 506, 484 A.2d 1079, 1081 (1984) (quotation omitted); *see Gagnon v. Frank,* 83 N.H. 122, 123, 139 A. 373, 374 (1927).

[1] The strict liability imposed by the statute is not unlimited. Although the statute suggests no qualifications to the liability of owners or keepers for the damage done by their dogs, it does not confer a right of action on all persons indiscriminately. It should be given a reasonable interpretation. *Noyes v. Labrecque,* 106 N.H. 357, 358, 211 A.2d 421, 422 (1965); *see Gagnon,* 83 N.H. at 123, 139 A. at 374.

[2,3] Statutes are not to be construed as changing the common law unless that intention is clearly expressed. *Bolduc v. Herbert Schneider Corp.,* 117 N.H. 566, 568, 374 A.2d 1187, 1189 (1977). Generally, at common law, when negligence served as the legal source of liability, it gave "rise only to an obligation to compensate the person immediately injured, not anyone who predictably suffer[ed] loss in consequence of that injury, unless liability for that person's consequential loss [had] a legal source besides its foreseeability." *Siciliano v. Capitol City Shows, Inc.,* 124 N.H. 719, 725, 475 A.2d 19, 21 (1984) (quotation omitted). New Hampshire did not afford a cause of action for the negligent infliction of emotional distress under facts such as those in this case before 1979. *See Corso v. Merrill,* 119 N.H. 647, 659, 406 A.2d 300, 308 (1979). As the cause of action did not exist in New Hampshire when the statute was enacted, we cannot

conclude that the legislature intended the statute's wording to encompass the plaintiff's claim. *See Siciliano,* 124 N.H. at 724, 475 A.2d at 21; *cf. Bolduc,* 117 N.H. at 568, 374 A.2d at 1189. We believe that under a reasonable interpretation the statute was not intended to cover a bystander's claim for emotional distress. *See Noyes,* 106 N.H. at 358–59, 211 A.2d at 422.

The plaintiff cites other jurisdictions which have extended liability for a bystander's emotional distress in strict liability cases to argue that the statute should provide him with a cause of action. We note that the cases relied upon by the plaintiff all involve claims based on strict *products* liability and are distinct from the facts of the case at hand. We leave the question of liability for a bystander's emotional distress under strict products liability for another time.

The plaintiff also contends that the principles we enunciated in *Corso* should apply to his claim under the statute. He argues that it would be illogical to allow bystander recovery for emotional distress in a negligence case, and deny that same recovery under the strict liability of the statute. In *Corso* we stated:

> "Recovery should not be barred for the serious emotional injury to parents who contemporaneously perceive or witness a serious injury to their child that is caused by defendant's negligence.
>
> * * *
>
> In summary, we hold that a mother and father who witness or contemporaneously sensorially perceive a serious injury to their child may recover if they suffer serious mental and emotional harm that is accompanied by objective physical symptoms. Any action for negligent infliction of emotional distress must be based on the criteria of foreseeability outlined in this opinion and on the causal negligence of the defendant."

Corso, 119 N.H. at 658–59, 406 A.2d at 307–08. The criteria of foreseeability were specifically adopted in order to maintain a balance between the fear of unlimited liability and "a plaintiff's serious emotional injury that is directly caused *by defendant's negligence.*" *Id.* at 653, 406 A.2d at 304 (emphasis added).

In the fifteen years since *Corso,* we have applied these criteria for recovery only in cases alleging negligence on the part of the defendants. *See, e.g., Wilder v. City of Keene,* 131 N.H. 599, 602–03, 557 A.2d 636, 638 (1989); *Waid v. Ford Motor Co.,* 125 N.H. 640, 640–41, 643, 484 A.2d 1152, 1152–53, 1154 (1984); *Nutter v. Frisbie Mem. Hosp.,* 124 N.H. 791, 794–95, 474 A.2d 584, 585–86 (1984); *Siciliano,* 124 N.H. at 726–27, 475 A.2d at 22–23.

We agree that the plaintiff has met the foreseeability factors of proximity of time, location, and relationship adopted in *Corso. See Siciliano,* 124 N.H. at 727, 475 A.2d at 23. Not every foreseeable injury to a legally recognized relationship necessarily postulates a cause of action, however. *Id.* at 724, 475 A.2d at 21. "A defendant's duty not to inflict emotional distress on a bystander is breached *only* when the defendant, *through his negligence,* physically injures a loved one of the bystander." *Waid,* 125 N.H. at 643, 484 A.2d at 1154 (emphasis added). Here, the defendant has not breached any duty owed the plaintiff.

The strict liability under the statute is a legislative creation, and not a judicially created principle. *Cf. Allgeyer,* 125 N.H. at 507, 484 A.2d at 1081. We need not determine if recovery for a bystander's emotional distress would have been included under a judicial creation of strict liability. Rather, we need only determine what the legislature intended in their creation of strict liability. In light of our interpretation of the statute, above, we decline to apply the principles enunciated in *Corso* to this case. If the legislature determines that the principles governing bystander recovery should be extended to actions brought under the statute, it may do so. *Cf. id.*

Affirmed and remanded.

All concurred.

(Reprinted with the permission of West Publishing Company.)

EXAMPLE

Douglas v. Fulis

CITATION:
Douglas v. Fulis, 138 N.H. 740, 645 A.2d 76 (1994)

Parties

Following the citation is information regarding the parties. Three components are needed to identify the parties: the first and last names of the lead parties, a categorization of the parties that is most relevant to the case, and the litigation titles of the parties on both the trial and appellate levels. Providing this information serves two needs. First, a judge will sometimes switch, within the opinion, the titles and names she uses to refer to parties. Understanding up front all of the possible titles and names that can be used to refer to an individual will help in understanding the case. Secondly, often a person reading a briefed case will question whether a certain individual they are representing would have standing in court. If the client is in the same category as a party in the briefed case, then the client could be a party and therefore have standing.

EXAMPLE

PARTIES:

Robert Douglas/father of victim/plaintiff, appellant
Kimon Fulis/owner of attacking animal/defendant, appellee

Issues

The next component of a brief is an indication of the issue or issues in the case. Locating the issue can be a difficult process, especially in older opinions. You will need to read the case several times before you can identify and understand the issue fully. Often, reading the headnotes can be helpful. In more recent opinions, courts tend to state issues more clearly. For instance, language such as "we are here to decide" or "the question before us" will likely identify an issue. The issue in the *Douglas* case is not so obvious; it can be ferreted out only by reading the facts carefully.

EXAMPLE

ISSUE:
Can a bystander father bring action under the theory of strict liability claiming mental injuries as a result of witnessing an attack by a dog on his daughter?

Facts

Next is a discussion of key and context facts. Key facts should be determined after the issue has been identified. Remember, key facts are a precondition to a particular issue. When determining context facts, strive to make the brief readable for the person for whom you are preparing it. In the brief, it is preferable to use the names of the parties and individuals rather than their titles. This makes for easier reading and better comprehension.

EXAMPLE

FACTS:
Douglas and his daughter Lindsay approached a golden retriever owned by Fulis. The dog attacked Lindsay, who was subsequently treated at a hospital. Douglas, who was not physically injured, claimed that he was mentally and emotionally injured as a result of the attack.

Prior Proceedings

A discussion of the prior proceedings—that is, all relevant court action leading up to the present appeals case—is the next component. It is helpful to know the legal avenues taken in the event the same maneuvers are taken in the case at bar. In addition, the prior proceedings will indicate the possible outcomes if the same avenues are taken.

EXAMPLE

PRIOR PROCEEDINGS:
Douglas brought a three-**count** strict liability action against Fulis in the Superior Court,

--------------------------------- LEGAL TERMS ---------------------------------

count † 1. A statement of a cause of action in a complaint. There may be several counts in one complaint. 2. A separate and distinct part of an indictment or information stating a

Rockingham. Counts I and II were for injuries suffered by his daughter. Count III was for his mental and emotional injuries. Fulis filed a **motion to dismiss** count III, which was granted. Douglas took an appeal to the Supreme Court of New Hampshire.

Holdings

Following the prior proceedings is a summary of the case's legal holdings. Each issue must have a corresponding holding (unless an issue is moot). It is a good idea to number each holding in multiple-holding cases to correspond to the appropriate issues. Remember, a holding without an issue would be dictum. In locating the holdings, take a common-sense approach by looking for the answers to the issues. The end of the opinion is the most likely place to find the holding in a one-issue case. In cases with multiple issues, it is more difficult to locate the holdings. The headnotes are sometimes, though not always, broken down by holdings.

EXAMPLE

HOLDING:
When a bystander father brings a strict liability action pursuant to RSA (Revised Statutes Annotated) 466.19 for mental injuries he incurs while witnessing a dog attack on his daughter, the father has no right of recovery.

Reasoning

The statement of the holding is followed by a short discussion of the court's reasoning in reaching the holding. In the case opinion's reasoning, the court will evaluate the various authorities (generally persuasive in nature) submitted by counsel. The brief's reasoning is a summarization of the logic the court employed in reaching its judgment.

EXAMPLE

REASONING:
The statute that created the strict liability action did not confer a right of action on all

----------------------------------- LEGAL TERMS -----------------------------------

separate and distinct offense. Division into counts is necessary when two or more offenses are charged in a single indictment or information.

motion [†] An application made to a court for the purpose of obtaining an order or rule directing something to be done in favor of the applicant. The types of motions available to litigants, as well as their form and the matters they appropriately address, are set forth in detail in the Federal Rules of Civil Procedure and the rules of civil procedure of the various states, as well as in the Federal Rules of Criminal Procedure and the various states' rules of criminal procedure. Motions may be written or oral, depending on the type of relief sought and on the court in which they are made.

dismiss [†] To order a case, motion, or prosecution to be terminated. A party requests such an order by means of a motion to dismiss.

individuals. A court should give the statute a "reasonable interpretation" to see if it would include Douglas.

Though the statute changed the common law, it did so at a time when a **cause of action** for mental or emotional distress did not exist. Consequently, the legislature could not have intended the present statute to encompass Douglas's claim.

Thus, based on a "reasonable interpretation," the statute was not designed to cover a bystander's claim for emotional distress.

Judgment

Finally, the court's disposition of the case should be indicated, generally referred to in the brief as the judgment. When searching the case, the judgment can often be found at the very end of the opinion, sometimes printed in capital or italicized letters.

EXAMPLE

JUDGMENT:
Affirmed and remanded.

Incidently, this opinion includes a statement that might be considered dictum. The court indicates that Douglas met the factors necessary to bring an action in negligence, but because the basis of the suit is strict liability, there is no duty (an element of negligence) that Fulis owes Douglas. This judicial commentary is irrelevant to whether Douglas can bring a strict liability claim. It appears that Douglas would have had better success bringing an action in negligence.

Also, the court appears to declare moot an issue raised by Douglas. He cites authority from jurisdictions that have extended liability for a bystander's emotional distress in strict liability cases to argue that the New Hampshire statute should provide him a cause of action. The court notes that these authorities are based on strict **product liability**—different from the case at bar, in which no "product" is involved. The court says: "We leave the question of liability for a bystander's emotional distress under strict products liability to another time." In the end, the court's final decision is based on very different grounds: the intention of the legislature when the statute was enacted.

Because the brief represents a summarization of a case opinion, making it as concise as possible is important. For this reason, it is not critical that the entire brief be in full complete sentences. Short phrases or even abbreviations are sufficient. See Figure 8-4 for the full brief.

--- LEGAL TERMS ---

cause of action † Circumstances that give a person the right to bring a lawsuit and to receive relief from a court.

product liability † The liability of a manufacturer or seller of an article for an injury caused to a person or to property by a defect in the article sold. A product liability suit is a tort action in which strict liability is imposed.

DOUGLAS V. FULIS

CITATION:

Douglas v. Fulis, 138 N.H. 740, 645 A.2d 76 (1994)

PARTIES:

Robert Douglas/father of victim/plaintiff, appellant

Kimon Fulis/owner of attacking animal/defendant, appellee

ISSUE:

Can a bystander father bring action under the theory of strict liability claiming mental injuries as a result of witnessing an attack by a dog on his daughter?

FACTS:

Douglas and his daughter Lindsay approached a golden retriever owned by Fulis. The dog attacked Lindsay, who was subsequently treated at a hospital. Douglas, who was not physically injured, claimed that he was mentally and emotionally injured as a result of the attack.

PRIOR PROCEEDINGS:

Douglas brought a three-count strict liability action against Fulis in the Superior Court, Rockingham. Counts I and II were for injuries suffered by his daughter. Count III was for his mental and emotional injuries. Fulis filed a motion to dismiss count III, which was granted. Douglas took an appeal to the Supreme Court of New Hampshire.

HOLDING:

When a bystander father brings a strict liability action pursuant to RSA (Revised Statutes Annotated) 466.19 for mental injuries he incurs while witnessing a dog attack on daughter, the father has no right of recovery.

REASONING:

The statute that created the strict liability action did not confer a right of action on all individuals. A court should give the statute a "reasonable interpretation" to see if it would include Douglas.

Though the statute changed the common law, it did so at a time when a cause of action for mental or emotional distress did not exist. Consequently, the legislature could not have intended the present statute to encompass Douglas's claim.

Thus, based on a "reasonable interpretation," the statute was not designed to cover a bystander's claim for emotional distress.

JUDGMENT:

Affirmed and remanded.

FIGURE 8-4   Sample case brief

Legal Analysis of Statutory Law

Because statutes are written by legislative bodies, they reflect political deal-making done during the drafting process. A compromise may require that a statute be written in vague terms in order to appease two sides having opposite views on its interpretation and application. In addition, authors attempt to anticipate future circumstances that might involve a particular law. Unfortunately, they often forecast incorrectly, and the result is a statute that does not "fit" easily. Furthermore, the statutory law of any government evolves over long periods of time. The laws are not compiled on the basis of chronology, like case opinions, but by subject matter. One statute might use language typical of the 19th century (see Figure 8-5), whereas the one following uses contemporary language. This makes it difficult to determine current applications of some laws. The result of all these problems is that statutes are often very difficult to interpret.

Legal Analysis Applied

The best way to understand a statute is by breaking it down into elements or parts. Reconsider the statute discussed in Chapter 3, 39 U.S.C.A. § 3003, the federal postal law discussing mail bearing a fictitious name or address (see Figure 8-6).

In the process of breaking down a statute for analysis the statute should be tested with facts from the case at bar, not unlike a mathematical formula. Sometimes this process is called "working" the statute.

Many times the appearance of the statute itself indicates a starting point for breaking it down. The illustrated statute is divided into two parts: (a) and (b). Each should be interpreted separately at first, then considered together as a unit.

The first section of part (a) describes a set of circumstances that must exist before subparts (1) and (2) can take effect. Writing this first section of the statute out in the following fashion will make it easier to understand:

EXAMPLE

Upon evidence
satisfactory to the Postal Service
that any person is using
a fictitious, false or assumed
name, title or address in
conducting, promoting, or carry on or assisting therein,
by means of the postal services of the United States,
an activity in violation of section 1302, 1341, and 1342
    of title 18, it may—

Many times the statute will separate naturally, based on punctuation or word groupings. Other times, you will need to set apart important concepts. This technique provides a visual aid to comprehension. As a result, it reveals terms that may have to be defined, such as: What constitutes "evidence?" Is a corporation a "person?" By the term "title," does the statute mean a professional title such as "Dr.," or simply "Mr."? In many instances, these questions will be answered in the annotations, in a definitional section found in the statute or a nearby statute, in other provisions that should be read with the statute, or in C.F.R. For instance, reference is made to 18 U.S.C.A. §§ 1302, 1341, and 1342 when considering acts that could be committed by using fictitious mail.

---

§ 245. Playing "thimbles," "little joker," "crap," etc.

Any person who shall play for money or any other thing the game called "thimbles" or what is called the "little joker" or at dice, or the game commonly called "crap," or any other device or fraudulent trick whatsoever, on conviction thereof, shall be imprisoned not less than six months nor more than two years in the Maryland House of Correction or fined not exceeding one hundred dollars, or both, in the discretion of the court. (An. Code, 1951, § 315; 1939, § 300; 1924, § 256; 1912, § 226; 1904, § 212; 1888, § 129; 1853, ch. 265, § 2; 1900, ch. 348; 1904, ch. 183.)

FIGURE 8-5 Old statutory language (Maryland statute). (Reproduced with permission of The Michie Company. Further reproduction without permission is strictly prohibited.)

The subparts (1) and (2) of section (a) discuss the consequences: withholding mail, and requiring the party to furnish proof of its identity and right to receive the mail. The word *and* indicates that if the Postal Service pursues this course (which is optional because of the word *may*), it must do both. If the word *or* had been used, then a choice would exist. Here, more questions about the meanings of terms arise. The statute does not provide insight as to the type of proof of identification that is necessary. Could this be a driver's license? Voter's registration card?

In considering part (b), we see that these provisions are not activated until part (a) has been triggered. In fact, (b) presents other options for the Post Office regarding mail of this type. The Postal Service may order that the mail be forwarded to a "dead letter office" or be returned to the sender, provided one of two conditions are met. The first is when (a)(2) cannot be met; there is failure to provide proof of identity and the right to receive the mail. The second is if "the Postal Service determines that the mail is addressed to a fictitious, false, or assumed name, title, or address," which is the condition that must apply before the statute can be considered in the first place.

Charting all the possible options available to the Post Office can be beneficial in analyzing the statute. See Figure 8-7.

Interpretation Theories

In addition, several interpretation theories are applied by courts in the analysis of statutory law.

The first is a literal reading of the statute. Sometimes called the **plain meaning rule**, the court interprets statutory terms in light of common, everyday meanings. For example, "person" in 39 U.S.C.A. § 3003 may appear not to mean

---
── **LEGAL TERMS** ──

plain meaning rule †   The rule that in interpreting a statute whose meaning is unclear, the courts will look to the "plain meaning" of its language to determine legislative intent. The plain meaning rule is in opposition to the majority view of statutory interpretation, which takes legislative history into account.

§ **3003.**   Mail bearing a fictitious name or address

(a) Upon evidence satisfactory to the Postal Service that any person is using a fictitious, false, or assumed name, title, or address in conducting, promoting, or carrying on or assisting therein, by means of the postal services of the United States, an activity in violation of sections 1302, 1341, and 1342 of title 18, it may—

(1) withhold mail so addressed from delivery; and

(2) require the party claiming the mail to furnish proof to it of the claimant's identity and right to receive the mail.

(b) The Postal Service may issue an order directing that mail, covered by subsection (a) of this section, be forwarded to a dead letter office as fictitious matter, or be returned to the sender when—

(1) the party claiming the mail fails to furnish proof of his identity and right to receive the mail; or

(2) the Postal Service determines that the mail is addressed to a fictitious, false, or assumed name, title, or address.

Pub.L. 91–375, Aug. 12, 1970, 84 Stat. 746.

Historical Note

Effective Date. Section effective July 1, 1971, pursuant to Resolution No. 71–9 of the Board of Governors. See section 15(a) of Pub.L. 91–375, set out as an Effective Date note preceding section 101 of this title.

Cross References

Fictitious name and address, penalty for using, see section 1342 of Title 18, Crimes and Criminal Procedure.

Library References

Post Office ⚮23.   C.J.S. Post Office § 31.

137

FIGURE 8-6   39 U.S.C.A. § 3003. (Reprinted with permission of West Publishing Company.)

corporation. However, consulting a legal dictionary reveals that the legal definition of *person* includes corporations.

Another analysis involves considering the law as a whole. This is called a **contextual analysis.** In a sense, the "four corners" of the statute or other referenced

---

contextual analysis   A method of legal analysis whereby disputed words are considered in light of the meaning of other similarly situated words or provisions.

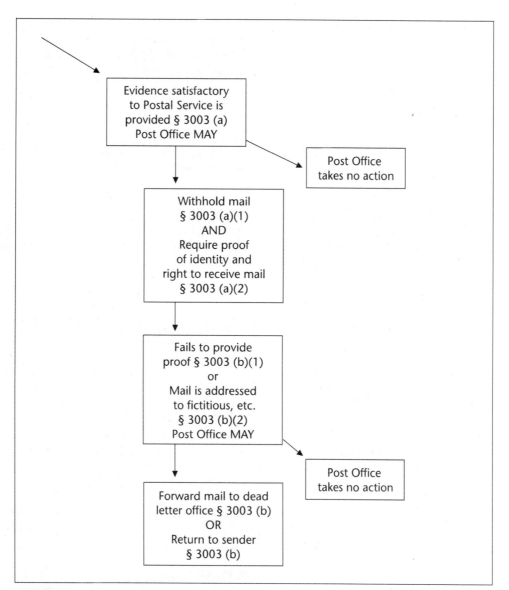

FIGURE 8-7   Chart of options in statute

statutes are examined to see if they assist in an understanding of a particular word or term. For instance, to completely comprehend 39 U.S.C.A. § 3003, you must also consult 18 U.S.C.A. §§ 1302, 1341, and 1342. The overall goal here is to make sure that various statutes do not conflict with one another. Interpretations should be sought that avoid conflict.

The third theory involves considering legislative history. This is especially helpful when the statute has never before been considered by a court. (This would be an example of a case of first impression.) The records of legislative committee hearings, committee reports, and debates on the floor of the legislature are among the sources for legislative history. What better place to find what congressional members intended than from their actual speeches and reports made during legislative sessions? As you recall, USCCAN is a good resource for federal legislative history.

Legal Analysis of Ordinances

Ordinances are passed by local levels of government: towns, cities, and counties. They deal primarily with functions best handled at the local level, such as zoning, business permits, and public education. They are rarely, if ever, housed in annotated publications. Because ordinances are set up similar to statutes, the same methods of analysis can be utilized.

Legal Analysis of Administrative Law

Administrative regulations have many of the same features as statutes. However, they are usually located in nonannotated codes. The fact that they are promulgated by agencies does not change the techniques of analysis to be employed. Separating the regulation into component parts can be helpful in gaining a complete comprehension. Because most regulations are enacted as a result of **enabling legislation** passed by legislatures, reading the corresponding statutory law is sometimes helpful in analyzing meaning.

Legal Analysis of Constitutional Law

Reading a constitution and using a plain meaning analysis might initially lead you to conclude that interpretation is clear. Nothing could be further from the truth.

The First Amendment of the U.S. Constitution provides that "Congress shall make no law respecting an establishment of religion, or prohibiting the free exercise thereof ... ." At first, this provision might seem straightforward and

---

LEGAL TERMS

enabling act (legislation) † 1. A statute that grants new powers or authority to persons or corporations. 2. A statute that gives the government the power to enforce other legislation or that carries out a provision of a constitution. The term also applies to a clause in a statute granting the government the power to enforce or carry out that statute.

thus not to require much analysis. However, constitutional analysis is not restricted to the document itself. It includes considering thousands of court opinions, mostly from the U.S. Supreme Court, that have interpreted its provisions under the authority of judicial review. Probably no document in history has been the subject of more political and judicial interpretation than the U.S. Constitution.

A major debate exists today in constitutional interpretation. Some legal scholars suggest that, when considering a provision, the intentions of the participants of the Constitutional Convention in 1787 should be the primary consideration. This is called the *original intent theory.* Another group believes that the U.S. Constitution is a *living document* that should be interpreted in light of current societal norms and expectations. For example, the Second Amendment appears to guarantee an unrestricted "right to bear arms." Those advocating original intent argue that this amendment guarantees every American the unfettered right to own a firearm, as was the case at the time of the drafting of the Second Amendment. However, most Americans and the current U.S. Supreme Court favor an interpretation that would grant individuals limited rights to own firearms, subject to reasonable and necessary restrictions by state and federal governments.

IRAC Method of Analysis

Law students and lawyers have long used a method of analyzing legal problems referred to as *IRAC.* IRAC is an acronym for issue, rule, application/analysis, and conclusion. This method is best used in answering a legal problem either as part of a work assignment or an examination question. The IRAC method could be employed when discussing in a document the legal principles of the *Knapp* case as they apply to the Ricardo problem.

The elements of IRAC are as follows.

Issue

When examining a legal problem or answering an exam question, the starting point is stating the issue to be considered. The issue is always stated as a question. It need not be complex, though sometimes this is unavoidable. To ensure precision, the issue might include facts pertinent to the case at bar. In the Ricardo case the issue was stated previously as:

> When parties are married and they, as well as the officiating clerk, believe that the clerk had proper authority to perform the ceremony, but it is later found that no such authority existed, is the marriage valid?

However, provided the facts are assumed, the shorter form is perfectly acceptable:

> Is the marriage valid?

Rule

The rule is the legal authority that will bring about a specific result desired by the client. Once a complete understanding of the facts and issues is achieved, location of applicable rules becomes the focus of research.

As a result of research, the rule in *Knapp v. Knapp* was determined to be appropriate. The rule could be stated as:

> Where persons are married in a ceremony by one whom they believe to be an ordained minister with authority to marry, who later is found to not have such authority, the marriage is nonetheless valid.

As you read previously, this is an application of the principle of apparent authority. A rule is any legal authority, whether mandatory or persuasive, that can be relied on to help answer the question presented. Rules are located not only in case law, but can also be found in statutes, ordinances, administrative regulations, and constitutional provisions.

Application/Analysis

In this step, the facts and law are, in a sense, melded together. The rule can be thought of as an equation. The formula must be tested with facts from the case at bar. If the test leads to a conclusion desired by the client, the rule works. If it does not lead to the preferred conclusion, a different rule must be found, if possible.

If the law is based on a statute, it will be necessary for you to analyze each and every element of the statute so that it can be tested with facts from the case at bar. If the law emanated from a case, you will want to show how the key facts in the case at bar are similar to the facts in the case being used as authority. Having done this, it would not be difficult then to conclude that the holding in that case controls your client's situation.

In considering the application of the *Knapp* case, you might indicate:

> In both the case at bar (the Ricardo matter) and the *Knapp* case, the parties reasonably believed they were married. Both officiating persons (in Ricardo a clerk and in *Knapp* a minister) honestly believed they had proper authority to perform the ceremony. In *Knapp* the court held that the marriage was valid. It follows, then, that the Ricardo marriage would likewise be held valid.

Conclusion

The "wrap-up" is found in the conclusion. Here you indicate what you believe the law justifies. It is your prediction of how the matter would be resolved by a court. In the Ricardo matter, the conclusion might be:

> Based on the holding in *Knapp v. Knapp*, it is my conclusion that the marriage of Mr. and Mrs. Ricardo is valid and legal.

Paralegal Tip

A good way to increase your analytical ability is to study written legal analyses made by others. Make sure you understand what their motivations are regarding the issues first.

Summary

- Legal analysis is the process of identifying and understanding legal principles and then applying these principles to factual situations.

- A rule embraces both factual conditions and a specific result.

- In a case opinion, holdings constitute the case's rules.

- For the principles in a case to be considered mandatory authority, the case must contain facts similar to the case at bar; its rules must relate to the same area of law as the case at bar; and it must emanate from the same jurisdiction as the case at bar.

- Cases not constituting mandatory authority are considered persuasive authority.

- Often a court will determine that an issue is moot and will not address it in a case opinion.

- Dictum is a court's commentary. As such, it does not respond to a legal issue and thus has no legal effect.

- Legal analysis of cases is helped by an objective summary of the case, known as a case brief.

- The components of a case brief are case identification, citation, parties, issues, facts, prior proceedings, holdings, reasoning, and judgment.

- To properly analyze a statute, reduce it to its component parts.

- Another way of understanding a statute is by interpreting its words literally.

- A contextual analysis looks at the four corners of the statute or other referenced statutes.

- Legislative history can also be a source for interpretation of a statute.

- Because they are drafted like statutes, administrative regulations and ordinances can be analyzed using the same methods employed for statutory law.

- The two theories of constitutional analysis are the original intent theory and the living document theory.

- One popular method of analysis used is referred to as IRAC. IRAC stands for issue, rule, application/analysis, and conclusion. It is best used when answering a legal problem or exam question.

Review Questions

1. Define legal analysis.

2. What are the component parts of a rule?

3. What is meant when a case is said to be on all fours with the case at bar?

4. Describe the criteria for mandatory authority.

5. Why is persuasive authority likely to be employed in a case of first impression?

6. What is dictum?

7. What are key facts? Why are they important?

8. Describe the types of briefs used in legal practice.

9. What are the two reasons for case briefing?

10. List the components of a case brief.

11. What are the two competing theories of constitutional analysis?

12. Describe the steps in the IRAC method.

Chapter Exercises

1. Prepare a case brief for *Stuart v. Board of Supervisors,* reprinted in Chapter 3. In the decision, the court refuses to decide an issue. What is that issue? Is this an application of the mootness doctrine?

2. Shepardize the case of *Knapp v. Knapp* to determine if it is still good law. What did you find?

3. Determine whether your state has a statute or common law principle similar to that applied in *Douglas v. Fulis.* Use a digest to accomplish this.

4. In your state code, locate the law concerning first-degree murder. Analyze the statute by breaking it down, as was done in this chapter with 39 U.S.C.A. § 3003.

5. Review the following provision of the U.S. Constitution:

   AMENDMENT VII: Excessive bail shall not be required, nor excessive fines imposed, nor cruel and unusual punishments inflicted.

   Consider this in light of the two competing theories of constitutional interpretation. If a state legislature enacted a law permitting "caning" for some offenses, would this law violate the Eighth Amendment?

6. Read either *Brown v. State,* 134 Ga. App. 771, 216 S.E.2d 356 (1975) or *Fisher v. Lowe,* 122 Mich. App. 418, 333 N.W.2d 67 (1983). Brief the case you have chosen using the same literary style as the court.

||||
CHAPTER 9

STRATEGIES FOR RESEARCH

OVERVIEW

Thus far this book's emphasis has been on introducing the various tools used to conduct legal research. In Chapter 8, legal analysis was introduced. Here, in discussing strategies for research, basic techniques needed to conduct legal research are examined.

A process for research was first introduced in Chapter 2. The Ricardo problem, dealing with the validity of a marriage ceremony, was used to demonstrate how such a plan could be implemented. This scenario was revisited in Chapter 8 to illustrate legal analysis. A detailed examination of the research plan applied to a different set of facts is the focus of this chapter. Now that the tools to conduct research have been covered, implementation of the plan should be easier to comprehend.

Before we address the plan, though, it is important to consider note taking. Suggestions are made for your use as a beginning researcher. Ultimately, however, you will develop your own style and method of note taking.

To review, successful research requires the implementation of a three-part process. As a threshold consideration, you must have a full understanding and appreciation of the legal problem at hand. This may be no easy task; you may have to undertake extensive follow-up with the client or the superior who made the assignment. Second, a sufficient understanding of the law is necessary. This, at a minimum, may require you to review a general text on the subject matter. A broad-based understanding of the basics of the legal specialty that applies brings confidence and provides structure to the research experience. Finally, actual researching is conducted. In most situations, this involves using secondary sources and primary law finders to locate primary law. Case law, in particular, can rarely be successfully researched by accessing reporters directly. Going to a primary law finder, such as a digest, is usually more efficient. Statutory law, however, can be accessed directly because codes are usually comprehensively indexed. Just the same, secondary sources are often preferred for locating statutes because they discuss laws in the context of their applicability.

In this chapter, four commonly known formulas for accessing legal materials are introduced: the Cartwheel, TAPP Rule, TARP Rule, and West's Descriptive Word Method. Though all are based on brainstorming, each is slightly different in its approach and thus its application.

Because the law is constantly evolving, verification of proper authority is of continual concern to the researcher. There are two aspects of verification: (1) checking for accuracy—whether the principle located has been correctly interpreted and used; and (2) validity—whether the legal principle remains applicable. Guidelines for completing these tasks are addressed in this chapter.

A final consideration in researching is knowing when to bring the research effort to a close. A number of factors may affect this decision, including time restraints, priority conflicts, and legal resource constraints.

PARALEGAL PRACTICE SITUATION

Your firm has been retained by Dr. B. Warren Krup, president of Smoke Free America, Inc. (SFA), a national antismoking organization. Recently, Dr. Krup was the guest on the Ray Lardbaugh radio call-in program. During the interview, Mr. Lardbaugh smoked cigarettes continuously and blew the smoke in Dr. Krup's direction. It is Dr. Krup's opinion that this was done intentionally. After the interview, Dr. Krup suffered from a headache and nausea for the remainder of the day. He also was required to have his suit dry cleaned.

SFA and Dr. Krup would like to take the radio station to court over the matter. Dr. Krup feels he was injured by the intentional smoking of Ray Lardbaugh. He is not interested only in monetary damages, but also in sending a message that would discourage similar activity and encourage smoking bans.

You are asked to conduct preliminary research to determine the feasibility of such a lawsuit.

Taking Effective Notes

The ability of an individual to retain and organize detailed information solely through memorization is limited. On average, most people can retain only seven items in short-term memory. Legal principles can be especially intricate and lengthy, and the differences between two case opinions can be minute. Consequently, relying exclusively on memory alone as a depository of legal research can be both foolish and dangerous. An effective method of note taking is essential to ensure the proper recollection and organization of material. Thus, it is imperative that you take effective written notations of your findings, leads, and even dead ends.

Besides the limitations on memorization, there are additional reasons justifying effective note taking. You must have a comprehensive and reliable record of your findings. Often a research assignment is interrupted by other, more pressing projects. If the completed work is written and well organized, picking up at a later date will not be difficult. Having a permanent record is also critical later when you transfer your findings into formal legal documents.

Maintaining focus is another reason. Keeping copious notes helps you focus on the task at hand, be it finding a simple legal definition or analyzing a complex legal issue. It is easy to get sidetracked in research. Because of the premium that law firms place on available research time, maintaining focus is critical.

There is no one method of note taking used throughout the legal profession. Law school students are rarely instructed as to the best methods of note taking. Only during initial employment do prospective attorneys receive insight and suggestions on note taking from experienced mentors. Of course, a "correct" method of note taking does not exist. Over time, each legal professional develops her own style, integrating valuable suggestions and discarding wasteful concepts.

Tools

Before you begin research, assemble the minimum basic tools: a pen and a writing pad. You may prefer to use a pencil so that you can erase when making changes. Unfortunately, when you are doing massive amounts of writing, a pen is easier to manage. Some researchers choose to use multicolored pens, each color signaling a different emphasis. To others, this might seem cumbersome.

REASONS FOR NOTE TAKING

1. Ability to memorize is limited
   - Legal principles are intricate and lengthy
   - Small differences may exist between two cases
2. Comprehensive record of findings is necessary
   - You or another can pick up from where you left off
   - Good notes are easier to transpose
3. Focus is maintained

Paralegal Tip

It might be risky to erase or discard material that at first glance seems inapplicable to the matter you are researching. When authority is located that at first appears not to be useful, save it separate from your other notes. After researching more or determining additional facts, the previously discarded authority may in fact turn out to be right on point. Unless saved you would be required to reconstruct the sources that you used. You will ask yourself: "Now where did I see that?" This can be a most frustrating experience!

The size of legal writing pads was traditionally 8½ inches wide by 14 inches long. This corresponded with the measurements of most other legal papers. However, today downsizing is the norm, with 8½ -inch by 11-inch paper used for nearly all documents. Likewise, the preferred writing tablet size is 8½ inches by 11 inches.

SIDEBAR   **CONFIDENTIALITY AND THE ENVIRONMENT**

Today, all businesses, including law offices, are becoming environmentally sensitive. Fortunately, most of the waste produced by legal professionals is easily recyclable, as pointed out in the following guest editorial.

However, confidentially is critical in the attorney-client relationship. Not only are oral discussions privileged, but the contents of many written documents must be kept confidential. Does this mean that you are not permitted to recycle your notes and other documents containing private information? You can, but you must carefully ensure confidentiality. For instance, in 1992, the North Carolina State Bar Association issued an ethics opinion (No. 133) that allowed lawyers to recycle paper products containing confidential matters, provided the lawyer ascertains that the recycler's procedures minimize the risk of disclosure. The opinion said that there may be occasions when confidential material is so sensitive that it cannot be recycled.

Many researchers typically employ index cards to record their notes and keep them well organized. This appears to be encouraged in English composition classes. Unfortunately, it is more difficult to get an aggregate picture of the

G U E S T   E D I T O R I A L

A Tree Hugger's Lament

John F. Rohe

John F. Rohe is a sole practitioner in Petoskey. A 1977 graduate of Thomas M. Cooley Law School, he is involved in a number of conservation projects in Northern Michigan. Reproduced with permission of the author. Further reproduction without permission is strictly prohibited.

Do you know the type? Unwilling to use a fresh sheet of paper, they retrieve indecipherable messages inscribed on fragmented corners of restaurant napkins from their pockets. They'll also jot you a message on the reverse side of junk mail, type a two-page letter on the front and back of a single sheet of paper, or fax a note on a fractional page. We're often called tree huggers. There is a measure of truth to the appellation.

Even if you are not a dedicated conservationist, at least some of the following suggestions can improve your efficiency, save you money, and, at the same time conserve paper. They might also endear you to your clients. Many, if not most, clients will conscientiously reuse their grocery bags and recycle newspapers. To such clients, unnecessary consumption of paper may be considered an affront. Thus, whether inspired by concern for the ecology, or motivated by sound marketing principles, paper conservation efforts make good sense for the legal professional. It's only reasonable for a client to expect that concern for the world around us reflects sympathy for their cause.

Easily implemented paper-saving techniques include the following:

Captions. A plethora of captions unnecessarily enhances the volume of a legal document. The caption on a motion is not required to be duplicated on the supporting affidavit, brief, the notice of hearing and again on the proof of service. A single caption can reference all components of a legal document. This will also minimize the risk of an accidental paper shuffle when the document is organized for mailing. The caption of a case with numerous parties only requires "... the name of the first party on each side with an appropriate indication of other parties, such as et al." MCR 2.113(D). The limited purpose of captions can typically be well served on less than a full page.

Redundancies. How often does the affidavit supporting a motion merely duplicate the motion itself? Such duplications could be considered offensive by a court buried beneath an overburdened docket. A supporting affidavit of this sort can simply attest to the accuracy of the "facts stated in the preceding motion." This practice demonstrates respect for not only the value of paper, but also of the court's time.

Page Formatting. A minute quantity of writing on the last page of a letter can often be consolidated in the preceding page by minor formatting changes to the side or top margins.

Type Face. Using a 12 cpi (characters per inch) rather than the 10 cpi type face will reduce paper quantities by as much as 20%. Twelve cpi is larger than the print in the *Michigan Bar Journal*.

Flip Side. Paper consumption is reduced 50% by discovering the reverse side of a sheet of paper. Where in the court rules does it say that we can only use one side of a sheet of paper? Where in the rules of jurisprudential etiquette is it said that one side of a sheet of paper must always remain blank? How does one select which side of a sheet of paper merits the craft of our trade? Paper consumption norms have been developed in a world without perceptible limits. As we become more sensitive to the transition to sustainability, it is understandable that our norms will also undergo a reevaluation. One of the first conventions to be discarded is the notion that one-half of all trees must be needlessly sacrificed to perpetuate the tradition than one-half of the paper must remain unblemished.

Reused Paper. A law office accumulates an incredible volume of unsolicited junk mail with printing on only one side. If a client regularly engages in the underrated activity of simply walking their dog through the woods, they are likely to develop a bonding relationship with their neighbors in the forest. Before long they will be knowledgeable of characteristics of vegetation in high-water table areas, growth patterns of the hemlock, characteristics of the canopy, diversity of life on decaying trees, and the list goes on.

No amount of advertising can duplicate the goodwill generated with this client by reusing the blank side of your junk mail. Office practices can make a compassionate statement for conservation. Recently, clients expressed their appreciation of our reusing the flip side of junk mail by sending their payment in a reused envelope. Admittedly, remolding the reverse side of junk mail into a cherished legal product is perhaps not yet a conservation technique to be used on the client with a fainthearted commitment to our natural resources and future generations. On the other hand, some clients may be offended if we use virgin paper on their legal projects. Even if you are not ready to reuse paper in client correspondence, it could be used in preparing a rough draft for review and correction.

Double Spacing. Word processing systems allow line spacing at finite increments. Where an expanded view is either warranted or required, word processing systems will allow spacing less than double. In other words, one and a half spacing may fulfill the objectives of double spacing. Double-spacing is, however, sometimes required. See, e.g., MCR 7.212(B).

Internal Memos. Even the reverse side of confidential documents may be cut into note pads for internal use only.

Note Pads. 8½″ × 11″ note pads (or even the more anachronistic 8½″ × 14″) frequently provide more space than is needed to document a particular meeting or phone conference. 5″ × 7″ miniature legal pads with perforated tops suffice

for most cases. They have the added advantage of conveniently fitting in the inside pocket of most sport coats.

Proof of Service. To avoid repeating names and addresses, a proof of service may be abbreviated to one or two lines by referencing the names of appearing parties or attorneys listed beneath the caption, as required by MCR 2.113(C).

Plain Language. As if there aren't already enough good reasons to avoid obsolete formalisms and redundancies, here are two more: your pocketbook and paper conservation.

Depositions. Most court reporters have computer programs enabling them to provide "condensed transcripts" which reduce four pages of text to a single page. It's less time consuming to locate a section of text when rummaging through fewer pages. Paper transcripts can even be entirely eliminated by requesting the reporter to only provide a floppy disk. The disks are functionally superior because they allow us to "search" for a section of text with incredible speed and precision. The search for truth can be enhanced when the cross examiner is armed with computerized transcripts. Deposition transcripts can also be shortened by going off the record for extended nonsubstantive intervals, e.g., when documents are organized. Eliminating such nonsubstantive, tedious sections is also welcome relief for the reader.

Signatures. Where in the court rules is it stated that a motion must be "Respectfully submitted" under a separate signature from the brief, and another "Respectfully submitted" signature for the Notice of Hearing? There is no reason that a single signature cannot be used for all components of a document (with the exception of an affidavit).

Cover Page. In many instances, the cover page has no substantive value. Explaining the identity of a self-explanatory enclosure may be considered an insult to the intelligence of a literate client. A cordial handwritten message on a Post-it brand note is often a suitable substitute.

Fax Cover. The endless ooze spewing from a fax machine is unnecessarily enhanced by the typical 8½″ × 11″ cover sheets. The 1.5″ × 4″ Post-it brand fax transmittal memos commonly suffice.

Heavy Bond. Use of heavy bond paper is an anachronistic tribute to the bygone era of unlimited forests. Thinner, lightweight, recycled paper can communicate a sense of accountability and responsibility to caring clients.

Billing Copies. Retaining hard copies of monthly billings is an unnecessary duplication of material already stored in the computer. Your lower desk drawer can probably store over 50 years of billings on floppy disks. There is no need to stretch the limits of your legal archives with hard copies of all billings when copies on floppy disks are functionally superior and more readily accessible. In our office, the paper storage area is euphemistically referred to as the "archives." Our interior decorator more accurately characterizes it as one notch above a haunted bat cave. Eliminating unnecessary trips to the archives is truly a noble goal.

Recycling. All papers in an office can be recycled. Bonded recyclers will preserve the confidentiality of privileged information. Even though not all paper is harvested from the rain forest, the mere removal of timber from tree farms can lead to soil erosion and nutrient depletion. Fertilizer is only a short-term fix for the symbiotic relationships among the diversity of life thriving on decaying trees. Recycling simply makes good common sense.

Modem. Communications between law offices can often be consummated by modem. Admittedly, it may be necessary to await a new generation of computer literacy and the standardization of software before the modem offers a universally accepted means of transmission. But, if the machines can speak to one another why not let them, and save the paper? Nothing in the court rules prohibits a stipulation allowing electronic service of papers.

Disks. Where law offices are known to use similar computer software programs, or where they have conversion programs, a floppy disk with lengthy documentation may be mailed. In the interest of professional civility, by mailing the floppy disk, your opponent is relieved of the obligation to retype all of the questions in your interrogatories. Most offices would be willing to stipulate to the receipt of a disk in lieu of the more labor-intensive written interrogatory copies. See MCR 2.302(F).

Fax. The need to document a matter can often be accomplished by faxing a correspondence. For every such telecopy, another envelope is spared. Fractional sheets of reused paper are ideal for this purpose.

Proofreading. By networking your computer with your support staff, it is possible to proofread documents at your terminal. I find that minor revisions are well within my rudimentary typing capabilities.

Envelopes. Envelopes may be eliminated by placing a stamp and address on the exterior of a folded and stapled paper. This technique is particularly useful when mass mailing non-confidential information on charitable projects.

CD-ROM. A handful of CD-ROMs have the capacity of a massive legal library. Technology now enables us to search the equivalent of a library shelf in a matter of seconds from a desktop computer. The paper waste stream generated by obsolete law books and updates can be entirely eliminated by CD-ROM libraries. It's just a matter of time before law offices are liberated from cumbersome and difficult-to-update law books. The waste stream originating from law offices can be substantially reduced by substituting cases, digests and statutes with the CD-ROMs which are now becoming available. If you enjoy channel surfing with your TV-remote, CD-ROMs hold promising opportunities for you.

Incentives. Typically, the personnel most capable of identifying paper-saving measures are not necessarily the attorneys, but the support staff. Incentives, such as an afternoon off, etc., may be used to reward the staff member submitting the best paper-saving measure.

The ideas expressed in this article are just the beginning. A paper conserving discipline can be made compatible with the idiosyncrasies of every office. Paper reduction is not only environmentally sound, but it also makes good business sense.

In some environmental circles it is said that Americans wipe their noses on their ancient forests. Most of us would take umbrage to extending this analogy to the legal profession, yet the point is well taken. Paper conservation promotes a valuable symbiotic relationship with natural resources. There's no reason for legal professionals to be bringing up the rear on conservation efforts currently sweeping the country. Environmental panache and savior faire are likely to translate into grateful recognition by the client. It's tough for a client to be critical of your efforts to build a better world. ▟

---

entire problem and its possible ramifications with index cards. Consequently, writing tablets are preferred in legal research.

Small laptop computers may eventually be of great assistance in conducting research. When permitted, many legal professionals take laptops with them into law libraries. Unfortunately, their current cost limits most researchers from taking advantage of this new technology. As laptops become more affordable, their use will become a more frequent occurrence.

Note Taking

Assume at this point that you have a sufficient understanding of the facts and primary issue. Dr. Krup's problem was most likely presented to you as follows: "I want you to find out if cigarette smoking can constitute the tort of **battery**." Your attorney either orally informed you of the facts or presented them to you in a short missive.

At the top of the first page of the writing tablet, indicate the client's name, the date, and, if it is necessary to keep a time sheet, the starting time. The facts provided, as well as the relief requested by the client, should then be recorded. Using abbreviations for terms and shorthand can be helpful. For instance, K is used to mean contract, T is used to mean tort, P means plaintiff, and D means defendant. Should you discover additional facts at a later date, they can be easily integrated. Leave this as the fact page (see Figure 9-1). On the second page, indicate the issue or the most significant issue if there are multiple issues (sometimes called subissues). In multiple-issue assignments, the first question will likely be a *foundation question,* one that must be resolved prior to examining other issues. It might deal with the constitutionality of a law or the standing of a client to bring suit. Whether cigarette smoking can constitute a battery and hence a cause of action is a foundation issue in our sample case that must be

---

────────────────────── **LEGAL TERMS** ──────────────────────

battery † The unconsented-to touching or striking of one person by another, or by an object put in motion by [the other], with the intention of doing harm or giving offense. Battery is both a crime and a tort.

5/1   Krup, B.W.

2:00

Krup (P) guest on Lardbaugh Show (D)
D smokes, blows at P
P suffers headache, nausea

P wants $ and message sent
discouraging smoking

FIGURE 9-1   Page one of notepad, with facts

answered first. An affirmative answer would necessitate research on the following issues: Who is the proper plaintiff, Dr. Krup individually or Smoke Free America? What types of damages are possible? Is Ray Lardbaugh personally liable, or is only the radio station liable? If smoking does not constitute a tort, there may be no need to explore the other issues. Usually for purposes of initial research, you must assume that the foundation issue can be answered favorably. Later on you can eliminate issues based on their lack of viability.

On the third page, list the second issue; on the fourth page, the third issue; and so forth until every issue has been accounted for (see Figure 9-2). The balance of each page is devoted to note taking.

Taking notes must be carefully done. It is important to correctly record legal principles in a neat and clear fashion. Too often, valuable research is lost merely because of sloppy handwriting.

5/1   Krup, B.W.

Does the intentional smoking of
cigarettes constitute battery?

FIGURE 9-2   Notepad page showing issue

Finally, it is important to indicate the full and correct citation for each authority used. You should not have to go back at the end of the research process to verify sources; they should be recorded correctly the first time.

Application of the Research Plan

Step One: Understanding the Problem

Before you commence research, it is important that you have a firm understanding of the legal problem at hand and its ramifications. You need to know *why* this concern is important. This may involve seeking additional key or context facts from either the client or the attorney making the assignment. Recall that *key facts* are facts that will affect the final outcome of the research; *context facts* help you to humanize and understand the situation. Context facts include the parties' names, dates, place names, and the like.

Suppose further investigation revealed that, as a result of the smoking incident, Dr. Krup developed an allergic reaction resulting in his hospitalization. Because this might affect the damage award and therefore the final outcome of the case, it is a key fact. As such, it should be added to the fact page.

Step Two: Understanding the Law

Step two involves acquiring an understanding of the law. Your prior knowledge in the area will dictate how extensive an understanding will be necessary. For an experienced paralegal, just knowing where to turn in the event of difficulties might be sufficient. The novice researcher will need to review a basic resource in the area prior to starting work. A basic text, such as a hornbook or Nutshell, will provide a broad overview of the extent and scope of the law.

In the instant case, you may want to obtain an understanding of the legal definition of the tort of battery. Knowing that a battery consists of offensive contact by one person upon any part of the body of another would be important. The instrumentality could be a part of the defendant or a weapon of contact such as a knife or club. The ultimate question is whether smoke can be a weapon of contact. Furthermore, the law says that actual physical injury is not required—unpermitted contact is enough. Though the plaintiff need not prove loss or damage, injury is essential to be entitled to a monetary award. These elements would certainly be covered in a hornbook such as *Prosser and Keeton on the Law of Torts* or West's *Torts in a Nutshell.*

You should list the elements of battery and the sources you used. It is also beneficial to note sources and legal principles that were *not* helpful. This way, if another paralegal must continue or assist in the research, he will not have to reconsider ground that you already covered.

TYPICAL SOURCES FOR TORT LAW UNDERSTANDING

Torts in a Nutshell (2d ed. 1992)	*Prosser and Keeton on the Law of Torts* (5th ed. 1984)
	CJS
Am. Jur. 2d	*Restatement (Second) of Torts*
State legal encyclopedia	

Step Three: Conducting Legal Research

In the final step, the actual techniques of legal research are utilized. Through the application of various methods, you access legal resources to locate legal answers.

In legal research, the ultimate goal is to secure primary law that has mandatory effect and that brings about a favorable result for your client. When applicable mandatory authority cannot be located, persuasive authority can be used to convince a court of the client's position. It is important that you never settle for applying principles found in secondary sources or primary law finders. These materials only comment on, analyze, or summarize the law. They do not have the effect of law.

As a researcher, you will employ primary law finders and secondary law sources as a means of locating primary law. Using sources such as digests and legal encyclopedias is the key to locating appropriate case opinions and statutes. If these resources can be bypassed, it is likely because the primary law source is well indexed. Examples of primary law with good indexes include statutory codes and administrative regulatory compilations.

A second consideration is that the law used to support your argument should be mandatory authority. Recall that to constitute mandatory authority, the law must be from a jurisdiction that has binding effect, the substantive area of law must be the same as the case at bar, and, finally, the key facts considered in the authority must be the same as in the case at bar. In the end, your findings will consist of either mandatory authority (in which situation the answer will be easy to determine), or persuasive authority from other jurisdictions.

Through the use of various methodologies that focus on factual understanding, you learn where and how to begin the research process. Each method is premised on employing your creative abilities to locate answers. All methods take the form of word association games. Each requires that you utilize "brainstorming" to create an exhaustive list of terms that can be used to access legal sources.

Once a word list has been created, you then use secondary sources and primary law finders to find appropriate authority. Review Chapters 4 and 5 to refresh your understanding on how to use a particular resource.

THREE-STEP PROCESS

STEP ONE: Understanding the Problem

- Get more facts from Dr. Krup
- Why is this issue important to the client?
- Additional injuries

STEP TWO: Understanding the Law

- Use secondary sources to understand tort Law

STEP THREE: Conducting Legal Research

- Apply the techniques of research to look for primary law that is mandatory authority

The Cartwheel

William P. Statsky, in his book *Legal Research and Writing: Some Starting Points* (4th ed. 1993), recommends use of the *Cartwheel*. Described as "a word-association technique," the object of this method is to put major words related to the problem into multiple alternative words and phrases. The researcher uses important or significant words in the client's problem to find other words that can be used to access indexes, encyclopedias, and other sources.

The first step is to determine a word or phrase that most aptly describes the legal problem. This will often be a nonlegal phrase such as, in the example from the paralegal practice situation, *cigarette smoke*. This phrase is then placed in the center of the Cartwheel. Each of the eight spokes of the Cartwheel represents either contexts of the phrase or a synonym or antonym (see Figure 9-3). Applying the steps to the phrase *cigarette smoke* would result in the following.

1. Identify broader words or phrases that describe cigarette smoke: *battery, assault, nuisance, pollution, smoke.*
2. Identify narrower words or phrases that describe cigarette smoke: *burning, fire, heat, cigarette.*
3. Identify synonyms for cigarette smoke: *pipe smoke, cigar smoke, marijuana smoke, tobacco smoke.*
4. Identify antonyms for cigarette smoke: *smokeless cigarette, fresh air.*
5. Identify words or phrases closely related to cigarette smoke: *lung cancer, emphysema, heart disease, second-hand smoke, health problems.*
6. Identify procedural terms related to cigarette smoke: *injunction, ban, damages, tort.*
7. Identify agencies (public and private) that might deal with cigarette smoke: Department of Health and Human Services, U.S. Surgeon General, health department, fire department, American Cancer Society.

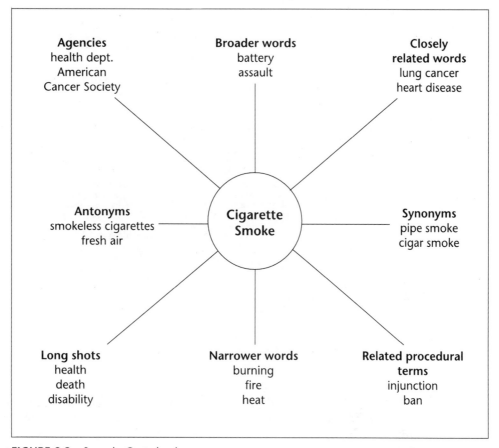

FIGURE 9-3 Sample Cartwheel

8. Identify "long-shot" words related (but not very closely) to cigarette smoke: *health, death, disability.*

Standard English dictionaries and thesauri can be helpful resources in searching for related words and phrases. Because categories overlap, the words listed are often repeated. Once a complete list of words is obtained, secondary sources and primary law finders can be utilized to locate definitions and principles related to the terms.

The descriptive word index of a West digest might be an appropriate starting place. You would start by picking a word or words that you feel are most likely to be used by the index to describe or categorize cigarette smoking. For instance, if from the Cartwheel you used "assault and battery," you would be led to a Topic and Key Number entry from Ohio that addresses your issue (see Figure 9-4).

You would then locate and read the case of *Leichtman v. WLW Jacor Communications,* 92 Ohio App. 3d 232, 634 N.E.2d 697 (1994) (see Figure 9-5).

⟨⟩2 ASSAULT & BATTERY

(A) ACTS CONSTITUTING ASSAULT OR BATTERY AND LIABILITY THEREFOR.

⟨⟩2. —— In general.

Ohio 1994. Cause of action premised upon acts of sexual abuse is subject to one-year statute of limitations for assault and battery.—Ault v. Jasko, 637 N.E.2d 870, 70 Ohio St.3d 114.

Ohio App. 1 Dist. 1994. Radio talk show guest stated "battery" claim against host by alleging that, at host's urging, second host repeatedly blew cigar smoke in guest's face. R.C. §§ 3704.01(B), 5709.20(A).—Leichtman v. WLW Jacor Communications, Inc., 634 N.E.2d 697, 92 Ohio App.3d 232.

Radio talk show guest stated claim for "battery" against radio station by alleging that he was invited to appear on talk show to discuss full effects of smoking and breathing secondary smoke and that, while in studio, talk show host lit cigar and repeatedly blew smoke in guest's face. R.C. §§ 3704.01(B), 5709.20(A).—Id.

FIGURE 9-4 Digest entry. (Reprinted with the permission of West Publishing Company.)

The next step would be to apply the principles of legal analysis from Chapter 8. You should brief the case to achieve a better understanding. After comparing it with Dr. Krup's situation, the *Leichtman* case appears very helpful. If Dr. Krup were in Ohio, the case would be *on all fours*: primary law that is mandatory authority. If you are in another jurisdiction, you would have a case representing persuasive authority.

The benefit of the Cartwheel method is that it presupposes no legal knowledge before application. In addition, it requires you to think about the problem in uncommon ways. On the down side, developing a complete Cartwheel is time-consuming. Nonetheless, for a beginning researcher it is probably the best method, because of its comprehensiveness.

TAPP Rule

A second research technique is the *TAPP Rule*. Developed by Lawyers Cooperative Publishing, the TAPP Rule is also referred to as the "fact/word approach." It was designed to be used with LCP publications such as ALR and Am. Jur. 2d. TAPP is an acronym standing for: *T*hing, *A*ct, *P*erson, and *P*lace. The method is premised on the belief that the researcher should be able to find the law by looking up terms representing those elements, which are present in nearly every legal problem. Applying the TAPP Rule to Dr. Krup's case would result in many of the same words located using the Cartwheel.

LEICHTMAN v. WLW JACOR COMMUNICATIONS, INC.   Ohio **697**
Cite as 634 N.E.2d 697 (Ohio App. 1 Dist. 1994)

92 Ohio App.3d 232

|232|LEICHTMAN, Appellant,

v.

WLW JACOR COMMUNICATIONS,
INC. et al., Appellees.

No. C–920922.

Court of Appeals of Ohio,
Hamilton County.

Decided Jan. 26, 1994.

Radio talk show guest (an antismoking advocate) sued radio talk show hosts and radio station for battery, invasion of privacy, and violation of municipal regulation making it illegal to smoke in designated public places. Guest alleged that he was invited to appear on talk show to discuss full effects of smoking and breathing secondary smoke and that, at host's urging, second host lit cigar and repeatedly blew smoke in guest's face. The Court of Common Pleas, Hamilton County, dismissed action for failure to state claim. Guest appealed. The Court of Appeals held that: (1) guest stated claim for battery; (2) guest failed to state claim for invasion of privacy; and (3) there is no private right of action for violation of municipal regulation.

Affirmed in part, reversed and remanded in part.

1. Pretrial Procedure ⚬⟶679

When construing complaint for failure to state claim, court assumes that factual allegations on face of complaint are true. Rules Civ.Proc., Rule 12(B)(6).

2. Pretrial Procedure ⚬⟶622

Court cannot dismiss complaint for failure to state claim merely because it doubts plaintiff will prevail. Rules Civ.Proc., Rule 12(B)(6).

3. Assault and Battery ⚬⟶24(1)

Antismoking advocate sufficiently alleged that radio talk show host committed "battery" by intentionally blowing cigar smoke in advocate's face when advocate was in studio to discuss harmful effects of smoking and breathing secondary smoke. R.C. §§ 3704.01(B), 5709.20(A).

See publication Words and Phrases for other judicial constructions and definitions.

|233|**4. Assault and Battery** ⚬⟶2

Radio talk show guest stated "battery" claim against host by alleging that, at host's urging, second host repeatedly blew cigar smoke in guest's face. R.C. §§ 3704.01(B), 5709.20(A).

5. Master and Servant ⚬⟶302(1)

Employer is not legally responsible for intentional torts of its employees that do not facilitate or promote its business.

6. Master and Servant ⚬⟶332(2)

Whether employer is liable under doctrine of respondent superior because its employee is acting within scope of employment is ordinarily question of fact.

7. Assault and Battery ⚬⟶2

Master and Servant ⚬⟶302(3)

Radio talk show guest stated claim for "battery" against radio station by alleging that he was invited to appear on talk show to discuss full effects of smoking and breathing secondary smoke and that, while in studio, talk show host lit cigar and repeatedly blew smoke in guest's face. R.C. §§ 3704.01(B), 5709.20(A).

8. Torts ⚬⟶8.5(4)

Antismoking advocate failed to state claim against radio talk show hosts and radio station for tortious invasion of privacy by alleging that he appeared on first host's radio talk show to discuss harmful effects of smoking and breathing secondary smoke, and that second host, at first host's prompting, lit cigar and repeatedly blew smoke in guest's face, as there was no substantial intrusion into guest's solicitude, seclusion, habitation, or affairs; guest willingly entered studio to make public radio appearance with first host, who was known for his blowtorch rhetoric.

FIGURE 9-5 *Leichtman v. WLW Jacor Communications.* (Reprinted with permission of West Publishing Company.)

698 Ohio   **634 NORTH EASTERN REPORTER, 2d SERIES**

9. Action ⬦3

Health and Environment ⬦25.15(4.1)

There is no private right of action under municipal regulation that makes it illegal to smoke in designated public places.

Kircher, Robinson, Cook, Newman & Welch and Robert B. Newman, Cincinnati, for appellant.

Strauss & Troy and William K. Flynn, Cincinnati, for appellees WLW Jacor Communications, Inc. and William Cunningham.

Waite, Schneider, Bayless & Chesley, Stanley M. Chesley and Paul M. DeMarco, Cincinnati, for appellee Andy Furman.

⌊234PER CURIAM.

The plaintiff-appellant, Ahron Leichtman, appeals from the trial court's order dismissing his complaint against the defendants-appellees, WLW Jacor Communications ("WLW"), William Cunningham and Andy Furman, for battery, invasion of privacy, and a violation of Cincinnati Bd. of Health Reg. No. 00083. In his single assignment of error, Leichtman contends that his complaint was sufficient to state a claim upon which relief could be granted and, therefore, the trial court was in error when it granted the defendants' Civ.R. 12(B)(6) motion. We agree in part.

In his complaint, Leichtman claims to be "a nationally known" antismoking advocate. Leichtman alleges that, on the date of the Great American Smokeout, he was invited to appear on the WLW Bill Cunningham radio talk show to discuss the harmful effects of smoking and breathing secondary smoke. He also alleges that, while he was in the

studio, Furman, another WLW talk-show host, lit a cigar and repeatedly blew smoke in Leichtman's face "for the purpose of causing physical discomfort, humiliation and distress."

[1, 2] Under the rules of notice pleading, Civ.R. 8(A)(1) requires only "a short and plain statement of the claim showing that the pleader is entitled to relief." When construing a complaint for failure to state a claim, under Civ.R. 12(B)(6), the court assumes that the factual allegations on the face of the complaint are true. *O'Brien v. Univ. Community Tenants Union, Inc.* (1975), 42 Ohio St.2d 242, 71 O.O.2d 223, 327 N.E.2d 753, syllabus. For the court to grant a motion to dismiss, "it must appear beyond doubt from the complaint that the plaintiff can prove no set of facts entitling him to recovery." *Id.* A court cannot dismiss a complaint under Civ.R. 12(B)(6) merely because it doubts the plaintiff will prevail. *Slife v. Kundtz Properties, Inc.* (1974), 40 Ohio App.2d 179, 69 O.O.2d 178, 318 N.E.2d 557. Because it is so easy for the pleader to satisfy the standard of Civ.R. 8(A), few complaints are subject to dismissal. *Id.* at 182, 69 O.O.2d at 180, 318 N.E.2d at 560.

Leichtman contends that Furman's intentional act constituted a battery. The Restatement of the Law 2d, Torts (1965), states:

"An actor is subject to liability to another for battery if

"(a) he acts intending to cause a harmful or offensive contact with the person of the other * * *, and

"(b) a harmful contact with the person of the other directly or indirectly results[; or] [1]

⌊235"[c] an offensive contact with the person of the other directly or indirectly results." [2] (Footnote added.)

---

1. Harmful contact: Restatement of the Law 2d, Torts (1965) 25, Section 13, cited with approval in *Love v. Port Clinton* (1988), 37 Ohio St.3d 98, 99, 524 N.E.2d 166, 167.

2. Offensive contact: Restatement, *supra,* at 30, Section 18. See, generally, *Love* at 99–100, 524 N.E.2d at 167, in which the court: (1) referred to battery as "intentional, offensive touching"; (2) defined offensive contact as that which is "offensive to a reasonable sense of personal dignity"; and (3) commented that if "an arrest is made by

a mere touching * * * the touching is offensive and, unless privileged, is a 'battery.'" *Id.,* 37 Ohio St.3d at 99, 524 N.E.2d at 167, fn. 3. See, also, *Schultz v. Elm Beverage Shoppe* (1988), 40 Ohio St.3d 326, 328, 533 N.E.2d 349, 352, fn. 2 (citing Restatement, *supra,* at 22, Chapter 2, Introductory Note), in which the court identified an interest in personality as "freedom from offensive bodily contacts"; *Keister v. Gaker* (Nov. 8, 1978), Warren App. Nos. 219 and 223, unreported (battery is offensive touching).

FIGURE 9-5   *(continued)*

LEICHTMAN v. WLW JACOR COMMUNICATIONS, INC.   Ohio **699**
Cite as 634 N.E.2d 697 (Ohio App. 1 Dist. 1994)

[3] In determining if a person is liable for a battery, the Supreme Court has adopted the rule that "[c]ontact which is offensive to a reasonable sense of personal dignity is offensive contact." *Love v. Port Clinton* (1988), 37 Ohio St.3d 98, 99, 524 N.E.2d 166, 167. It has defined "offensive" to mean "disagreeable or nauseating or painful because of outrage to taste and sensibilities or affronting insultingness." *State v. Phipps* (1979), 58 Ohio St.2d 271, 274, 12 O.O.3d 273, 275, 389 N.E.2d 1128, 1131. Furthermore, tobacco smoke, as "particulate matter," has the physical properties capable of making contact. R.C. 3704.01(B) and 5709.20(A); Ohio Adm. Code 3745–17.

[4] As alleged in Leichtman's complaint, when Furman intentionally blew cigar smoke in Leichtman's face, under Ohio common law, he committed a battery. No matter how trivial the incident, a battery is actionable, even if damages are only one dollar. *Lacey v. Laird* (1956), 166 Ohio St. 12, 1 O.O.2d 158, 139 N.E.2d 25, paragraph two of the syllabus. The rationale is explained by Roscoe Pound in his essay "Liability": "[I]n civilized society men must be able to assume that others will do them no intentional injury— that others will commit no intentioned aggressions upon them." Pound, An Introduction to the Philosophy of Law (1922) 169.

Other jurisdictions also have concluded that a person can commit a battery by intentionally directing tobacco smoke at another. *Richardson v. Hennly* (1993), 209 Ga.App. 868, 871, 434 S.E.2d 772, 774–775. We do not, however, adopt or lend credence to the theory of a "smoker's battery," which imposes liability if there is substantial certainty that exhaled smoke will predictably contact a nonsmoker. Ezra, Smoker Battery: An Antidote to Second–Hand Smoke (1990), 63 S.Cal.L.Rev. 1061, 1090. Also, whether the "substantial certainty" prong of intent from the Restatement of Torts translates to liability for secondary smoke via the intentional tort doctrine in employment cases as defined by the Supreme ⌊₂₉₆Court in *Fyffe v. Jeno's, Inc.* (1991), 59 Ohio St.3d 115, 570 N.E.2d 1108, paragraph one of the syllabus, need not be decided here because Leichtman's claim for battery is based exclusively on Furman's

commission of a deliberate act. Finally, because Leichtman alleges that Furman deliberately blew smoke into his face, we find it unnecessary to address offensive contact from passive or secondary smoke under the "glass cage" defense of *McCracken v. Sloan* (1979), 40 N.C.App. 214, 217, 252 S.E.2d 250, 252, relied on by the defendants.

Neither Cunningham nor WLW is entitled to judgment on the battery claim under Civ.R. 12(B)(6). Concerning Cunningham, at common law, one who is present and encourages or incites commission of a battery by words can be equally liable as a principal. *Bell v. Miller* (1831), 5 Ohio 250; 6 Ohio Jurisprudence 3d (1978) 121–122, Assault, Section 20. Leichtman's complaint states, "At Defendant Cunningham's urging, Defendant Furman repeatedly blew cigar smoke in Plaintiff's face."

[5–7] With regard to WLW, an employer is not legally responsible for the intentional torts of its employees that do not facilitate or promote its business. *Osborne v. Lyles* (1992), 63 Ohio St.3d 326, 329–330, 587 N.E.2d 825, 828–829. However, whether an employer is liable under the doctrine of *respondeat superior* because its employee is acting within the scope of employment is ordinarily a question of fact. *Id.* at 330, 587 N.E.2d at 825. Accordingly, Leichtman's claim for battery with the allegations against the three defendants in the second count of the complaint is sufficient to withstand a motion to dismiss under Civ.R. 12(B)(6).

[8] By contrast, the first and third counts of Leichtman's complaint do not state claims upon which relief can be granted. The trial court correctly granted the Civ.R. 12(B)(6) motion as to both counts. In his first count, Leichtman alleged a tortious invasion of his privacy. See, generally, Restatement, *supra,* at 376, Section 652B, as adopted by *Sustin v. Fee* (1982), 69 Ohio St.2d 143, 145, 23 O.O.3d 182, 183–184, 431 N.E.2d 992, 993. A claim for invasion of privacy may involve any one of four distinct torts. Prosser, Privacy (1960), 48 Cal.L.Rev. 383. The tort that is relevant here requires some substantial intrusion into a plaintiff's solitude, seclusion, habitation, or affairs that would be highly

FIGURE 9-5 *(continued)*

700 Ohio   **634 NORTH EASTERN REPORTER, 2d SERIES**

offensive to a reasonable person. See, *e.g.*, Restatement, *supra*, at 378–379, Section 652B, Comments *a* to *d*; *Killilea v. Sears Roebuck & Co.* (1985), 27 Ohio App.3d 163, 166, 27 OBR 196, 198–199, 499 N.E.2d 1291, 1294. Leichtman acknowledges that he willingly entered the WLW radio studio to make a public radio appearance with Cunningham, who is known for his blowtorch rhetoric. Therefore, Leichtman's[237] allegations do not support his assertion that Furman, Cunningham, or WLW intruded into his privacy.

[9] In his third count, Leichtman attempts to create a private right of action for violation of Cincinnati Bd. of Health Reg. No. 00083, which makes it illegal to smoke in designated public places. Even if we are to assume, for argument, that a municipal regulation is tantamount to public policy established by a statute enacted by the General Assembly, the regulation has created rights for nonsmokers that did not exist at common law. Bd. of Health Reg., *supra*, at Sections 00083–7 and 00083–13. Therefore, because sanctions also are provided to enforce the regulation, there is no implied private remedy for its violation. R.C. 3707.99, 3707.48(C); *Franklin Cty. Law Enforcement Assn. v. Fraternal Order of Police, Capital City Lodge No. 9* (1991), 59 Ohio St.3d 167, 169, 572 N.E.2d 87, 89–90; *Fawcett v. G.C. Murphy & Co.* (1976), 46 Ohio St.2d 245, 248–250, 75 O.O.2d 291, 293–294, 348 N.E.2d 144, 147 (superseded by statute on other grounds).

Arguably, trivial cases are responsible for an avalanche of lawsuits in the courts. They delay cases that are important to individuals and corporations and that involve important social issues. The result is justice denied to litigants and their counsel who must wait for their day in court. However, absent circumstances that warrant sanctions for frivolous appeals under App.R. 23, we refuse to limit one's right to sue. Section 16, Article I, Ohio Constitution states, "All courts shall be open, and every person, for an injury done him in his land, goods, person, or reputation, shall have remedy by due course of law, and shall have justice administered without denial or delay."

This case emphasizes the need for some form of alternative dispute resolution operat-ing totally outside the court system as a means to provide an attentive ear to the parties and a resolution of disputes in a nominal case. Some need a forum in which they can express corrosive contempt for another without dragging their antagonist through the expense inherent in a lawsuit. Until such an alternative forum is created, Leichtman's battery claim, previously knocked out by the trial judge in the first round, now survives round two to advance again through the courts into round three.

We affirm the trial court's judgment as to the first and third counts of the complaint, but we reverse that portion of the trial court's order that dismissed the battery claim in the second count of the complaint. This cause is remanded for further proceedings consistent with law on that claim only.

Judgment accordingly.

DOAN, P.J., and HILDEBRANDT and GORMAN, JJ., concur.

FIGURE 9-5 *(continued)*

THING   cigarette, pipe, marijuana, cigar
ACT   smoking, puffing, inhaling, exhaling, battery, assault
PERSON   smoker, bystander, children, nonsmokers, senior citizen
PLACE   restaurant, workplace, school, public place

You can now apply these additional words to an index to find legal principles that may be relevant to the legal problem.

Like the Cartwheel, the TAPP Rule is useful for the novice researcher. It is also less time-consuming and presents a more focused approach. Consequently, it is popular with paralegals. However, it is not as comprehensive as the Cartwheel.

TARP Rule

A third method, similar to the TAPP Rule, is called the *TARP Rule*. It was developed by Steven M. Barkan of Marquette University Law School and is discussed in J. Myron Jacobstein, Roy M. Mersky and Donald J. Dunn, *Fundamentals of Legal Research* (6th ed. 1994). TARP represents:

T   *Thing* or subject matter
A   Cause of *a*ction or ground of **defense**
R   *Relief* sought
P   *Persons* or parties involved

The "T" and "P" parts of the analysis are the same elements used in the TAPP method. However, two categories dealing with legal procedure are added. As a new researcher, you may be unfamiliar with these concepts, so this method might be difficult to apply without considerable legal knowledge in the area of litigation. In our cigarette smoke example, the cause of action terms might include *tort, battery, nuisance,* and *negligence*. Defense phrases might include **consent, assumption of risk,** and **contributory negligence**. Words for

--- **LEGAL TERMS** ---

defense [†] In both civil and criminal cases, the facts submitted and the legal arguments offered by a defendant in support of his or her claim that the plaintiff's case, or the prosecution's, should be rejected. The term "defense" may apply to a defendant's entire case or to separate grounds, called *affirmative defenses,* offered by a defendant for rejecting all or a portion of the case against him or her.

consent [†] Agreement; approval; acquiescence; being of one mind. Consent necessarily involves two or more persons because, without at least two persons, there cannot be a unity of opinion or the possibility of thinking alike.

assumption of risk [†] The legal principle that a person who knows and deliberately exposes himself or herself to a danger assumes responsibility for the risk, rather than the person who actually created the danger. Assumption of risk is often referred to as voluntary assumption of risk. It is a defense to negligence.

contributory negligence [†] In the law of negligence, a failure by the plaintiff to exercise reasonable care which, in part at least, is the cause of an injury. Contributory negligence defeats a plaintiff's cause of action for negligence in states that have not adopted the doctrine of comparative negligence.

relief sought might include ban, **injunction, temporary restraining order,** and damages.

West Method

Finally, West Publishing has developed its own method, called the *Descriptive Word Method*. Discussed previously in Chapter 4, it is described in *West's Law Finder* (1994). Because West editors use the same method when arranging the descriptive word indexes in their publications, this method works well when using West resources such as their digests and CJS. West recommends that the researcher consider one question: "What words describe the pertinent facts of the case or the legal questions involved?" It is suggested that the answer to this question is generally grouped around five elements common to every case: parties, places or things, basis of action or issue, defense, and relief sought. This method is only a slight variation of the TAPP and TARP Methods. As applied, it would result in the same pool of words. Like the TARP Rule, it might be difficult for you to use successfully at first, because of the prerequisite knowledge of litigation and substantive law. This method, though, would have been the most appropriate to use in Dr. Krup's case, because you were starting with a West digest.

Each method assists you in developing words that are of importance to the use at hand. As a beginning researcher, you should get into the habit of employing at least two of these methods. Because of its comprehensiveness, the Cartwheel should be one of the methods you use.

Finding the Law

Once you have developed a pool of terms or phrases related to the problem, you can use various resources to locate the law. (The particular techniques needed to use these sources were discussed in previous chapters.)

Your starting point would include primary law finders. Should you wish to search case law, a digest or ALR would be appropriate. As both are well indexed, words developed through the various brainstorming techniques can be easily used. If available, you could also employ computer-assisted legal research, such as LEXIS or WESTLAW.

─────────────────── **LEGAL TERMS** ───────────────────

injunction † A court order that commands or prohibits some act or course of conduct. It is preventive in nature and designed to protect a plaintiff from irreparable injury to his or her property or property rights by prohibiting or commanding the doing of certain acts. An injunction is a form of equitable relief.

temporary restraining order (TRO) † Under the Federal Rules of Civil Procedure, injunctive relief that the court is empowered to grant, without notice to the opposite party and pending a hearing on the merits, upon a showing that failure to do so will result in "immediate and irreparable injury, loss, or damage." TROs are similarly available under state rules of civil procedure.

In some instances, you may be able to go directly to primary law, such as statutes or administrative regulations. Because these sources are always indexed, a list of terms can be used to find relevant statutory or regulatory provisions.

Verification of Authority

During research, it is important to continuously update your references to law by frequently checking pocket parts, advance sheets, and legal newspapers to ensure that the most recent legal principles have been found and accurately interpreted. This, however, may not always be possible or convenient; because of time limitations, many researchers wait until the end of their work to check sources and authorities. Though it is preferable to update during the course of research, it most certainly must be done at the end.

Whenever it takes place, several steps are required in the process of verification. As a precondition, a certain mindset is required. During verification, you must play the role of devil's advocate. This means you must act as if you were working for the opposing party. You must examine your work for lapses in logic, conclusionary statements, inconsistent arguments, and outdated legal principles. In this way, you view your work with a skeptical and critical eye. As a result, legal errors will be revealed that can at this point be easily corrected.

The law must be considered in light of its accuracy and validity. *Accuracy* refers to whether you have correctly interpreted legal principles. Misinterpretation of a case opinion's holding or statute's meaning can be embarrassing in a minor matter and disastrous in a major one. *Validity,* in contrast, refers to whether the law is still applicable. This is important because case law principles are constantly modified by courts, statutes are frequently repealed or changed by legislatures, and regulations are updated by agencies. Remember, the law is constantly evolving.

There is a myriad of ways to ensure accuracy and validity. Applicable digests and their pocket parts should be consulted to ascertain if additional cases have been published that could impact your problem. Advance sheets and slip opinions should be reviewed for new cases. Pocket parts in statute books should be perused for new statutes or changes in old ones. Keep in mind, however, that these publications can themselves be outdated. For instance, pocket parts for encyclopedias are published once a year. After only a few months, the current supplement becomes obsolete. Only through using CALR, which is updated daily, can you be sure that you have the most current authority.

Shepard's Citations is probably the most valuable tool in verification. Used generally with primary law, many secondary sources, such as law reviews, can also be shepardized. Shepardizing every legal authority, primary or secondary, must become a habit.

Verification is the last step before you put your product into an appropriate written form, such as a memorandum or letter. Making sure that everything is covered is essential. Realize also that, in the writing stage, the law does not stop evolving. You must continue to verify legal principles while you are writing.

VERIFICATION STEPS

1. Play the role of devil's advocate.
2. Check validity.
3. Check accuracy.
4. Use Shepard's Citations and other tools.

Ending Your Research

As difficult as beginning research is knowing when to stop. Many times various restrictions placed on you will force you to stop. These restrictions include the following:

Time Limits   Having a time limit to complete a research task is quite typical in a law office. This might be caused by client demands or a trial date.

Library Limitations   You may feel that you have exhausted the library resources available. There may be no other place to look (at least, not easily).

Other Priority Conflicts   Should another assignment be given to you, an ordering of priorities may have to be made. The result may be that one project does not get completed in a timely fashion.

Your Own Sense of Completion   In the beginning, it will be difficult to determine when to stop. The massive amounts of material present may cause you to think that you will never finish. With experience, you will know when to bring the research to a close. If you feel you are spinning your legal wheels by using the same sources or by ending up with the same conclusions, it is probably time to bring your research to a close.

Summary

- Because human ability to memorize is limited, taking effective notes during legal research is crucial.

- The researcher who is conscious of note taking will have a permanent record of the findings, which will be needed in the event of interruptions and when presenting the research in another written form.

- A research plan requires application of a three-step process. The first step involves an understanding of the problem. The researcher may need to approach the attorney or client for additional information. The second step requires an understanding of the law. This might require the researcher to review a basic text in the legal area prior to starting work. In the third step, the actual techniques of research are utilized.

- The focus of research efforts is directed at locating primary mandatory law that favorably disposes of the issue or problem.

- Secondary sources and primary law finders are useful in locating relevant primary law.

- The four word-association techniques commonly used in the profession are the Cartwheel, the TAPP Rule, the TARP Rule, and West's descriptive word method.

- The pool of words located through use of the word-association techniques can be searched through indexes, tables of contents, dictionaries, and other secondary sources and primary law finders to find primary law.

- Before the research effort is complete, proper verification must be conducted. This involves determining whether a principle is accurate and valid. Using Shepard's Citations should always be a part of this verification process.

- Often, uncontrollable factors will affect the decision to stop researching. These include time limitations, library limitations, and priority conflicts.

Review Questions

1. Why is effective note taking important in legal research?

2. Why is it necessary to have a page of research devoted just to facts?

3. What is something a novice researcher can do to obtain a general understanding of a legal area?

4. What is the ultimate goal of legal research?

5. How are secondary sources useful when conducting research?

6. Describe the Cartwheel method of developing a pool of words and phrases.

7. How are the TAPP and TARP rules similar?

8. Why can secondary sources and primary law finders often be bypassed when searching a statutory code?

9. Explain the importance of verification.

10. What is meant by playing the role of devil's advocate?

11. Describe the various factors that may force a researcher to stop researching.

Chapter Exercises

1. Use the Cartwheel method to develop words useful in researching the following terms phases:
   a. narcotics
   b. computer
   c. scalpel
   d. semi-automatic weapon

2. Use either TARP, TAPP, or West methods to develop words useful in researching the following terms phases:
   a. paralegal liability
   b. health insurance
   c. rear-end collision
   d. murder

3. Brief the case of *Leichtman v. WLW Jacor Communications* (Figure 9-5). Shepardize the decision to determine if any other states have followed the decision. Notice that the case cites the *Restatement (Second) of Torts*. Do you personally feel that smoking should constitute a battery?

4. Conduct research to determine what other nontypical actions constitute a battery. Spitting? Coughing?

PART II

LEGAL WRITING

CHAPTER 10

INTRODUCTION TO LEGAL WRITING

CHAPTER OUTLINE

OVERVIEW

The importance of effective communication in the legal profession cannot be over-emphasized. In a real sense, every task an attorney performs involves communication. A lawyer communicates in the courtroom through oral argument, questioning witnesses, and offering evidence. She also communicates outside the courtroom through telephone conversations and conferences. Filing a lawsuit, proposing settlement, and other legal strategies are also forms of communication. Seemingly inconsequential matters, such as dress, language use, and office decorum, communicate various messages and impressions.

However, by far the most significant form of communication in the practice of law is the written word. This should come as no surprise. Recall that the law is not amorphous, but rather consists of words and phrases prescribing or proscribing social conduct, which are constantly being reinterpreted by courts and rewritten by legislatures. As a legal assistant, you will be expected to prepare various forms of legal writing. Consequently, it is of extreme importance that you develop and refine your writing skills.

In Chapter 1, the overall process of legal research and writing was compared to that of a recipe. Each subsequent chapter focused on particular tools that could be used in conducting research, much like utensils in cooking. This process is not completed until presentation. *Presentation* refers to the form the research takes when offered to a client, attorney, or court. If you consider how frequently written products are evaluated based on their appearance, it is easy to appreciate the importance of effective presentation. For example, in publishing, considerable time and effort are spent on the development of attractive covers that will invoke favorable reactions by prospective purchasers. Though the adage "don't judge a book by its cover" is preached, in reality it is seldom followed. The same could be said for an adaptation of this: "Don't judge the merits of legal research by the form in which it is presented!" In fact, this advice is rarely heeded.

Legal writing, like scientific or fiction writing, is an application of standard writing in a specialty setting. It builds on principles acquired in the study of English composition. A good foundation in the basics of composition is an absolute prerequisite to writing in the legal setting. Writing requires tremendous effort. William Zinsser, in his highly regarded work, *On Writing Well* (4th ed. 1990), comments:

> Writing is hard work. A clear sentence is no accident. Very few sentences come out right the first time, or even the third time. Remember this as a consolation in moments of despair. If you find that writing is hard, it's because it *is* hard. It's one of the hardest things that people do.

This difficulty is compounded by the fact that legal writing demands compliance with conventions that vary significantly from those of nonlegal writing.

Legal writing is differentiated by its dependence on words and phrases, known as *legalese,* that are unfamiliar to those who do not work in the legal field. It has been suggested that the use of legalese by attorneys has contributed to the suspicion and distrust in which the general public seems to hold the entire legal profession. Legalese, or *legal jargon* as it is sometimes called, is blamed for making legal documents incomprehensible to the people for whom they are often developed—the general public. In response to this, efforts have been launched by bar associations and law schools to encourage "plain English" writing. This requires the replacement of legalese with words and phrases familiar to the public at large. Even though success has been limited, efforts continue at all levels of the profession, including the paralegal field.

As with legal research, legal writing can best be understood as a three-step process. In Step One, the writer seeks to understand the purpose of the document, its audience, and any constraints that could affect its production. Step Two focuses on two matters. First is the development of an organizational structure through the application of an outline; second is the application of writing principles and conventions to prepare an initial draft. Finally, in Step Three, the writer edits, revises, and rewrites to assure that the work is accurate, complete, and professionally presented.

Legal writing has various applications and thus various forms. These forms include correspondence, instruments, office memoranda, pleadings, motions, discovery documents, litigation memoranda, and appellate briefs. Your role in drafting each will depend on such factors as the complexity of the legal matter and document, local practice and custom, paralegal and attorney ethics, and time and resource limitations.

PARALEGAL PRACTICE SITUATION

Pete Genesse has approached your law firm regarding legal assistance in opening a Chicago-style pizza parlor. At this point, he is making arrangements to obtain financing for his business. Parkville National Bank has tentatively agreed to lend him $15,000 to purchase start-up equipment.

Prior to signing the required documents, he has brought them to your employer for review. Your boss would like you to review the **promissory note** (see Figure 10-1) and translate any legalese into plain English so that Pete can better understand what he intends to sign.

Presentation as Communication

As has been discussed, books are frequently judged by their covers. This is unfortunate because many deficiently written works are artificially enhanced by slick and colorful covers, abundant photography, and sophisticated graphics. Of course, the converse also occurs. Thorough, well-written products are diminished because they are not presented in the best light. The way in which a written product is offered is a major factor in whether it succeeds.

The concept of presentation is just as relevant to legal writing. How a document appears often will determine whether its substance is regarded favorably. Here, presentation means more than the choice of vessel, such as a letter or memorandum; it also embraces how the vessel is constructed. Rules of grammar, spelling, punctuation, and word choice must be considered. Woe to the paralegal who completes quality research only to fail at drafting an effective pleading, letter, or memorandum in which to convey her results. The reader may pass harsh judgment based on its deficient presentation rather than its excellent substance. You should be thankful but greatly concerned if a superior comments: "I thought your research was well done in spite of your writing." The second time around,

---

LEGAL TERMS

promissory note † A written promise to pay a specific sum of money by a specified date or on demand. A promissory note is negotiable if, in addition, it is payable to the order of a named person or to bearer.

PARKVILLE NATIONAL BANK
100 Main Street
Parkville, Maryland 21234-1990

Parkville, Maryland
_____, 1995

FOR VALUE RECEIVED, I, the undersigned Borrower, promise to pay to PARKVILLE NATIONAL BANK, on order, FIFTEEN THOUSAND DOLLARS ($15,000.00) at its office in Parkville, Maryland, to-wit: FIVE HUNDRED DOLLARS ($500.00) together with interest on the unpaid principal balance from date until maturity, at the rate of 8 per cent per annum, said principal and interest payable at PARKVILLE NATIONAL BANK, 100 Main Street, Parkville, Maryland on the first day of each and every month.

Any installment of principal or interest not paid when due shall draw interest at the highest rate permitted by law until paid.

It is understood, agreed, and accepted that the failure to pay this note, or any installment when due, or any interest hereon, when due, shall at the option of the holder, mature the full amount of said note, and it shall at once become due, payable, and owing.

To secure payment of this note and all other indebtedness or liability, direct or indirect, joint or several, absolute or contingent, now existing or hereafter acquired or contracted, of Borrower to Bank, whether such obligations are created directly or acquired by Bank by assignment or otherwise, Borrower hereby pledges to Bank and grants to Bank a security interest in the following described property:

All equipment and fixtures used in the business known as
Pete's Preferred Parkville Pizza Parlor

and all other property now or hereafter in the possession or control of the Bank. Borrower agrees to deliver to the holder, immediately upon demand, additional collateral should the holder deem itself insecure.

The Borrower will pay on demand all costs of collection and attorneys' fees incurred or paid by the holder in enforcing this note upon default.

As herein used the word "holder" shall mean the payee or other endorsee of this note, who is in possession of it, or the bearer hereof, if this note is at the time payable to the bearer.

_____
DATE

_____
PETER J. GENESSE

FIGURE 10-1 Sample promissory note

your superior might not have the patience to search the haystack of poor legal writing for the needles of legal research.

It is said that communication is a two-way street. The sender (writer) must accurately and precisely convey to the receiver (reader) an intended message. The roles are then reversed when the receiver responds. Effective communication demands that the reader exert minimal effort in the process. Because the sender desires to induce the receiver to consider the "presentation" and the message, it is the sender's burden to make this as effortless as possible.

Writing therefore must be in a style that is easily understandable by the reader. The writer must do whatever is necessary to ensure that the reader is persuaded to accept the intended message. This is achieved through the application of good writing style. Words should be used with precision. Sentences should be clear and understandable. Logic should flow from one sentence to the next. Paragraphs should be concise and interesting. See Figure 10-2.

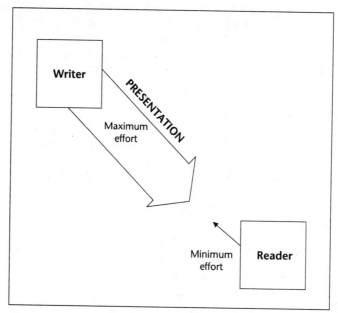

FIGURE 10-2 Presentation of writing

Expository Legal Writing

Before examining the details of legal writing, you should understand its overall purpose. The goal of legal writing is to discuss legal principles and explain how they affect or relate to particular factual situations. This style of writing can be referred to as *exposition*. Expository legal writing describes factual information and legal principles in a detailed and impersonal style. Though some forms of legal writing will take a subjective slant favoring the client, all in all, legal writing must be logical, factually detailed, and objective.

The best way to communicate an idea to other persons is to teach them. That is, you must guide the readers step by step from what they already know to what you want them to know. This can be done by developing bridges between concepts—an application of logic. The reader is carried along and persuaded if and only if each step in the argument follows from the last. For example, indicating the existence of a cause of action is not expository unless the specific elements of the cause of action are presented and substantiated. This is essential in legal writing.

Factual details not only assure the document's accuracy but also base the argument in human experience. Long, esoteric arguments quickly bore the reader and mask the reality of the situation. Relating the argument to real life is always more interesting and persuasive than discussing concepts in theoretical terms. The more detailed the facts that are provided, the better chance the reader has to understand the relevance of the legal principles applied.

An impersonal style can also be thought of as one that is objective. Though there is a role for subjectivity in legal writing, the overall tone must be objective, to convey the professionalism that is expected in law. Readers of legal writing expect an honest rendition of the facts and the relevant legal principles. Because this style is expected, maintaining it assures the writer's credibility.

Legal Archaisms

Legal writing is characterized by the use of terms and phrases unfamiliar to the general public. In this way, law is much like medicine and science, each having its own unique language.

Legalese

These unfamiliar legal words fall into two groups: legalese and terms of art. Sometimes referred to as *legal jargon,* **legalese** is characterized by the frequent use of Latin, old English, and French terms applied in no other professional setting. Legalese is also characterized by use of convoluted and archaic phrases and long-winded explanations to describe what often could be done in only a few words. A sentence employing legalese frequently is impossible to understand. Because effective communication is the goal of legal writing, legalese should be eliminated and avoided.

Terms of Art

Terms of art, in contrast to legalese, are necessary and accepted shorthand for long, complex concepts, which are needed to conduct legal business. These terms are often expected or required to be used in legal documents by court

---

LEGAL TERMS

legalese [†]   The use by lawyers of specialized words or phrases, rather than plain talk, when it serves no purpose; legal jargon. Contemporary commentators eschew legalese in favor of direct, effective use of language.

terms of art [†]   Technical words; words or expressions that have a particular meaning in a particular science or profession.

EXAMPLES OF LEGALESE

Phrase/Pronunciation	Root Language	Translation
aforesaid	Old English	the preceding
assumpsit (a *sump* sit)	Latin	a cause of action for breach of contract
heretofore	Old English	until now
mensa et thoro (*men* sa et *thoh* roh)	Latin	bed and board
oyez (*oi* yez)	Old English/French	attention
sua sponte (*soo* ah *spon* tay)	Latin	of his own will
wherefore	Old English	for what reason

EXAMPLES OF TERMS OF ART

Phrase/Pronunciation	Root Language	Translation
habeas corpus (*hay* bee ess *kore* pus)	Latin	"you have the body"; an order whose purpose is to obtain immediate relief from illegal imprisonment
heir (air)	Old English/ French	a person who inherits or is legally entitled to inherit property by will
landlord	Old English	a person who rents land or housing to another
per stirpes (per *ster* peez)	Latin	"by the root"; describes the method of dividing an estate in which the heirs share the portion of the estate that the deceased heir would have received had he or she lived
voir dire (vwar deer)	French	"look speak"; the process of oral examination of potential jurors

rule, statutory law, or custom. Frequently, it is a matter of dispute whether a particular word is unacceptable legalese or an acceptable term of art. One way of differentiating between the two is that legalese can easily be converted to common, everyday English. The translation of a term of art is often longer and more complex than the term itself; it may resemble an explanation of a concept rather than the definition of a word. The use of terms of art is also justified because these terms are more readily accepted by attorneys and judges. Regardless, terms of art, like legalese must also be interpreted and translated for clients. Their continued use presents the same problems as legalese.

Double-Meaning Words

A third suspect group includes terms that can be classified neither as legalese nor as terms of art. These are words that have common, everyday definitions, but, when used in law, take on different meanings. These *double-meaning words* can be very misleading to a client, so limited use by the attorney or paralegal is encouraged. Obviously, when use is required, translation is necessary.

DOUBLE-MEANING WORDS

Term	Legal Definition
complaint	the first document filed in a lawsuit
consideration	a required element for formation of a contract; defined as bargained-for legal detriment
deed	a document that transfers property
discovery	the process by which one party provides the other with facts about a case in advance of trial

Plain English versus Legalese

As has been mentioned, the prolific use of legalese by the legal profession has contributed to the low esteem in which lawyers and other legal professionals are held. The problem of legalese can best be understood through historical analysis.

As the English legal system evolved, so did legal language. Originally brought to England by the Romans, Latin was the language of the law and of the church, even though a form of English was in use by the Anglo-Saxon people.

In 1066, William, Duke of Normandy (a French province), claimed the English throne after the death of his cousin, Edward the Confessor, and invaded England. He defeated King Harold, formerly Earl of East Anglia, at the Battle of

Hastings. William was crowned the first king of modern England on Christmas Day, 1066. His accession to the throne introduced a period of French influence on English language, custom, and law. Among the more significant changes made by the Normans was establishment of the **jury** system. English society soon was bifurcated between the lower-class Anglo-Saxons and upper-class Norman French. French was the language of the victorious Normans, the landed upper classes, clergy, scholars, and the common law courts. Still, legal documents were issued by the king in Latin. The lower class Anglo-Saxons spoke a form of English. It was not until the 16th century that French was replaced in the courts with English.

As English gained more and more acceptance in the courts, lawyers feared that detailed meanings would be lost in the process of translating French into English. To remedy this, the legal profession often retained the French word or phrase together with the new English version. The result was long phrases with words strung together all appearing to say the same thing. Examples include: *remise, release, and discharge; give, devise, and bequeath; rest, residue, and remainder.* Latin phrases, in contrast, remained for most part unchanged. Most Latin phrases defined legal rules or doctrines, such as *res ipsa loquitur* ("thing speaks for itself"), rather than particular acts or objects. Such legal rules are still standard fare in law school. However, many of the rules have been translated into English.

Of late, a trend has emerged among many legal professionals and institutions to counter the use of legalese. Consumer groups have been in the forefront of this movement. The proponents believe that, whenever possible, **plain English** should be used instead of legal jargon. Legalese should be replaced with common, everyday English words having the same literal meanings. The overall goals in legal writing should be simplicity and clarity; redundancy and verbosity are to be avoided.

A number of state and local bar associations have launched campaigns among their membership to encourage plain English. Many legal specialty magazines (including those marketed to the paralegal profession, such as *Legal Assistant Today*) feature regular columns on the benefits of writing in plain English. In law school writing courses, the emphasis is now on reducing legal jargon. Some states, including New York, have passed laws requiring that "plain language" be used in consumer agreements, leases, and other types of documents heavily relied on by the general public.

The movement has met with resistance from some corners. Many legal scholars and attorneys argue that not all documents can be written plainly enough for all to understand and still remain accurate. They also argue that eliminating legalese erodes the English common law tradition that is the centerpiece of the American legal system. However, efforts to reduce legalese continue, especially among newer generations of attorneys and paralegals.

LEGAL TERMS

---

jury † A group of women and men selected according to law to determine the truth. Juries are used in various types of legal proceedings, both civil and criminal.

plain English Common, everyday English terms used to replace legalese.

MIXED-LANGUAGE LEGAL PHRASES

free
  (Old English)
	and	clear
		  (French)

give,
  (Old English)
	devise, and
	  (Old English/French)
		bequeath
		  (Old English)

heirs
  (Old English/French)
	and	assigns
		  (Old English/French)

remise,
  (French)
	release, and
	  (Old English/French)
		discharge
		  (Old English/French)

rest,
  (Old English/French)
	residue, and
	  (French)
		remainder
		  (Old English/French)

will
  (Old English)
	and	testament
		  (French/Latin)

A Writing Plan: Overview and Application

Legal writing, like research, lends itself to a broad three-step approach. If implemented correctly, this plan assures a high-quality written product.

Suppose that you have completed research in the Ricardo case. As determined in Chapter 8, Tom and Gail Ricardo have a valid marriage, notwithstanding the fact that the officiating clerk lacked proper authorization to preside over the ceremony. This result flows from the legal authority found in *Knapp v. Knapp,* 149 Md. 263, 131 A. 329 (1925). Your supervising attorney has asked you to prepare a letter to the client explaining the results. Because the substance of this letter constitutes legal advice, your supervisory lawyer will ultimately review and sign the letter.

Step One: Understanding the Document's Purpose, Audience, and Constraints

Three considerations must be made in Step One of legal writing. You must understand the purpose of the document, its audience, and any constraints that may exist.

Before a document can be drafted, its function must be determined. Is it to request information from an agency? Convey a legal position to an attorney? Update a client on the status of her case? Memorialize the terms of a verbal agreement? In the Ricardo case, you have been instructed to draft a letter to inform the clients of the results of the research completed on their behalf. The letter's purpose is to communicate legal principles to the clients and show how these principles affect their factual situation.

In drafting the document, you must first focus on the precise objective of the document. If more than one message is to be conveyed in a document, consider whether each can be covered without causing confusion. If it is not possible to eliminate purposes, it might be more fitting to draft more than one document. For instance, suppose that, in the Ricardo case, two matters had to be discussed with the parties: the results of the research and the fact that the fee for the matter was past due. Both matters deserve proper attention by the client. Dealing with both in the same letter might dilute the forcefulness of each one. In that situation, two letters would be more appropriate.

To carry out the purpose, an overall strategy for preparing the document is necessary. If your purpose is "to elicit information," you must first determine in precise terms what the needed information is. If the purpose is "to memorialize an agreement," you will need to obtain information from the client as to the terms of the oral agreement. For example, for the Ricardo letter, your strategy would include:

1. Review previous information provided to the clients.
   (Have the Ricardos been provided with any information regarding the research results? If so, you would not want to be redundant.)
2. Determine and verify new information to be given.
   (What do you want to tell them? In how much detail do you want to discuss your findings? You will need to verify the law up through the date the letter is sent.)
3. Consider any restrictions, ethical or otherwise, that might affect the document.
   (Can you sign the letter? Should you make any guarantee that their marriage is valid?)
4. Consider the limitations and expectations of the document itself.
   (What is appropriate language for a letter such as this? How formal should you be?)

Each goal dictates its own particular strategy. This process of deciding a strategy will become easier as you gain experience in drafting particular documents.

The second consideration is identification of the audience or audiences. Frequently, a document has two audiences, a primary audience and a secondary audience. The most usual primary audience is the client. If the client is not the primary audience, she will likely be the secondary one. That is, although the document is not addressed to the client, it is likely that a copy will be sent to her. Other likely audiences for legal writing include court clerks, laypersons other than clients, judges, attorneys, and, of course, other paralegals.

There are a number of audience characteristics that must be evaluated. These include but are not limited to the reader's expertise and knowledge in the document's subject matter, level of education, occupation, age, and previous relationship with the firm. By analyzing the audience's characteristics, you can write in a style to which the reader is receptive. For instance, if the audience is a client who is also a paralegal, it might not be necessary to go to great lengths to define and explain legal terminology. In contrast, a letter to a client with little legal background may involve considerable explanation of terms and concepts.

In legal writing, it is difficult not to make assumptions about the audience. Unfortunately, an erroneous assumption can insult, patronize, or confuse a client or attorney. You must be careful to base your writing on solid, objective information about the matter and client, as well as a thorough understanding of the applicable legal principles.

Paralegal Tip

Most firms have a policy of sending clients copies of every document prepared in their cases. This includes correspondence sent to opposing counsel. There is sometimes a risk in this procedure. When clients review copies of letters addressed to opposing counsel, they may find the tone belligerent and threatening or, alternatively, overly friendly. Unless you anticipate this, you might be put in a precarious situation with your client. You must be prepared to justify or explain to the client the reason for the tone of the letter. A good practice with all documents is to leave a postscript (P.S.) on the copy sent to the client, explaining any matters you feel the client might interpret erroneously.

Finally, various constraints that could beset you as a writer must be considered. The most significant constraint affecting a writer's work is time. Law practices are inherently hectic. Turnaround time is short, and results are expected promptly. It is important for you to look realistically at the time needed to complete an assignment. A paralegal's job often demands juggling many projects, constantly reprioritizing one before another. This is compounded by the fact that work schedules are influenced greatly by the priorities of others involved in the completion process. An attorney may not have time available to review a draft letter; a secretary may not be able to type a document in final form right away. Care must be taken to balance the requirements of a thorough job with the demand to be time-frugal.

A second constraint is limitations on resources. Sometimes this is factored by time. Certain resources may be available only at certain times. For example, a local bar library may only be open during certain periods of a day. Frequently, time must be reserved to use CALR such as LEXIS or WESTLAW.

Depending on the form of legal writing, further constraints may be imposed by rule. All jurisdictions have court rules governing the structure of litigation documents (See Figure 10-3). These rules may have to be strictly observed. Things such as paper size, headings, and margins may be prescribed by rule, so you are well advised to check your jurisdiction's rules of court before drafting a pleading or motion. A document not in compliance with format rules may be rejected by the court or successfully challenged by the opposing side.

Besides court rules, most localities have conventions based on tradition or common usage. Although locating rules governing documents can be easily done, customs are not so easily determined. You will have to make a habit of finding this out from an experienced co-worker or supervisor.

Rule 33.   Form of Jurisdictional Statements, Petitions, Briefs, Appendices, Motions, and Other Documents Filed with the Court

.l. (a) Except for typewritten filings permitted by Rules 42.2(c), 43, and 46, all jurisdictional statements, petitions, briefs, appendices, and other documents filed with the Court shall be produced by standard typographic printing, which is preferred, or by any photostatic or similar process which produces a clear, black image on white paper; but ordinary carbon copies may not be used.

(b) The text of documents produced by standard typographic printing shall appear in print as 11-point or larger type with 2-point or more leading between lines. Footnotes shall appear in print as 9-point or larger type with 2-point or more leading between lines. Such documents shall be printed on both sides of the page.

(c) The text of documents produced by a photostatic or similar process shall be done in pica type at no more than 10 characters per inch with the lines double-spaced, except that indented quotations and footnotes may be single-spaced. In footnotes, elite type at no more than 12 characters per inch may be used. Such documents may be duplicated on both sides of the page, if practicable. They shall not be reduced in duplication.

(d) Whether duplicated under subparagraph (b) or (c) of this paragraph, documents shall be produced on opaque, unglazed paper 6⅛ by 9¼ inches in size, with type matter approximately 4⅛ by 7⅛ inches, and margins of at least ¾ inch on all sides. The paper shall be firmly bound in at least two places along the left margin so as to make an easily opened volume, and no part of the text shall be obscured by the binding. However, appendices in patent cases may be duplicated in such size as is necessary to utilize copies of patent documents.

.2. (a) All documents filed with the Court must bear on the cover, in the following order, from the top of the page: (1) the number of the case or, if there is none, a space for one; (2) the name of this Court; (3) the Term; (4) the caption of the case as appropriate in this Court; (5) the nature of the proceeding and the name of the court from which the action is brought (*e.g.,* On Appeal from the Supreme Court of California; On Writ of Certiorari to the United States Court of Appeals for the Fifth Circuit); (6) the title of the paper (*e.g.,* Jurisdictional Statement, Brief for Respondent, Joint Appendix); (7) the name, post office address, and telephone number of the member of the Bar of this Court who is counsel of record for the party concerned, and upon whom service is to be made. The individual names of other members of the Bar of this Court or of the Bar of the highest court in their respective states and, if desired, their post office addresses, may be added, but counsel of record shall be clearly identified. The foregoing shall be displayed in an appropriate typographic manner and, except for the identification of counsel, may not be set in type smaller than 11-point or in upper case pica.

(b) The following documents shall have a suitable cover consisting of heavy paper in the color indicated: (1) jurisdictional statements and petitions for writs of certiorari, white; (2) motions, briefs, or memoranda filed in response to jurisdictional statements or petitions for certiorari, light orange; (3) briefs on the merits for appellants or petitioners, light blue; (4) briefs on the merits for appellees or respondents, light red; (5) reply briefs, yellow; (6) intervenor or *amicus curiae* briefs (or motions for leave to file, if bound with brief), green; (7) joint appendices, tan; (8) documents filed by the United States, by any department, office, or agency of the United States, or by any officer or employee of the United States, represented by the Solicitor General, gray. All

FIGURE 10-3 U.S. Supreme Court Rule 33

other documents shall have a tan cover. Counsel shall be certain that there is adequate contrast between the printing and the color of the cover.

.3.   All documents produced by standard typographic printing or its equivalent shall comply with the page limits prescribed by these Rules. See Rules 15.3; 16.3, 16.5, and 16.6; 21.4; 22.2, 22.5, and 22.6; 27.1, 27.2(b), 27.3(b), and 27.4; 34.3 and 34.4; 36.1 and 36.2. Where documents are produced by photostatic or similar process, the following page limits shall apply:

Jurisdictional Statement (Rule 15.3)	65 pages;
Motion to Dismiss or Affirm (Rule 16.3)	65 pages;
Brief Opposing Motion to Dismiss or Affirm (Rule 16.5)	20 pages;
Supplemental Brief (Rule 16.6)	20 pages;
Petition for Certiorari (Rule 21.4)	65 pages;
Brief in Opposition (Rule 22.2)	65 pages;
Reply Brief (Rule 22.5)	20 pages;
Supplemental Brief (Rule 22.6)	20 pages;
Petition Seeking Extraordinary Writ (Rule 27.1)	65 pages;
Brief in Opposition (Rule 27.2(b))	65 pages;
Response to Petition for Habeas Corpus (Rule 27.3(b))	65 pages;
Brief in Opposition (Rule 27.4)	65 pages;
Brief on the Merits (Rule 34.3)	110 pages;
Reply Brief (Rule 34.4)	45 pages;
Brief of *Amicus Curiae* (Rule 36.2)	65 pages.

.4.   The Court or a Justice, for good cause shown, may grant leave for the filing of a document in excess of the page limits, but such an application is not favored. An application for such leave shall comply in all respects with Rule 43; and it must be submitted at least 15 days before the filing date of the document in question, except in the most extraordinary circumstances.

.5. (a)   All documents filed with the Court which exceed five pages, regardless of method of duplication (other than joint appendices, which in this respect are governed by Rule 30), shall be preceded by a table of contents, unless the document contains only one item.

(b)   All documents which exceed three pages, regardless of method of duplication, shall contain, following the table of contents, a table of authorities (*i.e.,* cases (alphabetically arranged), constitutional provisions, statutes, textbooks, etc.) with correct references to the pages where they are cited.

.6.   The body of all documents at their close shall bear the name of counsel of record and such other counsel identified on the cover of the document in conformity with Rule 33.2(a) as may be desired. One copy of every motion and application (other than one to dismiss or affirm under Rule 16) in addition must bear at its close the manuscript signature of counsel of record.

.7.   The Clerk shall not accept for filing any document presented in a form not in compliance with this Rule, but shall return it indicating to the defaulting party wherein he has failed to comply: the filing, however, shall not thereby be deemed untimely provided that new and proper copies are promptly substituted. If the Court shall find that the provisions of this Rule have not been adhered to, it may impose, in its discretion, appropriate sanctions including but not limited to dismissal of the action, imposition of costs, or disciplinary sanction upon counsel. See also Rule 38 respecting oral argument.

FIGURE 10-3   *(continued)*

Step Two: Structure and Draft

Deciding the organizational structure of the document and producing a first draft are the goals of Step Two. Both are assisted by the drafting of an outline.

An outline accomplishes several things. First, it will help you organize your main points in a logical fashion. Logic can relate to both *substance* (the legal points of your document) and *format* (the layout of your document). Different documents and purposes demand different logic. Outlining forces you to think about what is required in the particular circumstance before you write.

Outlining also helps prevent the omission of important arguments, legal principles, or facts. In a sense, the outline becomes the skeleton on which the flesh of your draft is placed. Because the document may be read by an opposing party, it must leave no gaps open to possible attack nor illustrate a weakness in your position.

Finally, an outline builds confidence. Sitting in front of a blank sheet of paper (or screen) can be overwhelming. An outline will psychologically help you over this initial hurdle.

An outline can be a simple list or an elaborate plan with topics and subtopics. The more complex the document, the more important the need to have a comprehensive outline. The IRAC method is often useful in developing an outline.

EXAMPLE

OUTLINE OF RICARDO LETTER
(using IRAC)

  I. Purpose of letter
 II. Facts provided by client
III. Issue: Is the marriage valid?
 IV. Rule: *Knapp v. Knapp*
  V. Application/Analysis: Marriage is valid
 VI. Conclusion
VII. Closing

After preparing the outline, you are ready to prepare your first draft. Before writing, help maximize your efforts: make sure you have sufficient time, the proper tools (pen, paper, or word processor), and an appropriate setting (such as a library or a quiet office). Keep both a legal dictionary and a standard English dictionary and thesaurus close by for easy reference. (Chapter 11 is devoted to the necessary background of the mechanics needed for proper writing.)

Step Three: Editing and Rewriting

Step Three focuses on the process of editing and rewriting. Editing involves the fine-tuning of your writing. There are two types of editing, editing for grammar and style and editing for legal substance. When editing for grammar and style, you focus on the mechanics of writing: logical development, tone, sentence structure, punctuation, spelling, and citation format. Editing for substance involves carefully reconsidering the document's purpose, issues, and legal analysis. Having another person objectively review a document can be helpful as part of the editing process. If the document requires extensive editing, rewriting the entire work may be more efficient (especially if someone else has the task of retyping the document after editing). See Figure 10-4. Most professional writers would say that the difference between mediocre writing and good writing is editing. Editing is considered in more detail in Chapter 11.

June 1, 1995

Mr. and Mrs. Thomas Ricardo
7501 Perring Avenue
Baltimore, Maryland 21234-1909

        Re: File Name: Tom and Gail Ricardo
             File No.: 95.125

Dear Mr. and Mrs. Ricardo:

The purpose of this letter is to respond to your inquiry regarding the validity of your marriage. You indicated to me you were married by a deputy clerk at the Howard County Court House on April 4, 1994. Recently, you read in the Baltimore *Evening Sun* that the clerk that married you might not have had authority to do so. Evidently, the clerk believed he had the prerequisite authority. As a consequence, you might not be married.

We have completed research into whether your marriage might be valid even though the deputy lacked authority to marry you. It is our belief that your marriage is valid.

A similar circumstance as yours was presented before the Court of Appeals in the 1925 case of *Knapp v. Knapp*. In that case, the parties were married by a minister whom they believed had authority to do so. The minister, like the clerk in your case, believed he had proper authority. After her husband's death Mrs. Knapp requested her widow's allotment: an amount paid at that time to a wife from the proceeds of a husband's estate. Mr. Knapp's family opposed the request. The court determined that even if the minister did not have proper authority, the parties nonetheless were still validly married. As a result, Mrs. Knapp was entitled to her allotment. You should also know that the Attorney General of Maryland recently ruled that in a circumstance such as yours, the marriage is valid. The Attorney General also looked to the *Knapp* case as controlling.

As you can see, the facts in the *Knapp* case and your own are similar. You were both married by an official who honestly believed he had proper authority. Based on this factual similarity, the same result would exist in your case.

I hope that your fears are now settled regarding the validity of your marriage. Please telephone me if you have further questions regarding this matter.

        Very truly yours,

        Perry L. Matlock

PLM/SW

FIGURE 10-4 Sample client letter

Word Processing and Computers

Regardless of the document to be produced, word processing will likely be the means employed to achieve the finished product.

Technology started to revolutionize the law office about 40 years ago with the introduction of electric typewriters. This was soon followed by typewriters with memory capability. Dedicated word processors then replaced all forms of typewriters. Today, firms use computers with word-processing capabilities.

As technology advanced, the process of document preparation changed. For instance, an understanding of the proper use of hyphens to divide words into syllables is no longer relevant, as margin justification eliminates this need. Nearly all software programs have a spell checker and thesaurus, which can assist in preparation. Just the same, no word-processing program can think for you. You must ultimately make decisions regarding word choice, punctuation, and sentence structure. It is never acceptable to use the failure of a software program to catch errors as an excuse for a mediocre product.

Formerly, one of the great debates in law practice management was whether nonsecretaries should play a role in the typing (now referred to as "creation") of documents. This is now a moot point, as it is generally accepted that all members of a modern, technologically equipped firm should play a role in document creation. Because the private practice of law is ultimately a business, economizing to ensure profits is a major goal. In the past, the attorney would dictate a letter to a secretary, who would then type several drafts, each one edited by the attorney. The dictation might have been taken live by shorthand or by microtape-recording. Attorneys today now realize that it often makes more sense for them to initially create their documents through word processing and have a secretary play the role of editor. If attorneys are typing their own work, why not paralegals? Paralegals are in fact doing their own typing, which means taking on jobs that in the past were secretarial in nature.

Because of the competitive nature of the job market today, all paralegals must be on the technological cutting edge. You should take courses in the various technologies discussed in Chapter 6, as well as word processing. If possible, take these courses early in your education so that your new skills can be applied and refined in other courses.

Forms of Legal Writing

There are many different forms of legal writing. Legal correspondence includes letters sent to clients, attorneys, judges, and agencies. Generally, four types of letters are used in legal practice. A *confirmatory letter* confirms matters discussed over the telephone or in person. When documents are forwarded to court, often a *cover letter* provides instructions regarding the enclosures. In an *informational letter,* the writer is either asking for information from or providing information to the reader. The information in such a letter is nonlegal, whereas in an *advisory letter* legal advice is provided. Though a paralegal might be involved in drafting all four types, her signature would never appear on the advisory letter. For a paralegal to sign an advisory letter would imply that she is providing legal advice—which is clearly unethical and illegal. A paralegal could ethically sign any of the other letters, provided they had been reviewed by an attorney. Correspondence is addressed in detail in Chapter 12.

As a result of an interview, investigation, or research, a paralegal might be required to produce an office memorandum (the subject of Chapter 13). After an interview, it is always wise to memorialize the substance of the meeting in an *interview memorandum.* To update an attorney as to the status of an investigation, an *investigatory memorandum* might be required. Finally, a *research memorandum* presents the results of research in an acceptable form.

Instruments are documents that record the responsibilities or interests of the parties to a particular legal transaction. For example, in a business setting, a contract is an instrument. When a husband and wife separate, they often sign a *marital* or *separation agreement;* this is another form of an instrument. An instrument that transfers a piece of property is known as a *deed.* Chapter 14 is devoted to understanding instruments.

Most court rules define a *pleading* as a complaint, answer, counterclaim, cross-claim, or third-party complaint. A *motion,* also filed with a court, is a request made to a court for specific relief. Though not considered a pleading, it must still comply with the same court rules.

Discovery is a critical part of the litigation process. A litigation paralegal is frequently asked to draft interrogatories, answers to interrogatories, requests for production of documents and inspection of property, requests for admissions of fact and genuineness of documents, requests for depositions, and motions for physical or mental examinations. Motions filed to enforce or prevent discovery requests are also often necessary. Pleadings and discovery documents are addressed in Chapter 15.

A *litigation memorandum* is prepared in support of a motion; thus, it is filed in a trial court. An *appellate brief,* in contrast, is filed in an appeals court. Like a litigation memorandum, it presents the legal arguments in support of a specific legal proposition. Both types of documents are considered in Chapter 16.

Summary

- Written communication is the most common form of legal communication, and for this reason time and effort must be spent assuring that documents are presented properly.

- Expository legal writing is focused on explaining and describing factual information and principles in a detailed and impersonal style.

- Legalese consists of unnecessary Latin, French, and old English terms and other archaic language that can be readily replaced by common, everyday English words.

- Terms of art are necessary and accepted (though sometimes obscure) terms and short-hand needed to conduct legal business.

- Double-meaning words have common, everyday meanings but take on different meanings when applied to law.

- The use of legalese has been countered by the plain English movement, whose proponents advocate the use of common English words to replace legal jargon.

- There are three steps to legal writing. In Step One, the writer reaches an understanding of the purpose of the document, its audience, and any constraints that affect its preparation. In Step Two, the organizational structure and draft of the document are completed. The use of an outline greatly assists this effort. Step Three deals with editing and rewriting. The writer needs to edit for grammar, style, and substance. The difference between mediocre writing and good writing is editing.

- Today, attorneys as well as paralegals need to have word-processing skills for document preparation.

- The forms of legal writing include legal correspondence, office memoranda, instruments, pleadings, motions, discovery documents, litigation memoranda, and appellate briefs.

Review Questions

1. Why is presentation important to communication?

2. Describe some of the ways in which attorneys communicate.

3. What are the differences and similarities between terms of art and legalese?

4. Describe the historical influences on English legal language.

5. What is the plain English movement?

6. Describe the steps in legal writing.

7. What are some of the characteristics of an audience?

8. What are some of the constraints that could affect legal writing?

9. Discuss the impact of word processing and computers on document preparation.

Chapter Exercises

1. Obtain a copy of the deed to your home or the home of a friend. Review the document for legalese, terms of art, and double-meaning words. Look up all terms in a legal dictionary. Draft a new deed using plain English.

2. Check your state rules of civil procedure. Is there a rule similar to that in Figure 10-3 for documents filed in your state trial court?

3. Assume that the "smoking" battery of which Dr. Krup was a victim (see Chapter 9) took place in Ohio. Describe the strategy considerations for a letter you might send him advising him of his rights. Prepare an outline of the letter. Draft the letter.

4. Eliminate all legalese in the following document:

Greetings: Know ye that I, William S. Alfred of Philadelphia, Pennsylvania, for and in consideration of Five Hundred Dollars ($500.00), to me in hand paid by Joseph Davidson do by these presents for myself, my heirs and assigns, remise, release, and further discharge Joseph Davidson.

5. Read and brief the case of *Henderson v. Mississippi*, 445 So. 2d 1364 (Miss. 1984). Why did the court conclude that the rules of English grammar are not a part of the law of Mississippi? What were the problems in the indictment? Do you think the court was correct in its decision? Why or why not?

CHAPTER 11

LEGAL WRITING MECHANICS AND STYLE

CHAPTER OUTLINE

OVERVIEW

An effectively written document can be created only by paying close attention to writing mechanics and style. *Mechanics* refers to the basics of writing: word choice, punctuation, sentence structure, and paragraph formation. An understanding of these rules of grammar is required to communicate proficiently in written form. It is also important to develop a legal style of writing. *Style* is the diction and tone that reveal the expository nature of legal writing, differentiating it from other forms of prose.

Legal writing must be logical in both substance and format. A logical discussion of the substance of a matter in terms of time may have to present the points chronologically. The IRAC method of legal analysis is considered a logical approach because it discusses a problem in a practical fashion. Logical development can be assured by drafting and following an outline. Finally, in partisan forms of writing, putting the strongest arguments before weaker ones seems logical as an approach to convincing a reader.

Proper editing is critical to achieving an impressive written end product. There are two types of editing: editing for grammar and style, and editing for legal substance. Grammar and style editing focuses on the mechanics of writing: logical development, tone, sentence structure, punctuation, spelling, and citation format. When you reconsider a document's purpose, issues, and legal analysis, you are editing for substance. Most writers say that good writing is always the result of tenacious editing and rewriting.

PARALEGAL PRACTICE SITUATION

Your firm has been contacted by Ismail Chawdhari, the owner of Chawdhari Electronics, Inc. His company sells electronic supplies to various industries. Last month Ismail hired James Wong to join the company's sales force. Last week he was required to terminate James because of poor sales performance.

James then retained an attorney, who has contacted Ismail. James is claiming that he had a two-year employment contract with Chawdhari Electronics, Inc. The contract allegedly precluded his termination for performance reasons within that period of time. Evidently he is threatening a lawsuit against Chawdhari Electronics, Inc. Ismail claims that such a contract never existed.

You have been asked to draft a letter to James's attorney, explaining Ismail's position. Of course, this letter must be reviewed and signed by your supervisory attorney.

Legal Writing Mechanics

Mechanics, often called *grammar,* refers to the technical aspects of writing. It deals with the form and structure of words, both individually and as grouped together in sentences and paragraphs.

There are a myriad of grammar rules, all of which must be considered when writing. The rules most relevant to legal writing are discussed here. For other questions, you should seek guidance from an English composition instructor or a respected handbook such as *The Elements of Style* (3d ed. 1979) by William Strunk, Jr. and E.B. White.

Word Choice

Making the appropriate word selection is all the more important when you consider the critical impact words have in law. Consider a word such as *reasonable*. In a contract, it could be interpreted various ways, depending on the context and the interpreter. For instance, the term *reasonable visitation* in a custody agreement might mean a subjective definition that the parties themselves determine: visitation every other weekend is one possible interpretation. In contrast, *reasonable due care* is an objective standard usually determined by a court. This term might appear in an agreement dealing with liability: "The dealer is to use reasonable due care with the manufacturer's products." Careless word selection can contravene the intentions of the parties or the entire meaning of a document.

Names and Titles

Attorneys are the most frequent authors and readers of legal writing. An individual who is admitted to a state bar may add "Esquire" to his or her name. Though it is proper to abbreviate *Esquire* as *Esq.*, many attorneys prefer to spell it out. When addressing a lawyer in correspondence (not the salutation), do not use title abbreviations such as Mr. or Ms.

EXAMPLE

INCORRECT

      Mr. David J. Smith, Esq.

CORRECT

      David J. Smith, Esquire

To give legal writing a lifelike feel, it is important to humanize individuals. Do not use *plaintiff* or *defendant* when you are attempting to emphasize the "human" side of a person; rather, use the individual's surname.

EXAMPLE

INCORRECT

Plaintiff will deliver his daughter for visitation on Friday.

CORRECT

Mr. Martin will deliver his daughter for visitation on Friday.

In correspondence and instruments, always use surnames to identify people. In pleadings and other court-filed papers, it is best to use both the litigation status and the surname initially. Subsequently, it is permissible to refer to the parties by their litigation status only.

EXAMPLE

COUNT I

1. James Wong, Plaintiff, and Chawdhari Electronics, Inc., Defendant, entered into a contract on October 18, 1995.

2. Pursuant to the terms of the contract, Defendant was to employ Plaintiff for two years.

Capitalization

The capitalization of words and letters can effectively provide needed emphasis or distinguish particular terms in legal writing. Headings in all legal documents, especially pleadings, contracts, and memoranda, should be in capital letters, unless a specific court rule requires a different format.

EXAMPLE

JAMES WONG	)	IN THE
PLAINTIFF	)	CIRCUIT COURT
v.	)	FOR
CHAWDHARI ELECTRONICS, INC.	)	BALTIMORE COUNTY
DEFENDANT	)	CASE NO. 12345-95

MOTION TO DISMISS

The first letter in each major word of a government agency or office name should be capitalized. (Also see *Bluebook* Rule 8 on capitalization.)

EXAMPLE

U.S. Department of Justice
State's Attorney for Allegheny County

It is inappropriate to capitalize the names of seasons in legal writing.

EXAMPLE

INCORRECT
Mr. Bell started his business in the Spring of 1992.
CORRECT
Mr. Bell started his business in the spring of 1992.

The terms *plaintiff* and *defendant* should be capitalized when you are referring to a particular party in a formal document such as a contract or pleading.

EXAMPLE

The Plaintiff in this action is a Nevada corporation.

It would not be capitalized when the reference is to a generic plaintiff or defendant.

EXAMPLE

The plaintiff is usually required to pay the filing fee in advance when bringing a lawsuit.

These rules, however, are not applied consistently. Often, especially in pleadings, the words *plaintiff* and *defendant* are not capitalized. You will have to determine the proper usage in your jurisdiction.

Finally, words of importance in legal documents (especially pleadings) should be capitalized.

EXAMPLE

IT IS this 28th day of November, 1995 by the Circuit Court for Anne Arundel County; ADJUDGED, ORDERED, and DECREED ...

Abbreviations

Except when using a title or term that is never written in full, such as Mr., Ms., or P.M., avoid abbreviations in legal writing. Abbreviated words and phrases give legal writing an undesirable informality.

Numbers and Dates

If a number begins a sentence, it should always be written out.

EXAMPLE

Sixty paralegal students attended the monthly meeting of the association.

In legal writing, a date appears in the order month, day, and year, as in March 5, 1994. If the day is not indicated, then the month and year appear with no comma separating them: March 1994.

Unfortunately, there is little consistency in the use of numbers in legal writing. Generally speaking, numbers from zero to nine are spelled out, whereas numbers 10 and greater are written in arabic numerals. However, when two or more numbers are used in a sentence, they should appear in the arabic form.

EXAMPLE

There were 30 interrogatories posed, but only 9 complete responses.

Ages of individuals are usually written numerically.

EXAMPLE

The victim, a 9-year-old child, suffered a broken back as a result of the beating.

Finally, when complex numbers such as dollar amounts are used in contracts and pleadings, they should be spelled out first and then the amount stated using arabic numerals in parentheses. In other forms of legal writing, indicating the amount in arabic numerals only is preferred.

EXAMPLE

THIS COURT enters judgment in the amount of Thirty-One Thousand Five Hundred Fifty-Five Dollars ($31,555.00) for the Plaintiff.

Italics

Developed by Italians, the use of italics is appropriate in legal writing in two situations. The first is in citation. If italics are unavailable as a word processing option, underscoring is used. Consult the *Bluebook* Practitioners' Note 1 for particular applications.

Italics should also be used to indicate a word or phrase in a foreign language that has not been incorporated into common English usage. *Bluebook* Rule 7 indicates that there is a strong presumption that Latin words and phrases commonly used in legal writing have been incorporated.

EXAMPLE

This transformation has now touched the very core of an attorney's *raison d'être:* the practice of law.

The Plaintiff's theory is based on the doctrine of res ipsa loquitur.

However, in practice, many legal professionals develop the habit of italicizing all Latin terms. This is usually acceptable.

Contractions

A contraction is the shortening of a word or phrase, such as *can't* for *cannot* and *won't* for *will not*. Contractions are never acceptable in legal writing. They are considered too informal for legal use.

Shall, Will, and May

Shall, will, and *may* have distinct differences in meaning and thus in application. The term *shall* imposes an immediate duty to perform. It is always given an imperative interpretation.

EXAMPLE

Defendant shall pay the child support on a timely basis.

The term *will,* though often used interchangeably with *shall,* actually imposes a futuristic rather than immediate duty.

EXAMPLE

Defendant will pay the child support on a timely basis.

Though this distinction might be slight, judges and attorneys nevertheless adhere to it.

The word *may* conveys only the possibility that an act might take place. It is used to indicate permissiveness.

EXAMPLE

Defendant may pay the child support on a timely basis.

The effect of this sentence should be obvious. It implies that the Defendant "may not" pay child support on a timely basis as well.

That and Which

It is accepted that clauses beginning with *which* are nonrestrictive; those beginning with *that* are restrictive. In the following example, the second clause places a restriction on the first. The restrictive clause, in this case "that lacks an index," is never set off by commas.

EXAMPLE

A code that lacks an index is useless.

But consider:

EXAMPLE

Indexes, which are often found in codes, are the best way of locating statutory law.

Here the clause merely provides additional information, giving the sentence more specificity. If the clause is omitted, the sentence would still retain its basic meaning. In the prior sentence, removing the restrictive clause destroys the meaning of the sentence.

Spelling

Not enough can be said about the importance of proper spelling in legal documents. Incorrect spelling is the single biggest thing that can destroy the effectiveness of an otherwise superior presentation.

Most writers tend to consult a dictionary only when utilizing an unusual word or variation. You should get into the habit of checking every word that you have the slightest inkling might be incorrect. The following are a few of the words that are typically misspelled in legal documents.

INCORRECT	CORRECT
admissable	admissible
alledge	allege
affadavit	affidavit
bankrupcy	bankruptcy
breech	breach
circut	circuit
defendent	defendant
judgement	judgment
morgage	mortgage
priviledge	privilege
statue	statute
supercede	supersede
tenent	tenant

In a few situations, you might mistakenly use a British or Canadian variant of a word. Unless you are working in one of those countries, use American spellings.

AMERICAN	CANADIAN/BRITISH
center	centre
defense	defence
theater	theatre
gray	grey
traveling	travelling

One word of caution. With the increased use of word processing and computerization, software programs commonly known as *spell checkers* are now heavily relied upon. Unfortunately, many writers tend to employ a spell checker rather than relying on their own spelling abilities. You should never fall into the trap of relying on a spell checker to correct spelling; it should be used only as a double-check. Look carefully at every word used. Though English is not particularly logical in its spelling, often you can get a feel as to whether the word is correct or not. You might inadvertently misspell a word that is in fact another word correctly spelled. The spell checker would certainly not pick this up. Examples of this include words such as "statue" for "statute" and "site" for "cite."

Punctuation

In speech, pauses, intonation, and inflection are used to communicate meaning to the listener. In writing, these cues are provided through punctuation. The goal of punctuation is simple: to create only one possible interpretation for a given sentence. "Tight" punctuation should always be strived for in legal writing. The alternative, "loose" punctuation (where words and sentences might have several meanings), is appropriate for fiction writing, especially poetry.

Comma

Next to the period, the comma (,) is the most familiar form of punctuation. Because they are needed so frequently, commas are often used instinctively.

The overall purpose of a comma is to separate two distinct concepts within a sentence so as to reduce misunderstanding. If there is a chance that a sentence could be open to more than one interpretation, a comma should be employed.

A comma can be used to set off an introductory word or phrase. Such a phrase consists of information that is additional or qualifying in nature; if the phrase were removed, the sentence would still retain its basic meaning.

EXAMPLE

After Judge Ito instructed the jury, the jurors began their deliberations.

On his first day of work, the paralegal made a good impression.

If the phrase is short, the use of a comma is a matter of preference.

EXAMPLE

In July I will be sworn in as a judge.
OR
In July, I will be sworn in as a judge.

Commas are needed to set off a phrase within a sentence.

EXAMPLE

The paralegal's research, though not extensive, was critical to the success of the case.

A clause beginning with *that* is not set off by commas.

EXAMPLE

The paralegal that attracts the most clients for the firm will be promoted.

If the clause "that attracts the most clients for the firm" is removed, the meaning of the sentence is completely changed.

A comma should be used before a conjunction, such as "and," "but," "or," or "for," when two sentences are brought together (referred to as a *compound sentence*).

EXAMPLE

The attorney was experienced in trying murder cases, but he lost just the same.

If a comma is not placed before the conjunction *and* when introducing a list, a different meaning will result.

EXAMPLE

The firm had softball teams made up of attorneys, clerks, paralegals, and secretaries. (There were four groups playing softball)

The firm had softball teams made up of attorneys, clerks, paralegals and secretaries. (There were three groups playing softball)

When a prefix or suffix is used in legal writing, a comma should be used both before and after the abbreviation.

EXAMPLE

Lorenzo C. Smith, D.D.S., has his office in the suburbs.

One common error in employing a comma is using it to separate a verb from its subject (the requirements of having verb and subject in a sentence are discussed later in this chapter).

EXAMPLE

INCORRECT

The Governor, granted the Petitioner's request for a pardon.
   (subject)   (verb)

CORRECT

The Governor granted the Petitioner's request for a pardon.
   (subject)   (verb)

When used with quotation marks, commas are placed inside the marks rather than outside.

EXAMPLE

"Never have I been so impressed," said the attorney of the paralegal's efforts.

Semicolon

The semicolon (;) is a useful, yet underutilized, punctuation mark. When properly employed, it can strategically indicate a subtle relationship between two parts of a sentence.

A semicolon can be used between two parts of a compound sentence when a conjunction is not used.

EXAMPLE

Discovery is completed; a trial date can be set.

The same sentence could be written with a conjunction or divided into two sentences.

EXAMPLE

Discovery is completed, and a trial date can be set.
Discovery is completed. A trial date can be set.

The use of the semicolon creates a longer pause than a comma, but a shorter one than a period.

A semicolon is often used in a sentence to link a clause to a main clause already containing a prepositional phrase (a phrase beginning with a preposition such as "in," "by," "during," or "for").

EXAMPLE

During the trial, the defendant conceded liability; only damages had to be assessed.

In a series of items, both commas and semicolons are required.

EXAMPLE

The attorneys were Carl Silver, Esquire, of Towson, Maryland; Rhonda Limpert, Esquire, of Bel Air, Maryland; and Patricia Miata, Esquire, of Baltimore, Maryland.

Unlike commas, semicolons are placed outside of quotation marks.

EXAMPLE

The witness replied, "I saw the murder"; however, other testimony indicated that she was not present at the crime scene.

Colon

The most appropriate use of a colon (:) in legal writing is to introduce a list. In that case, the phrase preceding the colon must be a complete sentence.

EXAMPLE

The following members will be serving on the panel: Judge Mohammad, Judge Cohen, and Judge Hernandez.

Similarly, a colon can be used to introduce a phrase that either explains or summarizes what has preceded.

EXAMPLE

The jury reached its verdict: innocent.

In legal correspondence, a colon is always placed after the salutation.

EXAMPLE

Dear Ms. Lechner:
Dear Judge Nielsen:
Dear Dr. Bellantoni:

A colon is also used to introduce a quotation (discussed later in this chapter) and when separating hours and minutes in time designations, as in 11:30 P.M.

Parentheses

The use of parentheses (( )) is a method of setting apart text for special consideration. Parentheses are generally used to set off phrases, as an alternative to commas, when the enclosed clause is less important, somewhat tangential to the subject, or interjected.

EXAMPLE

Probably the largest professional group affected by California's Affordable Legal Services Act (besides attorneys) is paralegals.

Often, the reader incorrectly assumes that the writer does not want the reader to consider the set-off phrase. Consequently, use parentheses in this way sparingly.

Parentheses can also be appropriately utilized when introducing an abbreviation.

EXAMPLE

Alternative dispute resolution (ADR) is a viable option to litigation.

Parentheses can also be used to explain an unknown term or phrase such as a term of art.

EXAMPLE

The judge conducted *voir dire* (a French phrase for the process of selecting a jury) without the assistance of counsel.

Finally, parentheses can be used in structured enumeration.

EXAMPLE

The elements of a contract are: (a) agreement, (b) consideration, (c) legal capacity, and (d) legal purpose.

Brackets

In legal documents, brackets ([ ]) are generally used to show a departure from quoted text. When text is quoted and a letter must be changed from upper to lower case (or vice versa), the letter should be enclosed in brackets.

EXAMPLE

The judge noted that "[d]efendant's AA involvement" mitigated his sentence.

Brackets may also be used to add or make a change in a quotation when text is missing in the original. In that case, the word *sic* (meaning, thus or so) is placed within brackets after the correction.

EXAMPLE

"The statue [sic] did not provide any punishment for the crime."

Finally, brackets can be used in limited circumstances to set off extraneous information, much like parentheses.

EXAMPLE

The partners [the Plaintiffs] settled the lawsuit.

Ellipses

When you desire to include some, but not all, of a quoted text, use of the ellipsis (. . .) allows you to extract only as much as is needed. It is formed by three dots, each a space apart.

EXAMPLE

The court ordered that "the motion for reconsideration be denied . . . and defendant immediately incarcerated."

A fourth dot would be added if the ellipsis appeared at the end of a sentence. The ellipsis is often used when quoting material out of context.

Hyphen

In the past, the most typical use of a hyphen (-) was to divide words between syllables at the end of a line. Because right-justified word processing avoids this need, today hyphens are rarely used for this purpose.

Hyphens are still needed with a compound adjective when clarity is important.

EXAMPLE

> well-prepared attorney
> ill-equipped secretary

Hyphens should also be used when spelling out numbers.

EXAMPLE

eight-year lease

Hyphens are not used in most titles.

EXAMPLE

> vice president NOT vice-president
> commander in chief NOT commander-in-chief

Some phrases that once required use of the hyphen have evolved to use of separate words or being spelled solid. For instance, *paralegal* originally appeared as *para-legal*. Hyphens have been replaced by spaces for separate words such as *attorney at law* (not *attorney-at-law.*).

Dash

If the writer's desire is to create a dramatic effect, using a dash (—) may be appropriate. Fiction, rather than law, is the most suitable writing setting to show dramatic effect. There are, nonetheless, some circumstances when drama or emphasis is important in the law.

EXAMPLE

The Defendant—a priest—was charged with child abuse.

An en dash (a shorter dash) is appropriate when used in lieu of *to* to indicate a period of time or a range.

EXAMPLE

He served as a magistrate from 1965–1973.

Slash

A slash or virgule (/) in legal writing is used to mean "either-or." It is most typically used in "and/or." When used this way, it means either but not both. It is also used as punctuation with some commonly accepted legal abbreviations.

EXAMPLE

> a/k/a meaning "also known as"
> d/b/a meaning "doing business as"
> t/a meaning "trading as"

Quotation Marks

Materials are frequently quoted in memoranda. If the quoted material is in excess of 49 words, quotation marks (" ") are not used. Rather, the block quotation style described in *Bluebook* Rule 5.1 is employed. The quoted text is single-spaced, as opposed to the balance of the document, which is double-spaced.

EXAMPLE

Maryland Rule 2-326 addresses "Transfers from District Court on Demand for Jury Trial." Subsection (c) of that Rule provides:

> *Action Not Within Exclusive Original Jurisdiction* of the District Court.—When the action transferred is one over which the District Court does not have exclusive original jurisdiction, a complaint complying with Rules 2-303 through 2-305 shall be filed within 30 days after the date the clerk sends the notice required by section (a) of this Rule.

When presenting a quotation of 49 or fewer words, 2 sets of quotation marks are always used: a set at the beginning and at the end. If the quote ends the sentence, the period comes before (inside) the closing quotation mark.

If the quote is within a quote, a single quote mark is employed.

EXAMPLE

The witness testified, "I heard him say, 'I shot the cop.' "

Quotation marks can also be used to set apart a word or phrase for special emphasis.

EXAMPLE

The court interpreted the word "indigence" to mean below the poverty level.

Question Mark

Questions marks (?), of course, are used only at the end of a question. In legal writing, the only time a question mark is used is at the end of an issue statement, which is posed as a question, or in an interrogatory (a form of discovery discussed in Chapter 15). Rhetorical questions are not proper.

Exclamation Point

Because of their informality, exclamation points (!) are inappropriate in legal writing. The only time they may be used is when quoting material that contains one.

Apostrophe

An apostrophe (') is used in three circumstances: to show possession, plurality, and contractions. It has already been established that contractions are not used in legal writing.

To show possession, the apostrophe plus an "s" (for a single subject) or apostrophe alone (for plural or multiple subject) is added.

attorney's	judges'
client's	clerks'
Jones's	Lena's

An apostrophe can also be used in limited situations to show plurals of numbers and letters.

EXAMPLE

A's   5's

Professor Lee granted seven B's in his legal research class.

BUT

The 1970s saw great changes in the acceptance of paralegals.

Ampersand

The ampersand (&) is rarely used except in citations. In legal writing, its most likely application is in the name of a law firm or company. If the ampersand is part of name of the firm, it must be used rather than "and."

EXAMPLE

INCORRECT

Algier, Smolka, and Warnken

CORRECT

Algier, Smolka & Warnken

In the case of a firm name, a comma is not placed before the ampersand.

Sentence Structure

The sentence is the primary vehicle in which written thoughts are conveyed. Because the sender of a message has the burden of persuasion, all sentences must be clearly written. The easier a sentence is to read, the more likely it is to capture the audience's attention.

A sentence is essentially made up of two components: structure and substance. Dr. George D. Gopen, Director of Writing Programs at Duke University, conducts seminars for attorneys throughout the country on legal writing. He contends that readers focus on structure when analyzing a sentence much more than substance. If the structure is not what a reader expects, the reader might not have sufficient energy or interest to analyze the substance. For this reason, the writer must use structure that is expected by the reader. That way, the reader works less in determining the structure and can devote his efforts to the substance.

Subject-Verb-Object Structure

A sentence must contain at least a subject and a verb. When a sentence is just a subject and a verb, it is referred to as a *simple sentence.*

EXAMPLE

The prisoner escaped.
  (subject) (verb)

Because of the complexity of most legal concepts, this sentence pattern has limited utility in legal writing. The preferred sentence structure is subject, verb, object. In this pattern, the agent (subject) commits an act (verb) on or to the receiver (object). The verb and object are collectively referred to as the *predicate.*

EXAMPLE

The police officer shot the assailant.
  (subject) (verb)   (object)
            (predicate)

Readers generally expect this sentence structure. Consequently, it should be used in most cases. It is straightforward and forceful. For this reason, it is known as the *active voice.*

The *passive voice* results when the subject and object are in reversed order: object, verb, subject. This pattern is less direct and therefore has limited utility in legal writing.

EXAMPLE

> The assailant was shot by the police officer.
> (object)   (verb)   (subject)
> (predicate)

A form of the verb "to be" is often required to complete a sentence that uses the passive voice. The preceding example used the past tense of "to be." A result of using the passive active is that sentences are usually longer and less focused.

In circumstances when it is necessary to shift the focus from the "object" to the "subject" the passive voice might be preferred. Consider the following examples.

EXAMPLE

ACTIVE

> Chawdhari Electronics fired James Wong.
> *(subject)*   *(verb)* *(object)*

This example emphasizes the subject—the doer. If you represented James Wong, you might want to emphasize this action.

EXAMPLE

PASSIVE

> James Wong was fired by Chawdhari Electronics.
> *(object)*   *(verb)*   *(subject)*

Here, the writer wants to emphasize the object—the receiver. The attorney for Chawdhari Electronics might phrase the reference to the event this way.

Finally, it is important to be consistent in the use of active or passive voice in the same sentence. Shifting from one to the other leaves the sentence open to more than one interpretation.

EXAMPLE

INCORRECT

> The Defendant shot the clerk, robbed the store, and a customer was beaten.
> *(subject) (verb) (object) (verb) (object)   (object) (verb)*

CORRECT

> The Defendant shot the clerk, robbed the store, and beat a customer.
> *(subject) (verb) (object) (verb) (object) (verb) (object)*

Action Verbs

The preference for action verbs should be familiar if you have ever drafted a résumé. By using action verbs, the reader is led to visualize the activity. Again, this delivers the intended idea in a dynamic form.

EXAMPLE

INCORRECT

> The prosecutor questioned the witness.

CORRECT

> The prosecutor interrogated the witness.

Inert verbs, often a form of "to be," cloud activity. Always review your writing in an effort to replace inert verbs with action verbs.

INERT VERB FORM		*ACTION VERB FORM*
saw	change to	witnessed
found	change to	discovered
forms of "to be"	change to	the activity being done
is written		wrote/write
is prepared		prepared

Verb Overload

Verbs should not be overloaded; that is, required to handle too many subjects. Often this clouds the sentence's meaning. It is usually better to employ more than one sentence.

EXAMPLE

INCORRECT

Keeping the business open, expanding into new areas, and hiring new employees will be difficult with the current recession, until the economy improves.

CORRECT

Keeping the business open will be difficult with the current recession. Expanding into new areas and hiring new employees should be delayed until the economy improves.

Adjectives and Adverbs

Adjectives modify nouns; adverbs modify verbs. Both should be strategically used to provide the reader with additional information.

EXAMPLE

ADVERB USE

> The public defender *viciously* attacked the informant's credibility.

ADJECTIVE USE

> The *eager* public defender attacked the informant's credibility.

In both sentences, the addition of a modifier adds more information, helping the reader better visualize the occurrence.

You should be on guard for the misplaced modifier. A mispositioned adverb or adjective can change a sentence's meaning.

EXAMPLE

The attorney was interested in specializing in *only* family law. (She would specialize in no other area.)

The attorney was *only* interested in specializing in family law. (She was interested in one thing, specializing in family law.)

Modifiers should be placed as close as possible to the word they are modifying.

Clauses

To add interest in your writing, add clauses. Incorporating a subordinate clause into a subject, verb, object structure creates a complex sentence. A *subordinate clause* (sometimes called a *parenthetical phrase*) is one that is dependant on another clause called the *main clause*.

EXAMPLE

The defendant, who was not convicted, was impeached on the witness stand.
       (subordinate clause)   *(main clause)*

Often the subordinate clause will be linked by a conjunction.

EXAMPLE

The defendant, although he was impeached on the witness stand, was not convicted.
     (conjunction, subordinate clause)   *(main clause)*

Subordinate conjunctions include:

after	although
as	that
before	how
if	until
when	whether
whereas	unless

When two clauses that can stand independently are present, a compound sentence is created. The two clauses can be brought together either by a comma and conjunction or by a semicolon.

EXAMPLE

The police officer investigates, whereas the state's attorney prosecutes.

The two clauses present, "[t]he police officer investigates" and "the state's attorney prosecutes" can both stand alone as complete (though simple) sentences.

Run-On Sentences

A sentence with too many clauses is referred to as a *run-on sentence*. It improperly or unclearly combines two or more sentences into one. A run-on sentence is best corrected by breaking the run-on into separate sentences.

EXAMPLE

INCORRECT

The wife was helpless to prevent her husband from abusing her she received a black eye as a result of his battering.

CORRECT

The wife was helpless to prevent her husband from abusing her. She received a black eye as a result of his battering.

Sentence Fragments

A *sentence fragment* is a group of words put together in an attempt to create a sentence. The words fail to create a sentence because of the absence of a verb. Though sentence fragments are used in general conversation and fiction, they are never appropriate in legal writing.

EXAMPLE

Because the state police were pursuing him for murder.

Noun and Pronoun Ambiguity

It is important that the pronouns used in a sentence be in the same form as the nouns employed in the same sentence.

EXAMPLE

INCORRECT

When the prosecutor and the police detective arrived at court, *she* met with the judge.

CORRECT

When the prosecutor and the police detective arrived at court, *they* met with the judge.

Often, writers mistakenly believe collective nouns to be plural rather than singular. It is important to properly identify the noun on which the verb is acting.

EXAMPLE

INCORRECT

The members of the jury was housed in a local hotel.

CORRECT

The members of the jury were housed in a local hotel.

Members is the subject of the sentence, not *jury*.

Subject-Verb Agreement

The subject and verb must always agree within a sentence. That is, a plural subject must have a plural verb; a singular subject must have a singular verb.

EXAMPLE

INCORRECT

Kim, the secretary, and Mark, the paralegal, generally hostile toward each other, is now the best of friends.

CORRECT

Kim, the secretary, and Mark, the paralegal, generally hostile toward each other, are now the best of friends.

Parallelism and Balance

Parallelism refers to similar word structure within a sentence. Similar words, groupings, and phrases make for easier reading and comprehension.

EXAMPLE

INCORRECT

The judge ordered the defendant's assets seized, compensation given to the employees, and a jail sentence for his partner.

CORRECT

The judge ordered the defendant's assets seized, his employees compensated, and his partner jailed.

When sentences are written using parallel structure, they are easier to understand. The reader does not have to analyze the structure repeatedly. When the words used are approximately the same size and phrases the same length, the structure is said to be *balanced*.

EXAMPLE

He came, he saw, he conquered.

As previously noted, proper use of balanced structure permits the reader to focus on the substance of the sentence, rather than its structure.

The Stress Point

Dr. George Gopen contends that every sentence has a "stress position." This can be thought of as a focal point: where the reader expects to find the most important information in the sentence. Often this stress point is at the end of the sentence. This makes sense if you consider that information located at the end of a sentence is more likely to be remembered than information at the beginning. When crafting a sentence, make sure to place the most significant points in the sentence in the stress position.

EXAMPLE

The jury returned a verdict of guilty when they reassembled.
(The writer is emphasizing the fact that the jurors reassembled.)

The jury reassembled and returned a verdict of guilty.
(The writer is emphasizing the guilty verdict.)

Sentence Length

There is some debate in the legal community as to whether shorter sentences should always be encouraged. Some argue that shorter sentences are more easily read and therefore more effective. Others suggest that complex legal concepts cannot always be treated effectively in short sentences.

Because most sentences should convey only one concept, they can easily be limited to 25 words. As a result, shorter sentences tend to be the norm in paralegal writing. Shorter sentences also are advantageous when you remember the limitations of short-term memory. It is best, however, that sentence length vary. Though many long sentences are inappropriate, too many short sentences can make legal writing sound choppy. Varied writing will retain a reader's interest.

Paragraph Formation

A *paragraph* is a related group of sentences logically developed to convey a single idea or concept. It will include a topic sentence, a body, and occasionally a summation sentence. Both the beginning and end of the paragraph should be positions of emphasis.

Topic Sentence

A topic sentence at the beginning of a paragraph provides the reader with an overview of the substance of the paragraph. A topic sentence should indicate the connection between the various concepts considered in the paragraph.

A well-drafted topic sentence should stand alone. It could be extracted from the paragraph body and still provide sufficient information to be helpful. It also provides structure. All of the topic sentences of a document could be extracted and still provide a coherent, though choppy, discussion.

EXAMPLE

Legislation proposed in California recommends authorizing "legal technicians" to provide "legal assistance or advice" in defined areas of the law, including family law. The bills, introduced in both California houses and referred to collectively as the Affordable Legal Services Act, would create a Board of Legal Technicians to license, register, and regulate this new class of legal professionals. The legislation is bound to meet stiff resistance and scrutiny from traditional legal groups. Though the prospects of quick passage are bleak, the concept is likely to appear in other states and should be considered squarely by all attorneys.

The underscored topic sentence provides an overview of the paragraph. The body of the paragraph further develops the theme. A topic sentence used at the end of a paragraph is often referred to as a *summation sentence*.

Summation Sentence

A summation sentence can serve more than one purpose. In some cases, it is merely a topic sentence placed at the end of a paragraph. At other times, a summation sentence is needed to bring various concepts in a long paragraph together, even when there is a topic sentence.

EXAMPLE

In addition, the members of the legal team have changed. No longer does the team consist of a lawyer and secretary as dramatized by Perry Mason and Della Street. Paralegals, word processors, clerks, librarians, marketing directors, and other newly created positions are appearing. This transformation has now touched the very core of an attorney's raison d'être: the practice of law.

The last sentence brings the paragraph together by indicating the theme of the paragraph—changes in the legal profession that have affected the practice of law. It is not until this point that the reader knows for sure how the sentences are tied together. This type of paragraph is inductive, that is, the reader must infer the theme of the paragraph. Unfortunately, this requires patience on the part of the reader. For this reason, summation sentences should be used in this way sparingly.

Body: Using Paragraph Blocks

The definition of what constitutes the "body" of a paragraph varies with the application. Some short paragraphs appear to have no body at all, and consist of just a topic sentence. In larger paragraphs, the body will be the analysis or development that is described in the topic sentence. On a larger scale, the amorphous concept of a document's body is in reality a number of paragraphs logically developed to convey a specific analysis, argument, opinion, or factual scenario.

With memoranda and advisory letters, the body contains the legal analysis. The bodies of other types of legal documents, such as pleadings and instruments, will vary depending on the substance of the document itself. In an instrument, for instance, the contents will be based on the matters that were negotiated or desired by the parties.

To assist in developing documents, especially memoranda and letters, standard paragraph forms can be used. Marjorie Dick Rombauer and Lynn B. Squires, in their book *Legal Writing in a Nutshell* (4th ed. 1982), discuss these forms in detail. These patterns, called *paragraph blocks,* can be used within one paragraph or among several paragraphs.

A standard paragraph usually follows a typical pattern: topic sentence, elaboration, and conclusion. Here, the first sentence (topic sentence) introduces the topic. It is followed by a detailed discussion of the substance of the topic sentence. Finally, a conclusion or summation sentence summarizes the paragraph.

EXAMPLE

topic
sentence

    The confession, although damaging, is not in itself sufficient to prove the charge. There must be other evidence to corroborate the statements offered in the confession. The reasoning behind this thinking is set out in *Williams v. State,* 214 Md. 143, 132 A.2d 605

elaboration

(1957). There the court said that "[t]he salutary purpose of this rule is to protect the administration of criminal justice against errors of convictions based on untrue confessions alone." In two other cases, *Cooper v. State,* 220 Md. 183, 152 A.2d 120 (1957) and *Pierce v. State,* 227 Md. 221, 175 A.2d 743 (1961), the court stated, "[A]n extrajudicial confession of guilt by an accused person, standing alone, is insufficient to sustain a conviction of guilt."

conclusion

As a consequence, it will be necessary to submit evidence independent of the confession that establishes the guilt of the accused.

A variation—the Elaboration, Topic sentence pattern—is rarely recommended in legal writing applications. Here the elaboration (or support) is given first. The summation sentence, acting as a topic sentence, is at the end. As indicated previously, in this pattern a reader not knowledgeable about law might be left guessing until the end as to the theme of the paragraph.

EXAMPLE

elaboration

    The State could show the *corpus delicti* of murder by producing the body of the victim. This would not, however, connect our client to the crime. In considering the cases cited previously regarding the effect of the statement that Mr. Johnson made to the police, the State will have to show other corroborating evidence that confirms the facts of the

elaboration

statement in order for the statement to be admissible. The evidence at present is not sufficient to make this showing. If the State does produce evidence, direct or circumstantial, that verifies the statements made by Mr. Johnson, then there will be a direct link connecting our client to the crime. Although this situation would not be fatal to our case, it could be

topic sentence very damaging. The availability of corroborating evidence is a key factor in determining the extent of damage caused by the confession statement.

The IRAC method of analysis was discussed previously. As applied in legal writing, this pattern includes stating the Issue, establishing a Rule of law, Applying the facts to the law (analyzing them), and reaching a Conclusion. This is one of the most utilized writing patterns. It is employed in most forms of legal writing: correspondence, research memoranda, trial memoranda, and appellate briefs.

EXAMPLE

issue   The ultimate issue to be decided by the court deals with whether the biological mother is the proper custodial parent of the children. In deciding this issue, the court must be guided by "what is in the best interests of the child." *Montgomery County v. Sanders,* 38 Md. App. 406, 381 A.2d 1154 (1978). The court must also be mindful of the fact that *rule* under Maryland law it is presumed that the child's best interest is served by custody with a parent. This presumption is overcome if the parent is unfit to have custody, or if there are exceptional circumstances that make custody detrimental to the child's interests. *application/ analysis* *Ross v. Hoffman,* 280 Md. 172, 372 A.2d 582 (1977). In the present case, the facts reveal a mother who is caring, responsible, and concerned about her child's welfare. No evidence has been presented to indicate otherwise. As a result, it would appear that the best interests of *conclusion* the child are served by an award of custody to the biological mother.

In the Problem, Solution pattern, the problem is first stated, followed by the solution.

EXAMPLE

problem   The primary issue in this matter is whether our client is entitled to petition the court for guardianship of her brother's property. The statutory provision governing this is Md. Code Ann. Est. & Trusts § 13-207 (1991). The law permits several classifications of individuals to apply for guardianship status. Siblings are not specifically listed. However, it appears that *solution* our client might fall under two provisions: a person who would be his heir if he were dead, and any other person considered appropriate by the court.

In the Comparison and Contrast pattern, opposing fact patterns, legal principles, or theories are considered and analyzed. This pattern generally covers at least two paragraphs.

EXAMPLE

    In determining liability for injuries sustained by skiers on ski slopes, defending ski resorts must overcome claims of negligence by skiers and often use as a defense the skier's assumption of risk or contributory negligence. Resorts normally have a duty to clearly mark designated trails, indicate the degree of difficulty of the trails, and place warning markers at hazards of which the skier might not be aware.

contrast   Skiers, in contrast, must maintain that their behavior was reasonable under the circumstances and refute any charges of assumption of risk or contributory negligence.

Skiers have a duty to ski on trails within the limits of their ability, maintain control of their speed and course, watch for potential hazards, and avoid encounters with such hazards.

Finally, in a Definition pattern, the paragraph consists of a detailed definition or discussion of a legal rule.

EXAMPLE

In Maryland, the liability of a landowner to a person on the landowner's premises depends upon the status of the person while on the premises. This status may be that of an invitee, licensee by invitation, bare licensee, or trespasser. *Wagner v. Doehring,* 315 Md. 97, 553 A.2d 686 (1989). An *invitee* is defined as a person invited or permitted to enter or remain on another's property for purposes connected with or related to the owner's business. *Sherman v. Suburban Trust Co.,* 282 Md. 238, 384 A.2d 76 (1978). A landowner owes a duty to the invitee to keep the owner's premises in a reasonably safe condition and to protect the invitee against dangers of which the landowner knows, or which with reasonable care he should have discovered. *Maryland State Fair v. Lee,* 29 Md. App. 374, 348 A.2d 44 (1975).

Transitions

Transitions are needed to segue properly between sentences and paragraphs. A good transition will show the connection between the concept that preceded it and the one that follows it. Transitions are, in a sense, the glue that holds legal writing together. Transitions can consist of one- or two-sentence paragraphs, sentences at the beginning of a paragraph, and words such as *first, second, next,* and *since.*

Transitional paragraphs in legal writing are frequently used in large documents dealing with multiple or complex issues. They are usually short paragraphs whose purpose is to explain the relationship between two issues or concepts.

EXAMPLE

… Mr. Roland's next option is to have a magnetic resonance image (MRI) completed. However, in that he is uninsured, he is required to bear the entire cost of the procedure. The cost of the scan ranges from $1,000 to $1,200. Just the same, he anticipates depleting his savings to have the MRI completed.

Medical specials are only part of the damages Mr. Roland has suffered. He also lost considerable wages as a result of your company's faulty product.

It is Mr. Roland's belief that there were approximately 24 weeks in which he was out of work due to the injuries suffered on August 6, 1995. At a rate of $175 per week, his total loss of income was $4,200 … .

In shorter works, the effect can be accomplished through the use of a transitional sentence. Here, a sentence summarizing the previous paragraph is placed in the beginning of the subsequent paragraph.

In the following example, the previous paragraph discussed the faulty construction of a drummer's throne.

EXAMPLE

The faulty construction of the drummer's throne should now be obvious. Shortly after the accident, Mr. Roland began to suffer significant pain and discomfort. For the next several weeks he had difficulty lifting and frequently his back gave out ... .

One useful transitional device is the use of structured enumeration. This may be employed by use of the words *first, second,* or *third* in a sentence.

EXAMPLE

To establish a cause of action in strict liability in this case, Mr. Roland must prove four elements. First, he must show that the product was in a defective condition at the time it left the control of the seller. Second, he must demonstrate that the product was unreasonably dangerous to him as a user or consumer. Third, Mr. Roland must prove to the court that the defect in the product caused his injuries. Fourth, he must show that the product reached him without substantial change in its condition.

In addition, it is acceptable to use numbers in parentheses, such as (1), (2), (3), and (4), for purposes of showing transition.

EXAMPLE

The elements of a cause of action in negligence are (1) duty, (2) breach, (3) proximate cause, and (4) damages.

Paragraph Length

A key to writing convincingly is the use of short paragraphs. Professional fundraisers have long known that prospective donors tend to "glaze over" when they see long paragraphs. Thus the letters that fundraisers send are always made up of punchy, concise paragraphs. A long paragraph requires too many concepts to be retained in short term memory. The rule is: If the reader is required to reread the paragraph, it is too long.

Effective Legal Style

Of course, writing is not just arbitrarily putting words together. Conscious decisions must be made as to the appropriate legal style required for the document.

Uses to Avoid

The following uses should be guarded against in legal writing.

Ambiguity

Legal problems require specific legal answers by clients. Because laws are constantly changing and being reinterpreted, lawyers have a tendency to write in an ambiguous style, leaving open multiple interpretations. It should be kept in mind, however, that clients pay attorneys for specifics, not ambiguity. Why did the client want a one-handed lawyer? Because he was tired of lawyers saying "on the one hand" and "on the other hand" when providing answers. Legal answers must be presented in a straightforward fashion.

Ambiguity can be caused in numerous ways. The first is *personification*. This is when a thing is said to represent some ability, quality, thing, or idea. "The legal principle sprang to life" is an example. Here, a human or animate being's ability, "sprang," is attributed to a legal principle.

A second form of ambiguity is known as *metonymy*. This is the substitution of one label of a thing for that of another that is suggested by the first. An example would be to say that "the White House" issued a presidential proclamation, rather than "the President" issued it.

Another form of ambiguity is the use of an *oxymoron*. This is the combination of contradictory words to form a phrase. "Wise fool," "problematic solution," and "quiet thunder" are examples of oxymorons.

The use of clichés (expressions that have lost their novelty and effectiveness through overuse) can cause writing to be unclear. To say that "the attorney was as cool as a cucumber" adds little in the way of specificity as to the attorney's mannerisms.

Slang words not only create ambiguity, but are also too informal for legal writing. It would not be appropriate to say that "the judge got ticked off at Plaintiff's counsel."

Metaphors and similes are similar devices used for purposes of comparison. In a metaphor, one thing is stated to be another when the two are in actuality unrelated. For example, "all the world's a stage." A simile does not go as far as a metaphor, but tries to show how two concepts are alike. In a simile, one concept or thing is said to be "like" something else, as in "the judge was like a hungry bear" or "legalese should be avoided like the plague." Often, similes and metaphors appear as slang. Metaphors and similes are rarely useful in legal writing.

Sexism

Gender-specific language is not suitable for general legal writing. This is particularly important when using occupational nouns. You should pluralize when possible so you can use gender-neutral pronouns such as *they* or *them*. If it is necessary to use the pronouns *he* or *she* in writing, you should alternate usage within your document. However, changing from "he" to "she" frequently in a short document such as a letter will cause confusion. In those cases, stick to one form, conscious of the need to avoid sexism.

GENDER-SPECIFIC	*GENDER-NEUTRAL*
foreman	foreperson
fireman	firefighter
chairman	chairperson, chair
policeman	police officer
stewardess, steward	flight attendant
workmen's compensation	workers' compensation
cleaning lady	housekeeper
executor, executrix	personal representative
congressman	congressperson, member of Congress
housewife	homemaker

Of course, it is perfectly proper to refer to a particular individual with the appropriate pronoun.

Legalese, Terms of Art, and Double-Meaning Words

The problems with legalese were addressed in detail in Chapter 10. Legalese should always be avoided (but not "like the plague"). Terms of art, however, often must be used because their nonlegal explanations are too unwieldy. For example, there is no simple English definition for the Latin term **per stirpes**. Using the Latin phrase makes better sense. Double-meaning words must be properly translated or defined for the reader. Words that have a different meaning in the law than they do in standard English, such as **fee**, **consideration**, and **discovery**, are examples.

Verbosity and Redundancy

To be *verbose* is to be excessive in the use of words. Often writers use more words than are necessary in a phrase or sentence. Consider the following sentences:

——————————————————— LEGAL TERMS ———————————————————

per stirpes † *(Latin)* Means "by the root"; according to class; by representation. Per stirpes describes the method of dividing or distributing an estate in which the heirs of a deceased heir share the portion of the estate that the deceased heir would have received had he or she lived.

fee † An estate in real property that may be inherited. When "fee" is used without words of limitation, it always means fee simple.

consideration † The reason a person enters into a contract; that which is given in exchange for performance or the promise to perform; the price bargained and paid; the inducement. Consideration is an essential element of a valid and enforceable contract. A promise to refrain from doing something one is entitled to do also constitutes consideration.

discovery † A means for providing a party, in advance of trial, with access to facts that are within the knowledge of the other side, to enable the party to better try his or her case.

EXAMPLE

She was represented by an attorney in <u>regard to</u> her lawsuit. All <u>of</u> the candidates for judge were present at the debate. I will pay my <u>annual</u> dues on a yearly basis.

In these examples, the underscored words are unnecessary. The words either repeat already established facts or are unnecessary for structural purposes.

Wordiness is a form of verbosity. There is some truth to the common stereotype that lawyers write long sentences to explain simple issues. Much is due to the desire to be diplomatic in writing. Lawyers often place conditions in their writing, tone down their sentences, or use "waffle" words to lessen the blow of harsh consequences and results. Unfortunately, many attorneys habitually write in this way without considering if the purpose of the document is served by this approach. Learn to be stingy with words.

Often verbosity takes the form of redundancy. *Redundancy* refers to the unnecessary repetition of words or phrases (a form of legalese). Redundancy often exists in the pairing of legal words. Words such as "force and effect," "due and owing," "each and every," and "null and void" are needless repetitions.

Uses to Encourage

The following features of legal writing should be present in every sentence, paragraph, and document prepared.

Precision

A major requirement of all legal writing is precision. Because legal principles are often detailed and exact, the words used to describe them must also be precise. The words used to describe legal principles must be specific enough that only one interpretation is possible. Every individual who reads a legal document should take the same meaning from its contents. Striving for universal meaning is a critical goal in legal writing.

EXAMPLE

For purposes of this agreement, "weekend" is defined as Friday from 6:00 P.M. until Sunday at 6:00 P.M.

Consistency

The style and tone of writing in a document must be consistent throughout. Strive for consistency in word choice as well as in perspective. For instance, if a document refers to a party's husband, Admiral Jones, calling this individual alternatively "the Admiral," "Jones," and "Mr. Jones" in the letter would be inconsistent.

Completeness

Completeness, a form of comprehensiveness, is relative to the circumstances. There are times when it might not be critical to provide *all* the facts. Often, however, you must be complete to achieve other goals. For instance, to precisely describe a chain of events requires a comprehensive analysis of the facts. A client will not understand a legal alternative when she is only informed of some of the applicable principles. A court will not accept a legal position when it is informed of only half the relevant facts. (In addition, it might be unethical to tell only part of the story—in a sense, modifying the truth—to the court.)

Conciseness

Good legal writing is characterized by being concise. To be concise is to include what is important in as few words as possible without sacrificing clarity. Run-on sentences, by definition, are not concise. The use of legalese and other archaisms thwarts conciseness. To be clear is to write in a fashion that allows for only one interpretation of what is written.

EXAMPLE

NOT CONCISE

Lynette Thomas-Peters, Plaintiff, doing business as Creative Designs, submits this Memorandum of Law in support of her Amended Motion for New Trial or to Alter or Amend a Judgment filed on January 19, 1995, and in opposition to Defendant's Memorandum in Support of Its Motion for New Trial.

CONCISE

Lynette Thomas-Peters, Plaintiff, d/b/a Creative Designs, submits this memorandum in support of her amended motion filed January 19, 1995. It is also filed in opposition to Defendant's memorandum.

Positive Approach

Sentences should take a positive approach whenever possible. Readers understand direct, affirmative statements more readily than negative ones. Remember, sentences should be constructed in patterns familiar to readers.

EXAMPLE

INCORRECT

The attorney was not unfamiliar with trial procedure.

CORRECT

The attorney was familiar with trial procedure.

Familiar, Concrete Words

Because the law deals with abstract concepts, legal professionals tend to use abstract terms and phrases when more concrete words are more appropriate. Keep in mind that all legal writing should be clear. Establish the essential habit of seeking the most familiar and basic word or phrase. Stay away from unfamiliar words, many of which fall into the category of legalese.

UNFAMILIAR	*FAMILIAR*
in terms of	at, in, for, by, with
aforementioned	previous
in lieu of	instead
in light of	considering
hereafter	after this

Logical Development

Legal writing must be logical in its presentation. There is no such thing in law as a leap of faith. The reader cannot be left to guess about a concept, principle, or fact. If a legal principle is reduced to its elements, connection must be shown between each part. Facts must be presented chronologically, or at least in a way that is complete and makes sense to the reader. You must remember that every legal document is based on identifying goals or purposes, translating these goals to steps, and then putting these steps in meaningful order. This is often accomplished through an outline.

IRAC Method

The IRAC method, when applied to writing, can help you logically present a legal argument. To illustrate:

1. In analyzing a topic, the *issue* being considered is presented first.

EXAMPLE

Can newly discovered evidence located after a trial be the basis for granting a request for new trial?

2. A *rule* is offered or located which will be helpful in answering the issue. This rule is always a form of primary law.

EXAMPLE

If newly discovered evidence that directly contradicts material facts admitted at trial is found, and this new evidence would bring about a different result, then a new trial is required. *Angell v. Just,* 22 Md. App. 43, 321 A.2d 830 (1974).

3. The most critical part of the IRAC method is the *application/analysis* portion, in which the relevant law is juxtaposed with the facts. From this a certain result is prescribed by the rule.

EXAMPLE

In the case at bar, the newly discovered evidence is a cancelled check from Upper Dauphin High School. This evidence specifically contradicts testimony by a witness for Plaintiff that payment had not been made by Defendant. The newly discovered evidence would produce a different result. In this case, Defendant must be exonerated from failure to pay the commission because the check indicates that payment was made.

4. Finally, a *conclusion* is presented, summarizing the results of the application.

EXAMPLE

Based on the application of the rule from *Angell,* a new trial should be granted. Newly discovered evidence that would produce a different result has been located, thus requiring a new trial.

Chronological

The most coherent method of presenting facts is in a chronological fashion. This works because most individuals understand facts as they relate to the passage of time.

EXAMPLE

MOTION FOR A NEW TRIAL

1. On August 27, 1994, Peter Gray Entertainment, Plaintiff, filed suit in the District Court of Maryland against Willie James, d/b/a "The Rockers," Defendant, for failure to pay for services, claiming Two Thousand Dollars ($2,000) in damages.

2. Defendant filed a timely Notice of Intention to Defend on September 10, 1994.

3. Trial on the merits was held January 8, 1995.

4. At trial, judgment was entered against Defendant in the amount of Two Thousand Dollars ($2,000).

5. On January 12, 1995, Defendant filed a Motion for New Trial.

Importance of Outlining

The benefits of outlining were addressed in Chapter 10. Before you begin a legal or factual discussion, outlining is critical. Of all the advantages of an outline, the most important is helping you develop confidence in your writing.

EXAMPLE

I. (Topic) Motion for New Trial

A. (Issue) Procedure
   1. (Rule) Motion Rule 3-533
   2. (Application)
   3. (Conclusion)
B. (Issue) Basis: Newly discovered evidence
   1. (Rule) *Angell v. Just*
   2. (Application)
   3. (Conclusion)

Strongest Argument First

The reader usually expects to read your best argument first. Do not disappoint this expectation. Starting with a strong point gives the reader a positive impression about the entire document and the entire argument. Also, if the recipient reads only half of the paper, the most important points will have been made.

Editing Considerations

As you recall, the process of writing can be viewed as a three-step process. Step one involves understanding the document's purpose, audience, and any constraints present; step two focuses on structure and preparing a draft; and step three is editing and rewriting. This last step is probably the most important, because it gives you the opportunity to revisit the matters completed in steps one and two. Editing takes two forms: editing for grammar and style, and editing for substance.

Editing for Grammar and Style

Grammar must always be considered before style. Even if the style of writing is appropriate, a document containing many punctuation, spelling, or citation errors will be devalued.

Before editing, you must have the appropriate tools: a dictionary (both legal and standard), a grammar handbook, a thesaurus, the *Bluebook,* and sufficient time. Because of the hectic pace of work in many law offices, writers put off editing until the last moment, thinking that sufficient time will be available. Without careful planning, this is rarely so.

It is easiest to check the spelling of a document. For this reason, it should be done twice, at the beginning of the editing process and again after editing for substance. Do not rely on a computer's spell check program. Look at every word individually. It might take some time, but this way every word is considered. During this process, also evaluate word choice with the use of a thesaurus. Be wary of using the same word or phrase repeatedly, unless considerations of consistency demand it. Repetition can grate on the reader.

Paralegal Tip

The best way to proofread for spelling and citation is by reading the document backward. Because we tend to read words in groups, we often fail to pick up subtle spelling errors; we see what we expect to see. By reading the document backward, you focus on individual words and avoid getting caught up in the writing's structure or meaning.

After reviewing for spelling, read for punctuation and sentence structure. This can be an arduous process. All of the rules discussed in this chapter, as well as many others, must be considered. Common punctuation errors include the misuse of commas and apostrophes. Consider using semicolons where appropriate. Make sure that periods are placed appropriately in relation to punctuation marks. When considering sentence structure, examine every sentence to determine whether a subject, verb, and object are present. You should remove these words from the sentence and then reconstruct it word by word. Reduce the length of long sentences, but vary the overall length of sentences.

Then check for tone and logical development. If you are writing in the first person (that is, referring to yourself as "I" or "we"), is that voice being used consistently? Does the document sound condescending? Reconsidering the audience's characteristics will help you focus on tone. If a document requires considerable revision, determine if developing a new outline might be helpful.

Checking citations requires careful application of the *Bluebook* rules. Make sure that parallel citations, if needed, are present.

To edit effectively, it is important to know the language of editing—proofreader's marks (see Figure 11-1). If you are fortunate enough to have a secretary to assist you, he will be most grateful when you employ these standard marks. If you type your own documents, consistent use of proofreader's marks will help you recall your changes at a later date.

Editing for Substance

Editing for substance involves careful reconsideration of the purpose, issues, and legal analysis of the document. Often, by this point, you have reconsidered the issues that you began with. This is often the situation when you prepare a research memorandum. Make sure the issues are consistent with the authority you have located. Ask yourself if this authority responds to the issues. If it does not, you must search for new legal authority.

Revising the analytical portion of the document may be a difficult undertaking. The best method is to reemploy step three from the plan for legal research. This requires that you ensure that the legal principles employed are up-to-date. Shepardizing is the most effective way of accomplishing this.

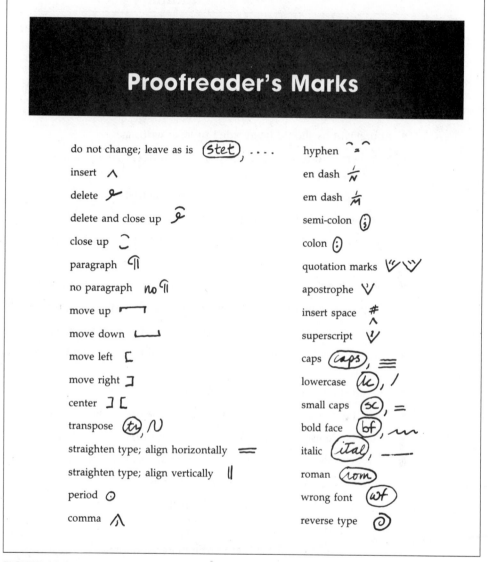

FIGURE 11-1 Proofreader's marks

Benefits of Another's Objectivity

Most writers develop a paternalistic attitude toward their writing. They are very protective of what they have created and do not want to make modifications. Unfortunately, this attitude often ignores deficiencies in grammar and substance. For these reasons, ask a third person (preferably a co-worker) to objectively review your document and suggest changes. You will soon find this individual asking you to review his work!

Summary

- Mechanics refers to word choice, punctuation, sentence structure, and paragraph formation.

- Style refers to the diction and tone of legal exposition.

- An individual who has been admitted to the bar may add Esquire to his or her name.

- The capitalization of words can add precision and emphasis in legal writing.

- Abbreviations should be avoided in legal writing.

- Numbers zero to nine are spelled out; numbers 10 and above are written in arabic numerals.

- Latin legal terms generally need not be italicized.

- Contractions should never be used in legal writing.

- *Shall, will,* and *may* have distinct differences in meaning and application.

- A clause beginning with *that* is restrictive; one beginning with *which* is unrestrictive.

- Poor spelling destroys the effectiveness of an otherwise well-written document.

- The goal of punctuation is to create only one possible interpretation for a sentence.

- The overall purpose of a comma is to separate two distinct concepts within a sentence.

- A semicolon can strategically indicate a subtle relationship between two parts of a sentence.

- The most appropriate use of a colon is to introduce a list.

- Parentheses are used to set apart text for special consideration.

- Brackets are usually used to show departure from quoted text.

- Ellipses show where the writer has extracted only a portion of quoted material.

- Hyphens are used with compound adjectives.

- Use of the dash creates a dramatic effect.

- A slash is used to mean either/or.

- Quotation marks are used when the material quoted is 49 words or fewer.

- A question mark is only used at the end of an issue or interrogatory.

- Exclamation points are not used in legal writing.

- In legal writing, an apostrophe is used to show possession or plurality.

- The ampersand can be used in a firm name.

- The primary vehicle in which written thoughts are conveyed is in a sentence.

- A sentence is made up of structure and substance.

- A sentence must have a subject and a verb. Most sentences have a subject, verb, and object.

- The subject-verb form of sentence is known as the active voice. The object-verb form is known as the passive voice.

- Action verbs are preferred in legal writing.

- Verbs should not be overloaded.

- Adjectives modify nouns; adverbs modify verbs.

- Clauses make writing more interesting.

- A run-on sentence is a sentence with too many clauses.

- A sentence fragment is a group of words that lacks a verb.

- Nouns and pronouns must be in the same form in a sentence.

- The subject and verb in a sentence must always agree.

- Parallelism should be observed in sentence structure.

- Significant points should be placed in the sentence's stress point.

- Sentence length should vary in legal writing.

- A paragraph includes a topic sentence, a body, and occasionally a summation sentence. A topic sentence provides the reader with an overview of the paragraph's substance. A summation sentence is located at the end of a paragraph.

- Paragraph blocks can help in structuring the body of paragraphs. Paragraph block patterns include Topic sentence, Elaboration, and Conclusion; Elaboration, Topic sentence; IRAC; Problem, Solution; Comparison and Contrast; and Definition.

- Transitions are needed to connect sentences and paragraphs. Words, sentences, and paragraphs can serve as transitions.

- Paragraphs should be kept short.

- Ambiguity should be avoided in legal writing.

- Gender-biased language is not suitable for legal writing.

- Legalese should be avoided in documents; terms of art and double-meaning words should be used cautiously.

- Verbosity and redundancy should be avoided.

- Legal writing should be precise.

- The style and tone in a document should be consistent.

- Completeness should be strived for in legal writing.

- Good legal writing is characterized by being concise.

- Sentences should take a positive approach.

- Familiar, definite words should be used in legal writing.

- Legal writing must be logical in presentation. Use of the IRAC method helps ensure logic. A chronological development is appropriate when discussing facts.

- Outlining helps the writer develop confidence and a logical presentation.

- The strongest argument should be placed first in a document.

- There are two aspects of editing: editing for grammar and style, and editing for substance.

- Having another individual review your document is a good editing technique.

Review Questions

1. Why might a writer want to use a party's name rather than the party's litigation status?

2. Are seasons of the year capitalized in legal writing?

3. What is the rule regarding writing out numbers?

4. Would italics be used for the word res judicata? Why or why not?

5. Are contractions used in legal writing?

6. If a judge were ordering a defendant to jail immediately, would she use the word *shall, will,* or *may* in her order?

7. Are the following words correctly spelled?
   defendent   supersede
   bankrupcy   tenant
   Correct them if they are not.

8. What is tight punctuation? Why is it preferred over loose punctuation in legal writing?

9. What is the overall purpose of a comma?

10. Are semicolons placed inside or outside closing quotation marks?

11. Indicate two appropriate uses of parentheses.

12. Why are hyphens less used today than in the past?

13. Why would a slash be used?

14. How does a quote within a quote appear?

15. Why is sentence structure of more importance than sentence substance to readers?

16. Define the passive voice. In what situation might it be preferred?

17. Why is there a preference for using action verbs?

18. What is the best way of rewriting a run-on sentence?

19. What is the significance of the "stress position" in a sentence?

20. What is the purpose of a topic sentence?

21. List the standard paragraph blocks employed in legal writing.

22. What is the purpose of a transition?

23. Why are short paragraphs preferred over long paragraphs?

24. List several causes of ambiguity in legal writing.

25. What is a metaphor? Give an example.

26. What is meant by being concise in legal writing?

27. What is meant by taking the positive approach in legal writing?

28. What is the best way to present facts in a legal document?

29. What tools should the writer have before starting to edit?

30. What is involved in editing for substance?

Chapter Exercises

1. The letter in Figure 11-2 has been drafted by the attorney for Chawdhari Electronics, Inc. concerning James Wong's allegations of illegal termination. Correct all errors in the letter.

March first, 1996

Ms. Marie LeClaire, Esquire
101 Wilson Avenue
Salt Lake City, Utah 84119-3567

Dear Ms. LeClaire,

This office has been retained to represent Chawdhari Electronics, Inc. regarding a claim made by your client Mr. James Wong.

Evidently, your client allegdes that he and the president of Chawdhari Electronics entered into a contract for his employment for 2 years that prohibited his being dismissed during that period of time. This was'nt the case at all!

Your client was hired by Chawdhari Electronics on October 18, 1995 to commence immediately Mr. Wong's position was that of customer sales representative. An agreed condition of his employment was maintaining a saled quoto as determined jointly by Mr. Chawdhari and your client. Unfortunately Mr. Wong has failed to maintain the quotos set, even after adjustments in the figures was agreed to by my client. As a consequence James was terminated.

To reiterate, though there was an agrement of employment, it was conditioned on sale performance. Wong's allegations are totally without merit. How about dropping this case? Bringing this lawsuit is just not kosher!

Thank you for your consideraton.

Very truly yours,

Margaret W. Greatbear

FIGURE 11-2 Letter to Wong's attorney

2. Consider the language on the ski lift ticket shown in Figure 11-3. Edit, keeping in mind the principles of drafting good sentences, as discussed in this chapter.

The purchaser of any ticket purchases it and uses it with the understanding that skiing is a hazardous sport that there are spots, ice, changing snow bumps, stumps, stones, trees and obstructions exist in any ski area in purchasing a ticket the purchaser recognizes such dangers whether marked or unmarked and realizes that falls and collisions are common and numerous and that injuries can result and that he accepts the hazards of the sport and the danger of injury thereto including negligence and carelessness on the part of fellow skiers it is with this understanding that such ticket is sold all tickets may be revoked by the management at any time without refund and are non-transferable.

FIGURE 11-3 Ski lift ticket language

3. Consider the language from the Annotated Code of Maryland shown in Figure 11-4. Edit the statute with the goal of making it understandable to persons who might be subject to its provisions.

Art. 27, § 152　　　ANNOTATED CODE OF MARYLAND

FEMALE SITTERS

§ 152. Employment prohibited.

　　It shall be unlawful for any proprietor, lessee or manager of any variety entertainment or concert hall (whether an admittance fee is charged or not), to employ, engage or allow any female sitters (or by whatever other name they may be called) in or about said entertainment or concert hall, building, room or premises; and all females who are allowed in or about the said premises who shall drink, smoke or partake any kind of eatables or refreshments at the expense of others, or solicit others to purchase such things as may be purchased there, upon which they shall receive or expect to receive a commission, or who may be paid a regular salary therefor, or who participate in any way in the profits thereof, shall be deemed sitters under this section. (An. Code, 1951, § 175; 1939, § 160; 1924, § 148; 1912, § 128; 1904, § 116; 1888, § 85; 1886, ch. 171, § 1.)

FIGURE 11-4 Criminal statute

If Maryland's constitution had an equal rights amendment, do you think this statute would be constitutional?

4. Correct the following sentences.
   a. Mr. Brian Long, Esq., who has been practicing law for over twenty-five (25) years was not appointed to the position of judge because of incompetency.

    b. Officers O'Brien and Martinez of the Southwestern District is prepared to testify at the Trial.

    c. The corporation entered into the new contract, new employees were hired, and they decided to purchase new property.

    d. "I am ordering you to serve 5 days in the county jail: the judge said in Court.

5. Rewrite the following sentences using the subject, verb, object pattern.

    a. Carol's daughter was injured by Mark's lawn mower.

    b. A new trial was ordered by the intermediate appellate court.

    c. The paralegal was hired by the firm the same day she was interviewed.

IIII
CHAPTER 12

CORRESPONDENCE

OVERVIEW

The letter is the form of legal writing most frequently employed in a law practice. It is through correspondence that legal professionals communicate with those outside the office. In fact, attorneys often prefer letter writing to telephone contact because it provides a permanent record of the event for both participants.

Many observers note that the amount of correspondence has increased over the last several decades. There are two possible causes for this increase. First, the introduction of word processors and computers has shortened production time. As a consequence, letter writing has become more economical and, in a modest way, possibly more profitable. The second cause stems from the mood that exists in the practice of law today. Heightened concerns about malpractice actions and bar association investigations have caused attorneys to practice law "defensively," focusing much of their effort on protecting themselves from accusations of wrongdoing. One means of self-protection is to document every decision, agreement, or settlement reached with a client by letter.

As a paralegal, when you write to clients, you must describe matters in concrete terms. Never promise a specific outcome, though. Also, keep in mind that clients both deserve and expect to be treated with respect and courtesy. These concepts are developed further in this chapter.

In most practices, the basic format of a legal letter is known as modified semi-block. It is characterized by indented paragraphs and left margins that are either left-justified or five spaces to the right of center. In some offices, block form is preferred. In this form, every portion of the letter is left-justified.

This chapter examines the variety of letters composed in a legal practice. Letters fall into four categories, according to their overall purpose: cover, confirmatory, informational, and advisory. As a paralegal you may play a large role in composing all forms of correspondence. However, you are permitted to sign only cover, confirmatory, and informational letters, but never advisory letters. This is because advisory letters involve the offering of legal advice or the presenting of a legal position. Both of these acts constitute the practice of law and thus are prohibited activities for paralegals.

PARALEGAL PRACTICE SITUATION

You are employed as a paralegal in the office of your state's attorney general. The attorney general has been contacted by representatives of the Kirwin Community Association. They are concerned that the continual use of lawn herbicides by one of the members, Wilbur Hack, is endangering the neighborhood. Evidently, several of the children in the area have developed mild respiratory problems after playing on or near the property. This concern is further exacerbated by the fact that the public elementary school bus stop is adjacent to Hack's property.

The association members would like the attorney general to take legal action against the property owner and Good Grow Grass, Inc., the company that treats the property. They specifically would like an injunction against further use.

The assistant attorney general for whom you work would like you to compose a letter to the Environmental Protection Agency for her signature. Pursuant the provisions of the federal Freedom of Information Act, reports of any government-sponsored scientific studies performed on dichlorophenoxyacetic acid (known as 2,4-D), the active ingredient in the treatment used by Good Grow Grass, should be available for public review. If studies have shown that the chemical is harmful, this consideration would support taking action.

Factors Affecting Correspondence Today

Legal professionals draft correspondence for a variety of reasons. Most of these reasons are rooted in the traditional role of the attorney: to advocate, represent, advise, negotiate, and report.

Two factors in the practice environment have affected the quality and purposes of legal correspondence. The first is the advent of the computer age. The introduction of word processing and computers have made letter production quicker and easier to accomplish. In the past, every letter was written literally from scratch. The letter was usually dictated to a secretary, who would take it down by shorthand and then type a first draft on a typewriter. The attorney would make changes manually and return the corrected letter to the secretary for a second draft. Often there were subsequent drafts as well, depending on the complexity of the letter.

Word processing revolutionized this process. Now, if one letter is similar to a previous one, the earlier one can be retrieved from a database and changes needed for the new letter made right on the screen. Many letters are standard and thus can be set up as form fill-ins. To create a new letter, the base form is accessed and the new information is inserted. Thus, a new letter is created in a fraction of the time needed to compose it from scratch. Even complicated letters are easier to produce because of the ease of correction (no more messy correction fluid!) and the speed with which printing a draft can be accomplished.

Paralegal Tip

Today, few attorneys require their secretaries to take shorthand. Most firms rely on microcassette recorders and dictation machines. Many users are, unfortunately, unaware of the proper way to dictate. They tend to dictate into the microphone at the same speed as in normal conversation. Few secretaries can type as fast as attorneys and paralegals can speak! The transcriber is forever rewinding the tape to pick up missing portions. To make it easier for the secretary and shorten the letter writing time, adhere to the following guidelines:

1. Always speak slowly and clearly into the microphone.
2. If special instructions are to be included on the tape, make sure they are provided clearly and in detail.
3. Make sure the file to which the dictated document relates is either attached to the tape or is easily accessible.
4. Leave clear written instructions with the tape. Many offices use routing slips that provide information such as the name of the file/client, file number, name of document, date dictated, desired date of completion, and name of the attorney/paralegal dictating the letter.

The ease of production in legal writing today has economically impacted the practice of law. If an attorney charged by the letter, she could produce more correspondence in less time, thereby increasing her income. The majority of attorneys do not, however, charge in this manner. A second effect is that attorneys can let secretaries do much of the letter writing, thereby leaving the attorneys more time for more profitable tasks, such as preparing pleadings and other complex documents.

The second factor affecting the preparation of correspondence today is the increasingly defensive attitude many lawyers have taken in practicing law. In the past, complaints against attorneys were rare. Only the most incompetent attorneys had bar grievances lodged against them. Times have changed. With consumer power as the watchword, both malpractice actions and bar grievances are at an all-time high. A large percentage of these complaints stem from miscommunication and misunderstanding between attorney and client. Attorneys may either convey the wrong message or fail to communicate a message at all. Because clients under stress frequently misinterpret telephone conversations that deal with legal complexities, attorneys today regularly send confirmatory letters to clients reemphasizing or clarifying certain points or legal concepts. This is especially important when settlement offers are rejected or litigation strategies are determined. Clients often forget, after losing at trial, that they rejected an earlier settlement offer. They might also wonder why certain witnesses were not called to testify. The client might very well blame the attorney for not bringing the strategy change or settlement offer to the client's attention. If the attorney had confirmed these matters by letter, she would be protected.

Some Considerations About Writing to Clients

Several noteworthy considerations must be kept in mind when writing to clients, the most common audience for correspondence.

A particular outcome must never be promised. Words in a letter must be chosen with great care to avoid any impression of a guarantee. This does not prevent pledging to represent a client efficiently according to the highest legal standards. This language, in fact, often appears in **retainer letters** (see Figure 12-1). It would be difficult to interpret statements of this sort as creating an exact

FACTORS AFFECTING CORRESPONDENCE TODAY

1. Advent of the computer age
   - Production of correspondence is quicker and easier
   - Letter writing is more economical and profitable
2. Defensive practice of law
   - Attorneys confirm all oral communications by letter
   - Reduction in misunderstandings and complaints against lawyers

---

LEGAL TERMS

retainer †   1. The act of hiring an attorney. 2. A preliminary fee paid to an attorney at the time he or she is retained, in order to secure her services.

December 1, 1995

Mr. William R. Roland
1001 Old Southpoint Road
Baltimore, Maryland 21222-4372

Re: File Name: William R. Roland
     File No.: 95.401

Dear Mr. Roland:

It was a pleasure meeting with you yesterday. This letter will provide a written summary of our conversation regarding representation in your claim against Jensen Products, Inc. for injuries sustained from the use of a faulty throne.

Should you wish to retain this office, representation would be on the following terms and conditions:

1. Further representation shall be effective upon return of this letter signed by you along with a cost advance of Fifty Dollars ($50.00).

2. If settlement is reached without the need to file a lawsuit, the fee charged by this office for the representation of you in this matter will be one-third (1/3) of any amounts obtained. If the filing of a lawsuit is necessary, the fee will be forty percent (40%) of all amounts obtained by settlement or by way of court judgment. If there is no recovery for you, there will be no fee.

3. The above fee does not include the expenses of investigation and litigation. These costs include, but are not limited to, the costs of expert witnesses, medical and scientific reports, private investigators, filing of the lawsuit, and long-distance telephone. These expenses are your responsibility and will be subtracted from the cost advance. In the event the amount of the cost advance is depleted, an additional advance may be required.

4. You will be kept informed of the progress of your case. You will be sent copies of all relevant documents regarding this matter either received by or sent from this office. Your file will be available for inspection by you at any reasonable time.

5. While every effort will be made to represent you properly and efficiently according to the highest legal and ethical standards, it is not possible to determine in advance the amount of time that will be expended in this matter, nor is it possible to project what final result will be accomplished.

If the statements set forth are agreeable to you, please sign and date this letter below on the line above your name and return it with the aforementioned cost advance. Please keep the second copy for your records.

Should you have any questions, please do not hesitate to contact me. Thank you for your consideration.

Very truly yours,

Patricia A. Miata

Understood, accepted and agreed:

_____   _____
William R. Roland   Date

PAM/skw
Enclosure

FIGURE 12-1 Retainer letter

standard that must be met. Rather, the attorney merely promises to work at her best level.

A letter to a client should always speak in concrete terms. Clients are not interested in a "best guess." However, reporting all the possibilities and options may leave the client confused and anxious. It can be difficult to be exact without leaving the impression of creating a promise. The writer should strive for a middle ground. Laying out all the relevant choices and then recommending an appropriate one is a good approach. See Figure 12-2.

Finally, it is important that the style of the letter show courtesy and respect toward the client. A pompous and condescending tone must be avoided. Clients should feel that the attorney is approachable and, most importantly, is working on their behalf. Remember, confidence in one's representation is essential to an attorney's ability to resolve conflicts competently and efficiently.

The offer that has been presented to us by the insurance carrier must be acted upon within ten (10) days. In my opinion the offer is a fair one; however, the final decision whether to accept it or not is yours.

At this juncture your options are:

(1) To accept the offer (in which case my fee would be one-third (1/3) of the settlement amount), or

(2) To file a lawsuit (in which case my fee would be forty percent (40%) of the recovery, either by settlement or judgment).

Though the settlement offer is ample, there is no way of predicting whether a court would order a judgment for more or less than this amount. In fact, it is possible that the court could order a judgment in favor of the defendant. You should know, however, that it would be at least a year until a trial is scheduled. During that period of time there may be further discussions of settlement. However, since the filing of suit is the next step, my fee would be higher.

Understandably, this is not an easy decision for you. You have been egregiously injured by the actions of Jensen Products and should be generously compensated for your injuries. But you must consider in making your determination the speculative nature of litigation versus the certainty of this offer.

Having said this, it is my recommendation that you accept the offer and settle the matter. By making this recommendation, I am in no way inferring that your case would not merit a higher award in court. I am only acknowledging the reality of litigation. Of course, the final decision is yours.

FIGURE 12-2 Example of middle ground

Letter Format

The modified semi-block format is the most popular legal letter style. The format is characterized by both the inside address and salutation being flush at the left margin (called *left-justified*). The date, reference line, complimentary close, and writer's name are lined up five spaces to the right of center. Each paragraph of the letter is indented five spaces. If word processing is employed, each line often ends on the right margin (called *right-justified*). In block format, all parts of the letter are left-justified. This format is occasionally used in legal practice but is more popular in business and educational contexts.

Letterhead

Correspondence is always written on the firm's letterhead. In public practice settings, such as corporations or nonprofit organizations, specialized stationery for the legal department is used. In private firms, the attorneys of the firm are usually listed on the left-hand side of the letterhead; partners first, followed by associates. If attorneys are members of bars of states other than the one the firm is located in, this will be indicated. In an agency or legal department of a corporation, generally only the chief attorney or general counsel is listed. In many states, it is also permissible for paralegals to be listed on the firm's stationery (see Figure 12-3).

	MIATA, WHEELER & SILVER	
	ATTORNEYS AT LAW	
	406 ALLEGHENY AVENUE	
	TOWSON, MARYLAND 21204-4223	
	(410) 882-8099	
PATRICIA A. MIATA	FAX (410) 555-2345	RHONDA OVERBE
MAX W. WHEELER*		SUSAN B. BARNES
CARL SILVER		LEGAL ASSISTANTS
WALTER S. MAGUIRE		
MARY ABRAHAM JONES*		
* ADMITTED IN D.C. ALSO		

FIGURE 12-3   Sample letterhead

SIDEBAR   **ARE PARALEGALS REPRESENTING THEMSELVES AS ATTORNEYS WHEN THEY ARE LISTED ON THE FIRM'S LETTERHEAD?**

There is considerable debate within the legal profession as to whether paralegals and legal assistants should be listed on a firm's letterhead. A minority of state bars feel that this is improper. They argue that it creates the appearance that the paralegal is a member of the bar. Most states, however, permit listing provided the letterhead clearly indicates the paralegal's position in the firm. Consider the ethics opinion from the Kansas Bar Association permitting legal assistants to be listed on letterheads and business cards (Figure 12-4).

Besides the expected name, address, and telephone number, letterheads today include branch office addresses, fax numbers, and a space where a direct dial number can be listed. A *direct dial number* is an attorney's private line. In larger firms, an attorney might provide a preferred client with this number so that the client can bypass the secretary or receptionist when calling. Some firms that are on the technological cutting edge even provide their e-mail addresses on their letterhead.

No. 92-15
December 2, 1992

Topic: **May in-house corporate law firm list legal assistants on the corporate legal office letterhead; business cards for legal assistants.**

===

Digest: **Non-lawyer legal assistants may be listed on a law firm's letterhead if they have achieved some minimal training as a legal assistant over and above that customarily given legal secretaries, and such listing is explained fully on the letterhead as to their nonlawyer status. Supervised non-lawyer employees may use business cards or separate, non-letterhead stationery containing their name and a clear identification of their capacity. We make no distinction between private firms and corporate law departments.**

Kansas Bar Association Legal Ethics Opinion 88-2 is hereby withdrawn.

===

Ref: MRPC 7.1, 7.5
Date of Request: September 30, 1992

The function of the Kansas Bar Association's ethics advisory service is to respond to inquiries from Kansas lawyers concerning pro-posed conduct. The limitations on the service do not allow us to render an opinion regarding past conduct or the conduct of someone other than the inquirer. Any opinion approved for release by the Ethics-Advisory Committee of the Kansas Bar Association will be limited to interpretation of the Rules of Professional Conduct, as augmented by clear judicial case law statement. It is not within the committee's province to conduct extensive decisional research or express an opinion as to any question of law applicable to the contemplated conduct which is the subject of an inquiry.

The following constitutes only the opinion of the Committee on Ethics-Advisory Services, and is not in any way intended to be a guarantee of a particular result or a conclusion by appropriate legal or disciplinary authorities. Further, this letter constitutes the Committee's opinion based upon the facts and information contained in correspondence referenced above. It is based upon a review of the Model Rules of Professional Conduct, and applicable case law. This opinion is not a grant of immunity from any form of legal or discipli-

FIGURE 12-4   Kansas Ethics Opinion

nary proceeding. The Kansas Bar Association expressly disclaims any liability in connection with the issuance of this opinion.

Facts

A corporate law department has its own letterhead. In addition to the senior counsel and "staff attorneys" which are listed with those specific titles, the firm desires to list the names of two "legal assistants" under that heading. The corporation also wants to issue business cards to the legal assistants with their name and title.

Questions Presented

1.   May corporate legal assistants be listed on in-house corporate legal office letterhead?

2.   May legal assistants use business cards which unambiguously list their title and position?

Analysis

This Committee has previously reviewed this issue. The only factual distinction is that the requesting lawyer in this instance is senior counsel in a corporate law department instead of a private law firm.

In Kansas Legal Ethics Opinion 88-2, an extensive review was made of the just-issued Model Rules of Conduct compared with the older Model Code provisions in light of listing legal assistants on firm letterhead. In February, 1989, the ABA issued informal opinion 89-1527, which held that nonlawyer support personnel could be listed on letterheads because the Model Rules did not preclude such. Based on that ABA opinion, LEO 88-2 was reconsidered. Upon reconsideration, this Committee reaffirmed its initial decision, holding,

> "The potential for misleading, confusion, or creating an unjustified impression as to the capacity, extent of the authority, and function of legal assistants and paralegals precludes them from being named on the firm letterhead. Supervised non-lawyer employees may use business cards or non-letterhead stationery containing their name and a clear identification of their capacity."

Briefly, 88-2 holds that MRPC 7.5 and 7.1, read in tandem, indicates lawyers cannot use firm letterhead in a manner violating MRPC 7.1 That Rule states lawyers cannot make false or misleading communication about the lawyer or the lawyer's services. "False and misleading" is defined in MRPC 7.1 to mean:

> (a)   contains a material misrepresentation of fact or law, or omits a fact necessary to make the statement considered as a whole not materially misleading;

> (b)   is likely to create an unjustified expectation about results the lawyer can achieve, or states or implies that the lawyer can

FIGURE 12-4   *(continued)*

achieve results by means that violate the rules of professional conduct or other law, or,

(c) Compares the lawyer's services with other lawyer's services ..."

Research into LEO 88-2 indicates that while the ABA had withdrawn several older Model Code-based opinions regulating who could be listed on letterheads, and while there were numerous new U.S. Supreme Court advertising cases with which to deal, the ABA did not withdraw, as of that 1988 opinion, ABA Informal Opinions 1367 or 1437, dated June 15, 1976 and April 2, 1979, respectively. These opinions hold it is improper to list <u>paralegals or legal assistants</u> on firm letterheads, and that caution dictates deferral of the use of such designations when such a person is signing correspondence which is incident to the proper conduct of his or her responsibilities. The potential for misleading a reader was cited. Chief among the problems is the difficulty of defining a "iegal assistant." The Opinion held:

> "Although we do not interpret our former opinion to sanction or require a blanket or absolute ban on the inclusion of any nonlawyer personnel in the letterhead of an attorney or law firm, we are persuaded by the most recent U.S. Supreme Court decision on lawyer advertising that utmost caution must be exercised in this area as the lawyer letterhead First Amendment commercial free speech rights have not been, as yet, precisely defined in the MRPC 7.1 area. In <u>Peel v. Attorneys Registration and Disciplinary Commission of Illinois</u>, 495 U.S. ___, 110 L.Ed.2d 83 (1990), a fractured group of justices ... held that **an absolute or blanket ban prohibiting a lawyer from placing in his letterhead his certification by the national Board of Trial Advocacy, a private organization, was violative of the First Amendment absent evidence showing that anyone was <u>actually misled</u> or deceived. However, six of the nine ... believe it to be "potentially misleading ..."**

This Committee declined to change its opinion when reconsidering 88-2, primarily based on the fact that while ABA 89-1527 appeared to allow paralegal listing on letterheads as long as it was not misleading, key previous opinions dealing with that topic were not withdrawn. We have checked and as of this date, these ABA opinions have not been withdrawn.[1]

---

[1] *Peter Geraghty of the ABA Center for Professional Responsibility indicates, however, that these two opinions are "not generally accepted anymore." The Center believes current Rules make no distinction between types of nonlawyers going on letterheads. (Telephone Conversation, 10/23/92)*

FIGURE 12-4 *(continued)*

Since that reconsideration, consensus in other state bars remains illusory. There are states which allow legal assistants to be listed on letterheads,[2] and those which do not.[3]

---

[2]*New York State Ethics Opinion 500 (1978)(permits nonlawyers on letterheads if inclusion would not be deceptive and clearly identified as nonlawyers); Connecticut Ethics Opinion 85-17 (11/20/85)(listing helps eliminate client confusion about the status of employees); Florida Ethics Opinion 86-4 (8/1/86)(may list names and titles of paralegals and legal assistants); Hawaii Ethics Opinion 78-8-19(7/3/84)(may list paralegal or legal assistant provided information is not false, fraudulent, misleading or deceptive); Illinois Ethics Opinions 81-4 (undated), 87-1 (9/8/87)(nonlegal personnel may be listed if clearly identified as such); Mississippi Ethics Opinion 93 (6/7/84)(may include name of paralegal provided nonlegal status is clearly indicated); Virginia Ethics Opinion 970 (9/30/87)(may list firm's chief investigator so long as includes affirmative statement that investigator is not licensed to practice law); Wisconsin Ethics Opinion E-85-6 (10/85)(may list legal assistant's names: their employment is relevant to the lawyer's ability to provide legal services.); Nassau County (NY) Bar Association LEO 91-32 (undated)(nonlawyers may be included on letterhead if listing indicates status and function of employee and that employee is not attorney); Michigan Bar Association Informal EO RI-34 (10/25/89); Nebraska Bar Association Ethics Opinion 673 (10/23/89); Cleveland Bar Association EO 89-1 (8/8/89); Columbus Bar Association EO 6 (11/17/88). The Cleveland and Columbus Bar opinions appear inconsistent with the Ohio State Supreme Court opinion in the next footnote.*

[3]*Rhode Island Ethics Opinion 91-42 (7/18/91, because of the "potential misleading effect of placing a legal assistant's name on a list of lawyers;" Ohio Supreme Court Ethics Advisory Opinion 89-16 (7/16/89)(a firm may not list nonlawyers on letterhead, but may issue them business cards); Iowa Ethics Advisory Opinion 88-5 (9/9/88)(certified legal assistant may not sign a law firm's correspondence with "CLA" after it); accord Iowa Advisory opinions 88-19; 87-18; New Jersey Ethics Opinion 611 (2/23/88)(nonlawyer assistant under lawyer may sign correspondence so long as it relates to gathering or dissemination of routine information and identity of nonlawyer is clearly indicated; may not sign correspondence to clients, lawyers or courts); Arizona EO 82-3 (2/26/82)(even bans separate letterhead of legal assistant; possibility of public confusion); Idaho EO 109 (11/30/81)(creates misleading impression); Michigan EO CI- 942 (6/7/83)(law firm employ-*

(Footnote Continued)

FIGURE 12-4 *(continued)*

Our 1988 reasoning was based on the inability to define "legal assistants" with some form of commonality. Some legal assistants have college degrees; others take the name "legal assistant" more through a process which more resembles the old 19th practice of reading law than a formal training. The concern was that lawyers might allow a secretary to masquerade as a "legal assistant" on the letterhead when that might not be the person's duties. Thus, the committee opted for the more conservative advice in LEO 88-2.

Since that time great strides are being made in defining the role of legal assistants. Legal Assistants, through the KBA Legal Assistant's committee, are gaining professional stature. They are, for example, soon to be allowed associate status with an "associate membership" in the KBA. Future efforts at standardizing the training of legal assistants will, no doubt, continue. The trend is towards certification exams for legal assistants. We do believe, however, to properly list such persons on a legal stationary requires some sort of asterisk indicating that this category of persons are not licensed to practice law, or some other phrase which clearly indicates supervised, nonlawyer status.[4]

Given our decision herein regarding the firm's letterhead, there is no reason to limit legal assistants from having their own unambiguous letterhead, or business cards.

(Footnote Continued)
ing accountant cannot list him; purpose of letterhead is to provide a list of those who can provide legal services); Allegheny County (Pennsylvania) EO 1 (10/81) (may not list legal assistants; titles do not identify graduates of properly accredited courses of study).

[4]*In the case of In re Wilkerson, 251 Kan. 546, 834 P.2d 1356 (1992), the Kansas Supreme Court allowed disbarred attorneys to serve as legal assistants, however, notes that disbarred or suspended attorneys "remains a member of the Bar and subject to the MRPCs." This means since a disbarred attorney cannot practice law, s/he cannot appear on a firm's letterhead in any capacity. Wilkerson does allow disbarred or suspended attorneys to act as legal assistant employees. The limits are: the work must be exclusively the work of a preparatory nature and under the supervision of a licensed attorney, does not involve client contact, and they cannot talk with clients on the phone, sign correspondence, or "contact (clients) either directly or indirectly." 834 P.2d at 1362. For our opinion to be consistent with Wilkerson, we do not believe that licensed attorneys can communicate the nonlawyer status of suspended attorneys working as legal assistants to those who receive the firm's letterhead, e.g. clients. Thus our holding in this opinion does not include disbarred attorneys acting as legal assistants.*

FIGURE 12-4 *(continued)*

Opinion

Non-lawyer legal assistants may be listed on a law firm's letterhead if they have achieved some minimal training as a legal assistant over and above that customarily given legal secretaries, and such listing is explained fully on the letterhead as to their nonlawyer status. Supervised non-lawyer employees may use business cards or separate, non-letterhead stationery containing their name and a clear identification of their capacity. We make no distinction between private firms and corporate law departments.

Kansas Bar Association Legal Ethics Opinion 88-2 is hereby withdrawn.

FIGURE 12-4   *(continued)*

Generally, the quality of letterhead paper is high grade (20- to 24-lb. bond), with a watermark for a prestigious look. Environmentally sensitive firms have their stationery printed on recycled paper stock.

Only the first page of a letter is printed on letterhead bond. Subsequent pages use matching paper without the letterhead. The name of the addressee, date, and page number are indicated at the top left-hand margin of subsequent pages. This is called a *header.*

Date

In modified semi-block format, the date is placed five spaces beyond the mid-way point of the width of the page. Because letters go through a number of drafts before being finalized, it is important to make sure that the date on the letter reflects the date it is actually mailed. A recipient will be insulted by a letter typed a week before she receives it.

Special Mailing and Handling Instructions

The vast majority of letters are sent by first-class mail. This is always assumed, unless special mailing instructions are indicated at the left margin. Common instructions are "hand-delivered" and "certified mail, return receipt requested" (see Figure 12-5). If it is critical that correspondence be received on the same day it is prepared, having it hand-delivered by messenger would be appropriate. The need for this form of delivery has been reduced, however, by the advent of the fax machine. Sending a letter by certified mail is often required by court rule, as in the case of **service of process**, or by written agreement, as in the case of putting

---

LEGAL TERMS

service of process [†]   Delivery of a summons, writ, complaint, or other process to the opposite party, or other person entitled to receive it, in such manner as the law prescribes, whether by leaving a copy at his or her residence, by mailing a copy to him or her or his or her attorney, or by publication.

P 384 311 367

US Postal Service
Receipt for Certified Mail
No Insurance Coverage Provided
Do not use for International Mail (See reverse)

Sent to	
Street & Number:	
Post Office, State, & ZIP Code	
Postage	$
Certified Fee	
Special Delivery Fee	
Restricted Delivery Fee	
Return Receipt Showing to Whom & Date Delivered	
Return Receipt Showing to Whom, Date & Addressee's Address	
TOTAL Postage & Fees	$
Postmark or Date	

PS Form **3800**, April 1995

Fold at line over top of envelope to the right of the return address

CERTIFIED

P 384 311 367

MAIL

SENDER:
- Complete items 1 and/or 2 for additional services.
- Complete items 3, 4a, and 4b.
- Print your name and address on the reverse of this form so that we can return this card to you.
- Attach this form to the front of the mailpiece, or on the back if space does not permit.
- Write "Return Receipt Requested" on the mailpiece below the article number.
- The Return Receipt will show to whom the article was delivered and the date delivered.

Is your RETURN ADDRESS completed on the reverse side?

I also wish to receive the following services (for an extra fee):

1. ☐ Addressee's Address
2. ☐ Restricted Delivery

Consult postmaster for fee.

3. Article Addressed to:

4a. Article Number

4b. Service Type
☐ Registered   ☐ Certified
☐ Express Mail   ☐ Insured
☐ Return Receipt for Merchandise ☐ COD

7. Date of Delivery

5. Received By: (Print Name)

6. Signature: (Addressee or Agent)
X

8. Addressee's Address (Only if requested and fee is paid)

Thank you for using Return Receipt Service.

PS Form **3811**, December 1994   Domestic Return Receipt

UNITED STATES POSTAL SERVICE

First-Class Mail
Postage & Fees Paid
USPS
Permit No. G-10

● Print your name, address, and ZIP Code in this box ●

FIGURE 12-5   Certified mail cards

a tenant on notice as to the **default** on a lease. Also, if the matter is personal or confidential, that fact should also be indicated.

Inside Address

The *addressee* is the person to whom the letter is sent. Her name and address appear two lines below any special mailing and handling instructions. If an individual addressee has a title, it should be used, either as a prefix or suffix—but never both. It is important to be specific when providing an address. If the addressee is an attorney, the name of the firm should be indicated as well as the specific addressee's name.

You should be aware of changes in the ZIP (zoning improvement plan) code. In 1983, the U.S. Postal Service introduced the "ZIP + 4" system (see Figure 12-6). Under this plan, four add-on digits were assigned to all existing five-digit codes. The first two new digits represent a "sector," which could be several blocks or a large apartment building. The second two new digits denote one side of a block or a floor of a large apartment building.

Because it was designed to be used with modern mail automation, the use of "ZIP + 4" increases speed of mail processing. Officials have, however, indicated that it will never be mandatory for either business mailers or the general public. Just the same, if its use improves the chances of a letter arriving on a timely basis, to do so is a prudent move.

Finally, make sure to employ the appropriate state and street abbreviations on the envelope (see Figure 12-7). The inside address, however, should always have the state and street names spelled out in full.

Reference Line

All legal correspondence should include a reference line, sometimes called a *re line*. When a matter is not in the litigation stage, providing only the client name and file number is sufficient.

EXAMPLE

Re: Client Name: Fiancée, Inc.
      File No.:   93.504

If suit has been filed, it is appropriate to indicate the caption name, court name, and case number.

───────────────────────────── LEGAL TERMS ─────────────────────────────

default [†]   1. The failure of a person to pay money when due. 2. The failure to perform a duty or obligation. 3. The failure of a party to a lawsuit to appear in court when he or she is under a duty to appear or to plead when he or she is required to plead.

INTRODUCTION

To make the best of new technology and automated equipment for the benefit of all, the Postal Service introduced the ZIP + 4 code.

The ZIP + 4 code consists of the five-digit ZIP Code, a hyphen and four additional digits. The five-digit ZIP Code identifies an area of the country and, additionally, contains enough information for sorting to the delivery post office.

WHAT YOUR ZIP CODE MEANS

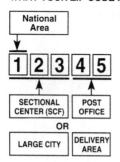

ZIP CODE NATIONAL AREAS

The first digit of a ZIP Code divides the country into national areas. Ten large groups of states numbered from 0 in the northeast to nine in the west.

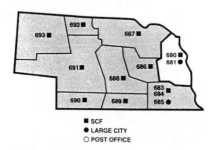

- ■ SCF
- ● LARGE CITY
- ○ POST OFFICE

Within these large areas, each state is divided into an average of ten smaller geographic areas, which are identified by the second and third digits of the ZIP Code. These digits, in conjunction with the first digit represent a sectional center facility or a mail processing facility or a mail processing facility area.

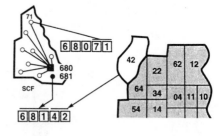

The fouth and fifth digits identify a post office, station, branch, or local delivery area.

P–7

FIGURE 12-6 Zip + 4 plan. (Reproduced with permission of the United States Postal Service.)

WHY THE ADDED FOUR NUMBERS?

The four additional digits enable automated equipment to sort mail to a specific mail carrier, the person who makes the actual delivery. The first two digits of the "+ 4" denote a delivery "sector," which may be several blocks, a group of streets, a group of post office boxes, several office buildings, a single high-rise office building with multiple firms, a large apartment building, or a small geographic area. The last two digits denote a delivery "segment," which might be one floor of an office building, one side of a street between intersecting streets, a firm, a suite, a post office box or a group of boxes, or another specific geographic location.

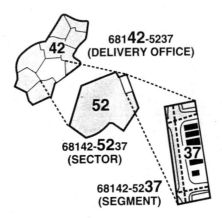

AUTOMATED MAIL SYSTEM

After an Optical Character Reader (OCR) "reads" the ZIP + 4 code and other address information from a typed or printed letter, it prints a bar code on the lower right portion of the envelope. When the letter reaches the post office that serves the addressee, a barcode sorter then reads and deciphers the bar code, and automatically sorts the letter.

P–8

FIGURE 12-6 *(continued)*

ADDRESS ABBREVIATIONS

The abbreviations listed here should be used in addresses on mail. By using the city-state abbreviations, it is possible to enter city, state, and five-digit ZIP Code on the last line of the address within a maximum of 28 positions: 13 positions for city, 1 space between city and state abbreviation, 2 positions for state, 2 spaces between state and ZIP Code, and 10 positions for ZIP + 4 code.

TWO-LETTER STATE AND POSSESSION ABBREVIATIONS

Alabama..............................AL	Illinois.................................IL	Nevada...............................NV	South Dakota.......................SD
Alaska................................AK	Indiana..............................IN	New Hampshire....................NH	Tennessee...........................TN
Arizona..............................AZ	Iowa...................................IA	New Jersey..........................NJ	Texas..................................TX
Arkansas............................AR	Kansas...............................KS	New Mexico.........................NM	Utah...................................UT
American Samoa..................AS	Kentucky............................KY	New York............................NY	Vermont..............................VT
California............................CA	Louisiana............................LA	North Carolina.....................NC	Virginia...............................VA
Colorado............................CO	Maine.................................ME	North Dakota.......................ND	Virgin Islands......................VI
Connecticut........................CT	Marshall Islands...................MH	Northern Mariana Islands......MP	Washington.........................WA
Delaware............................DE	Maryland............................MD	Ohio...................................OH	West Virginia.......................WV
District of Columbia.............DC	Massachusetts.....................MA	Oklahoma...........................OK	Wisconsin...........................WI
Federated States of Micronesia....FM	Michigan............................MI	Oregon...............................OR	Wyoming............................WY
Florida................................FL	Minnesota...........................MN	Palau..................................PW	Armed Forces the Americas....AA
Georgia..............................GA	Mississippi..........................MS	Pennsylvania.......................PA	Armed Forces Europe............AE
Guam.................................GU	Missouri..............................MO	Puerto Rico.........................PR	Armed Forces Pacific............AP
Hawaii................................HI	Montana.............................MT	Rhode Island.......................RI	
Idaho.................................ID	Nebraska............................NE	South Carolina.....................SC	

GEOGRAPHIC DIRECTIONAL ABBREVIATIONS

North.................................N	South..................................S	Northeast............................NE	Northwest...........................NW
East...................................E	West...................................W	Southeast............................SE	Southwest...........................SW

ABBREVIATIONS FOR STREET DESIGNATORS (STREET SUFFIXES)

Word	Abbreviation	Word	Abbreviation	Word	Abbreviation	Word	Abbreviation
Alley	ALY	Estates	EST	Lakes	LKS	Ridge	RDG
Annex	ANX	Expressway	EXPY	Landing	LNDG	River	RIV
Arcade	ARC	Extension	EXT	Lane	LN	Road	RD
Avenue	AVE	Fall	FALL	Light	LGT	Row	ROW
Bayou	BYU	Falls	FLS	Loaf	LF	Run	RUN
Beach	BCH	Ferry	FRY	Locks	LCKS	Shoal	SHL
Bend	BND	Field	FLD	Lodge	LDG	Shoals	SHLS
Bluff	BLF	Fields	FLDS	Loop	LOOP	Shore	SHR
Bottom	BTM	Flats	FLT	Mall	MALL	Shores	SHRS
Boulevard	BLVD	Ford	FRD	Manor	MNR	Spring	SPG
Branch	BR	Forest	FRST	Meadows	MDWS	Springs	SPGS
Bridge	BRG	Forge	FRG	Mill	ML	Spur	SPUR
Brook	BRK	Fork	FRK	Mills	MLS	Square	SQ
Burg	BG	Forks	FRKS	Mission	MSN	Station	STA
Bypass	BYP	Fort	FT	Mount	MT	Stravenue	STRA
Camp	CP	Freeway	FWY	Mountain	MTN	Stream	STRM
Canyon	CYN	Gardens	GDNS	Neck	NCK	Street	ST
Cape	CPE	Gateway	GTWY	Orchard	ORCH	Summit	SMT
Causeway	CSWY	Glen	GLN	Oval	OVAL	Terrace	TER
Center	CTR	Green	GRN	Park	PARK	Trace	TRCE
Circle	CIR	Grove	GRV	Parkway	PKY	Track	TRAK
Cliffs	CLFS	Harbor	HBR	Pass	PASS	Trafficway	TRFY
Club	CLB	Haven	HVN	Path	PATH	Trail	TRL
Corner	COR	Heights	HTS	Pike	PIKE	Trailer	TRLR
Corners	CORS	Highway	HWY	Pines	PNES	Tunnel	TUNL
Course	CRSE	Hill	HL	Place	PL	Turnpike	TPKE
Court	CT	Hills	HLS	Plain	PLN	Union	UN
Courts	CTS	Hollow	HOLW	Plains	PLNS	Valley	VLY
Cove	CV	Inlet	INLT	Plaza	PLZ	Viaduct	VIA
Creek	CRK	Island	IS	Point	PT	View	VW
Crescent	CRES	Islands	ISS	Port	PRT	Village	VLG
Crossing	XING	Isle	ISLE	Prairie	PR	Ville	VL
Dale	DL	Junction	JCT	Radial	RADL	Vista	VIS
Dam	DM	Key	KY	Ranch	RNCH	Walk	WALK
Divide	DV	Knolls	KNLS	Rapids	RPDS	Way	WAY
Drive	DR	Lake	LK	Rest	RST	Wells	WLS

EXTENDED SUFFIX TABLE

The following table lists suffix forms that may appear in address files. The corresponding official USPS suffix (as coded in the ZIP + 4 National Directory File) is shown in the adjacent column.

Street Suffix Word or Suffix Abbreviation	Official USPS Street Suffix Abbreviation	Street Suffix Word or Suffix Abbreviation	Official USPS Street Suffix Abbreviation	Street Suffix Word or Suffix Abbreviation	Official USPS Street Suffix Abbreviation	Street Suffix Word or Suffix Abbreviation	Official USPS Street Suffix Abbreviation
ALLEE	ALY	AVN	AVE	BOTTM	BTM	BURG	BG
ALLEY	ALY	AVNUE	AVE	BOTTOM	BTM	BURGS	BG
ALLY	ALY	BAYOO	BYU	BOUL	BLVD	BYP	BYP
ALY	ALY	BAYOU	BYU	BOULEVARD	BLVD	BYPA	BYP
ANEX	ANX	BCH	BCH	BOULV	BLVD	BYPAS	BYP
ANNEX	ANX	BEACH	BCH	BR	BR	BYPASS	BYP
ANNX	ANX	BEND	BND	BRANCH	BR	BYPS	BYP
ANX	ANX	BG	BG	BRIDGE	BRG	BYU	BYU
ARC	ARC	BLF	BLF	BRG	BRG	CAMP	CP
ARCADE	ARC	BLUF	BLF	BRIDGE	BRG	CANYN	CYN
AV	AVE	BLUFF	BLF	BRK	BRK	CANYON	CYN
AVE	AVE	BLUFFS	BLF	BRNCH	BR	CAPE	CPE
AVEN	AVE	BLVD	BLVD	BROOK	BRK	CAUSEWAY	CSWY
AVENU	AVE	BND	BND	BROOKS	BRK	CAUSWAY	CSWY
AVENUE	AVE	BOT	BTM	BTM	BTM	CEN	CTR

FIGURE 12-7 State and street abbreviations. (Reproduced with permission of the United States Postal Service.)

EXTENDED SUFFIX TABLE — Continued

Street Suffix Word or Suffix Abbreviation	Official USPS Street Suffix Abbreviation
CENT	CTR
CENTER	CTR
CENTERS	CTR
CENTR	CTR
CIR	CIR
CIRC	CIR
CIRCL	CIR
CIRCLE	CIR
CIRCLES	CIR
CLB	CLB
CLF	CLFS
CLFS	CLFS
CLIFF	CLFS
CLIFFS	CLFS
CLUB	CLB
CMP	CP
CNTER	CTR
CNTR	CTR
CNYN	CYN
COR	COR
CORNER	COR
CORNERS	CORS
CORS	CORS
COURSE	CRSE
COURT	CT
COURTS	CTS
COVE	CV
COVES	CV
CP	CP
CPE	CPE
CRCL	CIR
CRCLE	CIR
CRECENT	CRES
CREEK	CRK
CRES	CRES
CRESCENT	CRES
CRESENT	CRES
CRK	CRK
CROSSING	XING
CRSCNT	CRES
CRSE	CRSE
CRSENT	CRES
CRSNT	CRES
CRSSING	XING
CSWY	CSWY
CT	CT
CTR	CTR
CTS	CTS
CV	CV
CYN	CYN
DALE	DL
DAM	DM
DIV	DV
DIVIDE	DV
DL	DL
DM	DM
DR	DR
DRIV	DR
DRIVE	DR
DRIVES	DR
DRV	DR
DV	DV
DVD	DV
EST	EST
ESTATE	EST
ESTATES	EST
ESTS	EST
EXP	EXPY
EXPR	EXPY
EXPRESS	EXPY
EXPRESSWAY	EXPY
EXPW	EXPY
EXPY	EXPY
EXT	EXT
EXTENSION	EXT
EXTN	EXT
EXTNSN	EXT
EXTS	EXT
FALL	FALL
FALLS	FLS
FERRY	FRY
FIELD	FLD
FIELDS	FLDS
FLAT	FLT
FLATS	FLT
FLD	FLD
FLDS	FLDS
FLS	FLS
FLT	FLT
FLTS	FLT
FORD	FRD
FORDS	FRD
FOREST	FRST
FORESTS	FRST
FORG	FRG
FORGE	FRG
FORGES	FRG
FORK	FRK
FORKS	FRKS
FORT	FT
FRD	FRD
FREEWAY	FWY
FREEWY	FWY
FRG	FRG
FRK	FRK
FRKS	FRKS
FRRY	FRY
FRST	FRST
FRT	FT
FRWAY	FWY
FRWY	FWY
FRY	FRY
FT	FT
FWY	FWY
GARDEN	GDNS
GARDENS	GDNS
GARDN	GDNS
GATEWAY	GTWY
GATEWY	GTWY
GATWAY	GTWY
GDN	GDNS
GDNS	GDNS
GLEN	GLN
GLENS	GLN
GLN	GLN
GRDEN	GDNS
GRDN	GDNS
GRDNS	GDNS
GREEN	GRN
GREENS	GRN
GRN	GRN
GROV	GRV
GROVE	GRV
GROVES	GRV
GRV	GRV
GATEWAY	GTWY
GTWAY	GTWY
GTWY	GTWY
HARB	HBR
HARBOR	HBR
HARBORS	HBR
HARBR	HBR
HAVEN	HVN
HAVN	HVN
HBR	HBR
HEIGHT	NTS
HEIGHTS	HTS
HIGHWAY	HWY
HIGHWY	HWY
HILL	HL
HILLS	HLS
HIWAY	HWY
HIWY	HWY
HL	HL
HLLW	HOLW
HLS	HLS
HOLLOW	HOLW
HOLW	HOLW
HOLWS	HOLW
HRBOR	HBR
HT	HTS
HTS	HTS
HVN	HVN
HWAY	HWY
HWY	HWY
INLT	INLT
IS	IS
ISLAND	ISS
ISLANDS	ISS
ISLE	ISLE
ISLES	ISLE
ISLND	IS
ISLNDS	ISS
ISS	ISS
JCT	JCT
JCTION	JCT
JCTN	JCT
JCTNS	JCT
JCTS	JCT
JUNCTION	JCT
JUNCTN	JCT
JUNCTION	JCT
KEY	KY
KEYS	KY
KNL	KNLS
KNLS	KNLS
KNOL	KNLS
KNOLL	KNLS
KNOLLS	KNLS
KY	KY
KYS	KY
LANE	LN
LAKES	LKS
LANDING	LNDG
LANE	LN
LANES	LN
LCK	LCKS
LCKS	LCKS
LDG	LDG
LDGE	LDG
LF	LF
LGT	LGT
LIGHT	LGT
LIGHTS	LGT
LK	LK
LKS	LKS
LN	LN
LNDG	LNDG
LNDNG	LNDG
LOAF	LF
LOCK	LCKS
LOCKS	LCKS
LODG	LDG
LODGE	LDG
LOOP	LOOP
LOOPS	LOOP
MALL	MALL
MANOR	MNR
MANORS	MNR
MDW	MDWS
MDWS	MDWS
MEADOW	MDWS
MEADOWS	MDWS
MEDOWS	MDWS
MILL	ML
MILLS	MLS
MISSION	MSN
MISSN	MSN
ML	ML
MSL	MLS
MNR	MNR
MNRS	MNR
MNT	MT
MNTAN	MTN
MNTN	MTN
MNTNS	MTN
MOUNT	MT
MOUNTAIN	MTN
MOUNTIN	MTN
MSN	MSN
MSSN	MSN
MT	MT
MTIN	MTN
MTN	MTN
NCK	NCK
NECK	NCK
ORCH	ORCH
ORCHARD	ORCH
ORCHRD	ORCH
OVAL	OVAL
OVL	OVAL
PARK	PARK
PARKS	PARK
PARKWAY	PKY
PASS	PASS
PATH	PATH
PATHS	PATH
PIKE	PIKE
PIKES	PIKE
PINE	PNES
PINES	PNES
PKWAY	PKY
PKWY	PKY
PKWYS	PKY
PKY	PKY
PL	PL
PLACE	PL
PLAIN	PLN
PLAINES	PLNS
PLAZA	PLZ
PLN	PLN
PLNS	PLNS
PLZ	PLZ
PLZA	PLZ
PNES	PNES
POINT	PT
POINTS	PT
PORT	PRT
PORTS	PRT
PR	PR
PRARIE	PR
PRK	PARK
PRR	PR
PRT	PRT
PRTS	PRT
PT	PT
PTS	PT
RAD	RADL
RADIAL	RADL
RADIEL	RADL
RADL	RADL
RANCH	RNCH
RANCHES	RNCH
RAPID	RPDS
RAPIDS	RPDS
RD	RD
RDG	RDG
RDGE	RDG
RDGS	RDG
RDS	RD
REST	RST
RIDGE	RDG
RIDGES	RDG
RIV	RIV
RIVER	RIV
RIVR	RIV
RNCH	RNCH
RNCHS	RNCH
ROAD	RD
ROADS	RD
ROW	ROW
RPD	RPDS
RPDS	RPDS
RST	RST
RUN	RUN
RVR	RIV
SHL	SHL
SHLS	SHLS
SHOAL	SHL
SHOALS	SHLS
SHOAR	SHR
SHOARS	SHRS
SHORE	SHR
SHORES	SHRS
SHR	SHR
SHRS	SHRS
SMT	SMT
SPG	SPG
SPGS	SPGS
SPNG	SPG
SPNGS	SPGS
SPRING	SPG
SPRINGS	SPGS
SPRNGS	SPG
SPUR	SPUR
SPURS	SPUR
SQ	SQ
SQR	SQ
SQRE	SQ
SQU	SQ
SQUARE	SQ
SQUARES	SQ
ST	ST
STA	STA
STATION	STA
STATN	STA
STN	STA
STR	ST
STRA	STRA
STRAV	STRA
STRAVE	STRA
STRAVEN	STRA
STRAVENUE	STRA
STRAVN	STRA
STREAM	STRM
STREET	ST
STREETS	ST
STREME	STRM
STRM	STRM
STRT	ST
STRVN	STRA
STRVNUE	STRA
SUMIT	SMT
SUMITT	SMT
SUMMIT	SMT
TER	TER
TERR	TER
TERRACE	TER
TPK	TPKE
TPKE	TPKE

FIGURE 12-7   *(continued)*

EXTENDED SUFFIX TABLE — Continued

Street Suffix Word or Suffix Abbreviation	Official USPS Street Suffix Abbreviation	Street Suffix Word or Suffix Abbreviation	Official USPS Street Suffix Abbreviation	Street Suffix Word or Suffix Abbreviation	Official USPS Street Suffix Abbreviation	Street Suffix Word or Suffix Abbreviation	Official USPS Street Suffix Abbreviation
TRACE	TRCE	TUNEL	TUNL	VIEW	VW	VST	VIS
TRACES	TRCE	TUNL	TUNL	VIEWS	VW	VSTA	VIS
TRACK	TRAK	TUNLS	TUNL	VILL	VLG	VW	VW
TRACKS	TRAK	TUNNEL	TUNL	VILLAG	VLG	VWS	VW
TRAFFICWAY	TRFY	TUNNL	TUNL	VILLAGE	VLG	WALK	WALK
TRAIL	TRL	TURNPIKE	TPKE	VILLE	VL	WALKS	WALK
TRAILER	TRLR	TURNPK	TPKE	VILLG	VLG	WAY	WAY
TRAILS	TRLR	UN	UN	VILLIAGE	VLG	WAYS	WAY
TRAK	TRAK	UNION	UN	VIS	VIS	WELL	WLS
TRCE	TRCE	UNIONS	UN	VIST	VIS	WELLS	WLS
TRK	TRAK	VALLEY	VLY	VISTA	VIS	WELS	WLS
TRKS	TRAK	VALLEYS	VLY	VL	VL	WY	WAY
TRL	TRL	VALLY	VLY	VLG	VLG	XING	XING
TRLA	TRLR	VDCT	VIA	VLGS	VLG		
TRLRS	TRL	VIA	VIA	VLLY	VLY		
TRLS	TRL	VIADCT	VIA	VLY	VLY		
TRNPK	TPK	VIADUCT	VIA	VLYS	VLY		

COPYRIGHT—U.S. POSTAL SERVICE 1995

FIGURE 12-7 *(continued)*

EXAMPLE

Re: Fiancée, Inc. v. Peterson
District Court of Maryland for Caroline County
Case No.: 0001043-92

The *re* line provides a quick overview of the letter, enabling the receiving secretary, paralegal, or attorney to quickly match it to the corresponding file.

Salutation

The salutation appears two lines below the inside address on the left margin. It always begins with "Dear" followed by the appropriate title prefix, then the surname of the addressee followed by a colon. "Mr." is the prefix for a man unless he has another specific title. The prefixes for women in the past were "Mrs." or "Miss." Both of these forms are now out of fashion; use "Ms." unless the addressee has another specific title. However, if a client expects to be addressed in a certain way, convention should give way to this consideration. Occasionally, if you know the reader well, addressing him by his first name may be appropriate.

Paralegal Tip

In most cases, the client will receive a copy of every letter prepared in her case. You should be careful when sending a copy of a letter written to the opposing attorney or paralegal to the client if the salutation is informal, such as "Dear Jane." Some clients do not appreciate this informality. They may not want their attorney becoming too chummy with the opposing side. A better approach is to have the salutation typed formally and then cross out the surname with pen and replace it with a first name on the original but not the copy.

Dear Mr. Smith:

Make every possible effort to avoid sending correspondence without the name of a specific individual addressee. Using a person's name, even if it is a person unlikely to read the letter (like the head of an agency), will personalize the letter and give the perception that the letter is important. A client who receives a courtesy copy of a letter will be more impressed if the letter opens "Dear Dr. Ungerford" rather than with "To Whom It May Concern" or "Dear Sir or Madam."

Body

The body is the most important part of the letter because it contains the information you intend to convey. The beginning and end of the body should be places of emphasis. First and last impressions are usually the most memorable.

The purpose of the letter should be indicated in the beginning. If the letter answers a question posed by the client, it should be answered briefly up front and then in more detail further on. Like all legal documents, letters must be logically presented. If the problem to be answered deals with multiple parts, foundation concerns should be answered first. For instance, if the letter responds to a client's inquiry as to the ability to obtain an increase in child support from a former spouse, it is logical to discuss the legal basis supporting the client's position before discussing the measures that could be taken to collect the child support.

You will want to recapitulate the purpose or theme of the letter at the end. The end of the letter is also the appropriate place to inform the reader of what she should expect in the future. This might include a follow-up telephone call, further investigation, or a decision by the court. (See Figure 12-8; also review Figure 10-8 for another example.)

Closing and Complimentary Closing

The closing consists of a courteous one- or two-line statement such as "Please contact me if you have any questions" or "Thank you in advance for your cooperation and consideration." The closing is always ended with a period, not a comma.

The most popular complimentary closing in legal writing is "Very truly yours." Other closings include "Sincerely yours" or, if the letter is addressed to a judge, "Respectfully yours." "Sincerely" alone is not appropriate in legal writing.

You must not sign a letter without indicating your position as a paralegal. To do otherwise would leave the reader with the impression that you are an attorney. The specific types of letters paralegals are permitted to sign are discussed further later in this chapter. Most paralegals customarily use the term "Legal Assistant" rather than "Paralegal" to describe themselves in correspondence. Consider the two state bar opinion excerpts in Figure 12-9, which both address the issue of paralegals signing letters.

February 14, 1995

Ms. Mary McFann
1900 Proctor Lane
Carney, Maryland 21234-1908

Re: Client Name: Mary McFann
File No.: 12389-95

Dear Ms. McFann:

You have asked if there is a way to increase the amount of child support your ex-husband, Michael McFann, is paying for your children, Michael, Jr., and Emily. Based on income information you provided this office, I believe that you can have the present amount that he pays increased.

Your former husband's obligation to pay child support is both contractual and legal. Pursuant to the separation agreement entered into five years ago, child support was set at the amount of $100.00 per child per week. This agreement requires your ex-husband to support your children until they reach the age of 18. The court has authority to modify the original contracted amount when it feels there has been a material change in financial circumstances.

Based on an analysis of your and your ex-husband's income, it is my opinion that an increase is justified. Based on a analysis of the applicable law, it is likely that the court would order an increase of between $25.00 and $50.00 per week per child.

The procedure for requesting an increase in child support is to file a motion for increase in child support with the court. A hearing would be held after this motion is served on your ex-husband. At that time, the court would make an independent decision as to the merits of your request.

My paralegal, Susan, will telephone you by the end of the week regarding a time when you can come in and sign the necessary documents.

Thank you for your consideration.

Very truly yours,

Max W. Wheeler

FIGURE 12-8 Sample letter

Copies and Enclosures

Copies of all letters are regularly sent to clients. If a copy is sent, the original addressee is so informed by "cc:" followed by the name of the second receiver of the letter at the bottom left margin. This designation meant "carbon copy" at one time, but in the computer age stands for "courtesy copy." Some writers use merely "c:" for copy. Others have urged using "pc:" to indicate photostatic

---

MARYLAND STATE BAR ASSOCIATION, INC.

Docket 76-5
September 25, 1975

* * *

(2) We do not believe that a paralegal or other staff member of a law firm who is not a member of the Bar should ever sign a letter on firm stationery unless his or her status is clearly indicated beneath the signature (as, for example, "Legal Assistant"...) and the subject matter of the letter is ministerial, involving no legal opinions or legal advice. ...

IOWA BAR ASSOCIATION

Ethics Opinion 89-22
December 8, 1989

You have requested an opinion as to whether a paralegal may sign correspondence "Joe Smith, Legal Assistant to Attorney _____."

* * *

The Committee is of the opinion that "legal assistant," or "legal assistant to _____," or "paralegal," or "paralegal to _____," are not improper.

FIGURE 12-9 Ethics opinions

copy. Because of its current double meaning (also meaning politically correct), this abbreviation is unlikely to gain general acceptance.

Occasionally, you may not want the reader of the original letter to know who is receiving a copy. In such a case, indicating "bcc:", meaning blind courtesy copy, and then the name of the second receiver on the copy only is required. In practice, "bcc:" is rarely used because it gives an inappropriate impression of secretiveness.

Copies of correspondence are generally not signed. Rather, the symbol "/S/" is used to indicate that the original was signed.

If you are enclosing a document, the abbreviation "Encl." or "Enclosure" is indicated. If there are several enclosures, then either "Encls." or "Enclosures" can be used. Always make sure that all copies are actually enclosed before the letter is mailed.

Finally, the initials of the letter's author and typist are denoted. If the writer is Lucy T. Chander and the secretary Susan Cartwright, then the reference "LTC/sc" would be indicated beneath any reference to copies and enclosures.

Today, paralegals are frequently both composing and typing their own correspondence. In those cases, either indicating the author's initials only in capitals or omitting the indication is appropriate.

Cover Letter

A *cover letter,* sometimes called an *enclosure letter,* is the shortest and simplest letter drafted in a law office. This letter describes the document enclosed and provides direction (i.e., file the pleading, read the document, sign the agreement) for processing it. A cover letter may not be needed when it is obvious from the document how it should be processed. However, with the defensive attitude that pervades the profession nowadays, many lawyers habitually include cover letters with all documents. They do not want to take the chance that a document might be misfiled or lost.

Because the subject matter of these letters is administrative or ministerial in nature, they are often both composed and signed by paralegals. Though brief, they must still conform to all the features of good writing. See Figure 12-10.

February 14, 1996

Ms. Sharon Wick
Clerk of Court
Circuit Court for Baltimore County
401 Bosley Avenue
Towson, Maryland 21204-0754

Re: Roland v. Jensen Products, Inc.
     Circuit Court for Baltimore County
     File No.: 95.401

Dear Ms. Wick:

Enclosed please find a complaint to be filed in the above-referenced matter. Also find the required filing fee. Please prepare the complaint and summons for sheriff's service.

Thank you for your consideration.

Very truly yours,

Susan B. Barnes
Legal Assistant

SBB
Enclosures

FIGURE 12-10   Sample cover letter

Confirmatory Letter

Should you wish to confirm a decision or agreement reached over the telephone or at an in-person conference, a confirmatory letter is in order. In such a letter you recapitulate the substance of what was previously determined. If the matter is a serious one, the letter may reemphasize certain consequences or options. Such a letter is always a good way to confirm a court, deposition, or meeting date with the client. (See Figure 12-11.)

Attorneys greatly reduce the chance of miscommunication by committing to writing verbal discussions with clients and others. Reducing misunderstanding lessens the possibility that clients will feel slighted and maintains good will. This, in turn, diminishes the chance of malpractice and bar grievance claims.

February 3, 1996

Mr. William R. Roland
1001 Old Southpoint Road
Baltimore, Maryland 21222-4372

Re: Client Name: William R. Roland
File No.: 95.401

Dear Mr. Roland:

This is to confirm that you have an appointment with this office for Monday, February 13, 1996 at 3:00 p.m. in order to go over documents related to filing suit in your case. If you cannot make the appointment, please telephone this office to reschedule.

Thank you for your consideration.

Very truly yours,

Rhonda Overbe
Legal Assistant

RO

FIGURE 12-11   Sample confirmatory letter

Informational Letter

An informational letter takes two forms. In the first type, the writer shares information with the reader. For example, you may want to share with a client the status of negotiations for settlement or the status of an investigation.

In the second form, the writer requests information. For example, an attorney might request information from an agency in the course of representation. In some types of cases, such as personal injury matters, paralegals prepare a number of informational letters requesting police reports, medical records, and the like. Because of their frequent use, your firm may have a standard form letter for such requests. In medical situations, you often will need to have the client sign an authorization giving you permission to obtain confidential information about her (see Figure 12-12). Generally, health care providers charge a fee for providing medical records. The client should always be informed of this fact before the request is made. (See Figure 12-13.)

AUTHORIZATION FOR MEDICAL RECORDS AND REPORTS

I, the undersigned, authorize any physician, nurse, or other health care provider who has attended me, or any hospital or health care facility to which I have been confined, to furnish to Patricia A. Miata, Esquire, 406 Allegheny Avenue, Towson, Maryland 21204-4223 or her duly authorized agent, copies of any and all information regarding my physical or psychological condition and treatment rendered. I also give permission to allow her or any health care provider appointed by her to examine and/or copy any x-ray pictures taken of me or records regarding my physical or psychological condition or treatment.

_____   _____
Client   Date

Witness:

_____

FIGURE 12-12 Sample authorization

December 15, 1995

Abdul Shams, M.D.
4000 Frederick Road
Catonsville, Maryland 21228-3456

Re: Client Name: William Roland
Date of Injury: August 6, 1995

Dear Dr. Shams:

Enclosed is an Authorization for Medical Records and Reports executed by your patient William R. Roland.

Please be advised that this office has been retained to represent Mr. Roland regarding injuries he suffered on August 6, 1995. It is this firm's understanding that he has been treated by you for these injuries. We would greatly appreciate your providing this office with a report as to Mr. Roland's diagnosis, treatment, and prognosis.

If there is a charge for the preparation of this report, please forward a statement along with the report in care of this office.

Should you have any questions, please do not hesitate to contact me. Thank you for your consideration.

Very truly yours,

Rhonda Overbe
Legal Assistant

RO
Enclosure

FIGURE 12-13 Sample informational letter

A specific type of informational letter is a request pursuant to the federal **Freedom of Information Act** (FOIA) (see Figure 12-14). The FOIA (5 U.S.C. § 552) was passed by Congress in 1966. Its purpose is to allow public access to material held by the federal government. Basically, the FOIA gives anyone the right to request and receive records that are in the possession of federal agencies. There are nine exceptions, which permit an agency to withhold requested information. These exceptions are documents related to national security, internal agency rules, information exempted by other federal laws, trade secrets, internal agency memoranda, personal privacy information, investigatory records, certain banking information, and oil well information. Most states have their own version of the FOIA to provide for access to state records.

SAMPLE REQUEST LETTER

Date

Freedom of Information Unit
(Name and Address of Government Agency)

Dear Sir or Madam:

Re: Freedom of Information Request

Pursuant to the Freedom of Information Act, 5 U.S.C. 552, [and/or the Privacy Act, 5 U.S.C. 552a,] I hereby request access to (or a copy of) all records pertaining to (describe the subject or document containing the information that you want).

I am requesting these records (as a representative of the news media, for non-commercial personal use, for an educational institution, etc.)

[If any expenses in excess of $_____ are incurred in connection with this request, please obtain my approval before any such charges are incurred.] or

[I request a waiver of fees because my interest in the records is not primarily commercial and disclosure of the information will contribute significantly to public understanding of the operations or activities of the government because _____
_____.]

I will expect a response within 10 working days as provided by law. If my request is denied in whole or in part, I expect a detailed justification for withholding the records. I also request any segregable portions that are not exempt to be disclosed.

Thank you for your prompt attention to this matter.

Very truly yours,

FIGURE 12-14 Sample FOIA letter. (Courtesy of Freedom of Information Clearinghouse.)

LEGAL TERMS

Freedom of Information Act (FOIA) [†] A federal statute that requires federal agencies to make available to the public, upon request, material contained in their files, as well as information on how they function. The Act contains various significant exemptions from disclosure, including information compiled for law enforcement purposes.

Advisory Letter

The focus of an advisory letter is to provide legal advice. Such letters may take one of three different forms: demand letters, settlement letters, or opinion letters. Paralegals may draft, but never sign, advisory letters.

Demand Letter

In a demand letter, the attorney indicates her opinion as to the existence of a debt and advises the **debtor** of planned efforts to collect the amount. If the demand letter is for a client, it must comply with the federal **Fair Debt Collection Practices Act**, 15 U.S.C. § 1692. This law requires that a person who is in the business of collecting the debt of another (such as an attorney or a collection agency) inform the debtor of certain rights and provide certain information. This includes:

1. The amount of the debt.
2. The name of the **creditor**.
3. A statement that the attorney will assume the debt is valid unless the amount is disputed within 30 days.
4. A statement that the attorney will send the debtor verification of the debt if requested within 30 days.
5. A statement that the attorney will provide the debtor with the name and address of the original creditor (if different than the current one) if requested within 30 days.
6. A statement that the attorney is attempting to collect a debt and that any information received from the debtor will be used only for that purpose.

A debt collector who violates this act can be liable for damages, including actual damages and punitive damages up to $1,000.00.

The purpose of a demand letter is to motivate the debtor to pay the debt quickly and without objection. To achieve this, the letter should have a no-nonsense yet courteous tone. The letter must communicate to the debtor three things: first, any time limits for payment (i.e., within seven business days); second, any requirements as to the form of payment (i.e., cash, certified check); and third, the action to be taken should payment not be made (i.e., filing suit in small claims court) (see Figure 12-15). Remember, it would be unethical for an attorney to make threats of civil action that she had no intention of carrying out.

LEGAL TERMS
---

debtor [†] A person who owes another person money.
Fair Debt Collection Practices Act [†] One of the federal consumer credit protection acts, whose purpose is to eliminate improper collection practices by debt collection agencies.
creditor [†] A person to whom a debt is owed by a debtor.

April 15, 1994

Ms. Carol Shaftner
President
Shaftner Printing Company
100 Main Street
Denton, Maryland 21629-4321

Re: Client Name: National Business, Inc.
File No.: 92.516

Dear Ms. Shaftner:

This office has been retained to represent National Business, Inc. with regard to an unpaid invoice for services rendered in February 1993. The amount due and owing is $1,845.50. Enclosed please find an invoice dated February 14, 1993 reflecting this outstanding balance.

Unless this amount is disputed in writing and the letter is received by this office within 30 days, this debt will be assumed to be valid. Within that 30-day period you may also request verification of the debt. You should know that any information received from you will be used only for the purposes of attempting to collect this debt and for no other purposes.

Unless payment is received in full within 45 days from the date of this letter, suit will be filed in the District Court of Maryland to recover the amount due and owing. Once suit has been filed you will no longer be privileged to settle this for the above amount, in that court costs will have been incurred.

You must know that it is only a question of time in collecting the full amount. If you wish to avoid this course of action and save added costs and the inconvenience of a court trial, please send a certified check for the entire amount to this office made payable to National Business, Inc.

Thank you for your consideration.

Very truly yours,

Carl Silver

CS/skw
Enclosure
cc: National Business, Inc.

FIGURE 12-15 Sample demand letter

Settlement Letter

In a **settlement** letter (see Figure 12-16), the writer is giving an opinion as to the value and basis of a claim. The letter proposes a way in which to "settle" the matter and as a result keep it out of court. The dispute need not deal with a financial claim, but more often than not it does. If settlement of a personal injury case is the subject matter, the likely recipient is an insurance adjuster. To

---
LEGAL TERMS
---

settlement [†]   The ending of a lawsuit by agreement.

January 15, 1996

Mr. Mark Roberts
Columbia Insurance Group
160 Belmont Avenue
Baltimore, Maryland 21203-5698

Re: Client Name: William R. Roland
     File No.: 95.401
     Your Insured: Jensen Products, Inc.
     Claim No. 89-86-32-MR

Dear Mr. Roberts:

This is in follow-up to our conversation of January 4, 1996 concerning injuries suffered by William R. Roland as a result of the faulty manufacture of a drum stool purchased from Jensen Products, Inc.

Mr. Roland is the drummer for the musical group "Mirage." In addition, he is also a technician for Second Floor Productions. He is a 30 year old single male, approximately 180 pounds in weight.

In July, 1995 he purchased from the Carney Music Center on behalf of Second Floor Productions a drummer's throne for $300.00. This throne was manufactured by your insured, Jensen Products, Inc. The throne was used for normal studio use. During a session on August 6, 1995 the legs of the throne suddenly buckled. Mr. Roland landed on his back. Enclosed with this letter find photographs which indicate how the stool cracked.

Subsequently, Mr. Roland experienced significant pain and discomfort. For the next several weeks he had difficulty lifting small items and occasionally his back would give out. He, nonetheless, refused to seek treatment. He felt that his back would heal on its own. Also, he was medically uninsured and realized that it would be costly to be evaluated and treated.

On September 13, 1995 the pain was so great that Mr. Roland was taken to the emergency room of Bel Air General Hospital. At the hospital he was seen by Juan Rivera, M.D. who diagnosed him as having low back pain and recommended that he rest and not lift any heavy items. He was scheduled for follow-up with a neurosurgeon two weeks later. Enclosed please find discharge instructions from the hospital. Also find a statement for services rendered at Bel Air General Hospital in the amount of $86.83.

On October 1, 1995 Mr. Roland was seen by Abdul Shams, M.D. for a consultation and evaluation. Dr. Shams, a neurosurgeon, believed that the injury was a result of Mr. Roland's falling off the drum stool. It was Dr. Shams's opinion that Mr. Roland was suffering from musculoligamentous strain to the low back. Dr. Shams recommended that Mr. Roland have a magnetic resonance image (MRI) scan. Enclosed find Dr. Shams's report and his statement for services rendered in the amount of $250.00.

Mr. Roland's next option is to have the MRI completed. However, in that he is uninsured, he is required to bear the entire cost of the procedure. The cost of the scan ranges from $1,000.00 to $1,200.00. Just the same, he anticipates depleting his savings to have the MRI completed.

Medical specials are only part of the damages Mr. Roland has suffered. He also lost considerable wages as a result of your company's faulty product.

FIGURE 12-16 Sample settlement letter

Roberts, Mark
January 15, 1996
Page 2

It is Mr. Roland's belief that there were approximately 24 weeks in which he was out of work due to the injuries suffered on August 6, 1995. At a rate of $175.00 per week, his total loss of income was $4,200.00.

In order to conclude this matter without the need for litigation we would propose a settlement amount of $12,000.00. This amount would be in consideration of a full and final release given to Jensen Products, Inc. by Mr. Roland. The alternative would be to file a suit in the Circuit Court for Baltimore County. Understand that this offer is made without prejudice to my client and will only be open for the next 14 days.

It would be appreciated your considering this offer and responding at your earliest convenience, but no later than January 30, 1996.

Thank you for your consideration.

Very truly yours,

Patricia A. Miata

PAM/skw
Enclosures
cc: Mr. William R. Roland

FIGURE 12-16 *(continued)*

write this type of letter, the author must have an understanding of necessary medical terminology and concepts. This letter recites chronologically the chain of events that resulted in the client's injury. In the last paragraph, a proposal for settlement is made. It is important to include language indicating that the proposal is made without prejudice so that the offer cannot be subsequently raised at trial. Finally, it is important to make sure that the letter indicates a date on which the offer for settlement terminates. An open offer might allow negotiations to drag on indefinitely.

Opinion Letter

Finally, an attorney may provide a written legal opinion. The attorney may attempt to accomplish a number of things with this type of letter. She may be providing a client with an assessment of the possibility of success in court. A legal opinion letter could be sent to another attorney to convince her that the opinion writer has a better position and that settlement of the case may be in order. Finally, a legal opinion letter could be sent to a third party who needs a legal opinion as to a legal claim or matter.

Regardless of the receiver and purpose, legal opinion letters have common components. The following elements should be included in every letter.

Date

The date of the opinion letter is critical. The research must be current through that date. Changes that take place in the law after that date will not be the writer's responsibility.

Introduction

Every opinion letter should include an introduction identifying the relevant issues researched or reasons for issuing the letter.

Facts

It is important to discuss the facts that are the basis of the opinion. These facts may be obtained from various sources: the client, an investigation, or an opposing party. The facts should be provided in great detail. Even if a client reveals an additional fact, after the letter has been prepared, that would change the legal outcome, the attorney would only be responsible for researching the facts with which she was originally provided.

Ultimate Conclusion

A client may not have the patience to read a lengthy letter to determine the chances of success. If the letter is written to persons other than the client, they may want to know up front where the writer stands. For this reason, it is good practice to provide a short answer in the beginning.

Legal Issue

Here the legal question is presented in a concise, understandable fashion.

Legal Analysis

The legal analysis is the basis for the ultimate conclusion. Applicable laws are reviewed to determine how they impact the facts presented. The IRAC method and other paragraph blocks discussed in Chapter 11 could be used here to provide a proficient legal analysis.

Recommendation

The analysis is followed by the attorney's recommendation based on her findings. For the client, this is generally the most important portion of the letter, because the attorney puts herself on the line by taking a position—this is what the client pays for. For other recipients, the position the attorney takes here becomes a starting point for further investigation or discussion. It also is the manifestation of the attorney's legal acumen and reputation.

Instructions

Finally, the attorney provides the recipient information on what to expect or do based on the letter's findings. This may include filing suit, meeting with the attorney, or paying a retainer fee.

See Figure 12-17 for a sample opinion letter.

April 5, 1995

Mr. and Mrs. John S. Petrillo
1021 Miller's Lane
Pikesville, Maryland 21208-2345

Re: File Name: Peter Petrillo
File No.: 95.412

Dear Mr. and Mrs. Petrillo:

On March 20, 1995 we met to discuss the possibility of your bringing legal action against the Carroll County Board of Education for the death of your son, Peter, who died on May 10, 1994. What follows is a summarization of the status of the law as to wrongful death and an application to your particular situation.

FACTS

On May 10, 1994, your son Peter was killed by an automobile operated by Susan Lynn Johnson at the intersection of Station Road and Canary Parkway in Westminster, Maryland. The accident occurred sometime between 3:30 and 3:40 P.M. of that day.

At the time, Peter was a seventh-grade student at Sheehan Middle School. Peter was an exemplary student, having made the honor roll the previous semester. He was also involved in Little League baseball, as well as student government.

It was sometime after the death of your son that you suspected that he had not been in class the day he was killed. You came to find that he had "cut" last period with another student, Michael Robinson. The reason for Peter skipping class is unknown; it is your opinion that he had never previously done this. Michael Robinson was not injured on May 10; rather, he journeyed in a different direction prior to the accident.

It was Mr. Petrillo, a former police officer, who determined during the course of his own investigation that Peter might not have been in class the time of the accident. Evidently, last period would have commenced at 2:45 P.M. School would have concluded about 50 minutes later, or 3:35 P.M. Mr. Petrillo concluded that Peter could not have been in the area in which he was killed unless he had left school prior to the end of the school day. Evidently, Peter's cutting class was rumored by other students at the school after his death.

The case against Susan Lynn Johnson is still in litigation. You are represented by other counsel in that matter. The attorney representing you in that matter, Thomas Lerner, Esquire, referred you to me because of his current work load.

ULTIMATE CONCLUSION

Based on my analysis, it would appear that a suit against the Carroll County Board of Education would not be successful.

FIGURE 12-17 Sample opinion letter

Petrillo, Mr. and Mrs. John S.
April 5, 1995
Page 2

ISSUE NO. 1

Can parents maintain an action to recover damages for the death of a child?

LEGAL ANALYSIS

The Maryland Wrongful Death Act provides that parents as "primary beneficiaries" can bring an action to recover for the death of a child. Md. Code Ann., Cts. & Jud. Proc. § 3-904 (1995). The action must be brought within three years of the date of death. Courts Art. § 3-904(g). A wrongful act is any "act, neglect, or default ... which would have entitled the injured party to maintain an action and recover damages had death not ensued." Courts Art. § 3-901(e). This would presumably include an action in negligence.

Damages would include "damages for mental anguish, emotional pain and suffering, loss of society, companionship, comfort, protection, marital care, parental care, filial care, attention, advice, counsel, training, guidance, or education where applicable." Courts Art. § 3-904(d).

It seems clear that we have a factual case that can be brought under this law. In fact, it is this statute which is the basis of your current suit against Ms. Johnson.

ISSUE NO. 2

Can an action be brought against the Carroll County Board of Education for wrongful death?

LEGAL ANALYSIS

Historically, governmental entities were immune from liability for the negligent acts of their employees and agents. This included wrongful death actions, which generally take the form of negligence. There has in recent years been a movement among states and municipalities to waive immunity in limited instances. This trend has also included school boards.

Pursuant to Maryland law, sovereign immunity has been waived by a Maryland county board of education in any claim of $100,000.00 or less. If the claim is greater than that amount, sovereign immunity can be raised as a defense and the suit barred. Md. Code Ann., Educ. § 4-105 (1992). If an action is brought against a school board employee (in this case, the seventh-period teacher), the county board is automatically joined as a party in the action. The county board will ultimately only be liable for the actions of an employee who acts within the scope of her authority. *Carroll v. Hillendale Golf Club, Inc.*, 156 Md. 542, 144 A. 693 (1929). The issue of whether the instructor acted within the scope of her employment may be litigated as a separate issue. Educ. Art. § 4-105.1. School employees are, nevertheless, immune from lawsuits resulting from making a report required by law, and participating in a judicial proceeding that results from the report. Md. Code Ann., Educ. § 6-109 (1992). Also, school board employees are immune from lawsuits stemming from participating in the breaking up of fights and other disciplinary matters. Md. Code Ann., Educ. § 7-306 (1992).

FIGURE 12-17 *(continued)*

Petrillo, Mr. and Mrs. John S.
April 5, 1995
Page 3

In this particular case, it would appear that you would not be barred by immunity from bringing suit against the Carroll County Board of Education and its employee provided your suit is under $100,000.00. However, problems may arise if the school board is successful in arguing that the instructor's actions—for instance, in failing to timely report the absence in class of Peter—were either a report required by law or a disciplinary action. In addition, if it is determined that the teacher was not acting within the scope of her employment, the board might not be liable.

ISSUE NO. 3

Has Maryland permitted actions to be brought against school board employees for negligent acts?

LEGAL ANALYSIS

It appears that the basis of the wrongful death action would be negligence. Any type of neglect, unless intentional in nature, would likely be classified as negligence. The factual basis would be either the failure of the instructor to properly report that Peter was absent to the school administration, or the breach of the school's duty to keep him in school.

Negligence is defined as the failure to exercise that degree of care that circumstances reasonably require. The following would have to be established: (1) a specific duty imposed on the teacher; (2) a breach or failure to perform that duty; (3) an occurrence which would not have taken place but for the teacher's failure to perform the duty; and (4) damages arising from the occurrence attributable to the failure to adhere to the duty. *Myers v. Montgomery Ward & Co.*, 253 Md. 282, 252 A.2d 855 (1969).

It would seem that the school board might take the position that though a duty might have been breached, the occurrence and death of Peter were not proximately caused by the teacher's conduct. That is, there was no connection between the teacher's failure to report or keep Peter in school and his death. The school board would argue that it was the actions of Ms. Johnson, and not the teacher, that caused your son's death. The school board would argue the failure to establish the third element of negligence, sometimes referred to as proximate cause.

Courts in Maryland have held that a school board cannot be held liable for failing to properly test a student. *Hunter v. Board of Education*, 292 Md. 481, 429 A.2d 582 (1982). However, a school board and its employee could be held liable for intentional acts such as battery. *Doe v. Board of Education*, 295 Md. 67, 453 A.2d 814 (1982). In your case, we have no indication that the teacher committed any intentional acts against Peter.

The court of appeals in *Lunsford v. Board of Education*, 280 Md. 665, 374 A.2d 1162 (1977), was asked to decide the question of a school's duty to care for a specific student. In that case, a student had been assaulted by fellow students. Suit was brought against the school board and principal. The court rejected the argument that a school is under a special duty to exercise reasonable care to protect a specific pupil from harm. Rather, the school has a duty to exercise reasonable care to look out for the safety of all school children.

FIGURE 12-17 *(continued)*

Petrillo, Mr. and Mrs. John S.
April 5, 1995
Page 4

Reading these decisions together, it seems that the court might be reluctant to find that an instructor was negligent in failing to act during seventh-period class to report or locate Peter. The court would likely hold that the duty to exercise reasonable care extended to all students generally, and not to Peter in particular.

RECOMMENDATION

Based on my findings, you can bring an action under the Maryland Wrongful Death Act. Suit must be brought on or before May 10, 1997. In addition, provided your suit is less than $100,000.00, sovereign immunity is waived by the Carroll County Board of Education.

The problems with the case rest on establishing liability. If the teacher is working within the scope of her employment, the Board of Education would be liable. However, if the court determined that the teacher's actions constituted either the making of a report or student disciplinary action, neither the teacher nor the Board would be liable.

Should the Board of Education be unsuccessful in making this argument, it could still argue that Peter's death was not proximately caused by the teacher's negligence. In my opinion, this is the most persuasive defense.

Finally, though teachers have a duty of reasonable care for their students, it does not extend to a specific student such as Peter. The standard of reasonable care is a general one extending to all students.

After a thorough legal analysis of this case, it is my opinion that the chances of success are minimal. Even if we could convince a court that the teacher had a specific duty to Peter, it is unlikely that a court would find that the teacher's action proximately caused his death.

Please feel free to telephone me should you have questions concerning this letter. Unfortunately, much of this letter discusses legal theories with which you might not be familiar. I would be glad to discuss them with you in more detail.

Very truly yours,

Max W. Wheeler

MW/skw

FIGURE 12-17   *(continued)*

SIDEBAR **THE EPA: A SOURCE OF ENVIRONMENTAL INFORMATION**

The mission of the Environmental Protection Agency is to enhance the environment to the fullest extent possible under the laws enacted by Congress. Specifically, its function is to study, control, and abate pollution in the areas of air, water, solid waste, noise, radiation, and toxic substances.

Various experts can be contacted directly at the EPA concerning various types of environmental concerns. Some of the areas include: drinking water, toxic substances and pesticides, radiation, and research and development health. In addition, there are approximately 75 various divisions, branches, programs, grants, libraries, and publications designed to assist the EPA in fulfilling its mission. The EPA is located at 401 M Street, SW, Washington, DC 20460. The telephone number is (202) 260-2090. The EPA can be located on the Internet at http://www.epa.gov/.

Summary

- The letter is the form of legal writing most frequently used in the practice of law.

- The computer age has affected correspondence production by making it more economical and easier.

- Because attorneys today are increasingly concerned with malpractice actions and bar grievance investigations, attorneys depend on letter writing as a way of confirming decisions reached with clients and thus reducing misunderstanding.

- When writing to a client, the writer must never promise a particular outcome. Because clients expect concrete answers, letters should also avoid giving a "best guess." A middle ground should be sought.

- A pompous and condescending tone must be avoided.

- The format for legal letters is known as modified semi-block.

- All correspondence must appear on the firm's letterhead.

- The letterhead lists various information, including the firm members, address, fax, and telephone number.

- Occasionally, special mailing and handling instructions must be provided.

- If the case is not in litigation, the reference line includes only the client name and file name. If the case is in litigation, the caption name, court, and case number are indicated.

- The letter's body provides the essential message that the writer desires to communicate.

- If the letter includes an enclosure, this must be indicated.

- A cover letter describes a document that is enclosed and provides information as to its processing.

- A confirmatory letter confirms a decision or agreement reached between the attorney or paralegal and another individual.

- An informational letter either provides or requests information.

- The focus of an advisory letter is to provide a legal opinion.

- One form of an advisory letter is a demand letter. If the demand deals with a debt, it must comply the federal Fair Debt Collection Practices Act.

- In a settlement letter, a attorney provides an opinion as to the value and basis of a claim.

- In an opinion letter, an attorney provides a client, attorney, or third party with a legal analysis.

Review Questions

1. How have computers affected letter writing in the law office?

2. What are the characteristics of the modified semi-block format?

3. Besides the firm name, address, and telephone number, name two other things that often appear on a letterhead.

4. Describe the "ZIP + 4" system.

5. What does "cc:" indicate?

6. What are the purposes of a cover letter?

7. What are the purposes of a confirmatory letter?

8. What is the federal Freedom of Information Act?

9. What are the possible penalties for a debt collector who violates the federal Fair Debt Collection Practices Act?

10. Why is a paralegal prohibited from signing an advisory letter?

Chapter Exercises

1. What has your state's bar association said regarding paralegals being listed on letterheads and signing correspondence?

2. Locate your state's version of the Freedom of Information Act. Draft a letter under your state's act requesting information on a topic of interest to you. (You will have to determine the appropriate agency first.)

3. Review Figure 12-1. Can you identify any phrase that might constitute legalese?

4. Assume that your firm represents someone who was been involved in an automobile accident. Draft a letter to the hospital (pick the one nearest your home) requesting that it provide your firm with the client's records. Call the hospital first and find out who the appropriate addressee would be.

5. Assume you are employed in your state's attorney general's office. Prepare a letter to be sent to Wilbur Hack requesting that he stop using lawn herbicides, because of their potential danger. The letter would be signed by an assistant attorney general.

IIII

CHAPTER 13

OFFICE MEMORANDA

OVERVIEW

Paralegals are commonly requested to research and organize information critical to the practice of law. Once the material is obtained, it must be communicated to the supervising paralegal or attorney who requested the search. This presentation is most effectively accomplished by the use of an office memorandum. The term *memorandum* literally means (translated from Latin) "that which must be remembered." The primary purpose of such a document is apparent: to create a permanent record of legal material.

Some memoranda are circulated only within the firm and consequently are referred to as *office* or *internal memoranda*. Others are filed with the court and are considered by those outside the office, such as judges and opposing counsel. These forms of memoranda are referred to as *trial* or *external memoranda*. In this chapter, the focus is on the various forms of office memoranda that may be used in a law practice. Trial memoranda are the subject of Chapter 16.

Three different types of office memoranda are utilized in a law practice. The first is the *interview memorandum*. The second is referred to as an *investigatory memorandum*, and the third a *research memorandum*.

Should you wish to convey the results of an interview to a supervisor, you would draft an interview memorandum. There are three types of interviews in which you could participate as a paralegal: an initial client interview, a follow-up interview, and a field interview. The memorandum's purpose in each situation is to record in detail the substance of the interview, as well as your impressions of the person being interviewed.

In an investigative memorandum, you communicate to another the status of a legal investigation. The document's purpose is to provide your supervising paralegal or attorney with an objective and honest account of your efforts on the project to date.

The third type, the research memorandum, sometimes called a *law office memo*, presents research on a particular legal problem or question. Of the three forms of office memoranda, this type is the most complex, intellectually demanding, and time-consuming. Your answer to a legal question, and your presentation of that answer in a research memorandum, may help your attorney decide whether to represent the client; or the need for the research memorandum may arise during the course of representation. This memo is a highly analytical document demanding careful planning and execution. If asked to draft a research memorandum, you will be required to apply your best research and writing skills.

PARALEGAL PRACTICE SITUATION

Your firm is the local counsel for the Perpetual Insurance Company. Perpetual has assigned your firm a case dealing with the potential liability of property owners for injuries suffered in their swimming pool by a guest. The property owners, Blanche and Antonio Fulwood, are being sued by Jamal Brown for injuries he sustained in the Fulwoods' built-in swimming pool.

You have been requested to draft a research memorandum examining the Fulwoods' liability for Brown's injuries. Because you have not been provided with many facts, you will need to talk to various individuals, including Mr. and Mrs. Fulwood, to get a complete picture of the situation. You should prepare an interview memorandum for each person you question.

Interview Memoranda

There is no ethical prohibition on the practice of paralegals interviewing clients and other individuals as part of their professional responsibilities. In fact, paralegals can be most effectively and economically used in this capacity, as they can conduct many of the interviews that attorneys traditionally handled. This frees the attorney's time to handle more complex matters. Keep in mind that the focus of the paralegal profession is to assist attorneys in all activities not constituting the practice of law. Conducting interviews clearly falls into this category.

Three types of interviews are typically conducted by paralegals. These are the initial client interview, the follow-up interview, and the field interview.

Initial Client Interview Memorandum

Paralegals are increasingly requested to participate in initial client interviews. Sometimes this process of obtaining preliminary information is called *intake*, and for this reason this memo is sometimes called an *intake memorandum*. In many instances the interview is jointly conducted by the attorney and the paralegal. The paralegal obtains the factual background and information; the lawyer advises the client of her legal rights and responsibilities and suggests a legal avenue. This is analogous to the roles of doctor and nurse, where the nurse records a patient's symptoms and complaints, while the doctor makes a diagnosis and prescribes treatment.

When the attorney is unavailable, as a paralegal you may be asked to conduct the entire interview. In those instances, you must be extremely careful not to offer any legal advice. This would constitute the unauthorized practice of law and therefore be both unethical and illegal.

The importance of this interview cannot be overemphasized. It is at this time that the client reaches an initial opinion of the firm's competence. The impression the client acquires will likely be the single most important factor in whether she will retain the firm. It is important that a professional atmosphere be created. It is also critical that you obtain an accurate and complete picture of the client: her characteristics, legal needs, and expectations. If the attorney is not at the interview, you are acting as his eyes and ears. An important fact or angle not uncovered at this point can be lost forever.

Often you will be in a better position to obtain information from a client. The formal atmosphere of the law office, coupled with the serious nature of the problem for which legal counsel is required, can be quite intimidating for a client. Additionally, an attorney can appear as a distant and aloof individual who has difficulty "connecting" with the client. As a result, you as a paralegal often can act as the bridge or liaison between client and attorney. Sometimes your ability to relate to a client stems from your having personal characteristics similar to those of the client or from having the time to focus on the client as an individual.

After the interview, you would be required to produce an interview memorandum summarizing the consultation for your supervisor. There are generally four parts to such a memorandum.

The first section deals with objective information about the client, such as the client's name, address, telephone number, and relevant facts related to the problem. For instance, if you were interviewing Mr. and Mrs. Fulwood, you would want to obtain their full names, places of employment, the year they moved into the house, the year the pool was built and the builder, among other facts. If the client is charged with a crime, it is important that you ask questions regarding any previous criminal convictions. This portion of the memo can be presented either in a sentence format or as a completed questionnaire. (See Figure 13-1.)

The second section of the memorandum records the client's story. Here, the client's rendition of the events leading to her need for legal assistance is noted. It is generally recorded in a third-person style, and often parts of the story are summarized. If a precise statement is necessary, then you may be required to take a first-person narrative statement. A first-person narrative discusses an event from the point of view of the interviewee. The statement is taken down

---

GRANDPARENT RIGHTS CUSTODY/VISITATION QUESTIONNAIRE

1. Name(s) of child(ren): _____

   _____

   _____

   _____

2. Date(s) of birth: _____

   _____

3. Address(es) of child(ren): _____

   _____

   _____

   _____

4. Name of grandfather: _____

5. Date of birth: _____

6. Name of grandmother: _____

7. Date of birth: _____

8. Address of grandparent(s): _____

   _____

   _____

(continued on back)

FIGURE 13-1 Sample questionnaire

in the form of a transcript. (See Figure 13-2.) This type of statement is particularly useful should the interviewee subsequently be called to testify as a witness and not be able to recall what he indicated previously. The witness's memory can easily be refreshed with the statement.

STATEMENT OF MR. ANTONIO A. FULWOOD

I, Antonio A. Fulwood, live at 5398 New Court Road, Baltimore, Maryland 21208. I am married to Blanche Fulwood. We have two children, Jacquetta, age 16, and Davon, age 8. I am employed as an 11th grade social studies teacher in the Baltimore County Public School System.

On July 16, 1996, we hosted a swimming birthday party for our daughter. It was a surprise "Sweet 16" birthday party. There were around 25 of her friends and relatives in attendance. Included in that group was Jamal Brown, a friend of hers from school. The party started about 5 P.M. ....

FIGURE 13-2 First-person statement

The third part of the memorandum focuses on the interviewer's subjective impressions of the client. Often these impressions are instinctive or "gut" feelings. These observations are important because they provide a personal profile of the client that will enable the attorney to provide better representation. Impressions such as "client appeared nervous" or "client was very angry at his wife" are frequently of considerable value. You must, however, avoid drawing observations from inappropriate stereotypes. For instance, to say "client is unsophisticated" merely because she belongs to a certain ethnic group is wrong—both as a stereotype and likely as fact.

The final portion of the memorandum consists of your recommendations to the supervisor as to a possible course of action. To advise that "it appears that the client has grounds for divorce" or that "suit should be filed in order to **toll** the **statute of limitations**" might be appropriate. Though in doing so you are rendering legal advice, because it is to a superior and not a client, it is permitted. If you are competent, your boss will carefully consider your recommendations.

See Figure 13-3 for a sample interview memorandum.

Follow-Up Interview Memorandum

The second type of interview, the *follow-up interview*, is frequently conducted by a paralegal. The interviewee could be a client or a nonclient such as a potential witness. The purpose of this type of interview is usually limited. It is often held to cover only one particular subject or a select number of matters. For example, a client might be scheduled for a follow-up interview to review financial documents, such as tax returns, expense worksheets, and bank statements, in a divorce case. In an initial interview, clients are unlikely to bring such records with them. A follow-up interview could be scheduled with a paralegal to go over these papers.

A follow-up interview might also double as a trial preparation meeting during which the client is instructed as to trial procedure. The format of the memorandum will depend on the complexity and purpose of the follow-up interview. In simple interviews, the memorandum may merely appear as a note to be placed in the client's file (see Figure 13-4).

Field Interview Memorandum

The final type of interview is often called a *field interview*. A field interview differs from both an initial client interview and a follow-up interview because

---

LEGAL TERMS

tolling the statute [†]   A term referring to circumstances that, by operation of law, suspend or interrupt the running of the statute of limitations.

statutes of limitations [†]   Federal and state statutes prescribing the maximum period of time during which various types of civil actions and criminal prosecutions can be brought after the occurrence of the injury or the offense.

INITIAL CLIENT INTERVIEW MEMORANDUM

To: Mark Washburn, Esquire

From: Tamara Jones, Paralegal

Date: July 30, 1996

Re: Client Name: Blanche and Antonio Fulwood
        File No.: 96.401

You asked me to meet with Mr. and Mrs. Antonio Fulwood concerning a claim that has been brought against them for injuries sustained by Jamal Brown on their premises on July 16, 1996. I met with them yesterday, July 29, 1996, at 2:00 P.M.

Though you had originally been scheduled to meet with the Fulwoods, due to an emergency hearing in another matter I was requested to conduct the interview individually. I explained this change in plans to the clients. They had no objection to my meeting with them.

CLIENT INFORMATION

The Fulwoods live at 5398 New Court Road, Baltimore, Maryland 21208. They purchased their home in 1990. It is a rancher design with a 15 ft. by 30 ft. built-in swimming pool in back. When they purchased the home, the pool was already there. They do not know the builder. Also living with them are their children: Jacquetta, age 16, and Davon, age 8. Mr. Fulwood is a teacher with the Baltimore County School System. Mrs. Fulwood is the manager of a branch of Parkville National Bank.

The Fulwoods' home phone number is (410) 555-1212; Mr. Fulwood's work number is (410) 836-4000; Mrs. Fulwood's work number is (410) 555-1000.

The Fulwoods have been referred to us because we are local counsel for their homowner's carrier, Perpetual Insurance.

DISCUSSION OF EVENTS

The Fulwoods came to us because a claim has been brought against them by Jamal Brown for injuries he sustained at their swimming pool during a party on July 16, 1996. The Fulwoods indicated that they had planned a surprise sweet 16 party for their daughter. Approximately 20–25 friends and relatives were in attendance; among them was Jamal Brown. Jamal is a friend of Jacquetta's from high school.

The party started about 5:00 P.M. By 5:30 P.M., most of the guests had arrived. From the time the party started until about 8:00 P.M., the pool was closed to guests. The intent of the Fulwoods was that the guests would eat, rest an appropriate period of time, and then swim. Food was served in their club basement.

Unknown to the Fulwoods, Jamal Brown, at some time while everyone was eating, ventured out into the pool area. There is a question as to whether the pool gate was locked: Mr. Fulwood says it was not; Mrs. Fulwood thinks it was. Evidently, Jamal dove, jumped, or slipped into the shallow end (about one foot in depth) of the pool and injured his neck and back. He received bruises and lacerations on his head, neck, and back. He was taken by ambulance to Baltimore County General Hospital.

FIGURE 13-3 Interview memorandum

Though the Fulwoods do not know for sure, they suspect that Jamal may have consumed alcoholic beverages before arriving at the party. Evidently their son, Davon, indicated that he had smelled alcohol on Jamal's breath.

IMPRESSIONS

Both Mr. and Mrs. Fulwood seemed sincerely concerned about the lawsuit and about Jamal's injuries. They sent him flowers when he was at home recuperating. They indicated that no one has been injured before by use of the pool.

Mr. Fulwood seemed somewhat angered at his wife during the interview. He feels that it was her responsibility to monitor the guests and make sure no one was in the pool area. Mrs. Fulwood seemed to accept this responsibility. The issue of whether the pool gate was locked or not seems important to him. The lock is a combination lock, and only members of the family know the combination.

RECOMMENDATIONS

This case requires more investigation at this point. I recommend that a visit be made to the Fulwood home to inspect the pool area. Interviewing all possible witnesses should be done immediately.

Though the Fulwoods have not been served with a complaint, I suspect that the lawsuit will be brought on the grounds of negligence. Because there is a possibility that Jamal Brown was drinking and/or knew of the limitations as to the pool depth, there is a possibility of contributory negligence on his part. In addition, if he was aware of the fact that the pool area was not monitored at the time and he entered by jumping over the fence, he may also be liable under assumption of risk. Both of these theories will have to be considered and investigated thoroughly.

If there is anything else you would like me to do in this matter, please let me know. The Fulwoods seemed anxious to talk to you about the case. I indicated that you would give them a call by the end of the week.

FIGURE 13-3 *(continued)*

it is held where the interviewee either works or resides (in the "field"). Often the conditions for conducting this type of interview are less than ideal. In order to accommodate the interviewee's work commitments, the interview may be conducted early in the morning or late in the evening. In some instances, the individual will be reluctant to answer questions. This occurs particularly when

August 2, 1996

Mrs. Fulwood stopped by today and provided us with a comprehensive list of the guests' names, addresses, and telephone numbers in the event we needed to talk to anyone. She also provided us with some photographs of the pool area. I indicated that we would want to stop by and look at the pool ourselves in the near future.

FIGURE 13-4 Follow-up note

the interviewee is a potential witness for the opposing side (referred to as a **hostile witness**). For example, if Jamal Brown's girlfriend witnessed the accident, she is likely to be hostile to the interests of the Fulwoods. You will need to accurately convey the results of your findings. Here impressions can be critical. Comments such as "the witness used profanity when referring to our client" or "he never looked me directly in the eyes, indicating that he had something to hide" might reveal a lot about both the person and the circumstances of the case. See Figure 13-5 for a sample field interview memorandum.

FIELD INTERVIEW MEMORANDUM
(Kyisha Mitchell)

To: Mark Washburn, Esquire

From: Tamara Jones, Paralegal

Date: August 15, 1996

Re: Client Name: Blanche and Antonio Fulwood
          File No.: 96.401

One of the guests at the Fulwood party was Kyisha Mitchell. She is evidently Jamal Brown's girlfriend. To the best of our knowledge, she is the only individual to witness Jamal being injured in the pool. It appears that both she and Jamal snuck out of the party to go into the pool area.

I interviewed her yesterday afternoon, August 14, 1996. She was not anxious to be interviewed at our office after I explained to her whom our firm represented. She indicated that she would answer a few questions if I came to visit her at work. After she finished her shift at McDonald's, I talked to her for about five minutes.

She was very reluctant to talk to me, only providing answers in one- or two-word phrases. She indicated that she was Jamal's girlfriend and that they had been dating for about one year. She indicated that she had gone into the pool area with him. She indicated that he did not dive into the pool but rather slipped in. She did not know if there were any numbers indicating depth located on the edge of the pool. She denied that they had been drinking.

Her answers were very evasive and at times rude. She used profanity in referring to Jacquetta Fulwood. It appears that at one time Jacquetta had been interested in Jamal Brown. Kyisha believes that he had been invited to the party so that Jacquetta could "move in on him." Kyisha went to the party reluctantly, as Jamal's guest. She and Jacquetta, to put it mildly, are not good friends.

She could not provide me with any additional information. Her address and telephone number are in the file should we want to talk to her again.

FIGURE 13-5   Field interview memorandum

───────────────────── **LEGAL TERMS** ─────────────────────

hostile witness † A witness who may be cross-examined or impeached by the party who called him or her, because of malice or prejudice he or she displayed toward that party in ... direct examination.

Paralegal Tip

You might consider tape-recording a field interview. Often, the interviewee is walking (or even running) away when you are attempting to ask questions. In those cases, neatly taking down the facts on a writing tablet will be impossible. When you do record, it is preferable to inform the interviewee of that fact. But recording without permission is permissible if the recording will not be used in any court proceeding. In some instances, it might even be advantageous to videotape an interview. For instance, if it would be helpful for your attorney to see how a potential witness reacts to questions, videotaping should be used. (Not unlike a "60 Minutes" interview!)

Regardless of the type of interview conducted, the memorandum must be completed immediately after the interview. It is important that it be done while the facts are still fresh in your mind. You should not take the chance that your memory will fail. Also, the longer the period of time between the interview and memorandum writing, the greater the chance that your notes will be difficult to decipher when you do review them.

Investigatory Memorandum

An investigatory memorandum is submitted to an attorney in response to an inquiry as to the status of an investigation. Its purpose is to provide the supervising attorney with an objective account of the investigation to date. For example, it may be requested if you are investigating the circumstances surrounding an automobile accident. The investigation might include taking photographs of the accident scene, talking to witnesses, obtaining police documents, and securing various medical records. At some point, your supervisor may want a comprehensive report indicating the progress of the investigation. In the Fulwood case, taking photos of the pool area and talking to the party guests would be expected. In some offices, investigatory memoranda may be required on a periodic basis, as a method of quality assurance. These "status reports" will assist an attorney in determining what further action must be taken in preparation for trial.

It is important that an investigatory memo be objective in perspective and present an honest rendition of all the work accomplished up to that point. The memorandum should also indicate what tasks have yet to be completed. Like an interview memorandum, there is no particular format that must be employed in preparing an investigatory memorandum. If the memorandum is provided in response to a specific inquiry, such as "What is the status of preparing witnesses for trial?," this must be the focus of the report. Often the memorandum will cover a broad area. It may be helpful to divide the memorandum with headings so that the supervising attorney can easily locate the section dealing with any specific inquiry or concern he may have. See Figure 13-6 for a sample investigatory memorandum.

INVESTIGATORY MEMORANDUM

To: Mark Washburn, Esquire

From: Tamara Jones, Paralegal

Date: October 1, 1996

Re: Client Name: Blanche and Antonio Fulwood
         File No.: 96.401

You asked me to provide you with an update on the investigation in the Fulwood case. As you know, suit was recently filed in this case.

I originally met with the Fulwoods in July 1996. At that time I obtained information from them and took statements regarding the events of July 16, 1996, the date of the party. Mrs. Fulwood provided me with a list of 18 individuals who had attended the pool party, with their addresses and telephone numbers. I decided to interview a select few based on Mrs. Fulwood's recommendations. Copies of the interviews are in the file. One person of note that I interviewed was Kyisha Mitchell, evidently the only witness to the accident. It appears that she is backing her boyfriend's version of the story.

On August 10, 1996, I visited Mr. and Mrs. Fulwood at their home. At that time I also met their daughter, Jacquetta. I inspected the pool area. I found that, though the pool depths are marked, the markings are somewhat faded. In good light, one would be able to see them, but if there was less than full light there might be difficulty in discerning the depth. I also inspected the combination lock on the gate. There was nothing remarkable about it. I took photographs, which are included with this memorandum.

I have made efforts to contact Jamal Brown through his attorney, but his attorney has indicated that his client will be interviewed only by deposition. I recommend that we schedule him for deposition as soon as possible. I also have not been able to obtain consensually from his attorneys copies of medical reports indicating the extent of his injuries. I recommend that a request for production of documents be completed so that we can obtain and review all medical records generated as a result of his treatment at Baltimore County General Hospital.

Please advise as to the next step in this matter.

FIGURE 13-6 Investigatory memorandum

Research Memorandum

You will need to muster all your analytical and writing abilities to produce a research memorandum. In many instances, this critical document will dictate strategic decisions in a case.

General Considerations

Frequently, an attorney is unsure whether he should represent a particular client in a specific matter. At other times, there is some question as to the appropriate litigation strategy to pursue after a case has been accepted. At still other times, the attorney needs a comprehensive overview of the matter to help him determine the next step: further negotiation or litigation. All these situations will likely result in the need for a research memorandum.

Regardless of the motivating force behind the drafting of the memorandum, its primary purpose is the same. A research memorandum, first and foremost, must furnish an objective analysis of the legal situation. An honest look at the chances for success or failure will be important to the attorney making the assignment. Inherent in this is the need for a balanced analysis of both sides of the matter. The attorney must know not only the strengths of the case, but also its weaknesses. This is especially important if the attorney is undecided as to whether to represent the client at all. If representation has commenced, the research memorandum can help the attorney decide whether to litigate or settle.

The memorandum must be comprehensive. It is better to include a possibly irrelevant fact or potential issue than to mistakenly omit a possibly important one. If you are unsure as to whether a fact or issue is germane, include it. In a sense, the memorandum must be an encyclopedia of information for the reviewing attorney. He will determine the relevance of its contents.

The research memorandum's primary goal is to present authority to either support or defeat a legal position. To that end, the memorandum must identify primary law relevant to the facts at hand. Applicable cases, statutes, and administrative regulations must be located, analyzed, summarized, and finally applied to the available facts.

It is most important to remember that the office research memorandum presents the best opportunity to bring together your full array of research and writing skills in one document. This memorandum requires writing excellence, research competency, and an overall analytical approach to the task. Here, you will be required to employ every ounce of brainpower to produce a professional final product.

GENERAL CONSIDERATIONS IN PREPARING A RESEARCH MEMORANDUM

1. An objective analysis must be presented.
2. The memorandum must be comprehensive.
3. The memorandum must identify primary law relevant to the facts at hand.

Format

There is no universally accepted format used in law firms for the research memorandum, although some firms might prescribe a specific form. Frequently, the structure of the memo will be determined by the attorney or supervising paralegal who requested it. Regardless of its structure, in most cases such a memorandum includes the following components.

Heading

The memorandum should always have a detailed heading. The heading should include the name of the individual for whom the memo was produced, the author's name, the date of completion, the client's name, the file number, and an indication of the subject matter. (See Figure 13-7.)

RESEARCH MEMORANDUM

TO: Mark Washburn, Esquire

FROM: Tamara Jones, Paralegal

DATE: September 15, 1996

CLIENT: Blanche and Antonio Fulwood
File No.: 96.401

RE: Liability of swimming pool owners
for injuries to guest

FIGURE 13-7 Heading

Legal principles change rapidly; therefore, the date on which the research was completed is very important. Should the law change after the memorandum is completed, its author would not be expected to have included the change. Of course, validation of research should continue up through the date on which the final memo is produced (that is, typed up). One way this is accomplished is by shepardizing all sources through the date that the memo is completed.

The client's name and file number are important in the event the memorandum and file are separated. The current client will soon become a former client and his file closed. The research completed in the memorandum, though, will still be valid and may be useful in other cases. It will be important to maintain a copy in a research file for easy access in the event it is needed in the future. Though it will not be current indefinitely, it would be fairly easy for you to update if necessary.

Statement of Assignment

After the heading, insert a short statement as to the purposes of the assignment (see Figure 13-8). This statement assists you in focusing on the overall reason for the memorandum. Also, for the attorney, it refreshes memory and

---

STATEMENT OF ASSIGNMENT

You requested that I conduct research to determine the potential liability of Blanche and Antonio Fulwood for injuries that Jamal Brown received in their swimming pool on July 16, 1996.

FIGURE 13-8   Statement of assignment

provides the context in which to consider the memo. If you fail to cover a certain aspect that he expected, this statement will indicate that it was not communicated to you.

Ultimate Conclusion

An attorney often does not have the time or patience to read an entire memorandum at one sitting. Therefore, providing the ultimate conclusion up front will tell him what he really wants to know. The ultimate conclusion is not necessarily the answer to the legal issues, though it may be. The ultimate conclusion responds to the statement of assignment. (See Figure 13-9.) For example, if the statement deals with whether a lawsuit could be successfully defended, the ultimate conclusion will respond either affirmatively or negatively that the suit can be defeated.

Statement of Facts

After the ultimate conclusion, the facts are then presented in an objective fashion. Because this is an objective document, all facts, whether favorable or unfavorable, must be indicated. Facts must not be slanted positively for the client's benefit. They must be presented in a nonopinionated fashion.

The most practical and logical way is to present them chronologically. Often the facts will be incomplete and you may have to conduct interviews to obtain additional facts and information. All information that in any way affects the final legal outcome must be discussed. Legal results turn on minor factual changes; therefore, the facts must be presented in great detail.

ULTIMATE CONCLUSION

As a result of my research, I have concluded that the Fulwoods most likely would not be held liable under the theory of negligence for Jamal Brown's injuries. The risk of liability to the Fulwoods is further reduced if certain defenses, such as contributory negligence and assumption of risk, are successfully raised.

FIGURE 13-9   Ultimate conclusion

Issues

The next portion deals with the legal issues. There may be one major issue or several related issues that must be addressed. Often a complex issue is more manageable if broken down into various subissues.

If there are several issues, they must be prioritized, with threshold or foundation issues appearing first. For example, if the legal matter deals with the applicability of a statute to the facts, one possible foundation issue might be determining whether the statute is constitutional. If the matter concerns the bringing of a lawsuit, determining who is a proper party might be a threshold issue.

Another method of ordering issues is by chronology. In a chain of events, the legal issues should be ordered in the same way as the events to which they are tied. This is often the situation in criminal matters. For instance, in a case that involves a search, seizure, and arrest, if the search (which likely took place first) is illegal, then the subsequent seizure and arrest may be invalid. Take the sensational O.J. Simpson case: if the court found that the search of his home was illegal, then any seizure of evidence there would also be illegal, and there possibly would be no **probable cause** to arrest the defendant.

During the course of research, the issues may be modified or replaced with other issues. In the beginning, it is only possible to get a general idea of what the final issues might be. You should be prepared to change the focus of your research as you proceed.

The issues should be presented as yes-or-no questions. In law school, students are often taught to draft issues that include facts and are very particularized. For example:

EXAMPLE

Are pool owners liable for the injury to a guest, if the guest entered the pool while others were not watching and there were signs marking the pool depth?

The more particularized the issue, the more exact the answer that is required. Often, because the facts are provided in detail with the memorandum, a simpler statement of the issue is sufficient.

EXAMPLE

Are the pool owners liable for a guest's injuries?

──────────────── **LEGAL TERMS** ────────────────

probable cause † A reasonable amount of suspicion, supported by circumstances sufficiently strong to justify a prudent and cautious person's belief that certain alleged facts are probably true. A judge may not issue a search warrant unless he or she is shown probable cause to believe there is evidence of crime on the premises. A police officer may not make an arrest without a warrant unless he or she has reasonable cause, based upon reliable information, to believe a crime has been or is being committed.

Discussion and Analysis

Discussion and analysis are the focal point of the memorandum. Here the applicable law is discussed and applied to the facts presented. The facts are carefully reviewed to determine if any applicable constitutional provisions, statutes, administrative regulations, or court cases affect them.

When statutes and regulations are considered, they are often quoted directly. In such situations, the appropriate citation must be placed at the end of the quote, as shown in Figure 13-10.

Passages from cases are less often quoted verbatim. When they are, you are indicating that you can do no better through paraphrasing what a court has written. Generally, then, case authority is paraphrased and then cited. The citation to the source follows the point taken from that case. Never start a sentence with a full citation; it makes for difficult reading. Generally, limit yourself to citing primary law in a research memorandum. Facts in case law should also be restated when they are relevant to the legal principles discussed. Remember, it is improper to cite dictum to support a legal position. Secondary sources should be cited only when primary law is unavailable or when the secondary source discusses a legal principle in a particularly succinct or eloquent fashion.

It is important to review the law objectively. This means considering the strengths and weaknesses of the matter being researched. An attorney can accomplish more for a client if he realistically understands the weaknesses in the client's case, as well as the defenses available to the opposing party. The research memorandum presents the best opportunity for these vulnerabilities to surface and be assessed; then counterarguments can be developed to minimize their effect.

Maintaining focus is critical in the discussion and analysis portion of the memorandum. The memo should not drift off into tangential issues or concepts. Use of the paragraph blocks discussed in Chapter 11 will assist you in maintaining focus.

In Maryland, a violation of a statute, administrative regulation, or ordinance may be evidence of negligence. McLhinney v. Lansdell Corp., 254 Md. 7, 254 A.2d 177 (1969). The Baltimore County Code specifies the type of enclosure and lock that a pool must have:

> (a) Every person owning land on which there is situated a swimming pool which contains twenty-four (24) inches (610 mm) or more of water in depth at any point, shall erect and maintain thereon an adequate enclosure either surrounding the property or pool area sufficient to make such body of water inaccessible to small children. Such enclosure, including gates therein, shall be not less than four (4) feet above the underlying ground. *All gates shall be self-latching* with latches placed four (4) feet above the underlying ground and otherwise made unaccessible from the outside to small children.

Baltimore County, Md., Code § 20-5(a) (1988) (emphasis added).

FIGURE 13-10 Statute quotation (pool regulation)

IRAC paragraph blocks can be applied effectively in a research memorandum. The issue is addressed in the issue statement. The discussion and application portion can easily be presented in what is referred to as a "Facts plus RAC" form. First is a discussion of the facts, followed by a statement of the rule to be considered. This is followed by an analysis of the rule in relation to the facts. The question in your mind should be: Is the rule, by a reading of its terms, addressing the facts in the matter being researched? This portion of the application could be quite extensive and run several paragraphs. In the process, you answer the legal issue.

You should consider both affirmative and negative responses. Whichever answer is supported by the most compelling primary law is the objective result, which is then discussed in the conclusion. The conclusion may be one sentence or several paragraphs, depending on the complexity of the legal matter.

Presentation of Subsequent Issues

Thereafter, the same pattern is followed: presentation of an issue and then discussion and analysis, until all the issues have been addressed. Issues should be presented logically. A chronological format may be appropriate if the issues follow in that way.

Conclusion

Finally, the conclusions reached as to the various issues are brought together. This summary should show how each issue is related to or affects the others. The complexity of this section will depend on the complexities of the subject issues.

Recommendations

Finally, you provide your recommendations for further action. A recommendation might urge further investigation into a particular aspect or the filing of a lawsuit. Be sure that your recommendations are founded on the results of your research.

Figure 13-11 shows a complete research memorandum.

RESEARCH MEMORANDUM

TO: Mark Washburn, Esquire

FROM: Tamara Jones, Paralegal

DATE: September 15, 1996

FIGURE 13-11   Complete research memorandum

CLIENT: Blanche and Antonio Fulwood
             File No.: 96.401

RE: Liability of swimming pool owners
             for injuries to guest

STATEMENT OF ASSIGNMENT

You requested that I conduct research to determine the potential liability of Blanche and Antonio Fulwood for injuries that Jamal Brown received in their swimming pool on July 16, 1996.

ULTIMATE CONCLUSION

As a result of my research, I have concluded that the Fulwoods most likely would not be held liable under the theory of negligence for Jamal Brown's injuries. The risk of liability to the Fulwoods is further reduced if certain defenses, such as contributory negligence and assumption of risk, are successfully raised.

STATEMENT OF FACTS

The injuries that resulted in the claim against our clients, Blanche and Antonio Fulwood (Fulwoods), occurred during a private pool party on Saturday, July 16, 1996. The injured party and potential plaintiff, Jamal Brown (Brown), was a guest at the party. To the best of my knowledge, suit has not been filed in this case.

The Fulwoods decided to have a surprise pool party for their daughter Jacquetta on her 16th birthday. About 20–25 friends and relatives attended. The guests first were treated to a buffet dinner, cake, and ice cream. This portion of the party was held in the Fulwoods' club basement. The plan was that, at about 8:00 P.M., the Fulwoods' built-in swimming pool would be opened for swimming. Prior to that, the pool area was closed. The lock on the pool gate at the time was a combination lock. Mr. Fulwood believes the gate was not locked; Mrs. Fulwood believes that it was.

One of Jacquetta's guests was Jamal Brown. He arrived at the party about 5:00 P.M., along with his girlfriend Kyisha Mitchell. (All of the guests had to arrive by 5:15 P.M.; Jacquetta was to be surprised at 5:30 P.M.) Sometime during the serving of birthday cake, Brown and Kyisha ventured into the pool area. The exact time is difficult to pinpoint; sometime between 7:00 and 7:30 P.M. is the best estimate. At the time, no one else was in the pool area.

Brown's attorney has indicated that his client believed that the gate was unlocked. Mr. Fulwood additionally believes that it was unlocked when he entered to assist Brown. Brown claims that he approached the shallow end of the pool, about 4–5 inches from the edge, and slipped into the pool. At that point the pool was about one foot deep. Kyisha apparently confirms his version of the facts. There were no other witnesses.

After Brown went into the water, Kyisha screamed for help and Mr. Fulwood quickly arrived. Brown was taken from the pool by Mr. Fulwood and several friends. He appeared stunned, but was conscious. Within minutes an ambulance arrived and took Brown to Baltimore County General Hospital.

At the hospital Brown was seen by an emergency room physician. He received lacerations to the top of his head, neck, and back. Because of injury to his neck, he was given a neck brace to wear for several days. He is currently being seen on a

FIGURE 13-11   *(continued)*

weekly basis by an orthopedic specialist. The full extent of his injuries is still unknown to us.

Additional information indicates that Brown might have been drinking before the party. Evidently Davon, the Fulwoods' 8-year-old son, smelled alcohol on Brown's breath. We have not been able to confirm this or any matter regarding injuries; Brown's attorney is unwilling to provide the hospital records consensually.

Also, it should be noted that the depth of the pool is marked in concrete at eight different spots. The markings are faded, but still readable in good lighting. The pool area is surrounded by six high-intensity outdoor lights.

ISSUE

Can the Fulwoods be held liable under a theory of negligence for the injuries to Brown?

DISCUSSION AND ANALYSIS

Negligence has been defined as the failure to exercise that degree of care required by the circumstances. *State, ex rel. Bell v. Eastern Shore Gas & Electric Co.*, 155 Md. 660, 142 A. 503 (1928). For a cause of action in negligence to be sustained, the defendant must fully prove the following elements by a preponderance of the evidence to the trier of fact:

1. A duty on the part of defendant to use due care;
2. A failure by defendant to perform the duty;
3. Damage or injury to plaintiff;
4. Which damage or injury was caused by defendant's failure to perform the required duty. *Davis v. Johns Hopkins Hospital*, 330 Md. 53, 622 A.2d 128 (1993).

The specific duty of care required depends on the particular circumstances. In Maryland, the standard of care owed by an owner of land to a person entering upon the land depends on the status of the one entering. *Casper v. Chas. F. Smith & Son*, 71 Md. App. 445, 526 A.2d 87 (1987). A plaintiff can be classified in one of several categories for purposes of establishing the defendant's standard of care.

An *invitee* is one invited or permitted to enter or remain on another's property for purposes connected with or related to the owner's business. *Pahanish v. Western Trails, Inc.*, 69 Md. App. 342, 517 A.2d 1122 (1986). The owner of the property must use ordinary and reasonable care to keep its premises safe for invitees and to protect them from hazards which, by the exercise of ordinary care, they would not have discovered. *Id.*

There are two categories of licensees: a bare licensee and a licensee by invitation, or social guest. *Fitzgerald v. Montgomery County Board of Education*, 25 Md. App. 709, 336 A.2d 795 (1975). A person privileged by consent for his own purpose or convenience to enter the property of another is considered a *bare licensee. Mech v. Hearst Corp.*, 64 Md. App. 422, 496 A.2d 1099 (1985). A bare licensee takes the property as he finds it and is owed no duty by the owner except that of not being wantonly injured. *Id.*

A licensee by invitation or social guest takes the premises as the owner uses them. The legal duty owed by the owner is to take care of his guest as he takes care of himself or members of his family. He must exercise reasonable care to make the premises safe for his guest, or he must warn the guest of known dangerous conditions

FIGURE 13-11 *(continued)*

that cannot reasonably be discovered and which, in fact, are not discovered by the guest. *Bramble v. Thompson*, 264 Md. 518, 287 A.2d 265 (1972).

Finally, a *trespasser* is one who intentionally or without consent enters upon the property of another. The only duty owed by the property owner is that of not wantonly injuring the intruder. *Id.* at 522, 287 A.2d at 267.

To determine the appropriate status of Brown, *Telak v. Maszczenski*, 248 Md. 476, 237 A.2d 434 (1968) must be examined. The facts in that case are similar to those in the present case. The Maszczenskis hosted a swimming party on July 4, 1962. Among the 40–50 guests in attendance were Telak and his wife. At one point, Telak mounted the diving board, dove into the pool, and struck his head against the bottom. As a result, he became totally paralyzed below the waist. *Id.* at 479, 237 A.2d at 435.

In determining the standard of care owed by Maszczenski to Telak, the court considered *Stevens v. Dovre*, 248 Md. 15, 234 A.2d 596 (1967). There the court determined that the following conditions must exist before liability can be placed on a defendant for injuries to a social guest:

> (1) the host knows or has reason to to know of the condition and should realize that it involves an unreasonable risk of harm to such guests, and should expect that they will not discover or realize the danger, and (2) the host fails to exercise reasonable care to make the condition safe, or to warn the guests of the condition and the risk involved, and (3) the guests do not know or have reason to know of the condition and the risk involved.

Id. at 18, 234 A.2d at 598–99. In addition, certain limitations are placed on the plaintiff's expectations:

> [T]he guest is expected to take the premises as the host uses them, and he may not expect that they will be prepared for his reception or that precautions will be taken for his safety in any manner in which the host did not prepare or take precautions for his own safety or the safety of the members of his family.

Id. After determining this to be the proper standard, the court of appeals in *Telak* upheld the trial court's finding that the defendant had no knowledge of any unreasonable risk of harm and thus had no liability. *Telak*, 248 Md. at 484, 237 A.2d at 438.

In the case at bar, the facts are similar. At a pool party, an invited guest injured himself upon entry into the pool. A court would likely find Brown to be a licensee by invitation. The same standard used for the Maszczenskis would be applied to the Fulwoods.

Due to a lack of exact information concerning Brown's entry into the pool, certain facts must be assumed. Though the Fulwoods disagree as to whether the pool gate was locked, it could be assumed (based on Mr. Fulwood's observation) that it was not. If a trier of fact determines that the failure to lock the gate created an unreasonable risk of harm, the Fulwoods may be held to have been negligent.

In Maryland, a violation of a statute, administrative regulation, or ordinance may be evidence of negligence. *McLhinney v. Lansdell Corp.*, 254 Md. 7, 254 A.2d 177 (1969). The Baltimore County Code specifies the type of enclosure and lock that a pool must have:

> (a) Every person owning land on which there is situated a swimming pool which contains twenty-four (24) inches (610 mm) or more of water in depth at any point, shall erect and maintain thereon an adequate enclosure either

FIGURE 13-11 *(continued)*

surrounding the property or pool area sufficient to make such body of water inaccessible to small children. Such enclosure, including gates therein, shall be not less than four (4) feet above the underlying ground. *All gates shall be self-latching* with latches placed four (4) feet above the underlying ground and otherwise made inaccessible from the outside to small children.

Baltimore County, Md., Code § 20-5(a) (1988) (emphasis added).

An examination of the Fulwood pool revealed that the gate was not self-latching. The gate is locked by a combination lock. Only family members know the combination. Based on the county ordinance, the Fulwoods' failure to maintain a self-latching gate may be evidence of negligence. However, the court would have to determine that the failure to have the self-latching gate was the cause of the injury (the fourth element in negligence). This is generally known as *proximate cause*. There must be a reasonable connection between the plaintiff's injuries and defendant's omission. *Sun Cab Co. v. Carter*, 14 Md. App. 395, 287 A.2d 73 (1972). This can be understood as the "negligence that caused the accident." Richard J. Gilbert & Paul T. Gilbert, *Maryland Tort Law Handbook* § 11.7 (2d ed. 1992).

Because the absence of an appropriate latch permitted Brown entry only into the pool area, and not the pool itself, it could be argued that this failure in itself did not cause the accident. This same logic can be applied regarding the failure to lock the gate. The unlocked gate in itself did not cause the injury. Both points might fail because of the lack of proximate cause.

Another factual dispute centers around whether Brown slipped or dove into the pool. Though he contends that he slipped, his injuries seem to indicate that he dove. Brown's injuries were to the top of his head, neck, and back. This would appear to be inconsistent with someone who, presumably feet first, slipped into a pool.

Assuming that he in fact slipped, he would have to prove that the Fulwoods created an unreasonable risk by their failure to prevent invitees from slipping into the pool. However, Brown cannot expect that the Fulwoods would take safety precautions on his behalf that they would not take for their own family. A licensee by invitation is placed on the same footing as one of the family, and must take the premises as the owner himself uses them. W. Page Keeton et. al., *Prosser and Keeton on the Law of Torts* § 60 (5th ed. 1984). If taking measures to prevent slippage is not something the Fulwoods would do for their own family, they would not be required to do so for Brown.

However, if in fact Brown dove into the pool, the defenses of contributory negligence and assumption of risk might be employed. Contributory negligence applies whenever the injured person acted or failed to act in a manner consistent with the knowledge or appreciation, actual or implied, of the danger or injury that his conduct involved. *Chudson v. Ratra*, 76 Md. App. 753, 548 A.2d 172 (1988). Contributory negligence bars recovery, theoretically at least, even though by comparison the negligence is minuscule. Gilbert & Gilbert, *supra*, at § 11.4.1.

Although many states have judicially or statutorily eliminated the defense of contributory negligence, Maryland has refused to do so. *Id.* at § 11.4; *Schwier v. Gray*, 277 Md. 631, 357 A.2d 100 (1976). States that continue to use contributory negligence apply it to swimming pool liability cases. *See Davis v. Larue Enterprise, Inc.*, 246 S.E.2d 515 (Ga. Ct. App. 1978).

In addition, proof of intoxication may be used as evidence of negligence. *Smith v. Branscome*, 251 Md. 582, 248 A.2d 455 (1968). If Brown was in fact intoxicated, this fact could be used to show his contributory negligence.

FIGURE 13-11   *(continued)*

A motion for summary judgment was granted to defendant in *Mucowski v. Clark*, 590 A.2d 348 (Pa. Super. Ct. 1991), in which the plaintiff brought suit to recover for injuries sustained when he dove off a three-and-one-half-foot rail into four feet of water. The court found that the swimmer's conduct, rather than the host's failure to warn guests of the dangers of diving into shallow water, was the legal cause of the plaintiff's injuries. *Id.* at 351.

The defense of assumption of risk might also be used to the Fulwoods' benefit. When a plaintiff with full knowledge and understanding of an obvious danger exposes himself to that danger, he is said to assume the risk of all injuries. *Liscombe v. Potomac Edison Co.*, 303 Md. 619, 495 A.2d 838 (1985). Although contributory negligence does not relieve a defendant of the duty to use due care, assumption of risk negates the question of defendant's negligence because plaintiff has abandoned his right to maintain an action. *Gilbert & Gilbert, supra,* at § 11.6.

The court of appeals denied recovery to a plaintiff who dove off a pier, hit bottom, and was paralyzed. The water was only three-and-one-half feet deep. The plaintiff could not see the bottom and thus could not tell if it was safe to dive or not. The court found that the plaintiff had assumed the risk. *Pinehurst Co. v. Phelps*, 163 Md. 68, 160 A. 736 (1932).

Should it be proven at trial that Brown dove into the pool, either theory might be used. Contributory negligence and assumption of risk often arise from the same set of facts. *Maryland Sales & Service Corp. v. Howell*, 19 Md. App. 352, 311 A.2d 432 (1973). The depth markings were indicated and illuminated sufficiently that Brown should have known the risk of diving. By diving, he assumed the risk of his injuries. Additionally, it can be argued that he was contributorily negligent.

CONCLUSION

Based on my research, I would conclude that the Fulwoods would not be held liable for the injuries to Brown. Even though they failed to maintain an appropriate latch on the pool gate, this failure is only evidence of negligence. Proximate cause must still be proven. Even the failure to lock the pool would be insufficient without proximate cause.

The twin theories of contributory negligence and assumption of risk can both be employed by the Fulwoods. If Brown is found to have dived into the pool (as the evidence seems to indicate), then he probably assumed the risk of his injuries. In the alternative, Brown contributed to his injuries by failing to maintain a reasonable standard of care. Both theories would bar his recovery against the Fulwoods.

RECOMMENDATIONS

I recommend first that we obtain copies of all pertinent hospital reports. These records would help determine whether Brown dove or slipped into the pool (we might have to hire an expert to review the records), and, if a blood test was taken, whether he was intoxicated. As Brown's attorney is not providing these records voluntarily, we will have to wait until suit is filed and obtain them through discovery.

After suit is filed, we will want to depose both Brown and Kyisha Mitchell. I will begin to develop questions that could be asked of them.

FIGURE 13-11   *(continued)*

Summary

- Three types of interviews may be conducted by paralegals: initial client interview, follow-up interview, and field interview.

- The purpose of the initial client interview is to obtain objective information from the client, as well as to leave a favorable impression of the firm.

- An interview memorandum drafted after an initial client interview consists of four parts; objective client information, the client's story, subjective impressions about the client, and recommendations to the attorney.

- A follow-up interview is often scheduled to cover a particular item, such as reviewing financial records.

- A field interview is often conducted at the interviewee's place of employment or home.

- An investigatory memorandum is submitted in response to an inquiry as to the status of an investigation.

- A research memorandum provides an objective analysis of a legal situation. A research memorandum could be requested in a number of circumstances, including when a decision about accepting a case has to be made. It is a comprehensive document, containing an encyclopedia of information for the requesting attorney.

- Though there is no universal format for a research memorandum, commonly it contains: heading, statement of assignment, ultimate conclusion, statement of facts, issues, discussion and analysis, conclusion, and recommendations.

Review Questions

1. List the component parts of an initial interview memorandum.

2. What are the goals of an initial client interview?

3. What is the purpose of a follow-up interview?

4. Why is it important to complete the memorandum immediately after the interview?

5. What should be the perspective of an investigatory memorandum?

6. List some of the circumstances in which a research memorandum might be appropriate.

7. What must be included in the heading portion of a research memorandum?

8. What is the purpose of the ultimate conclusion section?

9. How can the IRAC format be applied to the discussion and analysis section of a research memorandum?

10. What is the purpose of the recommendation section of a research memorandum?

Chapter Exercises

1. Prepare an initial client interview memorandum for Ray Lardbaugh, the smoking radio station personality discussed in Chapter 9.

2. Prepare a research memorandum on behalf of Dr. Krup from Chapter 9. Assume that you have located the *Leichtman* case and that the event took place in your state.

3. Prepare an investigatory memorandum for Peter Houck, the father fighting for custody discussed in Chapter 4. Assume that he is your client and that you have uncovered the *Atkinson* case.

IIII
CHAPTER 14

INSTRUMENTS

CHAPTER OUTLINE

OVERVIEW

An *instrument* is a written document that records the responsibilities or interests of participants in a legal transaction. When an agreement or understanding is reached, an instrument is often drafted to memorialize its terms. There is a common misconception that general practice attorneys spend most of their time in court. In fact, the majority of most lawyers' time is devoted to drafting the numerous instruments that are part of a legal practice: wills, leases, articles of incorporation, and separation agreements, to mention only a few.

Because of their training, paralegals are uniquely positioned to play a pivotal role in the preparation of these documents. In many law offices, paralegals initially prepare all instruments, with attorneys performing an editing role. In order to assure success, instrument preparation demands self-motivation and persistence. As the preparer, you must be adept at utilizing a number of sources, especially form books. Drafting instruments requires considerable emphasis on detail and clarity.

A variety of instruments are prepared in a legal practice. All instruments discuss either responsibilities or interests important to the client in a particular legal transaction. A *deed* is a document that marks the transfer of an interest in real property. A landlord and tenant enter into a *lease* to put in writing their understanding. A *separation agreement,* sometimes referred to as a *marital agreement,* discusses not only the responsibilities of parties (such as custody of children), but also memorializes the parties' interests in certain property (such as bank accounts and real estate). A *will* describes, among other things, the responsibilities of the personal representative and the property interests that pass to the legatees and devisees. Finally, business documents, such as articles of incorporation, indicate the responsibilities of officers, directors, and stockholders of a corporation.

The utilization of forms can greatly assist in the preparation of instruments. A *form* is a printed document with blank spaces for the insertion of required relevant data. "Freestanding" forms can be purchased from paper suppliers or office supply stores. These forms are popular because they can be used without rewriting or retyping. Most forms used, though, are found in form books. These books may be either large encyclopedic series or single, compact volumes. Form books are generally divided between those with an emphasis on litigation documents (such as pleadings and motions) and those for instruments. Litigation form books are discussed in Chapter 15.

Though form books are convenient and comprehensive, they are not without disadvantages. One major problem is the boilerplate language frequently used in many forms. *Boilerplate* is language that is common to all legal documents of the same type. It is language that is difficult for laypersons to understand because of its reliance on legalese and terms of art. Generally, boilerplate reflects a general legal perspective, one that does not take into consideration the nuances of individual jurisdictions or circumstances. These conditions demand that the paralegal always check a form's content against the jurisdiction's current law, and not employ any language unless it is completely understood, intended, and useful.

A model can also assist in the drafting of an instrument. *Models* are documents previously prepared for similar cases. Many experienced paralegals routinely maintain a sample file of important documents they have prepared, with the expectation of referring to them again in the future.

Finally, checklists can be useful in the preparation of instruments. Checklists are especially useful when drafting complex documents such as leases or separation agreements. Often they serve as valuable double-checks, to ensure that documents are comprehensive and complete.

Keep in mind that, as with all written documents, any instrument you draft must be reviewed by your supervising attorney. Drafting an instrument and then providing it directly to a client without oversight would most likely constitute the unauthorized practice of law.

PARALEGAL PRACTICE SITUATION

Your neighbor, Amelia Juarez, recently purchased a multiunit dwelling for investment purposes. She would like to rent out rooms in the building to local college students. Because she is within a mile of a local college, she feels she has a lucrative market. She has approached you to see if your firm would prepare a lease that she could use with prospective tenants.

The attorney you work for has given you permission to put together an initial draft for his review. You are to draft a lease that meets Amelia's needs.

General Considerations

Though the types of instruments produced in legal practice vary greatly, some general considerations apply to all documents in this category.

A client's need for an instrument is often based on practical, nonlegal concerns, such as increasing income, excluding certain individuals from property, or limiting authority over certain individuals, to mention a few. Consequently, clients may sometimes request provisions that are not realistic or even legal. You must have a sufficient legal background to determine what can appropriately be placed in an instrument. Remember, though, only an attorney can select the appropriate document for a client or advise as to its limitations. Advising a client concerning an instrument would constitute the provision of legal advice and thus would be unethical activity for a legal assistant.

Often clients, when considering the implications of an instrument, are only interested in the problems and factors immediately affecting their legal situation. It is important that legal professionals not only direct their clients to immediate solutions, but also identify future problems that could arise if precautions are not taken and provided for in a particular document. Sometimes this is called "looking at the big picture." Clients must always anticipate future changes in their circumstances. The instruments they sign must always be flexible enough to stand the test of time.

Another consideration centers on writing style. When preparing instruments, you should strictly adhere to the principles discussed in Chapter 11. The importance of clarity is reemphasized here. No part of an instrument can be left vague or confusing. Words must be carefully selected to reflect the true intentions of the client. This can be achieved through the use of plain English instead of legalese. Unfortunately, this is easier said than done. Forms especially tend to use legalese profligately. Consequently, archaic language finds its way into documents more often than it should. If you must use terms of art, make sure they are clearly defined (even though the definitions may be quite long). Remember that instruments should be drafted in such a way that they can be used, interpreted, and applied by clients rather than legal professionals. A client should not have to call his lawyer every time he reads a contract.

A final consideration is that you should resourcefully and creatively craft instruments. Before beginning, secure all available forms, models, and checklists. You should not feel constrained by any previously developed format. Provided you understand the legal parameters and the client's desires, you may pursue new and innovative ways of preparing instruments.

GENERAL CONSIDERATIONS IN PREPARING INSTRUMENTS

1. A client's needs may be based on nonlegal concerns
   - Client may not realize that what is being asked for is illegal
   - Client may be unrealistic
2. A client may be interested only in immediate implications
   - Get client to look at the "big picture"
3. Good writing style is important
   - Document must be clearly written
   - Words should be carefully selected
   - Eliminate all legalese; define terms of art
4. Be resourceful in creation
   - Locate all possible models, forms, checklists
   - Consider new and innovative ways and resources

Deeds

When real estate passes from one individual (**grantor**) to another (**grantee**), the transfer is documented by a **deed**. The deed is recorded in the local land records office. Residential property transactions often use preprinted (freestanding) form deeds (see Figure 14-1). Commercial land transaction deeds, in contrast, tend to be created from forms and models.

There are three types of deeds, each of which provides a different level of protection for the buyer. In addition, a fourth document, an assignment of leasehold, is sometimes considered a deed.

LEGAL TERMS

grantor [†] The person who makes a grant; the party in a deed who makes the conveyance.

grantee [†] The person to whom a grant is made; the party in a deed to whom the conveyance is made.

deed [†] A document by which real property, or an interest in real property, is conveyed from one person to another.

DEED — FEE SIMPLE — INDIVIDUAL GRANTOR — LONG FORM

This Deed, MADE THIS

day of

in the year one thousand nine hundred and

by and between

of

of the first part, and

of the second part.

WITNESSETH, That in consideration of the sum of

the said

do   grant and convey to the said

personal representatives/successors and assigns   , in fee simple, all

lot   of ground situate in

and described as follows, that is to say:

FIGURE 14-1 Freestanding deed

Quitclaim Deed

In a **quitclaim deed**, the transferor makes no assurance to the transferee as to the quality of interest he may have in the land. He transfers only whatever interest he holds. It is possible that the grantor's interest is encumbered and, as

—————————————— **LEGAL TERMS** ——————————————

quitclaim deed † A deed that conveys whatever interest the grantor has in a piece of real property, as distinguished from the more usual deed which conveys a fee and contains various covenants, particularly title covenants. A quitclaim deed is often referred to simply as a "quitclaim."

TOGETHER with the buildings thereupon, and the rights, alleys, ways, waters, privileges, appurtenances and advantages thereto belonging, or in anywise appertaining.

To HAVE AND To HOLD the said described lot   of ground and premises to the said

personal representatives/successors

and assigns   , in fee simple.

AND the said part   of the first part hereby covenant   that   not done or suffered to be done any act, matter or thing whatsoever, to encumber the property hereby conveyed; that   ,will warrant specially the property hereby granted; and that   will execute such further assurances of the same as may be requisite.

WITNESS the hand   and seal   of said grantor

Test:

_____

_____(SEAL)

_____(SEAL)

STATE OF MARYLAND,   , to wit:
   I HEREBY CERTIFY, That on this   day of   in the year one thousand nine hundred and   , before me, the subscriber, a Notary Public of the State aforesaid, personally appeared

known to me (or satisfactorily proven) to be the person   whose name   is/are subscribed to the within instrument, and acknowledged the foregoing Deed to be   act, and in my presence signed and sealed the same.
   IN WITNESS WHEREOF, I hereunto set my hand and official seal.

_____
                                    Notary Public

My Commission expires:

_____

FIGURE 14-1 *(continued)*

DEED

FROM

. . . .

. . . .

TO

. . . .

. . . .

BLOCK No. . . . .

Received for Record, ... , 19 . . . . . . ,

at . . . . . . o'clock . . . M. Same day recorded

in Liber . . . . . No. . . . . . Folio . . . . . . &c.,

one of the Land Records of . . . .

. . . . , and examined per

. . . . , Clerk.

Cost of Record, $. . . . .

TOWSON STATIONERS, INC., TOWSON, MD.

FIGURE 14-1   *(continued)*

a result, that there is a **cloud on the title**. This means that the **title** is defective in some way. As a result, taking property by quitclaim can be risky for a buyer. Quitclaim deeds are frequently employed in divorce practice, where both spouses convey the entire interest to one spouse as part of a property settlement. In these cases a **title search** is usually not done (to avoid unnecessary additional cost).

Special Warranty Deed

In a **special warranty deed**, the grantor guarantees that she has not committed any act that would harm the quality of title. She warrants that she will be responsible should there be a cloud on the title which is later found to be her responsibility. Special warranty deeds are popular for residential property transactions.

Warranty Deed

Finally, in a **warranty deed** the transferor guarantees the title without condition. He promises to the transferee not only that he has good title, but also that he will protect the buyer from defects, whether caused by him or previous property owners.

Assignment of Leasehold

A fourth instrument, often referred to as an **assignment** of **leasehold**, is similar to a deed. Whereas a deed transfers all of the interest in the property to the grantee for eternity, an assignment of leasehold only permits the grantee to use the property for a specific period of time (typically 99 years), provided the rent is paid. The grantee is permitted to build on the land. Any improvements made, such as a house, are owned by the grantee. This results in the peculiar

--- **LEGAL TERMS** ---

cloud on the title [†] An outstanding potential claim against real estate somewhere in the chain of title, which reduces the market value of the property.

title [†] The rights of an owner with respect to property, real or personal, i.e., possession and the right of possession.

title search [†] An examination of all documents of record relating to the status or condition of the title to a given piece of real estate (including deeds reflecting past ownership and outstanding mortgages and other liens) in order to verify title.

special warranty deed [†] A deed that contains a special warranty rather than a general warranty.

warranty deed [†] A deed that contains title covenants.

assignment [†] 1. A transfer of property, or a right in property, from one person to another. 2. A designation or appointment.

leasehold [†] The interest or estate of a lessee under a lease. The lessee's interest or estate is also referred to as a leasehold interest or leasehold estate.

situation in which the land is owned by one person and the improvements by another. Frequently referred to as **ground rents**, these instruments became popular in residential properties after World War II because they encouraged the building of affordable housing. With a ground rent, the buyer was not required to bear the additional expense of purchasing the land. The assignee's expenses were limited to the costs of construction. Assignments of leasehold are seen in commercial situations as well as residential ones.

Property Description

The most important part of the deed is the property description. The property description must be exact; otherwise, confusion may later arise as to the precise boundaries and ownership interest. This may result in the need to bring an action for **quiet title**, a lawsuit wherein the exact interest and ownership in a piece of land is disputed.

In older deeds, a description method known as **metes and bounds** is commonly used. This system incorporates the location of natural objects, such as streams and trees, with compass directions and measurements of the land. (See Figure 14-2.) Often, this method appears archaic and difficult to understand.

In areas where properties are laid out in subdivision tracts, **plat** indications have replaced metes-and-bounds descriptions. The plat, with its specific boundary marking determined by a survey, is recorded in the land records office.

Leases

An agreement that deals with the rental of real property is referred to as a **lease**. The parties to a lease are the property owner, called the **landlord** or **lessor**, and the renter, called the **tenant** or **lessee**. Leases are used in both commercial and residential settings.

─────────────── **LEGAL TERMS** ───────────────

ground rent lease [†]   A long-term lease of land, commonly for 99 years, typically entered into by the tenant so that it can construct income-producing buildings.

quieting title [†]   Bringing an action to quiet title, i.e., a lawsuit brought to remove a cloud on the title so that the plaintiff and those in privity with him or her may forever be free of claims against the property.

metes and bounds [†]   A property description, commonly in a deed or mortgage, that is based upon the property's boundaries and the natural objects and other markers on the land.

plat [†]   A map of a tract of land, showing the boundaries of the streets, blocks, and numbered lots. A plat is also referred to as a "plat map" or a "plot."

lease [†]   A contract for the possession of real estate in consideration of payment of rent, ordinarily for a term of years or months, but sometimes at will. The person making the

BEGINNING for the same at a wild cherry tree standing at the end of the North 63¼ degrees West 51-3/4 perches line of that parcel of said land heretofore bequeathed by William Matthews, Sr., to William Matthews, and running thence and binding on said part the three following courses: North 36 degrees West 65½ perches to two Spanish Oak stumps North 53 degrees West 117 perches South 88½ degrees West 5½ perches to a stone standing in the county road leading by Kenney's Mill; thence binding on said road the two following courses South 44 perches, South 1¼ degrees West 104.7 perches, thence North 60½ degrees East 11 perches to the end of the last measured line of the whole tract called "Smith's Prospect"; thence binding on the given line of said tract South 5 degrees East 49.7 perches to the beginning of said tract; thence North 70½ degrees West 12.1 perches to a corner of Jacob M. Hamshire's land; thence South 35 degrees East 76¼ perches to a stone; thence North 64-3/4 degrees East 9.7 perches to a stone near the Mill Dam; thence North 81¼ degrees East 32 perches to a stone; thence North 85¼ degrees East 68 perches to a stone on the West side of the County Road, thence binding on said road North 13¼ degrees East 40½ perches until it intersects the third line of the whole tract called "Smith's Prospect"; thence North 6½ degrees West 3½ perches to the end of said line; thence North 21½ degrees East 33½ perches until it intersects Jacob Stabler's part of said land; thence reversing said part North 68½ degrees West 24½ perches to a stone; thence North 36½ degrees West 2.6 perches North 29 degrees East 16-3/4 perches; thence North 63¼ degrees West 26-3/4 perches to the first place of beginning. Containing 174 acres 1 rood and 20 perches of land, more or less.

FIGURE 14-2 Typical metes-and-bounds description

Residential Lease

Residential leases are typically form leases provided by apartment management companies for their agents to use with prospective tenants. In most instances, the provisions are not negotiable by the lessee—it is a take-it-or-leave-it situation. However, residential lease transactions are fairly closely regulated; the consumer protection movement has resulted in the granting of considerable rights for tenants. State statutes now often limit the types of provisions that a landlord can include in a lease. For instance, in many states, a landlord

--- LEGAL TERMS ---

conveyance is the landlord or lessor; the person receiving the right of possession is the tenant or lessee.

landlord (lessor) † An owner of real property who leases all or a portion of the premises to a tenant.

tenant (lessee) † A person who occupies realty under a lease with a landlord.

cannot, in the lease, require tenants to waive their right to a jury trial in the event of a lawsuit over the lease.

Residential leases include sections dealing with rent, security deposit, lease purpose, utilities, and repairs. See Figure 14-3.

Commercial Lease

A commercial lease differs from a residential lease in a number of ways. The first is that the parties are usually both represented by counsel. As a result, the lease is more fully negotiated. The second difference is that the term of the commercial lease is often longer than that of a residential lease. This means that more issues must be dealt with than in a residential lease. For instance, a residential lease usually does not have a rent escalation clause. A commercial lease for 10 years is not atypical. In that instance, annual rent increases tied to the **Consumer Price Index** or some other baseline may be requested by the landlord. A point of contention in commercial lease negotiations is whether the business entity, such as a corporation, or the tenant personally will be liable for the lease. The landlord always prefers personal liability because such a tenant is less likely to file **bankruptcy** to avoid responsibility under the lease. The tenant prefers the business to be liable, for the same reason.

Wills

An individual who wishes to pass certain property to her loved ones upon her death can effectuate her intentions through a **last will and testament**, generally referred to simply as a *will*. Under early English law, a will disposed of real property and a testament disposed of personal property. This distinction is no longer made, however; a will accomplishes both transfers. The existence of a properly drafted and executed will facilitates the passing of property from the **testator** (the maker of the will) to both **legatees** (recipients of personal property) and **devisees** (recipients of real property). To die with a will is to die **testate**, whereas an individual who has not made a will is said to be **intestate**. In the latter case, state statutory law governs how the decedent's property is disposed.

Besides disposing of assets, a will can provide for the guardianship of minor children and the custody of their property. A will can also include provisions creating a **trust**, a separate legal entity formed to hold property for others.

LEGAL TERMS

Consumer Price Index [†] Statistics compiled and published by the government on a regular basis, which reflect the current cost of living.

bankruptcy [†] The system under which a debtor may come into court (voluntary bankruptcy) or be brought into court by his or her creditors (involuntary bankruptcy), either seeking to have his or her assets administered and sold for the benefit of ... creditors

Some individuals even specify their burial and funeral desires and arrangements in their wills.

Paralegal Tip

It may be unwise to indicate burial and funeral arrangements in a last will and testament. Commonly, there is no reading of the will until after the burial has taken place. It is possible that survivors could make arrangements that vary from the desires of the decedent. Imagine if a person wanted to be buried, but the surviving children decided to have the remains cremated. It could be very distressing for the children once they learned of the burial provisions in the will. Individuals who desire specific burial or funeral plans should make those plans known to their loved ones in other ways. For example, a separate letter or written instructions could be placed with other important papers.

SIDEBAR   **HOW ABOUT A WILL VIDEOTAPING BUSINESS?**

Keep in mind that a paralegal is not permitted to prepare instruments, including wills, for clients. If the legal assistant is working under the supervision of an attorney, provided the attorney reviews the paralegal's work and is the only one making legal decisions, the paralegal may draft any document. Consider the language in an ethical opinion (No. 90-37) issued by the Maryland State Bar Association Committee on Ethics in response to a question concerning a paralegal will business that was to include videotaping. The opinion stated that the "mere determination of whether or not there are legal questions to be answered is in itself the practice of law." Does that mean paralegals are prohibited from even advising a client to speak to an attorney, because legal issues may be present?

─────────── **LEGAL TERMS** ───────────

and to be discharged from his or her debts (a straight bankruptcy), or to have his or her debts reorganized (a business reorganization or a wage earner's plan).

last will †   Same as will. The word "last" may connote "final wishes," or it may signify that the will is the most recent in a series of wills made by the testator.

testament †   A will. The terms "testament," "will," "last will," and "last will and testament" are synonymous.

testator †   A person who dies leaving a valid will.

legatee †   A person who receives personal property as a beneficiary under a will, although the word is often loosely used to mean a person who receives a testamentary gift of either personal property or real property.

devisee †   The beneficiary of a devise.

testate †   Pertaining to a person, or to the property of a person, who dies leaving a valid will.

intestate †   Pertaining to a person, or to the property of a person, who dies without leaving a valid will.

trust †   A fiduciary relationship involving a trustee who holds trust property for the benefit or use of a beneficiary. Property of any description or type (real, personal, tangible, intangible, etc.) may properly be the subject of a trust. The trustee holds legal title to the trust property (also called the *res* or *corpus* of the trust); the beneficiary holds equitable title. A trust is generally established through a trust instrument, such as a deed of trust or a will, by a person (known as the *settlor*) who wishes the beneficiary to receive the benefit of the property but not outright ownership. A trust may, however, also be created by operation of law.

FORM 3A-1 ▬▬▬▬▬▬
House Lease

CONTENTS

CLAUSE

Agreement between ...., of .... (Landlord), and ....,
of .... (Tenant), made ...., 19 ....

3A-26   12/92

FIGURE 14-3 Residential lease. (Copyright © 1994 by Warren, Gorham & Lamont, One Penn Plaza, New York, NY 10119 (1-800-999-9336). All rights reserved. Reprinted by permission of Warren, Gorham & Lamont from *Basic Legal Transactions,* by Vincent DiLorenzo.)

1. Agreement to Lease. Landlord agrees to lease to Tenant, and Tenant agrees to lease from Landlord, the premises on the terms and conditions stated in this Lease.

2. Premises. The premises leased are located at .... (the Premises).

3. Term. The term of this Lease begins on ...., 19 ...., and ends ...., 19 .... (the Term).

4. Rent. Tenant will pay Landlord, without demand, an annual rent of $............ Such rent is payable monthly in advance on the first day of each month during the Term, in monthly installments of $............, at Landlord's address stated above (or at such other address as Landlord may require). However, the first month's rent is payable when Tenant signs this Lease.

5. Additional Rent. Tenant may be required, under this Lease, to pay additional sums to Landlord. Any such sums are additional rent under this Lease. All additional rent is to be paid together with the next monthly installment of rent payable under this Lease. If Tenant does not pay additional rent when due, Landlord has the same rights against Tenant as if Tenant had failed to pay the rent.

6. Use of Premises. The Premises may be used as a single-family residence only. Only the Tenant and his immediate family may occupy the Premises.

7. Landlord's Failure to Give Possession. Landlord is not liable to Tenant if he fails to give Tenant possession of the Premises on the commencement date of this Lease. However, if Landlord is unable to give Tenant possession, rent will begin to be payable only from and after the date Tenant is given possession of the Premises. In such event, the end of the Term will not change.

8. Security. Tenant has deposited $............ with Landlord as security for his obligations in this Lease. If Tenant does not comply with all the terms of this Lease, Landlord may use the security deposit to pay any sum payable by Tenant, and to reimburse Landlord for any damages and costs arising by Tenant's default, under this Lease. Landlord will give Tenant written notice of use of all or any part of the security deposit. On receipt of notice, Tenant will immediately pay to Landlord an amount sufficient to restore the security deposit in full.

After the end of the Term or earlier termination of this Lease, if Tenant has performed all of the terms and conditions of this Lease, Landlord will

FIGURE 14-3 *(continued)*

return the security deposit (or any remaining portion not used by Landlord in accordance with this Clause) to Tenant, without interest.

If Landlord sells the Premises, he may transfer the security deposit to the purchaser. Thereafter, only such purchaser will be liable to return the security deposit to Tenant, under the terms of this Lease.

9. Utilities. Tenant is responsible for making arrangements for, and paying when billed, all utility and other services for the Premises, including electricity, gas, fuel oil, water, and gardening, except ...., for which Landlord will be responsible for payment.

10. Condition of Furniture and Furnishings. The furniture and other furnishing, appliances, equipment, and other personal property located on the Premises are accepted by the Tenant "as is."

11. Condition of the Premises. Tenant has inspected the Premises, including the grounds and building, acknowledges that they are in good order and repair, and accepts them "as is."

12. Repairs. Tenant must keep the Premises, including the grounds and all appliances, equipment, furniture, furnishings, and other personal property clean and in good repair. In the event of a default by Tenant, Landlord may make the necessary repairs and charge the cost of such repairs to Tenant as additional rent under this Lease.

13. Alterations. Tenant may not alter or decorate the Premises without the prior written consent of Landlord in each instance. All alterations made by Tenant will, unless Landlord requests removal, become Landlord's property and remain on the Premises at the termination of this Lease without any compensation to Tenant. If Landlord demands or permits removal, Tenant will put that part of the Premises into the same condition as existed prior to the alteration.

14. Fire and Casualty.

a. Notice. In the event of fire or other damage to the Premises Tenant will immediately notify Landlord.

b. Partial Damage and Conditions to Continued Effectiveness. If the Premises are only partially damaged and are inhabitable and Landlord makes full repairs within .... days, this Lease will continue without abatement or apportionment of rent.

c. Conditions to Termination. If the Premises are rendered uninhabitable, continued occupancy would be illegal, or Landlord cannot or does not repair within .... days, Tenant may immediately vacate the Premises and

FIGURE 14-3 *(continued)*

notify Landlord in writing within .... days after vacating of his intent to terminate, in which case this Lease will terminate as of the date of vacating and all prepaid rent and unapplied security deposit will be returned to Tenant.

15. Liability. Landlord is not liable for any loss, damage, or expense suffered by any person on or about the Premises, except that which is caused by Landlord's negligence. If Landlord incurs any damage or expense due to any claim, other than a claim arising from Landlord's negligence, Tenant will reimburse Landlord for the damage or expense, as additional rent under this Lease.

16. Assignment or Subletting. Tenant may not assign this Lease, sublet all or any part of the Premises, or allow any other person to occupy the Premises.

17. Insurance Requirements. Tenant agrees not to do anything that will increase the insurance premiums payable with respect to the Premises, and if any insurance company insuring the Premises does increase its premium because of Tenant's actions or use, Tenant will pay the additional premium, as additional rent under this Lease.

18. Right of Entry. Landlord may enter the Premises at reasonable times in order to examine the Premises or make repairs or alterations. In the event of an actual or apparent emergency, Landlord may enter the Premises at any time without notice. Tenant will not change any lock or install additional locks without Landlord's prior written consent and without providing Landlord a copy of all keys.

19. Future Tenants and Purchasers. During the last .... months of the Term, Landlord may enter the Premises at reasonable times to show the Premises to possible tenants, purchasers, and lenders, and may display "FOR SALE" or "FOR RENT" signs on the Premises.

20. Subordination. This Lease and Tenant's right under it are subject and subordinate to all existing and future (1) mortgages on the Premises and (2) leases of the land underlying the Premises, if any (including any renewals, extensions, and modifications of such mortgages and leases). Tenant will execute and deliver immediately upon demand any certeificates Landlord may require to evidence such subordination.

21. Eminent Domain Proceedings.

  a. Entire Premises. If all or almost all of the Premises are condemned by any governmental authority, this Lease and Tenant's rights and obliga-

FIGURE 14-3 *(continued)*

tions under it will terminate as of the date such governmental authority takes title.

b. Part of Premises. If part of the Premises is condemned by any governmental authority, Landlord may, at his option (to be exercised with reasonable promptness), terminate this Lease on .... days' prior written notice to Tenant. If Landlord cancels this Lease, Tenant's rights and obligations under it will terminate as of the termination date contained in Landlord's notice. Tenant will pay all rent due under this Lease until such termination date, without reduction or abatement. If Landlord does not cancel this Lease, the rent payable from and after the date title vests in such governmental authority will be prorated to encompass the portion of the Premises not taken or condemned.

c. Award. The entire award for any condemnation of the Premises is the sole property of Landlord. Tenant will have no interest in such award and will make no claim for the unexpired Term of this Lease.

22. Notices. All notices under this Lease must be in writing and either delivered personally or mailed by certified mail to the address of Landlord and Tenant stated above (or at such other address as Landlord may designate by notice to Tenant). Notices that are sent by mail will be deemed delivered two days after they are mailed.

23. Default and Remedies.

a. Notice of Default. Landlord agrees to provide .... days' written notice to Tenant to correct any default under this Lease, other than a failure to pay rent or additional rent.

b. Termination of Lease. If Tenant fails to correct any default, other than a failure to pay rent or additional rent, within such ....-day period, or if Tenant fails to pay rent or additional rent provided for in this Lease on its due date plus a grace period of .... days, then Landlord may cancel this Lease by .... days' prior written notice to Tenant. On the date stated in Landlord's notice, this Lease and Tenant's rights under this Lease will terminate, and Tenant must surrender the Premises. Tenant remains liable, after such termination, for rent, additional rent, costs, and damages provided in this Lease.

c. Rent for Unexpired Term. If this Lease is terminated because of Tenant's default, all rent and additional rent payable by Tenant during the entire Term as provided in this Lease become immediately due and fully payable. Landlord may thereafter lease the Premises to another tenant for any term and at any rent. Tenant is responsible for all costs incurred by

FIGURE 14-3 *(continued)*

Landlord in reletting the Premises (including attorney fees, advertising expenses, and repairs). Any rent received by Landlord from a new tenant will reduce the amount for which Tenant is liable to pay to Landlord.

    d. Other Remedies. If this Lease is terminated because of Tenant's default, Landlord may, in addition to any other rights and remedies available to him, (1) enter the Premises and have Tenant and Tenant's property removed, and (2) use any dispossession, eviction, and similar legal proceedings available.

    24. Curing Tenant's Defaults. If Tenant does not correct a default after .... days' notice by Landlord, Landlord may remedy such default on behalf of Tenant, and any costs incurred by Landlord will be payable by Tenant, as additional rent under this Lease.

    25. Surrender. At the end of the Term or earlier termination of this Lease, Tenant will quit and surrender the Premises in as good order and condition as they were on the commencement date of this Lease, except for ordinary wear and tear and damage by the elements.

    26. Rules. Attached to this Lease are written rules regarding Tenant's use and care of the Premises and appliances, equipment, furniture, furnishings, and other personal property located on the Premises. Tenant agrees to comply strictly with such rules.

    27. Quiet Enjoyment. If Tenant is not in default under this Lease, Tenant may peaceably and quietly enjoy the Premises during the Term.

    28. No Waiver. If Landlord fails to enforce any provision of this Lease, he is not deemed to waive such provision and is not prevented from enforcing such provision thereafter.

    29. Separability. If any provision in this Lease is invalid or unenforceable, the balance of this Lease shall remain effective, absent such provision.

    30. Successors. This Lease is binding on all persons who may succeed to the rights of Landlord or Tenant, including heirs, executors, and purchasers, as applicable.

    31. Merger. This Lease represents the entire agreement between Landlord and Tenant. Landlord has made no representations other than what is contained in this Lease.

    32. Amendments. No change in this Lease shall be effective unless it is in writing and signed by both Landlord and Tenant.

FIGURE 14-3 *(continued)*

33. Powers of Landlord's Agent. All rights and remedies of Landlord under this Lease or at law may be exercised by Landlord or by Landlord's agent in his name.

....

Landlord

....

Tenant

FIGURE 14-3 *(continued)*

When drafting a last will and testament, there are two matters to consider. First and foremost, you must make a complete and comprehensive inventory of all property of the testator. You must be able to differentiate between property that passes under a will and property that passes by title. For instance, property titled in either **joint tenancy** or **tenancy by the entireties** will pass to the other co-tenant automatically, without the necessity of directions in a will. Also, life insurance passes directly to the beneficiaries. This, of course, requires a basic understanding of property and insurance, as well as probate, law.

Secondly, the will must reflect the true intentions of the testator. This requires a careful and methodical process of communication and recordation of the client's preferences regarding specific items of property. An individual must be mentally competent to make a will. If there is a question as to competency, a medical evaluation may be necessary to determine if the client is legally able to make a will.

Most individuals have jointly titled property or very modest holdings. In these cases, the will drafted is often referred to as a *simple will,* because of its straightforwardness and lack of complexity. Also, with a simple will, maximizing tax benefits and avoiding probate assessments are not important concerns.

The typical components of a simple will include an introductory clause in which the testator is identified; a section appointing a **personal representative**

———————————————— LEGAL TERMS ————————————————

joint tenancy † An estate in land or in personal property held by two or more persons jointly, with equal rights to share in its enjoyment. The most important feature of a joint tenancy is the right of survivorship, which means that upon the death of a joint tenant the entire estate goes to the survivor (or, in the case of more than two joint tenants, to the survivors, and so on to the last survivor).

tenancy by the entirety † A form of joint tenancy in an estate in land or in personal property that exists between husband and wife by virtue of the fact that they are husband and wife. As with a conventional joint tenancy, a tenancy by the entirety is a tenancy with right of survivorship.

personal representative † Ordinarily, the executor or administrator of a decedent's estate, although the term may also include others who have the responsibility to manage the property or affairs of a person who is unable to manage them for himself or herself due to incapacity, incompetency, or insolvency.

and indicating his duties; several paragraphs specifying **bequests** (gifts of personal property) and **devises** (gifts of real property); a **residuary clause** (to distribute the remainder of the property), and a signature and witness block. (See Figure 14-4.) The more complex the will, the more provisions are required.

In addition to wills, other testamentary documents are typically prepared by a general legal practice. These include trusts, **durable powers of attorney**, **living wills**, and **codicils**. In a trust, a **fiduciary** relationship is created when property is transferred by an individual to a trust governed by a written agreement for the benefit of specific individuals. The **trustee** holds legal title to the property and has the power and responsibility to manage it. In a durable power of attorney, an individual gives the responsibility for health care and property decisions in the event of his incapacity to another person, the **attorney in fact** (usually a family member). A living will expresses an individual's wish to be permitted to die a natural death without the intervention of artificial life support (see Figure 14-5). Finally, a *codicil* is a written amendment to a will.

Contracts

Attorneys frequently prepare contracts on behalf of clients. Because there are so many variations in contract types, purposes, and provisions, it is impossible

---

LEGAL TERMS

bequest [t]   Technically, a gift of personal property by will, i.e., a legacy, although the term is often loosely used in connection with a testamentary gift of real estate as well.

devise [t]   A gift of real property by will, although it is often loosely used to mean a testamentary gift of either real property or personal property.

residuary clause [t]   A clause in a will that disposes of the part of the estate that is left after all other legacies and devises have been paid and all claims against the estate are satisfied. Residuary clauses frequently contain the phrase "rest, residue, and remainder."

durable power of attorney [t]   A power of attorney that remains effective even though the grantor becomes mentally incapacitated. Some durable powers of attorney become effective only when a person is no longer able to make decisions for himself or herself.

living will [t]   A document in which a person sets forth directions regarding medical treatment to be given if he or she becomes unable to participate in decisions regarding his or her medical care.

codicil [t]   An addition or supplement to a will, which adds to or modifies the will without replacing or revoking it. A codicil does not have to be physically attached to the will.

fiduciary duty [t]   A relationship between two persons in which one is obligated to act with the utmost good faith, honesty, and loyalty on behalf of the other. A fiduciary relationship is often loosely but inaccurately considered to be the equivalent of a confidential relationship.

trustee [t]   The person who holds the legal title to trust property for the benefit of the beneficiary of the trust, with such powers and subject to such duties as are imposed by the terms of the trust and the law.

attorney in fact [t]   An agent or representative authorized by [the agent's] principal, by virtue of a power of attorney, to act for [the principal] in certain matters.

LAST WILL AND TESTAMENT
OF
SCOTT WILLIAM CARR, II

I, SCOTT WILLIAM CARR, II, of Baltimore City, State of Maryland, being of sound and disposing mind, memory and understanding and being desirous of settling my worldly affairs, do hereby make, publish, and declare this as and for my Last Will and Testament, in the manner and form following, that is:

FIRST: I do hereby annul and revoke any and all other and former Wills or Codicils by me at any time heretofore made and hereby ratify and confirm this and none other as and for my Last Will and Testament.

SECOND: Definitions and Designation of Fiduciary—The provisions set forth below shall apply in connection with the administration of my estate and the construction of this will.

2.01 Any reference to the "child," "children," "descendant," or "descendants," however expressed, shall be construed as including legitimate descendants only, including a child or descendant by adoption if such child or descendant was adopted prior to attaining the age of eighteen (18) years. Any such term shall also include a descendant in gestation at any time specified in connection with the administration, division, or distribution of any portion of my estate. The term "descendant" includes "child."

2.02 Any reference to my "Executor" or "Personal Representative," whether in the singular or plural, is intended to refer to such person or persons to whom letters of administration are granted after my death. For convenience, I shall refer to such fiduciary or fiduciaries as my "Personal Representative," with the intention that any and all powers granted to such fiduciary shall be appurtenant to the fiduciary office.

2.03 Any reference to a distribution "per stirpes" shall be construed in such manner as shall preserve, at the time of distribution, equality between or among those lines of descent having one or more then-living members closest in relationship to the person of whom the "stirpes" are to be determined.

THIRD:

3.01 I direct that all my legally enforceable claims as may not be barred by limitations, including the expenses of the administration of my estate, be paid by my Personal Representative, hereinafter named, out of the first monies coming into her hands.

3.02 I direct my Personal Representative to pay the expenses of my last illness and my funeral expenses as my Personal Representative may deem proper, without regard to any limitation on such expense imposed by statute and without the necessity of obtaining the approval of any court having jurisdiction over the administration of my estate and without regard to any applicable statutory limitation.

3.03 My Personal Representative shall not, however, be required to pay prior to maturity any debts secured by a mortgage, pledge, or similar encumbrance on property owned by me at my death, and such property shall pass subject to such mortgage, pledge, or similar encumbrance.

FOURTH: My residuary estate shall consist of (a) all property or interests therein of whatever type and wherever located not otherwise effectively disposed of in this Will, including any property over which I may have a power of appointment and any insurance proceeds which may be payable to my estate, less (b) all valid claims

FIGURE 14-4 Simple will

asserted against my estate, all expenses incurred in administering my estate and including expenses of administering nonprobate assets.

FIFTH: All inheritance, estate, succession, and other transfer taxes occasioned by my death, together with the reasonable expenses of determining the same and any interest or penalties thereon not caused by negligent delay, paid with respect to all probate and nonprobate property included in my gross estate or taxable by reason of my death (whether payable to my estate or by the recipient of any such property), shall be paid, without any apportionment, by my Personal Representative out of my residuary estate.

SIXTH: I give, devise, and bequeath unto my mother, MARGARET MARY CARR, my dog, "Bijou."

SEVENTH:

7.01 If my mother, MARGARET MARY CARR, survives me, in that event I give, devise, and bequeath unto her, absolutely, all of the rest, residue, and remainder of my estate and property, real, personal, and mixed, of whatsoever kind, nature, and description, however acquired and wheresoever situated. Should my mother, MARGARET MARY CARR, predecease me, then and in that event, I give, devise, and bequeath as follows.

7.02 My estate shall be divided into four (4) equal shares. Two (2) shares shall pass to my sister ELIZABETH JOAN CARR; one (1) share shall pass to my brother MICHAEL JOHN CARR; one (1) share shall pass to my sister MARGARET CAROL EASTBURN.

EIGHTH:

8.01 I hereby constitute and appoint my sister ELIZABETH JOAN CARR Personal Representative of this my Last Will and Testament. I hereby excuse my Personal Representative from the necessity of giving bond, save the nominal bond required by law. My Personal Representative shall have full power in her discretion to do any and all things necessary for the complete administration of my estate, including the power to sell at public or private sale any or all of my estate, without application to any court of any jurisdiction in the State of Maryland or elsewhere, for authority to make such sale or sales and without the necessity of the purchaser or purchasers seeing to the application of the purchase money.

8.02 My Personal Representative shall have all powers conferred by Maryland law.

8.03 My Personal Representative is authorized to execute on my behalf or on behalf of my estate any tax return which may be filed.

8.04 My Personal Representative shall have, in addition to any other powers, the specific powers to invest, reinvest, sell, mortgage, or otherwise dispose of any part or all of my estate, without necessity of obtaining prior or subsequent court approval.

8.05 Distributions may be made in cash or in kind (and if in kind, may be made non-pro rata) in the discretion of my Personal Representative.

IN TESTIMONY WHEREOF, I have hereunto set my hand and affixed my seal this _____ day of _____ , in the year one thousand nine hundred ninety-six.

_____
SCOTT WILLIAM CARR, II

FIGURE 14-4 *(continued)*

SIGNED, SEALED, PUBLISHED, AND DECLARED by the testator SCOTT WILLIAM
CARR, II, his Last Will and Testament in the presence of us, who at his request, in his
presence, and in the presence of each other have hereunto subscribed our names as
witnesses.

_____ Residing at _____

_____

_____ Residing at _____

_____

FIGURE 14-4 *(continued)*

to address them all in this short space. In fact, we have already discussed some
types previously. A lease is a form of contract. In Chapter 9, the retainer agreement—a contract for legal services—was described. Two of the most typical
contracts drafted in a legal practice will serve for purposes of explanation.
These are a contract for sale of real estate and a separation agreement. Both can
be long, complex documents, the terms of which may be negotiated over long
periods of time. They can also be replete with legalese.

Contract for the Sale of Real Estate

A prerequisite for the sale of land is a written contract. An oral agreement
to sell land is unenforceable pursuant to the **Statute of Frauds**. This law requires that any agreement to transfer an interest in real estate be in writing.
Real estate agencies have standard freestanding forms which they use in the
preparation of contracts. Individuals selling real estate without the assistance of
agents may approach lawyers about writing real estate contracts. In those cases,
sale contracts are often drafted with the help of forms or models.

A real estate contract contains a variety of provisions, the most important
of which are as follows. See Figure 14-6 for a sample real estate contract.

Names of Parties

The names of the parties selling and buying the property must be clearly and
accurately stated. It is important that the names of the sellers be the same as
that of the owners on the deed. If the property is owned by spouses, each spouse

--------------------------------- LEGAL TERMS ---------------------------------

Statute of Frauds †   A statute, existing in one or another form in every state, that requires
certain classes of contracts to be in writing and signed by the parties. Its purpose is to
prevent fraud or reduce the opportunities for fraud.

DECLARATION ON LIFE-SUSTAINING PROCEDURES

On this _____ day of _____ , 19 _____ ,
I, _____ , being of sound mind, willfully
and voluntarily direct that my dying shall not be artificially prolonged under the circumstances set forth in this Declaration:

If at any time I should have an incurable injury, disease or illness certified to be a
terminal condition by two (2) physicians who have personally examined me, one (1) of
whom shall be my attending physician, and the physicians have determined that my death
is imminent and will occur whether or not life-sustaining procedures are utilized and where
the application of such procedures would serve only to artificially prolong the dying process, I direct that such procedures be withheld or withdrawn, and that I be permitted to die
naturally with only the administration of medication, and the performance of any medical
procedure that is necessary to provide comfort, care or alleviate pain. In the absence of
my ability to give directions regarding the use of such life-sustaining procedures, it is my
intention that this Declaration shall be honored by my family and physician(s) as the final
expression of my right to control my medical care and treatment.

I (do) (do not) (draw a line through word(s) that does not apply) want food and
water or other nutrition and hydration administered to me by tube or other artificial means
in the event that I am in a terminal condition.

I am legally competent to make this Declaration, and I understand its full import.

_____
(Signature of Declarant)

_____

_____

Under the penalty of perjury, we state that this Declaration was signed by
_____ , in the presence of the undersigned who, at re-
quest, in our presence, and in the presence of each other, have herein signed our names
as witnesses this _____ day of _____ , 19____ . Further, each of us, individually, states that: The Declarant is known to me, and I believe the Declarant to be of
sound mind. I did not sign the Declarant's signature to this Declaration. Based upon
information and belief, I am not related to the Declarant by blood or marriage, a creditor of
the Declarant, entitled to any portion of the estate of the Declarant under any existing testamentary instrument of the Declarant, entitled to any financial benefit by reason of the death
of the Declarant, financially or otherwise responsible for the Declarant's medical care, nor
an employee of any such person or institution.

_____ Address _____

_____

_____ Address _____

_____

FIGURE 14-5 Declaration on life-sustaining procedures

---

§ 219:201   Contract of sale of residential property—General form

This agreement is made at _____ , on _____ [date], by _____ , of _____ [address], _____ [city], _____ County, _____ [state], referred to as seller, and _____ , of _____ [address], _____ [city], _____ County, _____ [state], referred to as purchaser.

RECITALS

1.   Seller is the owner of the lot or parcel of real property situated in _____ [city], _____ County, _____ [state], and described as follows: _____ [set forth legal description]. The real property consists of a residential site at _____ [address], _____ [city], _____ County, _____ [state], with improvements on the property as follows: _____ [describe briefly, such as: a seven-room brick house with attached two-car garage and detached frame workshop]. Located on the real property are the following items of equipment and other articles of personal property, owned by seller and used on and in connection with the real property: _____ [describe generally, such as: gas-fire furnace, air conditioning system, gas cooking range, electric dishwasher, and drapes, curtains and carpeting in living room, dining room, hallways, and bedrooms of the dwelling]. The described real and personal property is referred to as property.

2.   Seller desires to sell and purchaser desires to buy property, for the purchase price and on the terms and conditions set forth below.

In consideration of the mutual and reciprocal promises of the parties, the parties agree:

SECTION ONE
PURCHASE PRICE AND TERMS OF PAYMENT

The purchase price for property is _____ Dollars ($____), which shall be paid as follows:

(a)   By cash on the signing of this agreement, receipt of which is hereby acknowledged by seller: $_____

(b)   By assumption of an existing encumbrance on property in the form of a _____ [mortgage or deed of trust] owned by _____ , at _____ [address], _____ [city], _____ County, _____ [state], which purchaser hereby expressly assumes and agrees to pay. Present principal balance outstanding on the encumbrance: $_____

(c)   By a purchase money _____ [mortgage or deed of trust] to be executed by purchaser to seller, securing purchaser's _____ [note or bond] payable in equal installments of _____ Dollars ($____), or more, including interest, commencing on the _____ day of the month following the close of this transaction and continuing at monthly intervals thereafter on the same day of each successive month. Interest: _____ per cent (_____%) per year. The _____ [note or bond and mortgage or deed of trust] shall be in form substantially as set forth in the attached Exhibits _____ and _____ , which are incorporated by reference. Principal amount: $_____

(d)   Additional cash on settlement, in the exact balance of purchase price after crediting the above items, with the principal balance on existing encumbrances to be computed exactly to close of transaction. Estimated amount: $_____

TOTAL: $_____

FIGURE 14-6   Contract for real estate

SECTION TWO
TITLE

Title to property to be conveyed by seller shall be good and marketable title, clear of all liens, encumbrances, defects, and burdens, except: _____ [*state exceptions, such as:* utility easements, and agreements with utility companies of record; zoning ordinances; existing rights of way for streets and alleys bordering property; taxes and assessments not delinquent].

Title as required by this agreement shall be evidenced by: _____ [*specify, such as:* a standard form policy of title insurance issued by a title company acceptable to purchaser, doing business in the _____ *(city or county)* where property is situated. The policy shall be issued as of the date of closing, shall be in the amount of the purchase price, and shall be a joint owner-mortgagee policy insuring seller and purchaser as their interests may appear].

Seller shall convey title at the closing of the transaction to _____ [*state exact names of grantees and identify, and specify form of tenure, such as:* _____ *(name of purchaser)* and _____ *(full name)*, _____ (his *or* her) spouse, as _____ (joint tenants *or* tenants in common *or* as the case may be)].

SECTION THREE
COSTS

The following costs shall be borne equally by the parties: _____ [*specify, such as:* recording fees, escrow fees, notarial fees, and transaction stamp tax of _____ [*state*].

The following costs shall be paid by seller: _____ [*specify, such as:* title insurance premium, charges of seller's attorney for drawing instruments and advising].

The following costs shall be paid by purchaser: _____ [*specify, such as:* mortgage tax, assumption charges of holder of existing encumbrance, if any, and charges of purchaser's attorney for drawing instruments and advising].

The following costs shall be prorated to the date of closing: _____ [*specify, such as:* taxes and assessments due but not delinquent].

SECTION FOUR
INSURANCE

Risk of loss or damage to property by fire, storm, burglary, vandalism, or other casualty, between the date of this agreement and the closing, shall be and is assumed by purchaser. No such loss or damage shall void or impair this agreement. If the improvements or personal property, or both, are damaged or destroyed, in whole or in part, by casualty prior to closing, the agreement shall continue in full force and effect, and purchaser shall be subrogated to seller's right of coverage with respect to any insurance carried by seller.

All existing insurance covering property now in effect shall be continued by seller, and shall be transferred to purchaser at closing. Premiums on the insurance shall be prorated to the time of closing. All such policies shall be exhibited forthwith to purchaser who may secure additional insurance on property, or any part of property, if purchaser so desires. Any additional insurance shall name seller and purchaser as co-insureds as their interests appear.

FIGURE 14-6   *(continued)*

SECTION FIVE
TRANSFER OF PROPERTY

Seller shall maintain property, including improvements, the personal property described above, and lawns, shrubs, and trees, in its present condition pending the closing of this transaction, normal and reasonable wear excepted.

Prior to transfer of possession, purchaser shall cause property to be cleaned and placed in a neat, sanitary, and habitable condition. Property shall be transferred to purchaser, as provided in this agreement, in such condition, and clear of all trash, debris, and the personal effects, furnishings, and belongings of seller.

Possession of property shall be transferred to purchaser within _____ days after the closing of the sale. All keys shall be delivered to purchaser at the time of transfer of possession. If the transfer is delayed for any cause beyond the period specified, seller shall pay to purchaser _____ Dollars ($_____) for each day of the delay, as agreed rental, but this provision shall not be construed as barring or limiting any remedy available to purchaser, in law or equity, for the recovery of possession.

SECTION SIX
TIME OF ESSENCE; CLOSING

Time is expressly declared to be of the essence of this agreement. The agreement shall be executed and completed, and sale closed, on or before _____ *[date]*, or such other date as the parties may in writing agree. Each party shall fully perform all the party's obligations under this agreement at such times as to insure that the closing takes place within the period specified, or any agreed-on extension of that period.

SECTION SEVEN
REMEDIES OF PARTIES

(1) If purchaser fails or refuses to comply with the conditions assumed by purchaser, or to perform all of purchaser's obligations under this agreement, seller may at seller's option: (a) hold and retain the initial deposit money and any additional funds paid or deposited by purchaser, as liquidated damages for breach of this agreement, and rescind and terminate the agreement, whereupon all rights and obligations under the agreement shall cease and determine; or (b) enforce this agreement by appropriate action, including an action for specific performance, or for damages for breach, and retain all monies paid or deposited by purchaser pending the determination of the action. Seller shall give buyer written notice of election with respect to seller's exercise of either of these options.

(2) If seller fails or refuses to perform seller's obligations under this agreement, including the furnishing of good title and transfer of possession, purchaser may either: (a) rescind the agreement and recover all deposits and other amounts paid by purchaser under this agreement, and all expenses paid or incurred by purchaser; or (b) pursue any remedy available to purchaser, in law or equity, including an action to compel specific performance of this agreement, or one for damages for breach, separately or alternatively.

SECTION EIGHT
ASSIGNMENT; MODIFICATION; ENTIRE AGREEMENT OF PARTIES EXPRESSED

No right or interest of purchaser under this agreement shall be assigned without the prior written consent of seller, which consent shall not be unreasonably withheld.

FIGURE 14-6 *(continued)*

No modification of this agreement shall be valid or binding unless the modification is in writing, duly dated and signed by both parties.

This instrument constitutes the entire agreement between the parties. Neither party shall be bound by any terms, conditions, statements, or representations, oral or written, not contained in this agreement. Each party hereby acknowledges that in executing this agreement the party has not been induced, persuaded, or motivated by any promise or representation made by the other party, unless expressly set forth in this agreement. All previous negotiations, statements, and preliminary instruments by the parties or their representatives are merged in this instrument.

SECTION NINE
SIGNATURE AND EFFECTIVE DATE

This instrument shall not be effective as an agreement until duly signed by both parties. The date of execution and the effective date of the agreement is the date first above set forth. The date of signature by each party is the date set forth unless otherwise indicated after the party's signature.

In witness whereof, the parties have executed this instrument, in duplicate, on the day and year first above written.

[Signatures]

[Acknowledgment]

FIGURE 14-6 *(continued)*

must be listed as a seller. The proper legal name must be indicated for a corporation or partnership. It is also important to indicate when land is sold by an agent under the authority of a power of attorney, as may occur when the owner lives out of town.

Description of Property

The property may be described in several ways, including by lot number, street address, plat description, or metes and bounds. To eliminate any confusion, it is always best to take the legal description from the deed. If personal property is to be included, such as appliances, these items must be itemized and identified accurately.

Deposit and Purchase Price

The purchase price should be stated in both words and numerals. Commonly, a deposit is required from the purchaser. In that case, an **escrow agent** is appointed to hold the funds until settlement. These matters must be clearly spelled out in the contract.

───────────── **LEGAL TERMS** ─────────────

escrow agent   An individual holding property conditioned on a certain act or event.

Settlement Date

The settlement date (also called the *closing date*) must be carefully selected and stated, after taking into consideration various factors, including financing availability for the buyer, buyer and seller short-term living requirements, building timelines (if a new home), and tax concerns.

Contingencies

The most important provisions of a real estate contract deal with the contingencies that must be met prior to settlement. These may include buyer financing, termite inspection, sale of the buyer's home, radon testing, zoning, and home inspection. The failure to meet any contingency may delay settlement or, in a serious failure, cause **rescission** of the contract.

Separation Agreement

When a marriage ends, the parties often enter into a **separation agreement**. (See Figure 14-7 for a sample.) Sometimes known as a *marital* or *postnuptial agreement,* this instrument puts in writing agreements dealing with custody of minor children, spousal support, child support, division of property, and other issues related to the marriage and its dissolution.

Custody of Minor Children

Typical custody arrangements include sole custody to one parent and visitation to the other; joint custody to both; or, when there is more than one child, split custody. Many attorneys, especially those who specialize in divorce **mediation**, use the term *parenting* to encompass all the responsibilities related to raising children, including custody and visitation. Parenting provisions are often spelled out with precision and as a result frequently appear very detailed and complex. This is usually a better practice than using a general statement

---
————————————————————————————— LEGAL TERMS —————————————————————————————

rescission † The abrogation, annulment, or cancellation of a contract by the act of a party. Rescission may occur by mutual consent of the parties, pursuant to a condition contained in the contract, or for fraud, failure of consideration, material breach, or default. It is also a remedy available to the parties by a judgment or decree of the court. More than mere termination, rescission restores the parties to the status quo existing before the contract was entered into.

separation (marital, postnuptial) agreement † An agreement between husband and wife who are about to divorce or to enter into a legal separation, settling property rights and other matters ... between them. Separation agreements are subject to court approval.

mediation † The voluntary resolution of a dispute in an amicable manner. ... Mediation differs from arbitration in that a mediator, unlike an arbitrator, does not render a decision.

MARITAL AGREEMENT

THIS MARITAL AGREEMENT, hereafter called "Agreement," is made this _____ day of _____ , 1996, by and between WAYNE STEPHEN HAUSEN, hereinafter called "Husband," and ANN KAREN HAUSEN, hereinafter called "Wife." The Husband and Wife hereafter are referred to as "Parties."

EXPLANATORY STATEMENT

The Parties were legally married on March 5, 1978 in a religious ceremony in the City of Baltimore, State of Maryland. As a result of the marriage two (2) children were born, Marie Carol Hausen, date of birth July 10, 1981 and Michelle Karen Hausen, date of birth November 20, 1984. The Parties have agreed to separate on June 1, 1996 and will live separate and apart from one another from that date, voluntarily and by mutual consent in separate abodes, without cohabitation, with the purpose and intent of ending their marriage.

Without waiving any ground for divorce which either of them may now or hereafter have against the other, the Parties deem it in their best interest to enter into this Agreement to formalize their voluntary separation from one another, to adjust and settle all questions pertaining to their respective property rights, child support and custody, spousal support, alimony, maintenance, counsel fees and to resolve other matters growing out of their marital relationship. Husband's social security number is 123-45-6789. Wife's social security number is 987-65-4321.

NOW, THEREFORE, IN CONSIDERATION of the mutual promises and mutual covenants and understandings of each of the Parties, the Parties do hereby, and agree with each other and for their respective heirs, personal representatives, and assigns as follows:

SECTION 1   RESERVATION OF GROUNDS

Nothing contained in this Agreement shall be construed as a waiver by either party of any ground for divorce which either party may now or hereafter have against the other, the same being hereby expressly reserved.

SECTION 2   TERMS OF SEPARATION

2.1   The Parties mutually and voluntarily agree with the intention of terminating the marriage to live separate and apart, in separate places of abode, without any cohabitation, which mutual and voluntary separation has continued without interruption from June 1, 1996.

2.2   Each party shall be free from interference, direct or indirect, by the other as fully as though unmarried. Neither party shall molest or malign the other or attempt to compel the other to cohabit or dwell with the other by any means whatsoever. Each party may for his/her separate benefit engage in any employment, business, or profession he/she may choose. Further, each party may reside in such place as he/she may choose.

SECTION 3   RECONCILIATION OF PARTIES

The Parties recognize the possibility of a reconciliation. It is their intention that a reconciliation, either temporary or permanent, shall in no way affect the provisions of this Agreement having to do with both the disposition of their property rights in their respective realty and personalty and the settlement of their financial obligations, unless

FIGURE 14-7   Marital separation agreement

a new agreement is entered into in writing, executed in the same manner as this Agreement, mutually revoking and rescinding this Agreement.

SECTION 4 CHILD CUSTODY

4.1 The Parties shall have the joint care and custody of the minor children, with Wife to have primary physical custody.

4.2 Husband is hereby granted reasonable visitation. "Reasonable visitation" is to be given a liberal interpretation as agreed to by the Parties and means that the Parties, using fair, mature, and practical judgment, shall schedule visitation from time to time on a reasonable basis such that the interest of all Parties are adequately and properly served. Due regard shall be given to school and work schedules; the convenience, health, and other schedules of the persons involved; the occurrence of holidays and special events; the existence of inclement weather; the geographic relationship of the residences of the Parties; and all other relevant factors. Nevertheless, each of them pledges that he or she will make all appropriate efforts to establish and comply with a workable schedule of reasonable visitation. In addition, reasonable visitation to the Husband shall not be unreasonably withheld by the Wife.

SECTION 5 SUPPORT OF CHILDREN

5.1 Husband agrees to pay Wife the amount of Four Hundred Dollars ($400.00) per child per month (or Eight Hundred Dollars [$800.00] total) directly to Wife for the support and maintenance of the minor children.

5.2 Said amount will be paid per child until each child reaches the age of 18, dies, marries, or becomes self-supporting, whichever occurs first.

SECTION 6 SUPPORT AND MAINTENANCE OF HUSBAND AND WIFE

6.1 Husband hereby waives any and all right to alimony, support, and maintenance, past, present, or future, from Wife, with the understanding that he may never apply for alimony or support.

6.2 Wife hereby waives any and all right to alimony, support, and maintenance, past, present, or future, from Husband, with the understanding that she may never apply for alimony or support.

SECTION 7 WAIVER OF MARITAL PROPERTY RIGHTS AND ESTATE RIGHTS BY WIFE

Except as otherwise herein provided by this Agreement, Wife hereby relinquishes and releases unto Husband, his heirs, personal representatives, and assigns all right and claims of inheritance by descent or otherwise to any and all of his real or personal property, or other property of any nature whatsoever now of his estate as surviving spouse under the Maryland Estates and Trusts Code Annotated (1991) or any amendments thereto. Except as herein provided by this Agreement, Wife also relinquishes and releases unto Husband, his heirs, personal representatives, and assigns all rights growing out of or incident to the marriage relationship, including, but not limited to, any claim arising under Maryland Family Law Code Annotated §§ 8-201 through 8-213 (1991), or any amendments thereto. Wife further agrees she will execute or join as a party in any deed or other instrument which may be required by Husband, his heirs, personal representatives, or assigns for the purpose of divesting

FIGURE 14-7 *(continued)*

any claim, either of dower or curtesy, inchoate or otherwise, or of the distributive share or otherwise in said property.

SECTION 8   WAIVER OF MARITAL PROPERTY RIGHTS AND ESTATE RIGHTS BY HUSBAND

Except as otherwise herein provided by this Agreement, Husband hereby relinquishes and releases unto Wife, her heirs, personal representatives, and assigns all rights and claims of inheritance by descent or otherwise to any and all of her real or personal property, or other property of any nature whatsoever now held or hereafter acquired by her, including any rights he might have to a share of her estate as surviving spouse under the Maryland Estates and Trusts Code Annotated (1991) or any amendments thereto. Except as herein provided by this Agreement, Husband also relinquishes and releases unto Wife, her heirs, personal representatives, and assigns all rights growing out of or incident to the marriage relationship, including, but not limited to, any claim arising under Maryland Family Law Code Annotated §§ 8-201 through 8-213 (1991), or any amendments thereto. Husband further agrees he will execute or join as a party in any deed or other instrument which may be required by Wife, her heirs, personal representatives, or assigns for the purpose of divesting any claim, either of dower or curtesy, inchoate or otherwise, or of the distributive share or otherwise in said property.

SECTION 9   PERSONAL PROPERTY AND FAMILY USE PROPERTY

9.1   The Parties agree that Wife shall be entitled to select that furniture and household belongings owned jointly for her use and that of the children within a reasonable period of time of her vacating the marital home. After Wife has made her selections, Husband shall have the right to make his choices of the furniture and household belongings he desires. All furniture and belongings remaining thereafter shall be sold and proceeds divided equally.

9.2   Notwithstanding the above, Husband shall be entitled to all tools owned jointly by the Parties.

9.3   The Parties own jointly a 1995 Ford van which is valued at Fifteen Thousand Five Hundred Dollars ($15,500.00). Notwithstanding § 9.1 of this agreement, the Parties have agreed to immediately sell the van and divide equally the proceeds.

9.4   The Parties agree that Wife shall have all right, title, and interest in stock owned by the Parties in Ridge Swim Club, Inc. Said stock shall be held by Wife for the benefit of the children. Husband will take steps necessary to transfer said stock. This transfer will take place on or about September 1, 1996.

9.5   The Parties agree that some monies will be distributed in advance of the final settlement of the house. These monies include, but are not limited to, such items as funds for car purchase, insurance, legal fees, security deposits, and so on. A full and complete accounting of all funds shall be kept and funds advanced deducted from the Parties' share of the proceeds from the house.

SECTION 10 REAL PROPERTY

10.1   The Parties own as tenants by the entireties real property known as 1000 Main Street, Flinstone, Maryland 21255-0123. Said property is subject to a mortgage held by Marian Hausen with an outstanding balance of approximately Twenty Thousand Two Hundred Dollars ($20,200.00) and a home equity loan with Signet Bank with an outstanding balance of approximately Thirty-two Thousand Dollars ($32,000.00).

FIGURE 14-7   *(continued)*

10.2 The Parties have agreed to immediately place the Main Street house on the market for private sale.

10.3 Upon the sale of the house, and after the payment of all settlement charges and the satisfaction of all liens on the house, the proceeds will be divided equally between the Parties.

10.4 Until the house is sold, Husband shall have the right to reside therein. During this period Husband shall be responsible for making all repairs necessary, the funds for which shall come from the sale of the van and household belongings. Should additional funds be necessary for house repairs, said funds shall be borrowed from existing lines of credit. A complete record and accounting shall be kept and all monies advanced will be by mutual agreement.

10.5 From the proceeds from the sale of the house, all existing debts incurred by either party, including credit cards, shall be paid. Debts incurred individually by the Parties after June 1, 1996 will not be paid from these proceeds.

10.6 During the pendency that Husband resides in the house, he shall be responsible for the mortgage payments. He shall not be permitted to take in renters or boarders or other residents.

10.7 Notwithstanding § 10.5 of this agreement, Wife shall, prior to the payment of joint debts, be entitled to Five Thousand Dollars ($5,000.00) to be used by her to purchase a vehicle.

SECTION 11 CREDIT/DEBTS

11.1 Husband, hereafter, shall neither contract nor incur any debt or liability for which Wife or her personal property or estate may be responsible. Husband shall indemnify and save harmless Wife against any and all liability, including, but not limited to, any claim made against her by reason of debts or obligations incurred by Husband from or after the date of the signing of this Agreement.

11.2 Wife, hereafter, shall neither contract nor incur any debt or liability for which Husband or his personal property or estate may be responsible. Wife shall indemnify and save harmless Husband against any and all liability, including, but not limited to, any claim made against him by reason of debts or obligations incurred by Wife from or after the date of the signing of this Agreement.

11.3 The Parties hereto expressly agree that they shall immediately either cancel each joint line of credit and/or retract the nonresponsible party's name from any and all lines of credit in the other party's name and each shall apply for credit solely in his or her own name. Each party shall furnish the other written proof of the action taken to effectuate this obligation within thirty (30) days of the date of this Agreement.

11.4 Husband shall hold harmless and indemnify Wife against any and all liability, including, but not limited to, attorneys' fees and costs in connection with each bill and/or debt that he is obligated to pay as a result of this Agreement.

11.5 Wife shall hold harmless and indemnify Husband against any and all liability, including, but not limited to, attorneys' fees and costs in connection with each bill and/or debt that she is obligated to pay as a result of this Agreement.

SECTION 12 PENSION RIGHTS

12.1 Husband hereby waives any and all rights to any interest now or in the future in Wife's pension, profit-sharing plan, or IRA.

FIGURE 14-7 (continued)

12.2 Wife hereby waives any and all rights to any interest now or in the future in Husband's pension, profit-sharing plan, or IRA.

SECTION 13 FORWARDING OF MAIL AND MESSAGES

Each party will use all reasonable efforts to see that all mail, deliveries, messages, inquiries, and the like which come to his/her attention and which are directed to the other party shall be forwarded to the other party, and the originator, shipper, inquiring party, etc., is to be advised of the last known address and telephone number of the party.

SECTION 14 MEDICAL AND DENTAL COVERAGE

14.1 Husband shall continue coverage for Wife until the granting of an absolute divorce, provided coverage is available through his employer-sponsored group plan at substantially the same cost as is being charged presently. Husband shall continue coverage for the children until they are 18 years of age or 21 and attending college on a full-time basis, as allowed by his health care provider, provided coverage is available through his employer-sponsored group plan at substantially the same cost as is being charged presently. All expenses not covered by insurance or deductibles will be equally divided between the Parties.

14.2 The Parties agree to divide equally all normal and typical dental expenses for the children.

SECTION 15 INCOME TAX RETURNS

Husband and Wife agree to file joint federal and state income tax returns for tax year 1996. Thereafter they shall file separate returns with the Parties splitting the children as dependents for 1997 and 1998. Thereafter Wife will claim both children as dependents.

SECTION 16 TO BE GOVERNED BY THE LAWS OF THE STATE OF MARYLAND

This Agreement has been drafted and executed in the State of Maryland and the validity, construction, meaning, and effect thereof shall be governed and determined by the laws of the State of Maryland.

SECTION 17 SUBMISSION TO COURT—BINDING EFFECT

17.1 It is covenanted and agreed by and between the Parties that this Agreement shall be submitted to the Court having jurisdiction thereof for its approval and any decree entered shall make no other provision for the Wife or Husband except as hereinabove provided and the said court shall be requested by the Parties to incorporate this Agreement by reference in any decree which may be entered.

17.2 Should the Court fail or decline to incorporate this Agreement or any provisions in said decree, then, and in that event, the Parties, for themselves and their respective heirs, personal representatives, and assigns, agree that they will nevertheless abide by and carry out all of the provisions herein. It is specifically understood and agreed that the incorporation of this Agreement or any provision herein in any decree shall not operate as a merger but that all of the terms of this Agreement as well as of said decree shall continue to inure to the benefit of and be binding upon the Parties and their respective heirs, personal representatives, and assigns.

FIGURE 14-7 *(continued)*

SECTION 18 INDEMNIFICATION FOR BREACH OF AGREEMENT

18.1 Husband shall hold harmless and indemnify Wife against any and all liability, including, but not limited to, attorneys' fees and costs for enforcement of any of the provisions of this Agreement, if Husband is determined to have breached said Agreement and a court determines that Wife is entitled to such award.

18.2 Wife shall hold harmless and indemnify Husband against any and all liability, including, but not limited to, attorneys' fees and costs for enforcement of any of the provisions of this Agreement, if Wife is determined to have breached said Agreement and a court determines that Husband is entitled to such award.

SECTION 19 COUNSEL FEES AND COURT COSTS

19.1 Each party shall be responsible for his/her own counsel fees for all services rendered through the granting of an absolute divorce.

19.2 All court costs, including deposition and Master's fees, shall be divided equally between the parties.

SECTION 20 REPRESENTATION—UNDERSTANDING OF AGREEMENT

20.1 Wife has been represented throughout the negotiation of this Agreement by David J. Smith, Esquire. Husband has not received nor relied on any legal advice from Wife's counsel.

20.2 The Parties declare that each has read this Agreement and each fully understands the facts upon which this Agreement is based and has been fully informed of the rights and liabilities created hereunder and that after such knowledge and advice, each believes the Agreement to be fair, just, and reasonable. Each party signs this Agreement freely and voluntarily and not as the result of any duress or undue influence and certifies that it contains the full and final settlement between the Parties.

SECTION 21 FURTHER ASSURANCES

The Parties for themselves and their respective heirs, personal representatives, and assigns do mutually agree to join in and execute any instruments and to do any other act or thing that may be necessary or proper to carry into effect any part of this Agreement or to release any dower, curtesy, or other right in any property which either of said Parties may now have or hereafter acquire, including the execution and delivery of such deeds and assurances as may be necessary to carry out the purposes of this Agreement.

SECTION 22 SEVERABILITY

All of the terms in this Agreement shall be severable from one another, and in the event any court should determine that any clause is void or unenforceable, the balance of the Agreement shall nevertheless remain in full force and effect.

SECTION 23 ENTIRE AGREEMENT AND MODIFICATION OF AGREEMENT

23.1 This Agreement contains the final and entire understanding of the Parties. There are no representations, terms, conditions, statements, warranties, promises, covenants, or understandings, oral or written, other than those expressly set forth herein.

23.2 Any modification of this Agreement must be in writing and executed by the Parties in the same manner as this Agreement.

FIGURE 14-7 *(continued)*

IN WITNESS WHEREOF, the Parties hereto have hereunder set their hands and seals to three counterparts of this Agreement, each of which shall constitute an original, on the date first above written.

WITNESS:

_____   _____ (SEAL)

                                                     WIFE

_____   _____ (SEAL)

                                                     HUSBAND

STATE OF _____ ; CITY/COUNTY OF _____ , to wit:

I HEREBY CERTIFY, that on this _____ day of _____ , 1996, before me, the subscriber, a Notary Public of the State of _____ , in and for the _____ of _____ , personally appeared _____ , Husband, and he made oath in due form of law that the matters and facts set forth in the foregoing Agreement are true and correct.

AS WITNESS my hand and Notarial Seal.

_____
Notary Public

My Commission Expires:

STATE OF _____ ; CITY/COUNTY OF _____ , to wit

I HEREBY CERTIFY, that on this _____ day of _____ , 1996, before me, the subscriber, a Notary Public of the State of _____ , in and for the _____ of _____ , personally appeared, _____ , Wife, and she made oath in due form of law that the matters and facts set forth in the foregoing Agreement are true and correct.

AS WITNESS my hand and Notarial Seal.

_____
Notary Public

My Commission Expires:

FIGURE 14-7 *(continued)*

such as "reasonable visitation," which each party will interpret subjectively. (Using the term *reasonable visitation* can work, however, if the children are nearly **emancipated**.)

──────────────── **LEGAL TERMS** ────────────────

emancipated minor [†]   A person who has not yet attained the age of majority who is totally self-supporting or married. A parent emancipates [a] minor child when he or she surrenders

Child Support

Except in rare cases, the parent with whom the children live receives financial support from the noncustodial parent. Support generally ceases once the children reach the age of 18. Today all states determine child support through the application of standardized income-based guidelines.

Spousal Support

Today, the phrase *spousal support* is used, rather than *alimony* or *maintenance,* to describe financial assistance from one spouse to the other. Traditionally, spousal support was for an indefinite period of time. Most states have adopted statutes that encourage rehabilitative alimony for a limited period of time. This is support intended to help a spouse until it is reasonable to believe that he can support himself.

Division of Property

For many parties, the most important and intricate provisions of a separation agreement deal with the division of assets. Property interests that typically have to be divided include houses and other real estate, motor vehicles, household furnishings, bank accounts, and other financial assets. Many assets are bought on credit and thus carry a debt that must be satisfied. Consequently, property division not only concerns the assets, but also apportionment of the debts between the parties.

Other Provisions

Other provisions in a typical separation agreement include those dealing with tax matters, payment for children's education, health and life insurance, and payment of attorney fees. Whether these areas are covered depends on the needs of the parties as well as the results of negotiations.

Paralegal Tip

Many instruments, including deeds and separation agreements, must be notarized before they can become valid and enforceable. In many states, the requirements to become a **notary public** are minimal. For instance, in Maryland, there is no examination. The only requirements are that the applicant be at least 18 years of age, complete an application, pay a modest fee, and take an oath. There is usually at least one notary public in every law office. The notary public may be a secretary, an attorney, or a paralegal. To make yourself more marketable, consider becoming a notary public.

LEGAL TERMS

control and authority over the child and gives [the child] the right to [the child's] earnings. Emancipation also terminates the parent's legal duty to support the minor child.

notary public [†] A public officer whose function is to attest to the genuineness of documents and to administer oaths.

Business Documents

Drafting documents for **corporations** and other forms of business, such as **partnerships**, are the mainstay of many attorneys' practices. Typically prepared instruments include articles of incorporation, meeting minutes, and bylaws.

Articles of Incorporation

When a corporation is formed, three different documents are typically prepared by an attorney. First, and most important, is the corporation's **articles of incorporation**. (See Figure 14-8.) Sometimes referred to as its *charter*, this document describes the corporation's purpose and powers. It also contains other provisions required by state law, including the corporation's proper name, address, **resident agent**, and the amount of stock initially issued. The corporation does not come into existence until the articles have been accepted by the state agency charged with overseeing corporations.

Organizational Meeting Minutes

After the articles of incorporation have been accepted by the state agency regulating corporate matters, the organizational meeting of the corporation is held. State corporation law will likely require that specific resolutions be taken up at this meeting. Frequently, the corporate counsel is present to ensure that all necessary matters are covered. All meeting resolutions must be documented in minutes; this is especially important when critical issues such as the election of officers are taken up. After the organizational meeting, the attorney might prepare the minutes for the corporate secretary to sign. See Figure 14-9.

LEGAL TERMS
---

corporation [†] An artificial person, existing only in the eyes of the law, to whom a state or the federal government has granted a charter to become a legal entity, separate from its shareholders, with a name of its own, under which its shareholders can act and contract and sue and be sued. A corporation's shareholders, officers, and directors are not normally liable for the acts of the corporation.

partnership [†] An undertaking of two or more persons to carry on, as coowners, a business or other enterprise for profit; an agreement between or among two or more persons to put their money, labor, and skill into commerce or business, and to divide the profit in agreed-upon proportions. Partnerships may be formed by entities as well as individuals; a corporation ... may be a partner.

articles of incorporation [†] The charter or basic rules that create a corporation and by which it functions. Among other things, it states the purposes for which the corporation is being organized, the amount of authorized capital stock, and the names and addresses of the directors and incorporators.

resident agent [†] A person residing in a state who is authorized by a ... corporation to accept service of process on its behalf.

HAIRSMITH, INC.
ARTICLES OF INCORPORATION

FIRST: I, JANE A. BROWN, whose post office address is 13 Hill Road, Williamsville, Maryland 21010-5678, being at least eighteen (18) years of age, hereby form a corporation under and by virtue of the General Laws of the State of Maryland.

SECOND: The name of the corporation (which is hereafter referred to as the "Corporation") is HAIRSMITH, INC.

THIRD: The Corporation shall be a close corporation as authorized by Title Four of the Corporations and Associations Article of the Annotated Code of Maryland, as amended.

FOURTH: The purposes for which the Corporation is formed are:

(1) To operate a hair dressing salon and to engage in any other lawful purpose and/or business; and

(2) To do anything permitted by Section 2-103 of the Corporations and Associations Article of the Annotated Code of Maryland, as amended.

FIFTH: The post office address of the principal office of the Corporation in this State is 123 Valley Road, Williamsville, Maryland 21555-1234. The name and post office address of the Resident Agent of the Corporation in this State is DAVID J. SMITH, 406 Allegheny Avenue, Towson, Maryland 21204-4255. Said Resident Agent is an individual actually residing in this State.

SIXTH: The total number of shares of capital stock which the Corporation has authority to issue is Five Thousand (5,000) shares of common stock, without par value.

SEVENTH: The following individuals shall constitute the Board of Directors: ALLEN BROWN, JANE A. BROWN, SUSAN SMITH, BETTY JONES, and CAROL O'BRIEN.

EIGHTH: The Corporation shall provide any indemnification required or permitted by the laws of Maryland and shall indemnify directors, officers, agents, and employees as follows:

(1) The Corporation shall indemnify any director or officer of the Corporation who was or is a party or is threatened to be made a party to any threatened, pending, or completed action, suit, or proceeding, whether civil, criminal, administrative, or investigative (other than an action by or in the right of the Corporation) by reason of the fact that he is or was such director or officer or an employee or agent of the Corporation, or is or was serving at the request of the Corporation as a director, officer, employee, or agent of another corporation, partnership, joint venture, trust, or other enterprise, against expenses (including attorney's fees), judgments, fines, and amounts paid in settlement actually and reasonably incurred by him in connection with such action, suit, or proceeding if he acted in good faith and in a manner which he reasonably believed to be in or not opposed to the best interests of the Corporation, and, with respect to any criminal action or proceeding, had no reasonable cause to believe that his conduct was unlawful.

(2) The Corporation shall indemnify any director or officer of the Corporation who was or is a party or is threatened to be made a party to any threatened, pending, or completed action or suit by or in the right of the Corporation to procure a judgment in its favor by reason of the fact that he is or was such a director or officer or an employee or agent of the Corporation, or is or was serving at the request of the Corporation as a director, officer, employee, or agent of another corporation,

FIGURE 14-8 Articles of incorporation

partnership, joint venture, trust, or other enterprise, against expenses (including attorney's fees) actually and reasonably incurred by him in connection with the defense or settlement of such action or suit if he acted in good faith and in a manner reasonably believed to be in or not opposed to the best interests of the Corporation, except that no indemnifications shall be made in respect of any claim, issue, or matter as to which such person shall have been adjudged to be liable for negligence or misconduct in the performance of his duty to the Corporation unless and only to the extent that the court in which such action or suit was brought, or any other court having jurisdiction in the premises, shall determine upon application that, despite the adjudication of liability but in view of all circumstances of the case, such person is fairly and reasonably entitled to indemnity for such expense which such court shall deem proper.

(3) To the extent that a director or officer of the Corporation has been successful on the merits or otherwise in defense of any action, suit, or proceeding referred to in paragraphs 1 or 2 of this Article EIGHTH or in defense of any claim, issue, or matter therein, he shall be indemnified against expense (including attorney's fees) actually and reasonably incurred by him in connection therewith, without the necessity for the determination as to the standard of conduct as provided in paragraph 4 of this Article EIGHTH.

(4) Any indemnification under paragraphs 1 or 2 of this Article EIGHTH (unless ordered by a court) shall be made by the Corporation only as authorized in the specific case upon a determination that indemnification of the director or officer is proper in the circumstances because he has met the applicable standard of conduct set forth in paragraphs 1 or 2 of this Article EIGHTH. Such determination shall be made (a) by the Board of Directors of the Corporation by a majority vote of a quorum consisting of directors who were not parties to such action, suit, or proceeding, or (b) if such a quorum is not obtainable, or, even if obtainable, if such a quorum of disinterested directors so directs, by independent legal counsel (who may be regular counsel for the Corporation) in a written opinion; and any determination so made shall be conclusive.

(5) Expenses incurred in defending a civil or criminal action, suit, or proceeding may be paid by the Corporation in advance of the final disposition of such action, suit, or proceeding, as authorized by the Board of Directors in the specific case, upon receipt of an undertaking by or on behalf of the director or officer to repay such amount unless it shall ultimately be determined that he is entitled to be indemnified by the Corporation as authorized in this section.

(6) Agents and employees of the Corporation who are not directors or officers of the Corporation may be indemnified under the same standards and procedures set forth above, in the discretion of the Board of Directors of the Corporation.

(7) Any indemnification pursuant to this Article EIGHTH shall not be deemed exclusive of any other rights to which those indemnified may be entitled and shall continue as to a person who has ceased to be a director or officer and shall inure to the benefit of the heirs, executors, and administrators of such a person.

NINTH: The Corporation is hereby empowered to authorize the issuance from time to time of shares of its common stock, whether now or hereafter authorized, subject to the restrictions of Title Four of the Corporations and Associations Article of the Annotated Code of Maryland, as amended.

FIGURE 14-8 *(continued)*

IN WITNESS WHEREOF, I have signed these Articles of Incorporation this _____ day of _____ ,199___ , and I acknowledge the same to be my act.

_____   _____ (Seal)
Witness   JANE A. BROWN

FIGURE 14-8 *(continued)*

HAIRSMITH INC.

MINUTES OF ORGANIZATIONAL MEETING OF THE CORPORATION

The first meeting of the Board of Directors named in the Articles of Incorporation of Hairsmith, Inc., a corporation organized under the laws of the State of Maryland (the "Corporation") was commenced at 123 Valley Road, Williamsville, Maryland 21010-1234 on Monday, November 28, 1996 at 2:00 P.M. pursuant to a Notice served on each and every member of the Corporation.

There were present at the meeting the following persons, including all Directors of the Corporation named in the Articles of the Corporation including: Allen Brown, Jane A. Brown, Susan Smith, Betty Jones, and Carol O'Brien.

Upon motion duly made, seconded, and unanimously carried, Allen Brown was named Chair of the meeting. Betty Jones, was named Secretary of the meeting.

The Chair announced that the original Articles of the Corporation were filed with the office of the State Department of Assessment and Taxation of Maryland on November 19, 1996. He presented to the meeting a certified copy of the Articles of Incorporation and thereupon the following resolutions were offered, seconded, and unanimously adopted:

Resolved: That the Articles of Incorporation of the Corporation filed with the State Department of Assessment and Taxation on November 19, 1996 be and the same hereby are approved and accepted.

Resolved: That a certified copy of the Articles of Incorporation be annexed to the minutes of this meeting and be made a part of the corporate records of the Corporation.

The Chair then presented to the meeting a set of Bylaws for the conduct and regulation of the business and affairs of the Corporation. The Bylaws were read and the following resolutions were offered, seconded, and unanimously adopted:

Resolved: That the Bylaws submitted to and read at this meeting of the Board of Directors of the Corporation be and the same are hereby declared to be the Bylaws of the Corporation.

Resolved: That the Secretary be and she is hereby instructed to cause the Bylaws referred to in the foregoing resolution to be annexed to the minutes of this meeting and made a part of the corporate records of the Corporation.

* * *

FIGURE 14-9 Corporate minutes

> There being no further business to come before the meeting, on motion duly made, seconded, and carried the meeting was adjourned.
>
> Witness my signature this _____ day of November, 1996.
>
>
> BETTY JONES,   SECRETARY

FIGURE 14-9   *(continued)*

Bylaws

The third mandatory document is the **corporate bylaws**. These rules govern the day-to-day operation of the corporation. The bylaws discuss the powers, duties, and election of officers; when and where meetings are held; rules of procedure for meetings; and other matters. (See Figure 14-10.) Attorneys will either provide standardized bylaws or, in some cases, tailor-make bylaws. Acceptance of the bylaws is a matter that must be addressed at the organizational meeting of the corporation.

Other corporate documents drafted by corporate counsel include **shareholders' agreements**, **stock certificates**, purchase agreements, and employment agreements.

Forms, Models, and Checklists

Forms, models, and checklists are often used to prepare instruments. Forms, found in form books, are popularly used to draft documents such as deeds, notes, and contracts. Models, (original but previously developed documents) can be useful in preparing subsequent letters and pleadings. Checklists can be used by themselves or in conjunction with forms or models. Complex instruments such as separation agreements can be improved by employing checklists.

LEGAL TERMS

by-laws † Rules and regulations created by corporations, associations, clubs, and societies for their governance.

shareholders' agreement An agreement among owners of a corporation.

stock certificate † An instrument issued by a corporation stating that the person named is the owner of a designated number of shares of its stock.

HAIRSMITH, INC.
BYLAWS
ARTICLE I

Stockholders

SECTION 1. Annual Meeting. The annual meeting of the stockholders of the Corporation shall be held on a day duly designated by the stockholders on the third Monday of November, if not a legal holiday, and if a legal holiday, then the next succeeding day not a legal holiday, for the transaction of such corporate business as may come before the meeting.

SECTION 2. Special Meetings. Special meetings of the stockholders may be called at any time for any purpose or purposes by the President, by a Vice-President, or by any stockholder, and shall be called forthwith by the President, by a Vice-President, or the Secretary upon the request in writing of any holder of shares outstanding and entitled to vote on the business to be transacted at such meeting. Such request shall state the purpose or purposes of the meeting.

Business transacted at all special meetings of stockholders shall be confined to the purpose or purposes stated in the notice of the meeting.

SECTION 3. Place of Holding Meetings. All meetings of stockholders shall be held at the principal office of the Corporation or elsewhere in the United States as designated by the stockholders.

SECTION 4. Notice of Meetings. Written notice of each meeting of the stockholders shall be mailed, postage prepaid, by the Secretary to each stockholder of record entitled to vote thereat at his or her post office address, as it appears upon the books of the Corporation, at least ten (10) days before the meeting. Each such notice shall state the place, day, and hour at which the meeting is to be held and, in the case of any special meeting, shall state briefly the purpose or purposes thereof.

SECTION 5. Quorum. The presence in person or by proxy of the holders of record of a majority of the shares of the capital stock of the Corporation issued and outstanding and entitled to vote thereat shall constitute a quorum at all meetings of the stockholders, except as otherwise provided by law, by the Articles of Incorporation, or by these Bylaws. If less than a quorum shall be in attendance at the time for which the meeting shall have been called, the meeting may be adjourned from time to time by a majority vote of the stockholders present or represented, without any notice other than by announcement at the meeting until a quorum shall attend. At any adjourned meeting at which a quorum shall attend, any business may be transacted which might have been transacted if the meeting had been held as originally called.

SECTION 6. Conduct of Meetings. Meetings of stockholders shall be presided over by the President of the Corporation or, if he or she is not present, by a Vice-President, or, if none of said officers is present, by a chairman to be elected at the meeting. The Secretary of the Corporation, or, if he or she is not present, any Assistant Secretary, shall act as secretary of such meetings. In the absence of the Secretary and any Assistant Secretary, the presiding officer may appoint a person to act as secretary of the meeting.

SECTION 7. Voting. At all meetings of stockholders, every stockholder entitled to vote thereat shall have one (1) vote for each share of stock standing in his or her name on the books of the Corporation on the date for the determination of stockholders entitled to vote at such meeting. Such vote may be either in person or by proxy

---

FIGURE 14-10 Corporate bylaws

appointed by an instrument in writing, subscribed by such stockholder or the stockholder's duly authorized attorney, bearing a date not more than three (3) months prior to said meeting, unless said instrument provides for a longer period. Such proxy shall be dated, but need not be sealed, witnessed, or acknowledged. All elections shall be had and all questions shall be decided by a majority of the votes cast at a duly constituted meeting, except as otherwise provided by law, in the Articles of Incorporation, or by these Bylaws.

If the chair of the meeting shall so determine, a vote by ballot may be taken upon any election or matter, and the vote shall be so taken upon the request of the holders of ten percent (10%) of the stock entitled to vote on such election or matter. In either of such events, the proxies and ballots shall be received and be taken in charge and all questions touching the qualification of votes and the validity of proxies and the acceptance or rejection of votes shall be decided by the tellers. Such tellers shall be appointed by the chair of said meeting.

* * *

FIGURE 14-10 *(continued)*

Forms

There are a number of established form books on the market today. Probably the most popular are the resources published by Lawyers Cooperative Publishing: *Am. Jur. Legal Forms 2d, Am. Jur. Pleading and Practice Forms, Revised,* and *Federal Procedural Forms, Lawyers Edition,* all part of the TCSL. These three sources contain alphabetically organized forms for all practice situations (see Figure 14-11). West Publishing also publishes a set comparable to *Am. Jur. Legal Forms 2d,* called *West's Legal Forms, 2d.* In addition, other legal publishers produce form books useful in preparing instruments, including comprehensive one-volume works that include both instruments and pleadings such as Warren, Gorham and Lamont's *Basic Legal Transactions.* There are also numerous state-specific form books, usually published by local companies.

Models

Because models are unique documents created by lawyers or paralegals for particular legal matters, published sources do not exist. You should get into the habit of collecting models that you feel may be useful. They should be organized in an easily accessible fashion. If a central location for models does not yet exist in your firm, set one up. When a document is located that can be used as a model, all confidential information must be erased. Also, it is a good idea to date each model, as laws change. Out-of-date models should be discarded or updated.

Checklists

Finally, checklists can be used either individually or in combination with forms and models. Often form books include checklists along with their forms.

§ 39:14 Contract of sale—Barbershop or beauty parlor

Agreement made effective as stated below, by and between _____ , of _____ [address], City of _____ , County of _____ , State of _____ , referred to as seller, and _____ , of _____ [address], City of _____ , County of _____ , State of _____ , referred to as buyer.

SECTION ONE
TRANSFER OF BUSINESS

For the consideration of _____ Dollars ($_____), to be paid by buyer in the manner set forth in this agreement, seller agrees to sell and assign to buyer a _____ [barbershop or beauty parlor] business, now solely owned and operated by seller under the name of _____ , located at _____ [address], City of _____ , County of _____ , State of _____ , together with the goodwill of the business, the right to continue use of the business name, and the fixtures, equipment, furniture, utensils, supplies, and inventory used by seller in connection with the business, all of which assets and their assigned values are listed in attached Schedule "_____ ".

SECTION TWO
PAYMENT

Buyer agrees to pay to seller, on or before _____ , 19___ , the initial sum of _____ Dollars ($_____), and to pay the balance of _____ Dollars ($_____), with interest at the rate of _____ percent (___%) per annum, in _____ [number] monthly installments of _____ Dollars ($_____) each, due and payable on the 6th day of each month. The first such installment shall be due and payable on _____ , 19_ . _____ [If purchaser is to obtain third-party financing, rather than to use seller financing, appropriate provisions should be inserted.]

SECTION THREE
SELLER'S RIGHTS ON DEFAULT

In the event buyer fails to pay any installment within _____ days of the date such installment is due, seller, at _____ [his or her] option, may _____ [declare the entire balance then outstanding immediately due and payable or rescind this contract and retake title to and possession of the business transferred after refunding to buyer the amount theretofore paid, less liquidated damages in the amount of _____ Dollars ($_____)].

SECTION FOUR
ASSIGNMENT OF LEASE

On the effective date of this agreement, seller agrees to assign to buyer the lease of the premises in which the business referred to herein is located, as described above.

SECTION FIVE
SELLERS' WARRANTY

Seller warrants that the business and its assets are free and clear of any liens, encumbrances, and indebtedness of any nature whatsoever, and that all fixtures, equipment, and other personal property sold will be delivered to buyer in as good condition as they now exist, ordinary wear from reasonable use excepted.

FIGURE 14-11 Sample Am. Jur. 2d form

SECTION SIX
EFFECTIVE DATE OF CONTRACT; DELIVERY OF POSSESSION

This agreement shall become effective at the time buyer makes the initial payment as herein provided, at which time seller shall deliver to buyer possession of the business and assets sold hereunder, together with all records and documents necessary for buyer to carry on the business.

SECTION SEVEN
ABSENCE OF WAIVER

The failure of either party to this agreement to insist on the performance of any of the terms and conditions of this agreement, or the waiver of any breach of any of the terms and conditions of this agreement, shall not be construed as thereafter waiving any such terms and conditions, but the terms shall continue and remain in full force and effect as if no such forebearance or waiver had occurred.

SECTION EIGHT
GOVERNING LAW

This agreement shall be governed by and construed in accordance with the laws of the State of _____ .

SECTION NINE
ENTIRE AGREEMENT

This agreement shall constitute the entire agreement between the parties and any prior understanding or representation of any kind preceding the date of this agreement shall not be binding on either party except to the extent incorporated in this agreement.

SECTION TEN
MODIFICATION OF AGREEMENT

Any modification of this agreement or additional obligation assumed by either party in connection with this agreement shall be binding only if in writing signed by each party or an authorized representative of each party.

SECTION ELEVEN
ATTORNEY FEES

In the event any action is filed in relation to this agreement, the unsuccessful party in the action shall pay to the successful party, in addition to all sums that either party may be called on to pay, a reasonable sum for the successful party's attorney fees.

SECTION TWELVE
PARAGRAPH HEADINGS

The titles to the paragraphs of this agreement are solely for the convenience of the parties and shall not be used to explain, modify, simplify, or aid in the interpretation of the provisions of this agreement.

SECTION THIRTEEN
ASSIGNMENT OF RIGHTS

The rights of each party under this agreement are personal to that party and may not be assigned or transferred to any other person, firm, corporation, or other entity without the prior, express, and written consent of the other party.

FIGURE 14-11   (continued)

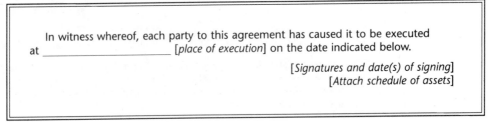

In witness whereof, each party to this agreement has caused it to be executed at _____ [*place of execution*] on the date indicated below.

[*Signatures and date(s) of signing*]
[*Attach schedule of assets*]

FIGURE 14-11   *(continued)*

Checklists can be helpful after an instrument has been drafted to double-check for comprehensiveness.

Most checklist publications focus on trial preparation rather than instrument preparation. For instance, *Am. Jur. Proof of Facts* is an encyclopedic collection of checklists focusing on elements of causes of action, defenses, and damages. (See Figure 14-12.) Though it can be used in document creation, it is most effectively employed in trial preparation.

The best checklists are those developed by the legal practitioner after considerable repetition in preparing specific instruments.

Boilerplate

Boilerplate is standard language that appears in every instrument (see Figure 14-13). It is often included without consideration of whether it achieves a particular purpose or is in compliance with the law. When using forms, it is important to carefully eliminate all language that is not appropriate for the particular document. If certain language seems to be appropriate, you should make certain it is in compliance with the laws of the jurisdiction in which the document is being drafted. Unfortunately, many attorneys and paralegals automatically include language because it appears to be appropriate when in fact it is outdated or even illegal.

In addition, you should not assume that a particular form is in compliance with the laws of the jurisdiction. Most forms are developed from a general perspective and consequently do not take into consideration the particular law of the state in which you work. You can often use your state code or regulatory compilation as a checklist.

LEGAL TERMS

boilerplate language †   Language common to all legal documents of the same type.

II. ELEMENTS OF PROOF; DAMAGES

§ 12. Elements of proof checklist

The following facts and circumstances, among others, tend to establish that a beauty salon or operator was negligent in the choice or administration of a product or treatment given to a patron:

☐ Selection of inappropriate product or treatment by beauty operator [§ 4]

☐ Failure of beauty operator to conduct preliminary tests before undertaking treatment [§§ 17, 24]

☐ Failure of beauty operator to conduct treatment or apply product in accordance with manufacturer's directions [§§ 19, 25]

☐ Careless or sloppy application of product or performance of treatment by beauty operator [§§ 18, 25]

☐ Healthy condition of patron's skin and hair before commencement of treatment [§ 21]

☐ Damaged condition of patron's skin and hair after completion of treatment [§§ 21, 22, 30]

☐ Violation of relevant statute by beauty salon or beauty operator [§ 6]

§ 13. Elements of damages checklist

Testimony as to the following elements of damages should be elicited, when applicable, from the plaintiff and his witnesses in an action seeking the recovery of damages for personal injury allegedly sustained during a treatment in a beauty salon:

☐ Necessary and reasonable medical expenses
 —Actual past expenses for physician, hospital, nursing, laboratory fees and, medicines
 —Anticipated future expenses

☐ Loss of past and future earnings

 —Actual wages lost
 —Loss of profits or net income by person engaged in business

☐ Cost of hiring substitute or assistant

☐ Harm from prolonged inactivity

☐ Harm from loss of sleep

☐ Past and future impairment of ability to enjoy life

☐ Pain and suffering from physical injuries

☐ Mental anguish or suffering
 —Fright and shock
 —Anxiety, depression, and other mental suffering or illness
 —Humiliation and embarrassment

III. PROOF OF BEAUTY SALON OR OPERATOR'S NEGLIGENCE IN PERFORMANCE OF BEAUTY TREATMENTS ON PATRON

[It is assumed in the following proof that a patron of a beauty salon has brought an action against the salon and an operator employed there to recover both for chemical burns she received on her scalp and forehead and for damage to her hair resulting from the administration of a permanent wave.]

A. Testimony of Injured Patron

§ 14. Introductory testimony

[After introduction and identification of witness]

Q. Would you please tell us your age?

A. ———

Q. What is your occupation?

A. I am the personnel director for a company here in town.

FIGURE 14-12 Sample checklists

Q. What company is that?
A.

Q. How long have you worked for that company?
A. ___ years.

Q. Are you married?
A. Yes, I am.

Q. Do you have any children?
A. Yes. My husband and I have three children.

Q. What ages are your children?
A.

Q. Do you patronize beauty salons on a regular basis?
A. Yes.

Q. For how many years have you done so?
A. Since shortly after my marriage, about 23 years ago.

Q. Is there any one particular beauty salon you patronize on a regular basis?
A. Yes.

Q. What salon is that?
A.

Q. Why do you patronize that particular salon?
A. Partly out of habit and partly because they generally do quite a good job.

Q. What do you mean by "partly out of habit"?
A. Well, I've been going there for the last 10 years or so. After a while, you get to know the people who work there and you can feel confident that they'll do the job correctly.

Q. Is there a particular operator at this salon who regularly does your hair?
A. Yes.

Q. Who is that?
A.

Q. Does he always do your hair?
A. Not always, but probably 7 times out of 10.

Q. Do you ever go to any other salons than the one where he works?
A. Generally not. On rare occasions, I do have to go to some other shop.

§ 15. Initial contact with defendants

Q. Have you ever had any treatment done at ___ Salon [defendant salon]?
A. I should say so.

Q. What do you mean?
A. It's the place that gave me the permanent wave that this whole mess is about.

Q. So you went there to get a permanent wave?
A. Yes.

Q. Why did you go there and not to your regular salon?
A. I phoned up my regular operator at the salon I usually patronize and told him that I needed a permanent wave on a particular day. He told me that he was going to be on vacation on that particular day and asked a number of the other operators whether they would be able to do the perm. Unfortunately, it was around the Christmas holidays, and at that time of year beauty salons are very busy and it is difficult to get an appointment for something like a permanent. So, I had to find another place to get the permanent.

FIGURE 14-12 (continued)

5. The rent for each item of Equipment shall be the amount designated on the face hereof or on any modification provided for in number 1. (hereinafter
called "Rent"). Lessee hereby agrees to pay Lessor without notice on demand at the address set forth above, or to such other person and/or such other place as
Lessor may from time to time designate in writing, said Rent, in the amounts and at the times set forth on the face hereof or on any modification provided for
in number 1, in immediately available U.S. funds. The obligation of the Lessee to pay Rent shall be absolute and unconditional and shall not be subject to any
abatement, reduction, set-off, defense counterclaim or recoupment whatsoever, by reason of any past, present or future claims which Lessee may have aga[illegible]
Lessor, the manufacturer of the Equipment or against any person for any reason whatsoever. Upon the failure of Lessee to pay timely any Rent or any other amou[illegible]
required to be paid hereunder, Lessee shall also pay a late charge computed at the rate of 5% of such delinquent rent (or such other maximum contractual rate
as may be imposed by applicable law). Lessee authorizes Lessor to draft any account of Lessee at any bank, savings institution, credit union or other financial institution for payments under this Equipment Lease as they mature (or by accelleration) and Lessee appoints Lessor, its officers, agents or attorneys as Lessee's
attorneys-in-fact with full authority to sign such drafts and to execute any other instruments in order to carry out the provisions of this paragraph.

6. Lessee shall inspect the Equipment within forty-eight (48) hours after receipt thereof. Within seventy-two (72) hours after receipt of the Equipment, Lessee
shall deliver to Lessor a certificate of acceptance in form acceptable to Lessor or written notice of non-acceptance specifying the reasons for non-acceptance.
Issuance by Lessee of a certificate of acceptance shall be conclusive presumption as between Lessor and Lessee that the Equipment has been delivered, installed,
inspected and found to be in good condition and repair, that Lessee is satisfied with and has accepted the Equipment, and for such other matters as are covered
in said certificate.

7. Lessee agrees to keep the Equipment in good condition and to make all necessary repairs and maintenance thereto without expense to Lessor. The Equipment will be used by Lessee in a careful manner for its intended use and in accordance with all applicable laws and regulations and will be kept at the location
specified herein (unless the Equipment is mobile or normally used in more than one location in the conduct of Lessee's business) and shall not be removed from
said location without the prior written consent of Lessor. Lessor shall have the right during regular business hours to enter upon any premises where the Equipment is located for the purpose of inspecting and observing its use. Lessee shall make no alterations, additions or improvements to said Equipment without prior
written consent of Lessor. Furthermore, any alterations, additions, or improvements made to said Equipment shall become the property of the Lessor.

8. Lessee agrees to provide Lessor with such information as Lessor may request from time to time with respect to the location, condition and maintenance
of any item of leased equipment, and with respect to the location of any of Lessee's places of business. Lessee will promptly notify Lessor of any change in any
of its offices or places of business. Lessee will provide Lessor with any financial or other information Lessor may request, and Lessee will permit Lessor, during
normal business hours, to have access to and examine all property, minute books, and other records, books of account and financial records, and to copy all such
information and records.

9. Lessee will pay promptly when due all fees, taxes, (sales, use, excise, personal property, or other taxes or assessments incurred), and all other charges upon
or related to the purchasing, ownership, use, operation, leasing, installation or delivery of the equipment; provided however, that lessee is not obligated to pay
any federal and (to the extent assessed by the State of MD.) state taxes imposed on the net income of the lessor. In the event that any fee, tax or assessment payable by Lessee hereunder is, by law, required to be assessed or billed to, or paid by, Lessor, Lessee at its own expense will do any and all things required to be
done by Lessor in connection with the levy, assessment, billing or payment of such charge and is hereby authorized by Lessor to act for and on behalf of Lessor
in any and all respects, including (but not limited to) the contest or protest, in good faith and for a reasonable period of time, of the validity of any such levy or
assessment, or the amount thereof. Lessee will cause all billings of such charges to Lessor to be made to Lessor in care of Lessee and will, in preparing any report
or return required by law, show the ownership of the Equipment in Lessor, and shall send a copy of any such report or return to Lessor. If Lessee fails to pay
any such charges when due, except any levy or assessment being contested in good faith as above provided for a reasonable period of time, Lessor at its option
may do so, in which event the sums so paid (including any penalties or interest incurred as a result of Lessee's failure) plus reasonable interest thereon shall be
deemed to be additional rent, and shall be paid by Lessee to Lessor with the next periodic payment of rent. The obligations of Lessee under this paragraph shall
survive the termination of this Lease.

10. Title to the Equipment shall at all times remain in Lessor, and Lessee shall have no right, title or interest therein except as expressly set forth herein. The
Equipment shall remain personal property, notwithstanding the manner in which it may be affixed to any real property, and Lessee shall obtain, at its own expense, from each landlord, owner or mortgagee or any person having an encumbrance or lien on the premises where the Equipment is to be located, waivers of
any lien, encumbrance or interest which such person might have or hereafter obtain or claim with respect to said Equipment. Lessee further agrees to maintain
said Equipment free from all claims, liens and legal proceedings of creditors of Lessee and will defend, at its own expense, Lessor's title to said Equipment free
from such claims, liens or legal proceedings. Lessee shall also notify Lessor immediately upon receipt of notice of any lien, attachment or judicial proceeding affecting said Equipment in whole or in part.

11. Lessee shall purchase and maintain insurance against loss or damage by fire, storm, theft, public liability and such other risks as are customarily insured
against, with responsible carriers acceptable to Lessor in an amount not less than the full replacement value thereof, and shall also purchase and maintain such
other insurance as Lessor may from time to time require. All policies covering the Equipment shall have loss payable clauses in favor of Lessor as its interest may
appear, and shall provide for not less than thirty (30) days notice of cancellation to Lessor. Lessee hereby appoints Lessor, its officers, agents and attorneys, as
Lessee's attorneys-in-fact, with full authority to receive any unearned premiums due under such policy or policies as well as to receive any and all proceeds payable by said insurance company or companies on account of loss or damage to the Equipment and the aforementioned policy or policies of insurance. Lessee
hereby expressly waives any and all notice of cancellation by Lessor and agrees that any monies received by Lessor for any unearned premiums or for any losses
under such policies shall be applied toward the reduction of, or in full payment of, any or all of the Rent or other obligations due hereunder and the surplus, if
any, shall be paid to Lessee. Should Lessee fail to provide insurance coverage, then Lessor may, at its option, purchase such insurance and add the total cost thereof to the amount owed to Lessor and Lessee, and within five (5) days from the date of demand, shall immediately reimburse Lessor for such sums expended.

12. In the event of loss of or damage to any item of the Equipment, Lessee shall promptly notify Lessor of such event and, at Lessor's option, immediately
place said item of Equipment in good repair or replace same with like Equipment in good working condition, without abatement of Rent. If Lessor determines
that said item of Equipment is lost or stolen, or destroyed or damaged beyond repair, Lessee shall pay Lessor in cash, on the next Rent payment due date following such determination, in addition to the Rent due and payable on such date, with respect to said item of Equipment the sum of (i) the present value of the unpaid Rent for the term of the Lease attributable to said item of Equipment computed by discounting such unpaid Rent in the manner described in Paragraph 16
and (ii) the Reversionary Value as set forth on the face hereof. Upon Lessor's receipt of such payment, this Lease will terminate with respect to such item of Equipment for which Lessor receives such payment, and Lessee shall be entitled to whatever interest Lessor may then have in said item of Equipment in its then condition and location, without warranty, express or implied.

13. Lessee shall indemnify Lessor against, and hold Lessor harmless from any and all claims, actions, costs, expenses, damages and liabilities, including attorney's fees, arising out of, connected with, or resulting from the Equipment or this Lease, including, without limitation, the manufacture, selection, delivery, possession, use, condition, operation or return of the Equipment. Lessee shall, at its own cost and expense, defend any and all such suits which may be brought against
Lessor and shall satisfy, pay and discharge any and all judgments and fines that may be recovered against Lessor in any such action; provided, however, that Lessor
shall give Lessee written notice of any such claim, damage or suit. Lessee agrees to execute any further instruments and to do any acts necessary to carry out the
terms of this lease and ensure its enforceability or to cure any invalidity. The obligation of Lessee under this paragraph shall survive the termination of this Lease.

14. Lessee, its owners and principal officers, hereby warrant and agree to indemnify and save harmless Lessor, its successors and assigns from any loss, damage,
liability, cost and expense arising from the breach hereof, that (a.) all information, statements, reports and representations made to Lessor are now and shall hereafter be true, correct and complete; (b.) the present officers, owners, partners, or others actively in charge of the management and affairs of Lessee shall continue
to serve in their present capacity so long as this lease remains in force; (c.) Lessee is duly organized and existing and is authorized to conduct its business at all
its offices, and the execution of this equipment lease and any related instruments is the duly authorized act of Lessee and is enforceable in accordance with its
terms; (d.) Lessee will not dispose of or encumber the leased equipment or enter into any contract or documents for the sale or transfer thereof, and will not
yield up possession thereof without written approval of Lessor; (e.) except with prior written consent of Lessor, Lessee will not enter into any merger or consolidation, or sell all or substantially all of its assets, or sell, mortgage or otherwise dispose of or encumber its property except in the normal course of business;
(f.) Lessee will not dissolve, liquidate or cease the active conduct of its business operations, and (g.) Lessee will not take any action or fail to take any action which
results in preferring any other creditor to Lessor.

15. Lessee shall be in default under this Lease upon the occurrence of any of the following events or conditions (hereinafter called Events of Default): (a.) Lessee's refusal, without good cause, to accept delivery of Equipment; (b.) the nonpayment of any Rent or any other amount payable pursuant to the terms of this
Lease within 10 days after the same becomes due and payable or the failure to perform any agreement of Lessee contained herein; (c.) Lessor's deeming itself
insecure; (d.) the breach or violation of any of Lessee's warranties set forth above or otherwise contained herein; (e.) the existence of any uncured event of default under the terms of any instrument or writing evidencing a debt (other than a trade debt) payable on demand or over a period in excess of one year; (f.) loss,
theft, substantial damage, destruction, sale or encumbrance of any of the Equipment or any material impairment of the value thereof, unless adequately covered
by then existing insurance; (g.) insolvency of Lessee, the making of any general assignment for the benefit of creditors, the filing of any petition by or against
Lessee under any provision or chapter of any bankruptcy or insolvency statute, or the (h.) existence of any judgment against or an attachment of the property
of Lessee; and (i.) the death of an individual Lessee or the dissolution, merger, consolidation, liquidation or reorganization of any Lessee which is a corporation.

16. Upon the occurrence of any Event of Default, Lessor may, without further notice to Lessee and in its sole discretion, exercise any one or more of the
following remedies: (a.) declare Lessee's obligations hereunder immediately due and payable; (b.) Proceed by appropriate court action or actions either at law or
in equity, to enforce performance by Lessee of the applicable covenants and terms of this Lease or to recover damages for the breach thereof; (c.) terminate this
Lease, and take possession of said Equipment with or without notice to Lessee and without order of court or other legal process, and without incurring any liability to Lessee for any damages incurred by reason of such taking. LESSEE HEREBY WAIVING ANY AND ALL RIGHTS TO PRIOR NOTICE AND TO A
JUDICIAL HEARING WITH RESPECT TO REPOSSESSION OF THE EQUIPMENT BY LESSOR; (d.) lease said Equipment for a term and rental which may
be less than, equal to, or greater than the rental and term herein provided, or use the Equipment or sell or otherwise dispose of the same for cash or credit, and
upon such terms as Lessor may determine, free of any rights of Lessee; (e.) recover immediately as liquidatad damages for Lessee's default, and not as a penalty,
an amount equal to the difference between: (i) Lessee's total obligation for Rent for the remainder of the term (discounted to then present value as hereinafter
provided) and (ii) the then fair market rental value to Lessor of said Equipment for the remaining term of this Lease. If Lessor sells or re-lets said Equipment within sixty days after taking possession thereof, the proceeds thereof shall conclusively be presumed to represent the fair market rental value of said Equipment.
If any statute governing the proceeding in which such damages are to be proved specifies the amount of such claim, Lessor shall be entitled to prove as and for
damages for the breach an amount equal to that allowed by such statute. For purposes of computing then present value of Rent, said Rent shall be discounted
at an annual rate of six percent (6%). Lessor may also recover in full all unpaid Rent, and other sums which accrued or became payable prior to Lessor's taking
possession of said Equipment. In addition, Lessor shall be entitled to recover from Lessee upon default, (i) any and all further damages which Lessor might suffer
as a result of said default, (ii) reasonable attorney's fees and, (iii) other expenses as are incurred in repossession, rental, repair, refurbishment, seizure, storage,
sale or reletting of said Equipment.

17. Upon expiration of the term or upon earlier termination of this Lease, Lessee shall return the Equipment in good repair, condition and working order,
ordinary wear and tear resulting from normal use expected, at its own expense by delivering the same to a location specified by Lessor which is within the state
wherein the Equipment was delivered or wherein the Equipment was located at such expiration or termination (if a change of location was made with consent
of Lessor as provided herein) or, at Lessee's expense, by loading the Equipment on such carrier as Lessor shall specify and by shipping the same, freight collect,
to the destination specified by Lessor. In the event repairs are necessary, Lessee shall do so at its own expense, paying Lessor a reasonable rent for the period of
time reasonably necessary to accomplish such repair beyond the termination date.

18. Except with Lessor's prior written approval, Lessee shall not assign, transfer, pledge or dispose of this Lease or any interest therein or permit the Equipment to be used by anyone other than Lessee or Lessee's authorized agents and employees. Lessor may assign this Lease and, subject to Lessee's interest therein,
may mortgage or otherwise encumber the Equipment in whole or in part without notice to Lessee, and any such assignee shall have all the rights but none of the
obligations of Lessor under this Lease, free from any defense, counterclaim or set-off which Lessee may have against Lessor.

19. This Lease and the Schedules attached hereto constitute the entire agreement of the parties. All notices, consents and communications under this Lease
shall be in writing and shall be sufficient if delivered personally or mailed to the other party at the address set forth above or at such other address as such party
shall specify in writing. No provision, term or condition of this Lease may be waived, amended or altered except with the written consent of Lessor. Waiver by
Lessor of any default by Lessee hereunder shall not be construed as a waiver of any other or subsequent default. If any part of this Lease shall be adjudged invalid, then such partial invalidity shall not cause the remainder of this Lease to be or to become invalid, and if a provision hereof is held invalid in any one or more
of its applications; the parties hereto agree that said provision shall remain in effect in all valid applications that are severable from the invalid application or applications. This Lease has been delivered in the State of Maryland and shall in all respects be governed by and construed in accordance with the laws of the State of
Maryland.

FIGURE 14-13 Sample boilerplate

Summary

- Any written document that records the responsibilities and interests of individuals in a legal transaction is considered an instrument. Examples of instruments are deeds, wills, leases, articles of incorporation, and separation agreements.

- Among the considerations that must be addressed when preparing instruments are: realizing the document's limitations, impressing upon the client the importance of anticipating future problems, writing the document in a clear and unambiguous style, and applying creativity in its preparation.

- A deed documents the passing of real estate from one party to another.

- A lease memorializes an agreement between two parties as to the rental of real property.

- An individual who wishes for certain property to pass to his loved ones upon his death can see that his intentions are effectuated through use of a will. Typical components of a simple will include introductory clause, section appointing a personal representative, sections indicating bequests and devises, residuary clause, and signature and witness block. Other testamentary instruments include trusts, durable powers of attorney, living wills, and codicils.

- Typical contracts seen in a law office include contracts for the sale of real estate and separation agreements.

- An agreement for the sale of land must be in writing. Components of a typical real estate contract include: a section indicating the names of the parties, a description of the property, a section discussing the purchase price and any deposit required, an indication of a settlement date, and sections on various contingencies.

- A separation agreement generally discusses the custody of minor children, child support, spousal support, and the division of property.

- Articles of incorporation must be filed with a state agency. This document describes a corporation's purpose and powers.

- The organizational meeting of the corporation must be memorialized by written minutes.

- Corporate bylaws are the rules that govern the day-to-day operations of a corporation.

- Forms, models, and checklists can assist in the preparation of instruments.

- Boilerplate, standard language that appears in many forms, should be avoided.

Review Questions

1. What considerations must be addressed in preparing an instrument?

2. Name the three types of deeds.

3. What is an assignment of leasehold?

4. Indicate one difference between a residential and a commercial lease.

5. Explain the importance of the property description in a deed.

6. Besides the disposition of property, indicate other matters typically addressed in a will.

7. List some of the other testamentary documents seen in a typical law practice.

8. What are some of the components of a real estate contract?

9. What term is frequently used today to describe custody and visitation responsibilities?

10. What is the significance of a corporation's articles of incorporation?

11. List the various form books published by LCP.

12. What is a model?

13. Define boilerplate. Why should it be avoided?

Chapter Exercises

1. Review Figure 14-4. Edit and rewrite the last will and testament so that it is easier to understand. Research your state code to determine your state's law in this area.

2. Both Figures 14-7 and 14-8 are typical instruments in law practice. Unfortunately, they are both replete with legalese and poor sentence structure. Edit and rewrite one of the documents.

3. Does your state require that certain provisions be included in residential leases?

4. Develop a general checklist for drafting a separation agreement.

5. Survey attorneys in your area to determine the most popular state-based form books.

CHAPTER 15

PLEADINGS, MOTIONS, AND DISCOVERY

OVERVIEW

Once the determination has been made to bring a lawsuit, the lawyer must file with the court a variety of documents necessary to prosecute the claim. The documents that present the formal allegations and defenses of the parties are referred to as *pleadings.* Pleadings include complaints, answers, counterclaims, cross-claims, and third-party complaints. Although criminal litigation utilizes pleadings, they are more extensively found in civil litigation. For this reason, the focus here is on civil cases.

A *complaint* is the initial document filed in a civil action. It sets forth the cause of action that is the basis for the lawsuit, the facts upon which the cause of action is based, and the relief requested by the plaintiff. Because it lays out the parameters of the lawsuit, it is the most important pleading filed in the case.

The defendant responds to the specific allegations in the complaint by filing an *answer.* In the answer, the defendant can also raise certain specific claims, called *affirmative defenses,* against the plaintiff.

Besides filing an answer, the defendant can bring a *counterclaim.* The counterclaim sets forth a separate action by the defendant against the plaintiff, usually based on the same set of facts stated in the plaintiff's complaint. The response to a counterclaim, generally known as a *reply,* is styled similar to an answer.

A *cross-claim* is an action brought by the defendant against a co-defendant. Finally, a *third-party complaint* is a suit brought by the defendant against an individual who was not an original defendant in the action.

When a party makes a request of the court, it does so by way of a motion. Whereas pleadings are generally filed in the initial stages of civil litigation, motions can be brought at any time. There are numerous types of motions, all for different purposes. A *preliminary motion* is generally filed after a complaint has been filed but before an answer is due. It raises a technical defense to the complaint's service or substance. A particular kind of motion known as a *motion for summary judgment* can be filed if a party feels that a judgment should be entered in its favor as a matter of law. Other motions include a motion for new trial, a motion for continuance, and a motion to strike or enter appearance of counsel.

Litigation documents that are not pleadings or motions include summonses, subpoenas, and proofs of service. A *summons* is issued by the clerk of court and is served upon the defendant along with the complaint. It commands the defendant to take certain action (usually to file a responsive pleading to the complaint within a specified period or face the consequences of a default judgment). A *subpoena* orders an individual to appear for a hearing. Once a summons or subpoena has been served, a *proof of service* must be filed by the process server, indicating the date and manner of service.

At the end of litigation, it is necessary to prepare a *judgment,* which puts in writing the oral determination of the court. An *order,* in contrast, is a court's decision on the merits of a motion.

The final types of litigation documents to be discussed are used during discovery. The goal of discovery is to obtain information regarding an opponent's case. There are several methods of discovery. *Interrogatories* are questions asked by one party of the other which must be answered under oath. A *request for admissions of fact and genuineness of documents* presents either factual statements or documents to the opposing party and asks him to admit or deny their accuracy. In a *request for production of documents and inspection of property,* one party asks that the other party produce certain documents or make available for inspection certain property related to the case. A *motion for physical or mental examination* may be filed during discovery requesting either a physical or a psychological examination of a party. If a party wishes to take the testimony of a party or nonparty prior to trial, she can hold a deposition. Finally, if discovery is not complied with, certain enforcement motions, including a *motion to compel* and a *motion for sanctions,* can be filed.

PARALEGAL PRACTICE SITUATION

After considerable efforts at negotiation, the attorney you are employed by has decided to bring suit in a personal injury matter. Your client, Claire Johnson, was involved in a collision with Steven Carmine at a major intersection. The defendant was following your client as she approached a red light. He failed to reduce speed and crashed into her vehicle from behind. She suffered injuries to her neck and had to be transported by ambulance to County Medical Center. Upon examination by emergency room physicians, it was determined that her injuries were of a soft tissue nature, which required her to participate in physical therapy over the course of several months. Jefferson Mutual Insurance Company, the defendant's insurance company, has refused to settle the case for an amount your attorney feels is reasonable.

You have been asked to draft the initial complaint to be filed in the trial court.

Characteristics of Litigation Documents

Because pleadings, motions, and (in most jurisdictions) discovery documents are all filed in court, they all share similar characteristics. The first three attributes deal with the perspective that the documents must take; the second four deal with document format.

All documents filed in court are governed by rules of pleading developed by legislatures and courts. These rules govern substance, style, and format. Each jurisdiction has its own very specific set of rules, and many courts strictly enforce their rules. Failure to follow pleading requirements can result in the opposing party successfully challenging a court document. For instance, if a complaint is handwritten rather than typed, or is on the wrong-size paper, it might be stricken by a court. Consequently, it is in a paralegal's interest to thoroughly know the pleading rules in his particular jurisdiction.

The attorney's objective is to show that her client is entitled to relief based on specific legal authority. To assist in this goal, facts and legal arguments must be offered that present the client and the cause in the best possible light. Though the truth must always be adhered to, lawyers often color their writing with language that tends to present their client in a sympathetic manner. Rather than stating "Plaintiff's car was hit by Defendant's vehicle," the lawyer for Ms. Johnson might write "Defendant rear-ended Plaintiff." The action verb "rear-ended" is more visual than "hit" and leaves a clearer impression that Mr. Carmine was at fault. Also, the subject, verb, object format emphasizes the negligent actions of Mr. Carmine.

Recall from Chapter 10 the discussion of the importance and benefits of using plain English. By reducing legalese and terms of art, documents are made easier to understand. Unfortunately, when it comes to litigation documents, the plain English movement has had only modest success. Few pleadings, even those written by the most conscientious attorneys, are free of all legalese. In fact, court rules often require the use of terms of art in litigation documents. This, of course, makes pleadings and other court documents difficult to comprehend. As a paralegal, you must be sensitive to the fact that the client will likely be perplexed by terms and phrases used in the pleadings in his case. You must always be prepared to translate these unknown words.

CHARACTERISTICS OF LITIGATION DOCUMENTS
(Perspective)

1. Governed by rules of procedure
2. Positively, though truthfully, portrays client
3. Replete with legalese and terms of art

The following characteristics deal with format.

Caption Every pleading, motion, discovery document, or other paper filed in court must have a caption at the top of the first page. The caption indicates the parties' names, their litigation status, the name of the court, and the docket number. (See Figure 15-1.) Many court rules require that the complaint include addresses of the parties. The caption will be the same for every document filed in the case.

Title Each document that is filed with the court must have a title. The title gives the reader an indication as to the document's substance and purpose.

```
CLAIRE JOHNSON              )    IN THE
101 Main Street            )    CIRCUIT COURT
Hamilton, Maryland 21019-1563  )  FOR
        PLAINTIFF          )    HARFORD COUNTY
    vs.                    )
STEVEN CARMINE             )    CASE NO.:
2 Oak Avenue               )
Jefferson, Maryland 21091-5361  )
        DEFENDANT          )

                    COMPLAINT
```

FIGURE 15-1 Caption and title

Because court rules dictate time limits within which to respond to pleadings and motions, knowing the title of the document helps opposing counsel to easily determine time constraints and the response required. Some attorneys not only indicate the title of the document but also cite the court rule that supports the filing of the document in the title.

Signatures   All documents filed in court must be signed. In most cases the only signature needed is that of the lawyer, but with some documents, such as answers to interrogatories, the party must also sign. By signing, the signatory is attesting to the truthfulness and "good faith" of the matters contained in the document.

Certificate of Service   Finally, all courts require that an affidavit or **certificate of service** be included with the document. This is verification furnished by the attorney that a copy of the document being filed in court has also been provided to opposing counsel or to the other party, if not represented by counsel. (See Figure 15-2.)

CHARACTERISTICS OF LITIGATION DOCUMENTS
(Format)

1. Caption
2. Title
3. Signature of attorney and/or client
4. Certificate of service

CERTIFICATE OF SERVICE

This is to certify that on this _____ day of May 1996, a copy of this answer was mailed postage prepaid to Melissa White-Jackson, Esquire, 1045 Chesapeake Avenue, Towson, Maryland 21204-4223, Attorney for Defendant.

David J. Smith

FIGURE 15-2 Certificate of service

———————————————— **LEGAL TERMS** ————————————————
certificate of service [†]   A verification, usually provided by an attorney, that a pleading or motion has been mailed or delivered to the opposing side.

Pleadings

The complaint, answer, counterclaim, cross-claim, and third-party complaint collectively are referred to as **pleadings**. The purpose of pleadings is to set forth specific legal and factual allegations that constitute or defend against a cause of action. In a sense, pleadings frame the issues for trial. Several philosophies affect the drafting of pleadings.

In **fact pleading**, the facts necessary to allege a valid cause of action must be provided. The failure to provide sufficient facts would cause the pleading to be defective and subject to attack by opposing counsel. By its nature, fact pleading is very detailed. Fact pleading is also referred to as *code pleading,* because the provisions governing this type of pleading are found in state codes.

The alternative philosophy is **notice pleading**. Notice pleading requires only a short statement as to the grounds on which the party is basing its claim, a statement indicating why relief should be granted, and the relief requested. Notice pleading does not require the extensive factual presentation required for fact pleading. Federal courts permit notice pleading. As a paralegal, you will need to determine which form is required in your jurisdiction. (See Figure 15-3.)

A third theory of pleading is rarely used today. In **common law pleading**, documents are drafted pursuant to technical rules developed not by courts or legislatures but by common law principles. One form of common law pleading is the use of **common counts**. These standardized phrases had to be used in order to state a particular cause of action. Common law pleading has been replaced in all states with either code or notice pleading. Some attorneys, however, still occasionally use common law pleading to allege basic causes of action such as breach of contract.

It is important that attorneys not violate the rule of **variance**. This rule prohibits an attorney from offering evidence at trial or raising issues at trial not alleged in her pleadings. For this reason, pleadings must be amended when new

---

 LEGAL TERMS

pleadings † Formal statements by the parties to an action setting forth their claims or defenses. The various kinds of pleadings, and the rules governing them, are set forth in detail in the Federal Rules of Civil Procedure and, with respect to pleading in state courts, by the rules of civil procedure of the several states. These rules of procedure abolished common law pleading.

fact pleading When detailed facts necessary to allege a cause of action are provided.

notice pleading When only a short statement as to the grounds for bringing a cause of action are provided.

common law pleading † A highly formal process of pleading a case, both claim and defense, the object of which was to put the matter in dispute at issue as precisely as possible.

common counts Standardized phrases used in common law pleading.

variance † In pleading, an inconsistency between the allegations of a complaint or an indictment and the evidence offered at trial. A fatal variance will result in the dismissal of an action or the reversal of a conviction.

STATE RULES

Rule 8. General Rules of Pleading. (a) *Claims for relief.*—A pleading which sets forth a claim for relief, whether an original claim, counterclaim, cross-claim, or third-party claim, shall contain (1) a short and plain statement of the claim showing that the pleader is entitled to relief, and (2) a demand for judgment for the relief to which he deems himself entitled. Relief in the alternative or of several types may be demanded. Every such pleading shall be accompanied by a completed civil case information statement in the form prescribed by the Supreme Court of Appeals.

FIGURE 15-3 Notice pleading rule (West Virginia). (Reproduced with permission of The Michie Company. Further reproduction without permission is strictly prohibited.)

theories or facts are advanced. There are limitations as to when pleadings can be amended. You will need to check the rules in your jurisdiction for guidance.

Complaint

The **complaint** is the initial pleading filed in every lawsuit. Occasionally, a complaint will be called a *petition* or *declaration*. Its component parts include a statement as to the cause of action; the facts (only a few facts in notice pleading, detailed facts in fact pleading) necessary to support the cause of action; and the relief being requested by the parties. Some jurisdictions may also require a statement that establishes the court's ability to hear the case, referred to as *jurisdiction*. These statements include the residency of the parties or the location where the cause of action arose.

The complaint begins with a short introductory paragraph indicating the names of the parties bringing the suit and their attorney. This might be followed by one or more statements presenting the jurisdictional basis for bringing the suit. Next, facts that relate to all aspects of the complaint are discussed.

Pursuant to most court rules, the complaint is divided into counts. (See Figure 15-4.) A *count* is a group of separately numbered paragraphs that discuss a particular cause of action and the facts supporting it. Each count is followed by a prayer for relief. This is also known as a *wherefore clause* because it begins with the word "wherefore." Here is indicated the damages or other relief, such as an injunction, that the plaintiff is seeking in the matter. See Figure 15-5.

LEGAL TERMS

complaint [†] The initial pleading in a civil action, in which the plaintiff alleges a cause of action and asks that the wrong done him or her be remedied by the court.

Rule 2-303. FORM OF PLEADINGS

(a) Paragraphs, Counts, and Defenses. — All averments of claim or defense shall be made in numbered paragraphs, the contents of each of which shall be limited as far as practicable to a statement of a single set of circumstances; and a paragraph may be referred to by number in all succeeding pleadings. Each cause of action shall be set forth in a separately numbered count. Each separate defense shall be set forth in a separately numbered defense.

(b) Contents. — Each averment of a pleading shall be simple, concise, and direct. No technical forms of pleadings are required. A pleading shall contain only such statements of fact as may be necessary to show the pleader's entitlement to relief or ground of defense. It shall not include argument, unnecessary recitals of law, evidence, or documents, or any immaterial, impertinent, or scandalous matter.

(c) Consistency. — A party may set forth two or more statements of a claim or defense alternatively or hypothetically. When two or more statements are made in the alternative and one of them if made independently would be sufficient, the pleading is not made insufficient by the insufficiency of one or more of the alternative statements. A party may also state as many separate claims or defenses as the party has, regardless of consistency and whether based on legal or equitable grounds.

(d) Adoption by Reference. — Statements in a pleading or other paper of record may be adopted by reference in a different part of the same pleading or paper of record or in another pleading or paper of record. A copy of any written instrument that is an exhibit to a pleading is a part thereof for all purposes.

(e) Construction of Pleadings. — All pleadings shall be so construed as to do substantial justice.

(Amended Mar. 22, 1991, effective July 1, 1991.)

FIGURE 15-4 Maryland pleading rule. (Reproduced with permission of The Michie Company. Further reproduction without permission is strictly prohibited.)

Answer

An **answer** responds to the allegations presented in the complaint. Each numbered paragraph of an answer addresses a corresponding paragraph in the complaint. (See Figure 15-6.) The defendant may admit, deny, or indicate a lack of knowledge as to each allegation. Should the defendant want to present new facts which show that he is not responsible, he can do so in the form of an

---

LEGAL TERMS

answer † A pleading in response to a complaint. An answer may deny the allegations of the complaint, demur to them, agree with them, or introduce affirmative defenses intended to defeat the plaintiff's lawsuit or delay it.

Form 2-303.27

Complaint—Product Liability

[Full Caption for Complaint: Form 1-301.1]

Complaint [and Demand for Jury Trial][1]

John Q. Public and Mary Q. Public, plaintiffs, sue Amalgamated Widget Corporation ("Amalgamated") and Widget World, Inc. ("World"), defendants, and say:

Count I (Special Liability in Tort)[2]

1. The plaintiffs are residents of [insert location].

2. Amalgamated is a [insert appropriate description] corporation engaged in the manufacture and sale of [product name] throughout the United States.

3. World is a Maryland corporation engaged in the distribution and sale of [product] in Maryland.

4. On [date of purchase], the plaintiffs purchased a new [product] from [immediate seller].

5. On [date of accident], John Q. Public, while using the [product] in a reasonably foreseeable manner, sustained physical harm to his person and property approximately caused by a latent, defective condition in the [product]. Also as a direct result of the product defect, the plaintiffs have sustained economic hardship, emotional trauma, and other damages.

---

1. Rule 2-325 requires that a demand for jury trial be filed either as a separate paper or separately titled at the conclusion of a pleading and immediately preceding any certificate of service. However, the authors suggest that the jury trial demand be titled *both* at the beginning of the complaint and at the end (as required by Rule 2-325) so that the demand is readily apparent to the reader.

2. Although commonly called "*strict* liability in tort," the title to Section 402A of the Restatement (Second) of Torts, which embodies this concept as adopted in Maryland, refers to the theory as "*special* liability in tort," a term less apt to confuse juries.

FIGURE 15-5 Complaint. (Reproduced with permission of Michie Butterworth.)

6. The [product] was in a defective condition unreasonably danger-ous to users of the product at the time it left the control of each defendant. [Describe nature of defect alleged.]

7. The [product] was expected to, and did, reach the plaintiffs with-out substantial change in its condition at the time of Mr. Public's injury.

WHEREFORE, John Q. Public claims compensatory damages against the defendants in the amount of [insert amount], plus interest and the costs of this action.

Count II (Negligence)

8. Plaintiffs incorporate the allegations of Count I.[3]

9. The defendants owed plaintiffs a duty to exercise reasonable care to [design], [manufacture], [test] and [inspect][4] the [product] so as to render it free of defects and reasonably safe for its reasonably fore-seeable uses.

10. The defendants further owed a duty to warn plaintiffs of any dangerous condition of the product which was not obvious to the user.

11. The defendants negligently breached these duties owed plaintiffs, and as a result proximately caused the plaintiff's damages set forth in paragraph 5 of this Complaint.[5]

WHEREFORE, John Q. Public claims compensatory damages against defendants in the amount of [insert amount], plus interest and the costs of this action.

---

3. Rule 2-303(d) provides that statements in a pleading may be adopted by reference in a different part of the same pleading or in another pleading or in any motion.

4. A seller of a product owes a variety of duties to a product user, some or all of which duties may have been breached. *See* MPJI (Civil-3d Edition) 26:1.

5. Although the pleading of the absence of contributory negligence appears to have become a convention among Maryland practitioners, such an al-legation is *not* required by the Rules or by the substantive law of negligence in Maryland. In the authors' view, the better practice is *not* to plead the absence of contributory negligence, inasmuch as it is not an element to be proved in the plaintiff's case. Rather, contributory negligence is an affir-mative defense required to be pleaded in answer to a complaint by Rule 2-323(g).

FIGURE 15-5 *(continued)*

Count III (Breach of Warranty)

12. Plaintiffs incorporate the allegations of Counts I and II.

13. The defendants expressly warranted that the [product] was [set forth essential terms of any express warranty].

14. The defendants impliedly warranted that the [product] was merchantable and fit for the ordinary purposes for which such products are intended.

15. The defendant [immediate seller][6] also impliedly warranted to plaintiffs that the [product] was fit for the particular purpose for which plaintiffs intended to use the [product], namely, [describe any particular purpose]. Plaintiffs communicated that purpose to [immediate seller] at the time of purchase and relied on the [immediate seller's] skill and judgment in selecting a product similar for that particular purpose.

16. The defendants breached these express and implied warranties to plaintiffs and as a result proximately caused the plaintiffs' damages set forth in paragraph 5 of this Complaint.

WHEREFORE, John Q. Public claims compensatory damages against defendants in the amount of [insert amount], plus interest and the costs of this action.

Count IV (Loss of Consortium)

17. Plaintiffs incorporate the allegations of Counts I through III.

18. Plaintiffs were married to each other on [date of marriage] and were married at the time of the events giving rise to this action.

19. The defective condition of the [product] proximately caused plaintiffs to suffer a loss of consortium for which they jointly make claim in this action.

---

6. Although it is theoretically possible for a manufacturer to impliedly warrant that a product is fit for a particular use intended by the purchaser other than the ordinary uses to which such a product would be put, in practice it is more likely that the purchaser's immediate seller would have given any such warranty since purchasers seldom communicate their intended uses of a product directly to a manufacturer.

FIGURE 15-5 *(continued)*

WHEREFORE, plaintiffs jointly claim compensatory damages against defendants in the amount of [insert amount], plus interest and the costs of this action.

/S/ _____

[Attorney name]

[Address][7]
[Telephone]

Attorney for Plaintiff

[Insert Demand for Jury Trial, if any: Form 2-325.1]

---

7. Rule 1-311(a) requires that every pleading and paper of a party represented by an attorney be signed by at least one attorney admitted to practice law in Maryland and who complies with Rule 1-312. The Rule also requires that every pleading or paper contain the address and telephone number of the person who signed it.

FIGURE 15-5 *(continued)*

IN THE ___(court name)___, DISTRICT COURT OF ___(county name)___
COUNTY
STATE OF ___(state name)___

(Jane Roe and Mary Roe) Plaintiffs, vs. (Retail Store, Inc. & John Does 1 and 2) Defendants.	ANSWER Civil No. _____

___(Retail Store, Inc.)___ in answering plaintiffs' complaint admits, denies and alleges as follows:

FIRST DEFENSE

Plaintiffs' complaint fails to state a cause of action against this defendant upon which relief can be granted.

SECOND DEFENSE

Answering plaintiffs' General Allegations:

1. This defendant has insufficient information upon which to form a belief as to the allegations contained in paragraph 1 of plaintiffs' complaint and for that reason denies the same.

2. This defendant admits paragraph 2 and 3 of plaintiffs' complaint.

THIRD DEFENSE

3. In answering paragraph 4 of plaintiffs' complaint except for admitting that on or about ___(date)___, the plaintiffs were on the premises of ___(retail)___, ___(address)___, this defendant denies that the plaintiffs were lawfully on the premises or on the premises with lawful intentions.

4. Defendant admits paragraph 5.

5. Defendant denies paragraphs 6, 7, and 8 of plaintiffs' complaint.

6. Defendant admits paragraph 9.

FIGURE 15-6 Answer. (Reproduced from *Causes of Action,* Volume 1, © 1983. Used by permission of Shepard's/McGraw-Hill, Inc. Further reproduction of any kind is strictly prohibited. For subscription information, please contact Shepard's/McGraw-Hill, Inc., 555 Middle Creek Parkway, Colorado Springs, CO 80921, 1-800-525-2474.)

7. In answering paragraph 10 of plaintiffs' complaint, except for admitting that the _____(name of police department)_____ Police were contacted and custody of the plaintiffs transferred to the _____(name of police department)_____ Police, this defendant denies each and every remaining allegation in said paragraph.

8. This defendant denies paragraphs 11, 12, 13, 14, 15, 16, 17, 18, 19, 20 and 21 of plaintiff's complaint.

9. Defendant denies each and every allegation in plaintiffs' complaint not heretofore admitted or denied.

FOURTH DEFENSE

As a separate and affirmative defense, this defendant alleges that any detention of the plaintiffs was based upon reasonable and probable grounds and that the manner in which the detention was accomplished, if any, was reasonable and for a reasonable length of time, all pursuant to
_____(citation to merchant's privilege statute)_____

FIFTH DEFENSE

As a further separate and affirmative defense, this defendant alleges that any arrest of the plaintiffs was based upon reasonable and probable grounds for believing that the plaintiffs committed larceny of goods held or displayed for sale, all pursuant to _____(citation to merchant's privilege statute)_____

SIXTH DEFENSE

As a further separate and affirmative defense, this defendant alleges that the taking into custody of the detention of the plaintiffs, if any, was done in a reasonable manner and for a reasonable length of time, all pursuant to
_____(citation to merchant's privilege statute)_____

WHEREFORE, having fully answered plaintiffs' complaint, this defendant prays that the same be dismissed and that this defendant be granted its costs of Court incurred herein and such other and further relief as the Court may deem just and equitable.

DATED this __(date)__ day of __(month)__, __(year)__

_____
(signature)
Attorney for Defendant
(address)

MAILED POSTPAID a copy of the foregoing to __(name)__, Attorney for Plaintiffs, __(address)__, and __(name)__, Co-counsel for defendant, __(address)__ this __(date)__ day of __(month)__, __(year)__.

_____
(signature)

FIGURE 15-6 *(continued)*

affirmative defense. For instance, if the defendant in the Johnson-Carmine automobile accident believes that the plaintiff committed **contributory negligence**, he would raise this affirmative defense to try to get a dismissal of the case. Other affirmative defenses include failure to meet the statute of limitations, bankruptcy, **estoppel**, **duress**, and illegality.

Request for Default

If an answer or preliminary motion is not filed within the court-prescribed period of time, the plaintiff has the option of requesting the entry of a **default judgment** against the defendant. A *default judgment* is a judgment in the plaintiff's favor based upon the defendant's failure to dispute the complaint. Once ordered by a judge, the proceedings come to an end in favor of the plaintiff. (See Figure 15-7.)

Counterclaim

The complaint alleges some compensable action taken by the defendant. If the defendant, however, feels that the plaintiff has committed some act for which the defendant should be compensated, he has the option to bring a **counterclaim**—literally, a complaint brought against the plaintiff by the defendant. (See Figure 15-8.) In most situations, the claim the defendant raises is based on the same set of facts as the original complaint. In the paralegal practice

-- **LEGAL TERMS** --

affirmative defense [†] A defense that amounts to more than simply a denial of the allegations in the plaintiff's complaint. It sets up new matter which, if proven, could result in a judgment against the plaintiff even if all the allegations of the complaint are true.

contributory negligence [†] In the law of negligence, a failure by the plaintiff to exercise reasonable care which, in part at least, is the cause of an injury. Contributory negligence defeats a plaintiff's cause of action for negligence in states that have not adopted the doctrine of comparative negligence.

estoppel [†] A prohibition imposed by law against uttering what may actually be the truth. There are two classes of estoppel. A person may be estopped by his or her own acts or representations (that is, not be permitted to deny the truth or significance of what he or she said or did) if another person who was entitled to rely upon those statements or acts did so to his or her detriment. This type of estoppel is also known as *equitable estoppel* or *estoppel in pais*. The second type of estoppel is *legal estoppel*. It includes matters of record such as marriage, divorce, judgments, and deeds, as well as the findings of a court. Estoppel must be distinguished from waiver, which is the voluntary surrendering of a known right.

duress [†] Coercion applied for the purpose of compelling a person to do, or to refrain from doing, some act. ... Duress may be a defense in a civil action.

default judgment [†] A judgment rendered in favor of a plaintiff based upon a defendant's failure to take a necessary step in a lawsuit within the required time.

counterclaim [†] A cause of action on which a defendant in a lawsuit might have sued the plaintiff in a separate action. Such a cause of action, stated in a separate division of a defendant's answer, is a counterclaim.

_____

_____

VS.

_____

_____
(Last known address required)

IN THE CIRCUIT COURT

FOR

BALTIMORE CITY

CASE NUMBER _____

REQUEST FOR ORDER OF DEFAULT

The plaintiff herein requests an Order of Default against the defendant, for failure to plead as provided by the Maryland Rules.

Date _____

_____
Attorney for Plaintiff

NON MILITARY AFFIDAVIT

1. The defendant is not in the military service of the United States;

2. The defendant is not in the military service of any nation allied with the United States;

3. The defendant has not been ordered to report for induction under the Selective Training and Service Act;

4. The defendant is not a member of the Enlisted Reserve Corps who has been ordered to report for military service.

I solemnly affirm under the penalties of perjury that the contents of the aforegoing paper are true to the best of my knowledge, information, and belief.

_____
AFFIANT

ORDER OF DEFAULT

It is ORDERED this   day of   19   that an Order

of Default is entered against the Defendant for failure to plead, [and that the testimony to support the alle-

gations of the Complaint be taken before one of the Standing Examiner/Masters of this court.]

_____
JUDGE

FIGURE 15-7   Request for default judgment

---

§ 1:421 Answer containing counterclaim—General form [FRCP 13]

UNITED STATES DISTRICT COURT

FOR THE _____ DISTRICT OF _____

_____ DIVISION

_____ Plaintiff, v. _____ Defendant.	))))) Civil Action, File No. _____) ANSWER AND COUNTERCLAIM)

Defense

1. Defendant denies each and every allegation contained in Paragraphs _____ , _____ , and _____ of the complaint.

2. Defendant admits the allegations contained in Paragraphs _____ , and _____ of the complaint, _____ [except for _____].

Counterclaim

As a counterclaim against plaintiff, defendant alleges:

1. _____ [State jurisdictional allegations in manner similar to that used in complaints, if required].

2. _____ [State further allegations of counterclaim in numbered paragraphs].

Wherefore, defendant demands:

1. That plaintiff take nothing on plaintiff's claim;

2. That defendant have judgment against plaintiff in the amount of $_____ ;

3. That defendant be awarded costs herein;

4. _____ [That defendant be awarded reasonable attorneys' fees]; and

5. That the court grant such other and further relief as the court may deem proper.

Dated _____ , 19___.

[Signature and address]

FIGURE 15-8 Counterclaim

situation, Mr. Carmine might contend that he suffered an injury caused by Ms. Johnson. As a result, he could bring a counterclaim alleging a cause of action in negligence against her. When a counterclaim is brought, the plaintiff is required to respond by filing a **reply**. Often a counterclaim is brought as part of an answer.

LEGAL TERMS

reply [†]   In pleading, the plaintiff's answer to the defendant's setoff or counterclaim.

Cross-Claim

Should a defendant feel that a co-defendant is responsible for the damages alleged by the plaintiff, he is permitted to file a **cross-claim** against another defendant. (See Figure 15-9.) If it is alleged that another driver caused Mr. Carmine's vehicle to collide with Ms. Johnson's car, Mr. Carmine might bring a cross-claim against the other driver. However, to do so, the other driver must have originally been named a co-defendant in suit by Ms. Johnson. Like a counterclaim, a cross-claim can be filed as part of an answer.

ANSWER AND CROSS CLAIM

Defense

_____ *[Set forth denials, admissions, etc.; see, e.g., § 1:421]*

Cross Claim

As a cross claim against defendant _____ , hereinafter referred to as cross defendant, defendant and cross claimant _____ , hereinafter referred to as cross claimant, alleges:

1. _____ *[Set forth jurisdictional allegations, if required.]*

2. _____ *[State allegations of cross claim against cross defendant.]*
   _____ *[If applicable, add:* 3. Cross defendant is liable to cross claimant for all claims asserted by plaintiff against cross claimant.]

Wherefore, cross claimant demands:

1. That plaintiff take nothing on plaintiff's action against cross claimant;
2. That cross claimant be awarded judgment in the amount of $_____ against cross defendant;
3. That in the event that cross claimant is held liable to plaintiff in any amount, that cross claimant be awarded judgment against cross defendant in that amount;
4. That cross claimant be awarded costs of this action _____ *[If applicable:* and reasonable attorneys' fees]; and
5. That the court grant such further relief as it may deem proper.

Dated _____ , 19___.

[Signature and address]

FIGURE 15-9 Cross-claim

─────────────── **LEGAL TERMS** ───────────────

cross-claim A claim against a co-defendant brought by a defendant.

Third-Party Complaint

A **third-party complaint** presents the final option open to the defendant. Should he feel that an individual not presently a party to the action is responsible, he can elect to bring an action against this party by way of a third-party complaint (see Figure 15-10). For instance, if Mr. Carmine believes that his collision with Ms. Johnson was caused by his faulty brakes, he might bring a third-party complaint against the repair shop that last serviced his car. This new party will then be required to respond as a defendant.

[Title of Court]

_____ , Plaintiff   )
     vs.   )
_____ , Defendant and Third-Party Plaintiff)   Civil Action File No. ___
     vs.   )
_____ , Third-Party Defendant   )

Third-Party Complaint

I

Plaintiff _____ has filed against defendant _____ a complaint, a copy of which is attached hereto as Exhibit "_____."

II

_____ *[State grounds on which defendant as third-party plaintiff is entitled to recover from third-party defendant all or part of what plaintiff may recover from defendant. The statement should be framed as an original complaint.]*

Wherefore, third-party plaintiff _____ demands judgment against third-party defendant _____ for all sums recovered by plaintiff from third-party plaintiff as defendant.

Dated _____ , 19___.

[Signature and address]

FIGURE 15-10   Third-party complaint

LEGAL TERMS

third-party complaint † A complaint filed by the defendant in a lawsuit against a third person whom he or she seeks to bring into the action because of that person's alleged liability to the defendant.

Motions

Should a party wish an order by the court directing that something be done in his favor, such application would be made by use of a **motion**. Though motions requesting specific types of relief are provided for in court rules, an attorney can often tailor a standard motion to fit his needs.

Preliminary Motions

Certain motions can be filed only during the period between the service of the complaint and the filing of an answer. These are referred to in many jurisdictions as **preliminary motions**.

After a complaint has been served, the defendant has the option of filing either an answer or a preliminary motion attacking a procedural defect in the complaint. These motions include a motion questioning whether there is jurisdiction over the defendant; a motion alleging that the action has been brought in the wrong **venue**; a motion asserting ineffective **service of process**; and a motion alleging failure to state a claim upon which relief can be granted. (See Figure 15-11.) In this last motion, once commonly called a **demurrer**, the defendant alleges that the facts stated in the plaintiff's complaint do not amount to a legal cause of action. For example, suppose parents promise to make a gift to a child, but later change their minds. If the child filed a complaint alleging these facts

─────────────── **LEGAL TERMS** ───────────────

motion † An application made to a court for the purpose of obtaining an order or rule directing something to be done in favor of the applicant. The types of motions available to litigants, as well as their form and the matters they appropriately address, are set forth in detail in the Federal Rules of Civil Procedure and the rules of civil procedure of the various states, as well as in the Federal Rules of Criminal Procedure and the various states' rules of criminal procedure. Motions may be written or oral, depending on the type of relief sought and on the court in which they are made.

preliminary motion A motion challenging a procedural defect in a complaint or its service.

venue † The county or judicial district in which a case is to be tried. In civil cases, venue may be based on where the events giving rise to the cause of action took place or where the parties live or work. ... Venue is distinguishable from jurisdiction because it is an issue only if jurisdiction already exists and because, unlike jurisdiction, it can be waived or changed by consent of the parties.

service of process † Delivery of a summons, writ, complaint, or other process to the opposite party, or other person entitled to receive it, in such manner as the law prescribes, whether by leaving a copy at his or her residence, by mailing a copy to [the opposite party] or his or her attorney, or by publication.

demurrer † A method of raising an objection to the legal sufficiency of a pleading. A demurrer says, in effect, that the opposing party's complaint alleges facts that, even if true, do not add up to a cause of action and that, therefore, the case should be dismissed. Demurrers have been replaced in many, but not all, jurisdictions by motions or answers, which perform the same function.

[Caption]

1. Plaintiff denies defendant's allegations in _____ [his *or* her] motion to transfer venue and states that exceptions to exclusive venue in the county of defendant's residence, or in which the cause of action arose, as provided by _____ *[cite statute or rule]*, exist in this cause. Plaintiff further denies all grounds alleged in defendant's motion made in support of _____ [his *or* her] efforts to have this cause transferred to the County of _____ , State of _____ .

2. On _____ , 19_____ , plaintiff filed _____ [his *or* her] petition in this action, a copy of which is attached, marked Exhibit "_____ ," and incorporated by reference.

3. This action is brought as a suit on a sworn account and on the face of the account it is stated that the amount due is payable in the City of _____ , County of _____ , State of _____ , and that an action may be maintained against defendant in the County of _____ , State of _____ , under the provisions of _____ *[cite statute or rule]*.

[Signature]

FIGURE 15-11 Preliminary motion response (venue)

and requesting relief, a motion to dismiss would be the appropriate response by the defendant parents. A breach of promise to make a gift is not, in most instances, a valid cause of action.

If a judge grants a preliminary motion, she is likely to permit the plaintiff to refile, redraft, or re-serve the complaint.

Motion for Summary Judgment

A trial may be avoided if a party feels there is no dispute as to the facts in the case, and the only question before the court is the appropriate law to be applied. In such a situation, the party would file a motion for **summary judgment** requesting a final judgment in its favor. In this motion, the applicant alleges two important points: (1) that there is no dispute as to any material fact, and (2) that the applicant is entitled to a judgment as a matter of law. To support the position that there is no factual dispute, the moving party may submit with the motion affidavits signed by the party or potential witnesses. A litigation memorandum (discussed in Chapter 16) might be submitted to support a party's position that an interpretation of the law should result in a judgment in his favor. (See Figure 15-12.)

─────────────── **LEGAL TERMS** ───────────────

summary judgment [†] A method of disposing of an action without further proceedings. Under the Federal Rules of Civil Procedure, and the rules of civil procedure of many states, a party against whom a claim, counterclaim, or cross-claim is asserted, or against whom a declaratory judgment is sought, may file a motion for summary judgment seeking judgment in his or her favor if there is no genuine issue as to any material fact.

To understand fully the purpose of this motion, an explanation of the role of a trial court is necessary. A court is presented with facts that allegedly amount to a cause of action, as well as legal principles that, if applied to those facts, would result in a decision favorable to one party over the other. At trial, facts are presented through testimony and other forms of evidence. Lawyers offer to the court their opposing legal theories; however, the court makes its own independent decision. In a **bench trial**, the judge interprets the facts and determines

---

State of Maryland

Circuit Court for the County of _____

_____
[Plaintiff (Name 1)]

        [Name 2]

    v.

_____
[Defendant (Name 2)]

Case No. _____

    [Firm]

Docket No. _____

Hon. _____
      [Judge]

Motion for Summary Judgment

Defendant, _____ , by its attorneys, _____ , moves the court for

the entry of an order for summary judgment in favor of Defendant and against Plaintiff

for failure of Plaintiff to establish any genuine issue of material fact as to this

Defendant and in support of the motion Defendant states as follows:

   1. (State facts upon which motion for summary judgment is based.)

In support of the above allegations, the affidavit of _____ is attached to

and made a part of this motion.

Defendant, _____ , prays that this court enters summary judgment in its

favor for failure of Plaintiff to show any genuine issue of material fact existing between

Defendant and Plaintiff.

_____
[Attorney (Bar No.)]

Attorney for Defendant

FIGURE 15-12 Motion for summary judgment (with affidavit)

──────────── LEGAL TERMS ────────────

bench trial †   A trial before a judge without a jury; a nonjury trial.

State of Maryland

Circuit Court for the County of _____

_____

[Plaintiff (Name 1)]

v.

_____

[Defendant (Name 2)]

Case No. _____

Docket No. _____

Hon. _____

[Judge]

Affidavit in Support of

Motion for Summary Judgment

_____ , on oath, states:

[Name 2]

1. I am the Defendant in this action brought for *[state basis or character of plaintiff's claim]*.

2. The facts on which this claim are not in genuine dispute as: *[set forth facts with particularity and explain why they are not genuinely disputed]*.

3. Attached is a sworn [or, certified] copy of the paper [or, each of the papers] on which I rely, which is [are]: *[describe paper or papers attached]*.

4. This affidavit is made on my personal knowledge, and, if sworn as a witness, I can testify competently to the facts as stated.

_____

[Affiant]

Signed and sworn to before me _____

[Date]

_____

Notary Public

_____ County, MD

My commission expires: _____

[Date]

FIGURE 15-12 *(continued)*

the applicable legal principles. In a **jury trial**, the jurors interpret the facts, while the judge applies the law.

Occasionally, both sides appear to present the same version of the facts. If a judge finds this to be so, he need not weigh the merits of the opposing stories or request the jury to do so. In this situation, one party will contend that because the facts are not contested, the judge need only consider the legal principles that should be applied. Of course, this same party will argue that the principles that should be applied favor her client. The opposing attorney will argue either that the facts are different or, if they are the same, that the controlling law to be applied results in a judgment favorable to his client.

After a response to the motion for summary judgment has been filed, a hearing is held. At that time the judge considers the written motion and the response, as well as oral arguments. In rendering a decision, the judge is required to give a high degree of deference (sometimes thought of as the benefit of the doubt) to the party against whom the motion is filed. For this reason, there is a heavy burden on the party filing the motion to prove his claim.

Additional Motions

Another motion typically filed in litigation is a request to reschedule a trial date, referred to as a *motion for continuance*. This motion is filed when there is a legitimate reason to postpone the date of a trial. A *motion to enter or strike appearance* is filed when an attorney wishes either to enter her appearance on behalf of a client or remove herself from a case. A *motion for new trial* is filed after a judgment has been entered by the court, requesting that a new trial be granted because of some irregularity that took place during the first trial.

TYPICAL MOTIONS

Motion to Strike Appearance	Motion to Compel Discovery
Motion to Suppress Evidence	Motion for Sanctions
Motion for Continuance	Motion for Change in Venue
Motion for Summary Judgment	Motion to Dismiss
Motion for New Trial	Motion to Amend a Judgment

LEGAL TERMS

jury trial † A trial in which the jurors are the judges of the facts and the court is the judge of the law. Trial by jury is guaranteed in all criminal cases by the Sixth Amendment, and in most civil cases by the Seventh Amendment.

Other Court Documents

Other court documents typically dealt with by legal assistants include summonses, subpoenas, and proofs of service.

Summons

A **summons** is issued by the clerk of court. It is served upon the defendant along with the complaint. The summons gives the defendant official notification that a suit was filed and informs him of the time period within which he must respond. Usually, the court provides a form summons, which is completed by the court clerk. (See Figure 15-13.)

Subpoena

To ensure that a witness shows up at trial or a deposition, a **subpoena** is issued. A subpoena can either be issued by a clerk of court or be prepared by an attorney and then affixed with the clerk's seal. (See Figure 15-14.) If a **subpoena** *duces tecum* (Latin for "bring with you") is issued, the witness will be required to bring specific documentation and records with him.

Proof of Service

Finally, a **proof of service** must be completed by the process server who delivers or attempts to deliver a summons, subpoena, or other court document. This is evidence that the document was actually delivered. (See Figure 15-15.) In most jurisdictions, process servers must be over the age of 18 and not a party to the action. Service can also be effectuated by a sheriff or constable. In that case, the document filed is referred to as a *sheriff's return*.

──────────────────── **LEGAL TERMS** ────────────────────

summons † In a civil case, the process by which an action is commenced and the defendant is brought within the jurisdiction of the court.

subpoena † A command in the form of written process requiring a witness to come to court to testify; short for subpoena ad testificandum.

subpoena duces tecum † The Latin term *duces tecum* means "bring with you under penalty." A subpoena duces tecum is a written command requiring a witness to come to court to testify and at that time to produce for use as evidence the papers, documents, books, or records listed in the subpoena.

return (proof) of service † A short account in writing, made by an officer, with respect to the manner in which he or she has executed a writ or other process.

CIRCUIT COURT FOR HARFORD COUNTY

Charles G. Hiob, III,
Clerk of the Circuit Court
Courthouse
Bel Air, Maryland 21014

WRIT OF SUMMONS

Case Number _____

STATE OF MARYLAND, HARFORD COUNTY TO WIT:

TO:

Name _____

Address _____

County _____

    You are hereby summoned to file a *written* response by pleading or motion in this Court to the attached

complaint filed by _____
                                  (Name and Address)

_____

_____

within _____ days after service of this summons upon you.

WITNESS The Honorable Chief Judge of the Third Judicial Circuit of Maryland.

Date Issued _____ _____
                                              CLERK

TO THE PERSON SUMMONED:

   1. PERSONAL ATTENDANCE IN COURT ON THE DAY NAMED IS NOT REQUIRED.

   2. FAILURE TO FILE A RESPONSE WITHIN THE TIME ALLOWED MAY RESULT IN A JUDGMENT BY DEFAULT OR THE GRANTING OF THE RELIEF SOUGHT AGAINST YOU.

SHERIFF'S RETURN

_____

_____

FEE $ _____ SHERIFF _____

NOTE:

   1. This summons is effective for service only if serve within 60 days after the date it is issued.

   2. Proof of service shall set out the name of the person served, date and the particular place and manner of service. If service is not made, please state the reasons.

   3. Return of served or unserved process shall be made promptly and in accordance with Rule 2-126.

   4. If this summons is served by private process, process server shall file a separate affidavit as required by Rule 2-126(a).

CV-1

FIGURE 15-13 Summons form

CIRCUIT COURT FOR HARFORD COUNTY

CHARLES G. HIOB, III
Clerk of the Circuit Court
Courthouse
Bel Air, Maryland 21014

_____   Case Number _____

_____

Vs.   ( ) Civil   ( ) Criminal

_____

STATE OF MARYLAND, HARFORD COUNTY TO WIT:

SUBPOENA

To (Name, Address and County):

YOU ARE HEREBY COMMANDED TO: ( ) Personally appear; ( ) Produce documents and or objects

only; ( ) Personally appear and produce documents or objects; at _____
                                                    (Place where attendance is required)

_____

on _____ the _____ day of _____, 19_____ at _____ a.m./p.m.

YOU ARE COMMANDED TO produce the following documents or objects:

Subpoena requested by ( ) Plaintiff; ( ) Defendant; and any questions should be referred to: _____

_____
                (Name of Party or Attorney, Address and Phone Number)

Date Issued _____   _____
                                    CLERK   (Signature and Seal)

N O T I C E :
(1) YOU ARE LIABLE TO BODY ATTACHMENT AND FINE FOR FAILURE TO OBEY THIS SUBPOENA.
(2) This subpoena shall remain in effect until you are granted leave to depart by the Court or by an officer acting on behalf of the Court.
(3) If this subpoena is for attendance at a deposition and the party served is an organization, notice is hereby given that the organization must designate a person to testify pursuant to Rule 2-412(d).

SHERIFF'S RETURN

( ) Served and copy delivered on date indicated below.

( ) Unserved, by reason of _____.

Date: _____ Fee: $_____   _____
                                            SHERIFF

ORIGINAL AND TWO COPIES NEEDED FOR EACH WITNESS

CV-4

FIGURE 15-14 Subpoena form

DISTRICT COURT OF MARYLAND FOR ....
City/County

Located at...
Court Address .... Case No. ....

.... vs. ....
Plaintiff/Judgment Creditor   Defendant/Judgment Debtor

Trial Date................ Issue Date .... Expiration Date............... Received From................ County

REQUEST FOR SERVICE
Please serve the attached process on the person shown.

ORDER FOR SERVICE
You are hereby commanded to serve the attached process and to make your return promptly on this Order if served, and if you are unable to serve, you are to make your return on this Order and return the original process to the Court no later than ten days following the termination of the validity of the process.

Case No. ....

Type of Paper ....

If service is not effected, send refund to:

....
....
....

....
Date   Clerk

PROOF OF SERVICE

I CERTIFY

☐ that I served a Summons by ☐ restricted delivery mail, return card attached ☐ delivery to ....
Name

.... on...
Title   Date   Time

Description of Defendant: Race .... Sex .... Ht ....
Wt. .... Age.................. Other ....

☐ and left with him a copy of the Complaint and all supporting papers.
☐ I posted the premises at...
☐ I was unable to serve because ....
....
☐ I served the Writ of Garnishment on Wages on the Garnishee by ☐ restricted delivery mail, return card attached ☐ delivery to ....
☐ I served the Writ of Garnishment on Property on the Garnishee by ☐ restricted delivery mail, return card attached ☐ delivery to ....
and promptly after service mailed a copy of the Writ to the Judgment Debtor's last known address.
☐ I served an Order to Appear for Oral Examination in Aid of Enforcement by ☐ restricted delivery mail, return card attached ☐ delivery to ....
☐ I served a Show Cause Order by ☐ restricted delivery mail, return card attached ☐ delivery to ....
If return is made by an individual other than a sheriff or constable, I solemnly affirm under the penalties of perjury that the contents of the foregoing paper are true to the best of my knowledge, information and belief and do further affirm I am a competent person over 18 years of age and not a party to the case.

☐ Serve on
Garnishee/Agent.................................
Address ....
City, State, Zip...............................
Serve in .... County
Special Instructions:...........................
....
....

....
Date   Signature   Title

....
Time   Address if Private Process Server

Telephone Number if Private Process Server

Plaintiff ....

Plaintiff's Attorney ....

Address ....

City, State, Zip ....

Defendant .... ☐ Serve on

Address ....

City, State, Zip ....

Serve in...................................... county.

ATTEMPT	
1 .... Date/Time	
2 .... Date/Time	
3 .... Date/Time	
4 .... Date/Time	

DC/CV 2 (Rev. 2/89)   COURT COPY

FIGURE 15-15 Proof of service form

Judgments and Orders

Once a court has ruled on a motion, it indicates its decision in the form of a written **order**. Most courts require that when a motion is filed, a proposed order must accompany it. (See Figure 15-16.) A **judgment**, in contrast, is prepared after the final determination of the merits of a case. It is often difficult to know what the judgment will be until after the trial. At the end of trial, the judge often instructs the winning attorney to draft a judgment reflecting the court's decision. Because it normally covers a variety of legal issues, a judgment is usually more complex than an order. (See Figure 15-17.)

IN THE MATTER OF	)	IN THE
DENNIS A. MARTIN	)	CIRCUIT COURT
FOR THE APPOINTMENT OF A	)	FOR
GUARDIAN OF THE PERSON	)	BALTIMORE COUNTY
AND THE PROPERTY	)	Case No.: 96T012

<u>ORDER</u>

Upon the foregoing Motion for Attorney's Fee in Lieu of Commission herein filed it is this _____ day of _____ 1996;

ORDERED by the Circuit Court for Baltimore County;

That Mary E. Crawford, guardian of the property of Dennis A. Martin, be paid the sum of Six Hundred Eighty Dollars ($680.00) as reasonable fees for services rendered as fully described in the Motion filed in this matter.

_____
JUDGE

FIGURE 15-16 Order

Discovery

After a complaint and answer have been filed and all preliminary motions ruled on, the focus of a litigator's work is on the **discovery** process. In discovery,

─────────── LEGAL TERMS ───────────

order † A determination made by a court; an order of court.

judgment † In a civil action, the final determination by a court of the rights of the parties, based upon the pleadings and the evidence; a decision.

discovery † A means for providing a party, in advance of trial, with access to facts that are within the knowledge of the other side, to enable him or her to better try his or her case.

LYNN A. LEMIRE) IN THE
     PLAINTIFF) CIRCUIT COURT
vs.) FOR
THOMAS J. LEMIRE) HARFORD COUNTY
     DEFENDANT) Case No.: 12/345/67

JUDGMENT OF DIVORCE

Plaintiff's Complaint for Absolute Divorce having come for hearing before this Court on the _____ day of November, 1996, both parties represented by counsel, and testimony heard and considered, it is this _____ day of November, 1996, by the Circuit Court for Harford County;

ADJUDGED, ORDERED and DECREED that Plaintiff, Lynn A. Lemire be and is hereby granted an absolute divorce from the Defendant, Thomas J. Lemire; and is further

ORDERED that the Agreement between the parties dated the 9th day of August, 1996, filed in these proceedings is hereby approved and incorporated by reference, but not merged, as is fully set forth herein and the parties shall abide by and perform in accordance with its terms; and is further

ORDERED that Plaintiff be, and she is hereby awarded alimony as provided for in the Agreement; and it is further

ORDERED that Plaintiff be granted the right to resume her former name, that is, Lynn A. Robinson; and it is further

ORDERED that the costs of these proceedings be equally divided between the parties.

_____
JUDGE

FIGURE 15-17 Judgment

each side hopes to obtain facts relevant to the case that are held by the other party. Generally, five discovery methods are available to an attorney: interrogatories, requests for admissions of fact and genuineness of documents, requests for production of documents and inspection of property, motions for physical or mental examination, and depositions. With the exception of depositions, all other discovery methods can be directed only at parties.

Because pleadings do not always provide the factual detail necessary to understand a case, the primary purpose of discovery is to acquire missing information that further assists in understanding the cause of action and its underlying facts. As a result, parties obtain a realistic view of their own and each other's cases through discovery. This often leads to settlement. Also, facts established and matters resolved through discovery can save time at trial. A consequence of discovery is that the element of surprise at trial, so often romanticized in movie dramas, is eliminated.

Discovery is not without limitations. All forms of discovery must limit inquiry to areas that are relevant to the case at hand. For instance, discovery asking Ms. Johnson about her political views would clearly be beyond the scope of discovery.

Also, questions cannot be asked about matters protected by the **work product doctrine**. This rule protects discussions and notes that an attorney has prepared in the course of representing a client.

The decision to use any particular form of discovery is often dictated by expense and time. Some forms, such as depositions, can be costly; others, such as interrogatories, are inexpensive. Also, discovery must be completed before a trial begins. There may be insufficient time to issue a request for production of documents and inspection of property, but a deposition can be set on a few days' notice.

Interrogatories

Interrogatories are written questions submitted by one party to another which must be answered under oath. The total number of interrogatories asked is often limited by court rule. The propounding of interrogatories is by far the most commonly utilized form of discovery. This is, in part, because forms and models can be easily accessed to develop questions. Because of this ease in preparation, drafting interrogatories is a quick and inexpensive method of discovery. Also, it is in the drafting and answering of interrogatories that paralegals play their most significant discovery role.

There are two considerations to keep in mind when preparing interrogatories. First, it is important to look at the particulars of the case in which they are being used and not rely solely on copying questions from another case or form book. Though cases may look similar, each one has its own unique facts and issues. Realize also that forms are often based on a general perspective and do not take into consideration the law of your jurisdiction. Second, avoid composing questions that require only yes or no answers. A full, detailed answer is always preferred because of the important factual information that it contains. An explicit answer may lead you to new facts and issues and as a result require you to follow up with other methods of discovery. For instance, if in an answer to an interrogatory the name of a witness is revealed, a deposition might thereafter be scheduled of this person.

Once the questions are received by the opposing attorney, she will assist her client in preparing appropriate responses. Interrogatories are very exacting and thus require detailed responses. In many firms, paralegals are exclusively assigned the role of both composing and answering interrogatories.

The instructions and definitions section is a critical component of interrogatories. (See Figure 15-18.) *Instructions* inform the receiver when a response is due and where it should be filed. The *definitions* section defines terms used throughout the interrogatories. By defining certain words or phrases at the

---

LEGAL TERMS

work product rule (doctrine) † The rule that an attorney's work product is not subject to discovery.

interrogatories † Written questions put by one party to another ... in advance of trial. Interrogatories are a form of discovery and are governed by the rules of civil procedure.

INSTRUCTIONS:

A. These interrogatories are deemed to be continuing in character, so as to also require the filing of supplementary answers after a change in any of the circumstances questioned herein, if any, and that any such supplementary answers shall also be subjected to and filed in accordance with the Maryland Rules.

B. If you fail to file complete answers to these interrogatories within thirty (30) days or fail to mail a copy of said answers to the attorney(s) for the Plaintiff(s) at the time of said filing, an order may be passed in these proceedings compelling you to complete discovery and/or imposing sanctions for your failure to do so.

C. Where knowledge, information, or possession of a party is requested, such request includes knowledge of the party's agents, representatives, and, unless privileged, his/her attorney. When an answer is made by a corporate defendant, state the name, address, and title of the person supplying the information and making the affidavit as well as the source of the person's information.

D. Where the name or identity of a person is requested, state full name, home address, and also business address, if known; otherwise, note the fact that any or all of these is unknown.

E. Unless otherwise indicated, these interrogatories refer to the time, place, and circumstances of the occurrence mentioned or complained of in the pleadings.

F. Each interrogatory shall be answered to the fullest extent of the person's present knowledge. Each interrogatory answer is to be set forth separately. Interrogatories should not be combined for the purpose of supplying a common answer thereto.

G. Where an interrogatory cannot be answered in full, state why, but furnish all available information. Estimated data should be given when, but only when, exact data cannot be supplied. Any estimated data should be identified as such. The source(s) and means of derivation of each estimate should be specifically set forth. If you do not have the information necessary to answer an interrogatory, but know where such information may be procured, the source and availability of such information shall be disclosed and the person in possession or control thereof identified with the particularity specified in clause D.,

DEFINITIONS:

a. The pronoun "you" refers to the party to whom these interrogatories are addressed, and any persons mentioned in clause D.

b. The word "document" shall include, without limitation, the original and any copy, regardless of origin or location, of any: book, pamphlet, periodical, letter, memorandum, telegram, record, business record, bill, check, receipt, invoice, note, agreement, contract, study, handwritten note, working paper, chart, paper, graph, index, tape, data sheet, data processing card, or any other written, recorded, transcribed, punched, taped, filmed, or graphic matter, however produced or reproduced.

c. "Identify" or "identity," as used herein with reference to a document, shall mean to state the date, author(s), the person(s) to whom it was directed, the type of document, its present location, the location of each copy thereof, and the identity of its custodian. If any of the above-described information is unavailable, some alternative means of identifying the document must be supplied. If any such document was, but

FIGURE 15-18 Instructions and definitions section of interrogatories

is no longer in your possession or subject to your control, state what disposition was made of it.

d. "Identify" or "identity," as used herein with reference to an individual, a corporation, or other entity (referred to hereinafter in this subsection as "person"), whether connected with description of documents, oral communications, or otherwise, shall mean to set forth the name, the present or last known home address, the present or last known employment address, the resident agent, the resident agent's address, the job title, and by whom employed, of the person or any of the areas of inquiry applicable. Once a person has been identified in an answer to an interrogatory, it shall be sufficient thereafter when identifying that person to state merely the person's name and the number of the interrogatory answer in which the person is fully identified.

e. "Date" shall mean the exact day, month, and year, if ascertainable, or, if not, the best approximation thereof, including relationship to other events.

f. The word "or" is used in its inclusive sense. If, for example, an interrogatory requests indentification of all documents indicating A or B, you should identify all documents that indicate A and all documents that indicate B, as well as all documents which indicate both A and B. In other words, "or" may be read as "and/or." Similarly, the word "any" may be read as "any and all."

FIGURE 15-18   *(continued)*

start, you make it unnecessary to repeat a meaning throughout the document every time a particular word appears. Questions can then be written more concisely, and as a result are easier to read.

To efficiently and effectively draft appropriate interrogatories, you must have complete knowledge of the client's case. Only with a full understanding of the particulars of the case can you properly determine what information is needed. Often interrogatories carelessly request information that has already been ascertained or is easily available without discovery. Because the number of interrogatories allowed is limited by court rule, it is imperative to request only information of critical importance.

The questions themselves usually fall into several categories. Some interrogatories request basic biographical information: names, addresses, telephone numbers, and work information, for example. Other interrogatories seek out factual information. For instance, Mr. Carmine's lawyer could propound an interrogatory asking specifics about Ms. Johnson's injuries. He might ask about her medical diagnosis, treatment, and prognosis. This way he can get a clearer picture of the damages she is claiming.

Factual questions can also include inquiry about potential witnesses, including those considered to be **experts**, who might be called to testify. Interrogatories can also be used to identify contentions and legal theories. Ms. Johnson's

---

LEGAL TERMS

expert †   A person who has special skill or knowledge in a given field.

attorney might ask whether Mr. Carmine is contending that Ms. Johnson was contributorily negligent.

Finally, in some jurisdictions interrogatories can be used to discover documents. For example, in the practice situation, Mr. Carmine's attorney might ask Ms. Johnson to attach medical reports to her answers to interrogatories to support her responses. In this form, the interrogatory acts as a subpoena duces tecum.

Each question must be clear and unambiguous. Otherwise, the question will be objected to on the ground of vagueness. Each question must also comply with the general discovery requirement of relevancy. See Figure 15-19 for sample interrogatories.

Request for Admissions of Fact and Genuineness of Documents

A **request for admissions of fact and genuineness of documents** is formatted like a set of interrogatories. It differs, however, in that the questions only require the receiving party to admit or deny the truthfulness of various statements or the authenticity of specified documents. (See Figure 15-20.)

The importance of requests for admissions lies in their ability to resolve disputed issues before trial. If parties can admit to certain facts prior to trial, there will be no need to prove these matters at trial, thereby saving costs and time. For instance, Ms. Johnson might request that Mr. Carmine either admit or deny the fact that he owned the vehicle he was operating at the time of the action. If admitted, this point would not have to be proven at trial.

Request for Production of Documents and Inspection of Property

Through a form of discovery known as a **request for production of documents and inspection of property**, a party can gain access to documents and other items that are not currently in that party's possession for purposes of inspection, examination, and copying. In a production of documents, one attorney submits a list of items she desires to inspect. A date, time, and place is scheduled for the inspection when a representative of the requesting attorney (possibly the paralegal) reviews and copies any relevant documents. A production of documents can also request the inspection of property, including personal effects and real property. (See Figure 15-21.)

LEGAL TERMS
---

request for admission † Written statements concerning a case, directed to an adverse party, that he or she is required to admit or deny. Such admissions or denials will be treated by the court as having been established, and need not be proven at trial.

request for production of documents and inspection of property A discovery request that certain documents be provided or property be inspected.

1. Identify all persons who were eyewitnesses to all or any part of the occurrence, and state the location of such person at the time of the occurrence.

2. Identify all persons (other than those identified in your answer to the previous Interrogatory) who arrived at the scene of the occurrence within two hours after its happening.

3. Identify all persons whom you expect to call as expert witnesses at trial, and for each such expert state the subject matter on which the expert is expected to testify, the substance of the findings and opinions to which the expert is expected to testify and a summary of the grounds for each opinion; also, attach to your answers copies of all written reports of such expert concerning those findings and opinions.

4. Identify all persons who have investigated the occurrence or its consequences.

5. Identify all persons who have given written or recorded statements concerning the subject matter of this action, state the date of each such statement, identify the person taking the statement, and identify its present custodian.

6. State whether you are aware of any written or oral statement concerning the subject matter of this action made by this party or any agent, representative or employee of this party; if so, state the substance of each such statement, the place and date when that statement was made, and identify the person making the statement, the person to whom it was made, and all documents concerning the statement.

7. Identify all persons having or claiming a subrogation interest in the outcome of this litigation and, for each such person, state the alleged dollar value of that subrogation interest.

8. Identify all persons not identified in your answers to the other Interrogatories who have personal knowledge of facts pertinent to the subject matter of this litigation.

FIGURE 15-19 Interrogatories. (Reproduced with permission of Michie Butterworth.)

Motion for Physical or Mental Examination

Should the mental or physical condition of a party be at issue in a case, the opposition might request that party to undergo an examination by medical

Case II. Slip and Fall

NO. 2

DEFENDANT'S REQUESTS

to

Plaintiff—Fall While Boarding Aircraft

THE FACTS

Plaintiff brought an action to recover for injuries sustained while boarding defendant's aircraft. The court dismissed the action after finding it was barred by the applicable statute of limitations.

Summary of Form

Details of Flight (Q's 1–3)
Circumstances of Accident (Q 4)
Plaintiff Attended by Stewardess (Q 5)
Plaintiff Taken to Hospital (Q 6)

> [*Names of court and parties, description of action, introduction, and usual formal parts, see* CAPTIONS AND FORMAL PARTS.]

Details of Flight

1. On _____, 19____, the plaintiff purchased a ticket from _____ at _____ for Flight No. _____ to _____, ticket No. _____.

2. _____, plaintiff, was a passenger on board said Flight and did travel from _____ to _____ on _____ Airlines.

3. On _____, after having traveled on _____ Flight No. _____ from _____ to _____, landing at the _____ Airport, plaintiff debarked from the plane in

FIGURE 15-20 Request for admissions. (Reproduced with permission of Matthew Bender and Co., Inc. Further reproduction without permission is strictly prohibited.)

4. At the time of plaintiff's accident defendant had exclusive control of every part of the store.

5. A shopping cart to which defendant had title was being pushed by _____, an employee of defendant, who was acting within the scope of his employment and who was operating the cart with the consent of defendant.

Accident

6. The cart struck plaintiff on the back, hip, and leg.

7. Immediately prior to the cart's striking plaintiff the employee lost control of the cart.

8. Prior to plaintiff's being struck, no one warned him of the cart's approach.

9. The accident was in no way caused by plaintiff's negligence.

FIGURE 15-20 *(continued)*

personnel. This request is made by motion and consequently must be agreed to by the court. Because the request is often strongly opposed, the moving party must provide the judge with sufficient justification for ordering a **physical or mental examination**. (See Figure 15-22.)

This motion is often made in personal injury litigation, where it is common practice to request that the plaintiff be examined by a physician designated by the defendant. This could easily apply to the Johnson-Carmine case. When parents litigate the issue of custody of their children, one party may allege that the other is mentally unfit. In that case, an examination by a mental health professional may be appropriate.

Deposition

A **deposition** is an oral rendering of testimony given outside of a courtroom. The participants are the attorney requesting the deposition, the person being

---
LEGAL TERMS
---

motion for physical or mental examination A discovery motion requesting the court to order an evaluation of a party by medical personnel.

deposition † The transcript of a witness's testimony given under oath outside of the courtroom, usually in advance of the trial or hearing, upon oral examination or in response to written interrogatories.

PLAINTIFFS' REQUEST FOR PRODUCTION OF DOCUMENTS—ACTION ALLEGING DENIAL OF DUE PROCESS IN WITHHOLDING OF DIPLOMA FOR FAILURE TO PAY SCHOOL FEES

UNITED STATES DISTRICT COURT
_____ DISTRICT OF _____

_____ DIVISION

Civil Action No. _____

(*Title of Action*)

Plaintiffs' Request for Production of Documents

Pursuant to Rule 34 of the Federal Rules of Civil Procedure, the plaintiffs hereby request that the defendants produce and permit counsel to inspect and copy the following documents at the offices of defendant _____ beginning at _____ on Thursday, _____:

1. All documents regarding plaintiff _____.

2. All documents regarding all high school students since _____ who have attended or presently attend school within the _____ School District in _____ and who have unpaid school fees.

3. All documents which relate in any manner to _____ School District in _____'s school policy, practice or custom concerning the withholding of any educational benefit due to nonpayment of school fees.

Dated at _____ this _____ day of _____, 19____.

_____
Attorney for Plaintiffs

(*Certificate of Service*)

FIGURE 15-21 Request for production of documents. (Reproduced with permission of Matthew Bender and Co., Inc. Further reproduction without permission is strictly prohibited.)

State of Maryland

Circuit Court for the County of _____

_____

[Plaintiff (Name 1)]

Case No. _____

v.

Docket No. _____

_____

[Defendant (Name 2)]

Hon. _____

[Judge]

Defendant's Motion to Compel Examination

Defendant, by counsel, pursuant to Md Rule 2-423, moves the court to enter its order compelling Plantiff _____ to submit to a physical examination by a

[Name 1]

physician, based on the following grounds:

1. Plaintiff's complaint alleges that as a result of Defendant's negligence, Plaintiff

_____ sustained continuing and permanent injury and loss of function to his

[Name 1]

left knee.

2. Defendant denies that Plaintiff sustained any injury as a proximate cause of Defendant's negligence and therefore Plaintiff's alleged physical condition is in controversy.

3. Defendant seeks to confirm or deny the existence and extent of Plaintiff's alleged left knee injury in order to evaluate and defend against Plaintiff's claim.

4. Given the physical condition alleged by Plaintiff and denied by Defendant, good cause exists for compelling Plaintiff to submit to an independent physical examination.

5. [If applicable] Plaintiff previously rejected Defendant's request to stipulate to the entry of the order sought by this motion and is therefore subject to assessment of

FIGURE 15-22 Motion for examination

costs and reasonable attorney fees pursuant to Md Rule 2-433. A copy of the

proposed order and affidavit establishing the rejection are attached.

_____
[Date]

_____

_____
[Attorney (Bar No.)]
Attorney for Defendant

[Certificate of Service]

FIGURE 15-22 *(continued)*

deposed (called the **deponent**), that person's lawyer or the lawyer for the other side, and a court reporter.

The deposition has significant benefits over other forms of discovery. Because it is live, the attorney gets an opportunity to evaluate the credibility of potential trial witnesses. She also obtains an understanding of the other attorney's style and techniques. Unlike other forms of discovery, a deposition can be taken of a party or a nonparty. Also, there is no set limit on the number of questions that can be asked of a deponent. In fact, many depositions take several days to complete.

The major disadvantage of depositions is their expense. This is caused by two factors. Though a paralegal might assist an attorney in preparing questions for a deponent, only an attorney can ask questions during a deposition. In other forms of discovery, paralegals, whose billable time usually costs considerably less than attorneys', do much of the work. Also, a court reporter must take verbatim testimony by stenographic shorthand. After the deposition, the reporter converts her shorthand into a transcript. It is not uncommon for a court reporter's fee for a two-hour deposition and transcript preparation to be several hundred dollars. This multiplied over several depositions can be quite costly for a client of modest means.

SIDEBAR

CAN A PARALEGAL TAKE A DEPOSITION?

The ethical opinion by the Pennsylvania Bar Association in Figure 15-23 addresses the issue of whether a paralegal who is also a third-year law student can take a deposition if all the involved participants agree.

LEGAL TERMS

deponent [†]   1. A person who gives a deposition. 2. A person who gives sworn testimony in any form; an affiant; a witness.

Paralegals are often requested to assist in the deposition process in two ways. First, they may assist in the preparation of questions to be asked of a deponent. For this, you will need to know the case extensively, especially the legal theory that is the basis of the client's position. Secondly, a paralegal can be asked to **digest** or summarize the transcript of a deposition. In digesting the deposition, you are asked to carefully examine the deposition and extract important concepts

---

Inquiry No. 91-137

You requested an opinion from the PBA Committee on Legal Ethics and Professional Responsibility concerning an experienced litigation paralegal's acting on an attorney's behalf at deposition of a client. According to your letter, you anticipate the paralegal's role at the deposition to include making objections, advising the client, and performing examination of the client as necessary. In addressing your inquiry, I have assumed approval of the judge, opposing counsel, and the client and availability of the attorney. Further, I have considered the paralegal's experience, in the area of law and in the office, and current status as a third year law student ranking fifth in his class. Nonetheless, I conclude that the paralegal's performance of the anticipated duties would constitute an ethical violation.

Such conduct on the part of a paralegal would be proscribed by Formal Opinion No. 87-127. In that opinion, the Committee concluded that a paralegal's conducting a deposition, following a pre-determined series of questions, would be unethical in that the need for lawyer functions, such as advising the witness or objecting to opposing counsel's conduct, could arise. The Committee stated that "[i]t is our opinion that each of these functions are uniquely lawyer functions and are not functions which can be engaged in by the paralegal." The anticipated duties addressed in your inquiry constitute lawyer functions which the Committee has previously determined cannot be performed by a paralegal.

The fact that the paralegal in question is a third year law student ranking fifth in his class does not affect the answer to your inquiry. In Formal Opinion 86-97, the Committee commented on the activities which a law student who had taken the Pennsylvania Bar Exam could engage in while awaiting the results. Excluding a Certified Legal Intern Program, as prescribed by Pa.B.A.R. 321 and Pa.B.A.R. 322, the Committee concluded that a law student may perform certain enumerated duties which do not involve the student's being held out as being an attorney or as being capable of rendering legal advice. Since your inquiry does not involve a Certified Legal Intern Program and since the anticipated duties involve the law student's rendering legal advice, such actions would also run contrary to Formal Opinion 86-97.

Permitting the paralegal to perform the duties outlined in the inquiry would also violate Rule 5.5 of the Pennsylvania Rules of Professional Conduct. The Rule provides, in pertinent part:

A lawyer shall not:

(a) aid a non-lawyer in the unauthorized practice of law ... .

FIGURE 15-23 Pennsylvania Bar opinion

LEGAL TERMS

digest [†]   To understand or synthesize.

Rule 5.5.

The Supreme Court of Pennsylvania has been vested with the power to govern the practice of law within the Commonwealth. Pa. Const. art. V, § 10(c). The Court has noted that delimiting the practice of law to those who are authorized to do so is for the protection of the public's interest in competent legal representation. *Dauphin County Bar Ass'n v. Mazzacaro*, 465 Pa. 545, ___ , 351 A.2d 229, 233 (1976). Judgments requiring an understanding of legal principles and a skill for applying those principles constitute the practice of law. *Id.*

Since the anticipated duties alluded to in the inquiry require an understanding of various legal principles and their applications, such conduct on the part of a lay person would constitute an unauthorized practice of law.[1] Condonation of this conduct on the part of an attorney would, therefore, violate Rule 5.5(a).[2]

Thus, the paralegal referred to in the inquiry may not act on the attorney's behalf at a client's deposition. Such conduct is proscribed by Formal Opinion #87-127, Formal Opinion #86-97, and Rule 5.5(a) of the Pennsylvania Rules of Professional Conduct.

Caveat: Each person requesting an opinion from this Committee must be informed that this is not an official opinion of the Disciplinary Board of the Supreme Court of Pennsylvania and that any opinion rendered will be afforded only as much weight as the reviewing authority may choose to give it. Furthermore, this is the opinion of only one member of the Committee and is not a formal opinion of the full Committee.

------

[1] This conduct is also subject to penalization by the legislature:

> Any person who within this Commonwealth shall practice law, or who shall hold himself out to the public as being entitled to practice law ... without being an attorney at law ... commits a misdemeanor of the third degree.

42 Pa.C.S.A. § 2524 (Supp. 1991).

[2] The attorney would also thereby violate Rule 8.4(a) which states:

> It is professional misconduct for a lawyer to:
>
> (a) Violate or attempt to violate the rules of professional conduct, knowingly assist or induce another to do so, or do so through the acts of another ... .

FIGURE 15-23 *(continued)*

and points that may be relevant at trial. These points are then categorized or indexed in a method considered useful by the attorney requesting the digest.

A deposition is initiated when a request for deposition is filed with the court. If the deposition is of a party, the request is sufficient. A subpoena, however, is necessary if a nonparty is to be deposed. Often a subpoena duces tecum is issued, requiring that the deponent bring certain documents with him to the deposition. Finally, a recent trend is for depositions is to taken by videotape. This may be necessary when it is important to retain the realism of the deponent's responses. (See Figure 15-24.)

State of Maryland

Health Claims Arbitration Office

_____

[Claimant (Name 1)]

    V.

_____ and

[Respondent (Name 2)]

HCA No. _____

_____

[Respondent (Name 3)]

Notice To Take Videotape Deposition

Notice is given, pursuant to the Maryland Rules, that the videotape deposition, upon

oral examination, of _____ will be taken for purposes of use at trial,
                        [Name 1]

pursuant to Md Rule 2-419(a)(4), on _____ , _____ , at _____ ,
                               [Day]   [Date]   [Time]

at the law offices of _____ , _____ , before a Notary Public, or
                   [Firm]   [Street Address]

some other officer authorized by law.

_____

_____

[Attorney (Bar No.)]

_____

[Street Address]

_____

[City, State ZIP]

_____

[Telephone No.]

Certificate of Service

I certify that on _____ a copy of the foregoing Notice to Take Videotape
                  [Date]

Deposition was sent by first class mail, postage prepaid, to _____ ,
                                         [Name 4]

FIGURE 15-24 Request for deposition

_____ , _____ , Attorney for Defendant, _____ , and to
   [Firm]   [Street Address]   [Name 2]

_____ , _____ , _____ , Attorney for _____ .
   [Name 5]   [Firm]   [Street Address]   [Name 3]

_____

_____
[Attorney (Bar No.)]

_____
[Street Address]

_____
[City, State ZIP]

_____
[Telephone No.]

FIGURE 15-24 _(continued)_

Discovery Enforcement Motions

There are three motions that can be used specifically in discovery situations. If a person believes that discovery is causing annoyance, embarrassment, oppression, undue burden, or expense, that person can file a **motion for a protective order**. In this motion, the person indicates the specific reasons he feels that discovery is inappropriate. The court then either denies discovery or provides a middle course whereby the individual is protected and some discovery is still provided.

Secondly, a party that fails to comply with requests for discovery can be subject to a **motion to compel discovery**. Through this motion, a party requests the court to issue an order requiring that discovery be held at a specific time and the consequences for failure to provide discovery.

Finally, in a **motion for sanctions**, a party requests that specific sanctions or punitive measures be taken against the opposing party for failure to provide discovery. Examples of not providing discovery might include not attending a

———————————————— **LEGAL TERMS** ————————————————

motion for protective order   A motion filed when discovery is intrusive.

protective order [†]   An order of court protecting a person from harassment by excessive discovery, process, or the like; it is requested by a party by means of a motion for protective order.

motion to compel discovery   A motion asking a court to order that discovery be provided.

motion for sanctions   A motion requesting that certain punitive measures be taken against a party who fails to provide discovery.

sanction [†]   1. Action taken by a tribunal ... by way of enforcing its judgment, decision, or order. ... 3. A punishment; a penalty.

deposition or failing to comply with a request for production of documents. Requested measures can include the preclusion of certain evidence at trial or the assessment of attorney fees. Often a motion for sanctions cannot be filed until an order on the motion to compel has been issued and then violated.

Forms, Models, and Checklists

Most of the examples used in this chapter are from form books devoted to pleadings and discovery documents. For paralegals, these sources provide invaluable guidance in the preparation of court documents. In fact, often drafting a pleading consists of completing a freestanding form (see Figure 15-25). Because pleading rules vary from state to state, the better publications are locally published. Examples of well-respected national publications include *Am. Jur. Pleading and Practice Forms, Revised,* published by Lawyers Cooperative, and *Forms of Discovery,* published by Matthew Bender. Remember, though: when using a form, make sure to check it against the law of your jurisdiction, and do not automatically include unfamiliar phrases unless you know their meaning and consequences.

Of course, personally created models are also an excellent source for preparing a pleading or discovery document. Once you have created a document that you feel can be used again, keep a copy in an easily accessible resource file.

Paralegal Tip

Court files are public records open to review by any individual. If you are at a loss as to how to create a document, approach a pleadings clerk at the courthouse and ask whether she knows of a model that might be helpful as guidance. Many court employees will be glad to give you a reference to a file containing documents that can be used as models in your case. Because these documents are filed publicly and not copyrighted, using them as models is not considered unethical activity. Use discretion, however, with the personal information you uncover. Though not privileged, there is still the expectation that only court officials will have knowledge of these matters.

Summary

- Pleadings, motions, and discovery documents are all governed by court rules, which cover substance, style, and format.

- Though court documents must be truthful, a lawyer might use language that presents her client in a sympathetic light.

- The plain English movement has made only modest gains when it comes to preparing court documents.

- Each litigation document must have a caption and title.

RW-3

IN THE ORPHANS' COURT FOR _____

BEFORE THE REGISTER OF WILLS FOR _____

In the Matter of: _____ Estate No. _____

Date _____

PETITION FOR PROBATE

The Petition of _____
            Name   Address

_____
            Name   Address

_____
            Name   Address

each being a citizen of the United States and of legal age, shows:

1. _____, the decedent who

was domiciled in _____ County, State of _____

died on the _____ day of _____, 19_____.

2. Petitioner is entitled to be personal representative of the decedent's estate because:

_____

_____

3. This is the proper office in which to file the petition because: _____

_____

4. Petitioner has made a diligent search for a will and to the best of his knowledge: (a) none exists (b) the will dated _____ accompanying this petition is the last will and it came into petitioner's hands in the following manner: _____

_____

5. Attached is a ☐ list of all interested persons and their addresses OR ☐ list setting forth: (a) the names and relationships to the decedent of all heirs (that is, surviving spouse and children, and, if none, all other persons who would inherit if there were no will) and legatees (persons who take under the will) and

    (b) the names and addresses of the witness to the will.

6. All other proceedings regarding the decedent's estate are as follows: _____

_____

_____

7. The reasons why any information required to be furnished in this petition has not been furnished are as follows:

_____

_____

8. Petitioner accepts the duties of the office of personal representative and consents to personal jurisdiction in any action brought in this State.

WHEREFORE, the petitioner prays that he be granted letters appointing him personal representative of the decedent's estate and that the will, if any, be admitted to (administrative) (judicial) probate, and that the following additional relief be granted: _____

_____

Petitioner solemnly declares and affirms under the penalties of perjury that the above information and representations are true and correct to the best of his knowledge, information and belief.

_____   _____
Attorney for Estate   Petitioner

_____   _____
Address   Petitioner

_____   _____
Phone Number   Petitioner

                                              Phone Number _____

            Personalty (approximate value) $ _____   Unsecured Debts

            Real (approximate value) $ _____   (approximate value) $ _____

FOR REGISTER'S USE ONLY

Safekeeping Wills _____ Custody of Wills _____ Petition Docket _____

            Bond Set $_____

                     Deputy _____

FIGURE 15-25 Freestanding probate form

- All documents filed in court must be signed by an attorney and often by the client.

- A certificate of service is required on court documents.

- The complaint, answer, counterclaim, cross-claim, and third-party complaint are referred to as pleadings. Pleadings set forth specific legal and factual allegations that constitute or defend against a cause of action. The two philosophies employed today in pleading are known as fact pleading and notice pleading.

- A complaint, the initial pleading filed in a case, includes a statement as to the cause of action, facts necessary to support the cause of action, and relief requested.

- An answer responds to the allegations presented in the complaint.

- If an answer or motion is not filed, a default judgment could be entered.

- In a counterclaim, a defendant makes allegations against the plaintiff.

- A cross-claim is brought by a defendant against a co-defendant.

- In a third-party complaint, a defendant alleges that an individual not presently a party is responsible for alleged injury.

- A motion is a written application to a court for specific relief.

- Preliminary motions are filed after the complaint is served but before an answer is required.

- A motion for summary judgment is filed when a party believes that there is no dispute as to facts and that the parties are entitled to a judgment as a matter of law.

- Other documents include a summons, which is filed with a complaint; a subpoena, which commands an individual to attend a hearing; and a proof of service, which is completed by a process server.

- A judgment is prepared by a court after a trial.

- An order is a court's decision on a motion.

- Through discovery, each side in litigation obtains information about the other side's case.

- Interrogatories are written questions submitted by one party to another which must be answered under oath.

- In a request for admissions and genuineness of documents, one party requests the other to admit or deny the truthfulness of certain statements or documents.

- In a request for production of documents and inspection of property, one party requests the other party to provide records for inspection and copying or to permit the viewing of certain property.

- Should a party feel that another party's physical or mental state is at issue, she can file a motion for an examination.

- A deposition is an oral rendering of testimony outside of a courtroom.

- A motion for protective order is filed when one party feels that discovery is intrusive or burdensome.

- A motion to compel discovery is filed to require a party to provide discovery.

- In a motion for sanctions, one party requests that certain punitive measures be taken against the opposing party for failure to provide discovery.

- Forms, models, and checklists are frequently used to prepare pleadings, motions, and discovery documents.

Review Questions

1. What is a certificate of service?

2. List the documents that are considered pleadings.

3. Describe the difference between fact pleading and notice pleading.

4. What are the component parts of a complaint?

5. What is an affirmative defense? Provide an example of one.

6. When would a default judgment be entered?

7. What are the differences among a counterclaim, a cross-claim, and a third-party complaint?

8. When would a motion for summary judgment be filed with the court?

9. List the five forms of discovery.

10. What is the purpose of the definitions section of a set of interrogatories?

11. Compare and contrast a request for admissions of fact and genuineness of documents and a production of documents and inspection of property.

12. How can a paralegal assist in preparing for a deposition?

13. What is the purpose of a motion for protective order?

Chapter Exercises

1. Locate your state's pleading rules. What affirmative defenses are permitted? When must an answer be filed in your state?

2. Draft five interrogatories that might be prepared by Mr. Carmine's lawyer in the paralegal practice situation.

3. What types of documents would Mr. Carmine's lawyer want Ms. Johnson to produce based on a request for production of documents and inspection of property?

4. Locate your state's pleading rules. Does your state permit the videotaping of a deposition?

CHAPTER 16

LITIGATION MEMORANDA AND APPELLATE BRIEFS

CHAPTER OUTLINE Litigation Memorandum

Appellate Brief

OVERVIEW

The outcome of a lawsuit often depends on the sufficiency of legal authority submitted to the court in oral or written form. Oral argument is a matter of trial advocacy—the subject of a different text. When authority is in written form, it is presented in one of two different documents: at the trial court level, in a *litigation memorandum;* and at the appellate court level, in an *appellate brief.*

At the trial court level, factual and legal arguments are summarily presented in pleadings and motions. Should a particular position require a detailed factual and legal discussion, a litigation memorandum would be prepared. A litigation memorandum is often referred to as a *trial memorandum,* an *external memorandum of law,* a *memorandum of points and authorities,* or a *trial brief.*

When a party feels that a trial court ruled unjustly in its case, that party might opt to file an appeal in a higher court. In such a situation, an appellate brief would be filed with the appropriate appellate court. The appellate brief presents, in highly analytical fashion, the legal authority needed to convince an appeals court that the trial court was in error in its decision and that a reversal of the decision is therefore warranted.

Both the litigation memorandum and the appellate brief are discussed in detail in this chapter.

PARALEGAL PRACTICE SITUATION

Recall from Chapter 13 that your firm represented the Perpetual Insurance Company and Mr. and Mrs. Antonio Fulwood. In that case, Jamal Brown brought suit against Mr. and Mrs. Fulwood for injuries sustained in their swimming pool. Assume that suit has been filed by Jamal Brown. The Fulwoods' attorney has decided to file a motion for summary judgment to have Mr. Brown's lawsuit dismissed. She would like to file a litigation memorandum in support of her motion. You have been assigned to assist in the preparation of a preliminary draft of this document.

Litigation Memorandum

To support a motion's factual and legal arguments with primary law, an attorney would prepare a **litigation memorandum**. This is sometimes referred to as a *memorandum of points and authorities* because it asserts particular legal points and supports each one with legal authorities. Some jurisdictions call this document a *trial memorandum* because it is often filed during a trial. It is also called an *external memorandum of law* because it is designed for those outside the office. Some jurisdictions use the term *trial brief* to describe any document arguing the facts and law of a case in detail. The phrase *litigation memorandum* is used here because, regardless of its localized name, this document is employed in litigation.

──────────── **LEGAL TERMS** ────────────

litigation memorandum A memorandum filed with a trial court.

Even though nomenclature varies, the characteristics of these memoranda are consistent. First, they are usually filed in support of motions. On some occasions, a memorandum might be filed at the request of a judge during trial without an accompanying motion, but this is rare. Second, because they are filed with a court, memoranda are governed by the same court rules and format conventions that govern pleadings and motions. Third, memoranda are highly analytical documents and thus attorneys rather than paralegals frequently have the primary responsibility for preparing them. The paralegal's role in drafting a memorandum will depend on its complexity as well as the paralegal's experience. Finally, because memoranda are filed with a court, they always take a partisan and adversarial stance as to the law and the facts of the case.

Purposes

The overall purpose of litigation memoranda is to put in writing a complex argument and to present it in such a way that it is favorably viewed by the court. Because motions generally discuss facts and law in a cursory fashion, a memorandum is often needed to "put meat on the bones" by providing the court with the detailed facts and authority necessary to warrant a favorable decision.

A litigation memorandum breaks down an intricate argument into easily understood component parts, each part supported by specific legal authority. This makes it easier for the court to appreciate the argument. A judge can focus on one point, obtain an understanding, then see how this relates to other points. It also assists the attorney in crystallizing his own position. Often lawyers only have a "gut feeling" for an issue when preparing a motion. By preparing a memorandum, the attorney himself digests the argument. As a result, the memo raises his confidence level in his abilities and in the position he has taken.

Frequently an attorney will feel that a motion in and of itself is sufficient to convince a court of her position. Or she may feel that what she lacks in the motion, she can compensate for through oral argument in open court. For these reasons, the vast majority of motions are filed without accompanying memoranda. However, an attorney may feel compelled to prepare a memorandum either when oral argument is unavailable or when her position is so complex that a detailed written argument is needed, even if there will be an opportunity to make an oral argument.

In recent years, many judges have complained about the proliferation of memoranda filed in cases. Most judges believe that when dealing with basic procedural issues, an attorney can make a better argument orally than in writing. A judge would rather listen to a live argument, with witnesses, emotion, and oral eloquence, than read a 50-page memorandum that puts her to sleep! A lawyer should realize that a judge may form a poor impression of him if he files a memorandum in a situation that does not merit one. Additionally, memoranda rarely go unchallenged. If one side files one, the other side will feel compelled to file a countermemorandum. "Papering" the opposition ad infinitum is not an ethical way to practice law.

Guidelines

When a litigation memorandum is appropriate, the following preparation guidelines should be strictly adhered to.

Be Short and Concise

The judge reviewing the memorandum is almost certainly a busy person. She may have little time to review a long and tedious litigation memorandum. In fact, many judges assign the responsibility for reading many memoranda to their law clerks. The shorter the memo, the better the chance that the judge herself will read it. Memos should be concise, short, and to the point. To be concise does not mean eliminating needed detail. Rather, it means choosing words carefully and not wasting time on matters that are unimportant to the reader. Also, only relevant material and precise language should be used in discussing facts and legal principles.

Follow the Rules of Logical Development

Recall the discussion on logical development from Chapter 11. These suggestions should also be followed when preparing litigation memoranda. Most memoranda follow the IRAC block paragraph method of analysis: issue, rule, application/analysis, and conclusion. However, other block paragraph forms can be used effectively. In the section of the memorandum that addresses facts, a chronological presentation should be employed.

Rephrase Rather Than Recopy Legal Authority

In the argument section of a litigation memorandum, legal authority is presented to support the legal position. However, as with research memoranda, these principles should be indicated not as direct quotes, but rather rephrased in a readable style. Remember to correctly cite all authority used.

Occasionally, it may be worth quoting directly when the material is precisely on point. You should quote case material directly when you cannot say better in your own words what the judge has indicated. Statutes and regulations are more frequently quoted verbatim. When they are quoted, strategically use ellipses to eliminate irrelevant provisions. Generally, quoted material is more difficult to read than the same material paraphrased, so use direct quotes sparingly. Of course, quoted material must also be cited.

Maintain a Partisan But Honest Third-Person Style

Only in correspondence is first-person narrative permitted. In litigation memoranda, the third person should be maintained. More importantly, because it is an adversarial document, the client's position and situation should be presented in a positive light. This follows the general characteristics of pleadings discussed in Chapter 15. Notwithstanding, the law must always be accurately recounted and the facts presented truthfully. Otherwise, the attorney may be accused of being less than honest with the court.

Applications

Memoranda can be prepared in a number of typical litigation situations. Suppose, as in the paralegal practice situation, that a motion for summary judgment is being filed by the defendant's counsel. The attorney has a sense that the plaintiff's acts constitute either contributory negligence or assumption of risk. He knows that the judge will not accept this argument without legal authority to support it. Though there will be oral argument on the motion, the complexity of the motion indicates a need for the memorandum.

Assumption of risk and contributory negligence are comprised of a number of elements, which can be discussed in detail in a litigation memorandum. In contributory negligence, the defendant alleges that the plaintiff has been negligent; that is, that the plaintiff breached a duty that contributed to the injury or loss for which the plaintiff is suing defendant. The assumption of risk doctrine contemplates a plaintiff who, with knowledge that a specific risk existed, entered that situation of his own free will and as a result was injured. The memorandum provides the framework for a discussion of these elements, thereby making it easier for the judge to fully understand the legal argument.

In the vast majority of situations, memoranda are filed to support or oppose the legal positions taken in motions. Because a memorandum presents legal authorities in support of a legal argument, it is considered only by the judge and not by the jury. Sometimes, during the course of litigation, a judge may be required to rule on a matter, but would like to consider written arguments by counsel before proceeding. In that case, she might request that counsel submit opposing memoranda of law.

Format and Contents

Though court rules place general restrictions on litigation memoranda, there are actually few rules that deal with their specific format and set-up. In fact, many state rule schemes do not even acknowledge the existence of memoranda. Just the same, local custom and practice have resulted in the emergence of guidelines.

Though the precise format will vary from jurisdiction to jurisdiction and even from office to office, most litigation memorandum include the following components. (Use the complete sample memorandum in Figure 16-1 to follow and identify these elements.)

MARK F. BROWN, JR.	)	IN THE
PLAINTIFF	)	CIRCUIT COURT
v.	)	FOR
MELISSA R. BROWN	)	BALTIMORE COUNTY
DEFENDANT	)	Case No. 12/96/12CSP34

MEMORANDUM IN SUPPORT OF DEFENDANT'S MOTION TO STRIKE JUDGMENT

Melissa R. Brown, Defendant, through her attorney David J. Smith, respectfully submits this memorandum in support of her Motion to Strike Judgment filed in this matter.

STATEMENT OF FACTS

On February 10, 1996 a Judgment of Absolute Divorce was granted to Plaintiff by the Honorable Preston L. Black. That under the terms of the judgment, care and custody of the parties' minor child, Robert Neil Brown, date of birth June 2, 1994, was granted to Defendant.

Subsequently, a Petition for Visitation by Grandparents was filed by Plaintiff's parents on or about January 12, 1997. In addition, a Complaint for Modification of Decree to Change Custody was filed by Plaintiff on or about February 25, 1997.

Defendant had in the interim moved with her child from Maryland to York County, Pennsylvania. She has lived uninterrupted in Pennsylvania since October, 1996.

Upon service of the petition and complaint, Defendant retained Catherine Anne Jones, Esquire, of York, Pennsylvania. Not being a member of the bar of Maryland, Jones attempted to obtain admission *pro hac vice* in Maryland. Her request was denied by the Honorable James M. Johnston on May 12, 1997. Thereafter, Defendant was without counsel, and as a consequence represented herself in proper person. However, she received no hearing date notices, pleadings, or other court papers regarding this matter from the clerk's office of the Circuit Court for Baltimore County.

A hearing was held on Plaintiff's Complaint for Modification of Decree to Change Custody and the Petition for Visitation by Grandparents on July 7, 1997. Said hearing was *ex parte,* in that neither Defendant nor counsel were present on her behalf. Recommendations were made by the hearing examiner which were incorporated into a judgment signed by the Honorable Margaret W. O'Reilly on July 13, 1997. The first time Defendant received the judgment of July 13, 1997 was when Plaintiff filed a Petition for Contempt on or about August 26, 1998.

ISSUE

In that Defendant never received notice of the hearing of July 7, 1997, due to an error of the clerk of court, is she entitled to have the judgment entered on July 13, 1997 stricken?

SHORT ANSWER

Defendant is entitled to have the judgment stricken. Md. Code Ann., Cts. & Jud. Proc. § 6-408 (1989) grants the court revisory power in cases in which a court employee fails to perform a duty required by rule. Maryland case law provides that the remedy for the failure of a clerk of court to send out a copy of a judgment as required

FIGURE 16-1 Litigation memorandum

by rule is to revise the judgment. Because Defendant also failed to receive a copy of the notice for the hearing where the judgment was issued, the only proper and reasonable remedy is to have the judgment stricken.

ARGUMENT

Md. Rule 2-535 provides in part that "[o]n motion of any party filed at any time, the court may exercise revisory power and control over the judgment in case of fraud, mistake, or irregularity." Md. Code Ann., Cts. & Jud. Proc. § 6-408 (1989) reiterates what is provided in Md. Rule 2-535 and in addition gives the court revisory power in the event of a "failure of an employee of the court or of the clerk's office to perform a duty required by statute or rule." This provision has been held to supersede Md. Rule 2-535. *Pacific Mortgage & Investment Group, Ltd. v. Wienecke,* 50 Md. App. 128, 436 A.2d 499 (1981). Finally, Md. Rule 1-324 provides, "[u]pon entry on the docket of any order or ruling of the court ... the clerk shall send a copy of the order or ruling to all parties entitled to service under Rule 1-321." Md. Rule 1-321 permits service upon an attorney who has entered his appearance on behalf of a client.

Defendant's argument is that the clerk failed to comply with Md. Rule 1-324 by not providing her with a copy of the judgment of July 14, 1997, as well as with the notice for the hearing that resulted in the order. As a result, she should be entitled to have the judgment stricken.

The Court of Special Appeals in *Government Employees Insurance Co. v. Ropka,* 74 Md. App. 249, 536 A.2d 1214 (1988) held that the trial court had authority to revise its judgment in order to give a party which had not received a copy of an original order an opportunity to appeal. In that case a suit was brought by personal representatives of several decedents against Conrail and the Pennsylvania Department of Transportation. *Id.* at 253, 536 A.2d at 1215. In addition, defendants filed a third-party claim against the estate of the driver of the vehicle, seeking contribution. The estate demanded that Government Employees Insurance Company (GEICO) defend against the third-party claim. GEICO refused to defend and brought a declaratory judgment action seeking a declaration that a policy exclusion was valid and that GEICO therefore would not be required to defend on the merits. The Court held the exclusion void as against public policy, and that GEICO would be required to defend and pay any judgment arising out of the third-party case. The 30-day appeal period ran without GEICO taking an appeal. Thereafter, GEICO filed a Motion to Revise Enrolled Judgment. The attorney for GEICO filed affidavits with the court stating they had not received copies of the judgment finding the exclusion void. The trial court granted that motion. *Id.* at 253, 536 A.2d at 1216.

In finding the trial court's decision a correct one, Judge Alpert, writing for the majority, held that "the express provision for notice to the litigants overrides our often stated proposition that it is the duty of the defendant to keep [him]self informed as to what [is] occurring in the case." *Id.* The Court found that GEICO had met its burden of proving that a copy of the judgment had not been sent to its counsel. In reviewing the circumstances, the Court noted:

> The notation on the docket stated that copies of the order were sent to "Plaintiff's Attorney" and "Defendant's Attorney," both in the singular. Thus, the docket entry appears to confirm GEICO's claim that copies of the order were mailed to only two of the three parties who should have received them.

Id.

FIGURE 16-1   *(continued)*

The Court of Special Appeals dealt with the problem of the failure of a party to receive court notice in *Dypski v. Bethlehem Steel Corp.*, 74 Md. App. 684, 539 A.2d 1165 (1988). Here the plaintiff took an appeal from a worker's compensation commission ruling to the Circuit Court for Baltimore City. Thereafter, the case was dormant for one year, so a notice was sent by the clerk indicating that dismissal would take place under Md. Rule 2-507. The plaintiff moved to suspend the rule, whereupon the Court deferred the dismissal for one year. No further action was taken. The matter was dismissed one year later with judgment in favor of Bethlehem Steel Corporation. Neither litigant was notified of the dismissal by the Court. The plaintiff learned of the docket entry after receipt of a statement of costs from the Court. Immediately, the plaintiff filed a Motion to Revise the Judgment and a Motion to Suspend the Rule. *Id.* at 695, 539 A.2d at 1166–67. In finding for the plaintiff, the Court cited *Alban Tractor Co. v. Williford*, 61 Md. App. 71, 484 A.2d 1039 (1984), *cert. denied*, 302 Md. 680, 490 A.2d 718 (1985) which upheld a trial court's decision to set aside a judgment in a condemnation case because of the clerk's failure to obey Md. Rule 1-324.

In the case at bar, Defendant has technically been without counsel since early 1996. At the time of her divorce in February, 1996 she had retained Sally Wilson, Esquire; however, pursuant to Maryland Rule 2-132(d), Wilson's appearance was automatically terminated after the period for taking an appeal from the divorce ended. Md. Rule 2-132(d) provides "[w]hen no appeal has been taken from a final judgment, the appearance of an attorney is automatically terminated upon the expiration of the appeal period unless the court, on its own initiative or on motion filed prior to the automatic termination, orders otherwise." Md. Rule 8-202 provides that an appeal must be filed within 30 days after the entry of the judgment.

As indicated, Catherine Anne Jones, Esquire, filed a request to be admitted *pro hac vice*. *Edwards v. Webb*, 182 Md. 60, 32 A.2d 702 (1943). However, her request was denied by Judge Johnston. As a result, Defendant was without counsel and represented herself in proper person. It is this fact that the clerk's office failed to note. It is possible that the clerk sent notices to Wilson, incorrectly assuming that she was counsel. Wilson, however, does not recall receiving court documents in this matter. Accompanying this memorandum find an affidavit (Exhibit A) from Wilson indicating this fact.

In the case at bar, the clerk of court failed to comply with Md. Rule 1-324 by not sending Defendant a copy of the July 13, 1997 judgment. Additionally, the court failed to provide the Defendant with a hearing date notice. Defendant's affidavit (Exhibit B) verifies that she was without notice of the July 13, 1997 hearing.

CONCLUSION

The clerk of court failed to provide Defendant with a hearing notice for the July 13, 1997 hearing as well as the judgment that resulted from that hearing. The failure to provide the judgment violated Md. Rule 1-324. Pursuant to the court's revisory power under Md. Rule 2-535 and Md. Code Ann., Cts. & Jud. Proc. § 6-408 (1989), Defendant is entitled to have the judgment stricken.

DAVID J. SMITH
406 Allegheny Avenue
Towson, Maryland 21204-4223
(410) 882-8099
Attorney for Defendant

FIGURE 16-1 *(continued)*

> CERTIFICATE OF SERVICE
>
> I HEREBY CERTIFY that on this 15th day of September, 1998, a copy of the foregoing Memorandum in Support of Defendant's Motion to Strike Judgment and accompanying exhibits were mailed postage prepaid to Rhonda Limpert, Esquire, 100 Main Street, Bel Air, Maryland 21015-1234, Attorney for Plaintiff.
>
> DAVID J. SMITH

FIGURE 16-1   *(continued)*

Caption, Title, and Introductory Paragraph

Basic information about the memorandum is presented first. Court rules require that every document filed in court have a caption, which must include the parties' names, their litigation status, the name of the court, and the case number (which was previously assigned by the court).

Most rules also require that the document have an appropriate title. A memorandum's title will probably be lengthy, because it will incorporate the name of the motion it is supporting.

An introductory paragraph reiterates the purpose of the motion and provides the attorney's and client's names. At one time, this paragraph used formal language, such as "To The Honorable, the Judge of said Court, to wit:." Today, this verbose formality has been replaced with a more direct opening.

Statement of Facts

The introductory paragraph is followed by the statement of facts. Here, a discussion of the facts in the case is presented in a partisan yet honest style. Though the attorney may not misrepresent the facts, he is permitted (and expected) to present the facts in a way that shows his client in the most favorable light.

Recall that when a case is briefed, the brief includes the key facts of the case. Similarly, the facts of the case that are critical to understanding the issues of the memo are included in the memo. To allow the court to better understand the case, the attorney might include some context facts that make the case realistic and immediate, such as names, dates, and places dealing with the case.

The facts themselves will vary based on when the memorandum is filed. If a litigation memorandum is filed to support a preliminary motion, the facts will be found in the complaint or from events outside of the pleadings. When facts have not been established by a court, personal affidavits are often necessary. Later in the case, the facts may be more developed and established. For instance, a motion for a new trial is filed when a party feels that procedural errors occurred during a trial. In this situation, a supporting memorandum could discuss facts developed at the trial itself.

Issue

The issue section first establishes the justification for the memorandum. It is important that the issues be clearly stated. As in the research memorandum, they should be stated as questions. Complex statements with multiple clauses make comprehension difficult. If an issue contains many components, then stating subissues might be appropriate in the memorandum.

The issues should be written in a direct, simplistic style. Though law school students are taught to write issues that include assumed facts, in order to create a very specific question, this is often not the best way of considering the issues. Consider the two statements of the issue in Chapter 13 as examples. The second form is clearer and more direct than the first.

If an issue involves determining the cause of action or a defense (such as contributory negligence), then each particular element must be analyzed separately. For example, contributory negligence would have to be reduced to its elements, with each element constituting a separate issue.

1. Did the plaintiff have a legal duty to act in a reasonable manner?
2. Assuming the plaintiff had such a duty, did he breach that duty?
3. Did the plaintiff's breach cause him to suffer injuries?
4. Were the injuries sustained by the plaintiff caused by his failure to perform the required duty?

Short Answer

As stated previously, judges rarely have time to read long, complicated memoranda. To encourage the judge to read a memorandum, attorneys often will provide a short answer section. Here (as in the research memorandum), the ultimate answer to the issue or issues is presented. This section appears conclusionary in nature. Its support is found in the argument section, which follows.

Argument

The argument section is the heart of the memorandum. All the rules of effective writing from Chapter 11 must be employed in this portion. Through the use of block paragraph methods such as IRAC, the client's position is set out in detail. If there is more than one issue, each should be discussed separately. Headings can also be employed to further distinguish between issues.

The aim of this section is to convince the reader of the client's position. To do this requires convincing a court that specific legal principles should be applied to the facts at bar. The evaluation of authority is made from a partisan standpoint; objectively looking at both sides of the case is not done. An attorney must convince a court that the legal principles he has selected to govern the outcome of the case are the only appropriate ones.

Conclusion

A summary of the argument is provided in the conclusion. This will be more extensive than the short answer, in that it ties together the various component parts of the argument to fashion a comprehensive answer. The summary also states in unequivocal terms what the client desires. Of course, the summary of the argument and the client's requested relief should be the same.

Signature Block and Certificate of Service

Because a litigation memorandum must comply with pleading rules, it must be signed by the attorney submitting it. In addition, a copy must be mailed to opposing counsel. A certificate of service is the affirmation that this has been done.

Exhibits

Frequently, it will be necessary for exhibits to accompany the memorandum and motion. The most typical exhibit is an affidavit that establishes facts not contained in the pleadings. See Figure 15-12 for an example.

Appellate Brief

Purposes and Applications

After a trial court judgment is entered in a case, the losing party may wish to take an appeal to the appropriate appellate court. This party, known as the *appellant,* must file a **notice of appeal** in the trial court, which then informs the opposing party (the *appellee*) of the appeal. Courts strictly enforce rules that require appeals to be filed within specific time limits. Most courts require that appeals be taken within 30 days of the entry of a judgment on the trial level.

Sometime after the notice is filed, the appealing party is required to file an *appellant's brief.* Thereafter, the opposing party is required to file an *appellee's brief,* which responds to the appellant's brief. Most jurisdictions allow for the appellant to file a *reply brief* responding to the appellee's arguments, and then the appellee is permitted to counter the appellant's reply brief. Court rules also permit the filing of *amicus curiae* briefs. *Amicus curiae* is Latin for "friend of the court"; the name shows that such a brief is filed not by a party but by one having a substantial interest in the outcome of the case.

──────── **LEGAL TERMS** ────────

notice of appeal † The process by which appellate review is initiated; specifically, written notice to the appellee advising him or her of the appellant's intention to appeal.

In essence, an **appellate brief** presents the legal arguments and supporting authority for a party's position. After the briefs are filed, the court will schedule a date and time for the attorneys to present oral arguments. This will often be before a panel of three or more judges. The purpose of the oral argument is to bring to life the positions taken in the briefs, as well as to point out new legal principles that might have emerged after preparation of the briefs. A number of weeks or months after the arguments are presented, the judges render their decision in the case. At that time they also decide whether the decision will be reported and as a consequence have precedential value.

In their briefs, the parties present facts, issues, and legal authority in a way most favorable to their clients' positions. The rules and customs that govern appellate practice require that briefs be highly analytical and be set up in a very specific and exact manner. Failure to comply with the rules of appellate practice can result in an appeal being dismissed by a court.

Though every party is entitled to take one appeal as a matter of right, not every losing party has the necessary grounds for a successful appeal. In a jury trial, the role of the jury is to determine the facts and apply these facts to the legal principles provided to them by the judge. In a bench trial, the judge determines the facts and the law. An appeals court will rarely reconsider the facts as decided by the factfinder. For instance, in the paralegal practice situation, if the jury determines that Jamal Brown had not been drinking prior to the time he was injured, an appeals court will not review this point. Only misapplication or misinterpretation of law can be reviewed by an appeals court. Errors of law may include inappropriate **jury instructions**, the allowance of **hearsay** evidence during trial, or the wrongful exclusion of evidence. If in the Brown-Fulwood case, the jury had been not been instructed as to the law of contributory negligence (an important defense for the Fulwoods), and as a result a decision was made against the Fulwoods, this might be the basis of an appeal.

A complete appellate brief is reproduced in Appendix B.

Guidelines

By and large, most state and federal jurisdictions have adopted similar format requirements for appellate practice. Normally, an appellate brief includes a cover page, a table of contents, a table of authorities, a statement as to the nature of the case, a statement of the questions presented, a statement of facts, an argument section, a conclusion, and one or more appendices.

--------- **LEGAL TERMS** ---------

appellate brief   A brief filed by a party in an appeals court.

jury instructions †   Directions given to the jury by the judge just before he or she sends the jurors out to deliberate and return a verdict, explaining the law that applies in the case and spelling out what must be proven and by whom.

hearsay †·   The testimony of a witness as to a statement made to him or her outside of court, or made to someone else who told him or her what was said, that is offered in court to prove the truth of the matter contained in the statement.

Because of its complexity, most appellant brief writing is done by attorneys. When paralegals play a role, it is likely to be either in assisting in gathering material and doing the research necessary to write the brief or in assisting in the editorial process. Legal assistants can play an important role by employing their skills in cite checking and shepardizing. Whatever your role, the guidelines identified for litigation memoranda, in addition to the three guidelines indicated here, should be kept in mind.

Know the Appellate Practice Rules

Knowledge of the rules of appellate practice is crucial, for two reasons. First, appellate rules are always different from trial court rules. (See Figure 16-2.) Because most attorneys rarely file or defend appeals, these rules are likely to be unfamiliar to you and your employer. Second, these rules are very strictly enforced. One missed deadline can cause a court to dismiss an appeal without recourse. A paralegal knowledgeable in appellate procedure can be a time and life saver for the general practice attorney.

Understand the Theory of the Appeal

Every appeal is based on a theory espoused by the attorney taking the appeal. Often, this theory is an evolving one. After a trial, the attorney may have only a feeling that something went wrong, although he usually can point to events that took place during trial as the basis for his belief. At times, however, the attorney files a notice of appeal before he fully understands why he is taking the appeal. As he researches, he starts to articulate specific justifications for taking the appeal. The paralegal must be privy to this theory. Your role, though a supporting one, will most likely involve reviewing the trial **transcript** for evidence of errors of law. You must know what to look for and how to use what is found.

Understand the Client's Position

Surprisingly, understanding the client's position does not always deal with the traditional aspects of representation. An appeal is a long process that requires a great deal of patience from attorney and client alike. It is also more mysterious than trial to the client because it does not involve her; there is no trial and no testimony. Frequently, the attorney puts her entire efforts into preparing the brief without informing the client as to the process and progress. You should take the primary role in keeping the client informed of what is going on. Of course, all contact with clients should be with attorney approval and oversight.

───────────────── **LEGAL TERMS** ─────────────────

transcript † A typewritten copy of the court reporter's stenographic notes of a trial, i.e., a record of the proceedings.

SECTION TWO. GENERAL PROVISIONS

RULE 3. DEFINITIONS; UNIFORM TERMINOLOGY

(a) Terms in Rules. Certain terms used in these rules are defined as follows: "Appellant" is the party taking the appeal or suing out a writ of error to the court of appeals. "Appellee" is the party adverse to "appellant." "Petitioner" is the party applying to the Supreme Court for a writ of error, "Respondent" is the party adverse to "petitioner" in the Supreme Court. "Court below" is the trial court from which the appeal or writ of error is taken. "Appellate court" includes the courts of appeals, the Supreme Court and the Court of Criminal Appeals. "Relator" is the person seeking relief in an original proceeding in the appellate court. "Respondent" is the party against whom relief is sought in an original proceeding in the appellate court. "Applicant" is a party seeking a writ of habeas corpus in the trial court.

(b) Uniform Terminology in Criminal Cases. [*Pub. Note: SUPREME COURT TEXT as promulgated effective Sept. 1, 1990. See also Court of Criminal Appeals text following this paragraph.*] In briefs and other papers in criminal appeals, the parties should be referred to as "the appellant" and "the appellee;" procedural labels such as "appellee," "petitioner," "respondent," "movant," etc. should be avoided unless they are necessary to clarify a question of procedural law. In habeas corpus proceedings the person for whose relief the writ is asked should be referred to as "the applicant."

(b) Uniform Terminology in Criminal Cases. [*Pub. Note: COURT OF CRIMINAL APPEALS TEXT as promulgated effective Sept. 1, 1990. See also Supreme Court text preceding this paragraph.*] In briefs and other papers in criminal appeals, the parties should be referred to as "the State" and "the appellant" unless the State has appealed pursuant to Article 44.01, C.C.P., in which event defendant is "the appellee;" otherwise procedural labels such as "appellee," "petitioner," "respondent," "movant," et cetera should be avoided unless they are necessary to clarify a question of procedural law. In habeas corpus proceedings the person for whose relief the writ is asked should be referred to as "the applicant."

(Adopted by Supreme Court and Court of Criminal Appeals effective Sept. 1, 1986; amended by Supreme Court effective Sept. 1, 1990, and by Court of Criminal Appeals effective Sept. 1, 1990.)

RULE 4. SIGNING, FILING AND SERVICE

(a) Signing. Each application, brief, motion or other paper filed shall be signed by at least one of the attorneys for the party and shall give the State Bar of Texas identification number, the mailing address, telephone number, and telecopier number, if any, of each attorney whose name is signed thereto. A party who is not represented by an attorney shall sign his brief and give his address and telephone number.

(b) Filing. The filing of records, briefs and other papers in the appellate court as required by these rules shall be made by filing them with the clerk, except that any justice of the court may permit the papers to be filed with him, in which event he shall note thereon the filing date and time and forthwith transmit them to the office of the clerk. If a motion for rehearing, any matter relating to taking an appeal or writ of error from the trial court to any higher court, or application for writ of error or petition for discretionary review is sent to the proper clerk by first-class United States mail in an envelope or wrapper properly addressed and stamped and is deposited in the mail on or before the last day for filing same, the same, if received by the clerk not more than ten days tardily, shall be filed by the clerk and be deemed as filed in time; provided, however, that a certificate of mailing by the United States Postal Service or a legible postmark affixed by the United States Postal Service shall be prima facie evidence of the date of mailing.

(c) Number of Copies.

(1) Each party shall file six copies of briefs, petitions, motions and other papers with the Clerk of the Court of Appeals in which the case is pending. Any court of appeals may by local rule authorize the filing of fewer or more copies.

(2) [*Pub. Note: SUPREME COURT TEXT as promulgated effective Sept. 1, 1990. See also Court of Criminal Appeals text following this paragraph.*] Each party shall file twelve copies of its application for writ of error or of its petition for discretionary review with the Clerk of the Court of Appeals.

(2) [*Pub. Note: COURT OF CRIMINAL APPEALS TEXT as promulgated effective Sept. 1, 1990. See also Supreme Court text preceding this paragraph.*] Each party shall file twelve copies of its application for writ of error with the Clerk of the Court of Appeals. In addition to filing an original petition for discretionary review with the Clerk of the Court of Appeals, the party shall deliver eleven copies. The State Prosecuting Attorney may deliver the eleven copies to the Clerk of the Court of Criminal Appeals.

(3) Each party shall file twelve copies of all other papers addressed to the Supreme Court or Court of Criminal Appeals with the clerk of the court to which it is addressed.

(d) Papers Typewritten or Printed. [*Pub. Note: SUPREME COURT TEXT as promulgated September 4, 1990. See also Court of Criminal Appeals text*

FIGURE 16-2 Appellate court rule (Texas)

following this paragraph.] All applications, briefs, petitions, motions and other papers shall be printed or typewritten. The use of recycled paper is strongly encouraged. Typewritten papers must be with a double space between the lines and on heavy white paper in clear type.

(d) **Papers Typewritten or Printed.** [*Pub. Note: COURT OF CRIMINAL APPEALS TEXT as promulgated effective September 1, 1986. See also Supreme Court text preceding this paragraph.*] All applications, briefs, petitions, motions and other papers shall be printed or typewritten. Typewritten papers must be with a double space between the lines and on heavy white paper in clear type.

(e) **Service of All Papers Required.** Copies of all papers filed by any party and not required by these rules to be served by the clerk shall, at or before the time of filing, be served by a party or person acting for him on all other parties to the appeal or review. Service on a party represented by counsel shall be made on counsel.

(f) **Manner of Service.** Service may be personal, by mail, or by telephonic document transfer to the party's current telecopier number. Personal service includes delivery of the copy to a clerk or other responsible person at the office of counsel. Service by mail is complete on mailing. Service by telephonic document transfer is complete on receipt.

(g) **Service.** Papers presented for filing shall be served and shall contain an acknowledgement of service by the person served or proof of service in the form of a statement of the date and manner of service and of the names and addresses of the persons served, certified by the person who made the service. Proof of service may appear on or be affixed to the papers filed. The clerk may permit papers to be filed without acknowledgement or proof of service but shall require such to be filed promptly thereafter.

(Adopted by Supreme Court and Court of Criminal Appeals effective Sept. 1, 1986. Rule 4(a), (b), (f) and (g) amended by Supreme Court and Court of Criminal Appeals effective Sept. 1, 1990; Rule (c)(2) amended by Supreme Court effective Sept. 1, 1990, and by Court of Criminal Appeals effective Sept. 1, 1990; Rule 4(d) amended by Supreme Court Sept. 4, 1990.)

Notes and Comments

Comment to 1990 change: Time period clarification, deletion of requirement of verification by a pro se litigant, provision for service by telephonic document transfer, and textual corrective changes.

FIGURE 16-2 *(continued)*

Format and Contents

Make sure to check your particular state appellate practice rules before beginning work. The contents of an appellate brief in most jurisdictions are typically specified as in the rule shown in Figure 16-3.

Cover Page

The cover page indicates the case caption, the trial court name, the trial court docket number, the appeals court name, and the submitting attorney's name and address. Most court rules require that the cover page for the appellant's brief and the appellee's brief be of different colors. For instance, in Maryland's Court of Special Appeals (the state's intermediate appellate court), the appellant's brief cover must be yellow and the appellee's brief cover must be green.

Table of Contents

As with other lengthy documents, a table of contents is helpful in directing the reader to specific sections of the brief. The table of contents lists the

Rule 8-504. CONTENTS OF BRIEF

(a) **Contents.**—A brief shall contain the items listed in the following order:

(1) A table of contents and a table of citations of cases, constitutional provisions, statutes, ordinances, rules, and regulations, with cases alphabetically arranged. When a reported Maryland case is cited, the citation shall include a reference to the official Report.

(2) A brief statement of the case, indicating the nature of the case, the course of the proceedings, and the disposition in the lower court, except that the appellee's brief shall not contain a statement of the case unless the appellee disagrees with the statement in the appellant's brief.

(3) A statement of the questions presented, separately numbered, indicating the legal propositions involved and the questions of fact at issue expressed in the terms and circumstances of the case without unnecessary detail.

(4) A clear concise statement of the facts material to a determination of the questions presented, except that the appellee's brief shall contain a statement of only those additional facts necessary to correct or amplify the statement in the appellant's brief. Reference shall be made to the pages of the record extract supporting the assertions. If pursuant to these rules or by leave of court a record extract is not filed, reference shall be made to the pages of the record or to the transcript of testimony as contained in the record.

Cross reference: Rule 8-111(b).

(5) Argument in support of the party's position.

(6) A short conclusion stating the precise relief sought.

(7) The citation and verbatim text of all pertinent constitutional provisions, statutes, ordinances, rules, and regulations except that the appellee's brief shall contain only those not included in the appellant's brief.

FIGURE 16-3 Appellate brief rule (Maryland). (Reproduced with permission of The Michie Company. Further reproduction without permission is strictly prohibited.)

page numbers of all component parts of the brief. It is a complete "road map" of everything covered in the document. It is usually the last part of the brief to be completed.

Table of Authorities

The table of authorities lists alphabetically the various statutes, cases, administrative regulations, and other legal authority cited in the brief. In an appellate brief, reference must be only to primary law.

Statement of the Case

The statement of the case contains a summary of the nature of the case and a discussion of the proceedings to date. It does not discuss the specific facts of the case; rather, it focuses on the court procedure the case has undergone to the present date.

Questions Presented

The issue is the basis on which the attorney has taken the appeal. After a trial court decision, an attorney may believe there to be multiple bases for taking an appeal. However, her chances are often improved if she focuses on only the most critical issues which would most likely result in a reversal. To attack every aspect of a trial would result in a cluttered and unfocused brief.

The question presented is likely to be drafted in the law school style, presented as a complex question consisting of facts and a specific legal proposition. In many appeals, there are several issues that the attorney feels have merit for appeal.

Statement of Facts

In the statement of facts, the facts relevant to the appeal are discussed. This section has three important characteristics. First, only key facts and those context facts that assist in a complete understanding of the case are presented. Second, the facts must be taken directly from the trial transcript. A reference must be given to the transcript when a fact is stated. Finally, because the facts are taken from the record, embellishment of the facts to show the client in the best light is not permitted. It is best to present the facts in a chronological fashion, unless a different format appears to make for better comprehension.

Argument

As with the litigation memorandum, this is the longest portion of the brief. This section focuses on rediscussing the facts within the context of applicable (and favorable) legal authority. It is partisan, detailed, logical, and convincing in its presentation. The IRAC method and other block paragraph methods are frequently employed in this section. If there are multiple issues, each is addressed individually. This section represents the highest form of persuasive writing.

Conclusion

In the conclusion, a concise summary of the basis for the reversal (or sustaining) of the lower court's decision is indicated. The attorney also indicates in this section what type of relief he wishes from the appellate court.

Appendix

The appendix is a collection of documents from the trial court that are relevant for the appeal. These documents together are referred to as the **record**. It will always include the transcript and pleadings from the trial court.

Summary

- A litigation memorandum is filed to support the factual and legal arguments presented in a motion. Because it asserts particular legal points and supports them with legal authorities, this memorandum is sometimes referred to as a memorandum of points and authorities.

- A litigation memorandum is usually filed with a motion, is governed by the same rules and writing conventions as pleadings, is a highly analytical document, and is always written in a partisan style.

- The purpose of a litigation memorandum is to set forth a complex argument in such a way that it will be favorably viewed by the court.

- A litigation memorandum should be concise. Its contents should be logically presented. Legal authority should rarely be quoted; rather, rules should be rephrased. The memo should take a partisan, yet honest, third-person approach.

- The component parts of a typical litigation memorandum include: caption, title, and introductory paragraph; statement of facts; issue; short answer; argument; conclusion; signature block and certificate of service; and exhibits.

- When an appeal is taken, the parties, known as the appellant and appellee, must file briefs with the appeals court.

- In their briefs, the parties present relevant facts, issues, and legal authority in a way most favorable to their client's position.

- Rules governing appellate procedure are strictly enforced.

- Paralegals who assist in the preparation of an appellate brief should know the appellate practice rules. They should understand the theory of the case. They should keep the client informed of the progress of the appeal.

- The component parts of the brief generally include: cover page, table of contents, table of authorities, statement of the case, questions presented, statement of facts, argument, conclusion, and appendix.

LEGAL TERMS
---

record on appeal [†]   The papers a trial court transmits to the appellate court, on the basis of which the appellate court decides the appeal. The record on appeal includes the pleadings, all motions made before the trial court, the official transcript, and the judgment or order appealed from.

Review Questions

1. By what names are litigation memoranda known?

2. In what situations is a litigation memorandum likely to be filed?

3. Why is it important that a litigation memorandum be short and concise?

4. What is included in the statement of facts of a litigation memorandum?

5. What is the procedure for taking an appeal?

6. What is an *amicus curiae* brief?

7. Why is it important for the paralegal to know the rules of appellate practice when assisting in the preparation of an appellate brief?

8. What are the component parts of an appellate brief?

Chapter Exercises

1. Check the rules of appellate practice in your state. How do the required contents of a brief differ from what was discussed in this chapter?

2. Check your state's rules concerning the filing of motions. Is there a mention of memoranda that might be filed in support of a motion? How about the rule that deals with motions for summary judgment? What do these rules provide for?

3. Note that Rule 4(d) of the Texas Rules of Appellate Procedure, Figure 16-2, encourages the use of recycled paper. Check your state's rules to see if recycled paper is advocated.

APPENDIX A

THE CONSTITUTION OF THE UNITED STATES OF AMERICA

We the People of the United States, in Order to form a more perfect Union, establish Justice, insure domestic Tranquility, provide for the common defence, promote the general Welfare, and secure the Blessings of Liberty to ourselves and our Posterity, do ordain and establish this Constitution for the United States of America.

ARTICLE I

Section 1 All legislative Powers herein granted shall be vested in a Congress of the United States, which shall consist of a Senate and House of Representatives.

Section 2 (1) The House of Representatives shall be composed of Members chosen every second Year by the People of the several States, and the Electors in each State shall have the Qualifications requisite for Electors of the most numerous Branch of the State Legislature.

(2) No Person shall be a Representative who shall not have attained to the age of twenty-five Years, and been seven Years a Citizen of the United States, and who shall not, when elected, be an Inhabitant of that State in which he shall be chosen.

(3) Representatives and direct Taxes shall be apportioned among the several States which may be included within this Union, according to their respective Numbers, which shall be determined by adding to the whole Number of free Persons, including those bound to Service for a Term of Years, and excluding Indians not taxed, three fifths of all other Persons. The actual Enumeration shall be made within three Years after the first Meeting of the Congress of the United States, and within every subsequent Term of ten Years, in such Manner as they shall by Law direct. The Number of Representatives shall not exceed one for every thirty Thousand, but each State shall have at Least one Representative; and until such enumeration shall be made, the State of New Hampshire shall be entitled to chuse three, Massachusetts eight, Rhode Island and Providence Plantations one, Connecticut five, New York six, New Jersey four, Pennsylvania eight, Delaware one, Maryland six, Virginia ten, North Carolina five, South Carolina five, and Georgia three.

(4) When vacancies happen in the Representation from any State, the Executive Authority thereof shall issue Writs of Election to fill such Vacancies.

(5) The House of Representatives shall chuse their Speaker and other Officers; and shall have the sole Power of Impeachment.

Section 3 (1) The Senate of the United States shall be composed of two Senators from each State, chosen by the Legislature thereof, for six Years; and each Senator shall have one Vote.

(2) Immediately after they shall be assembled in Consequence of the first Election, they shall be divided as equally as may be into three Classes. The Seats of the Senators of the first Class shall be vacated at the Expiration of the second Year, of the second Class at the Expiration of the fourth Year, and of the third Class at the Expiration of the sixth Year, so that one third may be chosen every second Year; and if Vacancies happen by Resignation, or otherwise, during the Recess of the Legislature of any State, the Executive thereof may make temporary Appointments until the next Meeting of the Legislature, which shall then fill such Vacancies.

(3) No Person shall be a Senator who shall not have attained to the Age of thirty Years, and been nine Years a Citizen of the United States, and who shall not, when elected, be an Inhabitant of that State for which he shall be chosen.

(4) The Vice President of the United States shall be President of the Senate, but shall have no Vote, unless they be equally divided.

(5) The Senate shall chuse their other Officers, and also a President pro tempore, in the Absence of the Vice President, or when he shall exercise the Office of the President of the United States.

(6) The Senate shall have the sole Power to try all Impeachments. When sitting for that Purpose, they shall be on Oath or Affirmation. When the President of the United States is tried, the Chief Justice shall preside: And no Person shall be convicted without the Concurrence of two thirds of the Members present.

(7) Judgment in Cases of Impeachment shall not extend further than to removal from Office, and disqualification to hold and enjoy any Office of honor, Trust or Profit under the United States: but the Party convicted shall nevertheless be liable and subject to Indictment, Trial, Judgment and Punishment, according to Law.

Section 4 (1) The Times, Places and Manner of holding Elections for Senators and Representatives, shall be prescribed in each State by the Legislature thereof; but the Congress may at any time by Law make or alter such Regulations, except as to the Places of chusing Senators.

(2) The Congress shall assemble at least once in every Year, and such Meeting shall be on the first Monday in December, unless they shall by Law appoint a different Day.

Section 5 (1) Each House shall be the Judge of the Elections, Returns and Qualifications of its own Members, and a Majority of each shall constitute a Quorum to do Business; but a smaller Number may adjourn from day to day, and may be authorized to compel the Attendance of absent Members, in such Manner, and under such Penalties as each House may provide.

(2) Each House may determine the Rules of its Proceedings, punish its Members for disorderly Behaviour, and, with the Concurrence of two thirds, expel a Member.

(3) Each House shall keep a Journal of its Proceedings, and from time to time publish the same, excepting such Parts as may in their Judgment require Secrecy; and the Yeas and Nays of the Members of either House on any question shall, at the Desire of one fifth of those Present, be entered on the Journal.

(4) Neither House, during the Session of Congress, shall, without the Consent of the other, adjourn for more than three days, nor to any other Place than that in which the two Houses shall be sitting.

Section 6 (1) The Senators and Representatives shall receive a Compensation for their Services, to be ascertained by Law, and paid out of the Treasury of the United States. They shall in all Cases, except Treason, Felony and Breach of the Peace, be privileged from Arrest during their Attendance at the Session of their respective Houses, and in going to and returning from the same; and for any Speech or Debate in either House, they shall not be questioned in any other Place.

(2) No Senator or Representative shall, during the Time for which he was elected, be appointed to any civil Office under the Authority of the United States, which shall have been created, or the Emoluments whereof shall have been encreased during such time; and no Person holding any Office under the United States, shall be a Member of either House during his Continuance in Office.

Section 7 (1) All Bills for raising Revenue shall originate in the House of Representatives; but the Senate may propose or concur with Amendments as on other Bills.

(2) Every Bill which shall have passed the House of Representatives and the Senate, shall, before it become a Law, be presented to the President of the United States; If he approve he shall sign it, but if not he shall return it, with his Objections to that House in which it shall have originated, who shall enter the Objections at large on their Journal, and proceed to reconsider it. If after such Reconsideration two thirds of that House shall agree to pass the Bill, it shall be sent, together with the Objections, to the other House, by which it shall likewise be reconsidered, and if approved by two thirds of that House, it shall become a law. But in all such Cases the Votes of both Houses shall be determined by Yeas and Nays, and the Names of the Persons voting for and against the Bill shall be entered on the Journal of each House respectively. If any Bill shall

not be returned by the President within ten Days (Sunday excepted) after it shall have been presented to him, the Same shall be a Law, in like Manner as if he had signed it, unless the Congress by their Adjournment prevent its Return, in which Case it shall not be a Law.

(3) Every Order, Resolution, or Vote to which the Concurrence of the Senate and House of Representatives may be necessary (except on a question of Adjournment) shall be presented to the President of the United States; and before the Same shall take Effect, shall be approved by him, or being disapproved by him, shall be repassed by two thirds of the Senate and House of Representatives, according to the Rules and Limitations prescribed in the Case of a Bill.

Section 8   (1) The Congress shall have Power To lay and collect Taxes, Duties, Imposts and Excises, to pay the Debts and provide for the common Defence and general Welfare of the United States; but all Duties, Imposts and Excises shall be uniform throughout the United States;

(2) To borrow Money on the credit of the United States;

(3) To regulate Commerce with foreign Nations, and among the several States, and with the Indian Tribes;

(4) To establish an uniform Rule of Naturalization, and uniform Laws on the subject of Bankruptcies throughout the United States;

(5) To coin Money, regulate the Value thereof, and of foreign Coin, and to fix the Standard of Weights and Measures;

(6) To provide for the Punishment of counterfeiting the Securities and current Coin of the United States;

(7) To establish Post Offices and post Roads;

(8) To promote the Progress of Science and useful Arts, by securing for limited Times to Authors and Inventors the exclusive Right to their respective Writings and Discoveries;

(9) To constitute Tribunals inferior to the supreme Court;

(10) To define and punish Piracies and Felonies committed on the high Seas, and Offenses against the Law of Nations;

(11) To declare War, grant Letters of Marque and Reprisal, and make Rules concerning Captures on Land and Water;

(12) To raise and support Armies, but no Appropriation of Money to that Use shall be for a longer Term than two Years;

(13) To provide and maintain a Navy;

(14) To make Rules for the Government and Regulation of the land and naval Forces;

(15) To provide for calling forth the Militia to execute the Laws of the Union, suppress Insurrections and repel Invasions;

(16) To provide for organizing, arming, and disciplining, the Militia, and for governing such Part of them as may be employed in the Service of the United States, reserving to the States respectively, the Appointment of the Officers, and the Authority of training the Militia according to the discipline prescribed by Congress;

(17) To exercise exclusive Legislation in all Cases whatsoever, over such District (not exceeding ten Miles square) as may, by Cession of particular States, and the Acceptance of Congress, become the Seat of the Government of the United States, and to exercise like Authority over all Places purchased by the Consent of the Legislature of the State in which the Same shall be, for the Erection of Forts, Magazines, Arsenals, dock-Yards, and other needful Buildings;—And

(18) To make all Laws which shall be necessary and proper for carrying into Execution the foregoing Powers, and all other Powers vested by this Constitution in the Government of the United States, or in any Department or Officer thereof.

Section 9   (1) The Migration or Importation of such Persons as any of the States now existing shall think proper to admit, shall not be prohibited by the Congress prior to the Year one thousand eight hundred and eight, but a Tax or Duty may be imposed on such Importation, not exceeding ten dollars for each Person.

(2) The Privilege of the Writ of Habeas Corpus shall not be suspended unless when in Cases of Rebellion or Invasion the public Safety may require it.

(3) No Bill of Attainder or ex post facto Law shall be passed.

(4) No Capitation, or other direct, Tax shall be laid, unless in Proportion to the Census or Enumeration herein before directed to be taken.

(5) No Tax or Duty shall be laid on Articles exported from any State.

(6) No Preference shall be given by any Regulation of Commerce or Revenue to the Ports of one State over those of another; nor shall Vessels bound to, or from, one State, be obliged to enter, clear or pay Duties in another.

(7) No Money shall be drawn from the Treasury, but in Consequence of Appropriations made by Law; and a regular Statement and Account of the Receipts and Expenditures of all public Money shall be published from time to time.

(8) No Title of Nobility shall be granted by the United States: And no Person holding any Office of Profit or Trust under them, shall, without the Consent of the Congress, accept of any present, Emolument, Office, or Title, of any kind whatever, from any King, Prince or foreign State.

Section 10 (1) No State shall enter into any Treaty, Alliance, or Confederation; grant Letters of Marque and Reprisal; coin Money; emit Bills of Credit; make any Thing but gold and silver Coin a Tender in Payment of Debts; pass any Bill of Attainder, ex post facto Law, or Law impairing the Obligation of Contracts, or grant any Title of Nobility.

(2) No State shall, without the Consent of Congress, lay any Imposts or Duties on Imports or Exports, except what may be absolutely necessary for executing its inspection Laws: and the net Produce of all Duties and Imposts, laid by any State on Imports or Exports, shall be for the Use of the Treasury of the United States; and all such Laws shall be subject to the Revision and Controul of the Congress.

(3) No State shall, without the Consent of Congress, lay any Duty of Tonnage, keep Troops, or Ships of War in time of Peace, enter into any Agreement or Compact with another State, or with a foreign Power, or engage in War, unless actually invaded, or in such imminent Danger as will not admit of Delay.

ARTICLE II

Section 1 (1) The executive Power shall be vested in a President of the United States of America. He shall hold his Office during the Term of four Years, and, together with the Vice President, chosen for the same Term, be elected, as follows:

(2) Each State shall appoint, in such Manner as the Legislature thereof may direct, a Number of Electors, equal to the whole Number of Senators and Representatives to which the State may be entitled in the Congress: but no Senator or Representative, or Person holding an Office of Trust or Profit under the United States, shall be appointed an Elector.

The Electors shall meet in their respective States, and vote by Ballot for two Persons, of whom one at least shall not be an Inhabitant of the same State with themselves. And they shall make a List of all the Persons voted for, and of the Number of Votes for each; which List they shall sign and certify, and transmit sealed to the Seat of the Government of the United States, directed to the President of the Senate. The President of the Senate shall, in the presence of the Senate and House of Representatives, open all the Certificates, and the Votes shall then be counted. The Person having the greatest Number of Votes shall be the President, if such Number be a Majority of the whole Number of Electors appointed; and if there be more than one who have such Majority, and have an equal Number of Votes, then the House of Representatives shall immediately chuse by Ballot one of them for President; and if no Person have a Majority, then from the five highest on the List the said House shall in like Manner chuse the President. But in chusing the President, the Votes shall be taken by States, the Representation from each State having one Vote; a quorum for this Purpose shall consist of a Member or Members from two thirds of the States, and a Majority of all the States shall be necessary to a Choice. In every Case, after the Choice of the President, the Person having the greatest Number of Votes of the Electors shall be the Vice President. But if there should remain two or more who have equal Votes, the Senate shall chuse from them by Ballot the Vice President.

(3) The Congress may determine the Time of chusing the Electors, and the Day on which they shall give their Votes; which Day shall be the same throughout the United States.

(4) No Person except a natural born Citizen, or a Citizen of the United States, at the time of

the Adoption of this Constitution, shall be eligible to the Office of President; neither shall any Person be eligible to that Office who shall not have attained to the Age of thirty five Years, and been fourteen Years a Resident within the United States.

(5) In Case of the Removal of the President from Office, or of his Death, Resignation, or Inability to discharge the Powers and Duties of the said Office, the Same shall devolve on the Vice President, and the Congress may by Law provide for the Case of Removal, Death, Resignation or Inability, both of the President and Vice President, declaring what Officer shall then act as President, and such Officer shall act accordingly, until the Disability be removed, or a President shall be elected.

(6) The President shall, at stated Times, receive for his Services, a Compensation, which shall neither be increased nor diminished during the Period for which he shall have been elected, and he shall not receive within that Period any other Emolument from the United States, or any of them.

(7) Before he enter on the Execution of his Office, he shall take the following Oath or Affirmation:—"I do solemnly swear (or affirm) that I will faithfully execute the Office of President of the United States, and will to the best of my Ability, preserve, protect and defend the Constitution of the United States."

Section 2 (1) The President shall be Commander in Chief of the Army and Navy of the United States, and of the Militia of the several States, when called into the actual Service of the United States; he may require the Opinion, in writing, of the principal Officer in each of the executive Departments, upon any Subject relating to the Duties of their respective Offices, and he shall have Power to grant Reprieves and Pardons for Offenses against the United States, except in Cases of Impeachment.

(2) He shall have Power, by and with the Advice and Consent of the Senate, to make Treaties, provided two thirds of the Senators present concur; and he shall nominate, and by and with the Advice and Consent of the Senate, shall appoint Ambassadors, other public Ministers and Consuls, Judges of the supreme Court, and all other Officers of the United States, whose Appointments are not herein otherwise provided for, and which shall be established by Law: but the Congress may by Law vest the Appointment of such inferior Officers, as they think proper, in the President alone, in the Courts of Law, or in the Heads of Departments.

(3) The President shall have Power to fill up all Vacancies that may happen during the Recess of the Senate, by granting Commissions which shall expire at the End of their next Session.

Section 3 He shall from time to time give to the Congress Information of the State of the Union, and recommend to their Consideration such Measures as he shall judge necessary and expedient; he may, on extraordinary Occasions, convene both Houses, or either of them, and in Case of Disagreement between them, with Respect to the Time of Adjournment, he may adjourn them to such Time as he shall think proper; he shall receive Ambassadors and other public Ministers; he shall take Care that the Laws be faithfully executed, and shall Commission all the Officers of the United States.

Section 4 The President, Vice President and all Civil Officers of the United States, shall be removed from Office on Impeachment for, and Conviction of, Treason, Bribery, or other high Crimes and Misdemeanors.

ARTICLE III

Section 1 The judicial Power of the United States, shall be vested in one supreme Court, and in such inferior Courts as the Congress may from time to time ordain and establish. The Judges, both of the supreme and inferior Courts, shall hold their Offices during good Behaviour, and shall, at stated Times, receive for their Services, a Compensation, which shall not be diminished during their Continuance in Office.

Section 2 (1) The judicial Power shall extend to all Cases, in Law and Equity, arising under this Constitution, the Laws of the United States, and Treaties made, or which shall be made, under their Authority;—to all Cases affecting Ambassadors, other public Ministers and Consuls;—to all Cases of admiralty and maritime Jurisdiction;—to Controversies to which the United States shall be a party;—to Controversies between two or more States;—between a State and Citizens of another State;—between Citizens of different States;—between Citizens of the same State claiming Lands under Grants of different States, and between a State, or the Citizens thereof, and foreign States, Citizens or Subjects.

(2) In all Cases affecting Ambassadors, other public Ministers and Consuls, and those in which a State shall be Party, the supreme Court shall have original Jurisdiction. In all the other Cases before mentioned, the supreme Court shall have appellate Jurisdiction, both as to Law and Fact, with such Exceptions, and under such Regulations as the Congress shall make.

(3) The Trial of all Crimes, except in Cases of Impeachment, shall be by Jury; and such Trial shall be held in the State where the said Crimes shall have been committed; but when not committed within any State, the Trial shall be at such Place or Places as the Congress may by Law have directed.

Section 3 (1) Treason against the United States, shall consist only in levying War against them, or in adhering to their Enemies, giving them Aid and Comfort. No Person shall be convicted of Treason unless on the Testimony of two Witnesses to the same overt Act, or on Confession in open Court.

(2) The Congress shall have Power to declare the Punishment of Treason, but no Attainder of Treason shall work Corruption of Blood, or Forfeiture except during the Life of the Person attainted.

ARTICLE IV

Section 1 Full Faith and Credit shall be given in each State to the public Acts, Records, and judicial Proceedings of every other State. And the Congress may by general Laws prescribe the Manner in which such Acts, Records and Proceedings shall be proved, and the Effect thereof.

Section 2 (1) The Citizens of each State shall be entitled to all privileges and Immunities of Citizens in the several States.

(2) A Person charged in any State with Treason, Felony, or other Crime, who shall flee from Justice, and be found in another State, shall on Demand of the executive Authority of the State from which he fled, be delivered up, to be removed to the State having Jurisdiction of the Crime.

(3) No Person held to Service of Labour in one State, under the Laws thereof, escaping into another, shall, in Consequence of any Law or Regulation therein, be discharged from such Service or Labour, but shall be delivered up on Claim of the Party to whom such Service or Labour may be due.

Section 3 (1) New States may be admitted by the Congress into this Union; but no new State shall be formed or erected within the Jurisdiction of any other State; nor any State be formed by the Junction of two or more States, or Parts of States, without the Consent of the Legislatures of the States concerned as well as of the Congress.

(2) The Congress shall have power to dispose of and make all needful Rules and Regulations respecting the Territory or other Property belonging to the United States; and nothing in this Constitution shall be so construed as to Prejudice any Claims of the United States, or of any particular State.

Section 4 The United States shall guarantee to every State in this Union a Republican Form of Government, and shall protect each of them against Invasion; and on Application of the Legislature, or of the Executive (when the Legislature cannot be convened) against domestic Violence.

ARTICLE V

The Congress, whenever two thirds of both Houses shall deem it necessary, shall propose Amendments to this Constitution, or, on the Application of the Legislatures of two thirds of the several States, shall call a Convention for proposing Amendments, which, in either Case, shall be valid to all Intents and Purposes, as Part of this Constitution, when ratified by the Legislatures of three fourths of the several States, or by Conventions in three fourths thereof, as the one or the other Mode of Ratification may be proposed by the Congress; Provided that no Amendment which may be made prior to the Year One thousand eight hundred and eight shall in any Manner affect the first and fourth Clauses in the Ninth Section of the first Article; and that no State, without its Consent, shall be deprived of its equal Suffrage in the Senate.

ARTICLE VI

(1) All Debts contracted and Engagements entered into, before the Adoption of this Constitution, shall be as valid against the United States under this Constitution, as under the Confederation.

(2) This Constitution, and the Laws of the United States which shall be made in Pursuance thereof; and all Treaties made, or which shall be made, under the Authority of the United States, shall be the supreme Law of the Land; and the Judges in every State shall be bound thereby, any Thing in the Constitution or Laws of any State to the Contrary notwithstanding.

(3) The Senators and Representatives before mentioned, and the Members of the several State Legislatures, and all executive and judicial Officers, both of the United States and of the several States, shall be bound by Oath or Affirmation, to support this Constitution; but no religious Test shall ever be required as a Qualification to any Office or public Trust under the United States.

ARTICLE VII

The Ratification of the Conventions of nine States, shall be sufficient for the Establishment of this Constitution between the States so ratifying the Same.

ARTICLES IN ADDITION TO, AND AMENDMENT OF, THE CONSTITUTION OF THE UNITED STATES OF AMERICA, PROPOSED BY CONGRESS, AND RATIFIED BY THE SEVERAL STATES, PURSUANT TO THE FIFTH ARTICLE OF THE ORIGINAL CONSTITUTION

AMENDMENT I (1791)

Congress shall make no law respecting an establishment of religion, or prohibiting the free exercise thereof; or abridging the freedom of speech, or of the press; or the right of the people peaceably to assemble, and to petition the Government for a redress of grievances.

AMENDMENT II (1791)

A well regulated Militia, being necessary to the security of a free state, the right of the people to keep and bear Arms, shall not be infringed.

AMENDMENT III (1791)

No Soldier shall, in time of peace be quartered in any house, without the consent of the Owner, nor in time of war, but in a manner to be prescribed by law.

AMENDMENT IV (1791)

The right of the people to be secure in their persons, houses, papers, and effects, against unreasonable searches and seizures, shall not be violated, and no Warrants shall issue, but upon probable cause, supported by Oath or affirmation, and particularly describing the place to be searched, and the persons or things to be seized.

AMENDMENT V (1791)

No person shall be held to answer for a capital, or otherwise infamous crime, unless on a presentment or indictment of a Grand Jury, except in cases arising in the land or naval forces, or in the Militia, when in actual service in time of War or public danger; nor shall any person be subject for the same offence to be twice put in jeopardy of life or limb; nor shall be compelled in any criminal case to be a witness against himself, nor be deprived of life, liberty, or property, without due process of law; nor shall private property be taken for public use, without just compensation.

AMENDMENT VI (1791)

In all criminal prosecutions, the accused shall enjoy the right to a speedy and public trial, by an impartial jury of the State and district wherein the crime shall have been committed, which district shall have been previously ascertained by law, and to be informed of the nature and cause of the accusation; to be confronted with the witnesses against him; to have compulsory process for obtaining witnesses in his favor, and to have the Assistance of Counsel for his defence.

AMENDMENT VII (1791)

In Suits at common law, where the value in controversy shall exceed twenty dollars, the right of trial by jury shall be preserved, and no fact tried by a jury, shall be otherwise re-examined in any Court of the United States, than according to the rules of the common law.

AMENDMENT VIII (1791)

Excessive bail shall not be required, nor excessive fines imposed, nor cruel and unusual punishments inflicted.

AMENDMENT IX (1791)

The enumeration in the Constitution, of certain rights, shall not be construed to deny or disparage others retained by the people.

AMENDMENT X (1791)

The powers not delegated to the United States by the Constitution, nor prohibited by it to the States, are reserved to the States respectively, or to the people.

AMENDMENT XI (1798)

The Judicial power of the United States shall not be construed to extend to any suit in law or equity, commenced or prosecuted against one of the United States by Citizens of another State, or by Citizens or Subjects of any Foreign State.

AMENDMENT XII (1804)

The Electors shall meet in their respective states and vote by ballot for President and Vice-President, one of whom, at least, shall not be an inhabitant of the same state with themselves; they shall name in their ballots the person voted for as President, and in distinct ballots the person voted for as Vice-President, and they shall make distinct lists of all persons voted for as President, and of all persons voted for as Vice-President, and of the number of votes for each, which lists they shall sign and certify, and transmit sealed to the seat of the government of the United States, directed to the President of the Senate;— The President of the Senate shall, in the presence of the Senate and House of Representatives, open all the certificates and the votes shall then be counted;—The person having the greatest number of votes for President, shall be the President, if such number be a majority of the whole number of Electors appointed; and if no person have such majority, then from the persons having the highest numbers not exceeding three on the list of those voted for as President, the House of Representatives shall choose immediately, by ballot, the President. But in choosing the President, the votes shall be taken by states, the representation from each state having one vote; a quorum for this purpose shall consist of a member or members from two-thirds of the states, and a majority of all the states shall be necessary to a choice. And if the House of Representatives shall not choose a President whenever the right of choice shall devolve upon them, before the fourth day of March next following, then the Vice-President shall act as President, as in the case of the death or other constitutional disability of the President—The person having the greatest number of votes as Vice-President, shall be the Vice-President, if such number be a majority of the whole number of Electors appointed, and if no person have a majority, then from the two highest numbers on the list, the Senate shall choose the Vice-President; A quorum for the purpose shall consist of two-thirds of the whole number of Senators, and a majority of the whole number shall be necessary to a choice. But no person constitutionally ineligible to the office of President shall be eligible to that of Vice-President of the United States.

AMENDMENT XIII (1865)

Section 1   Neither slavery nor involuntary servitude, except as a punishment for crime whereof the party shall have been duly convicted, shall exist within the United States, or any place subject to their jurisdiction.

Section 2   Congress shall have power to enforce this article by appropriate legislation.

AMENDMENT XIV (1868)

Section 1   All persons born or naturalized in the United States and subject to the jurisdiction thereof, are citizens of the United States and of the State wherein they reside. No State shall make or enforce any law which shall abridge the privileges or immunities of citizens of the United States; nor shall any State deprive any person of life, liberty, or property, without due process of law; nor deny to any person within its jurisdiction the equal protection of the laws.

Section 2   Representatives shall be apportioned among the several States according to their respective numbers, counting the whole number of persons in each State, excluding Indians not taxed. But when the right to vote at any election for the choice of electors for President and Vice-President of the United States, Representatives in Congress, the Executive and Judicial officers of a State, or the members of the Legislature thereof, is denied to any of the male inhabitants of such State, being twenty-one years of age, and citizens of the United States, or in any way abridged, except for participation in rebellion, or other crime, the basis of representation therein shall be reduced in the proportion which the number of such male citizens shall bear to the whole number of male citizens twenty-one years of age in such State.

Section 3   No person shall be a Senator or Representative in Congress, or elector of President and Vice-President, or hold any office, civil or military, under the United States, or under any State, who, having previously taken an oath, as a member of Congress, or as an officer of the United States, or as a member of any State legislature, or as an executive or judicial officer of any State, to support the Constitution of the United States, shall have engaged in insurrection or rebellion against the same, or given aid or comfort to the enemies thereof. But Congress may by a vote of two-thirds of each House, remove such disability.

Section 4   The validity of the public debt of the United States, authorized by law, including debts incurred for payment of pensions and bounties for services in suppressing insurrection or rebellion, shall not be questioned. But neither the United States nor any State shall assume or pay any debt or obligation incurred in aid of insurrection or rebellion against the United States, or any claim for the loss or emancipation of any slave; but all such debts, obligations and claims shall be held illegal and void.

Section 5   The Congress shall have power to enforce, by appropriate legislation, the provisions of this article.

AMENDMENT XV (1870)

Section 1   The right of citizens of the United States to vote shall not be denied or abridged by the United States or by any State on account of race, color, or previous condition of servitude.

Section 2   The Congress shall have power to enforce this article by appropriate legislation.

AMENDMENT XVI (1913)

The Congress shall have power to lay and collect taxes on incomes, from whatever source derived, without apportionment among the several States, and without regard to any census or enumeration.

AMENDMENT XVII (1913)

The Senate of the United States shall be composed of two Senators from each State, elected by the people thereof, for six years; and each Senator shall have one vote. The electors in each State shall have the qualifications requisite for electors of the most numerous branch of the State legislatures.

When vacancies happen in the representation of any State in the Senate, the executive authority of such State shall issue writs of election to fill such vacancies: *Provided,* That the legislature of any State may empower the executive thereof to make temporary appointments until the people fill the vacancies by election as the legislature may direct.

This amendment shall not be so construed as to affect the election or term of any Senator chosen before it becomes valid as part of the Constitution.

AMENDMENT XVIII (1919)

Section 1   After one year from the ratification of this article the manufacture, sale, or transportation of intoxicating liquors within, the importation thereof into, or the exportation thereof from the United States and all territory subject to the jurisdiction thereof for beverage purposes is hereby prohibited.

Section 2   The Congress and the several States shall have concurrent power to enforce this article by appropriate legislation.

Section 3   This article shall be inoperative unless it shall have been ratified as an amendment to the Constitution by the legislatures of the several States, as provided in the Constitution, within seven years from the date of the submission hereof to the States by the Congress.

AMENDMENT XIX (1920)

The right of citizens of the United States to vote shall not be denied or abridged by the United States or by any State on account of sex.

Congress shall have power to enforce this article by appropriate legislation.

AMENDMENT XX (1933)

Section 1   The terms of the President and Vice President shall end at noon on the 20th day of January, and the terms of Senators and Representatives at noon on the 3d day of January, of the years in which such terms would have ended if this article had not been ratified; and the terms of their successors shall then begin.

Section 2   The Congress shall assemble at least once in every year, and such meeting shall begin at noon on the 3d day of January, unless they shall by law appoint a different day.

Section 3   If, at the time fixed for the beginning of the term of the President, the President elect shall have died, the Vice President elect shall become President. If a President shall not have been chosen before the time fixed for the beginning of his term, or if the President elect shall have failed to qualify, then the Vice President elect shall act as President until a President shall have qualified; and the Congress may by law provide for the case wherein neither a President elect nor a Vice President elect shall have qualified, declaring who shall then act as President, or the manner in which one who is to act shall be selected, and such person shall act accordingly until a President or Vice President shall have qualified.

Section 4   The Congress may by law provide for the case of the death of any of the persons from whom the House of Representatives may choose a President whenever the right of choice shall have devolved upon them, and for the case of the death of any of the persons from whom the Senate may choose a Vice President whenever the right of choice shall have devolved upon them.

Section 5   Sections 1 and 2 shall take effect on the 15th day of October following the ratification of this article.

Section 6   This article shall be inoperative unless it shall have been ratified as an amendment to the Constitution by the legislatures of three-fourths of the several States within seven years from the date of its submission.

AMENDMENT XXI (1933)

Section 1   The eighteenth article of amendment to the Constitution of the United States is hereby repealed.

Section 2   The transportation or importation into any State, Territory or possession of the United States for delivery or use therein of intoxicating liquors, in violation of the laws thereof, is hereby prohibited.

Section 3   This article shall be inoperative unless it shall have been ratified as an amendment to the Constitution by conventions in the several States, as provided in the Constitution, within seven years from the date of the submission hereof to the States by the Congress.

AMENDMENT XXII (1951)

Section 1 No person shall be elected to the office of the President more than twice, and no person who has held the office of President, or acted as President, for more than two years of a term to which some other person was elected President shall be elected to the office of the President more than once. But this Article shall not apply to any person holding the office of President when this Article was proposed by the Congress, and shall not prevent any person who may be holding the office of President, or acting as President, during the term within which this Article becomes operative from holding the office of President or acting as President during the remainder of such term.

Section 2 This Article shall be inoperative unless it shall have been ratified as an amendment to the Constitution by the legislatures of three-fourths of the several States within seven years from the date of its submission to the States by the Congress.

AMENDMENT XXIII (1961)

Section 1 The District constituting the seat of Government of the United States shall appoint in such manner as the Congress may direct:

A number of electors of President and Vice President equal to the whole number of Senators and Representatives in Congress to which the District would be entitled if it were a State, but in no event more than the least populous State; they shall be in addition to those appointed by the States, but they shall be considered, for the purposes of the election of President and Vice President, to be electors appointed by a State; and they shall meet in the District and perform such duties as provided by the twelfth article of amendment.

Section 2 The Congress shall have power to enforce this article by appropriate legislation.

AMENDMENT XXIV (1964)

Section 1 The right of citizens of the United States to vote in any primary or other election for President or Vice President, for electors for President or Vice President, or for Senator or Representative in Congress, shall not be denied or abridged by the United States or any State by reason of failure to pay any poll tax or other tax.

Section 2 The Congress shall have power to enforce this article by appropriate legislation.

AMENDMENT XXV (1967)

Section 1 In case of the removal of the President from office or of his death or resignation, the Vice President shall become President.

Section 2 Whenever there is a vacancy in the office of the Vice President, the President shall nominate a Vice President who shall take office upon confirmation by a majority vote of both Houses of Congress.

Section 3 Whenever the President transmits to the President pro tempore of the Senate and the Speaker of the House of Representatives his written declaration that he is unable to discharge the powers and duties of his office, and until he transmits to them a written declaration to the contrary, such powers and duties shall be discharged by the Vice President as Acting President.

Section 4 Whenever the Vice President and a majority of either the principal officers of the executive departments or of such other body as Congress may by law provide, transmit to the President pro tempore of the Senate and the Speaker of the House of Representatives their written declaration that the President is unable to discharge the powers and duties of his office, the Vice President shall immediately assume the powers and duties of the office as Acting President.

Thereafter, when the President transmits to the President pro tempore of the Senate and the Speaker of the House of Representatives his written declaration that no inability exists, he shall resume the powers and duties of his office unless the Vice President and a majority of either the principal officers of the executive department or of such other body as Congress may by law provide, transmit within four days to the President pro tempore of the Senate and the Speaker of the House of Representatives their written declaration that the President is unable to discharge the powers and duties of his office. Thereupon Congress shall decide the issue, assembling within forty-eight hours for that purpose if not in session. If the Congress, within twenty-one days after receipt of the latter written declaration, or, if Congress is not in session, within twenty-one days after Congress is required to assemble, determines by two-thirds vote of both Houses that the President is unable to discharge the powers and duties of his office, the Vice President shall continue to discharge the same as Acting President; otherwise, the President shall resume the powers and duties of his office.

AMENDMENT XXVI (1971)

Section 1 The right of citizens of the United States, who are eighteen years of age or older, to vote shall not be denied or abridged by the United States or by any State on account of age.

Section 2 The Congress shall have power to enforce this article by appropriate legislation.

AMENDMENT XXVII (1992)

No law varying the compensation for the services of the senators and representatives shall take effect, until an election of representatives shall have intervened.

APPENDIX B

SAMPLE APPELLATE BRIEF

IN THE
COURT OF SPECIAL APPEALS OF MARYLAND

September Term, 1996

No. 000

John C. Doe

Appellant

v.

Jane B. Doe

Appellee

Appeal from the Circuit Court for
Anne Arundel County, Maryland
(The Honorable Allen Brown, Judge)

BRIEF OF APPELLANT, JOHN C. DOE

Monica R. Gates
101 East Potomac Avenue
Baltimore, Maryland 21212-1234

Attorney for Appellant

TABLE OF CONTENTS

TABLE OF AUTHORITIES

CASES

STATUTES

STATEMENT OF THE CASE

This appeal presents a number of questions concerning financial responsibilities, division of property, and visitation with minor children following a divorce. On May 16, 1993, the Appellee, Jane B. Doe (hereinafter "Mrs. Doe"), sued the Appellant, John C. Doe (hereinafter "Dr. Doe"), for a limited divorce or absolute divorce. On July 11, 1993, Mrs. Doe filed an Amended Complaint for Absolute Divorce, or in the alternative, a Limited Divorce and Dr. Doe filed an Answer to the Amended Complaint on August 10, 1993. The discovery phase of the case was initiated on July 11, 1993, with Mrs. Doe's Interrogatories and Request for Production of Documents. Discovery continued throughout the case until approximately April 29, 1995, when Mrs. Doe took her husband's deposition.

On May 2, 1994, Mrs. Doe filed an Amended Supplemental Complaint for Absolute Divorce and Other Equitable Relief. Dr. Doe filed his Answer to the Amended Supplemental Complaint on May 29, 1994. On August 2, 1994, Dr. Doe filed a Counterclaim to Enforce Visitation Rights. Mrs. Doe filed a Request for Emergency Hearing on Pendente Lite Alimony and Child Support on August 9, 1994. In addition, on August 15, 1994, Mrs. Doe filed her Answer to the Counterclaim to Enforce Visitation Rights Pendente Lite.

On September 27, 1994, the case was called for hearing on all pending motions before the Honorable Betty Black of the Circuit Court for Anne Arundel County. Testimony was taken and the case was continued to September 30, 1994. On the latter date, testimony resumed, exhibits were presented, and counsel for both parties were heard. After consideration of the testimony, evidence, and argument of counsel, Judge Black denied Mrs. Doe's request for alimony *pendente lite;* denied her request for a contribution to the mortgage payment *pendente lite;* awarded the care and custody, *pendente lite,* of the minor children to Mrs. Doe; awarded use and possession of the family home and family use personal property, *pendente lite,* to Mrs. Doe; ordered Dr. Doe to pay child support, *pendente lite,* of $1,427.00 per month; and awarded Dr. Doe visitation rights, *pendente lite,* of every other weekend from 6:00 P.M. Fridays until 5:00 P.M. Sundays. Judge Black ordered that the *pendente lite* relief would remain in effect until November 22, 1994, the date of the scheduled merits trial.

Dr. Doe filed a Counterclaim for Absolute Divorce on October 15, 1994. On October 18, 1994, Mrs. Doe filed a Motion for Voluntary Dismissal, asking that her Complaint for Absolute Divorce be dismissed. On November 18, 1994, the lower Court dismissed Mrs. Doe's Complaint. The case was called for a hearing on the merits on November 22, 1994 before the Honorable Charles Green. The case was continued, pending resolution of various motions, including Mrs. Doe's Motion to Strike Counterclaim and Mrs. Doe's attorney's request to strike his appearance. On December 18, 1994, Dr. Doe filed a second Motion to Enforce Visitation Rights Pendente Lite and Request for Emergency Relief.

On February 4, 1995, the case was reopened and on February 28, 1995, Mrs. Doe filed her Answer to the Counter Complaint for Absolute Divorce. On March 10, 1995, a Consent Order was filed granting *pendente lite* visitation to Dr. Doe. On May 26, 1995, Dr. Doe filed an Amended Counterclaim for Absolute Divorce. Mrs. Doe filed her Answer to said Amended Counterclaim on July 13, 1995. On July 20, 1995, Mrs. Doe filed a Second Amended Complaint for Absolute Divorce.

On July 31, 1995, the lower Court ordered a consolidation of the case involving Mrs. Doe's newly filed case containing the Second Amended Complaint for Absolute Divorce (Case No.: C-95-34567) with Dr. Doe's Counterclaim for Absolute Divorce (Case No.: C-94-12345). The consolidated case came on for hearing on July 31, 1995 and was continued to August 11, 1995 and August 12, 1995. The Honorable Allen Brown, Circuit

Court for Anne Arundel County, presided over the three days of testimony. At the close of the parties' cases on August 12, 1995, Judge Brown held the matter *sub curia.*

Judge Brown issued a written Opinion and Order on August 31, 1995. Dr. Doe appeals the Opinion ordering him to pay alimony, child support, health insurance, and the mortgage and other costs of the family home, all totalling the sum of approximately $2,845.00 per month; appeals the Opinion of the lower Court requiring him to pay twelve (12) years of rehabilitative alimony; appeals the Opinion of the lower Court entering a Judgment against him and in favor of Mrs. Doe in the amount of $60,000.00; appeals the Opinion of the lower Court entering a Judgment against him for $5,000.00 as a contribution to Mrs. Doe's attorney fees; and appeals the Opinion of the lower Court ordering a visitation schedule contrary to the schedule agreed upon by the parties and placed on the record before the lower Court.

Dr. Doe filed his Notice of Appeal on September 16, 1995. On October 16, 1995, Mrs. Doe filed a Petition for Contempt, Specific Performance, an Immediate Hearing, Attorneys' Fees and Other Relief. On November 27, 1995, Dr. Doe filed an Emergency Motion to Stay Execution of the Judgment. The Show Cause hearing on the contempt issue was held before the Honorable Daniel White on December 1, 1995. Judge White found Dr. Doe not guilty of contempt but capable of making the payments as ordered on August 31, 1995. By written Order dated December 17, 1995, Judge White entered the aforesaid findings, as well as others, including modifying the prior Order of August 31, 1995, which required Dr. Doe to obtain medical insurance on behalf of the parties' three minor children, to provide that Dr. Doe pay only the cost of the children's existing medical insurance coverage which Mrs. Doe had through her employer.

On December 22, 1995, Judge Brown, the presiding Judge at the merits hearing, entered an Order granting Dr. Doe's Emergency Motion to Stay Execution of Judgment. Pursuant to Judge Brown's December 22nd Order, Dr. Doe's total support payments were reduced to $1,800.00 per month pending the appeal. In addition, pursuant to the aforesaid Order, Dr. Doe was exempted from the requirement to post bonds or security pursuant to Maryland Rule 8-422 in order to stay execution of the Judgment.

QUESTIONS PRESENTED

1. Did the Circuit Court err in awarding Mrs. Doe a monetary award of Sixty Thousand Dollars ($60,000.00) and entering a Judgment against Dr. Doe in that amount when the parties stipulated that the marital equity in the family home was Eighteen Thousand Four Hundred Dollars ($18,400.00), which the lower Court divided equally among the parties, and the evidence revealed that the remaining marital property was valued at a minimum of $6,302.76 but no more than $42,302.76?

2. Did the Circuit Court err in ordering Dr. Doe to spend approximately eighty-one percent (81%) of his net monthly income for alimony, child support, health insurance, and mortgage payment and other costs of the family home during the three-year possession and use period?

3. Did the Circuit Court err in ordering Dr. Doe to pay rehabilitative alimony for a period of twelve (12) years where the evidence established that Mrs. Doe would need only three (3) to five (5) years to obtain her doctoral degree in her career field?

4. Did the Circuit Court err in ordering Dr. Doe to contribute to Mrs. Doe's attorney fees, deposition expenses, and court costs where there was insufficient evidence to establish that Mrs. Doe had substantial justification for withholding visitation, retaining seven attorneys, or that Mrs. Doe lacked financial resources to pay her fees?

5.   Did the Circuit Court err in ordering a visitation schedule that is contrary to the visitation schedule agreed upon by the parties and placed on the record before the lower Court?

STATEMENT OF FACTS

Dr. and Mrs. Doe had been married for twelve (12) years by the time their divorce trial began on July 31, 1995. (E.119). For more than two (2) years prior to the trial, the parties had lived apart in separate residences. (E.251). During the separation period, Mrs. Doe remained in the family home and Dr. Doe rented an apartment in Green City. (E.412). The parties have three children, Aye, born August 1, 1985, Bee, born November 1, 1988, and Cee, born March 1, 1992. (E.134). The children have remained with Mrs. Doe in the family home, located in Hill Valley. (E.417).

Dr. and Mrs. Doe are Zambian and were born in the same area of Zambia. (E.291). The couple met in the fall of 1981 in the library at the University of Connecticut, where Dr. Doe was a graduate student and Mrs. Doe was finishing college. (E.291, 237). After a brief courtship, the couple was married by a civil ceremony on March 10, 1982.

The parties did not have the benefit of a "honeymoon"—extended or otherwise—as they were both hard-working students during the early years of their marriage and because their first son was born the first year they were married. (E.238, 239). Dr. Doe began medical school at the Medical College in Bridgeport during the fall of 1982 and the couple lived in the married students' dormitory. (E.238). During this time, Mrs. Doe was a graduate student at the University of Connecticut School of Public Health. (E.238). Mrs. Doe received her Master of Science degree from that institution in 1985 and Dr. Doe graduated from medical school the following year. (E.238, 239).

The couple faced financial challenges as well as academic ones in the early years of their marriage. (E.242). Both parties took out loans to partially finance their respective educations; in addition, both have worked throughout the marriage. (E.237, 419). During the first four (4) years of the marriage, when both parties were students, their total annual family income ranged from $20,466.00 in 1982 to $9,014.00 in 1983, $2,949.00 in 1984, and zero in 1985. (E.532-533).

In addition to the academic and financial stresses which served to dampen the beginning of the marriage, the couple also had many "extended stay" visitors. (E.243). Relatives of both Dr. and Mrs. Doe stayed with them in Bridgeport and the couple always opened their home for these visits because they believe in the concept of the "extended family" and in helping out other family members. (E.154). Likewise, it was a benefit to Dr. and Mrs. Doe to have a relative stay with them to help after the birth of each child. (E.155).

In June 1986, after he graduated from medical school, Dr. Doe began his internship at Memorial Hospital at an annual salary of $18,000.00; Mrs. Doe worked full time that year and they had a joint annual income of $20,792.00. (E.244, 289).

Although the couple faced academic, financial, and other challenges in the first years of their marriage, their own marital problems, by both parties' accounts, did not surface until sometime in 1986. (E.292, 125). Prior to 1986, Dr. Doe thought that he and his wife had a good marriage; he was attracted to his wife because he found her to be charming and attractive and he felt that they had much in common because they were born and raised in the same area of Zambia and shared the same beliefs. (E.290, 291). In 1986, however, the same year the couple visited their respective families in Zambia, marital problems surfaced. (E.292). Mrs. Doe accused her husband of infidelity and physical abuse during that trip and he denied both claims; she also felt that their communication problems started back then. (E.294, 131). Dr. Doe attributes the estrangement partially to a pattern of false accusations of infidelity which he claims started in 1986. (E.297, 298). In addition, Dr. Doe began to see his wife as having very low self-esteem and he became increasingly isolated from her, as he felt that she wanted pity from others and that she drove away friends because she gossiped about them. (E.299).

In June 1987, Dr. Doe began his three (3) year residency at General Hospital in New York City. (E.244). During this time period, the couple's second child was born. (E.130). Dr. Doe supplemented his residency salary by moonlighting at another hospital on weekends and evenings. (E.245). After two (2) months, Mrs. Doe obtained a position as a dietician at Suburban Hospital in New York City. (E.130). Although this was a demanding time for Dr. Doe because of the residency, he felt that he and his wife took time to enjoy their two (2) children. (E.246). Mrs. Doe felt that her husband had no time to communicate with her or to help her with housework or child care. (E.131).

By the time Dr. Doe completed his residency in 1991, both parties knew that they did not want to raise their family in New York City. (E.247). Mrs. Doe was pregnant with their third child. (E.248). The Does moved to Hill Valley because Dr. Doe knew a doctor there who was selling his medical practice and both parties liked the location and thought that it would be a better place to raise their family. (E.248, 157).

In 1991, the couple purchased a two (2) bedroom condominium in Hill Valley, where Mrs. Doe and the children still reside. (E.249). After the Does had settled in Hill Valley, Dr. Doe learned that the deal involving the other doctor's practice was not a good one; accordingly, Dr. Doe joined a three (3) office optical company based in Annapolis and did eye examinations for them. (E.249). Mrs. Doe, meanwhile, was pregnant during this time and delivered their third child, another son, in March 1992. (E.145). After working at some temporary and part-time jobs following her pregnancy, Mrs. Doe obtained a position as a dietician at Delta Hospital in South Annapolis, where she is still employed. (E.58).

In March 1993, Dr. Doe opened his sole ophthalmology practice in Hill Valley, which he maintains to date. (E.251, 252). The couple's marital problems reached a peak at approximately this time. (E.257). Dr. Doe spoke to his pastor about how to deal with his feelings; in addition, he asked his wife's brother for his opinion and guidance. (E.297, 230). Mrs. Doe reported that her husband was abusive to her and the couple had a final argument in the marital home on April 12, 1993, when Dr. Doe wanted to take the children to "McDonalds" for lunch. (E.144, 145). Dr. Doe claimed that this incident was only a verbal argument precipitated by his wife's refusal to allow the children to leave the home without her. (E.303). Mrs. Doe reported that Dr. Doe was abusive and hit her. (E.144). Dr. Doe denies this claim. (E.303). Ultimately, Dr. Doe agreed to leave the family home and establish his residence elsewhere. (E.251, 302).

During the separation period, Mrs. Doe would not allow her husband to have the children visit with him because she claimed to be afraid that he would take the children to Zambia and not return. (E.145). Dr. Doe was finally able to see the children either at their school or at his pastor's home. (E.321). On September 30, 1994, following a *pendente lite* hearing, a regular schedule of nonsupervised visitation, including overnights, was established for Dr. Doe by Order of Judge Betty Black of the Circuit Court for Anne Arundel County. (E.2, 13). In late November 1994, Mrs. Doe again denied her husband visitation with the children. (E.319). Dr. Doe was not allowed to see his children for Thanksgiving or for Christmas in 1994. (E.320). Dr. Doe filed a Motion to Enforce Visitation Rights and Request for Emergency Relief shortly before Christmas 1994 but a hearing was not scheduled until March 13, 1995. (E.34). A Consent Order "reinstating" the visitation was filed on March 10, 1995 and Dr. Doe's visitation schedule with the parties' children was resumed. (E.16).

Immediately following the parties' separation, Dr. Doe continued to pay the mortgage on the parties' home, condo fees and other costs associated with the condo, real estate taxes, and the childrens' day care cost. (E.266). Dr. Doe stopped making the day care payment when he learned that Mrs. Doe's mother was watching the children and Mrs. Doe was not taking the children to the babysitter. (E.266). For a while, Dr. Doe also paid for the utilities on the family home. (E.266). Mrs. Doe felt that she needed additional financial support from her husband and on August 9, 1994, she filed a Request for Emergency Hearing on Pendente Lite Alimony and Child Support. (E.1). These issues, along with the visitation issue previously raised by Dr. Doe, were heard by Judge Black at the *pendente lite* hearing on September 27 and 30, 1994. (E.2). Mrs. Doe's attorney prepared a written order corresponding to the findings and order of Judge Black; however, her counsel did not file the Order with the Court. (E.13).

After September 30, 1994, Dr. Doe made payments directly to his wife pursuant to Judge Black's Order until January of 1995. (E.327). In January, Dr. Doe learned from the mortgagor on the parties' home that the company was going to foreclose on the home because the mortgage had not been paid. (E.325). At that time, Dr. Doe resumed paying the mortgagor directly and he deducted that amount from the support payments he made to his wife. (E.325).

ARGUMENT

I. THE CIRCUIT COURT ERRED IN AWARDING MRS. DOE A MONETARY AWARD OF $60,000.00 AND REDUCING THE TOTAL AWARD TO A JUDGMENT AGAINST DR. DOE.

A. The Circuit Court's award to Mrs. Doe exceeds the total value of marital property.

The lower court clearly erred in concluding that a $60,000.00 monetary award to Mrs. Doe was appropriate. The error is obvious in several respects. First, the monetary award exceeds the value of the total marital property; this is manifestly improper. *Ward v. Ward*, 52 Md. App. 336, 449 A.2d 443 (1982). The parties submitted a Joint Statement Concerning Marital and Non-Marital Property pursuant to Maryland Rule S-74 and stipulated to the identity, title, and value of all property *except* the medical practice and the property in Zambia. (E.497, 498, 171, 172, 173). Dr. and Mrs. Doe agreed that the equity in the family home was $18,400.00 (E.497). The lower court ordered that the home be sold and the net proceeds divided equally following the three (3) year possession and use period. Judge Brown proceeded to value[1] and credit the remaining property as follows (E.21,22):

Mrs. Doe		Dr. Doe	
'88 Sentra	585.46	Property in Zambia	unknown
Life Insurance	35.50	'90 Mitsubishi	-0-
Cash	880.48	Medical Practice	36,000.00
IRA	1,057.19	Cash	1,489.13
	2,558.63	IRA	2,255.00
			39,744.13

---

[1] All values listed are net equity figures.

As illustrated above, the lower court identified equity in marital property totalling $42,302.76 and "credited" Mrs. Doe with $2,558.63. Accordingly, factors itemized in Md. Code Ann., Fam. Law § 8-205(b) were considered along with the previous alimony award. (E.23). The lower court's opinion reveals that Judge Brown was apparently most impressed with Mrs. Doe's contributions to the marriage, Dr. Doe's medical practice, Mrs. Doe's role in ensuring that Dr. Doe obtained his education, the Zambian property and Dr. Doe's present income and potentiality for the future. (E.23). As in *Ward*, however, the other factors were largely irrelevant. As in *Ward*, factor 4 (circumstances contributing to estrangement of parties) should have no bearing in this case because Mrs. Doe's allegations of cruelty and adultery during the marriage were not corroborated. The only evidence of Dr. Doe's adultery was two (2) years after the parties' separation; accordingly, as in *Ward*, it should have no bearing on the monetary award in this case. In the case at bar, both parties are in their 30's and in good general health. The Does lived together in marriage for ten (10) years and both obtained advanced degrees during the marriage. In addition, both Dr. Doe and Mrs. Doe worked throughout the marriage.

In the case at bar, as in *Ward*, the proper conclusion resulting from a consideration of the nine (9) factors is that the balance is even and the marital property should be divided equally. Since the effect of the lower court's Order is to give Mrs. Doe 100% of the marital property, the decision constitutes clear error.

B. The Circuit Court's inclusion of Dr. Doe's family's property in Zambia as marital property was clearly erroneous.

Dr. Doe's family has property in Zambia. The property consists of a five (5) bedroom house and a small old house with an outdoor kitchen, both sitting on approximately one (1) acre of fenced-in land. (E.67, 282–286). Dr. Doe's mother still lives on the property, which the family calls "the compound." (E.67, 273). Dr. Doe and his six (6) sisters were born and raised in the older house, as was Dr. Doe's mother. (E.68, 284). In 1980, Dr. Doe's sister took charge of having the newer house built on the compound because the older house was falling apart and their mother needed a better shelter. (E.69). In northern Zambia, where Dr. Doe and his sisters grew up and where the compound is located, the tradition is that the eldest son of a family (or the eldest daughter if there is no son) is responsible for ensuring that the family property is preserved for the next generation so that there is always a home for anyone in the family to return to, if necessary. (E.279–282). The newer house was completed in 1981, before the Does were married. (E.79, 80, 286). Dr. Doe was living in the United States during construction of the new home and did not contribute money or assistance in any way. (E.72, 73). Dr. Doe has no interest in the property in Zambia save for that it belongs to "the family."(E.72). Mrs. Doe's own brother also testified that the home in Zambia is a family home, as long as Dr. Doe's mother is alive and living in it. (E.229). Dr. and Mrs. Doe did not see the newer house until 1986 when they visited Zambia with their children. (E.287).

The property in Zambia is not marital property because it was not acquired by the parties during their marriage. The lower court improperly considered this property in arriving at a monetary award for Mrs. Doe. In determining an equitable distribution of marital property, Maryland courts are required to engage in the three (3) step process outlined in Md. Code Ann., Fam. Law §§ 8-202, 8-203, 8-204, and 8-205. First, all the property owned by the parties must be classified as either marital or non-marital. Second, marital property must be valued. Finally, the Court determines a monetary award, if appropriate. *See e.g., Quinn v. Quinn,* 83 Md. App. 460, 575 A.2d 764 (1990) (quoting *Sharp v. Sharp,* 58 Md. App. 386, 473 A.2d 499 (1984)). The lower Court erred when executing the first step because the Zambian property was not acquired by the parties during their marriage. The party asserting a marital interest in property has the burden of proving its identity and value. *Melrod v. Melrod,* 83 Md. App. 180, 574 A.2d 1 (1990). Mrs. Doe was unable to sustain this burden because she offered no concrete evidence verifying that the property was acquired by the couple during their marriage.

Even if the judge was to liberally consider and find that improvements were made to the property with marital funds, characterizing the Zambian property as partly marital, the Court would still fail to execute the second step required by § 8-204, which is to value the property. Indeed, in the judgment appealed from, the Court states that "it cannot put a value on the property in [Zambia]." (E.23). The only evidence offered to show the Does' contribution to the construction of the Zambian home was Mrs. Doe's statement " ... we started sending money home." (E.122). *See Blake v. Blake,* 81 Md. App. 712, 569 A.2d 724 (1990) (holding that the trial court had properly declined to consider the costs of repairs or improvements to property when there existed no credible evidence of the level of costs of repair or improvements, labor or materials, or change in value resulting therefrom). Dr. Doe denied that he sent any money to help build the new home. (E.273, 274). Significantly, the evidence revealed that the couple had an extremely low joint income in the early years of their marriage; this corroborates Dr. Doe's testimony that there was not enough money for them to be "investing" in property overseas. (E.532, 533).

Without valuation, there is no means for judicial recognition and thus the property may not be considered marital property. *Unkle v. Unkle,* 305 Md. 587, 505 A.2d 849 (1985). *See also Rosenberg v. Rosenberg,* 64 Md. App. 487, 497 A.2d 485 (1985) (holding that Wife had not proven Husband's personal efforts had increased his interest in inherited property, and therefore, the accretion in interest was non-marital property). Because there is no sufficient evidence to conclude otherwise, the value of the non-marital property is not subject to equitable distribution and thus, the monetary award should be vacated as an abuse of discretion. *Harper v. Harper,* 58 Md. App. 193, 472 A.2d 1018 (1984).

C. The Circuit Court's acceptance of Mrs. Doe's valuation of Dr. Doe's sole medical practice was clearly erroneous where the valuation failed to itemize and specify the relevant elements of a sole medical practice.

The lower court valued Dr. Doe's three (3) year old sole ophthalmology practice in Hill Valley at $36,000.00. This valuation is clearly erroneous because the opinion submitted by the Appellee's expert lacks an itemization of the essential factors which must be considered in a proper evaluation. (E.490).

When valuing a professional practice, the value of the work in progress, in addition to other tangible factors, should be considered. *See Quinn v. Quinn,* 83 Md. App. 460, 470, 575 A.2d 764, 769 (1990) (quoting *Stern v. Stern,* 66 N.J. 340, 331 A.2d 257 (1975)). The expert's opinion must be based on facts sufficient to support a reasonable, accurate conclusion. *See Quinn v. Quinn,* 83 Md. App. at 471, 575 A.2d at 769 (holding that the wife's expert did not have an adequate basis on which to value her husband's law firm where her expert valued the contingent fee cases solely on the number of hours expended on the case multiplied by the hourly rate). Moreover, any goodwill contained in Dr. Doe's medical practice must be identified and valued; it is not considered marital property, however, unless it has a separate value from Dr. Doe's personal reputation. *Prahinski v. Prahinski,* 321 Md. 227, 582 A.2d 784 (1990).

Mrs. Doe's expert offered no support as to how he arrived at a final value of the medical practice. The opinion fails to itemize and specify the values of the relevant elements of a medical practice. Most significantly, the "goodwill factor" is not addressed. Given the absence of oral expert testimony at the hearing regarding the valuing of the practice, the written opinion of the Appellee's expert witness should have specifically delineated the bases for the valuation given. It is evident that the lower court erred in accepting the Appellee's expert valuation over the Appellant's, which did itemize relevant elements of the practice. *Compare John O. v. Jane O.*, 90 Md. App. 406, 601 A.2d 149 (1992) (holding that husband could not complain about valuation of wife's pension where he presented no alternative evidence). Dr. Doe described his current practice in detail for the lower court and he presented a detailed evaluation of its worth. (E.250–258, 492–496). Consequently, the lower court erred in valuing Dr. Doe's practice at $36,000.00.

In addition, the trial court failed to consider Dr. Doe's post-separation efforts to build his practice when determining the monetary award. In *Wilen v. Wilen,* 61 Md. App. 337, 486 A.2d 775 (1985), the Court of Special Appeals held that the extent to which efforts of one spouse may have led to acquisition of property or increase in its value without any monetary or non-monetary contribution by the other spouse after the parties separate, can and should be taken into account in determining what would constitute an equitable monetary award. Although Dr. Doe established a relationship with an Annapolis-based optical company in the fall of 1991 and collected fees for eye exams he did at their satellite offices, he did not open his sole practice until March 1993. Prior to 1993, he was simply using someone else's offices and equipment. (E.249-50). In April 1993, the Does began living apart. The practice was valued in July 1995. Accordingly, the practice was about three (3) years old when it was valued, and of those three (3) years, the parties were separated for two (2) years. The lower court erred in failing to consider this fact.

D. The Circuit Court's order that the total monetary award of $60,000.00 be reduced to a judgment was clearly erroneous pursuant to Md. Code Ann., Fam. Law § 8-205(c).

The lower court ordered Dr. Doe to pay Mrs. Doe a monetary award of $60,000.00 at a rate of $5,000.00 per year for twelve (12) years. In addition, the court reduced the $60,000.00 award to a judgment against Dr. Doe (E.23). The lower court's judgment is clearly erroneous because the court may only reduce a monetary award to a judgment to the extent that any part of the award is due and owing. Since the total amount of the judgment is not due and payable in the present case, the total amount cannot be reduced to a judgment. Md. Code Ann., Fam. Law § 8-205(c) (1991); *Ross v. Ross,* 90 Md. App. 176, 600 A.2d 891 (1991). *See also Cotter v. Cotter,* 58 Md. App. 529, 473 A.2d 970 (1984) (holding that reducing the alimony and marital award to a judgment was a clear abuse of discretion because no part was due and owing).

II.   THE CIRCUIT COURT ERRED IN ORDERING DR. DOE TO SPEND APPROXIMATELY 81% OF HIS NET MONTHLY INCOME FOR ALIMONY, CHILD SUPPORT, HEALTH INSURANCE, AND MORTGAGE AND OTHER COSTS OF THE FAMILY HOME DURING THE THREE-YEAR POSSESSION AND USE PERIOD.

The Court's Order requires, in pertinent part, that Dr. Doe make payments on behalf of his family totalling approximately $2,845.00 per month during the three (3) year possession and use period. (E.20, 21, 531). These payments represent approximately 81% of Dr. Doe's net (after-tax) monthly income or 54% of his gross monthly income. (E.525, 527). The total payment is broken down as follows: child support ($1,400.00); alimony

($400.00); mortgage payment, condo fees, insurance, taxes, and other costs associated with the family home ($770.00); and separate health insurance policy for the children (approximately $275.00). (E.315, 316, 536).

The parties stipulated at trial that Mrs. Doe's gross monthly income is $2,098.00 ($25,176.00 annual) and Dr. Doe's is $5,233.00 ($62,796.00 annual). (E.112, 113). Both parties submitted Child Support Guidelines including Dr. Doe's monthly gross income as $5,233.00 and concluding that the proper amount of monthly child support is approximately $1,430.00 (if $280.00 per month work-related child care is included). (E.499, 525). It is evident that the trial judge recognized and validated the parties' stipulation concerning their respective gross monthly incomes because the judge calculated and ordered approximately the same amount of child support as proposed by both of the parties, namely, $1,400.00 per month. (E.20).

Accordingly, upon receipt of the Court-ordered payments during the three (3) year possession and use period, Mrs. Doe will have $4,668.00[2] in pre-tax funds supplied for her household each month while Dr. Doe will have $2,663.00, before he pays for the children's health insurance.

The health insurance issue has changed since the merits trial before the lower court. In his Opinion and Order, Judge Brown required Dr. Doe to "provide medical insurance for his children." (E.20). At the time of the trial, however, Mrs. Doe maintained the children on the health insurance plan available through her employer at a cost of $86.60 per month. (E.525, 531). This amount was deducted from Mrs. Doe's gross income by both parties for purposes of the child support calculation. (E.499, 525). Dr. Doe is not covered under his wife's plan and therefore must, as a sole proprietor, maintain a separate policy for himself; this costs him approximately $275.00 per month. (E.529).

At the Contempt Hearing before Judge White on December 1, 1995, Dr. Doe explained that his health insurance premium would approximately double if he had to add the children. Judge White modified Judge Brown's Opinion and Order to provide that instead of requiring Dr. Doe to maintain a new and separate policy for the children, he must pay the cost of the children's existing medical coverage which Mrs. Doe has through her employer. (E.26). Since Mrs. Doe's employer deducts this sum from her pay, Dr. Doe is, in a sense, required to "reimburse" her each month in that amount. Accordingly, when the health insurance payment is considered, Mrs. Doe still has approximately $4,668.00 in monthly pre-tax funds supplied for her household, while Dr. Doe has approximately $2,576.00. In sum, as a result of Judge White's modification of the lower court's Order, Dr. Doe is currently required to make payments on behalf of his family representing approximately 75% of his net monthly income.

The Court's Order is excessive because it grossly exceeds Dr. Doe's financial ability. It is critical to note that immediately following the judgment appealed from, Dr. Doe could not keep up with the payments ordered and fell behind, triggering a contempt hearing; significantly, Judge Brown granted Dr. Doe's Emergency Motion to Stay Execution of Judgment and reduced Dr. Doe's support payments to their pre-merits trial level. (E.28). As there is no statutory mandate concerning support judgments, the Court is compelled to tailor the remedy *sui generis. Bowis v. Bowis*, 259 Md. 41, 267 A.2d 84 (1970) (quoting *Burton v. Burton*, 253 Md. 233, 252 A.2d 472 (1969)). The Court has traditionally considered the parties' financial circumstances, station in life, age, physical condition, ability to work, length of marriage and the circumstances leading up to the divorce in determining the proper amount of support. *Bowis v. Bowis*, 259 Md. 41, 267 A.2d 84 (1970).

---

[2] Mrs. Doe's income of $2,098.00 plus $1,800.00 in direct payments from Dr. Doe and Dr. Doe's $770.00 payment of the mortgage on the family home and related costs.

Additionally, the remedy must balance the child's needs and the spouse's financial capabilities. *Unkle v. Unkle,* 305 Md. 587, 505 A.2d 849 (1985).

This Court has previously considered support payment judgments excessive when they surpass the spouse's financial ability to pay. *See Newmeyer v. Newmeyer,* 216 Md. 431, 140. A. 2d 892 (1958) (holding that the stipulated alimony, support payments, and counsel fees were disproportionate to the husband's means and, therefore, grossly excessive regardless of the Newmeyers' prior considerably high standard of living). *See also Rubin v. Rubin,* 233 Md. 118, 195 A.2d 696 (1963) (holding that an Order requiring support payments totaling approximately 68% of husband's monthly income was too excessive). Although the Court has not set a standard as to what equates with "excessive," the Court considers the husband's financial capabilities in light of the wife's ability to be self-supporting. *See Provenza v. Provenza,* 226 Md. 63, 172 A.2d 503 (1961) (holding that alimony payments and counsel fees accounting for approximately 60% of husband's gross income was grossly excessive considering the couple's moderate standard of living before the divorce and the husband's modest income as a dentist).

In the case at bar, it is evident that the award is patently excessive. Under the lower court's order, the funds remaining in Dr. Doe's possession each month will not allow him to meet his basic living expenses and his required student loan and other liability payments. He will have only approximately $2,388.00 to pay taxes (totalling, an average, $1,700.00), leaving him $688.00 to pay for student loans ($279.00), netting only approximately $409.00 for rent, utilities, food, insurance, clothing, and other personal expenses. (E.527, 529). Mrs. Doe, on the other hand, will have approximately $3,898.00 (upon receipt of $1,800.00 in child support and alimony) each month, *after* paying taxes, to pay her expenses. (E.503). After Mrs. Doe pays her student loan of $130.00, she will still have approximately $3,449.00 left for her basic living expenses, and she is not required to make a mortgage or rent payment out of that.

It is evident that Mrs. Doe is capable of supporting herself, for she has a Master of Science degree in nutrition and is currently employed. Additionally, she is young and healthy and thus is able to maintain continued employment, should she so desire. Dr. Doe has a solo medical practice that is not yielding him the profits he anticipated; as a result, he lives a meager lifestyle. (E.412, 413). Indeed, the Does' standard of living throughout their marriage can only be described as very modest. (E.300, 301, 302). Consequently, the lower court's decision to order the Appellant to transfer 81% of his net monthly income to the Appellee is unconscionable and should be reversed.

III. THE CIRCUIT COURT ERRED IN ORDERING DR. DOE TO PAY REHABILITATIVE ALIMONY FOR A PERIOD OF TWELVE (12) YEARS WHERE THE EVIDENCE ESTABLISHED THAT MRS. DOE WOULD NEED ONLY THREE (3) TO FIVE (5) YEARS TO OBTAIN HER DOCTORAL DEGREE IN HER CAREER FIELD.

The Court's award of twelve (12) years of rehabilitative alimony to Mrs. Doe is inconsistent with the facts of the case. Mrs. Doe was never deprived of career growth; instead, she was continually encouraged by her husband to achieve her career goals and during their marriage, Mrs. Doe received her Master of Science degree in Nutrition. (E.203, 244, 258–260). During the trial below, Mrs. Doe expressed an interest in returning to school to obtain a Ph.D in Gerontology so that she may earn a higher salary. (E.202, 203).

Md. Code Ann., Fam. Law § 11-106 governs the calculation, distribution, and duration of an award of alimony. The present social policy behind an award of alimony, in accordance with this statute, is the need to rehabilitate the dependent spouse so that he or she can become economically self-sufficient. *Holston v. Holston,* 58 Md. App. 308,

473 A.2d 459 (1984). Thus, when awarding alimony, the Court is required to consider not only those factors relating to the financial situation, age and health of each party, his or her standard of living, duration of marriage and contribution of both to the well-being of the marriage, but also the ability of the party seeking alimony to obtain education or training that would enable that party to find suitable employment. *Rogers v. Rogers,* 80 Md. App. 575, 565 A.2d 361 (1989). As an essential purpose of the statute is to enable the spouse seeking alimony to be self-supporting, it is necessary to allot sufficient time to enable the spouse to obtain the requisite training or education. Mrs. Doe testified that it would take her three to five years to complete a Ph.D. program in Gerontology at State University and that she will probably be entitled to reduced tuition payments in exchange for teaching some courses. (E.203). Notwithstanding this fact, the lower court awarded her twelve (12) years of rehabilitative alimony. The Court itself stated in the Order that the function of the alimony award is to provide support "for sufficient time for the Plaintiff to conclude her educational pursuits in obtaining her Ph.D in her chosen field." (E.20). After completion of the Ph.D. program, Mrs. Doe will possess one of the most advanced degrees obtainable; therefore, any argument that she will be unable to support herself is without merit. Accordingly, the Order granting twelve (12) years of rehabilitative alimony to Mrs. Doe is unfounded and should be reversed.

IV.   THE CIRCUIT COURT ERRED IN ORDERING DR. DOE TO CONTRIBUTE TO MRS. DOE'S ATTORNEY FEES, DEPOSITION EXPENSES, AND COURT COSTS WHERE THERE WAS INSUFFICIENT EVIDENCE TO ESTABLISH THAT MRS. DOE HAD SUBSTANTIAL JUSTIFICATION FOR WITHHOLDING VISITATION, RETAINING SEVEN (7) ATTORNEYS, OR THAT MRS. DOE LACKED FINANCIAL RESOURCES TO PAY HER FEES.

Mrs. Doe consulted with and/or retained seven (7) attorneys during the course of the parties' separation and divorce, thereby substantially driving up the total cost of her attorney fees. (E.187–190). Further, Mrs. Doe prevented the Appellant from seeing their children for one lengthy period of time and then for a second block of time, forcing Dr. Doe to file two (2) pleadings to enforce his visitation rights. (E.31, 34). Mrs. Doe's explanation for her refusal to allow visitation during the first part of the separation (April 1993 through the September 27, 1994 *pendente lite* hearing) was that Dr. Doe would take the children and not return them. (E.137). Mrs. Doe failed, however, to offer a reasonable justification for this fear; her only explanation was that the oldest son has the "upper hand" in Zambia. (E.137). Zelda Zeta, a Zambian and a professional woman with young children who has lived in the United States almost as long as Mrs. Doe, completely contradicted Mrs. Doe's belief concerning child-snatching by Zambian men. (E.73–75).

Mrs. Doe never offered any explanation for her refusal to allow the children to see their father from late November 1994 until March 1995; in fact, when questioned about visitation during this time, Mrs. Doe claimed to believe that her husband was able to see the children, as scheduled. (E.195). In fact, this is not true at all and Dr. Doe absolutely confirmed that his wife denied him the visitation for no reason. (E.319–321). Mrs. Doe's attorneys were thus compelled to devote additional time and resources to the case as a result of her unjustifiable actions.

Under Md. Code Ann., Fam. Law § 11-110(c), when determining counsel fees, the trial court must consider the financial resources and needs of both parties and whether there was substantial justification to prosecute or defend in the proceeding before an award of attorney fees should be granted. Mrs. Doe had no substantial justification for withholding visitation. Moreover, her financial resources are adequate to cover her counsel fees, particularly in light of the totality of the alimony payments, child support, and monetary award she received. Consequently, the amount awarded to her for counsel fees is excessive and an abuse of the trial court's discretion.

V.   THE CIRCUIT COURT ERRED IN ORDERING A VISITATION SCHEDULE THAT IS CONTRARY TO THE VISITATION SCHEDULE AGREED UPON BY THE PARTIES AND PLACED ON THE RECORD BEFORE THE LOWER COURT.

Prior to the divorce proceeding, the parties reached an agreement on the issue of custody of the parties' minor children and the agreement was read into the record at the trial below. (E.174–176). The parties agreed to share joint legal custody of the three minor children and that Mrs. Doe would retain primary physical custody. Further, an agreement was reached regarding Dr. Doe's visitation schedule. First, he is to have visitation with the minor children every other weekend, from Friday at 7 P.M., until Sunday at 6 P.M. Second, the parties agreed that they would alternate the following holidays with the children: (1) Thanksgiving; (2) the first half of Christmas vacation (end of school through December 23rd); (3) Christmas Eve and Christmas Day through January 1st; (4) Martin Luther King's Birthday; (5) Presidents' Day; (6) Easter; (7) Memorial Day; (8) Fourth of July; and (9) Labor Day. The parties agreed to alternate time on the children's birthdays as well. Additionally, the parties agreed that Dr. Doe, in addition to a minimum of two weeks of summer vacation with the children, was entitled to take up to one-half ($^1/_2$) of the children's summer vacation if he can take time off or make special plans for the children. (E.175). The lower court failed to adhere to the aforesaid schedule and granted Dr. Doe only two weeks of summer vacation visitation, omitting the provision which entitles him to up to one-half ($^1/_2$) as outlined above. Moreover, the lower court's Order also sets forth a different holiday schedule, leaving out the time period described as the first half of Christmas vacation (end of school through December 23rd) and designating Christmas Eve and Christmas Day as two (2) separate holidays.

It is well established in Maryland that a valid settlement agreement between the parties is binding upon them. *E.g., Chernick v. Chernick,* 327 Md. 470, 610 A.2d 770 (1992). In *Chernick,* the Court of Appeals explains that as early as 1855, the Court has made it clear that settlement agreements are desirable and should be binding and enforceable. *Id.* at 481, 610 A.2d at 775.

In the instant case, the parties' complete and final agreement was clearly placed on the record before the Court and the parties themselves indicated their understanding of their agreement and voluntary participation in it. (E.176). Consequently, the lower court's failure to incorporate the visitation schedule as agreed to by the parties was clearly erroneous.

CONCLUSION

For all of the reasons stated herein, Dr. Doe respectfully requests that this Court vacate and reverse the judgment of the Circuit Court for Anne Arundel County and that the case be remanded to the Circuit Court for findings consistent with this Court's opinion.

Respectfully submitted,

Monica R. Gates
101 East Potomac Avenue
Baltimore, Maryland 21212-1234
Attorney for Appellant

GLOSSARY

Administrative Procedure Act † A statute enacted by Congress that regulates the way in which federal administrative agencies conduct their affairs and establishes the procedure for judicial review of the actions of federal agencies. The Act is referred to as the APA.

administrative regulation A law enacted by an agency, sometimes referred to as a *rule.*

adultery † Sexual intercourse by a married person with a person not his or her spouse.

advance sheets † Printed copies of judicial opinions published in loose-leaf form shortly after the opinions are issued. These published opinions are later collected and published in bound form with the other reported cases which are issued over a longer period of time.

affirmative defense † A defense that amounts to more than simply a denial of the allegations in the plaintiff's complaint. It sets up new matter which, if proven, could result in a judgment against the plaintiff even if all the allegations of the complaint are true.

agent † One of the parties to an agency relationship, specifically, the one who acts for and represents the other party, who is known as the *principal.* The word implies service as well as authority to do something in the name of or on behalf of the principal.

alimony † Ongoing court-ordered support payments by a divorced spouse, usually payments made by an ex-husband to his former wife.

American Bar Association † The country's largest voluntary professional association of attorneys, commonly referred to as the ABA. Its purposes include enhancing professionalism and advancing the administration of justice.

American Law Institute (ALI) † A nonprofit organization committed to clarifying legal principles and standardizing them throughout the country. Its best-known work [is] the Restatement of the Law ... .

American Law Reports A primary law finder and reporter published by Lawyers Cooperative Publishing Company. It is commonly known as ALR.

amicus curiae † [Latin for] "Friend of the court." A person who is interested in the outcome of the case, but who is not a party, whom the court permits to file a brief for the purpose of providing the court with a position or a point of view which it might not otherwise have. An amicus curiae is often referred to simply as an *amicus.*

annotated † Containing explanatory comments.

annotation † 1. A notation, appended to any written work, which explains or comments upon its meaning. 2. A commentary that appears immediately following a printed statute and describes the application of the statute in actual cases. Such annotations, with the statutes on which they comment, are published in volumes known as annotated statutes or annotated codes. 3. A notation that follows an opinion of court printed in a court report, explaining the court's action in detail.

answer † A pleading in response to a complaint. An answer may deny the allegations of the complaint, demur to them, agree with them, or introduce affirmative defenses intended to defeat the plaintiff's lawsuit or delay it.

apparent authority † Authority which, although not actually granted by the principal, he or she permits his or her agent to exercise.

appellant (petitioner) † A party who appeals from a lower court to a higher court.

appellate brief A formal structured document *(brief)* filed in an appeals court by either appellant or appellee.

appellee (respondent) † A party against whom a case is appealed from a lower court to a higher court.

Articles of Confederation † The document that governed the confederation of the original 13 states before the Constitution was adopted. It formed a mere association of states, not the union of states into a nation, which the Constitution created.

articles of incorporation † The charter or basic rules that create a corporation and by which it functions. Among other things, it states the purposes for which the corporation is being organized, the amount of authorized capital stock, and the names and addresses of the directors and incorporators.

assignment † 1. A transfer of property, or a right in property, from one person to another. 2. A designation or appointment.

associate † A person engaged in the practice of law with another attorney or attorneys, but not as a partner or member of the firm.

assumption of risk † The legal principle that a person who knows and deliberately exposes himself or herself to a danger assumes responsibility for the risk, rather than the person who actually created the danger. Assumption of risk is often referred to as voluntary assumption of risk. It is a defense to negligence.

attorney general † The chief law officer of the nation or of a state. The attorney general is responsible for representing the government in legal actions with which it is concerned, and for advising the chief executive and other administrative heads of the government on legal matters on which they desire an opinion.

attorney in fact † An agent or representative authorized by [the agent's] principal, by virtue of a power of attorney, to act for [the principal] in certain matters.

bankruptcy † The system under which a debtor may come into court (voluntary bankruptcy) or be brought into court by his or her creditors (involuntary bankruptcy), either seeking to have his or her assets administered and sold for the benefit of ... creditors and to be discharged from his or her debts (a straight bankruptcy), or to have his or her debts reorganized (a business reorganization or a wage earner's plan).

battered spouse (woman) syndrome † A psychological condition in which a woman commits physical violence against her husband or mate as a result of the continued physical or mental abuse to which he has subjected her. The courts are split with respect to the admissibility of expert testimony ... to prove the psychological effects of continued abuse.

battery † The unconsented-to touching or striking of one person by another, or by an object put in motion by [the other], with the intention of doing harm or giving offense. Battery is both a crime and a tort.

bench trial † A trial before a judge without a jury; a nonjury trial.

bequest † Technically, a gift of personal property by will, i.e., a legacy, although the term is often loosely used in connection with a testamentary gift of real estate as well.

bill † A proposed law, presented to the legislature for enactment; i.e., a legislative bill.

Bill of Rights † The first 10 amendments to the United States Constitution. The Bill of Rights is the portion of the Constitution that sets forth the rights which are the fundamental principles of the United States and the foundation of American citizenship.

binding (mandatory) authority † Previous decisions of a higher court or statutes that a judge must follow in reaching a decision in a case.

boilerplate language † Language common to all legal documents of the same type.

breach of contract † Failure, without legal excuse, to perform any promise that forms a whole or a part of a contract, including the doing of something inconsistent with its terms.

brief † 1. A written statement submitted to a court for the purpose of persuading it of the correctness of one's position. A brief argues the facts of the case and the applicable law, supported by citations of authority. 2. A text that an attorney prepares to guide him or her in the trial of a case. Called a *trial brief*, it can include lists of questions to be asked of various witnesses, points to be covered, and arguments to be made. 3. An outline of the published opinion in a case, made by an attorney or a paralegal for the purpose of understanding the case.

by-laws † Rules and regulations created by corporations, associations, clubs, and societies for their governance.

(court) calendar † A list of cases ready for the court to dispose of, whether by trial or otherwise … also referred to as a *docket*.

capital crime (offense) † A crime punishable by death.

case at bar The legal matter that is before the court.

case brief A concise, objective summary of a case opinion.

case law † The law as laid down in the decisions of the courts in similar cases that have previously been decided.

casebook † A book containing court decisions and other materials in a specific field of law, used for teaching law students.

cause of action † Circumstances that give a person the right to bring a lawsuit and to receive relief from a court.

certificate of service † A verification, usually provided by an attorney, that a pleading or motion has been mailed or delivered to the opposing side.

certiorari † *(Latin)* A writ issued by a higher court to a lower court requiring the certification of the record in a particular case so that the higher court can review the record and correct any actions taken in the case which are not in accordance with the law. The Supreme Court of the United States uses the writ of certiorari to select the state court cases it is willing to review. Commonly referred to as "cert."

charter † The basic law of a city or town.

circumstantial evidence † Facts and circumstances from which a jury or a judge may reason and reach conclusions in a case.

citation † Reference to authority (a case, article, or other text) on a point of law, by name, volume, and page or section of the court report or other book in which it appears.

cited case A known case that is being shepardized.

citing case A case located through shepardizing that makes reference to principles from the cited case.

cloud on the title † An outstanding potential claim against real estate somewhere in the chain of title, which reduces the market value of the property.

Code of Federal Regulations † An arrangement, by subject matter, of the rules and regulations issued by federal administrative agencies; commonly referred to as the CFR or abbreviated as C.F.R.

codicil † An addition or supplement to a will, which adds to or modifies the will without replacing or revoking it. A codicil does not have to be physically attached to the will.

common counts Standardized phrases used in common law pleading.

common law † 1. Law found in the decisions of the courts rather than in statutes; judge-made law. 2. English law adopted by the early American colonists, which is part of the United States' judicial heritage and forms the basis of much of its law today.

common law pleading †   A highly formal process of pleading a case, both claim and defense, the object of which was to put the matter in dispute at issue as precisely as possible.

complaint †   The initial pleading in a civil action, in which the plaintiff alleges a cause of action and asks that the wrong done him or her be remedied by the court.

computer-assisted legal research   Known as CALR, a method of research utilizing computers and databases.

concurring opinion †   An opinion issued by one or more judges which agrees with the result reached by the majority opinion rendered by the court, but reaches that result for different reasons.

conference committee †   A meeting of representatives of both houses of a legislature to resolve differences in the versions of the same bill passed by each, by working out a compromise acceptable to both bodies.

consent †   Agreement; approval; acquiescence; being of one mind. Consent necessarily involves two or more persons because, without at least two persons, there cannot be a unity of opinion or the possibility of thinking alike.

consideration †   The reason a person enters into a contract; that which is given in exchange for performance or the promise to perform; the price bargained and paid; the inducement. Consideration is an essential element of a valid and enforceable contract. A promise to refrain from doing something one is entitled to do also constitutes consideration.

constitution †   1. The system of fundamental principles by which a nation, state, or corporation is governed. A nation's constitution may be written or unwritten. A nation's laws must conform to its constitution. A law that violates a nation's constitution is unconstitutional and therefore unenforceable. 2. The document setting forth the fundamental principles of governance.

Constitution of the United States †   The fundamental document of American government, as adopted by the people of the United States through their representatives in the Constitutional Convention of 1787, as ratified by the states, together with the amendments to that Constitution.

constitutional law †   The body of principles that apply in the interpretation, construction, and application of the Constitution to statutes and to other governmental action. Constitutional law deals with constitutional questions and determines the constitutionality of state and federal laws and of the manner in which government exercises its authority.

Consumer Price Index †   Statistics compiled and published by the government on a regular basis, which reflect the current cost of living.

contextual analysis   A method of legal analysis whereby disputed words are considered in light of the meaning of other similarly situated words or provisions.

contract †   An agreement entered into, for adequate consideration, to do, or refrain from doing, a particular thing.

contributory negligence †   In the law of negligence, a failure by the plaintiff to exercise reasonable care which, in part at least, is the cause of an injury. Contributory negligence defeats a plaintiff's cause of action for negligence in states that have not adopted the doctrine of comparative negligence.

corporation †   An artificial person, existing only in the eyes of the law, to whom a state or the federal government has granted a charter to become a legal entity, separate from its shareholders, with a name of its own, under which its shareholders can act and contract and sue and be sued. A corporation's shareholders, officers, and directors are not normally liable for the acts of the corporation.

count †   1. A statement of a cause of action in a complaint. There may be several counts in one complaint. 2. A separate and distinct part of an indictment or information stating a separate and distinct offense. Division into counts is necessary when two or more offenses are charged in a single indictment or information.

counterclaim † A cause of action on which a defendant in a lawsuit might have sued the plaintiff in a separate action. Such a cause of action, stated in a separate division of a defendant's answer, is a counterclaim.

court of general jurisdiction † Generally, another term for trial court; that is, a court having jurisdiction to try all classes of civil and criminal cases except those which can be heard only by a court of limited jurisdiction.

court of limited jurisdiction † A court whose jurisdiction is limited to civil cases of a certain type or which involve a limited amount of money, or whose jurisdiction in criminal cases is confined to petty offenses and preliminary hearings. A court of limited jurisdiction is sometimes called a court of special jurisdiction.

creditor † A person to whom a debt is owed by a debtor.

crime † An offense against the authority of the state; a public wrong, as distinguished from a private wrong; an act in violation of the penal code; a felony or a misdemeanor.

cross-claim A claim against a co-defendant brought by a defendant.

debtor † A person who owes another person money.

deed † A document by which real property, or an interest in real property, is conveyed from one person to another.

default † 1. The failure of a person to pay money when due. 2. The failure to perform a duty or obligation. 3. The failure of a party to a lawsuit to appear in court when he or she is under a duty to appear or to plead when he or she is required to plead.

default judgment † A judgment rendered in favor of a plaintiff based upon a defendant's failure to take a necessary step in a lawsuit within the required time.

defense † In both civil and criminal cases, the facts submitted and the legal arguments offered by a defendant in support of his or her claim that the plaintiff's case, or the prosecution's, should be rejected. The term "defense" may apply to a defendant's entire case or to separate grounds, called affirmative defenses, offered by a defendant for rejecting all or a portion of the case against him or her.

demurrer † A method of raising an objection to the legal sufficiency of a pleading. A demurrer says, in effect, that the opposing party's complaint alleges facts that, even if true, do not add up to a cause of action and that, therefore, the case should be dismissed. Demurrers have been replaced in many, but not all, jurisdictions by motions or answers, which perform the same function.

deponent † 1. A person who gives a deposition. 2. A person who gives sworn testimony in any form; an affiant; a witness.

deposition † The transcript of a witness's testimony given under oath outside of the courtroom, usually in advance of the trial or hearing, upon oral examination or in response to written interrogatories.

desertion † As a ground for divorce, a voluntary separation of one of the parties to a marriage from the other without the consent of or without having been wronged by the second party, with the intention to live apart and without any intention to return to cohabitation.

devise † A gift of real property by will, although it is often loosely used to mean a testamentary gift of either real property or personal property.

devisee † The beneficiary of a devise.

dicta † Plural of dictum, ... short for the Latin term *obiter dictum*. Dicta are expressions or comments in a court opinion that are not necessary to support the decision made by the court; they are not binding authority and have no value as precedent.

digest † (noun) A series of volumes containing summaries of cases organized by legal topics, subject areas, and so on. Digests are essential for legal research. ... Digests cover virtually all cases ever decided in the United States; some digests are limited to specific jurisdictions or to specific fields in the law. Digests are updated continuously to ensure that they are current.

digest † (verb) To understand or synthesize.

discovery † A means for providing a party, in advance of trial, with access to facts that are within the knowledge of the other side, to enable the party to better try his or her case.

dismiss † To order a case, motion, or prosecution to be terminated. A party requests such an order by means of a motion to dismiss.

dissenting opinion † A written opinion filed by a judge of an appellate court who disagrees with the decision of the majority of judges in a case, giving the reasons for his or her differing view. Often a dissenting opinion is written by one judge on behalf of one or more other dissenting judges.

durable power of attorney † A power of attorney that remains effective even though the grantor becomes mentally incapacitated. Some durable powers of attorney become effective only when a person is no longer able to make decisions for himself or herself.

duress † Coercion applied for the purpose of compelling a person to do, or to refrain from doing, some act. ... Duress may be a defense in a civil action.

elective share (widow's allowance) † In some states, the share a surviving spouse may elect to take in the estate of the deceased spouse.

emancipated minor † A person who has not yet attained the age of majority who is totally self-supporting or married. A parent emancipates [a] minor child when he or she surrenders control and authority over the child and gives [the child] the right to [the child's] earnings. Emancipation also terminates the parent's legal duty to support the minor child.

enabling act (legislation) † 1. A statute that grants new powers or authority to persons or

corporations. 2. A statute that gives the government the power to enforce other legislation or that carries out a provision of a constitution. The term also applies to a clause in a statute granting the government the power to enforce or carry out that statute.

enactment † 1. A statute. 2. The process by which a legislative bill becomes law.

Equal Rights Amendment † A proposed constitutional amendment, passed by Congress in 1972, which failed for lack of ratification by three-fourths of the states. The proposed amendment, generally referred to as the ERA, provided that "equality of rights under the law shall not be abridged by the United States or any state on account of sex."

equitable parent doctrine A doctrine that permits a nonbiological parent to be considered a natural parent when certain circumstances exist between parent and child, including mutual acknowledgment of their relationship.

escrow agent An individual holding property conditioned on a certain act or event.

estate † 1. The right, title, and interest a person has in real or personal property, either tangible or intangible. Estates in real property (estates in land or landed estates) include both freehold estates ... and estates less than freehold. ... 3. The property left by a decedent; i.e., a decedent's estate.

estoppel † A prohibition imposed by law against uttering what may actually be the truth.

There are two classes of estoppel. A person may be estopped by his or her own acts or representations (that is, not be permitted to deny the truth or significance of what he or she said or did) if another person who was entitled to rely upon those statements or acts did so to his or her detriment. This type of estoppel is also known as *equitable estoppel* or *estoppel in pais*. The second type of estoppel is *legal estoppel*. It includes matters of record such as marriage, divorce, judgments, and deeds, as well as the findings of a court. Estoppel must be distinguished from waiver, which is the voluntary surrendering of a known right.

executive order [†] An order issued by the chief executive officer of government, whether national, state, or local.

expert [†] A person who has special skill or knowledge in a given field.

expert testimony [†] The opinion evidence of an expert witness; the testimony of a person particularly skilled, learned, or experienced in a particular art, science, trade, business, profession, or vocation who has a thorough knowledge concerning such matters that is not possessed by people in general.

fact pleading When detailed facts necessary to allege a cause of action are provided.

Fair Debt Collection Practices Act [†] One of the federal consumer credit protection acts, whose purpose is to eliminate improper collection practices by debt collection agencies.

family law [†] Area of the law concerned with domestic relations.

Federal Register [†] An official publication, printed daily, containing regulations and proposed regulations issued by administrative agencies, as well as other rulemaking and other official business of the executive branch of government. All regulations are ultimately published in the Code of Federal Regulations.

fee [†] An estate in real property that may be inherited. When "fee" is used without words of limitation, it always means fee simple.

fiduciary duty [†] A relationship between two persons in which one is obligated to act with the utmost good faith, honesty, and loyalty on behalf of the other. A fiduciary relationship is often loosely but inaccurately considered to be the equivalent of a confidential relationship.

first impression [†] Phrase referring to a case that has not arisen before and that is without precedent to govern it.

Freedom of Information Act (FOIA) [†] A federal statute that requires federal agencies to make

available to the public, upon request, material contained in their files, as well as information on how they function. The Act contains various significant exemptions from disclosure, including information compiled for law enforcement purposes.

general counsel The chief attorney in the legal department of a business.

grantee [†] The person to whom a grant is made; the party in a deed to whom the conveyance is made.

grantor [†] The person who makes a grant; the party in a deed who makes the conveyance.

ground rent lease [†] A long-term lease of land, commonly for 99 years, typically entered into by the tenant so that it can construct income-producing buildings.

handbook A "nuts-and-bolts"-oriented practice guide, often prepared by a bar association.

headnote [†] A summary statement that appears at the beginning of a reported case to indicate the points decided by the case.

hearsay [†] The testimony of a witness as to a statement made to him or her outside of court, or made to someone else who told [the witness] what was said, that is offered in court to prove the truth of the matter contained in the statement.

HLA testing [†] Abbreviation of human leukocyte antigen testing. An HLA blood test is a paternity test.

holding [†] The proposition of law for which a case stands; the "bottom line" of a judicial decision.

home rule [†] The right of a city, town, or county to self-government with respect to purely local matters. A state's constitution may or may not confer such a right upon its cities and towns.

hornbook [†] A book that explains the fundamental aspects of an area or field of the law in basic terms. A hornbook is usually concise.

hostile witness † A witness who may be cross-examined or impeached by the party who called him or her, because of malice or prejudice he or she displayed toward that party in ... direct examination.

injunction † A court order that commands or prohibits some act or course of conduct. It is preventive in nature and designed to protect a plaintiff from irreparable injury to his or her property or property rights by prohibiting or commanding the doing of certain acts. An injunction is a form of equitable relief.

interrogatories † Written questions put by one party to another ... in advance of trial. Interrogatories are a form of discovery and are governed by the rules of civil procedure.

intestate † Pertaining to a person, or to the property of a person, who dies without leaving a valid will.

jailhouse lawyer An inmate who represents himself or herself or assists other inmates in legal matters.

joint tenancy † An estate in land or in personal property held by two or more persons jointly, with equal rights to share in its enjoyment. The most important feature of a joint tenancy is the right of survivorship, which means that upon the death of a joint tenant the entire estate goes to the survivor (or, in the case of more than two joint tenants, to the survivors, and so on to the last survivor).

judgment † 1. In a civil action, the final determination by a court of the rights of the parties, based upon the pleadings and the evidence; a decision. 2. In a criminal prosecution, a determination of guilt; a conviction.

judicial review The power of courts to review decisions of another department or level of government.

jury † A group of women and men selected according to law to determine the truth. Juries are used in various types of legal proceedings, both civil and criminal.

jury instructions † Directions given to the jury by the judge just before he or she sends the jurors out to deliberate and return a verdict, explaining the law that applies in the case and spelling out what must be proven and by whom.

jury trial † A trial in which the jurors are the judges of the facts and the court is the judge of the law. Trial by jury is guaranteed in all criminal cases by the Sixth Amendment, and in most civil cases by the Seventh Amendment.

key facts Facts that are essential for a court in reaching its decision.

landlord (lessor) † An owner of real property who leases all or a portion of the premises to a tenant.

last will † Same as will. The word "last" may connote "final wishes," or it may signify that the will is the most recent in a series of wills made by the testator.

law dictionary A dictionary devoted to legal terms.

law outline A paperback summary of general legal principles.

law review † A publication containing articles by law professors and other authorities, with respect to legal issues of current interest, and summaries of significant recent cases, written by law students. ... Another name for a law review is law journal or legal periodical.

lease † A contract for the possession of real estate in consideration of payment of rent, ordinarily for a term of years or months, but sometimes at will. The person making the conveyance is the landlord or lessor; the person receiving the right of possession is the tenant or lessee.

leasehold † The interest or estate of a lessee under a lease. The lessee's interest or estate is also referred to as a leasehold interest or leasehold estate.

legal authority [†] 1. The power of the law to require obedience. 2. Precedent.

legal directory A resource containing lists of attorneys as well as other useful legal information.

legal encyclopedia An encyclopedia devoted to legal matters and subjects.

legalese [†] The use by lawyers of specialized words or phrases, rather than plain talk, when it serves no purpose; legal jargon. Contemporary commentators eschew legalese in favor of direct, effective use of language.

legatee [†] A person who receives personal property as a beneficiary under a will, although the word is often loosely used to mean a person who receives a testamentary gift of either personal property or real property.

legislative history [†] Recorded events that provide a basis for determining the legislative intent underlying a statute enacted by a legislature. The records of legislative committee hearings and of debates on the floor of the legislature are among the sources for legislative history.

litigation memorandum A memorandum filed with a trial court.

living will [†] A document in which a person sets forth directions regarding medical treatment to be given if he or she becomes unable to participate in decisions regarding his or her medical care.

looseleaf service A specialized form of legal publication used in areas subject to rapid change.

majority opinion [†] An opinion issued by an appellate court that represents the view of a majority of the members of the court.

manual [†] Written directions for performing a certain task or certain work.

mediation [†] The voluntary resolution of a dispute in an amicable manner. ... Mediation

differs from arbitration in that a mediator, unlike an arbitrator, does not render a decision.

medical malpractice [†] A physician's negligent failure to observe the appropriate standard of care in providing services to a patient; also, misconduct while engaging in the practice of medicine. Like legal malpractice, medical malpractice is a tort if it causes injury.

metes and bounds [†] A property description, commonly in a deed or mortgage, that is based upon the property's boundaries and the natural objects and other markers on the land.

Model Act A statute developed by the National Conference of Commissioners on Uniform State Laws.

moot [†] Of no actual significance.

motion [†] An application made to a court for the purpose of obtaining an order or rule directing something to be done in favor of the applicant. The types of motions available to litigants, as well as their form and the matters they appropriately address, are set forth in detail in the Federal Rules of Civil Procedure and the rules of civil procedure of the various states, as well as in the Federal Rules of Criminal Procedure and the various states' rules of criminal procedure. Motions may be written or oral, depending on the type of relief sought and on the court in which they are made.

motion for physical or mental examination A discovery motion requesting the court to order an evaluation of a party by medical personnel.

motion for protective order A motion filed when discovery is intrusive.

motion for sanctions A motion requesting that certain punitive measures be taken against a party who fails to provide discovery.

motion to compel discovery A motion asking a court to order that discovery be provided.

National Association of Legal Assistants (NALA) [†] A national organization of legal assistants and paralegals whose purpose is to enhance professionalism and the interests of those in the profession, as well as to advance the administration of justice generally. Among its other undertakings, NALA has established a "Code of Professional Responsibility" for paralegals and legal assistants and provides professional certifications, continuing education, and assistance in job placement. A person who receives certification through NALA is entitled to so indicate by the use of "CLA" (Certified Legal Assistant) after his or her name.

National Conference of Commissioners on Uniform State Laws   A group of legal scholars whose purpose is to develop uniform statutory law.

National Federation of Paralegal Associations (NFPA) †   An association of paralegal and legal assistant organizations nationwide whose purpose is to enhance professionalism and the interests of those in the profession, as well as to advance the administration of justice. Among its other undertakings, NFPA has established the "Affirmation of Responsibility," a code of professional conduct for paralegals and legal assistants, and provides continuing education and assistance in job placement.

National Reporter System   West's systematic reporting of decisions from all state appellate courts and many federal courts.

negligence †   The failure to do something that a reasonable person would do in the same circumstances, or the doing of something a reasonable person would not do.

notary public †   A public officer whose function is to attest to the genuineness of documents and to administer oaths.

notice of appeal †   The process by which appellate review is initiated; specifically, written notice to the appellee advising him or her of the appellant's intention to appeal.

notice pleading   When only a short statement as to the grounds for bringing a cause of action are provided.

on all fours †   Refers to a judicial opinion in a case that is very similar to another case, both with respect to the facts they involve and the applicable law.

order †   A determination made by a court; an order of court.

ordinance †   A law of a municipal corporation; a local law enacted by a city council, town council, board of supervisors, or the like.

override †   To exercise one's authority or will so as to nullify the action of another or others.

parallel citation †   A citation to a court opinion or decision that is printed in two or more reporters.

partner †   A member of a partnership.

partnership †   An undertaking of two or more persons to carry on, as coowners, a business or other enterprise for profit; an agreement between or among two or more persons to put their money, labor, and skill into commerce or business, and to divide the profit in agreed-upon proportions. Partnerships may be formed by entities as well as individuals; a corporation ... may be a partner.

per curiam opinion †   An opinion, usually of an appellate court, in which the judges are all of one view and the legal question is sufficiently clear that a full written opinion is not required and a one- or two-paragraph opinion suffices.

per stirpes †   (Latin) Means "by the root"; according to class; by representation. Per stirpes describes the method of dividing or distributing an estate in which the heirs of a deceased heir share the portion of the estate that the deceased heir would have received had he or she lived.

personal representative †   Ordinarily, the executor or administrator of a decedent's estate, although the term may also include others who have the responsibility to manage the property or affairs of a person who is unable to manage them for himself or herself due to incapacity, incompetency, or insolvency.

persuasive authority †   Authority that is neither binding authority nor precedent, but which a court may use to support its decision if it chooses.

pinpoint cite   A citation to a particular page in a report.

plain English   Common, everyday English terms used to replace legalese.

plain meaning rule †   The rule that in interpreting a statute whose meaning is unclear, the courts will look to the "plain meaning" of its language to determine legislative intent. The plain meaning rule is in opposition to the majority view of statutory interpretation, which takes legislative history into account.

plat †   A map of a tract of land, showing the boundaries of the streets, blocks, and numbered lots. A plat is also referred to as a "plat map" or a "plot."

pleadings †   Formal statements by the parties to an action setting forth their claims or defenses. The various kinds of pleadings, and the rules governing them, are set forth in detail in the Federal Rules of Civil Procedure and, with respect to pleading in state courts, by the rules of civil procedure of the several states. These rules of procedure abolished common law pleading.

pocket part   A periodically published pamphlet that supplements a bound volume. It is placed in a "pocket" in the back of a volume.

pocket veto †   The veto of a congressional bill by the president by retaining it until Congress is no longer in session, neither signing nor vetoing it. The effect of such inaction is to nullify the legislation without affirmatively vetoing it. The pocket veto is also available to governors under some state constitutions.

precedent †   Prior decisions of the same court, or a higher court, which a judge must follow in deciding a subsequent case presenting similar facts and the same legal problem, even though different parties are involved and many years have elapsed.

preliminary motion   A motion challenging a procedural defect in a complaint or its service.

private law †   1. The rules of conduct that govern activities occurring among or between persons, as opposed to the rules of conduct governing the relationship between persons and their government. 2. A private statute.

probable cause †   A reasonable amount of suspicion, supported by circumstances sufficiently strong to justify a prudent and cautious person's belief that certain alleged facts are probably true. A judge may not issue a search warrant unless he or she is shown probable cause to believe there is evidence of crime on the premises. A police officer may not make an arrest without a warrant unless he or she has reasonable cause, based upon reliable information, to believe a crime has been or is being committed.

probate †   1. To prove a will to be valid in probate court. 2. To submit to the jurisdiction of the probate court for any purpose.

product liability †   The liability of a manufacturer or seller of an article for an injury caused to a person or to property by a defect in the article sold. A product liability suit is a tort action in which strict liability is imposed.

promissory note †   A written promise to pay a specific sum of money by a specified date or on demand. A promissory note is negotiable if, in addition, it is payable to the order of a named person or to bearer.

protective order †   An order of court protecting a person from harassment by excessive discovery, process, or the like; it is requested by a party by means of a motion for protective order.

public defender †   An attorney appointed by the court to represent indigent persons in criminal cases.

public domain †   In copyright law, a literary composition or other work that has not been copyrighted or with respect to which the copyright has expired.

public law † 1. Body of law dealing with the relationship between the people and their government, the relationship between agencies and branches of government, and the relationship between governments themselves. 2. A statute dealing with matters that concern the community as a whole.

quieting title † Bringing an action to quiet title, i.e., a lawsuit brought to remove a cloud on the title so that the plaintiff and those in privity with him or her may forever be free of claims against the property.

quitclaim deed † A deed that conveys whatever interest the grantor has in a piece of real property, as distinguished from the more usual deed which conveys a fee and contains various covenants, particularly title covenants. A quitclaim deed is often referred to simply as a "quitclaim."

ratify † To give approval; to confirm.

reasoning As found in a case opinion, a court's analysis and justification for a specific holding.

record on appeal † The papers a trial court transmits to the appellate court, on the basis of which the appellate court decides the appeal. The record on appeal includes the pleadings, all motions made before the trial court, the official transcript, and the judgment or order appealed from.

remand † *n.* The return of a case by an appellate court to the trial court for further proceedings, for a new trial, or for entry of judgment in accordance with an order of the appellate court.
v. To return or send back.

reply † In pleading, the plaintiff's answer to the defendant's setoff or counterclaim.

reported case † A case which has been published.

reporters † Court reports, as well as official, published reports of cases decided by administrative agencies.

request for admission † Written statements concerning a case, directed to an adverse party, that he or she is required to admit or deny. Such admissions or denials will be treated by the court as having been established, and need not be proven at trial.

request for production of documents and inspection of property A discovery request that certain documents be provided or property be inspected.

rescission † The abrogation, annulment, or cancellation of a contract by the act of a party. Rescission may occur by mutual consent of the parties, pursuant to a condition contained in the contract, or for fraud, failure of consideration, material breach, or default. It is also a remedy available to the parties by a judgment or decree of the court. More than mere termination, rescission restores the parties to the status quo existing before the contract was entered into.

resident agent † A person residing in a state who is authorized by a ... corporation to accept service of process on its behalf.

residuary clause † A clause in a will that disposes of the part of the estate that is left after all other legacies and devises have been paid and all claims against the estate are satisfied. Residuary clauses frequently contain the phrase "rest, residue, and remainder."

Restatement of the Law † A series of volumes published by the American Law Institute, written by legal scholars, each volume or set of volumes covering a major field of the law. Each of the Restatements is, among other things, a statement of the law as it is generally interpreted and applied by the courts with respect to particular legal principles.

restitution † In both contract and tort, a remedy that restores the status quo. Restitution returns a person who has been wrongfully deprived of something to the position he or she occupied before the wrong occurred; it requires a defendant who has been unjustly enriched at the expense of the plaintiff to make the plaintiff whole, either, as may be appropriate, by returning property unjustly held, by reimbursing the plaintiff, or by paying compensation or indemnification.

retainer † 1. The act of hiring an attorney. 2. A preliminary fee paid to an attorney at the time he or she is retained, in order to secure her services.

return (proof) of service † A short account in writing, made by an officer, with respect to the manner in which he or she has executed a writ or other process.

right of survivorship † In the case of a joint tenancy or a tenancy by the entirety, the entitlement of the surviving tenant, upon the death of the other, to hold in his or her own right whatever estate or interest both previously shared.

rulemaking † The promulgation by an administrative agency of a rule having the force of law, i.e., a regulation.

rules of court † Rules promulgated by the court, governing procedure or practice before it.

sanction † 1. Action taken by a tribunal ... by way of enforcing its judgment, decision, or order. ... 3. A punishment; a penalty.

self-help book A book designed to explain legal procedures to nonlawyers.

separation (marital, postnuptial) agreement † An agreement between husband and wife who are about to divorce or to enter into a legal separation, settling property rights and other matters ... between them. Separation agreements are subject to court approval.

service of process † Delivery of a summons, writ, complaint, or other process to the opposite party, or other person entitled to receive it, in such manner as the law prescribes, whether by leaving a copy at his or her residence, by mailing a copy to him or her or his or her attorney, or by publication.

session † 1. As opposed to a "term," the time when a court, legislature, or other body is actually meeting or sitting for the purpose of conducting its business. A court that is sitting, or a legislature that is meeting, is said to be in session. 2. Synonymous with "term," i.e., the entire period during a particular year in which a court sits to conduct its business.

session laws † The collected statutes enacted during a session of a legislature.

settlement † The ending of a lawsuit by agreement.

shareholders' agreement An agreement among owners of a corporation.

Shepard's Citations A citator published by Shepard's/McGraw-Hill.

shepardizing † Using a citator.

signal A phrase indicating how a writer wants a reader to consider an authority.

slip law A statute issued in single sheet form and published shortly after it has been issued by the legislature.

slip opinion † A single judicial decision published shortly after it has been issued by the court and well before it is incorporated into a reporter.

special warranty deed † A deed that contains a special warranty rather than a general warranty.

specific performance † The equitable remedy of compelling performance of a contract, as distinguished from an action at law for damages for breach of contract due to nonperformance.

standing to sue † The legal capacity to bring and to maintain a lawsuit. A person is without standing to sue unless some interest of his or hers has been adversely affected or unless he or she has been injured by the defendant. The term "standing to sue" is often shortened simply to "standing."

star paging A pagination system to help a reader in an unofficial report locate the same page in the official report.

stare decisis † [Latin for] "standing by the decision." Stare decisis is the doctrine that judicial decisions stand as precedents for cases arising in the future. It is a fundamental policy of our law that, except in unusual circumstances, a court's determination on a point of law will be followed by courts of the same or lower rank in later cases presenting the same legal issue, even though different parties are involved and many years have elapsed.

statute † A law enacted by a legislature; an act.

Statute of Frauds † A statute, existing in one or another form in every state, that requires certain classes of contracts to be in writing and signed by the parties. Its purpose is to prevent fraud or reduce the opportunities for fraud.

Statutes at Large † An official publication of the federal government, issued after each session of Congress, which includes all statutes enacted by the Congress and all congressional resolutions and treaties, as well as presidential proclamations and proposed or ratified amendments to the Constitution.

statutes of limitations † Federal and state statutes prescribing the maximum period of time during which various types of civil actions and criminal prosecutions can be brought after the occurrence of the injury or the offense.

statutory law † Law that is promulgated by statute, as opposed to law that is promulgated by the judiciary.

stock certificate † An instrument issued by a corporation stating that the person named is the owner of a designated number of shares of its stock.

strict liability † Liability for an injury whether or not there is fault or negligence; absolute liability. The law imposes strict liability in product liability cases.

subpoena † A command in the form of written process requiring a witness to come to court to testify; short for subpoena ad testificandum.

subpoena duces tecum † The Latin term *duces tecum* means "bring with you under penalty." A subpoena duces tecum is a written command requiring a witness to come to court to testify

and at that time to produce for use as evidence the papers, documents, books, or records listed in the subpoena.

summary judgment † A method of disposing of an action without further proceedings. Under the Federal Rules of Civil Procedure, and the rules of civil procedure of many states, a party against whom a claim, counterclaim, or cross-claim is asserted, or against whom a declaratory judgment is sought, may file a motion for summary judgment seeking judgment in his or her favor if there is no genuine issue as to any material fact.

summons † In a civil case, the process by which an action is commenced and the defendant is brought within the jurisdiction of the court.

temporary restraining order (TRO) † Under the Federal Rules of Civil Procedure, injunctive relief that the court is empowered to grant, without notice to the opposite party and pending a hearing on the merits, upon a showing that failure to do so will result in "immediate and irreparable injury, loss, or damage." TROs are similarly available under state rules of civil procedure.

tenancy by the entirety † A form of joint tenancy in an estate in land or in personal property that exists between husband and wife by virtue of the fact that they are husband and wife. As with a conventional joint tenancy, a tenancy by the entirety is a tenancy with right of survivorship.

tenant (lessee) † A person who occupies realty under a lease with a landlord.

terms of art † Technical words; words or expressions that have a particular meaning in a particular science or profession.

testament † A will. The terms "testament," "will," "last will," and "last will and testament" are synonymous.

testate † Pertaining to a person, or to the property of a person, who dies leaving a valid will.

testator † A person who dies leaving a valid will.

third-party complaint † A complaint filed by the defendant in a lawsuit against a third person whom he or she seeks to bring into the action because of that person's alleged liability to the defendant.

title † The rights of an owner with respect to property, real or personal, i.e., possession and the right of possession.

title search † An examination of all documents of record relating to the status or condition of the title to a given piece of real estate (including deeds reflecting past ownership and outstanding mortgages and other liens) in order to verify title.

tolling the statute † A term referring to circumstances that, by operation of law, suspend or interrupt the running of the statute of limitations.

tort † A wrong involving a breach of duty and resulting in an injury to the person or property of another.

transcript † A typewritten copy of the court reporter's stenographic notes of a trial, i.e., a record of the proceedings.

treaties † A formal written agreement between two or more nations with respect to matters of common concern. The Constitution requires ratification, by a two-thirds vote of the Senate, of all treaties between the United States and foreign countries.

treatise † A book that discusses, in depth, important principles in some area of human activity or interest.

trial brief Either a memorandum submitted to court or a text that an attorney prepares to guide him or her at trial.

trust † A fiduciary relationship involving a trustee who holds trust property for the benefit or use of a beneficiary. Property of any description or type (real, personal, tangible, intangible, etc.) may properly be the subject of a trust. The trustee holds legal title to the trust property (also called the *res* or *corpus* of the trust); the beneficiary holds equitable title. A trust is generally established through a trust instrument, such as a deed of trust or a will, by a person (known as the *settlor*) who wishes the beneficiary to receive the benefit of the property but not outright ownership. A trust may, however, also be created by operation of law.

trustee † The person who holds the legal title to trust property for the benefit of the beneficiary of the trust, with such powers and subject to such duties as are imposed by the terms of the trust and the law.

unconstitutional † 1. In conflict with the Constitution of the United States. 2. In conflict with a constitution. 3. Not grounded in or based upon the Constitution or a constitution.

Uniform Commercial Code † One of the Uniform Laws, which has been adopted in much the same form in every state. It governs most aspects of commercial transactions, including sales, leases, negotiable instruments, deposits and collections, letters of credit, bulk sales, warehouse receipts, bills of lading and other documents of title, investment securities, and secured transactions.

Uniform Laws † Model legislation prepared and proposed ... by the [National Conference of Commissioners] on Uniform State Laws, the purpose of which is to promote uniformity throughout the country with respect to statutes governing significant areas of the law. Many Uniform Laws are adopted by many, most, or all of the states, with variations from state to state.

United States Code † The official codification of the statutes enacted by Congress.

United States Reports † The official court reports of the decisions and opinions of the Supreme Court of the United States.

vacate † As applied to a judgment, decree, or other order of a court, to annul, set aside, void, or cancel.

variance † In pleading, an inconsistency between the allegations of a complaint or an indictment and the evidence offered at trial. A fatal variance will result in the dismissal of an action or the reversal of a conviction.

venue † The county or judicial district in which a case is to be tried. In civil cases, venue may be based on where the events giving rise to the cause of action took place or where the parties live or work. ... Venue is distinguishable from jurisdiction because it is an issue only if jurisdiction already exists and because, unlike jurisdiction, it can be waived or changed by consent of the parties.

veto † The refusal of the executive officer of government to approve a bill passed by the legislature. A veto by the executive nullifies the bill unless the legislature is able to override the veto by the constitutionally required number of votes. In the case of a presidential veto, the requirement is two-thirds of the members of both houses of Congress.

warranty deed † A deed that contains title covenants.

work product rule (doctrine) † The rule that an attorney's work product is not subject to discovery.

INDEX